CH00701031

The Dictionary of
Football Club Nicknai
in Britain and Ireland

Thank you for all of
you hospitality,
Hope this raises a
few smiles.

Nicholas Cosh Q.C.
September, 2013

THE DICTIONARY OF FOOTBALL CLUB NICKNAMES
IN BRITAIN AND IRELAND

SHAUN TYAS

PAUL WATKINS

DONINGTON

2013

Published by

PAUL WATKINS
(An imprint of Shaun Tyas)
1 High Street
Donington
Lincolnshire
PE11 4TA

ISBN
978–1–907730–25–2 (paperback)
978–1–907730–26–9 (hardback)

DEDICATION
For my three brothers
Andrew, Christopher and Ian
and in memory of
Our Wonderful Mother
Jean Elizabeth Tyas

Printed and bound in Wales
by Gwasg Dinefwr Press, Llandybie, Carmarthenshire

CONTENTS

ACKNOWLEDGEMENTS

A great many people have helped with this book, with feedback, factual contributions and invaluable encouragement. In an alphabetical level playing-field they are: Bernard Adams, Geoff Almond, Hilary Baker, Edmund Bennett, John Bleach, Jim Blessett, John Burton, Clive Burgess, Matthew Campion, Ray Carroll, Howard Chandler, Richard Coates, Pam Combes, Charlie Cook, Peter Cox, Brian Crabb, the late Paul Craig, Paul Cullen, Alison and Mostyn Davies, Carrie Devine, Andrew Eadie, Richard Fairhurst, Ed Fancourt, Michael Gale, Alasdair Galloway, Anna Henderson, Peter Hodgkiss, Bruce Holdsworth, Richard E. Huws, Barry Ketcham, Roger Leitch, David Lepine, Chris Lewis, Markos Loullis, Clive Lurhs, Gilbert Márkus, Joanna Mattingly, Sam McKinstry, Ishobel McNab, Malcolm Mills, Richard Morgan, Kiran Nanchahal, Elizabeth New, Hywel Wyn Owen, Oliver Padel, Caroline Palmer, James Petre, Martin Pidd, Jason Potter, Rebecca Redmond, David Roffe, John and Sheila Rowlands, Jennifer Scherr, John Smith, Tim Smith, Edward Sproston, Christian Steer, Maureen Sutton, Simon Taylor, Kevin Troop (who also heroically proof-read the entire book and saved me from many typing errors), Alan Tutt, Michael Vetterlein, John Viner, David Walters, Paul Watkins, Marilyn Wood, Vanessa Young; and my three brothers: Andrew, Christopher and Ian, together with Alison, Carmen, Chris, Heather, Helen, Jake and Mark. I sincerely hope I have not left anyone out. The main sources of information are recorded in each dictionary entry and in the bibliography.

Of particular note in the above list has been the secondhand booksellers who have helped bring older books to my attention. The county and university libraries do not hold copies of the vast majority of the sources mentioned here, so this help has been invaluable.

During the production of this book contact was made with Richard E. Huws, who was compiling a study of the nicknames of football and rugby clubs in Wales. Inevitably, our work overlapped. We decided to keep our books separate (they do have a slightly different approach), to help each other with feedback, corrections and additions, and to publish both books simultaneously. It has been a delightful and fruitful exchange which has greatly improved both books. In some cases, our interpretations remain slightly different, and there are unique entries in each, so both books remain independent surveys. Richard's book shows that rugby club nicknames, at least in Wales, are just as interesting, and also that greater access to local sources of information can yield more nicknames.

I have been very fortunate with the feedback I've received, but am keen to hear of further corrections and additions for the possibility of future reprints.

Shaun Tyas

INTRODUCTION

The Dictionary serves two purposes. One is to record the nicknames which exist, the other is to explain them.

Recording the nicknames allows them to be identified, so the Dictionary records them whether the explanation is obvious or difficult. Sometimes a nickname is a genuine mystery and there are several theories about its origin; the Dictionary records the different ideas as well as attempting an answer. Nicknames change and sometimes they evolve into different expressions, the Dictionary attempts to provide dating evidence and variant forms. The Dictionary does not impose a strict definition of 'nickname', any name which is an alternative to the official or formal name of the club is eligible for inclusion. But it does impose a definition of 'football': that is Association Rules, named from football's governing body, established in 1863, and itself having the nicknames 'soccer' (adapted from the second syllable of the main word) and 'footy'.

The word 'nickname' comes from medieval English and means 'an extra name'. The Oxford English Dictionary records the earliest known use of the word from c.1440. Nicknames are not necessarily offensive or mocking or affectionate: they are simply alternative expressions to the normal name.

Many medieval 'secondary names' evolved into formal surnames, usefully distinguishing people with the same first name. So, 'John the Archer' became John Archer; 'John from York' and 'John the Tall' became John York and John Tall. In the same way football clubs can be usefully distinguished as 'The Blues' or 'The Reds', or other nicknames, ensuring the language used in match reports has variety, friendliness and brevity.

In some human activities, nicknames abound. In others, they are rare or non-existent. In the armed services, personnel, places and regiments have nicknames. In football and rugby, it is common for clubs and players to have nicknames, thoughout the world. In cricket they are rare. Nowadays, women's football could hardly be more popular, yet it is not so common for women's clubs to have nicknames. There appears to be a gender bias here, with men finding nicknames useful, or enjoyable, women seemingly having little use for them.

Nicknames have a social use, because they can express friendliness but with a certain distance: the affection is not directed towards the real name of the other person or group, so it is not too direct. When the nickname is derogatory, the same benefit of distance applies. Once the person or thing is so labelled, however, it also gives a means of relating, as if the other entity has been tied up with string, ready to be engaged with. So, the male preference for nicknames seems to be an aspect of the 'rough and tumble' of life, a means of making social engagement work more smoothly; but that still makes it difficult to explain why women's football clubs rarely have nicknames. Most women's clubs are affiliated to men's clubs, so they frequently share a nickname ... the difference, of course, may lie with the fans rather than the clubs (a reasonably-large fan base seems to be a factor in whether a club has a nickname or not). The Dictionary does include the known nicknames for women's independent football clubs, and for those affiliated with the men's clubs if they use different nicknames.

A nineteenth-century work on names by Harry Long coined the phrase that nicknames are 'biographies crowded into a word' (1883, p. 46), which illustrates how a nickname can record the most prominent characteristics of someone or something, as perceived by others who are engaged in some way with that other person or thing. So, when a locality develops a specialised industry, such as hat-making at Luton or steel-making at Corby, this characteristic stands out when seen by outsiders, and 'The Hatters' or 'The Steelmen' is naturally used for the football club from that place; the players may even have been employed in those industries, so they may have coined the nickname themselves. The nickname can stick with them long after the specialised industry has declined. Sometimes the characteristic can be entirely unique, so it strikes observers as really special, as in the case of the nicknames 'The Squirrels', 'The Bones', 'The Minstermen', or 'The Ghosts'. Sometimes a location has a traditional nickname of its own, recording the reputation the place had amongst outsiders, in days when travel was more difficult, culture was less uniform and each place had a uniqueness, and these, too, are often transferred to the local football club (examples are 'Belters', 'Cats', 'Cobbydalers', 'Shannocks', 'Shiners' and 'Sons of the Rock').

Abbreviation is another common motivation in the coining of nicknames. Some formal names are a mouthful – 'Albion Rovers Association Football Club (Newport)' is more easily referred to as 'Albion'. It is more euphonious to say 'QPR' than 'Queen's Park Rangers Football Club'.

In football, nicknames may not always be coined by rival sides or the club's own supporters. There seems something artificial about a committee inventing its own nickname and expecting the rest of the world to use it, but nicknames are now so much the norm that a new club, or a relaunched club, feels the need to promote this aspect of its public image from the outset. A spontaneous nickname may take too long to appear. A club may also have several unofficial nicknames and one officially-accepted one, raising the question whether any one of them is the *real* nickname of the club. And sometimes a nickname can be so popular, it raises the question whether it is actually the real, formal, name of the club. A team without a nickname does appear to be lacking something.

Some nicknames stemming from 'outsiders' may be considered insulting at first, but may be accepted decades later with pride. This has certainly happened with 'Baggies' for West Bromwich Albion, and 'Smoggies' for Middlesbrough.

There are many common nicknames, 'Blues' and 'Town' especially. Some clubs seem entirely happy to share a nickname, others desire something rare or unique.

There has long been a tradition in American sports for teams to adopt an animal as part of the club name, reappearing in the club's badge and also as a nickname, and there may be very little reason why one animal is chosen in preference to another, so long as it sets a club apart from its rivals. It is very popular to chose an animal which happens to have the same opening letter as the club's name (as in 'Bradford Bulls'). This fashion has now spread to British and Irish rugby clubs, but in proper football there is usually a reason for the choice of a badge, related in some way to local folklore, strip colour, heraldry or the place-name; but not always. The Dictionary attempts to explain the nicknames, when and why they were chosen and what they mean.

How the List was Made

Football is a well-researched subject as far as the mainstream clubs are concerned. Supporters have long memories and are proud of their history. So, football now has a vast literature, but there has never been a systematic survey of the club nicknames before; there are not even many essays on the subject (and the few that there are only examine the mainstream clubs).

This is a dictionary, so it was important to survey the subject systematically and attempt to include all the relevant material, or have a logical cut-off point. The first challenge was to find a list of clubs.

There are thousands of football clubs in Britain and Ireland. The English Football Association Pyramid contains some 7,000 clubs, and yet there are thousands more of amateur status which are not part of the Pyramid. They play in local leagues which are even smaller in geographical area than the county leagues at the very bottom of the Pyramid. The Channel Islands, the Isle of Man, Ireland, Northern Ireland, Scotland and Wales have fewer clubs, but just as many as England in proportion to their population size. The different nations also have their own league systems, with no obvious way of measuring common status across the nations. There is no list of clubs; even the Football Association does not publish a list, so a systematic search through them all is difficult.

The most comprehensive list of present-day clubs is that available on the Wikipedia website, gathered under their various leagues. The existence of this fantastic free internet encyclopedia provided the opportunity to start a systematic search through existing clubs, starting with the national league system for each country and moving through the whole of each system, one league at a time. Wikipedia also contains pages devoted to individual clubs which are linked to the League pages, and there are also links to the clubs' own websites, unofficial websites and supporters' websites. Wikipedia also includes references to printed material. Down to levels ten and eleven of the English Pyramid, the information is fairly even, but it soon peters out in the lower levels, with both Wikipedia and the Leagues' own websites displaying only very basic information, and rarely anything on individual clubs. A great many clubs do not have their own website, or have one with only limited information, and it soon became apparent that, lower down the league systems, a great many clubs either have no nickname or at least never publish it.

So, rather than adopting a cut-off point, the survey contains all the nicknames I could find in a systematic search through the mainstream printed and electronic sources in each of the several nations in Britain and Ireland. Sometimes the only nickname found was the same word as the club suffix (words like United and Wanderers), but I only included the suffix as a nickname if I found some evidence that it was being so used, in match reports for example. I did not wish to exclude anyone, but if a club had no published nickname and I could find no evidence of one being used anywhere, the club could not go in the Dictionary. Leaving a club out was actually a disappointment to me. I have made no distinction in importance for clubs based on their size or wealth or location; all nicknames are equal, and many of the smaller clubs have more interesting nicknames than the larger ones.

Wikipedia and other websites need to be supplemented by printed sources, because these record nicknames no longer in use, and for clubs which no longer exist. The British Library has published a bibliography of football (Peter J. Seddon, *A Football Compendium. An Expert Guide to the Books, Films & Music of Association Football*, 2nd edn, Boston Spa: the British Library, 1999), which shows the scale of the literature, essential for the history of the game, but most of the early sources do not record the nicknames. For example, a long-running annual has been the *News of the World Football Annual*, from 1887 to 2007–8, after which it renamed as the *Nationwide Football Annual*), but, disappointingly, nicknames have only been included in recent issues of this annual.

In most cases, nicknames will have been used by spectators and would be first recorded in match reports by local journalists; many may even have been invented by the journalists to add colour to their articles. The early books on football do not record them (many have been examined without discoveries). The earliest to record some, and then only 'in passing', is *The Book of Football. A Complete History and Record of the Association and Rugby Games*, which was issued in 12 parts, between October 1905 and March 1906. Even the earliest football encyclopedia (Johnston 1934) did not deliberately record them, but it also mentioned some in passing (both these works have been carefully checked for any).

The Rothman's Football Yearbook (first published for 1970–1) is the first to include nicknames for the mainstream clubs repeated on a regular basis. This series was renamed *The Sky Sports Football Yearbook* for the 2003–4 issue. It still only covers the mainstream clubs of England and Scotland, however; but it means there is a systematic record of nicknames for the main clubs from 1970 to the present.

A new series of annual directories for England began in 1978, the *Non-League Club Directory*, edited by Tony Williams. Sharing some characteristics with a football club in its own right, in that the series has often changed its home ground (publisher), sponsorship logos (on the spines), official name (title) and strip (colour), it has been at the top of the football reference book league for a long time, and the volume for 2013 is the thirty-fifth to appear. The first two issues were published by Playfair in pocket format with nicknames included in the second issue, for *1979–80*. The third edition was published by Tony Williams himself in the same format, and it is now extremely rare. Rothmans published the series for the next three issues, *1981–2, 1982–3* and *1983–4*, matching the appearance of their mainstream yearbook. Uniquely, the *1982–3* volume has profiles of 17 Scottish clubs with their nicknames, but this was never repeated. Newnes produced two volumes for 1985 and 1986, before Tony Williams himself again rescued the series, publishing the volume for 1987 and all later editions. Welsh clubs were included from 1987 to 2005, but their nicknames were only included since 1994. The volume for 1991 was the first to be more than a thousand pages long. Clubs in the lower leagues are only included in summary form, often without nicknames, but the series is a fantastic achievement and invaluable data for all aspects of the so-called 'non-league' clubs. The 25th anniversary issue, for *2003*, has a collage of the series wrappers on its back cover, which provides a useful checklist for those who are confused by the changing formats and titles.

The original volumes are confusingly the ancestors of two series, because there was an independent revival of the Playfair format in the 1990s, edited by Bruce Smith. Two Playfair volumes were published for *1991–92* and *1992–93*, and three appeared for Words on Sport for *1993–94, 1994–95* and *1995–96*, with nicknames recorded.

The entire runs of *Rothman's Football Year Books* and Williams' *Non-League Club Directories* have been examined for all recorded nicknames, and this dating evidence recorded in the Dictionary entries.

In 1993, John Robinson, of Soccer Books of Cleethorpes, started publishing a series of *Supporters' Guides* to the mainstream clubs in Wales, Scotland, Northern Ireland and the Irish Republic, which included nicknames, so the Celtic areas now had some regular directory coverage. These nations, of course, have their own long history of publications, but, frustratingly, the various yearbooks do not record the nicknames.

There have been other annual directories, such as the eleven volumes of the Tony Williams' *Football League Club Directory* from 1985, mutating in 1988 to *Barclays League Club Directory*, and finally to the *Endsleigh* directory in 1994 and 1995, which contain some variant nicknames to those in Rothmans. There was another competitor in the two editions of *Panini's Football Yearbook 1988/89* and *1989/90*, edited by Peter Dunk. These have also been quarried for evidence, and there was a one-off rival to the non-league directories, *The Non-League Football Year Book 1996–97* by Kerry Miller and James Wright, which also has unique information.

Although the earlier directories never included nicknames, there have been some non-conventional publications which made surveys of the mainstream clubs. In 1933, Ogden's Tobacco published a set of fifty cigarette cards devoted to football club nicknames. Each nickname was given an amusing cartoon and an explanation of the name. The Hignett company also issued the set in the same year, and 'Imperial' made a facsimile reprint in 1997, which is still widely available. It is the earliest survey of the nicknames, albeit of only fifty mainstream ones.

In 1936, the Dundee-based publisher D. C. Thomson issued an album of football 'stamps' with the children's magazine *Adventure*. There were 129 in the set, mostly showing players and colours, but 24 celebrated nicknames, with another amusing cartoon. The texts in the album also made references to a further 20 clubs and their nicknames. The set provides early appearances of several nicknames, including 'The Spiders'.

In 1959, the Sweetule confectionary company issued their own set of twenty-five 'cigarette cards' of football club nicknames which, although it has never been reprinted, is not rare and is easy to find. Also in 1959, Charles Harvey's *Encyclopædia of Sport* included nicknames of the mainstream English and Scottish clubs.

In 1960, Anglo-American Chewing Gum Ltd., based in Halifax, issued a series of colourful waxed wrappers featuring 'Famous Soccer Clubs', followed the next year by 'Noted Football Clubs'. Some of the texts included nicknames. Full sets have proved elusive, but about 70 of the wrappers have now been checked, revealing the earliest use of 'The Loons' in the Dictionary.

A small *Soccer Dictionary* was published by F. C. Avis in 1954. The first edition included only a few of the mainstream nicknames but the 1966 and 1970 editions included many more, covering the whole of Britain and Ireland and including many non-league clubs. Some 316 nicknames were recorded in the three editions, and the title is important because it was published so early. The book is often cited here as the earliest appearance of a nickname in print, and it includes some nicknames no longer heard of.

In 1956 Maurice Golesworthy published his *Encyclopaedia of Association Football*, which went through twelve editions between then and 1976. It cites nicknames for the mainstream clubs, and the first, seventh and last editions have been checked for references.

Another early work which contains some nicknames of the mainstream clubs is the 1958 'Penguin Special' by R. C. Churchill, *Sixty Seasons of League Football*. It has club profiles which mention the nicknames for many of the entries.

Although it is a recent title, David Pickering's *The Cassell Soccer Companion. History, Facts, Anecdotes* (1994; revised editions 1995, 1998) usefully contains many nicknames, and some unique ones.

Between 1963 and 1965 the monthly Boys' Brigade *Stedfast Magazine* included a regular series of cartoons based on football club nicknames, which have been occasionally useful for early datings. Three cartoons appeared in each issue, though the publishers later started repeating them.

The delightful Panini football stickers series included a set of nicknames in the 1986 album. Many of the cartoons from this series are now for sale as fridge magnets, but the coverage of nicknames was slight and there was no explanatory text.

Another unconventional source of information is the enamel badges sold to supporters by many hundreds (thousands?) of clubs. There is a Football Badge Collectors

Association and they have published a directory (actually a catalogue) in four volumes showing images of the badges known to members. Although no attempt has been made to date the badges, the images often record nicknames, some of which may not otherwise be known, and they illustrate how a nickname is seen by the club supporters.

Two on-line free databases provide excellent basic information about the clubs, though much of their content is duplicated in Wikipedia. The English Football Club History Database (FCHD) records official names, dates and league positions, but not nicknames; and the Scottish Football Historical Archive (SFHA) provides similar information for Scotland, but with more background information, including occasional references to nicknames. There is also an on-line Welsh Football Data Archive, but it is league-based, so less informative for invidual clubs.

So, the internet is invaluable as a source of knowledge for present-day nicknames, and there has been directory coverage since the 1970s and some reference book coverage from the 1950s. Before then, nicknames were certainly being used but were rarely recorded in mainstream print. Local newspapers, and the club's own programmes, however, still offer the potential to recover this culture from the darkness.

Although there has never been a previous attempt at a Dictionary of these names, there have been some short essays discussing the nicknames of the mainstream clubs, such as those by Peter Norris in 1959, Gordon Jeffrey in 1961, Basil Easterbooke in 1969, Leslie Vernon in 1970 (in the *Squelcher* series of pamphlets), Ken Ferris in 2005 and Michael Heatley in 2008 (the last is a book called *Football Club Origins and Nicknames*, but the nickname content is only a section of chapter three). General studies of names and nicknames, such as those by Andrew Delahunty, Leslie Dunkling, Adrian Room and Laurence Urdang, have included references to some of the mainstream football clubs, but have not proved useful. Basil Easterbrooke's 1969 essay began with the remark "The definitive history of dubbing first-class Soccer teams with alternative, easily recognisable titles has yet to be written, which is strange, for it seems to me a fascinating offshoot of the game. Nicknames are as old as the Football league itself..."

At a late stage in the production of this dictionary, contact was made with Richard Huws, who was preparing a guide to the football and rugby club nicknames of Wales. We had a slightly different approach. Richard included football and rugby but only for one nation, and his research had more emphasis on local sources, including direct contact with clubs and supporters. So, his work includes many nicknames which have not previously appeared in print. My own Dictionary is football-only, Britain- and Ireland-wide, but largely based on information available in mainstream printed and internet sources. We decided to help oneanother, keep our books as separate but complimentary works, and publish them together. Richard's book illustrates just how many more potential nicknames could be found if one could make a systematic study of local newspapers and draw on the long-term memories of the clubs themselves. It is hoped that enthusiasts with access to this material for their own clubs will forward information for future editions.

Unofficial Nicknames

One of the great advantages of Wikipedia over formal printed sources is that Wikipedia is written by the readers. It has protocols to prevent mischief, but if supporters themselves can record their own thoughts, it means that unofficial nicknames can also be recorded. The printed directories only include officially-sanctioned nicknames, which can sometimes be dull in comparison to the spontaneously-generated ones. The Dictionary includes unofficial nicknames where known; most of them are friendly, but including them raises the question whether offensive nicknames should also be included.

I decided to exclude only those unofficial nicknames which were openly offensive. For example, if a club is called 'City', rival fans may refer to it as 'Shitty'. This may be a clever rhyming phrase, but it seems too nasty to include, and it also raises the question whether it really is a nickname or just an insult. On the other hand, some references which might be offensive are left in because they are historically significant. It is bad taste to mock Manchester United as 'The Munichs', in reference to the 1958 tragedy, but the event was so historically significant, I decided to leave it in with a health warning. 'Dirty Leeds' was an unofficial nickname applied to Leeds United during a period of notoriously aggressive play in the 1960s and '70s. The club used to be nicknamed 'The Peacocks', but the *Rothman's Yearbook* shows that they preferred to have no nickname at all for most of the 1970s and '80s, before taking 'United' as their nickname. More recently 'Super Whites' has become popular. Intriguingly, one wonders if the club's rejection of *any* nickname was in some way motivated by a dislike of the 'Dirty Leeds' nickname.

Another word, normally considered racist, is 'Yids', though the related word 'Yiddish', for the German Jewish dialect, is widely accepted. 'Yids' is an unofficial nickname for Tottenham Hotspur, but the reasons for it are so historically significant, and the usage actually very heroic, that I never hesitated whether to include it or not. The nickname was adopted by the club's mainstream supporters in defiance of the racist agitations of Oswald Moseley and his British Fascists in the 1930s.

Some unofficial nicknames refer to specific sporting sides during a club's history, such as Busby Babes, Crazy Gang, Fergie's Fledglings, Iron Curtain, Lisbon Lions, Proud Preston, Sven's Men and Wembley Wizards (note the tendency to rhyme or alliterate!). Although ephemeral, they were too important to leave out.

The Football Fans Census website conducted a survey of traditional rivalries in 2003 and included questions about nicknames. The survey produced many new nicknames, stemming from supporters of rival clubs. Some of them were too clever not to include, such as the conceptually perfect 'Barcodes' and 'Skunks' for a certain club which plays in black-and-white stripes, and other sources include 'The Y-Fronts', for York City, during the 1970s, when they adopted a large Y-shape on their shirts. The list posted on the 2003 website had already been vetted, and I left a few more out of the Dictionary, but included most of them. A dictionary should record what exists. On the whole, I have preferred to include rather than exclude.

Changes in Nicknames

An advantage the printed sources have over the on-line is the recording of older short-lived nicknames with a clear date. The Airdrieonians club was normally called 'The Diamonds', then in 1974 'The Waysiders' appears as an alternative nickname in the *Rothman's Football Year Books*, but for two years between 1972–3 and 1973–4, 'The Onians' appears. This is clearly a short form of the official name, but I have only found it in this particular source. The Edinburgh City football club is recorded in the Robinson guides as 'City', but the first edition, for 1993, gives the rare nickname 'The City Slickers'. An extremely useful reference to 'The Sand Dobbers' is recorded for Leighton Town in Williams 1983–4.

The usual nickname for Celtic F.C. is 'The Bhoys', but the first two editions of the *Rothman's Yearbook* give a rarer alternative, 'The Tims'. Its appearance in print in this mainstream work of reference shows that it used to be more current as a nickname for the club than it is now.

I have included all the variant nicknames I have found. Interestingly, when many of the Wikipedia entries were rechecked during the final edit of the draft Dictionary, some nicknames were found to have changed and some new variants had been added. Football nicknames are still evolving.

Without doubt, most of the nicknames existed before they were recorded in print, and there are likely to be earlier appearances in local newspapers and match programmes, but the sheer bulk of the local material makes it impossible for a single person to survey. A late appearance in print *might* be because the nickname is recent, but it is equally likely that it is the printing which is late, the nickname being older. Using a wide variety of sources, I believe I have ensured a good 'capture rate' for the nicknames, even if the dates of the earliest use remain difficult to find.

Similarities and Differences across Britain and Ireland

Covering the whole of Britain and Ireland, it soon became apparent that there were similarities as well as differences between the cultural areas, and where different clubs used the same nickname, even if they were hundreds of miles apart, this offered help in explaining them. There are national differences: the English clubs are so numerous that they tend to display all patterns; but the Welsh clubs have a liking for bird nicknames, the Scottish ones are fond of flowers, rhyming phrases and 'friendly short forms', like 'Killie' for Killmarnock. But, however unique a nickname seemed to be, when it became possible to compare nicknames from different parts of Britain and Ireland, it became apparent just how unifying a cultural force football is, and how similar the cultures of Britain and Ireland actually are. For example, the northern Scottish club, Wick Academy in Caithness, takes the nickname 'The Scorries'. This is the Caithness dialect word for 'Seagulls', Wick being a seaside town, but the same idea is used for clubs in seaside towns throughout England, Wales and Ireland. And even nicknames based on history, such as 'The Vikings', are found throughout the islands.

The cultural similarities can also explain mysteries, when the same nickname appears in widely different locations. An example is 'The Ammies', the unexplained nickname of Salford City. A web search reveals that a small club in Barnstaple, Devon, is also nicknamed 'The Ammies' and that a Scottish junior club, Kilsyth Amateurs, also takes the nickname. The Kilsyth club usefully reveals the meaning of the two English nicknames. It is a friendly short form of 'Amateurs'.

The use of *U's* as a nickname for clubs called United, common in England, was useful in explaining the Scottish nickname, 'The Yowes', for Lanark United. In Scots, yowes are female sheep, called yews in English, and so the nickname puns on the sound of the abbreviation for United, but gives it a Scottish flavour.

Similarities are extremely useful, but differences are also interesting. The Irish club Bohemians is nicknamed 'The Gypsies', which needs to be explained in the context of the different cultural history for travellers in Ireland than in Britain. Local dialect is also unique to the area of the club and needs some care in interpretation, but even here 'Tane', 'Tarn', 'Tayn', 'Toon' and 'Town' all mean the same thing.

Sometimes, of course, different clubs take exactly the same nickname but for different reasons, such as the different reasons for 'The Peacocks'.

In complete contrast to localism, many football clubs adopt a name or nickname with international associations. 'Brazil' is a nickname for several clubs, 'Inter', 'Dynamo', and 'Athletico' are suffixes copied from world-famous teams. 'Olympic', 'Sparta' and 'Sporting' may not be direct copies but are certainly duplicated overseas, and 'Team' is a prefix normally associated with the international Olympic games.

The Importance of Dating and Variant Forms

Gathering the information is one thing, but a dictionary needs to explain the meaning. It soon became obvious that many names are mysterious, and subject to conflicting explanations. Once a nickname has become accepted, the reasons for it may be forgotten, and explanations are then 'found' which are not necessarily the correct answer. In fact, they are invented during heated discussions amongst supporters. Names which have been subject to many different attempts to explain them are Addicks, Baggies, Dabbers, Grecians, Pars, Posh, Pompey and Trotters. The dating of the nickname is often really useful in the search for an explanation.

The transition of 'Haddocks' to 'Addicks' as a nickname for Charlton Athletic is neatly traced in a series of cartoons in the *Kentish Independent* between 1908 and 1910. The club was only founded in 1905 and was soon nicknamed 'Haddocks' from its association with a local fishmonger. By 1910 the nickname had already mutated to 'Addicks', but soon afterwards theories began to appear which explained it as meaning 'Athletic' or even 'Adicts', but only tracing the mutation from 'Haddocks' to 'Haddicks' and then 'Addicks' makes the true meaning clear.

The great Scottish club, the Third Lanark, had a mysterious nickname, 'The Hi-Hi's', which is now also used by Haddington. The *Scots Dictionary* records its first mainstream use in a newspaper in 1951, yet it appears on an early postcard which can be dated to c.1902, in the form 'Hi! Hi! Hi!' This seems to confirm that the origin of the nickname is in an early supporters' chant. If it were not for the existence of the early postcard, and one believed that the nickname started around 1951, one might be tempted to look for an explanation in the Butlins Holiday camp expression, 'Hi-de-Hi', because the entertainment officials who used that phrase were called 'Redcoats', which was another nickname for The Third Lanark, and Butlins had opened a branch in Ayr in 1947, only four years before the nickname's alleged appearance. The existence of the early dating evidence makes this theory totally impossible.

Another Scottish mystery is 'The Pars', for Dunfermline Athletic. Theories based on 'parallel stripes', 'paralytic' performance and the parr fish are implausible in the context of other club nicknames for stripes, the late appearance of the word 'paralytic' (for drunk), and spelling. Some have even suggested an origin in an abbreviation ('Plymouth Argyle (Rosyth) Supporters') or as a mutated form of 'Athletic'. The nickname is clearly a pluralised form of the golfing expression, and for a specific historical reason.

A famous English nickname is 'Pompey', for the city and football club of Portsmouth. Many explanations for this nickname have been suggested, but most ignore the important dating evidence. Theories which suggest a coining for the naval base in Napoleonic times are confounded by the fact that the nickname only appears for the first time in 1899, and does so first in a football context.

Another mystery is 'The Grecians' for Exeter City, which is also explained by the scholarly study of the sources, rather than by invented folklore which claims either a Cornish language explanation or a colloquial English phrase based on 'The Greasy 'uns', for lads of a dishevelled appearance.

Classifying the Nicknames

The Dictionary reveals great diversity in club nicknames. To make sense of that diversity, and perhaps in the process explain more of the names, a classification system is needed. The names themselves often have double meanings, and the same name can be chosen by different clubs for entirely different reasons, so it is the reasons for the nicknames which we need to classify rather than the names themselves. For example, 'Swans' might be adopted as a metaphor for a riverside location (Walton & Hersham), or a play on the place-name (Swansea), or because the swan has long been a symbol of the club's county (Buckingham), but 'Robins' is only chosen as a metaphor for the club's colours, so classifying Robins and Swans as 'nicknames based on birds' would be irrelevant.

Football club nicknames can first be divided into two main categories: those based on aspects of the locality and those based on aspects of the club. The chart on page 15 helps make the arrangement clear.

Names Based on the Club

This section divides into four further sections: names based on aspects of the club's history or aspects of the club's home ground, names adapted from the club's official names and names based on the club's playing strip.

The club's own history offers three further divisions: memorable events, memorable people and the club's memorable (or perceived) qualities. The nickname 'Munichs' records the memorable tragedy of 1958; 'River Boys' looks like it merely records a riverside locality but it actually refers to an incident when a club manager said he would jump in the river if his team won the first match in their new strip: they did, so he kept his promise. Other examples include 'The Exiles', 'The Outcasts', 'The Rebels', and 'The Scabs'. 'Memorable people' includes nicknames based on famous managers ('Busby Babes', 'Sven's Men', 'Roy's Boys') or owners of the club ('The Fowlers') or particularly successful sides ('Crazy Gang', 'Famous Five', 'Invincibles', 'Lisbon Lions', or'Wembley Wizards'). 'Chelski' refers to the Russian ownership of Chelsea, without specifically using the chairman's name; 'France' and 'Sund-Ireland' are similar, but these nicknames are still referring indirectly to memorable people.

The 'perceived club qualities' includes nicknames based on memorable expressions in the club's history ('The Posh', from "Posh new players for a posh new club"), which stuck in the memory of supporters and commentators; the club's own declaration that they have qualities of prowess ('The Warriors' and probably 'The Pars', from the supporters' perspective at Dunfermline); or insults made against the club from rival sides ('The Council Housers', 'The Squatters', which are placed here because they still express alleged characteristics of the club); or names which are considered to be representative of the club as a whole, or of its status at the centre of its community ('The Baggies' [possibly], 'The Lads', 'The Locals', 'The Bhoys'; Sheffield F.C.'s use of 'The Club' perhaps also belongs here as marking the club's status as the oldest one in the world); or based on supporters' chants ('The Hi-Hi', 'The Ziggers'); or the club's own adoption of a symbol which it feels expresses the club's qualities ('The Lions' at Millwall, and 'The Bantams' at Coventry, arguably the same as 'prowess', but here using a metaphor rather than a description).

Football is fond of mascots and these are often based on the nickname, but the mascot never seems to be the actual origin of the nickname. In the case of 'The Ziggers', a mascot was adopted which was also celebrated in a supporters' chant, becoming a nickname, but this seems to be the only case where a mascot *might have* inspired a nickname: arguably the chant came first. In the case of 'The Friars', the friar mascot was based on the original name of the club, Greyfriars at Kettering, and it is not known for certain that the friar was ever used as a nickname. Mascots now have their own book: Rick Minter's *Mascots. Football's Furry Friends* (Tempus 2004).

Turning to nicknames based on the club's own ground, this divides into those based on the name of the ground, and those describing some feature of the ground. Names based on the ground usually mean 'those who come from that place', expressed with the endings *–ers* or *–ites* or *–men*, such as 'Cottagers', 'The Rokerites' or 'The Rokermen', but occasionally the location of the ground generates the nicknames: 'Seals' from Sealand Road, 'Paraders' from Valley Parade.

The ground's features can be commemorated: 'The Hedgemen' records an enormous yew hedge running alongside the ground at Brechin, and 'The Kopites' records the name of a particular stand at Liverpool's stadium. 'The Gas' refers to an adjacent gasworks for Bristol Rovers.

The club's official name is a common source of nicknames, which can draw on the place-name, the suffix or both. The club name can be expressed as abbreviations, acronyms or initialisms. Abbreviations include A's, F1, K's and T's. Acronyms are words made from abbreviations, and football examples include 'Chenecks', 'Save' and 'Scow'. An initialism is where an abbreviation becomes so familiar that it forms a name in its own right (as in the cases of the BBC or the RAF). Not everyone would agree that some of these have switched from abbreviation to initialism, it just depends on the sense of familiarity. Football examples include 'AFC', 'B's', 'PNE', 'QPR', 'U's' and 'WBA'. Sometimes an initialism can even generate a new word altogether. 'The B's' often grows into 'The Bees', 'The Yows' expresses 'United', using a Scots word for female sheep, punning with the English word, 'ewes', standing for 'The U's'. These could be called 'metaphors for initialisms'. The abbreviation for Football Club United Manchester, FCUM, deliberately suggests an entirely different, rude expression. It is difficult to categorise, but it is perhaps best seen as an acronym.

Initialisms like 'The U's' often use an inverted comma. The wrong use of inverted commas is something which really upsets the average pedant, but here it is not standing for possession, as in 'United's game', but correctly marks abbreviation.

There are plenty of playful adaptations of the club names in football nicknames. 'The Roosters' is adapted from the sound of the letters in the Welsh place-name *–rwst*, sounding like 'roost', generating the pun 'roosters'. 'Daggers' comes from Dagenham, 'Hammers' is often used to express *–ham* in the club's place-name. 'Lawyers' comes from Tow Law, 'Sarnies' is a playful nickname for 'egg and ham', for the club at Egham in Surrey. 'Shots' and 'Swans' are well-known puns based on Aldershot and Swansea. Nicknames based on rhyming slang belong here, as playful adaptations of the club's official name, but which are frequently difficult to interpret: Hibernian generating 'Cabbage' through the rhyme of 'cabbage and ribs' with 'Hibs'. This entertaining category is discussed in more detail below.

Short forms are also common sources of nicknames, such as 'Ton' for a club name ending in *–ton*, as in Greenock Morton. Other examples are 'Field', 'Ford', 'Gate', 'Gers', 'Villa' and 'Wands', where the full names are Mangotsfield, Hurlford, Highgate, Rangers, Aston Villa and Wanderers. Sometimes the short form will change in pronunciation: 'fud' returns to 'ford' when it is separated, 'Gers' is easier to say as 'Jairs' rather than 'juss', and sometimes the short form may be preceded by a short pause, almost as if the brain feels the need to pronounce the inverted comma which usually marks abbreviation, to emphasise that something has been omitted (try saying out loud "Tomorrow, we're playing 'Ton" and see if an extra stress appears on the T). This change of pronunciation has a strange effect: it is quite visceral, seemingly gripping the word in a wrestling hold; like a call to arms it can send a shudder down your spine. 'Point', for Hurstpierpoint, has the same effect.

The specialised 'friendly short forms' tag a new ending onto the extracted letters to make a different word: Tiverton becomes 'Tivvy', Darlington 'Darlo'. These forms are called 'friendly' because such endings are usually used to convey affection. They are encountered throughout Britain, but they are more apparent in Scotland because they are a common feature of the Scots language. Because they are friendly personal names, they tend not to be preceded by 'The'. Football itself has such a nickname: 'footy'. This is significant: footy connotes friendly fun.

Finally, for nicknames based on the official names, the club suffix can be copied as a nickname: 'Albion', 'City', 'Rovers', 'Town', 'United', 'Wanderers', and many other words are often used on their own. Appendix 1 lists the words used as suffixes for the clubs mentioned in the book, and many of them are also in the Dictionary when they have been encountered as nicknames. The suffix may also mutate to a different form when it becomes a nickname (such as Aths or Latics adapted from Athletic). Because suffixes are such an interesting aspect of football names, they are also discussed in more detail below.

The club's playing strip (or colours, or 'uniform' is used in Scotland) is also the source of many nicknames. Some are straightforward descriptions of the colour: 'The Reds', 'The Blues' or 'The Gold and Blacks'. Others are metaphors for the colours: 'Badgers', 'Blackbirds', 'Bloods', 'Bluebells', 'Cardinals' or 'Cards', 'Magpies', 'Mono-chrome', 'Peppermints', 'Robins', 'Royals', 'Satsumas', 'Tigers', and 'Undertakers'.

Some describe the shapes on the strip rather than the colours: 'The Diamonds', 'The Hoops', 'The Spiders', 'The Spots', 'The Stripes'; or the shapes can be referred to metaphorically, as in 'The Barcodes' and even 'The Y-Fronts'. Some record both colours and shapes in an overall metaphor: 'Bees', 'Hornets', 'Humbugs', 'Peppermints', 'Tigers', 'Wasps' and 'Zebras', each of which stand for stripes in particular colours.

The Historical Football Kits website illustrates how club colours were not necessarily fixed in the early years of a club, probably because they originally made do with what was available, what they could afford or what would not compete with other clubs in the same league. When clubs had a choice, the colours chosen might have been for a reason (as 'Blac and Ambers' for Llanberis), but a choice *had* to be made. Once made, a club tradition might follow. Usually the colours inspire the nickname, but sometimes the nicknames comes first (e.g. 'The Canaries' at Norwich).

Nicknames based on the Club's Locality

This second major category divides into aspects of the location's human history or its natural history.

F O O T B A L L C L U B N I C K N A M E S	NAMES BASED ON THE CLUB	Names based on the club's history	memorable events	documented	*Munichs*
				undocumented	*River Boys*
			memorable people	managers	*Busby Babes*
				owners	*Fowlers*
				specific sides	*Lisbon Lions*
			perceived club qualities	expressions	*Posh*
				insulting	*Squatters*
				prowess	*Warriors*
				representative	*Lads*
				supporters' chants	*Hi-Hi*
				symbols	*Lions*
		Names based on the club's home ground	ground name	name of locality	*Paraders*
				name of ground	*Rokerites*
			ground features	general	*Hedgemen*
				based on stands	*Kopites*
		Names based on the club's official names	place-name or suffix or both	acronyms	*FCUM*
				initialisms	*U's*
				metaphors	*Bees*
				for initialisms	*Yows*
				puns	*Roosters*
				rhyming slang	*Jambos*
				short forms	*Ton*
				friendly short forms	*Tivvy*
				suffix	*Wanderers*
				suffix mutated	*Latics*
		Names based on the club's playing strip	strip colours	descriptive	*Reds*
				colour metaphors	*Robins*
			strip design	descriptive	*Hoops*
				design metaphors	*Spiders*
			whole strip	metaphors	*Wasps*
	NAMES BASED ON THE LOCALITY	Names based on human history	cultural history	folklore tales	*Pedlars*
				literature	*Honest Men*
				local heraldry	*Rams*
				songs	*Poachers*
				television	*Wombles*
			economic and social history	general to area	*Hatters*
				associative	*Cheesemen*
				specific institutions	*Welfare*
				metaphors	*Sooty*
			general history	local history	*The Witches*
				national history	*Zeplins*
			identity	national	*Saxons*
				regional	*Fifers*
			language	local dialect	*Ar Tarn* / *Jaggy Bunnets*
				meaning of the place-name	*Cuckoos* / *Martyrs*
				nicknames for the place or people	*Shannocks* / *Tribesmen*
				proverbial phrases	*Bairns*
		Names based on natural history	local animal species	birds	*Swans*
				mammals	*Squirrels*
			local geography	descriptive	*Seasiders*
				metaphors for type of place	*Seagulls* / *Stags*

In alphabetical order, we can subdivide human history into cultural history, economic and social history, general history, identity or language.

Five subcategories come under 'Cultural History'. Local folktales are celebrated in nicknames which refer to these stories, such as 'Cuckoos', 'The Imps', 'Monkey Hangers' and 'Pedlars'. The presentation of the locality in literature can be an inspiration, as in 'The Honest Men', 'Hearts', 'Ivanhoe' and perhaps also 'The Ghosts'; 'The Pickwicks' is obviously adapted from the Dickens novel, but may be based initially on a local club with the same name. Cardiff's 'Bluebirds' perhaps belongs here because it is traditionally explained as based on a local production of a drama. Local heraldry, for civic or aristocratic or regimental coats of arms, can be copied as a club badge, which then inspires a nickname ('The Black Dragons' at Porth, 'The Eagles' at Bedford, 'The Lions' at Andover, 'The Rams' at Derby, 'The Seahorses' at Whitley Bay). Heraldic use can also be from national symbols ('Red Dragons', 'Harp', 'Three Lions' or 'Thistle'). Folksongs often have a strong local reference, and 'The Poachers' is based on 'The Lincolnshire Poacher' song. Finally, even the presentation of the locality in television can inspire a football nickname, certainly the case in 'The Wombles', possibly also 'The Wurzels', though that unofficial nickname may refer to a folkband rather than the television character Worzel Gummidge.

The Economic and Social history of the locality is strongly represented with a great many nicknames referring to local industry. First 'general' references refer to a particular industry which used to dominate the locality's economy, but which would have been represented in many different businesses, such as 'The Hatters', 'The Silkmen' or 'The Lacemen'. However, some clubs started as sides attached to specific businesses or institutions, illustrated by 'The Welfare' clubs attached to the Miner's Welfare Institutes, the school and university sides and clubs representing individual businesses, so the nickname may record a specific institution rather than the general economy. Halfway between 'general' and 'specific' is an 'associative' category, where a product is associated with the place, but it does not dominate the local economy, such as 'The Toffees' for Everton, 'The Cheesemen' for Cheddar and 'The Smokies' for Arbroath. Finally, the local economy can still be referred to metaphorically, which justifies a separate category, such as 'Sooty' for a mining community, and 'Harbour Rats' or 'Pirates' for a port.

General History can be divided into 'local general', where the nickname commemorates an important aspect of the town's history, such as 'The Curfews', 'The Gable Endies', 'The Minstermen', 'The Puritans' or 'The Witches'; and 'national local' where some aspect of local history is important in national history, such as 'The Admirals', 'The Alfredians', 'The Arrows', 'The Cromwellians', or 'The Pilgrims'.

'Identity' is a subject already expressed in club suffixes, but it can also appear in a nickname. A regional example is Carlisle's 'The Cumbrians' and a national one is Stockport Sports, nicknamed 'The Saxons' with 'Storm the Saxon' as a mascot.

The final 'human' category is local language. Obviously, expressions made in a local dialect make for a category, even if the content of the expression would also mean the nickname could fit elsewhere. Examples include 'Ar Tarn' (and several other dialect words for 'Town'), 'Barlick', 'Bonnie Oodle', 'Brig', 'Brum', 'Dokens', 'Jaggy Bunnets', 'Loons', 'Peasy' and 'Posset'. Sometimes, nicknames coined in one language mutate slightly to fit the expected spelling or pronunciation of words in another, such as 'Pennies' and 'Y Darans'.

Under language also comes the original meaning of the place-name, where a nickname refers back to this. Nicknames based on scholarly etymologies might imply that some research has gone into the choice of nickname, but they may also illustrate the reception of scholary conclusions in the place itself, or continuing local pronunciation based on the original meaning. Examples include 'The Cuckoos' (at Yaxley, other uses record a folktale), 'The Adders', 'Brig', 'Eagles' (in some cases), 'Martyrs' and 'Wolves' (indirectly based on personal names within the place-names). Included here are also false etymologies, where the place-name has been believed to carry a certain meaning, even if this idea has been superceded. So, 'The Badgers' might appear for places with 'Broc' in the place-name, 'The Buzzards' for Leighton Buzzard, 'Maglonians' for Machynlleth, 'Wolves' for Louth (because of the similarity of *Lupa* and *Luda*). Even some medieval scribal forms appear as nicknames, such as 'Barum', 'Cestrians' and 'Salop'.

Many places, or the people who live in them, also have nicknames of their own, and these often transfer to the football club and make for another category: 'Brandanes', 'Cobbydalers', 'Cockney Boys', 'Covies', 'Dabbers', 'Doonhamers', 'Geordies', 'Grecians', 'Kingdom Boys', 'Mackems', 'Niseachs', 'Queen of the South', 'Shannocks', 'Shiners', 'Sons of the Rock', 'Sunset City', 'Tribesmen', 'Tykes' and 'Yeltz' belong here.

Finally, some places also have proverbial phrases about them, which are celebrated in the club nickname. 'The Bairns' refers to a Scots phrase 'Better meddle with the Devil than the bairns of Falkirk', 'The Hares' at March adopts 'Mad as a March hare', even if *that* March is the month rather than the Cambridgeshire town.

The natural history category is simpler: it divides into names based on the local presence of certain animals (not necessarily those animals adopted as club badges), and ones based on local geography. Here, animals divide into just birds or mammals (there are names based on insects but these refer to the club colours so they are not in this category). Birds include Crows, Kingfishers, Linnets, Rooks, Swans, and Throstles, here because the birds are present in the immediate vicinity of the club, or because the locality may have a famous breed ('The Ducks', for Aylesbury). Mammals, for the same reason, include Moles, Stags and Squirrels. But animals reappear in the next section for a different reason. For local geography, we have nicknames which are descriptive of the type of place: 'Borderers', 'Hillians', 'Islanders', 'Riversiders', 'Seasiders' and 'Villagers', but types of place can also be referred to metaphorically, so we have another section where 'Eagles' might refer to a mountainous place, 'Pewits' a moorland,

'Seagulls' a seaside place and 'Stags' for a forest location, whether the animal is actually present or not. It can be difficult to distinguish whether the animal is used metaphorically (poetically) or descriptively (factually).

Place-name scholars are reluctant to accept metaphorical meanings in place-names, because it is difficult to find evidence to support such interpretations, but they have been noted on occasion: moorland locations in Cornwall, Shropshire and Fife have been recorded using the lapwing, or pewit, bird as a metaphor, for instance. The village of Hart in Co. Durham has long been controversial: it is a place called 'deer'. It would make sense if first there was a timber building so called because the roof timbers resembled the impressive antlers of stags (this appears to be why the hall in the Old English poem *Beowulf* is called *Heorot*). The settlement which grew up around the hall then took the same name. This has happened in modern times too, with Nelson in Lancashire named from a Lord Nelson hotel (see under 'Admirals'). So, football's use of metaphors contributes a great deal to the science of name study.

The attached diagram records these categories with just an example or two for each. There are, perhaps surprisingly, as many as fifty different categories of football club nicknames in this arrangement. It may be difficult to place some of the nicknames in a category, because some could fit in more than one place, or because the meaning is unknown so one cannot decide, but I believe there is a category for each possible interpretation.

Rhyming Slang

The old Morris Minor car is affectionately known as a Moggie, but there is no clear connection between nickname and original other than the first two letters. It appears to have a missing link: Morris became Morrie, then Moggie because it was easier to pronounce (and perhaps more affectionate). This illustrates the tendency of nicknames to undergo radical mutation, using only parts of the original name to form the basis of a new one. When names are based only on alliteration or rhyming slang, however, it makes them difficult to explain. The Glasgow side, Rangers F.C., illustrates the same mutation as Moggie: Rangers is abbreviated to *'Gers*, which, as a separate word, is easier to pronounce as 'Gairs' rather than 'Juss', and so it rhymes with 'Bears', offering an alternative nickname to the club. Some even expand the new word into 'Teddy Bears', but how do you trace the journey from Rangers to Teddy Bears without knowing the intervening words? Watching for rhyming slang may also lead you to conclusions which are false. London slang uses 'Abergavenny' for 'penny'. The nickname of the Abergavenny club is 'Pennies', but this is based on a local place-name, not on Cockney rhyming slang.

A junior Glasgow side, Yoker Athletic, has an unusual nickname, 'The Whe Ho', which appears to be a Glaswegian rendering of the northern expression 'Away' ("Ha' Way the Lads" in Sunderland, "Whe ho the wee Yoker" in Glasgow). There remains some doubt whether this really is the explanation, but it is plausible and illustrates the tendency for phrases to adjust to rhyming positions (...ho / Yo...). It's pure poetry, with, of course, poetry's ability to confuse as well as charm. The investigation of this name revealed another rhyming expression, that being the tendency of supporters to call their side 'Our Landlords'. This is based on the rhyme club / pub. It has only been encounted by this researcher for Yoker, but it could perhaps be applied to any Scottish club.

Two more Scottish examples are 'Cabbage', an unlikely and incomprehensible nickname for Hibernian F.C., until one understands the rhyme 'cabbage and ribs' / Hibs; and 'Jam Tarts' for Heart of Midlothian F.C. (Tarts / Hearts). A diagram helps explain this sort of development. Perhaps we should call it a 'scrabble diagram':

HIBERNIAN	RANGERS
HIBS	'GERS
CABBAGE AND RIBS	BEARS
CABBAGE	TEDDY BEARS

The English language offers bizarre rhyming phrases where one word carries the meaning but the other is there simply to confuse matters: phrases like 'hoity-toity', 'nitty-gritty' and 'itsy-bitsy', based on the words haughty, grit, and bits. When a nickname uses the same type of construction, it is likely that 50% of the phrase is only there as filler, making it even harder to decipher. A lost rhyming phrase appears to have inspired 'The Trickies' for Northwich Victoria F.C. ('Tricky Vickies' is assumed).

A Northern Ireland example appears to be 'Cock 'n' Hens' for Glentoran F.C., based on a probable transitional nickname 'Glens'. A possible Irish example is 'The Money Men', for Mount Merrion YMCA F.C., though it does not quite fit as a rhyme; it seems to work better from the visual appearance of the letters.

England is not immune to this either. 'Sweeney' is a bizarre nickname for A.F.C. Guildford City, but it follows the Cockney slang 'Sweeney Todd' for 'Metropolitan Police Flying Squad', and then makes a political comment on the fate of the Guildford Four (notorious for having confessed to crimes they did not commit when under pressure from 'The Sweeney'). An example which is easier to understand is 'Jo Row' for the York works side Nestlé Rowntree F.C. (based on Joseph Rowntree).

Welsh nicknames certainly include some word play but there do not appear to be any formed from rhyming slang.

The Suffixes

A suffix is an expression added on to the end of something else. In football club names, we use it for those words such as Albion, City, Rovers, Town, United, or Wanderers which appear at the end of club official names. They are often used as nicknames in their own right, and may even be official names on their own, so I have included an appendix after the Dictionary, listing the various words encountered.

A common meaning is that of travel: Bohemians, Rangers, Rovers, Strollers,

Vikings, Wanderers, all have this sense. Clubs have to travel to play 'away games'. Clubs may not originally have had their own home ground, so some always travelled to play. 'Trotters' and 'Walkers' also appear, but with alternative explanations. 'Crusaders' and 'Vikings' also suggest travel, but with the extra ideology for bands of roving warriors.

Another frequent occurrence is a word which expresses nationality: Albion, Caledonians, Celtic, Cumbrians, Druids, Hibernians, sometimes because the club was formed for members of a cultural minority who wished to play as a team, such as Irish people living in Scotland (and the occurrence of 'The Geordies' for a London club), or because the club wished to display patriotism because they felt they were playing for the whole nation. Although 'Albion' means Britain, and occurs throughout Britain, it is used as a nationality name in England because there is no obvious alternative word for the English to use. Nationalism can also be expressed through a symbol, which can appear as a suffix or a nickname: Dragons, Harp, Jags, Lions, Thistle.

A smaller nation is the home community, and the suffixes County, City and Town are popular, together with Villa and the nickname 'Villagers', and other suffixes for institutes, such as Academical, Academy, College, Institute, University or YMCA. From the outset, football clubs adopted names which suggested they were representatives of their home, usually using the place-name of their location for this purpose. There is certainly a profound sense that a football team *is* playing for its home, and is staffed by the best its home has to offer.

A club's status may be recorded in the modest suffixes Amateurs, Casuals, and Juniors, though suffixes often suggest that the club is grander than it really is. 'United' suggests that it is the only club in a locality, and so represents the whole community, even though it may have several rivals. 'Inter' or International do seem rather exaggerated when used in the name of a village side, and 'Team' suggests the club plays in the Oympic Games. 'Galaxy' has become familiar from David Beckham playing for that American team, but inter-planetary games are only known in science fiction.

Some important national movements, providing social improvements, are reflected in the suffixes or nicknames, where a club was founded as a branch of that movement; examples include Blue Cross, British Legion, Comrades, Rechabites, Welfare and YMCA.

The suffix may mutate to a different word when it becomes a nickname. Examples include Alb (for Albion), Accies (for Academicals), Ammies and Ammers (for Amateurs), Citizens (for City), and Ath or Aths, Latics and Tic (for Athletic).

A great many of the suffixes or nicknames based on them, and also the names of leagues, display 'Classicalism': words like 'Corinthian', 'Olympian' (or 'Olympic'), 'Isthmian', 'Roman', 'Romulus', 'Spartan', all suggesting the revival of the ancient Olympic Games in modern times, and the sense that sporting prowess is so fundamental a human activity that it is in itself 'classical'.

The Definite Article, Pluralities and Compounds

Most of the nicknames begin with 'The', the 'definite article'. Interestingly, some do not, and it is not always obvious why. The definite article is used in language to define things, to refer to them specifically, and it appears within communities where everyone is familiar with the matter referred to, or in sentences where the object has previously been mentioned so, again, it is already familiar: "I'm going to the station" (everyone knows which), "There's a table over there, put the parcel on the table" (everyone knows which table because it was mentioned before). So, why do some football club nicknames have 'The' and others do not? They are *names*, and names are not usually preceded by 'the' because they are already sufficiently unique to need no further definition (one would not normally say "The David Beckham", for instance).

Where the nickname is a 'friendly short form' it has no definite article because it is functioning the same way as a personal name: "I'm watching Tivvy tomorrow", "Pompey are playing The Reds" (not "The Pompey are playing Reds"). These names fully function like personal names or place-names.

An older reference book, Johnson 1934, regularly uses the expression 'The United'. This phrase is now very unexpected, because 'United' has become so familiar that we assume it means Manchester United, and because of the dominance of that name, all instances of United tend to lose the definite article as well. There is a further push in this direction because 'United' is so much easier to pronounce than 'The United', where the unexpected lack of a following noun makes one hesitate.

In the case of 'The Reds' or 'The Lads', the names are functioning in the same way as ordinary nouns rather than proper nouns, even though they are definitely names. Within the community of Sunderland, everyone knows who 'The Lads' are, but because the words are also ordinary nouns in everyday speech, the brain prefers them to continue functioning that way. What about 'The Posh'? Here, one does not quite expect the definite article, because 'posh' is never heard anywhere else as a noun. Even in the case of 'Posh Spice', it continues to function as an adjective, then becomes part of Mrs Beckham's name as soon as 'Spice' is mentioned, so it no longer needs 'the'. Language is happy to accept plural adjectives on their own as nouns because they are assumed to be followed by an unspoken noun, such as 'men', but it is unexpected to have an adjective in the singular, on its own, and preceded by 'the'. The definite article here marks 'The Posh' out as a unique entity, it makes it into a name, even if one would then expect it to lose its 'The'. It seems to need to keep it because it is an adjective. The construction needs that extra help to trigger the right response in the brain.

Indeed, sometimes the definite article can emphasise as well as refer. In 'The Club' for Sheffield F.C., it marks it out for special emphasis, a tribute to its unique position as the oldest football club in the world. It goes against what is normally expected in English, to have 'the' in a singular proper noun, but here this generates a sense of greater emphasis in the brain. It would be frightening enough to encounter 'Attila the Hun'. To encounter 'The Hun' would be to face overwhelming odds, the

21

entire barbarian nation acting as one.

The difference between singular and plural forms also appears in other nicknames. Usually, one expects 'The Black and Whites' to refer to the team, the players, but 'The Black and White' (singular) would refer to the club. Some clubs sport both plural and singular forms for the same nickname, there is not necessarily a consistent pattern. The same ambiguity is found with the noun 'club': is it a singularity or a plurality? 'The club plays in red' is just as acceptable as 'The club play in red'. So it is no surprise to find a lack of consistency in the nicknames also.

Another phenomenon is that compound nicknames often run as two words for several years before evolving into a single word. York City started using 'The Minster Men' (in Rothmans 1972–3), which eventually became 'The Minstermen' (in Rothmans 1982–3); other examples include 'Railwaymen', 'Bluebirds', and 'Chairboys'. If the first word ends in a soft sound such as –er, the joining process is made easier, but if it ends in a stressed sound suggesting finality, it is harder for it to evolve into a single word (e.g. 'Walnut Boys' cannot combine, but 'Blueboys' can), and if the combination would create a difficult spelling or pronunciation, it also tends to keep the two words apart ('Gable Endies', 'Merry Millers'). When it happens, though, it marks a development in the nickname's evolution, from a simple description made of common nouns into a unique proper noun, a name.

These observations raise interesting, but rather 'abstract', questions about how names function grammatically, and it is good to see football contributing to that debate.

Joy

Football brings out the best in people, and the nicknames reveal a sense of fun and merry banter, which seems to be less apparent in other sports. Today, the dominance of the money men seems to have stolen football from many of its supporters, with fewer matches being shown on mainstream television or even on the internet because the money men think they own the very photons bouncing off the players and entering the eyes of spectators! The nicknames seem to defy the cynical commercialism of the game, as genuine expressions of supporters' love for their team and, yes, a playful respect for other sides.

The births of rebel clubs such as Football Club United Manchester are protests against the theft of the game from the people, but the rise in popularity of the 'non-league' and 'junior' game must, surely, also be understood in this context. Football has a reputation as 'the people's game', but the 'top flight' game is snobby and elitist and expensive, and even has rules to exclude clubs from their own leagues when they have financial difficulties, as if wealth was remotely relevant to sporting ability. Few clubs survive this vicious treatment. Financial fines and penalty points, when a club ought to be given help, quickly remove the social embarrassment from the league. Football should not have the same snobbery which excluded non-aristocrats from medieval jousts, or athletes from the early Olympic Games because they were not 'gentlemen'.

There really is no reason at all why a club which has financial problems should be denied a share of the Premier League bounty (all coming from media 'fees'), when it has already earned a place in the league by its prowess.

But football still flourishes because everybody loves it. The use of classical names like 'Corinthians' and 'Spartans' for clubs and leagues, and the flamboyant use of heraldry (the coats of arms and badges that every club and league has throughout the world) shows how football has long believed itself to be just as important as, and perhaps more worthy than, the aristocracy, royalty and all the governments and churches of the world, with their meaningless, arbitrary rules, daft social pretensions and subtle corruption.

Two historical events from the First World War show how football expresses the best of mankind, and how football is sometimes 'against' the worst of mankind. In 1914, many soldiers in different parts of the Western Front stopped fighting on Christmas Day and in some places it is recorded that friendly free-for-all football matches took place between opposing sides in 'No-Man's Land', to the fury of the ruling elites. In 1999, a monument was erected near Ypres recording this event, and giving the players a nickname: 'the Khaki Chums'. There could be no better illustration of the integrity of football against an otherwise nasty world.

On the home front, women were employed in the armaments factories and began to play football matches against teams from other factories. In the First World War, women's football flourished. The most famous women's team of the time was the Dick Kerr Ladies from Preston. They were so popular that they even went on an overseas tour and played against men's teams. In 1921, the Football Association heartlessly suppressed the whole movement and women's football was banned from FA grounds until 1971; now it is flourishing again. Football needs disciplinary and administrative institutions, but the powers-that-be have not always acted in the interests of the game or supported those whose only offence was that they simply wanted to play football.

The late Bill Shankly (1913–81) was famously quoted as saying 'Someone said to me "To you, football is a matter of life or death!" and I said "Listen, it's more important than that".' Presumably he meant by this that football expresses human values which are universals, hence more important than the day-to-day concerns of individual lives; and this is correct. Whether one likes football or not, one cannot deny its social significance, its cultural impact and how much it matters to supporters. There is a further illustration of this idea in the nicknames: they seem to touch on every subject under the sun, as if, collectively, football really is a universe. No other sport on Earth can claim this.

They are 'the beautiful names'.

The Entries

Each entry in the Dictionary attempts to give the official name of the club, its year of foundation and its location. I have mostly used the modern county names and boundaries. 'London' in the entries means 'Greater London'. The county is not always given for famous places.

After a discussion or explanation for the nickname, there are details of any dating evidence from printed sources. In recent years, the number of printed references has increased enormously, so excessive duplication is avoided, but the earliest known reference, and records which appear in different decades, are always included. Because the nicknames in the Williams directories come and go from year to year, the span expressions (e.g. W1994–2013) do not necessarily mean the nickname appears in every single year, but if there are long gaps between the records, the dates are separated; otherwise, the references are only to the years in which the nickname is mentioned, not to where the club is mentioned without a nickname. Most of the sources record the nickname without an explanation, which often has to be interpreted from background information found elsewhere, so the reference is to the nickname's appearance, rarely to any explanation. Printed sources take priority over the internet because they are dated and unchanging, but sometimes a nickname is only recorded on the internet, which is acknowledged, but there can be no guarantee that the record will always be there. For the smaller clubs, the importance of Wikipedia cannot be overstated, as it is often the only source for a nickname in any media.

Older literature often uses different expressions for football kit. On the whole, simple modern expressions are used in the entries: 'shirts', 'shorts', 'socks' and 'strip' rather than 'jerseys', 'nickers', 'stockings' or 'uniform' (the last is still a popular word in Scottish football).

The entries finish with cross references to other nicknames for the same club.

Where several clubs share the same nickname, they are presented as subdivisions of the one entry, with a football bullet.

Repeated references to the club's official name in the discussions, or lists of its earlier names, are often abbreviated; frequently cited sources are also abbreviated, and there is a list of such abbreviations in the bibliography at the back.

The majority of nicknames begin with 'The', but this has been omitted in the headings.

THE DICTIONARY

A's is a nickname for three clubs which have a suffix beginning with A in their official names. The clubs are:

⚽ Banstead Athletic F.C. Founded in Surrey in 1944, originally as Banstead Juniors, the name changed to Athletic in 1947, from which the nickname comes; recorded in W1979/80–2013.

⚽ Headington Amateurs F.C., founded in Oxford in 1949, where the nickname is an abbreviation of the word Amateurs; W1994–2013.

⚽ Walthamstow Avenue F.C., founded in London in 1900 and closed in 1988, recorded in W1979/80. See also Avenue.

Abbey was the nickname of Waltham Abbey F.C., founded in Essex in 1944; recorded in W1994–2001; a short form of the place-name. See also Abbots.

Abbies is the nickname of Abercorn Amateurs F.C., founded at Paisley in 1877, closed 1920 but reborn in 2009; a pluralised friendly short form of the place-name, but also punning on the fact that Abercorn is the site of one of the most ancient abbeys in Scotland, mentioned by Bede (writing in 731). Although the original abbey is not in Paisley, the two names became associated in the seventeenth century when the Earl of Abercorn became also Lord Paisley, so it features in Paisley place-names.

Abbots is the nickname for two clubs with medieval Benedictine abbeys in their home town. An abbot was the head of such a monastery. The clubs are:

⚽ Abingdon Town F.C., founded in Oxfordshire in 1870. The nickname appears in W2000–13. See also Over the Bridge, Town.

⚽ Waltham Abbey F.C., founded in Essex in 1944; W2007–13. See also Abbey.

Aber is a common nickname in Wales for towns with a place-name that begins with *Aber–*, meaning a river mouth or estuary, and so might be used for any club from such a place. It has been noticed for the following:

⚽ Aberaman Athletic F.C., founded in Aberdare in Rhondda Cynon Taf in 1893; the club has gone through several name changes in successive mergers and separations with the neighbouring Aberdare Athletic or Town. A combined club was again founded in 1945, only to separate once more in 1947, and then Aberaman F.C. rebranded itself as Aberdare Town in 2012; the nickname is recorded in RW1994–2011.

⚽ Aberdare Athletic F.C., founded in Rhondda Cynon Taf in 1892, folding after a failed merger with the above club in 1928, but reformed in 1947 as Aberdare Town. This club is also called 'Aber' on the present club website. See also Darians.

⚽ Aberystwyth Town F.C., see also Black and Greens, Seagulls, Seasiders.

Aber Uni is the nickname of Aberystwyth University F.C., as a short form of the official name; recorded in RW2011. See also Students.

Academical is a football club suffix, for clubs associated with a school or an academy. The earliest are Scottish clubs, such as the surviving Hamilton Academical (1874), and Ayr Academicals (1876–9), but there is also a Northern Irish rugby club, Omagh A., the Welsh Cardiff Academicals and now the University College of London side. The word originally appears in the singular, but the pluralising –s has crept in, probably under the influence of the nicknames based upon it: Academicals, Acas and Accies.

Academy is the nickname for Cirencester Football Academy F.C., founded in Gloucestershire in 1996 in a partnership between C. College and C. Town F.C.; recorded in W1998–2003.

Academy of Football / Academy is now another official nickname for West Ham United F.C. The title was given to the club by the London media in recognition of the club's successful youth development system, established by the manager Ted Fenton in the 1950s. Pickering 1994 records the nickname as 'Academy of Soccer'. See also Claret and Blues, Cockney Boys, Eastenders, Hammers, Hamsters, ICF, Irons, Wet Sham.

Acas / Accies are nicknames for clubs with the word Academical or Academy in their official name. The clubs are:

☉ Cardiff Academicals F.C., founded in 1979; the nickname is used on the club's own website; also Huws 2013.

☉ Dumbarton Academy Former Pupils A.F.C., founded in 1911.

☉ Hamilton Academical F.C., founded in Lanarkshire in 1874, as a school side for the famous Hamilton Academy (founded in 1588). *Acas* was the earlier nickname. The 1975 club history used it in its title: *Acas Centenary Yearbook*. Recorded (as Accies) in the 1936 Thomson 'stamp' album, G1956–76, Avis 1966–70, through RY1972/3–SSY2012/13 and RS 1993–2012. The AFBC records enamel badges with 'Accies'.

☉ U.C.L. Academical F.C., founded in 1985 at University College, London.

Aces is the nickname of Pontymister F.C., founded in Gwent in the mid 1950s. Ancestor clubs with various names resulted in A.C. Pontymister in the late 1970s, from which the nickname comes (from the initials of Athletic Club); used on the club's own website; also Huws 2013.

Acorns was the nickname of two clubs. The clubs are:

☉ Newton Aycliffe F.C., founded in Co. Durham in 1965. The place-name Aycliffe means 'oak-tree wood or clearing' (Mills 1991), and Acorns is frequently used as a name for businesses and institutions in the town; W1985 and 1992–4. See also Aycliffe.

☉ Oakham United F.C., founded in 1969 and closed in 1996. The club was based in Sutton-in-Ashfield, Nottinghamshire, not in Oakham, the capital of Rutland. To add to the confusion, the nickname would have been entirely relevant to a club based in the tiny county, which uses the acorn as one of its symbols, because of the proverb 'From tiny acorns mighty oak trees grow'. The proverb may be the explanation for the nickname, or it may refer to the Sherwood Forest location of Sutton-in-Ashfield; the Williams directories do not record the nickname, but do give Major Oak Securities as one of the sponsors (W1995–6), which perhaps offers another possible explanation.

Adders is the nickname of two clubs, based on earlier interpretations of the meaning of the place-name. The clubs are:

- Adderbury Park F.C., founded in Oxfordshire in 1995. The club badge in AFBC displays the snake's open mouth, but the place-name records a personal name, Eadburh (Mills 1991).

- Atherstone Town F.C. founded in Warwickshire in 2004, but succeeding an old club of the same name, 1887–1979, and its successor A. United, 1979–2003. The club's badge displays two interlocking snakes and the club ground is called The Snake Pit. Nevertheless, the nickname is based on the place-name, in the belief that it referred to the snake (Mills 1991 gives the Domesday form as *Aderestone*). The nickname is inherited from the older club: recorded in Avis 1966–70, W1983/4–2004; W2007–13.

Addicks is the nickname of Charlton Athletic F.C. Founded in 1905, the club became nicknamed The Haddocks soon after. This is because a local fishmonger, Arthur Bryan, had a catering contract with the club and treated the players (visitors too) to a haddock and chip dinner, and he was also noted for parading haddocks on poles around the ground for publicity's sake before a match. A series of cartoons in the *Kentish Independent* traces the development of the nickname. On 31 October 1908 it is printed as Haddocks and by 1910 this had changed to Haddicks and then Addicks, due to local pronunciation beginning to dominate the spelling of the word. There are alternative explanations for the name, that it is a corruption of Addicts or Athletic (q.v.), but the printed cartoons discount these theories, which are in any case improbable: Addicts would more naturally apply to the fans rather than the club, and a more likely London mutation of *ath–* would be to *aff–*, but *haddocks* to *addicks* is entirely natural. Churchill 1958, Harvey 1959, Richards 1960, Avis 1966–70 and the Vernon 1970–1 pamphlet, record the name in the form Haddicks, half-way between the original and final forms, but itself confirming the origin of the word as Haddocks. Even more suprising is the late appearance of Haddocks itself in SWSCYB 1962–3. Pickering 1994 has both spellings but inexplicably regards the nickname as redundant. Both the Rothmans and Williams series of League yearbooks start with Haddicks but use Addicks from Williams 1991–5 and RY1991/2 to SSY2012/13. The Rothmans series include all four nicknames of the club in various editions but have listed Addicks alone since RY1994/5. See also Haddicks, Haddocks, Red Army, Robins, Valiants.

Admirals is a new nickname for Nelson F.C., founded in 1881. The Lancashire place-name was a fresh coining for a new textile town, and was taken from a nearby Lord Nelson Inn (see Mills 1991), itself named from the famous Admiral Horatio Nelson (1758–1805), who in this extraordinary circular process is now the source of the nickname; club website and Wikipedia. See also Blues, Seedhillers.

Aelwyd is the Welsh word for 'home', but used to mean 'youth club' in the national Urdd Gobaith Cymru movement, and it is the suffix and a nickname for Rhos Aelwyd F.C., founded in 1943 at Rhosllanerchrugog in Wrexham Co. Bor. The club merged with Ponciau Aelwyd in 1958 and is now based in Ponciau; Wikipedia, club's own website and Huws 2013. See also Rhos.

AFC / A.F.C. is the standard abbreviation for Association Football Club, but it is used as a nickname in its own right for the club called A.F.C. Wimbledon, founded in London in 2002 in protest against the original club's relocation to Milton Keynes and its subsequent renaming as Milton Keynes Dons F.C. The nickname is therefore in deliberate contrast to the other successor of this ancient club, originally founded in 1889. See also Crazy Gang, Dons, Wombles.

Afton is a nickname for Glenafton Athletic F.C., founded in Ayrshire in 1930; club's own website. See also Glens.

Aggie is the nickname for St Agnes F.C., founded in Cornwall before 1978 (FCHD). The nickname is a friendly short form of the saint's name, recorded in W1992–4.

Airmen is the nickname for RAF St Mawgan F.C., founded in Cornwall before 1959 (FCHD), for staff at this RAF station; printed in W1992–3.

Airportmen is a new nickname for Stansted F.C., founded in 1902. The village is dominated by the major international airport of Stansted, hence the nickname; Wikipedia. See also Blues.

Albatross is a popular bird, regarded as a symbol of good luck by seafarers. It was adopted as a club name by a Glasgow side between 1876 and 1880; SFHA.

Albert is the nickname for two Scottish clubs, for the same reason. The clubs are:

⚽ Hawick Royal Albert F.C., founded in Roxburghshire in 1947. The club plays at Albert Park, though only since 1963. The 'Royal Albert' phrase in the club name is actually borrowed from Royal Albert F.C., see next entry, because a founder member was from Larkhall; RS1993–7, 2000–1. See also Royalists, Sleeping Giants.

⚽ Royal Albert F.C., founded in the South Lanarkshire town of Larkhall in 1878. The club was originally a colliery works side and the owner of the mine, Captain Johns, named the club after his private yacht, *The Royal Albert*; Wikipedia, SFHA.

Albies is the nickname of Evans and Williams Sports A.F.C., founded in 1960, originally as Evans and Williams United, renaming in 1967. The club was originally a works side for the Evans and Williams Wagon Works in Llanelli, Carmarthenshire, and takes its nickname from one of the founders of the business, Albert Evans; a pluralised friendly form of Albert; club's own website and Huws 2013.

Albion is the ancient name for Britain, recorded by the Ancient Greeks. It became popular in the eighteenth and nineteenth centuries in poetry and street and pub names, and it became a football club suffix. It seems slightly odd that a football club should call itself 'Britain', but the explanation lies in English nationalism, which has taken 'Albion' to its heart because it lacks a suitable word of its own: the Welsh, the Scots and the Irish have nationalistic 'people' names (Celts, Cambrians, Caledonians, and Hibernians), but there has never been a fashion for English football clubs to call themselves Angles or Saxons. So, although 'Albion' definitely means 'Britain', and its use is not entirely confined to England, it is primarily used to express English nationalism because of its poetic charm and the lack of an attractive alternative word. Many of the clubs are Victorian foundations, but later coinings, around the time of the Second World War, are more suggestive of the whole of Britain as they are not confined to England. In Scotland, the name may be used to suggest that the club is non-sectarian, because the name appeals to everyone. Occasionally, there is the possibility that the Albion suffix was taken from another use, such as Albion in a business name. Two other possible explanations may be discounted. The possible origin of the word in the White Cliffs of Dover (Latin *albus*, white) would make it suitable for clubs which play in a white strip, but few of the 'Albion' clubs do so. The word could express a spirit of defiance, the phrase 'Perfidious Albion' occurring in a French work of 1793 and the expression was later popularised by being attributed to Napoleon, so in this spirit it makes some sense as a sporting name, but no such connection is ever suggested. The most famous, and early, adoption of the name is by West Bromwich Albion, and this certainly influenced more takers. There are plenty of clubs called Albion which do not use it as a nickname, but it has been noticed for the following (and see Huws 2013 for several more in Wales):

- Aberford Albion F.C., founded in West Yorkshire in 1906; club website.
- Albion Rovers A.F.C. (Newport), founded in 1937. The Welsh club was formed by Scottish coalminers from Coatbridge, who named the club after their local Scottish side. The Welsh club takes the Albion nickname, for the Scottish club see Wee Rovers.
- Brighton and Hove Albion F.C., founded in 1901. Johnston 1934 refers to the club as 'Albion', and the nickname appears in RY from 1971/2 to 1977/8. Pickering 1994 records it late. See also Dolphins, Flippers, Seagulls, Seasiders, Seaweed, Shrimps, Tesco's.
- Burton Albion F.C., founded in Staffordshire in 1950; recorded in Avis 1966–70. See also Brewers.
- Forfar Albion F.C., founded in Angus in 1974, in a merger between F. Celtic (1891) and F. East End (1881). For one season, the club was called Forfar East End Celtic before adopting the present name; SFHA.
- Grange Albion A.F.C., founded in Grangetown, Cardiff in 1942, in a merger of the football side (1933) of a baseball club (originally formed in 1907) with Stockland Rovers. The club is nicknamed 'The Albion' in the *South Wales Echo* on April 28 1988. The club still has a baseball image on its club badge; website, Huws 2013.

⚽ Ossett Albion A.F.C., founded in West Yorkshire in 1944; W1986–2013. See also Golds, Unicorns.

⚽ Ryton & Crawcrook Albion F.C., founded in Tyne and Wear in 1970, originally as Ryton, renaming as Albion in 2011.

⚽ Sandy Albion F.C., founded in Bedfordshire in 1909. The club was renamed 'Sandy F.C.' after a merger in about 2000; W1994.

⚽ Shepshed Albion F.C., founded in Leicestershire originally in 1890 or 1891, but the earlier club was reformed and renamed as S. Charterhouse in 1975. This club reverted to its Albion suffix in 1991 and appears so in W1992–3 with the nickname 'Albion'. The club then folded and was replaced in 1994 by S. Dynamo. See also Charterhouse, Dynamo, Raiders.

⚽ Splott Albion F.C., founded in the Splott area of Cardiff in 1968, when it broke away from an earlier called Bridgend Street (see Street); club website.

⚽ Stirling Albion F.C., founded in 1945. Recorded in RY1988/9–90/1 and in *Panini's Football Yearbook 1988/89–89/90*, and RS 1993–2011; and in Pickering 1994, who adds the story, under 'Annfield Park', that the club originally had no stands and was so named because officials used to watch the match from the back of Albion lorries. Albion Motors was a Scottish company, based in Scotstoun, Glasgow, absorbed into Leyland Motors in 1951, and certainly made commercial trucks. The previous club, King's Park (1875–1944), had suffered war damage to its stadium, and Annfield Stadium was built for the new club in 1945, the same year of foundation. The lorry story must be apocryphal, because the stadium opened promptly (in August) and there is no record that the club existed before it was called Albion. See also Binos, Yo-Yos.

⚽ West Bromwich Albion; founded in 1878 as West Bromwich Strollers, the suffix was changed to Albion in 1880. The usage derives from an early support base in the Albion Industrial Estate, which itself would be named from the traditional poetic usage (see www.baggies.com; this is also mentioned in BoF1905–6, p. 136, as 'Albion district'). All three main nicknames for the club (Albion, Baggies, Throstles) appear throughout RY1970/1–SSY2012/13, and the suffix is used early as a nickname, in BoF1905–6. See also Baggies, Bennies, Boing!, Nigger Minstrels, Sandwell Town, Stripes, Strollers, Tatters (for a possible connection), Team of Boys, Tesco's, Throstles, W.B.A.

⚽ Witton Albion F.C., founded in Cheshire in 1890; W1979/80–2013. See also Albs.

Albs is a pluralised short form of Albion, recorded as a nickname for Witton Albion F.C. (see previous entry), in Miller & Wright 1996. See also Albion.

Ale House Brawlers was a temporary unofficial nickname for Southampton F.C. during the 1970s when Bill Shankly of Liverpool labelled them so after a robust performance (Pickering 1994, Seddon 2004, p. 212).

Alex is a nickname for two clubs which have the personal name 'Alexandra' in their official name, either taken from the Princess of Wales (since 1863), who became queen in 1901, or from another institution named after her. The name makes sense in the context of other clubs called Albert or Victoria (which also might be for ambiguous reasons). There was an early club using the name, Alexandra Athletic F.C., founded in Glasgow in 1873, closed in 1884, but the club played at Alexandra Park, named after the Princess of Wales in 1870, leaving it unclear if the football club was named after the Princess or the Park. An early Northern Irish club to use the name was Coleraine Alexandra (see Bannsiders). This short form nickname neatly avoids the frequent confusion over the spelling of the name. The clubs are:

- Crewe Alexandra F.C. The Cheshire club was founded in 1877 as Crewe F.C. but soon adopted the second name, but no-one seems to know exactly when, and the reason is not quite clear either. The name may have been chosen directly from the princess, but the pub in which early meetings was held was called The Princess Alexandra, and for a while the club played on the Alexandra Recreation Ground. The current ground was only renamed Alexandra Stadium in 2000. G1976 has the nickname. See also Railwaymen, Robins.

- Mold Alexandra F.C., founded in Flintshire in 1929 from an earlier church mission side. The name is difficult to explain. The club tradition (on Wikipedia) is that the suffix in the club name was taken from the title of an *Alexandra Hymn Book*, a copy being nearby during a crucial meeting at the birth of the club. However, this tradition cannot be confirmed, not least because no hymn book of that name exists, or any other by Queen Alexandra. There is, however, an Alexandra Road in Mold (possibly relevant?), and the queen had died in 1925 (not long before the club was formed); there was a famous writer of hymns called Cecil Frances Alexander (author of 'All Things Bright and Beautiful'), whose evangelical hymns would certainly have been suitable for a club attached to a mission church. Alexander and Alexandra are easily and frequently confused (Alexandria even appears sometimes), but the contradiction in two very famous names still makes the story slightly difficult to accept. Nevertheless, the hymn book and the recent death of the queen could have provided the inspiration for the name, with further encouragement no doubt drawn from the fame of the long-established Crewe Alexandra, which is geographically not far from Mold; recorded in W1994–5 and RW1996–2011.

Alfredians is the nickname for Wantage Town F.C., founded in 1892. Wantage in Berkshire is the birthplace of King Alfred the Great (c.848), who is celebrated with a statue in the centre of the town, and the club's home ground is called Alfredian Park. At the time of the club's foundation, Alfred was a major cult figure for the Victorians; W1998–2013.

All Whites is the nickname of two clubs, for their distinctive strip. The clubs are:

- Caerau All Whites F.C., founded in Bridgend Co. Bor. and recorded on the internet with references from 1990 to 2010. An old enamel badge of the club is recorded in AFBC. The expression has an obvious meaning as a description of the strip colours but it is significant as a rare use of 'All' for a football club. It is commonly used in rugby, both in Britain and overseas, and this club is in a 'rugby' area.

☺ Clifton F.C., founded in Nottinghamshire in 1963, originally as Thistledown Rovers. The nickname is frequently used in online match reports. Wikipedia calls the club 'Clifton' and uses 'Clifton All Whites' as a nickname.

Alltudion is the Welsh word for 'Exiles', q.v.

Alma was the nickname of Alma Swanley F.C., founded in Swanley in Kent in 1963, but folding in 1994. The nickname and part official name appears to be the same word as that in the Latin expression 'alma mater', meaning nursery mother, used affectionately by graduates for their old school or college, but the reason for its use in the name of Swanley's former football club is not clear. W1983/4–5, 1989–94.

Almonds is the nickname of both Almondsbury UWE F.C., founded in 1969, originally as Patchway North End but now associated with the University of Western England; and Almondsbury Town A.F.C., founded in 1897, originally as A. Greenway (W1979/80–88), then A. Picksons (W1989–90, 1992–3), then Town (W1995–2011). The Bristol sides make a pun from the first element of their place-name, though originally this was a Saxon personal name (perhaps Æthelmond).

Alpha is a nickname of Cardiff Corinthians A.F.C., founded in 1898, when the Alpha Cricket Club formed a football side; the word is the name of the first letter in the Greek Alphabet, so not only suggesting 'first' but also another example of Greek Classicalism, like the Corinthian suffix itself; Wikipedia. See also Cards, Corinthians, Corries.

Alphas is a nickname for Alphington F.C., founded in Devon before 1992 (when it appears on FCHD); a pluralised short form used in *This is Devon*, 3 May 2010, and club's own website.

Amateurs is a football club name element, for clubs which do not have professional (that is, salaried) status. See also A's, Ammers and Ammies, for adaptations of the word. Four clubs using it as a nickname are:

☺ Blaenau Festiniog Amateurs F.C., founded in Gwynedd in 1980 (after a succession of previous clubs). The suffix and nickname are a deliberate response to the semi-professional status of the previous club; Wikipedia and club's own website. See also Comrades, Quarry Men.

☺ Caersws F.C., founded in Powys in 1887, originally as C. Amateurs, renaming in 1974; Wikipedia. See also Bluebirds.

☺ Corinthian Casuals F.C. Based in Tolworth near Kingston-upon-Thames, the club was formed in 1939 as a merger between Corinthian (1882) and Casuals (1878); Wikipedia. See also Casuals, Corinthians, Pink and Chocolate.

☺ Cottesmore Amateurs F.C., founded in Rutland and recorded in the FCHD from 1992; *Stamford Mercury* 5.10.2012.

☺ Girvan F.C. founded in Ayrshire in 1947, originally as Girvan Amateurs; recorded in RS1995–7, SFHA. See also Seasiders.

☺ Lincoln United F.C., founded in 1938 as Lincoln Amateurs, but the original name was abandoned in 1951 when they signed a player who was paid a salary (Wikipedia).

- Queen's Park F.C., founded in Glasgow in 1867, and the oldest surviving Association Football Club in Scotland. The club is also the only amateur side in Scottish senior football, so the word is occasionally used to describe them in internet forums because it refers to a unique characteristic. The club's motto is *Ludere causa ludendi*, 'to play for the sake of playing'. See also Glorious Hoops, Queen's, Q.P., Spiders.

Amber and Blacks is the nickname of Handsworth F.C., founded in South Yorkshire in 2003, for the strip colours; W2012.

Ambers is a nickname for clubs which play in this colour, a shade of yellow. The clubs are:

- Builth Wells F.C., founded in Powys in 1879 or 1883; recorded in RW2011. The club plays in amber shirts with black shorts. See also Black and Ambers, Bulls, Wyesiders.
- Cheshunt F.C., founded in Hertfordshire in 1946; W1994–2013.
- Falmouth Town F.C., founded in Cornwall in 1950; for their amber and black strip; W2008–13. See also Town.

Ammers is the nickname of Yorkshire Amateurs A.F.C., founded in 1918 and based in Leeds. The nickname chimes with the more famous 'Hammers' but means Amateurs; W1999–2013. See also Hammers.

Ammies is the nickname of Salford City F.C., founded in Greater Manchester in 1940. The nickname appears on the club's badge as well, and it is also used for clubs in Barnstaple and Kilsyth. It is a friendly short form of 'Amateurs', for a non-professional side. Salford is currently semi-professional, but old nicknames stick; W1983/4–2013.

Ams is a nickname for three clubs, which are:

- Lambourne Sports F.C., founded in Berkshire in 1946. The nickname (recorded on Wikipedia) seems to be either a short form of the place-name or of 'Amateurs', though it is not recorded that the club was officially called Amateurs.
- Wellington Amateurs F.C., founded in Shropshire in 1950, originally as Old Wellingtonians, by former pupils of Wellington Grammar School. The club website records that the club renamed after it was discovered that some players were not former pupils, and it took the Amateurs suffix to distinguish it from W. Town. The 'Ams' nickname appears on the club badge.
- Wythenshawe Amateurs F.C., founded in Greater Manchester in 1946. A club badge is illustrated in AFBC; Wikipedia.

Anchormen is the nickname of Darwen F.C., founded in Lancashire in 1870, and reformed in 2009 as A.F.C. Darwen. The name refers to that of their home turf, The Anchor Ground; recorded in W1979/80–90. See also Darreners, Salmoners.

Ancients is a nickname for four clubs, but it is often unclear exactly what it refers to. It can refer to the ancient history in the club's vicinity, or in its official name, or it can be used for a club of exceptionally long duration. The clubs are:

- ⚙ Cefn Druids F.C., founded in 1992 in a merger between Cefn Albion and Druids United (founded in 1869, renamed Druids in 1872); recorded in RW 1995–2011. The club is based at Cefn Mawr near Wrexham and both Ancients and Druids were nicknames used by Druids United. The word here seems more likely to refer to the ancient history of Albion and the Druids rather than the longevity of the football club, but the club is also the oldest surviving in Wales. See also Druids, Zebras.

- ⚙ Norton and Stockton Ancients F.C., founded in the historic county of Durham (Cleveland, now an unitary authority) in 1959 as Norton F.C., and assuming the place of Stockton F.C. (1882–1975) after its closure. The name and nickname are from the older Stockton club (see below). Norton itself can claim some ancient history, in that St Mary's church is one of the oldest Saxon churches in the North, and the club has adopted an Anglo-Saxon cross as its badge, but the nickname does not refer to this; W1985–2013.

- ⚙ St Andrews Ancient City Athletic, founded in Fife in 1893 and closed in 1901; here the official name ties the word specifically to the ancient history of the city.

- ⚙ Stockton F.C., founded in Cleveland in the historic county of Durham in 1882, closed in 1975; the nickname is printed in Avis 1966–70. It is said on Northumbria University's Communigate website that the nickname appeared around 1898, and was due to the club's longstanding presence in the town: a foundation in 1882, however, cannot justify this claim. However, the football started after a discussion at Stockton Cricket Club, founded as long ago as 1816, so the sense of longevity is entirely justified if the nickname refers to the cricket club.

Anfielders is an old nickname for Liverpool F.C., recorded in Moss 1983, from the long-established home ground of Anfield Stadium. See also Culture Club, Kop / Kopites, Liddellpool, Mariners, Merseysiders, Micky Mousers, Pool, Reds, Spice Boys.

Angels is a nickname for two clubs, for different reasons. The clubs are:

- ⚙ Rochdale Town F.C., founded in 1924, originally as St Gabriel's. The club was originally a Catholic church side for St Gabriel and the Angels in the town of Castleton in Rochdale borough, Lancashire. In 1990 they were renamed Castleton Gabriels, and then Rochdale Town in 2008; Wikipedia. See also Angels, Castlemen, Gabs, Garrison, Guardians, Messengers.

- ⚙ Tonbridge Angels F.C. Founded in Kent in 1947 as Tonbridge F.C., the club was based (until 1980) at The Angel Ground (itself named from the nearby Angel Hotel), and so the nickname was in use very early. In 1976 the club folded but was immediately succeeded by Tonbridge Angels; Avis 1966–70, W1979/80–2013.

Annies was an unofficial nickname for the Northamptonshire club Rushden and Diamonds F.C., from the perspective of Cheltenham and Northampton supporters, and recorded on the 2003 Football Fans Census website. The nickname is a pun on the official name Diamonds and the name of the popular television presenter Anne

Diamond. See also Diamonds, Russians.

Antelopes is the nickname and the suffix of Llandegfan Antelope F.C., founded in Anglesey in 2010, originally as Antelope but merging with Llandegfan in 2012. The antelope is one of the most graceful of African mammals and is here adapted from the name of the Antelope Inn on Holyhead Road, Bangor, used as the club base; club website, Huws 2013.

Ants is the nickname of St Anthony's F.C., founded in Cardonald, Glasgow, in 1902. The nickname takes the standard nickname for the personal name Anthony. The Catholic side has a great claim to fame: the famous 'Celtic' green and white hoops were first worn here; SFHA.

Anvils is a nickname for clubs associated in some way with a local blacksmithing industry. Two clubs are:

☉ Crawley Down Gatwick F.C., founded in Sussex in 1993 as C.D. Village, in a merger between C.D. United and two other local sides. The club renamed as just C.D. in 1999 and then took the present name in 2012. Here, the village has been a centre for iron furnace activity since the early seventeenth century, at the Myllwood Furnace, commemorated in the name of Furnace Wood. An anvil is also a badge for the village and appears on the village sign; W2009, W2013.

☉ Gretna F.C., founded in 1946 and closed in 2008. Gretna Green in Dumfries and Galloway was the famous centre for runaway marriages before a change in Scottish law in 1856. The tradition was that these could take place over a blacksmith's anvil, hence the nickname. The town continues to be a popular location for marriages simply for romantic reasons. An anvil appeared on the club's badge (and also on that of the successor side, Gretna F.C. 2008); Wikipedia. See also Black and Whites, Borderers, Celebrant, Monochrome, Weddingmakers.

Apollo is the nickname of Apollo Juniors F.C., founded in Greater Manchester in 1994. The nickname is a good example of classicalism, used on club's own website.

Ar Tarn is the nickname of the Northamptonshire side, Desborough Town F.C., founded in 1896. The affectionate nickname is 'our town' with a spelling reflecting the local pronunciation. Addis 1995 reprints newspaper articles of c.1949 which use the nickname (pp. 18–19); W1982/3–2013.

Arabs has been a football name suffix (the ancestor club of Bristol Rovers F.C. was founded in 1883 as Black Arabs F.C., named from the Arabs rugby team and the black strip they wore), but it is now only known as a nickname for Dundee United F.C., founded in 1909, originally as D. Hibernian, after the demise of D. Harp and D. Wanderers. Although some claim that the term refers to the fans, it is definitely also used for the team on a regular basis; it is in any case an unofficial nickname, so its use for neither fans nor team is fixed. The explanation given on several websites is that during the harsh winter of 1962–3, the club had been unable to play, so they hired a tar burner to clear the ice and then imported several lorry-loads of sand to cover the pitch. Commentators soon observed that the players took to the sand 'like

Arabs' and the expression has stuck. Supporters soon adopted it and even began wearing pretend Arab dress. Rumours that the nickname was introduced by the Respect M.P., George Galloway, who began his political career in Dundee, are entirely unfounded. Two enamel badges record the nickname (AFBC). See also Tangerines, Terrors.

Arcadians is a football club suffix, used in England for the short-lived Manchester Arcadians F.C., recorded in BoF1905–6, p. 242 and on Wikipedia for a famous match against Newton Heath LYR (the ancestor club of Manchester United) in 1883; and in Wales for Holywell Arcadians F.C., a temporary renaming in 1929 of H. United, recorded on Wikipedia and in Huws 2013. Arcadia was a district of Ancient Greece but the term has long had strange poetical and mystical associations (notably in the famous Poussin painting of 1647). It seems to be used in football, however, as simply another 'classical' suffix. The name survives in Manchester today as a nickname for the Manchester Roller Hockey Club, based at the Arcadia Sports Centre. For Holywell, see also Wellmen.

Archers is the nickname of University of Wales in Cardiff F.C., founded in 1957; recorded in RW1996 (for Cardiff Institute H.E. A.F.C.) and RW1998–2002. The club shows a medieval archer on its badge, which suggests that the club is assuming the reputation of the medieval Welsh archers, whose performance at Agincourt is celebrated in Shakespeare's *Henry V* and in many original medieval references. At the time of the club's foundation in the 1950s, the fame of the archers was well-known from the stunning visual effects in the 1944 Laurence Olivier film.

Ards is the nickname for Cornard United F.C., founded in Great Cornard in Suffolk in 1964. A pluralised short form of the name, but also suggesting 'hard'; W1995– 2013.

Argyle has been a suffix for at least three Devon clubs and a nickname for at least two of them. The clubs are:

☻ Dawlish Town A.F.C., founded in Devon in 1889, originally as Dawlish Argyle; the use of the word as a nickname has not been noticed for the club but is mentioned here because it is probably the first Devon club to adopt the suffix after Plymouth. See also Seasiders.

☻ Okehampton Argyle F.C., founded in Devon in 1926; the club's website records that the initial meeting of the club committee was held at the Plymouth Inn in Oke-hampton, which no doubt influenced the club to adopt the famous suffix of the Ply-mouth Argyle club; W1994–6.

☻ Plymouth Argyle F.C., founded in Devon in 1886. See the discussion under 'Pil-grims' for an explanation of the suffix; 'Argyle' as a nickname is recorded early, in BoF1905–6; and in Churchill 1958, Goodall 1982 (p. 134) and the Williams League Directories for 1985–6. See also Green Army, Pilgrims.

Aristocrats is recorded on Wikipedia as an alternative nickname for Newcastle Blue Star F.C., founded in Tyneside in 1930, originally as a works side. The nickname is not explained, but it has appeared before in a Newcastle context (see under Tyneside Professors). See also Star.

Arky-Penarky is the nickname of Penparcau F.C., founded in Ceredigion in 1909; recorded in RW2011. The place-name is pronounced 'Penparky', so the nickname plays on the general sound of the place-name. Richard Huws reports that the nickname frequently occurs as just 'Arky' and 'Pen'arkee' is also often heard as a nickname for the place, so the euphonious phrase actually combines two nicknames for the place. It may be that 'or' should have been inserted instead of a hyphen. 'Arky' is used by the BBC Wales online news service.

Armadillos is the nickname of Hallen Athletic F.C., founded in 1949, originally as Lawrence Weston Athletic, near Bristol. The present name dates from 1990 and the nickname appears on Wikipedia and the club's own website. Armadillos are American Spanish-named armour-plated mammals of the dasypodidae family, and thus have no connection with football whatsoever. The common nine-banded armadillo has a striped appearance, and the club plays in blue-and-black stripes but the colours do not match those of the animal. The nickname seems to copy the American fashion for sporting clubs to adopt an animal as a badge and nickname, without necessarily a specific reason for the choice ... though it is just possible that it is a punning adaptation of the club's motto: *absit invidio* ('let there be no envy', but misspelled on the badge with a final *–o* instead of an *–a*).

Army is a football club nickname element, often used with the club's colours to make 'Blue Army', 'Green Army' etc. It suggests both the size of the club's support (an army of fans), and the strength of the club's players.

Arnie is a nickname for Arniston Rangers F.C., founded in Gorebridge, Midlothian, in 1878; a friendly short form of the official name recorded on Wikipedia. See also 'Gers.

Arrad was a nickname for Great Harwood Town F.C., founded in Lancashire in 1966, originally as Harwood Wellington (after the Duke of Wellington pub), but renaming to G.H.Town in 1978 after the demise of another local club called G.H. F.C. The nickname is recorded in W1982/3–7. The club folded in 2006. Dobson 1973 records 'Gret 'Arrud' as a nickname for the town itself. See also Robins, Wellie.

Arrows is the nickname of two clubs, for different reasons. The clubs are:
- Harrowby United F.C., founded in Lincolnshire in 1949; clearly an adaptation of the place-name; W1995–2006.
- Hastings United F.C., founded in Sussex in 1894. The name 'Arrow' is a common one for businesses in the Hastings area and clearly relates to the Battle of Hastings in 1066, when an arrow was responsible for the death of the last English king, Harold II, and the subsequent Norman Conquest of England. It is also used for the radio station Arrow F.M., which was established in 1997 by Conqueror Broadcasting Ltd.; W2003–9. See also Claret & Blues, Town, U's, United.

Ash / Ashes are nicknames of the Greater Manchester team Ashton Athletic F.C., founded in 1978, using the first element of the place-name, which does refer to the ash tree (Mills 1991).

Ash Trees is the nickname of the Middlesex club, Ashford Town F.C. Founded in 1958 as A. Albion, switching to the current name in 1964. The pun expresses the meaning of the first element in the place-name, and an appropriate tree appears on the club's badge. W1994–2009, 2012–13. See also Tangerines.

Ashes is the nickname of Saltash United F.C., founded in Cornwall in 1946; a pluralised short form of the place-name; Avis 1966–70, W1979/80–2013.

Aston Village is an unofficial nickname for Aston Villa F.C., from the perspective of Birmingham City supporters (Football Fans Census, 2003). The nickname is a simple pun on the official name, but suggests a very small fan base. See also Claret and Blues, Lions, Seals, Villa.

Ath is the nickname of Buckingham Athletic, founded in 1933 as B. Juniors, changing to the present name in 1939; a short form of Athletic recorded on Wikipedia. See also Swans.

Athletic is a common football club suffix, with the obvious sense of being athletical. It perhaps suggests that the club is not exclusively for football, and many such clubs were founded as branches of general sports clubs. It is also a common name in continental clubs. See A's, Addicks, Ath, Aths, Latics, and Tics for discussions of athletic mutation. It is rarely used as a nickname on its own, but it is in the following cases:

- ✪ Annan Athletic F.C., founded in Dumfries and Galloway in 1942; SFHA. See also Black and Golds, Galabankies.
- ✪ Blaby and Whetstone Athletic F.C., founded in Leicestershire in 1993, originally as Whetstone Athletic.
- ✪ Brantham Athletic F.C., founded in Suffolk in 1887; recorded in W1982/3–6. See also Imps / Blue Imps.
- ✪ Briton Ferry Athletic F.C., founded in the Co. Boro. of Neath Port Talbot in 1925, originally as B.F. Ex-Schoolboys, the club renamed as Athletic in 1926. The club merged with Llansawel to form Briton Ferry Llansawel A.F.C. in 2009; 'Athletic' appears as a nickname in W1994–7. See also Ferry.
- ✪ Bryntirion Athletic F.C., founded in Bridgend Co. Bor. in 1956; recorded in RW2011. See also Bryn, Tirion.
- ✪ Cadbury Athletic F.C., founded for the chocolate factory in Bournville, Birmingham in 1994.
- ✪ Caerau F.C., founded in Bridgend Co. Bor. in 1901. The club is based at the Athletic Ground, and 'Athletic' is often added to the club name to distinguish it from other clubs. See also Riverboaters.
- ✪ Ferndale Athletic F.C. founded in Rhondda Cynon Taf in 1945; recorded in RW1994–5. See also Fern.
- ✪ Garw A.F.C., founded in Mid Glamorgan in 1945; recorded in RW1994–6.

⚽ Gresford Athletic F.C., founded near Wrexham in 1946; recorded in RW1994–2011.

⚽ Leith Athletic F.C., founded in Edinburgh in 1996. This club is a refounding of an older club of the same name (1887–1955). The new club expanded in a merger with Edinburgh Athletic F.C. in 2008 and is now a major club for youth football; SFHA. See 'Crew' for the Edinburgh Athletic side. See Black and Whites and Zebras for the earlier Leith club.

⚽ Mexborough Town Athletic, F.C., founded in South Yorkshire before 1885, as M. F.C., the club adopted the Town and Athletic suffixes in 1974. The club is now called A.F.C. Sportsman Rovers. See also Boro, Pockets, Town.

⚽ Milford Athletic F.C., founded in Pembrokeshire at an uncertain date, but the nickname appears in match reports from 1972–3 on the 'Pembrokeshiresport.co.uk' website. A modern club for youth sides was founded with the same name in 2008.

⚽ South Normanton Athletic F.C., founded in Derbyshire in 1980, W1995–6. See also Shiners.

⚽ St Margaretsbury F.C., founded in Hertfordshire in 1894, originally as Stanstead Abbots; W2006–13. Both Wikipedia and the club's own website give the nickname as Bury, but this alternative nickname is the one given by Williams, repeated for seven years now. It may, however, be a mistake. See also Bury.

⚽ Thorpe Athletic F.C., founded in Essex in 1946.

⚽ Tring Athletic F.C., founded in 1971 in Hertfordshire; W1994–2013.

⚽ Wigan Athletic F.C., see also County, Latics, Pie-Eaters / Pies, T'Colliers or T'Pit-men.

Aths is the nickname of Stornoway Athletic F.C., founded in 1891 on the Isle of Lewis. It is a pluralised short form of 'Athletic', the suffix the club adopted in 1909 and is recorded on Wikipedia.

Atomic Boys is the older nickname for the supporters of Blackpool F.C., used between the 1940s and 1960s, when atomic power had caught the public imagination. The name is recorded on Wikipedia and many other websites without explanation. It may have been a subtle reference to the orange overalls traditionally worn by atomic power workers, as Blackpool are 'The Tangerines', and the supporters are well known for their tendency to dress in orange. See also Donkey Lashers, Merry Stripes, 'Pool, Seasiders, Tangerines.

Aul Reds is a nickname for Shelbourne F.C., founded in Dublin in 1895; the club plays in red shirts and socks with white shorts. The nickname means 'The Old Reds' and is recorded on Wikipedia. See also Real Reds, Reds, Shels.

Aurora is the nickname and part official name of Sheffield Aurora F.C., founded in 1964, and based at the Aurora Sports and Social Club in Rotherham, originally called Crookes F.C. The name changed in 1990 (FCHD); W1994–5.

Avenue has been a nickname for at least two clubs, which are:

⚽ Bradford A.F.C. or Bradford Park Avenue, from the name of their home ground,

Park Avenue. The club existed between 1907 and 1974, and was reborn in 1988. Churchill 1958 calls the club 'Bradford' and adds "often called 'Bradford Park Avenue' to distinguish them from neighbours Bradford City", so the official name derives from an expression used as a nickname; G1956–65, Harvey 1959 and Richards 1960 record the name for the older club. Pickering 1994 adds the variant 'Avenuites'; W1994–2013 for the new club. See also Stans.

☉ Walthamstow Avenue F.C., founded in London in 1900 and closed in 1988. Early publicity on the commemorative website refers to the club as 'The Avenue', and this is the nickname printed in W1980/1–8 and Goodall 1982. See also A's.

Aycliffe is the nickname of Newton Aycliffe F.C., founded in Co. Durham in 1965. The post-war 'new town' used to be called Aycliffe before expansion and the nickname restores the original; W2010–13. See also Acorns.

B's is a nickname for clubs whose names begin with the letter B. Some of these nicknames mutate from the initialism into the word 'Bees'. The clubs are:

☉ Bustleholme F.C., founded in 1975 in the West Bromwich area. Unlike other nicknames which began as B's but mutated to Bees (q.v.), this example has not swarmed. Recorded on Wikipedia and the club's own website.

☉ Basildon United F.C., founded in Essex in 1967; the club is listed as B's in W1979/80–80/1. See also Bees.

BA is the nickname of Shotts Bon Accord F.C., founded in Lanarkshire in 1950, as an abbreviation of the second phrase in the club's official name. 'Bon Accord' is the motto of the City of Aberdeen, from its use in the medieval wars of Scottish independence; it was used as the name of a previous football club, from the city, which on 12 September 1885 suffered an extraordinary 36–0 defeat against Arbroath. Despite that, another team was founded with the name in 1890, and a junior team in the 1980s. The expression has a patriotic appeal throughout Scotland; Wikipedia cites the initialism, SFHA, however, gives the full 'Bon Accord' as the nickname. See also Bonny.

Babes used to be a nickname for Bristol City F.C. and is recorded on the 1933 Ogden card with the explanation that a cartoon of Bristol Rovers as a pirate nursing a baby labelled 'Bristol City' made such an impression on the City supporters that they adopted the nickname. However, Johnston 1934 uses the word several times (e.g. for Queen of the South, p. 186), where the meaning is simply a newcomer to a league. The word was also used in the 1930s for the Buckley Babes (q.v.), and later became far more famously used for the Busby Babes (q.v.) in the 1950s; also recorded in the 1936 Thomson 'stamp' album. See also Cider Army, City, Eighty-Twoers / 1982 Ltd, Reds, Robins, Slave Traders, Turnips, Wurzels.

Bacachs is a nickname for Back F.C., founded in 1933 on the Isle of Lewis. The nickname uses a Scots Gaelic word for beggars, but here it is a friendly pun on the sound of the official name, which is taken from the Back district of Lewis; Wikipedia. See also Blues.

Bad Boys is the nickname for Defaid Du F.C., founded at Llandrinio in Powys in 1999. The club's name is the Welsh for 'Black Sheep', a traditional expression for 'bad' members of an otherwise 'good' family. The nickname appears on Facebook and in several Youtube videos where the footballers like to play on their 'bad lad' image. The club's own website uses 'The Du' ('The Black'), and 'Du Boys' also appears. The club plays in black-and-red colours; websites and Huws 2013.

Bad Lions is a nickname for the Sark National Football Team. The semi-independent island in the Channel Islands has only 600 inhabitants but heroically assembled a team to play against other island nations in the international Island Games in 2003. The team played four times, scored no goals but had 70 scored against them. The nickname puns on the team's performance and the use of the lion as a national symbol in neighbouring Guernsey (see Green Lions for Guernsey); recorded on Wikipedia and several other websites. See also Mad Lions, Wasps.

Badgers is a nickname for several clubs, either because they play in the 'badger' colours of black and white, or because the word 'brock' (a nickname for the badger) appears in the club's official name. See also Barcodes, Humbugs, Magpies, Monochromes, Skunks and Zebras for other black-and-white nicknames. The 'badger' clubs are:

- Brockenhurst F.C., founded in 1898. The Hampshire club plays in blue, rather than the black and white stripes usually associated with the nickname. They have a badger head on their club badge and here the nickname puns on the place-name. Miller and Wright 1996, W2000–13.
- Brocton F.C., founded in Staffordshire in 1937; also have a badger on the club badge and a nickname punning on the place-name; W2005.
- Bugbrooke St Michaels F.C., founded in Northamptonshire in 1929, punning on the place-name (the club plays in blue and yellow); W1993–2013.
- Eastwood Town F.C., founded in Nottinghamshire in 1953. The club plays in black-and-white stripes with white shorts; W1982/3–2013.
- Fulham F.C. Founded in 1879, the club adopted an all-white strip in 1903, soon changing to black shorts. The black-and-white colours lie behind the recent choice of Billy the Badger as the club mascot. The previous mascot was a knight named Sir Craven of Cottage (after the stadium). See also Cottagers, Lilywhites, Whites.
- Goole A.F.C., founded in East Yorkshire in 1912 as Goole Town, changing to Goole in 1997; W2008–13. The nickname is a mystery and may simply be a mistake, though now appearing in print for six successive years. The club continues to display the 'Vikings' nickname on its badge, and it plays in all-yellow or all-red strips, not in black and white. See also Town, Vikings.
- Retford United F.C., founded in Nottinghamshire in 1987. The club plays in black-and-white stripes with black shorts and socks, W2010–13, though the nickname must be earlier because the club programme is called *The Badgers* in illustrations in W2008–9.

Baggies is a nickname for two clubs, for different reasons. The two clubs are:

⚽ Badshot Lea F.C., a Surrey village side founded in 1907. The nickname is not explained but almost certainly refers to the prominent local industry of open-cast sand and gravel extraction. The village today has many former pits, some made into lakes, others used as landfill, and it remains a significant employer. Because gravel is traditonally collected into bags, the nickname is plausibly one for those who did that work, so similar to 'Dabbers' and 'Dobbers', used elsewhere in the salt and sand extraction industries (and also forming nicknames for football clubs). Badshot is close to the town of Bagshot, but the places are too distinct for Bagshot to be the origin of the nickname. In the Williams directories the nickname goes through three spellings: Baggiy's (W2005), Baggys or Baggy's (2006–8) and Baggies (W2009–2013). Internet match reports use 'Baggies'.

⚽ West Bromwich Albion F.C., founded in 1878. The phrase is said to have been first heard at the Hawthorns ground in the 1900s, but its meaning is obscure. Eight theories have been proposed. The first few refer to the dress of the supporters: **(1)** is that it refers to the baggy trousers worn by workers with molten iron in the local foundries and factories (loose-fitting for coolness, though leather aprons are the traditional protection for metalworkers) or **(2)** that it refers instead to the baggy moleskin trousers worn by the workers on their days off, at matchdays; or **(3)** that it refers to the patches sewn on these trousers which had the appearance of flour bags; or **(4)** that it is a general term of rather snobbish contempt for the dishevelled appearance of the supporters, as perceived by the better-off supporters of other clubs (such as traditional rivals Aston Villa and Wolverhampton Wanderers); specifically, the term could refer to the baggy cloth caps worn by the supporters (the expression 'baggy caps' also has a sporting usage in cricket). This origin for the nickname would therefore work exactly the same way as 'The Hatters' did for Luton Town, originally referring to the headwear of supporters, later used for the club. There are also the money-bag theories: **(5)** favoured by club historian Tony Matthews is the idea that it refers to the 'bagmen' who carried the club's takings on matchdays, since someone in the crowd first shouted out "Here come the bagmen!". The unique aspect here is that the Hawthorns ground originally only had two entrances and the bags of money had to be carried from each side to an office which was near the centre line of the pitch; or **(6)** that it derives from the poverty of the club in 1905 when supporters took bags round local pubs to collect donations to ward off bankruptcy (though it would be more plausible if the nickname had become 'beggers') (this theory is recorded in Norris 1959); and lastly two ideas referring to players: **(7)** that it refers to the baggy shorts worn by the players in the early years (also recorded in Norris 1959 and Pickering 1994, but again that would not be distinctive to any particular club, though some argue that the poverty of the club meant that players often wore hand-me-downs which didn't always fit well). 'Baggies' was a popular word for voluminous shorts, surviving into 1960s American surfing slang; or **(8)** that it was a corruption of Magee, the name of a player in the 1920s (but this does not fit with the claim that the nickname appeared early). It is obvious that there is no evidence to clinch any particular interpretation. One cannot help wondering if there is a connection with the Throstles nickname, given that bagging birds is a sporting expression, though it is difficult to think of a specific explanation for how this could work (in the early years of the club they were *not* notorious for bagging trophies). Perhaps there may be a Black Country association here with coal bags, but the industrial associations have always been metalworking. Finally, the nickname has now inspired an amusing (but chronologically impossible) twist. Some local rival supporters suggest that the Baggies adopted their blue-and-white stripes after admiring the similar stripes on a Tesco carrier bag, from which the nickname has come … (In 1996 Bristol Rovers adopted a blue-and-white striped and quartered design which was also reminiscent of Tesco bags and was so nicknamed by their own supporters). This inexplicable name is commemorated today in the club mascots, Baggie Bird and Baggie Bird Junior. If obliged to favour one theory, this writer regards no. 4 as the most likely explanation. All three main nicknames for the club (Albion, Baggies, Throstles) appear throughout RY1970/1–SSY2012/13. See also Albion, Bennies, Boing!, Nigger Minstrels, Sandwell Town, Stripes, Strollers, Tatters (for a possible connection), Team of Boys, Tesco's, Throstles, W.B.A.

Bairns is the nickname of Falkirk F.C., founded in 1876. The Scots and Northern English word means 'children' and the nickname is taken from that for the people of Falkirk. The town's motto is 'Better meddle wi' the deil [Devil] than the Bairns o'Falkirk'; another old saying is 'You're like the bairns o'Falkirk, you'll end ere you mend', but there is an even older association between the town and the word. In the late seventeenth century, one of the Livingston earls of Callendar gave some money for the building of a well 'for the wives and bairns of Falkirk', since when the people of the town have called themselves 'The Bairns'. Recorded in Johnston 1934, the 1936 Thomson 'stamp' album, G1956–76, AA 1960, SWSCYB 1962–3, Avis 1966–70, throughout RY1970/1–SSY2012/13 and RS 1993–2012.

Baker Boys was a nickname for Martin Baker Sports F.C., at Denham in Buckinghamshire. The FCHD records the club between 1985 and 2004; W2001–4.

Bakers was the nickname of the works side for Baker Perkins Ltd., an engineering company based in Peterborough in Cambridgeshire since 1904; 'Baker' in the official name is a family surname, though the company has not only manufactured ovens, it also bakes confectionary. The football club is listed as Baker Perkins without a nickname in W1986–91, but it renamed as A.P.V. Peterborough City in 1992 and the nickname is recorded for that club in W1992–3. The A.P.V. initials came from another renaming of the engineering company to APV Baker, but the company has now restored its old name.

Banc is the nickname of Bancffosfelen F.C., founded at Pontyberem near Llanelli in 1957; a short form of the place-name; used on the club's own website for a match report from 1960–1; Huws 2013.

Bank of England Club was an unofficial nickname for Sunderland A.F.C. in the 1940s and '50s when the club was spending considerable amounts of money on transfer fees, twice breaking the record; though another suggestion is that the nickname records their dependability as a side. Recorded in Pickering 1994. See also Black Cats, Lads, Light Brigade, Mackems, Miners, Rokerites / Rokermen, Sols, Sund-Ireland, Team of All the Talents, Wearsiders.

Bankers is the nickname of South Bank F.C., founded in 1868. The Teesside club has a long and proud history. The nickname is in Appleton 1960, W1979/80–92 and Barton 1984 & 1985. Although this is a play on the place-name, in general sports lingo, 'bankers' is used to mean those who are likely to win, from the idea of 'safe money', or a 'good bet' (heard on a BBC News commentary at the Paralympics on 31 August 2012).

Bankies is a nickname for clubs in Scotland with the element –*bank* in their place-name, as a pluralised friendly short form. The clubs are:

- Annbank United F.C., founded in Ayrshire in 1939; Wikipedia and the club's own website and SFHA. See also White Brigade.
- Bankfoot Athletic F.C., founded near Perth in 1919; Wikipedia, SFHA.
- Clydebank F.C., founded in West Dunbartonshire in 2003 as a successor to the earlier club of the name (1966–2002). Recorded in RS 1993–2001 and through RY1972/3–2002/3, for the older club, SFHA.
- Sunnybank F.C., founded in Aberdeen in 1936; the nickname appears on various websites and SFHA. See also Black and Whites.

Bannsiders is the nickname of Coleraine F.C., founded in Co. Londonderry in 1927, in a merger between C. Olympic and C. Alexandra. Coleraine is a large town beside the river Bann. Recorded in RI1997–2007. See also Lilywhites.

Bantams is the nickname of at least two football clubs. The nickname is associated with the colours of the bantam cockerel and also the use of this bird in the once-popular sport of cock-fighting (in boxing, the term is used for fighters below 54 kg.). The two football clubs are:

- Bradford City F.C. Formed in West Yorkshire in 1903 as a successor to Manningham Rugby club, the new club also inherited the amber and claret strip and the home ground of Valley Parade (1886) from the old club. Bantam cockerels come in many colours, but amber and claret often appear, and the colour is regarded as the explanation. A bantam in the club colours appears as a crest above the club shield. Recorded in Avis 1954–70; the early Rothmans directories give 'Paraders' but the switch is made to 'Bantams' in RY1982/3, continuing through to SSY2012/13. See also Chickens, Citizens, Cocks, Gents, Paraders, Sadford.
- Coventry City F.C., as recorded by G1956, Churchill 1958, Harvey 1959, Norris

1959, Avis 1954–70, Richards 1960 and Easterbrooke 1969. However, the club has played almost entirely in various shades of blue since 1898. Norris 1959 suggests in explanation that "at one time their players were nearly always on the small side". This would connect the nickname to the boxing usage, but it is not a plausible idea. More convincingly, Wikipedia in 2012 states "Coventry were first called the Bantams in December 1908 after the local newspaper noted that they were one of the few clubs who did not have a nickname. Being the lightweights of the Southern League, the Bantams was suggested and stuck with the press and supporters. (They remained as the 'Bantams' until the summer of 1962, when Jimmy Hill re-christened them the 'Sky Blues' and the club switched to an all sky blue kit.)". So, it appears that the nickname is entirely based on the boxing usage and a comment on the club's performance in the years around 1908. The nickname makes an unexpected late appearance in RY1983/4. See also Blackbirds, Citizens, Peeping Toms, Singers, Sky Blues, Wheelmen.

Banw is the nickname of Dyffryn Banw F.C., founded at Llangadfan in Powys in 1982; a short form of the official name (for the river Banw), recorded in RW2011.

Baptists is the nickname of Battle Baptist F.C., founded in East Sussex before 2008, and no doubt used also by many other Baptist Church sides. The club website adopts the inspiring motto 'Football as God intended'.

Barcodes is a recent unofficial nickname for Newcastle United F.C., coined by supporters of traditional rivals Sunderland (and recorded on the 2003 Football Fans Census website). It refers to the influential black-and-white stripes of the club shirts. Although it is currently considered offensive in Newcastle, it is conceptually a very neat nickname (implying also technological sophistication) and seems likely, as with many other clever insults, to be adopted with pride in the future. This seems to be the earliest use of a computer expression in a football club nickname. See also Cartoon Army, Entertainers, Frenchcastle, Geordies, Magpies, Skunks, Toon, Tyneside Professors, Tynesiders.

Bardon is the nickname for Bardon Hill F.C., founded in Leicestershire in about 1945, in a merger of the village football and cricket clubs. A short form of the place-name, used in internet match reports.

Barlick is the nickname of Barnoldswick Town F.C., founded in Lancashire in 2003 in a merger between B. United and B. Park Rovers. The nickname uses the popular short dialect pronunciation of the rather long place-name Barnoldswick; Wikipedia. See also Town.

Barmy Army is the unexpected nickname of South Park F.C., founded in Reigate, Surrey, in 1897. The phrase is usually used for the England cricket team's supporters while the team is playing abroad, and describes eccentric behaviour, but there is another football usage, in Blackpool's Seaside Barmy Army (for supporters). Pickering 1994 lists the name as applying to large groups of supporters generally. The nickname appeared on Wikipedia in 2011, but in late 2012 it had been changed to 'Eric Cartman's Barmy Army', after a character in the unconnected American cartoon series *South Park*.

Barrowsiders is the nickname of F.C. Carlow, founded in Co. Carlow in 2008. The river Barrow flows through the town of Carlow; Wikipedia.

Barum is the nickname for Barnstaple Town F.C., founded in 1904, originally as Pilton Yeo Vale, but renamed as early as 1905. The nickname, like *Sarum* for Salisbury, takes a thirteenth-century abbreviated Latin scribal form of the place-name (see *The Place-Names of Devon*, 1931, I, pp. 25–6). The name was revived in Victorian times and is popular as a local business name; W1981/2–2013. See also Town.

Bash is the nickname for Bashley F.C., founded in Hampshire in 1947; a short form of the place-name, nevertheless suggesting an effective and playful team. The club's home is the Recreation Ground, but this is nicknamed Bashley Road; W1991–2013, but the nickname is earlier because it appears in a photograph in W1990 (p. 571).

Bassett is the nickname of Wootton Bassett Town F.C., founded in 1882. The second word in the name of the famous Wiltshire town originates in a family surname; cited on Wikipedia and used on the club's own website.

Batmans is an unofficial nickname for Newtown A.F.C., founded in Powys in 1875. The club plays in an all-red strip and its official nickname is 'The Robins'. After the popularity of the recent *Batman* films, building on the tradition of the much earlier comic character, this nickname makes an amusing pun on the official nickname (as Robin is Batman's young companion); cited on Wikipedia. See also Robins, Stars.

Battling Barnsley was an unofficial nickname for Barnsley, applied to the heroic side which won the FA Cup in 1912, referring to the hard campaign which the team waged. Recorded in Pickering 1994. See also Colliers, Reds, Saints, Tykes.

Bay is a nickname for clubs with 'Bay' in their official names, as a short form. Examples are:

- ⚽ Cemaes Bay F.C., founded in 1976 on Anglesey; Wikipedia. Huws 2013 reports an amusing variant on this from local nespapers, 'Bay Enders', referring to the troubles of the club in the 1990s and punning on the television soap opera *Eastenders*. See also Demolition Squad, Seasiders.
- ⚽ Colwyn Bay F.C., founded in North Wales in 1885; recorded in W1980/81, W1989–2003, RW1994–2011. See also Harbourmen, Seagulls, Seasiders.
- ⚽ Cruden Bay Junior F.C., founded in Aberdeenshire in 1934; Wikipedia, SFHA.
- ⚽ Herne Bay F.C., founded in 1886. The Kent club was later reborn in 1935 as Herne Bay Invicta, but reformed again in 1974 with the present name; W1983/4–2013.
- ⚽ Whitley Bay F.C., founded in Tyne and Wear in 1951, originally as Whitley Bay Athletic, recorded in Barton 1985 and W1979/80–2013. See also Seahorses.

Beach Boys is the nickname of Concord Rangers F.C. Founded in 1967 on Canvey Island in the Thames Estuary, the club takes its name from the Concord Beach on the seafront, where they used to play their early matches. No doubt the nickname was also influenced by the great popularity of the American pop group The Beach

Boys in the 1960s. The aeroplane *Concorde* is unconnected with the club name, as it did not fly till 1969. Recorded on Wikipedia and in W2013 as separate words, on the club's own website as 'The Beachboys'. See also Rangers.

Bears is a nickname for several clubs, for slightly different reasons. The clubs are:

- Broadbridge Heath F.C., founded in West Sussex in 1919; W1988–2008. The nickname is not explained. The club was formed by former soldiers in 1919, so there may have been a regimental significance. The street name Bearsden Way is very close to the club grounds, but this is probably named later. The club badge shows a magnificent snarling bear's head.
- Congleton Town F.C., founded in 1901. This Cheshire town is itself nicknamed Beartown. In the 1620s the town became a centre for the cruel sport of bear-baiting but, needing to raise money to buy a new bear, the town spent the money it had saved to buy a Bible, and soon Congleton was notorious as the town which had sold its Bible for the sake of sport. A bear, inevitably, is the club's mascot, and one appears on the club's badge; W1986–2013. See also Humbugs, Town.
- Fochabers F.C., founded in Moray in 1983. In this case, the nickname appears to be a pun on the last syllable of the place-name; Wikipedia, SFHA.
- Paget Rangers F.C., founded in Paget Road, Birmingham in 1938, but now based in Sutton Coldfield; W1998–2002. The club badge shows a heraldic bear, traditionally associated with the county of Warwickshire, and with the Neville family as earls of Warwick. See also P's.
- Wakefield F.C., founded originally as Emley A.F.C. in West Yorkshire in 1903. In 2002 the club became Wakefield and Emley F.C. and then Wakefield in 2004, while other members of the club returned to Emley as the new A.F.C. Emley. In 2004 the club adopted this new nickname and a badge featuring a growling bear's head. There was a famous incident in the early nineteenth century concerning a breakaway dancing bear at the Wakefield Orangery, but there seems no specific reason for the adoption of the nickname and badge. The explanation probably lies in Wakefield's rugby tradition, so the club has copied the rugby fashion of adopting an animal as both a symbol and a nickname; W2011–13. See also Pewits.

Beath is a nickname of Cowdenbeath F.C., founded in Fife in 1881, as a short form of the place-name; RY1970/1–72/3. See also Blue Brazil, Brazil, Cowden, Fifers, Miners.

Beau is the nickname for Beaumaris Town F.C., founded in Anglesey before 1908. The short form of the place-name, derived from the French for 'beautiful', is used on the club's own website; Huws 2013.

Beavers is a nickname for at least three clubs, each apparently as punning adaptations of place-names. The clubs are:

- Hampton and Richmond Borough F.C. Founded in London in 1921, the club changed its name from just Hampton F.C. in 1999. The home ground has been Beveree Stadium since 1959, which lies on Beaver Close. Beveree is actually a local surname, the origin of Beveree House on the High Street, but the nickname and street name play on this to forge an alternative meaning. The club's youth group is called Hampton Beavers, or the Beaver Patrol. W1982/3–2013. See also Borough.

⚽ Leicester YMCA F.C., founded in 1910; W2002–4. The club folded in 2004. Here, the nickname was based on the location of the YMCA sports ground in Belvoir Drive (Belvoir is a Leicestershire place-name, pronounced 'beaver').

⚽ Rhyl F.C., founded in Clwyd in 1878 and recorded in W1982/3–86. As with the previous entry, the nickname appears to have been an adaptation of the ground name, Belle Vue. See also Lilies / Lillies, Lillywhites, Seagulls.

Becks is a nickname for Beckenham Town F.C., founded in Kent in 1971; a pluralised short form of the place-name, recorded in Miller & Wright 1996. The nickname is possibly influenced by the popularity of David Beckham, who is often given this nickname. See also Reds, Town.

Bees is a nickname for clubs who wear amber and black colours, usually in stripes like the bee, or other combinations which also suggest the insect, or because they have a letter 'B' in their official name (and often for both reasons). The clubs are:

⚽ Barnet F.C., founded in London in 1888, though going through several name changes and mergers before the present club emerged in 1919; from the club's black and amber stripes (which had been used by ancestor club Alston Works, 1901–12). Recorded in Avis 1966–70 (and with B's as a variant in another part of the dictionary), W1981/2–91, W2002–5; RY1991/2–2001/2 and SSY2004/5–12/13. See also Dentals, Hillmen.

⚽ Basildon United F.C., founded in Essex in 1967. The club plays in amber and black stripes; W1982/3–4; Miller & Wright 1996. See also B's.

⚽ Brentford F.C., founded in London in 1889. The spelled-out version of the abbreviation for Brentford is considered to derive from a media misinterpretation of a terrace chant 'Buck up, B's', but the bee symbol was subsequently adopted on the club badge, and the club's red-and-white stripes are at least partly suggestive of bee colours. The nickname is recorded early, in BoF1905–6 (at a time of blue-and-gold stripes). The 1933 Ogden card records the nickname, and the 1936 Thomson 'stamp' album, which uses the form 'Busy Bees' and suggests that it derives from alliterative journalism ("Busy Bees beat bewildered opponents by brisk and brilliant bombardments"). Also recorded in Johnston 1934, G1956–76, Churchill 1958, Avis 1954–70, Richards 1960 and SWSCYB 1962–3. Norris 1959 records the nickname but unconvincingly claims it is derived from "a famous local brewery called 'The Beehive' [which] stood near Griffin Park ... Perhaps it should be the Bee-r-s!" The club colours have always been red and white; the nickname appears throughout RY and SSY from 1970/1 to 2012/13.

⚽ Bridport F.C., founded in Dorset in 1885, and wearing black and red stripes; W1979/80–85 and W1992–2013.

⚽ Studley F.C. The Warwickshire club was founded in 1971, originally as BKL F.C.

for employees of the BKL Fittings Company. When the firm folded in 2002, the club relaunched using the town name. The club's ground is called The Beehive and a bee appears on the club badge. The club colours, however, are pale blue and black, so the nickname must derive from the first letter of the original name; W1993–2013.

⚽ Trowbridge Town F.C., founded in Wiltshire in 1880, reformed in 1998. The club plays in yellow-and-black stripes, black shorts and socks; W1989–98 and W2012.

Beganifs is the nickname for Waunfawr F.C., founded in Gwynedd before 2007 when they joined the local league. The nickname is that for anyone from the village of Waunfawr and is pronounced 'Began-eves'. It is recorded for the club in the *Caernarfon and Denbigh Herald* for October 15, 2009. The nickname was adopted by a pop group from the village, formed in 1988, who later changed their name to 'Big Leaves' after a mistaken pronunciation by Belgian radio announcers. The most likely explanation is that it refers to a formidable lady from the village, one Began Ifan and her difficult 'problem family'. Began is a variant form of Megan, and Ifan is a common variant of Evan, but is pronounced 'Eevan'; the English pluralising –s has been added. The nickname spread from the family to the whole village, from the perspective of outsiders; thanks to Hywel Wyn Owen and Huws 2013.

Belles is a nickname and part official name for Doncaster Rovers Belles Ladies F.C., founded in 1969, originally as Belle Vue Belles, renaming as Doncaster Belles in 1971. Belle Vue was the original home ground of the club. The word means 'beautiful' and is also frequently used on its own to refer to ladies, so the nickname puns on ground name and players. It appears in the title of the club history by Pete Davies: *I Lost My Heart to the Belles* (London: Heinemann, 1996) and is used in W1989. See also Donny Belles.

Bels is the nickname for Belgrave Wanderers F.C., founded in Belgrave Bay on the Isle of Guernsey in 1897. The club shows three bells on its badge, but the nickname takes the spelling of the first syllable in the place-name and is so used on the club's own website. For Stamford Belvedere, see below, under 'Belvo'.

Belters is the nickname of Tranent F.C., founded in East Lothian in 1911. The nickname is that of the residents of Tranent, transferred to the football club. There are various theories for the nickname, the most likely of which is that it is a tribute to the town's reputation for making good quality leather goods, including belts. One website suggests that these could be industrial belts for agricultural machinery, rather than menswear belts. Another suggestion, however, is that it records the town's reputation for fighting, i.e., *belting* the living daylights out of opponents; and the Scots Dictionary does record a use of the word with this meaning as early as 1823, in Ayr: "I'll stand ahint a dike, and gie them a belter wi' stanes, till I hae na left the souls in their bodies, if ye approve o't". As with many such nicknames, both explanations could be true, if it is a pun which combines them. 'Belters' has been the name of a pub in the town since about 1990; Wikipedia, SFHA.

Belvo is the nickname of Belvedere F.C., a youth side formed in Dublin in 1971. The club is based in *Fairview* Park and the official name seems to have been adapted as a play on this, because Belvedere is Italian for 'beautiful view'. The nickname is a friendly short form; Wikipedia. In Lincolnshire, Stamford Belvedere F.C., dating from some time in the 1970s, is nicknamed 'The Bels' in local media (eg. *Stamford and Rutland Mercury* on 26 October 2012).

Bengal Tigers is a nickname for Sporting Bengal United F.C., founded in London in 1996. The club was founded to offer football to the Bangladeshi community and the club badge shows an outline map of Bangladesh. A Bengal tiger is a particular tiger subspecies found in the Bengal region, though the club colours are all-blue; W2009–13. See also Sporting.

Bennies is an unofficial derogatory nickname for West Bromwich Albion F.C., from the perspective of supporters of Wolverhampton Wanderers, as recorded in the 2003 Football Fans Census. The nickname refers to the simple character of Benny Hawkins, who appeared between 1975 and 1987 in the long-running television soap opera *Crossroads* (1964–81). The nickname is an insult because of Benny's notorious stupidity, and the series was set in a fictional location, but one which could be close to West Bromwich. Possibly, the nickname was encouraged as a slight pun on 'Baggies' (using 'bean bags'). See also Albion, Baggies, Boing!, Nigger Minstrels, Sandwell Town, Stripes, Strollers, Tatters (for a possible connection), Team of Boys, Tesco's, Throstles, W.B.A.

Bens is the nickname of Benburb F.C., founded in Govan, Glasgow, in 1900; a pluralised short form of the place-name; Wikipedia, club's own website and SFHA.

Beris, Y is a nickname for C.P.D. Llanberis, founded in Gwynedd in 1890, as a short form of the place-name (reported verbally from a local source). See also Blac and Amber, Darans, Llanbêr, Loco / Locomotives, Teigars.

Berko is a friendly short form nickname for Berkhamstead F.C., founded in Hertfordshire in 2009 as a successor to B. Town (1919). Recorded in W1988–90 and Miller and Wright 1996 for the older club. See also Comrades, Lilywhites.

Berrypickers is a nickname of Blairgowrie Junior F.C., founded in Perth and Kinross in 1946. The town is a major centre for the production of soft fruit, especially strawberries and raspberries, with a cannery and a jam-making factory as well, and related transport. Many bus-loads of migrant berrypickers come to the town for seasonal work; recorded on Wikipedia and SFHA. See also Blair.

Berts is the nickname for Lochgelly Albert Junior F.C., founded in Fife in 1926. The nickname is a short form of the second name. The source of Albert in the name is most likely to be the association between the town and the Battle of the Somme during the First World War. Many Lochgelly men took part and were stationed at the time in the town of Albert in Somme Département, Picardie. The foundation of the club in 1926 is too late for it to be a commemoration of Prince Albert (who is recalled in the Scottish club nicknames Alberts and Royalists, q.v.); Wikipedia.

Bhoys is the main nickname for Celtic F.C., founded in Glasgow in 1887. The spelling appears on an early postcard, which shows a player in the strip of 1898–9 in the form 'The Boald [or Bould] Bhoys', but 'Bold Boys' is said to be recorded earlier (the postcard is reproduced in McCarra's *Scottish Football*, 1984). The spelling is intended to convey an Irish pronunciation (but one coined in English, in Irish spelling the letters bh would be pronounced 'v', see also Hi-Hi's for this 'h' fashion). The nickname is recorded in the 1936 Thomson 'stamp' album and all issues of RS (1993–2012), and through RY1972/3–SS2012/13. The nickname has been copied by some youth sides, such as the Sandiacre Town under 12s team in Nottinghamshire, and by clubs which copy the Celtic style, such as Lurgan Celtic F.C., founded in Co. Armagh in the 1970s, reforming an older club established in 1903. See also Celts, Hoops, Lisbon Lions, Quality Street Kids, 'Tic, Tims.

Big Club is a nickname for Bohemians F.C., founded in Dublin in 1890. The club is one of the most successful in Ireland; Wikipedia. See also Bohs, Gypsies.

Billy Town is the nickname of the Co. Durham club Billingham Town F.C., founded in 1967, originally as B. Social F.C; W2008–13. See also Social, Sound.

Binners / Binmen is an unofficial nickname for Ipswich Town F.C., recorded on the Football Fans Census website for 2003, from the perspective of Norwich City supporters. The nickname records an episode in the television series *Lovejoy* in which a local authority refuse collector pulled an Ipswich Town scarf out of a bin and proceeded to wear it. See also Blues, Superblues, Town, Tractor Boys, Witches.

Binos (or Beanos) is a nickname for Stirling Albion F.C., founded in 1945. The nickname is almost certainly a pun on the Albion suffix of the official name, but it could also be a pun on the related word 'Albino', for an unusually white person or animal, from the club's adoption of a mainly all-white kit from 1957 to 1968 (and entirely white 1965–7). The adoption of the nickname is not directly related to the hugely popular and best-selling Dundee-published comic, *The Beano* (from 1938 and taking its own name from an English expression for 'a jolly time', derived from 'bean-feast'), but the words are pronounced the same and it cannot but have helped encourage the nickname. In fact, 'The Beanos' does appear as an alternative spelling on Wikipedia. The nickname is recorded in RY1990/1–SSY2012/13, Pickering 1994 (with Albion as the explanation), and RS2012. A plan launched in 2010 for the club to accept sponsorship from 'comparethemarket.com' in return for a rebranding as the Stirling Meerkats, has come to nothing. See also Albion, Yo-Yos.

Biscuit Boys was the nickname of Huntley & Palmers F.C. recorded in Avis 1966–70. This was a successful works side for the Reading biscuit company (1822–1976) which also inspired the nickname of the town's club (next entry).

Biscuit Boys / Biscuitmen / Biscuiteers were variants of the old nickname for Reading F.C. Founded in Berkshire in 1871, the nickname lasted till 1976 and was a tribute to the town's main industry, the massive Huntley & Palmers biscuit factory, which was founded in the town in 1822 but closed in 1976. The 1933 Ogden card gives the variant form of Biscuiteers; Avis 1966–70 has the form 'Biscuit Boys / Men' and in G1956–76, Churchill 1958, Richards 1960, AA 1960, and RY1970/1– 76/7 it is 'Biscuitmen'. The nickname makes a last appearance in *Panini's Football Yearbook 1988/89–89/90*. A fanzine is called *Taking the Biscuit*. See also Royals.

Bish is the nickname for Bishopmill United F.C., founded in Elgin, Moray, in 1882; a short form of the place-name recorded on Wikipedia and SFHA.

Bishops is a nickname for clubs with 'Bishop' in their place-names, recording an early ecclesiastical association for the place. The clubs are:

⚽ Bishop Auckland F.C., founded in Co. Durham in 1886. Recorded in Avis 1966– 70, Barton 1985, W1979/80–2006. This nickname is probably old: it is used in Appleton 1960 while discussing matches of the early twentieth century. See also Two Blues.

⚽ Bishop's Stortford F.C., founded in Hertfordshire in 1874. Recorded in Avis 1966– 70, W1983/4–2013. See also Blues.

⚽ Bishop Sutton A.F.C., founded in Somerset in 1977; W1994–2013.

Bit o'Red is the nickname of Sligo Rovers F.C., founded in Co. Sligo in 1928. The club plays in an all-red strip, ironically with a bit of white, but expressions in 'a bit of' usually mean 'a lot of'. Recorded in RI1997, as 'The Bit of Red'. See also Rovers.

Bitters / Bitter Blues are unofficial nicknames for two clubs, each playing in blue, from the perspective of rival supporters mocking alleged feelings of disillusionment from repeated failure. The clubs are:

⚽ Everton F.C., from the perspective of Liverpool supporters, recorded on the Football Fans Census website for 2003. See also Black Watch, Bluenoses, Blues, Dogs of War, Merseysiders, Moonlight Dribblers, People's Club, School of Science, Toffees/Toffeemen.

⚽ Manchester City F.C., coined by Manchester United supporters, and recorded on the 2003 Football Fans Census website, in the belief that City fans hate their rivals more than they love their own club (evidenced by the stadium never being full). Since then, rhyming slang has generated a cartoon character, 'Bertie McGoo the Bitter Blue' and City has reponded with 'Rags', for United. This is explained on a United fans website as "an ever so slightly outdated term from the 1930s when United had no money and were in financial trouble", but it should also be understood in the context of the recent wealth of the City club. 'Rags and Berties' is now often used as a single expression. See also Blues, Citizens, City, Council Housers, Man, Massives, Sheik City, Stockports.

Biz is the nickname of Chinnor F.C., founded in Oxfordshire in 1884. The nickname is a popular twentieth-century word for 'the business', meaning 'the real thing', though here it might have originated in an abbreviation describing the club's all- blue strip (the B's). Green 1998 adds that the word commands respect; Wikipedia.

Blac and Amber is a nickname of C.P.D. Llanberis, founded in Gwynedd in 1890. The club plays in black and amber colours and the nickname appears on the club website. Like some of the other nicknames for this club, the form is a slight mixture of Welsh and English. It takes the Welsh 'Y' for 'The', and Welsh spelling of the colours, but uses the English word for 'and'. There are two other aspects of the club colours worth mentioning. One is that the Assheton Smith family, who owned the local Dinorwig quarry and were the town's leading employers, owned several race horses and their jockeys also wore black and amber colours, almost certainly influencing the club's kit colours. Another is perhaps coincidental, but the meaning of the Darans nickname (q.v.) is 'thunder' and 'thunder and lightning' is known as a colloquial phrase for black and yellow colours (Weekley 1921). See also Darans, Llanbêr, Loco / Locomotives, Teigars.

Black and Ambers is a nickname for clubs playing in a combination of those two colours. Examples are:

- Bodmin Town F.C., founded in Cornwall in 1889; they adopted the present colours in 1925; W1994–2005.
- Builth Wells F.C., founded in Powys in 1879 or 1883; recorded in RW1994. The club plays in amber shirts with black shorts. See also Ambers, Bulls, Wyesiders.
- Crook Town A.F.C., founded in Co. Durham in 1889 in a merger of Crook F.C. and Crook Excelsior F.C. The nickname used to be the distinctive and easier to pronounce 'Black Ambers' (Barton 1984 & 1985 and W1982/3–94); W1995–2013 has the form with 'and'.
- Llanberis F.C., but see above, under Blac and Amber.
- Newport County F.C., for their playing colours; recorded on the 'This is South Wales' website on 16 February 2013, and in Huws 2013. Wikipedia has 'Amber Army' for the club's supporters. See also County, Cromwellians, Exiles, Ironsides, Port, Wasps.
- Stornoway United F.C., founded on the Isle of Lewis in 1945, according to the club badge. The club plays in black and amber stripes. See also United.

Black and Gold/s is a nickname for Scottish clubs which play in these colours. The examples are:

- Aberdeen F.C., founded in 1903. The club first played in black and gold stripes, changing to red stripes with red shorts in 1966. The strip also earned them the nickname Wasps; Wikipedia. See also Dandies, Dons, Red Devils, Reds, Wasps.
- Annan Athletic F.C., founded in Dumfries and Galloway in 1942; the club has worn black and gold since at least 1974; SSY2012/13. See also Athletic, Galabankies.
- Berwick Rangers F.C., founded in Northumberland in 1884. The club plays in the Scottish leagues and they have worn black and gold stripes since 1908. This particular club takes the nickname in the singular: The Black and Gold; SSY2012/13. See also Borderers, Dream Team, Rangers, Wee Gers, Wee Rangers.
- Huntly F.C., founded in Aberdeenshire in 1928. The club plays in black and gold stripes with black shorts and socks; Wikipedia.

Black and Gold Brigade was a nickname for Irvine Caledonia F.C., founded in

Ayrshire in 1896, closed in 1898, referring to the club colours. Despite its short life and early existence, the SFHA records two nicknames for the club. See also Caley.

Black and Greens is a nickname for Aberystwyth Town F.C., founded in Ceredigion in 1884. The club plays in green shirts and black shorts; recorded on various websites in this form, in W1994 as 'Old Black and Green'. See also Aber, Seagulls, Seasiders.

Black and Red Army is a nickname for Lower Maze F.C., founded in Maze, Co. Down in 1960; from the strip colour; Wikipedia. See also Maze, Mills.

Black and White Army is a nickname of St Mirren F.C., founded in Paisley, Renfrewshire in 1877. St Mirren is the patron saint of Paisley. The club plays in black and white stripes with black shorts and this unofficial nickname appears on several websites. See also Buddies, Paisley Brazilians, Saints.

Black and Whites is a nickname for some of the clubs which play in those colours (see also Badgers, Barcodes, Humbugs, Magpies, Skunks, Zebras). The clubs are:

- Elgin City F.C., founded in the Morayshire cathedral city in 1893. The club played in black and white striped shirts from the outset. Recorded in RY2000/1– SSY2012/13 and RS1993–2012. See also City.
- Gretna F.C., founded in Dumfriesshire in 1946 and closed in 2008. The club played in a white strip with black arms. Barton 1984 & 1985, W1983/4–2002; RS2003, AFBC. See also Anvils, Borderers, Celebrant, Monochrome, Weddingmakers.
- Gretna 2008 F.C., cited on the 'soccerwiki' website as the nickname for the new club, though there does not appear as yet to be an official nickname.
- Heybridge Swifts F.C., founded in Essex in 1880; W1987–91. See also Swifts.
- Leith Athletic F.C., founded in the Portobello district of Edinburgh in 1887, from the black and white stripes of the club shirts. Recorded in Johnston 1934. The club was wound up in 1955. See also Zebras, and Athletic for a new club of the same name.
- Sunnybank F.C., founded in Aberdeen in 1936. The club plays in black and white stripes with white shorts; Wikipedia. See also Bankies.

Black Arabs is an unofficial former nickname for Bristol Rovers F.C., from their foundation in 1883 as Black Arabs F.C. (named from the Arabs rugby team and the black strip they wore), the team renamed as Eastville Rovers in 1885, then to Bristol Eastville Rovers, before becoming Bristol Rovers in 1898. Recorded in Pickering 1994 as a nickname. See also Arabs, Gas / Gasheads, Pirates, Purdown Poachers, Rovers, Squatters, Tesco's.

Black Cats is a nickname of three clubs, for folklore reasons. The clubs are:

- Kidwelly Town A.F.C., founded in Carmarthenshire at an uncertain date, before 2009. The nickname is that of the townsfolk, widely used in local businesses and on the town's badge, from a local legend in which the animal became a symbol of hope after one of the medieval plagues; Wikipedia and Huws 2013.
- Kilkenny City A.F.C., founded in Co. Kilkenny in 1966 but dissolved in 2008. The

nickname uses that of the natives of Kilkenny ('Cats', q.v.) and refers to the black and amber strip worn by the club since 1989; a handsome black cat appeared on the club badge next to a football; Wikipedia. See also Cats, City.

⚽ Sunderland A.F.C., founded in Co. Durham in 1879. The nickname was chosen as the new official nickname by a vote in 1997. The main source of the name is the Black Cat artillery battery on the River Wear. The story is that in 1805 one of the Sunderland Loyal Volunteers called Joshua Dunn fled from the battery after seeing a black cat, convinced that he had seen the Devil Incarnate; the battery being renamed Black Cat after this, but since the 1960s the Black Cat has been on the badge of the Sunderland Supporters Club and two black lions are on the Sunderland coat of arms. The 1933 Ogden card does not give this as a nickname, but records the use of the black cat as a symbol and a mascot. It finally appears in a mainstream printed source as a nickname in SSY2007/8–12/13. See also Bank of England Club, Lads, Light Brigade, Mackems, Miners, Rokerites / Rokermen, Sols, Sund-Ireland, Team of All the Talents, Wearsiders.

Black Dogs is the nickname of Bungay Town F.C., founded in Suffolk in 1925 in a merger of B. United and B. Harriers. It refers to the legend of the ghostly hound called Black Shuck, or Snarleyow, who appeared and killed two and injured one member of the congregation at St Mary's church in 1577. The dog appears on the club badge.

Black Dragons is the nickname of Athletic F.C. Porth, founded at Porth in the Rhondda Valley in 1950, originally as Beatus United F.C., and changing briefly to A.F.C. Rhondda. Recorded in RW 1994–2011. The club plays in blue and red or maroon colours; the 'Black' of the nickname comes from the black dragons of the Rhondda civic heraldry, where the colour is chosen to represent the coal industry.

Black Watch was a nickname for Everton F.C., at the time when they wore an all-black strip during the 1981–2 season. The nickname was copied from the famous army regiment of that name and is recorded on the Historical Football Kits website. See also Bitters / Bitter Blues, Bluenoses, Blues, Dogs of War, Merseysiders, Moonlight Dribblers, People's Club, School of Science, Toffees/Toffeemen.

Blackbirds has been a nickname for clubs which play in black. The clubs are:

⚽ Ammanford A.F.C., founded in Carmarthenshire in 1992, in a merger between A. Town and A. Athletic (see next entry). The nickname was inherited from A. Town. The present club plays in black and white stripes with black shorts and socks.

⚽ Betws Blackbirds A.F.C., founded in Carmarthenshire in 1945 or 1946. The club renamed as Ammanford Town in 1960, and merged with Ammanford Athletic in 1992 to form the present club, Ammanford A.F.C. The present club plays in black and white stripes with black shorts and socks, and keeps the nickname. The original name records what must have also been the original colours, together with a salute to the popularity of bird names for football clubs in Wales. See also Town.

⚽ Coventry City F.C. The unexpected nickname makes a single appearance in

RY1983/4, along with other older nicknames for the club. The club has nearly always played in various shades of blue, but the Historical Football Kits website illustrates a near-all-black strip worn in the 1890–91 season, to which the nickname must refer. See also Bantams, Citizens, Peeping Toms, Singers, Sky Blues, Wheelmen.

Blades is a nickname for two clubs, one for a city's steel-making industry and one to suggest knife crimes. However, the word has also been used since the sixteenth century to suggest sporting youths. The clubs are:

⚽ Limerick F.C., founded in Co. Limerick in 1937. The unofficial nickname stems from Limerick's recent reputation for knife crimes, earning the city the horrible nickname 'Stab City'. There is a discussion of the name on the Foot.ie website, where the contributions are all dated April 2005. See also Blues, Lims.

⚽ Sheffield United F.C., founded in West Yorkshire in 1899, but in the nineteenth century Blades was used for more than one Sheffield club, including The Wednesday. It celebrates the major steel-working and cutlery-making businesses which made Sheffield a prosperous Victorian city; the 1933 Ogden card says the club lives up to their name "in their sharpness in pursuit of victory". Recorded for United in BoF1905–6 (pp. 58, 120), on the 1936 Thomson 'stamp', and in G1956–76, Churchill 1958, Norris 1959, Richards 1960, AA 1960, Avis 1966–70, and throughout RY1970/1–SSY2012/13. For other United nicknames, see also Blunts, Cutlers, Laneites, Pigs, Red and White Wizards, United. For Sheffield Wednesday nicknames, see also Groveites, Owls, Pigs, Wednesday, Wendys.

Blair is a nickname of Blairgowrie Junior F.C., founded in Perth and Kinross in 1946; a short form of the place-name, recorded on Wikipedia. See also Berrypickers.

Blanketmen is the nickname of Witney United F.C., founded in 2001 after the closure of Witney Town, founded in 1885. The Oxfordshire town has been famous for the production of woollen blankets since the Middle Ages. In 1721 Blanket Hall was built in the High Street for weighing and measuring them. However, the last blanket factory, Early's, closed in 2002; Miller & Wright 1996, W1998–2001 and W2008–13. See also Town.

Blast was the nickname for Pontlottyn Blast Furnace A.F.C., founded in Glamorgan in 1968; a short form of the official name but one which puns on the industry and the popular expression for a good time. Recorded in RW1994–6.

Blasties is the nickname of Kilbirnie Ladeside F.C., founded in Ayrshire in 1901. There are two sources of inspiration for the nickname. Initially, the phrase 'Kilburnie blastie' belongs to Robert Burns, occurring in his poem 'The Inventory' ("A damn'd red-wud Kilburnie blastie!", glossed as "A damned stark-mad Kilbirnie blasted!"). The word is a general term of contempt, usually applied to ill-tempered and unmanageable youths (literally 'blasted', 'damned'), but in the poem it is applied to a horse. The second source is the local blast-furnaces at the Glengarnock steel works, the major industry of the town between 1841 and 1985. The nickname is recorded on Wikipedia, which favours the Burns interpretation, but it probably puns on both definitions.

Bleachers is the nickname of Luncarty Junior F.C., founded near Perth in 1886. The village of Luncarty dates, more or less, from the foundation there of a major bleaching business by William Sandeman and Hector Turnbull in 1752. By 1790, some 80 acres of land were being used for the bleaching of linen cloth, in the place still called 'The Bleachfields'; the club's own website states that the club was founded for employees of James Burt Marshall, one of the bleaching companies.

Bloaters is the nickname for Great Yarmouth F.C., founded in Norfolk in 1897. A bloater is a smoked mackerel or herring, for which this major fishing port is famous. Recorded in Avis 1966–70, W1979/80–2005.

Bloods is a nickname for two clubs, seemingly because they play in bright red shirts. The nickname also puns on an old expression for enthusiastic young men (in Chappel 1811 it is defined as 'A riotous disorderly fellow'). The clubs are:

⚽ Droylsden F.C. Founded in Greater Manchester in 1892 as a village side to play behind the Butcher's Arms pub (and their home ground is still called The Butcher's Arms Ground), the team plays in a predominantly bright red strip. Does the nickname reflect the colour or the name of the ground? One website claims that fans nickname the ground as 'Under the Patio' or 'In the Cellar', suggesting that it is all a Gothic murder mystery. Recorded in W1979/80–2013 and SSY2008/9.

⚽ Saffron Walden Town F.C., founded in Essex in 1872. Although saffron is yellow and used in making dyes, the club plays in blood-red shirts with black shorts and socks. Recorded in W1979/80–2013. See also Saffron, Wardens.

BLose is an unofficial nickname for Birmingham City F.C., from the perspective of Aston Villa supporters (Football Football Fans Census, 2003). The nickname mocks the sound of the official nickname, Blues, by suggesting 'B. [will] Lose [this match]'. See also Bluenoses, Blues, Brum, Heathens, Smallheath.

Blue and Whites is a nickname for two clubs which play in these colours:

⚽ Blackburn Rovers F.C. Founded in Lancashire in 1875, their strip colours have long been blue and white in equal halves. Recorded early, in BoF1905–6 (p.63), and in G1956–76, Churchill 1958, Richards 1960 and Avis 1966–70, RY1970/1–1992/3. See also Dingles, Highwaymen, Jackburn, Plastics, Riversiders, Rovers.

⚽ Willington A.F.C., founded in Co. Durham in 1906. The club plays in blue and white striped shirts with blue shorts and socks; W1994–2005. See also Blues.

Blue Army can be a nickname for football clubs which wear blue strip, certainly used for Portsmouth F.C., founded in 1898; the club did not adopt the strong blue shirts till 1911 (see also Blues, Pompey, Sailors, Skates); and Carlisle United F.C., founded in 1904 and adopting a new striking blue strip at the same time (see also Cumbrians, Foxes).

Blue Belles is the nickname for Rangers Ladies F.C., founded in 2008, and freely adapting one of the nicknames used by the affiliated Glasgow side, 'The Blues';

Wikipedia.

Blue Boys is the nickname of Hatfield Town F.C., founded in Hertfordshire in 1886. The club plays in an all-blue strip. For this club the nickname usually appears as two words, with a different club taking the spelling as one (Blueboys), but in W2013 it appears as 'Blueboys'; Wikipedia. See also Town.

Blue Brazil is a nickname of Cowdenbeath F.C., founded in Fife in 1881, in a merger of C. Rangers and C. Thistle. The club has worn blue shirts since 1911 and the nickname complements the alleged standard of playing as comparable with that of Brazil, who play in yellow shirts and are just about the most successful national team ever. On the other hand, a supporter called Big Bob was quoted in Seddon 2004 (p. 202) as saying "Why the nickname 'Blue Brazil'? Easy. Cowden play in blue and have the same debt as a Third World country." Cowdenbeath itself is nicknamed The Chicago of Fife, due to its allegedly high level of industry. Recorded in RS1993–2012 and SSY2012/13. See also Beath, Brazil, Cowden, Fifers, Miners.

Blue Cross is the nickname of Wootton Blue Cross F.C., founded in Bedfordshire in 1887. The Blue Cross here is an international religious tee-total movement, founded in the nineteenth century, and with which many football clubs were originally affiliated; W1982/3–2010.

Blue Imps, see Imps

Blue Toon is the nickname of Peterhead F.C., founded in Aberdeenshire in 1891. The nickname is that of the town itself, traditionally explained as referring to the blue worsted stockings, or blue *mogganners*, worn by the fishermen there. In the old days of North Sea fishing, fishermen all along the East coast of Britain would wear clothes which had distinct patterns and colours, allowing their home port to be identified should they be lost at sea and their bodies washed up some distance away. The nickname appears on the club badge and the club itself has always played in various combinations of blue colours. Recorded in RS1993–2012 and through RY2000/1–SSY2012/13, SFHA, AFBC.

Bluebell is the nickname of Dundonald Bluebell F.C., founded at Cardenden, Fife, in 1938; a short form of the official name, appearing in the singular; Wikipedia.

Bluebells is the nickname for three clubs, which play in blue-and-white colours, like those of the popular spring flower. The clubs are:

⚽ Haywards Heath Town F.C., founded in West Sussex in 1888, adding the 'Town' suffix in 1989; W1983/4–96, white shirts with blue shorts and socks. See also Heath.

⚽ Lochee United Junior F.C., founded in Dundee in 1892. The club plays in an all-blue uniform (but with white socks); club website and Wikipedia.

⚽ Yate Town A.F.C. Founded in Gloucestershire in 1906, originally as Yate Rovers, the club was reformed in 1933, and again in 1946 as Yate YMCA, and then as Town in 1959. The club plays in white shirts with blue shorts; W1992–2013. See also Whites.

Bluebirds is a nickname for clubs who wear a blue strip, but prefer a more distinctive nickname than just 'Blues'. The nickname is particularly popular in Wales where there is a fashion for 'bird' nicknames. The examples are:

- Abertillery Bluebirds F.C., founded in the co. borough of Blaenau Gwent in 1989. The club has a badge showing a flying blue bird carrying a football. No doubt the nickname and official name were partly influenced by the long-established Cardiff usage (see below). The club plays in a blue strip. The word is used as a nickname on the club's own website, AFBC.
- Barrow A.F.C., founded in Cumbria in 1901, the club had certainly adopted the blue-and-white colours behind the nickname by 1912; RY1970/1–72/3; W1981/2—2013 and SSY2009/10–12/13. See also Shipbuilders, Strawberries, Ziggers.
- Caersws F.C., founded near Newtown in Powys in 1887, originally as C. Amateurs; recorded in RW1994–2011 and W1994–2005. The club plays in blue shirts. See also Amateurs.
- Cardiff City F.C., founded in 1899, the 'City' suffix and the blue shirts were both adopted in 1908. The modern badge features a blue bird, which appears to be a swift rather than a real bluebird (an American member of the thrush family). The story is that Maurice Maeterlinck's children's play *The Blue Bird* was performed in Cardiff in 1911 to great acclaim. In it, a boy and a girl pursue the 'Blue Bird of Happiness'. Only a week later, Maeterlinck was awarded the Nobel Prize for Literature. The publicity led to the fans calling the club the Bluebirds, and before long it became official. Nevertheless, the popular Victorian composer Stanford also wrote a choral song, *The Blue Bird*, in which one flies over a landscape of mountains and lakes, and the success of this piece might have given Cardiff an extra encouragement towards adopting the nickname. The 1959 Sweetule card simply refers to the blue shirts as the explanation. Recorded in G1956–76, Churchill 1958, Richards 1960, SWSCYB 1962–3, Avis 1954–70, RW 1994–2011, all as 'Bluebirds'. In Rothmans, the nickname first appears in RY1970/1 as 'Blue Birds', then as 'Bluebirds' throughout RY and SSY 1971/2–2012/13. See also Dwarfs, Redbirds, Welsh Bluebirds.
- Chippenham Town F.C., founded in Wiltshire in 1873; all-blue strip; W1982/3–90, W1997–2013.
- Dafen Welfare A.F.C., founded in Carmarthenshire in 1925; the nickname and date appear on the club badge and Huws 2013.
- Haverfordwest County A.F.C., founded in Pembrokeshire in 1899. The club has had various official names, including H. Town (1901) and H. Athletic (1936) and took the present name in 1956. The nickname is a popular one in Wales. The club plays in an all-blue strip and the club badge shows two bluebirds; recorded in Avis 1966–70, W1987, W1994 and W1999–2005, RW 1994–2011. See also County, West.
- Ilfracombe Town, founded in Devon in 1902, all-blue strip. The club added the

'Town' suffix in 1920 and there are blue birds on its badge; W1987–2013.

☺ Letchworth Garden City F.C., founded in Hertfordshire in 1906, closed in 2002; royal blue and white strip. Recorded in Avis 1966–70, W1979/80–2003. Adult football in Letchworth is now represented by Letchworth Garden City Eagles since 2008.

Blueboys is the nickname of London Colney F.C., founded near St Albans in 1907. The club plays in an all-blue strip. A different club spells the nickname Blue Boys; W1994–2013 (W1993 contains a unique reference to the nickname as The Blues).

Bluenoses is an unofficial nickname for two clubs, from rival supporters, recorded on the Football Fans Census website for 2003. The idea behind the nickname is mockery of the club in blue strip having been 'left out in the cold' by the success of others, though in the case of Birmingham the supporters were already calling themselves Bluenoses, because 'nose' can often be found in popular expressions of devotion, carrying the sense of being sufficiently close to sniff intimate smells. The clubs are:

☺ Birmingham City F.C., from the perspective of Aston Villa. See also BLose, Blues, Brum, Heathens, Smallheath.

☺ Everton F.C., from the perspective of Liverpool supporters. See also Bitters / Bitter Blues, Black Watch, Blues, Dogs of War, Merseysiders, Moonlight Dribblers, People's Club, School of Science, Toffees/Toffeemen.

Blues is the second-most common football club nickname (after 'Town') with well over a hundred examples recorded here; it always refers to the colour of the club strip, be it in variant shades or combinations, or the shirts alone. Examples are:

☺ Amesbury Town F.C., founded in Wiltshire in 1904; blue shirts. This side is noted for having played its first match in a field beside Stonehenge, spawning later stories that they had used the monument for goalposts. See also Town.

☺ Arlesey Town F.C., founded in Bedfordshire in 1891. The club plays in a mixture of dark and pale blue strip. Recorded in Avis 1966–70, W1982/3—2013. See also Two Blues.

☺ Armitage F.C., founded in Staffordshire in 1946, reformed in 1990 as Armitage 90 F.C., folded in 1996. The club played in blue shirts and white shorts; recorded in W1992–3. See also Tage.

☺ Aveley F.C., founded in Essex in 1927; royal blue strip; W1979/80–90. See also Millers.

☺ Back F.C., founded in 1933 at Upper Coll in the district of Back, Isle of Lewis. The club plays in blue shirts and socks, with white shorts; Wikipedia. See also Bacachs.

☺ Ballinamallard United F.C., founded in Co. Fermanagh in 1975; sky-blue shirts. Recorded in RI1997. See also Ducks, Mallards.

☺ Barking F.C., founded in London in 1880, originally as Barking Rovers. The club plays in an all-blue strip; recorded in Avis 1966–70, W1979/80–2001, W2007–13. For W2002–6 the club was listed as Barking and East Ham United, also nicknamed Blues.

☺ Basingstoke Town F.C., founded in Hampshire in 1896, for their blue and yellow strip; recorded in Miller & Wright 1996. See also Camrose Blues, Dragons, Stoke.

☺ Bettws F.C., founded in Bridgend Co. Bor. in 1995 in a merger of B. A.F.C. (1957) and B. Athletic (1981). The club plays in pale blue shirts, with dark blue shorts and socks; Wikipedia.

☺ Billericay Town F.C., founded in Essex in 1880, which plays in blue shirts; recorded in W1979/80, W2008–13 and Miller & Wright 1996. See also Ricay, Town.

☺ Birmingham City F.C., founded in 1875 as 'Small Heath Alliance', they adopted the name Birmingham in 1905 and have always had a blue strip. Fans of the club are known as Bluenoses, and the club mascot has always had a prominent nose. The current mascot is nicknamed Beau Brummie. A statue outside the home ground, St Andrew's Park, is often found to have been decorated with blue paint on its nose. The 1933 Ogden card records Blues but also gives Heathens; mentioned in the 1936 Thomson 'stamp' album, G1956–76, Churchill 1958, Norris 1959 and Richards 1960 have just 'Blues'; Avis 1966–70 has 'Blues' and 'Brum'; just 'Blues' occurs throughout RY and SSY from 1970/1 to 2012/13. See also BLose, Bluenoses, Brum, Heathens, Smallheath.

☺ Bishop's Stortford F.C., founded in Essex in 1874, which plays in an all-blue strip; recorded in W1979/80–2013. See also Bishops.

☺ Bletchley Town F.C., recorded in W2000 for an all-royal-blue strip. This club was a temporary renaming in 1999, just before it folded, of Milton Keynes F.C., founded in 1993 as a successor to M.K. Borough. See also Borough for the club of the previous name, and City for another comment.

☺ Brandon United F.C., founded in Co. Durham in 1968; recorded only in W1994. The club nowadays wears a red strip but is listed as wearing blue in 1994. See also United.

☺ Brentwood Town F.C., founded in Essex in 1954, originally as Manor Athletic. The team plays in pale blue shirts and socks with white shorts; W1986–2013.

☺ Burnham F.C., founded in Buckinghamshire in 1878. The club plays in blue shorts and socks, and blue and white quartered shirts. The club was known as Burnham & Hillingdon 1985–7; W1980/1–95; W2010–13.

☺ Bury Town F.C., founded in Bury St Edmunds, Suffolk, in 1872; all-blue strip; W1979/80–2013.

☺ Caledonian F.C., founded in Inverness in 1885, which merged with Inverness Thistle in 1994 to form Inverness Caledonian Thistle. The club wore blue shirts with white shorts; RS1993–4. See also Caley.

☺ Carlisle United F.C. Founded in Cumbria in 1904 in a renaming of Shaddongate F.C., the club adopted a striking blue strip at the same time. This alternative nickname to 'Cumbrians' is recorded in Williams League Directories 1985–6 and RY1987/8–SSY2012/13 and W2005. See also Blue Army, Cumbrians, Foxes.

☺ Causeway United F.C., founded in 1957 and now based at Stourbridge in West

Midlands. The club plays in blue shirts and socks and black shorts, and take their official name from the Causeway Green area of Oldbury; Wikipedia.

☺ Chelsea F.C, founded in London in 1905, their first strip was a pale blue and the current royal blue was adopted in 1912. It is recorded as an alternative nickname to 'Pensioners' on the 1933 Ogden card, but has since been the exclusive nickname for some time, recorded throughout RY and SSY from 1970/1 to 2012/13 with the single exception of the edition for 1971/2. See also Chelsea Headhunters, Chelski, Drake's Ducklings, Pensioners.

☺ Chessington and Hook United F.C., founded in a merger in Surrey between Chessington United and Hook Youth in 1986. The club plays in an all-blue strip; Wikipedia. See also Chessey.

☺ Chester F.C., founded in 1885, renamed City in 1983, and reformed in 2010, based on the various shades and combinations of blue which the club wore after 1930. The nickname and a similar blue-and-white striped shirt were re-adopted by the new Chester F.C. in 2010. In Rothmans, the nickname is recorded early, and late, in R1971/2–72/3 and RY1988/9–2000/1 and in SSY2004/5–09/10; W2001–4 and, for the new club, in W2010–13 and SSY2010/11. The Williams League Directories also include it, as the only nickname, 1985–95. See also Cestrians, City, Ivies, Magpies, Romans, Seals.

☺ Chesterfield F.C., founded in Derbyshire in 1919; the blue colours were adopted in 1921, first in stripes then as solid blue; recorded in G1976 and throughout RY and SSY1970/1–2012/13. See also Cheaterfield, Spireites, Team of Surprises, Town.

☺ Clitheroe F.C., founded in Lancashire in 1877 as Clitheroe Central. They play in blue and white quartered shirts, with blue shorts and socks; Miller & Wright 1996, W1998–2013.

☺ Croydon F.C., founded in London in 1953, originally as Croydon Amateurs. Listed in W1979/80–94. See also Trams.

☺ Curzon Ashton F.C., founded in Ashton-under-Lyne, Greater Manchester, in 1963 originally as Curzon Amateurs. They play in an all-blue strip; W2001–7. See also Curzon, Nash.

☺ Darlaston Town F.C., founded in West Midlands in 1874; W1995–2002. See also Darlo.

☺ Dundee F.C., founded in 1893. The traditional nickname is 'The Dark Blues' but this shorter form appears in G1956–65 and RY1970/1–73/4. See also Bonnets, Dark Blues, Dee, Dens Parkers.

☺ Dunstable Town F.C., founded in Bedfordshire in 1998, though recalling two older clubs in the town, of 1883–1975 and 1975–94. The club plays in blue-and-white stripes with blue shorts and socks. Recorded in W1979/80–96 for Dunstable F.C., W2005–13 for Town.

☺ Dynamo Blues F.C., founded at Tuam, Co. Galway, in 1978. The club plays in an all-blue strip; Wikipedia.

- Eastwood Hanley F.C., founded in Hanley, Stoke on Trent, Staffordshire in 1946; for an all-blue strip; W1986–97. The club folded in 1997. See also Potters.
- Evenwood Town F.C., founded in Co. Durham in 1890; W1980/1. See also Wood.
- Everton F.C., founded in Liverpool in 1878; since the club's adoption of a navy blue strip in 1901. Norris 1959 recorded the name and suggested it was more popular than 'Toffees'. Nevertheless, it is now supplanted by Toffees; recorded in RY1970/1–82/3 and surviving in the Williams League Directories for 1995–6. See also Bitters / Bitter Blues, Black Watch, Bluenoses, Dogs of War, Merseysiders, Moonlight Dribblers, People's Club, School of Science, Toffees/Toffeemen.
- Exmouth Town F.C., founded in Devon in 1933; blue shirts; W1994–2006. See also Town.
- Feltham F.C., founded in London in 1946, originally as Tudor Park, renaming in 1963. The club plays in a mainly all-blue strip. Recorded in W1979–82 and W2009–13. See also Boro, Flyers.
- Fleet Town F.C., founded in 1890. This Hampshire club plays in pale blue shirts and dark blue shorts and socks; W1986–2013. See also Tarn, Town.
- Frickley Athletic F.C. Founded in West Yorkshire in 1910 as Frickley Colliery, the club plays in blue shirts; W1979–2013, though Pickering 1994 and Smith 1991/2–1995/6 record the nickname as 'The Blue'.
- Gainsborough Trinity F.C., founded in Lincolnshire in 1873; blue shirts; recorded in Avis 1966–70, W1979/80–2013. See also Holy Blues, Recreationists, Trinity.
- GKN Sankey F.C., founded in Shropshire in 1910, for an all-blue strip. The club was a works side for the GKN Sankey engineering company, but disbanded in 1988; W1983/4–8.
- Glasshoughton Welfare A.F.C., established near Castleford in West Yorkshire in 1964 (originally as Anson Sports, the name changed in 1976). The club plays in blue-and-white hoops, blue shorts and socks, and the miners' welfare aspect of its history is represented by a pithead on the club badge; W2012. See also Welfare.
- Grays Athletic F.C., founded in Essex in 1890, originally as Grays Junior before a merger with G. Town; blue shirts; recorded in W1979/80–2013 and SSY2006/7–10/11. See also Boys from Rathbone Street, Gravelmen / G-Men, Grays.
- Hall Road Rangers F.C., founded in East Yorkshire in 1959; W2005–7. See also Rangers.
- Helston Athletic F.C., founded in Cornwall in 1896, for their all-blue strip; Avis 1966–70.
- Hertford Town F.C., founded in about 1900, in a merger between H. Rovers and Port Vale Rovers, renamed H. Town in 1904. The club plays in an all-blue strip; W1981/2–2013.
- Hillingdon Borough F.C., founded in Middlesex in 1872, originally as Yiewsley, renamed in 1964; sky-blue strip. The club folded in 1987 but was reformed in 1990. Recorded in Avis 1970, W1979/80 and W1985. See also Boro, Hillmen.

⚽ Ipswich Town A.F.C., founded in Suffolk in 1878; blue shirts. The nickname appears as an alternative to 'Town' throughout RY1970/1–SSY2012/13. See also Binners / Binmen, Superblues, Town, Tractor Boys, Witches.

⚽ Lancaster City, see under Dolly Blues.

⚽ Leek Town F.C., founded in Staffordshire in 1946; blue shirts and shorts with white socks; W1979/80–2013.

⚽ Leiston F.C., founded in Suffolk in 1880; blue shirts and socks with white shorts; W2012–13.

⚽ Limerick F.C., founded in Co. Limerick in 1937; all-blue strip; RI1997, 2006, Wikipedia records Blues and the variant 'Super Blues'. See also Blades, Lims.

⚽ Linfield Football and Athletic Club, founded in Belfast in 1882; blue shirts and socks with white shorts. The club was originally founded as a works side for the Ulster Spinning Company's Linfield Mill; recorded in *Stedfast* May 1963, Pickering 1994, RI1997 and RNI2007.

⚽ Liskeard Athletic F.C., founded in Cornwall in 1946, refounding an older club of 1888; all-blue strip; W1979/80–2013.

⚽ Llandrindod Wells F.C., founded in Powys in 1883; blue and white shirts; the supporters are nicknamed The Blue Army; RW1994–8. See also Spamen.

⚽ Long Eaton United F.C., founded in Derbyshire in 1956; all-blue strip; W1979/80–2013.

⚽ Lowestoft Town F.C., founded in Suffolk in 1890; all-blue strip. Recorded in Avis 1966–70, W1979/80–2013. See also Trawler Boys.

⚽ Maesglas F.C., founded in Ceredigion in 1974. The club has an all-blue strip; club's own website and Huws 2013.

⚽ Maghull F.C., founded in Merseyside in 1921; the club plays in blue-and-white hoops; Miller & Wright 1996.

⚽ Maine Road F.C., founded in Manchester in 1955, originally as 'City Supporters Rusholme'. Like City, the club plays in a pale-blue strip; W1994–2013. See also Road.

⚽ Maldon and Tiptree F.C., formed in Essex in 2009 in a merger between Maldon Town (1946) and Tiptree United (1933); blue-and-white hooped shirts with blue shorts and socks; Wikipedia. See also Hoops, Jam Makers, Strawberries, Town.

⚽ Maldon Town F.C., formed in Essex in 1946, merging with Tiptree United in 2009 to form Maldon and Tiptree (see Blues, Hoops, Jam Makers, Strawberries, Town); W1990 and W2008–10. See also Town.

⚽ Manchester City F.C., founded in 1880, renaming as Manchester City in 1894, but the club had certainly adopted the famous sky-blue shirts with white shorts by 1892. Recorded in G1965–76, Avis 1966–70 and the first Rothmans Yearbook: RY1970/1, then not repeated till RY1989/90–SSY2012/13, though it appears in the Williams League Directories 1985–95. See also Bitters / Bitter Blues, Citizens, City, Council Housers, Man, Massives, Sheik City, Stockports.

❂ Marlow F.C., founded in Buckinghamshire in 1870; all-blue strip; W1979/80–2013.

❂ Mercedes Benz F.C., founded in Milton Keynes, Buckinghamshire, in 1967 and renaming as Milton Keynes City in 1998. The club was the second to call itself M.K.City, and folded in 2003; it played in a combination of royal and navy blues; W1994–8 for M.B., W1999–2004 for this M.K.C.

❂ Metropolitan Police F.C., founded in London in 1919; all-blue strip; W1979/80 and W1983/4–2013. See also Met.

❂ Milton Keynes City F.C., the second Buckinghamshire club of that name, 1998–2003 (originally Mercedes Benz, also nicknamed Blues); nickname recorded in W1999–2004. For the earlier club called M.K.C., see City, Gladiators, Moles.

❂ Minehead A.F.C., founded in Somerset in 1889; all-blue strip; recorded in W1980/1–90. One of the club badges illustrated in AFBC records 'Royal Blues', but 'Sky Blues' appears as an alternative nowadays. See also Seasiders, Sky Blues.

❂ Morda United F.C., founded in 1897, folded 1954, reformed 1976. The club is based in Oswestry in Shropshire and plays in royal-blue shirts with yellow shorts; RW1994.

❂ Mount Merrion YMCA F.C., founded in Dublin in 1981. The club plays in blue and white stripes; Wikipedia. See also Money Men.

❂ Nelson F.C., founded in Lancashire in 1881; all-blue strip. Recorded in Avis 1966–70, W1995–2013. See also Admirals, Seedhillers.

❂ Newhall United F.C., founded in Derbyshire in 1926 according to the club's badge; W1985 and W1994–5. The club wore 'scarlet and navy halves' in the 1990s, but now has an all-blue shirt.

❂ North Greenford United F.C., founded in London in 1944. The club plays in an all-blue strip; W2007–13.

❂ Oldbury United F.C., founded in West Midlands in 1958, folded in 2009; W1996–2009. The club played in a mixture of sky and navy blues. See also Cricketts.

❂ Oswestry Town F.C., founded in 1860 in Shropshire but playing in the Welsh leagues; the club played in blue and white halves, and the nickname is recorded in Avis 1966–70, W1981/2–8 and RW1998. In 2006 the club merged with Total Network Solutions and is now called The New Saints (see under Saints). See also Town.

❂ Penrith F.C., founded in Cumbria in 1894; blue shirts and socks with white shorts; W1982/3–2013. See also Cumbrians.

❂ Port Talbot Athletic F.C., founded in 1901; recorded in RW1994–8. The club played in blue-and-white shirts and has now been reformed as Port Talbot Town. See also Steelmen.

❂ Portland United F.C., founded in Dorset in 1921; all-blue strip (club's own website).

❂ Portsmouth F.C., founded in Hampshire in 1898; the club did not adopt the strong blue shirts till 1911 (see Historical Football Kits website). See also Blue Army, Pompey, Sailors, Skates.

- Rangers F.C., founded in Glasgow in 1872; light-blue shirts; G1965–76, RY1970/1–87/8. See also 'Gers, Huns, Iron Curtain, Light Blues, Rangers, Teddy Bears.
- Ringmer F.C., founded in 1905. The Sussex club plays in a very dark all-blue strip; W2000–13.
- Rustington F.C., founded in West Sussex in 1903; all-blue strip; Wikipedia.
- Ruthin Town F.C., founded in 1951 in Clwyd; blue-and-white shirts; RW1994–8. See also Ruths / The Ruthless, Town.
- Scotland national football team, which wears blue shirts in the same shade as the Scottish national flag; recorded in Pickering 1994. See also Bravehearts, Tartan Army / Terriers, Thistle, Wembley Wizards.
- Selsey F.C., founded in West Sussex in 1903; all-blue strip; W1988 and W1994–2013. See also Seasiders.
- Shrewsbury Town F.C., founded in Shropshire in 1886; the club tradition is that the blue strip was adopted from that of the Shrewsbury public school team; RY1971/2–73/4 and RY1997/8–SSY2012/13. See also Salop, Shrews, Town.
- Sidley United F.C., founded in Sussex in 1906; all-blue strip in two shades; W1988–2013.
- Southend United F.C., founded in Essex in 1906; very dark blue strip; Avis 1966–70, RY1991/2–SSY2012/13. See also Seasiders, Shrimpers.
- St Leonards F.C., founded in East Sussex in 1971, originally as STAMCO F.C., as they were a works side for the Sussex Turnery And Moulding Company, renamed 1996 as St Leonards Stamcroft before adopting St Leonards, then folding in 2003; blue shirts; W1996 (for Stamco), Miller & Wright 1996 and W1997–8 (for St L.S), W1999–2001 for St L). See also Saints.
- Staines Lammas F.C., founded in Surrey in 1926; all-blue strip, but occasionally with yellow shorts; Wikipedia.
- Stamco, see under St Leonards, above.
- Stansted F.C., founded in Essex in 1902; all-blue strip; W1986 and W1997–2013. See also Airportmen.
- Storrington F.C., founded in West Sussex in 1920; blue strip; W1986 as 'The Blue', W1989–90 as Blues. See also Swans.
- Stranraer F.C., founded in Dumfries and Galloway in 1870. The club has always played in various shades and patterns of blue shirts, and adopted solid blue shirts in 1910; RY1988/9–SSY2012/13 and RS1993–2012, SFHA. See also Clayholers.
- Team Bury F.C., founded in Bury St Edmunds, Suffolk, in 2005, all-blue strip; Wikipedia. See also Team.
- The 61 F.C., founded in Luton, Bedfordshire, in 1961; combination of sky- and royal-blue strip; W1983/4. See also Two Blues.

⚽ Thornaby F.C., founded in 1980. The Teesside club plays in an all-blue strip; Wikipedia.

⚽ Trojans F.C., founded in Derry, Co. Londonderry, in 1938. The club wears a largely all-blue strip; Wikipedia. See also Trojans for a discussion of the official name.

⚽ Ware F.C., founded in Hertfordshire in 1892. The club plays in blue-and-white striped shirts with blue shorts and socks; Avis 1966–70, W1979/80–2013.

⚽ Waterford United F.C., founded in Co. Waterford in 1982, as a reformation of W. F.C. (1930–82). The club plays in an all-blue strip. Recorded in RI1997, 2006.

⚽ Watford F.C., founded in Hertfordshire in 1881, renaming after a merger between West Herts and St Mary's in 1898. The club adopted of an all-blue shirt in 1927 and until 1959, when the colour changed to gold (see Historical Football Kits website, which also mentions the change of nickname to Blues in 1927). See also Brewers, Golden Boys, Hornets, Horns / 'Orns, Saints, Wasps, Yellow Army.

⚽ Whitby Town F.C., founded in North Yorkshire in 1880, originally as Streaneshalch F.C., using the ancient name of Whitby, but the present name dates from 1882. The club plays in an all-blue strip (with a red and black narrow stripe); Wikipedia. See also Seasiders.

⚽ Willington A.F.C., founded in Co. Durham in 1906. The club plays in blue and white striped shirts with blue shorts and socks; W1987. See also Blue and Whites.

⚽ Wingate and Finchley F.C., founded in London in 1991, in a merger between Wingate (1946) and Finchley (1874); all-blue strip; W1994–2013.

⚽ Winsford United F.C., founded in Cheshire in 1883; all-blue strip; Avis 1966–70, W1991–2013. See also United.

⚽ Worcester City F.C., founded in 1902; blue shirts. See also City, Dragons, Faithfuls, Loyals, Royals.

⚽ Wycombe Wanderers F.C., founded in Buckinghamshire in 1887; the mixture of Oxford and Cambridge blue colours has been used from the outset, but in a variety of arrangements. Recorded in W1979/80–91 and RY1993/4–SSY2012/13. See also Chairboys, Wanderers.

⚽ Yiewsley F.C., founded in Middlesex in 1872; the club renamed as Hillingdon Borough in 1964, but the nickname is recorded for Yiewsley in Avis 1966. The club folded in 1987 but was reborn in 1990. For the new club see Blues, Boro, Hillmen.

Blunts is a derogatory unofficial nickname for Sheffield United F.C., as coined by supporters of the rival club, Sheffield Wednesday, and recorded on the 2003 Football Fans Census website. The nickname puns on United's official nickname 'The Blades'. See also Blades, Cutlers, Laneites, Pigs, Red and White Wizards, United.

Boars is the nickname of Eversley F.C., founded in Hampshire in 1910. The club has a strong image of a boar on its badge, and a boar is the symbol of the village. The place-name itself is believed to mean 'wood, or clearing, of the wild boar' (Mills 1991); W2010 has 'Boars', W2011–13 'The Wild Boars'. Usage on the club's own website is 'The Boars'. In 2012 the club was taken over by California Youth F.C. (established in 1975 in the California district of Wokingham, Berkshire) and renamed 'Eversley and California'; W2013 has 'Wild Boars' for the new club.

Boatmen is a nickname for three clubs associated with boats, for two different reasons. The clubs are:

- Dunkirk F.C., founded in 1946 in the Nottingham district of Dunkirk. Although the famous evacuation of British troops early in the Second World War was from a different Dunkirk, the nickname reflects the fame of that operation. The club badge shows a solitary man in a rowing boat; W2011–13.
- Hythe and Dibden F.C., founded in 1902. Hythe is a small port and ferry terminal for the service across Southampton Water to the main city of Southampton, and now also the location of a marina. The place-name even means 'landing place or harbour' (Mills 1991).
- Sholing F.C., originally founded in 1952 as a works side for the boat-building business of Thornycrofts (Woolston), the club reformed in 1960 as Vosper Thornycrofts; the name changed to VT in 2003, and then to Sholing in 2010. Sholing is a district of Southampton, a major sea port and sailing centre, though the modern VT company concentrate on defence services rather than boatbuilding; W2008–10 for VT, W2011–13 for Sholing. The nickname also appears on the new badge since 2010.

Boded is the nickname for Bodedern Athletic F.C., founded on Anglesey in 1946. A short form of the place-name, recorded on the club's own website and Huws 2013.

Bohs is a nickname for clubs in Ireland which have the name 'Bohemians' in their official name, as a short form of the word. For the idealogical meaning of 'Bohemians' in Ireland, see discussion under 'Gypsies'. The clubs are:

- Bohemians F.C., founded in Dublin in 1890. A group of fans are strangely called The Notorious Boo-Boys, the middle word clearly based on this nickname. Recorded in RI2006. See also Big Club, Gypsies.
- Cork Bohemians F.C., which played between c.1928 and c.1934. The club is briefly and dismissively mentioned in Johnston 1934.
- Galway Bohemians F.C., founded in 1932; Wikipedia.

Boing! is an unofficial nickname for West Bromwich Albion F.C., and also the official name of Boing F.C., the WBA supporters football team. The word expresses an exuberant bouncing and is known in general speech from the 1960s (see Green 1998). According to www.baggies.com the phrase may have originated in fans bouncing to keep warm during an extremely cold match against Hull. The 'Baggie Bounce' is a phrase that has also been used. See also Albion, Baggies, Bennies, Nigger Minstrels, Sandwell Town, Stripes, Strollers, Tatters (for a possible connection), Team of Boys, Tesco's, Throstles, W.B.A.

Bole is the nickname of Maybole F.C., founded in Ayrshire in 1946, from the second syllable of the place-name; Wikipedia.

Bones was the nickname of Rothwell Town F.C., founded in 1894 as Rothwell Town Swifts, but sadly closed in March 2012. This Northamptonshire town's Holy Trinity church contains one of the few bone crypts in Britain, containing the bones of some 1,500 people. It is famous, and it is to this that the nickname refers. Bones have also occasionally been featured on the club's badges, and the club had a pirate skull-and-crossbones flag. The club's social club was called The Rowellian, adapting the town's place-name. Addis 1995 reprints a newspaper article of 1954 which uses the nickname (p. 66); W1982/3–2012.

Bonnets is a nickname for Dundee F.C., founded in 1893. It is used in the title of the club history by Norrie Price, *Up wi' the Bonnets!* (1993) and refers to the traditional industry of Dundee as a centre for bonnet-making. See also Blues, Dark Blues, Dee, Dens Parkers.

Bonnie Oodle is a nickname of Wooldale Wanderers A.F.C., founded in West Yorkshire in 1919. The nickname copies that used for the picturesque village near Huddersfield, and means 'beautiful Wooldale', the second word representing the slurred West Riding pronunciation of the place-name. The nickname is recorded in the title of the club history by Simon Paul Berry: *Bonnie Oodle: Celebrating 75 years of Wooldale Wanderers AFC, 1919–1994* (Holmfirth, 1994).

Bonny is a nickname for Shotts Bon Accord F.C., founded in Lanarkshire in 1950. One could see this as a pun, playing the suffix in the club's official name, where it is French for 'good', against the standard Scots and northern English friendly word meaning 'beautiful'; or one could call it a friendly short form with no pun intended; Wikipedia. 'Bon Accord' is the motto of the city of Aberdeen but it has a general appeal in Scotland because it was used as a catchphrase during the fourteenth-century Wars of Scottish Independence. See also BA.

Bonny Blues was a nickname for Alnmouth F.C., founded in Northumberland in 1901, originally as A. United. The nickname is recorded on the club's website as an expression used by the local press (probably *The Alnwick and County Gazette*) in the early days when one journalist wrote "Alnmouth play by far the prettiest football in the tournament ... [and] ... they have a strong young lady following." The handsome side still plays in blue today.

Bont is an unofficial occasional nickname for Welsh clubs with the element *pont*, meaning a bridge, in their official name or for a nearby location. Clubs are:

- Acrefair Youth F.C., founded in 1992 at the site of the famous Pontcysllte Aqueduct in Denbighshire. The Aqueduct itself is nicknamed 'The Bont', so it is a natural transfer. The nickname is also used for the club's ground (see Huws 2009).
- Penybont United F.C., founded in Powys at an uncertain date, before 2009 when internet match reports start to appear. The nickname is used on the Presteigne St Andrews website for a match of 16 February 2013.
- Pontrhydfendigaid and District F.C., founded in Ceredigion in 1947, appearing also for the club on the BBC Wales website, and even used as the name of the club in

printed programmes (such as for Bont v. Llanfair United on 27 August 2011); Huws 2013.

Borderers is a nickname for three clubs which straddle the borders of countries in Britain. The clubs are:

⚽ Berwick Rangers F.C., founded in Northumberland in 1884. This English club plays in the Scottish leagues. Recorded in Barton 1985, RS1993–2012, RY1980/1– SSY2012/13, AFBC. See also Black and Gold, Dream Team, Rangers, Wee Gers, Wee Rangers.

⚽ Gretna F.C., founded in Dumfriesshire in 1946 and closed in 2008. This Scottish club played in the English leagues; Wikipedia, AFBC. See also Anvils, Black and Whites, Celebrant, Monochrome, Weddingmakers.

⚽ Knighton Town F.C., founded in Powys in 1887; the town straddles the English– Welsh border; Wikipedia. See also Radnor Robins, Town.

Bordermen is a nickname for two clubs in border locations. The clubs are:

⚽ Newry City F.C., founded in Co. Down in 1923, which straddles the Northern Ireland and Eire border. The club renamed from 'Town' in 2004 but folded in 2012. The nickname is recorded on many websites for City. See also Town.

⚽ Saltney Town F.C., founded in 2010 but with previous clubs dating from 1908; the town straddles the Flintshire / Cheshire border; Wikipedia and Huws 2013.

Boring Arsenal was an unofficial nickname for Arsenal F.C., in the years immediately before the coming of Arsène Wenger as manager (1996) (mentioned on BBC Radio 4, 21.8.2011). It used to be used as a taunt, but is now used ironically by the club's own supporters when they are playing well; the nickname is a complete contrast to 'The Invincibles' which was used in the 2003–4 season. See also France, Gooners, Gunners, Invincibles, Lucky Arsenal, Reds, Royals, Woolwich.

Boro or **Borough** is a popular nickname for clubs which have the element –*borough* (or –*brough*, or –*bury*) in their place-name, or appended to this as a suffx to emphasise the district or the local connection, or because the locality is a borough even if the club's official name does not record this. Originally, the element usually meant a fortified settlement. Most clubs adopt the 'Boro' spelling, but the spellings frequently vary and so have not been separated in the following list. The clubs are:

⚽ Bacup Borough F.C., founded in Lancashire in 1875. The Borough suffix was added to the club's name in 1922; W1994–2013. See also Buttercups, Lilywhites.

⚽ Bilston Town F.C., founded in West Midlands in 1894; recorded in W1991–2002. See also Steelmen.

⚽ Borough United F.C., founded in 1952 at Llandudno Junction in the Co. Bor. of Conwy. The club folded in 1969; Wikipedia and Huws 2013.

⚽ Broxbourne Borough V. and E. F.C., founded in Greater London in 1991. See discussion under SAVE.

⚽ Caernarfon Borough F.C., founded in Gwynedd in 1985; websites.

⚽ Collier Row and Romford F.C., formed in Essex in a merger in 1996. The Boro nickname comes from the Romford side and the name of the enlarged club reverted to Romford in 1997; Miller & Wright 1996, W1998.

🌐 Crowborough Athletic F.C., founded in East Sussex in 1894; W2009. See also Crows.

🌐 Eastbourne Borough F.C., refounded in a name change in 2001; W2007–13. See also Sports.

🌐 Farnborough F.C., founded in Hampshire in 1967 as F. Town, reformed in 2007; SSY2004/5–5/6 and the nickname runs for both clubs in W1981/2–2013. See also Town, Yellows.

🌐 Feltham and Hounslow Borough F.C. Feltham F.C. was founded in London in 1946, originally as Tudor Park, renaming in 1963; the nickname refers to the time of their merger with Hounslow from 1990 to 1995, when the club reverted to the name of Feltham F.C.. Recorded in W1993–5. See also Blues, Flyers.

🌐 Gateshead F.C., founded on Tyneside in 1977. The nickname is uniquely recorded in W1980/1, but Gateshead is certainly a Metropolitan Borough. See also Heed, Laides, Tynesiders.

🌐 Gosport Borough F.C., founded in Hampshire in 1944, originally as G. Borough Athletic Club; recorded in W1979–2013.

🌐 Greenwich Borough F.C., founded in Greater London in 1928, originally as Woolwich Borough Council Athletic Club; W1986–2013.

🌐 Hampton and Richmond Borough F.C., founded in London in 1921, as Hampton F.C., renaming in 1999. The nickname appears soon after the change of name: W2001–13. See also Beavers.

🌐 Haringey Borough F.C., founded in 1973 in a merger between Edmonton (1907) and Wood Green Town (1911); W1980/1–9 and W2006–13.

🌐 Harrow Borough F.C. Formed in Greater London in 1933 as Roxonian F.C. (from Roxeth, a hamlet within Harrow), it changed to Harrow Town in 1938, then to H. Borough in 1967; W1979/80–2013. See also Reds.

🌐 Havant and Waterlooville F.C. Formed in 1998 in a merger of the two Hampshire sides Havant F.C. (1883) and Waterlooville F.C. (1905); the new club appears in W1999 with the nickname 'Borough'. See also Hawks, Magnets, Ville.

🌐 Hillingdon Borough F.C., founded in London in 1872 as Yiewsley F.C., renamed as H. Borough in 1964 before the club folded in 1987; reborn in 1990 when Bromley Park Rangers assumed the name; W1979/80–83/4 and W1994–2013. See also Blues, Hillmen.

🌐 Hounslow Borough F.C., after Harrow Hill Rovers renamed itself as H. Borough in 1987. The club folded in 2007. The 'Pyramid Passion' website records the nickname as 'The Borough Boys'.

🌐 Mexborough Town Athletic, F.C., founded in South Yorkshire before 1885, as M. F.C., the club adopted the Town and Athletic suffixes in 1974. The club is now called A.F.C. Sportsman Rovers. Recorded in W1980/1–88. See also Athletic,

Pockets, Town.

◉ Middlesbrough F.C., founded in Cleveland in 1876. Recorded early, in BoF1905–6 (as 'The Borough'); and in Johnston 1934 (as Boro), G1956–76, AA 1960, Avis 1966–70; RY1970/1–71/2 as Borough, then through RY1972/3–SSY2012/13 as Boro. See also Cleveland Cowboys, Ironsiders, Nops, Riversiders, Scabs, Smoggies, Teessiders, Washers.

◉ Milton Keynes Borough F.C., founded in Buckinghamshire in 1966, originally as Belsize F.C. This club folded in 1993 and was replaced by a club called Milton Keynes F.C., which in 1999 renamed itself as Bletchley Town but folded soon after. The various relationships between clubs called Bletchley and Milton Keynes is a source of great confusion, not least because of this late appearance of the BT name in 1999; the Borough nickname is recorded in W1982/3–6 and W1994. See 'City' for the brief appearance of the late Bletchley Town.

◉ Nuneaton Town F.C., founded in 2008 as a successor to the bankrupt Nuneaton Borough A.F.C. Fans have loyally retained the Boro nickname and campaign for the full restoration of the old name; Avis 1966–70 and W1979/80–2008 for the old club, W2009–13 for the new club. See also Nuns, Saints, Townies.

◉ Pembroke Borough F.C., founded in Pembrokeshire in 1906, originally as Dock Stars. The nickname appears in match reports from 1972–3 on the 'Pembrokeshiresport.co.uk' website; also Huws 2013. See also Magpies, Stars.

◉ Penryn Athletic F.C., founded in Cornwall in 1963; Wikipedia. See also Pens.

◉ Radcliffe Borough F.C., founded in Greater Manchester in 1949. Recorded in W1979/80–2013.

◉ Romford F.C., founded in 1992 as a new team, unrelated to the older Romford clubs (1876–c.1914, 1929–78). The district of Romford is the headquarters of the London Borough of Havering, from which the Boro nickname comes; the club had a merger with Collier Row in 1996 but reverted to the simpler name of Romford in 1997. Recorded in Avis 1966–70 for the older club, and W1993–2013 for the new.

◉ Scarborough F.C. (1879–2007). Two teams have now replaced the bankrupt North Yorkshire side, one of which, Scarborough Town F.C., has assumed the Boro nickname; Avis 1966–70, W1979/80–87, RY1987/8–99/2000, SSY2004/5–06/7 and W2007 for the old club. See also Seadogs, Seasiders, Town.

◉ Solihull Borough F.C., founded in West Midlands in 1953, merging with Moor Green (1901) in 2007 to form Solihull Moors; W1983/4–2007. See Moors for the new club.

◉ Stafford Rangers F.C., founded in 1876; so nicknamed from their base in the hinterland of Stafford Borough Council. Recorded in W1979/80–2006 and SSY2007/8–08/9. See also Rangers.

◉ Stevenage F.C., founded in Hertfordshire in 1976 as a successor to previous clubs. Between 1980 and 2010 the club was named Stevenage Borough; W1982/3–2010 and SSY2004/5–12/13. See also Stripes.

⚽ Sudbury Town F.C. Founded in Suffolk in 1885, the club merged with Sudbury Wanderers in 1999 to form the new A.F.C. Sudbury. Recorded in Avis 1966–70, W1979/80– 83/4 as Boro, Borough in W1987–99; and as *Bury* in Smith 1995/6. See also Suds, Town, Wanderers, Yellows.

Bot is the nickname of Auchinlock Talbot F.C., founded in Ayrshire in 1909; as a short form of the second word in the official name, which was in honour of the man who donated Beechwood Park to the club, Lord Talbot de Maldahide (SFHA); Wikipedia.

Bourne is a nickname for clubs with this element in their place-name, as a short form. The clubs are:

⚽ Eastbourne Town F.C., founded in Sussex in 1881, originally as Devonshire Park, renaming as Eastbourne before 1890 and adding the Town suffix in 1971; Avis 1966–70, W1983/4–5 and W1994–2007. See also Town.

⚽ Sittingbourne F.C., founded in Kent in 1886; W1982/3 and in Smith 1992/3– 1995/6. See also Brickies.

⚽ Wellesbourne F.C., founded in Warwickshire in 1932; W1995–7.

⚽ Winterbourne United F.C., founded in the village near Bristol in 1911 (originally as Winterbourne Wasps); W2002–13.

Bowers is the nickname for Bowers and Pitsea F.C., founded in Essex in 2003 in a merger of Bowers United (1946) and Pitsea (1970); a short form of the club name used in internet match reports.

Boyds is a nickname for Bitton A.F.C., founded in 1892. The Gloucestershire River Boyd runs alongside the ground, but the nickname comes from an incident in 1934 when the chairman, Jonathan Crowe, said he would jump in the river if the team were to win the first match in their new red and white colours. They did, and he jumped in the river in front of the supporters; Wikipedia. See also River Boys, Ton.

Boynesiders is a nickname for Drogheda United F.C., founded in Co. Louth in 1975, in a merger of D. United (1919) and D. F.C. (1962); the town is located at a bridge over the River Boyne; Wikipedia. See also Drogs / Super Drogs, Turks.

Boyos is a nickname for Whitton United F.C., founded in Suffolk in 1926. The unusual pseudo-Welsh ending to the word seems out of place for a team as far away from Wales as Suffolk, but it is recorded on Wikipedia and one other web source. See also Greens.

Boys from Rathbone Street is a nickname for Grays Athletic F.C., founded in 1890 and currently based at Corringham in Essex. The nickname appears on Wikipedia and is the name of a small local chain of card shops, which presumably once sponsored the club though they are not current sponsors; Rathbone Street itself is in London. An enamel badge in AFBC records the nickname alongside the useful dating 'Champions 1984–1985'. See also Blues, Gravelmen / G-Men, Grays.

Boys from Up the Hill was an early nickname for Headington United F.C., the club which changed its name to Oxford United in 1960. Headington is a district of Oxford, and in a more elevated landscape compared to the city centre; the final element in the place-name was originally *dun*, meaning 'hill' (Mills 1991). See also Dons, U's, United, Yellows.

Boys in Green is the nickname for the Republic of Ireland National Football Team. Although the island of Ireland had a representative team since 1882, this was organised by the Belfast-based Irish Football Association and a new body was set up in Dublin for the Irish Free State in 1921, called The Football Association of Ireland. The Republic's side played its first international in 1924; Wikipedia.

Brad is the nickname of the Wiltshire side, Bradford Town F.C., founded in 1992; a short form of the place-name; Wikipedia. For an earlier club in Bradford, see Firm.

Braidmen is a nickname for Ballymena United F.C., founded in Co. Antrim in 1928. The nickname, recorded in RNI2007, refers to the Braid district in the town. In RI 1997 the nickname is recorded as 'United'. See also Light Blues, Sky Blues, United.

Brakes is the nickname for Leamington F.C. Founded in Warwickshire in 1891, the club was reformed as a works side, Lockheed Borg and Beck F.C. in 1944, taking the current name of the brake-making factory originally founded as the Lockheed Hydraulic Brake Co. Ltd in 1929, from which the nickname comes. The name changed to A.P. Leamington F.C. in 1973 when the company was taken over by Automotive Products, then to the current name in 1985. The nickname is recorded in Avis 1966–70, W1979/80–86, 87–8, 2005–7, 2010–13. In celebration of a 2005 F.A. Cup run, the Warwickshire Beer Co. brewed a celebration ale with the perfect name of Brakes Fluid.

Brandanes, see Danes.

Brants is the nickname of Brantwood F.C., founded in Belfast in 1901; a pluralised short form of the place-name. Recorded in RI1997, RNI2007.

Bravehearts is a nickname for the Scottish national team, as used on Sky Sports on 12 October 2012. The nickname refers to the popularity of the 1995 film *Braveheart*, based on the life of Scottish freedom fighter William Wallace (d. 1305), played by Mel Gibson in the film. The nickname is also used in Wales for Swansea City Bravehearts DFC, a successful special needs club founded in 2000 (thanks to Richard Huws for both examples). See also Blues, Tartan Army / Terriers, Wembley Wizards.

Braves is the nickname of Eton Manor F.C., founded in Essex in 1901. The club badge shows a strong image of a growling lion with the motto *Fortes Fortuna adiuvate*, or 'Fortune favours the Brave', and the nickname suggests a team of roving warriors. Ultimately a French word, it was used by the French in North America to describe the warriors of the native American tribes. The English word had the same meaning long before that, but the nineteenth-century North American usage certainly made it more popular. Wikipedia records the club nickname. See also Manor.

Braw Lads is a nickname for Gala Fairydean F.C., founded in Galashiels near

Edinburgh in 1907. 'Braw' is the Scots word for 'brave', which, as in standard English, does not necessarily mean 'courageous' but "handsome, of fine physique, stout, able-bodied, fit for warfare" (the Scots Dictionary). With either meaning, it makes a splendid nickname; SFHA. See also Dean, Fairies, Gala.

Brazil is a nickname for several football clubs, from claimed association with, or ironic contrast to, the successful Brazilian national side. The clubs are:

⚽ Clydebank Rovers F.C., founded in 2004 near Glasgow (but usually as 'Little Brazil').

⚽ Cowdenbeath F.C., founded in Fife in 1881 (but usually as 'Blue Brazil'). See also Beath, Blue Brazil, Cowden, Fifers, Miners.

⚽ Newcastle It's Just Like Watching Brazil F.C., founded in Heaton, Tyneside in 1998 and folded in 2007. The club was also often referred to as Newcastle I.J.L.W.B. F.C. The club's surviving website and online journalism use the nickname 'Brazil'.

⚽ St Mirren F.C., founded in Paisley in 1877 (but usually as 'Paisley Brazilians').

Brecklanders is the nickname for two Norfolk clubs, both based in the Breckland District in the centre of the county. The clubs are:

⚽ Thetford Town F.C., founded in 1883. The nickname appears on Wikipedia. See also Town.

⚽ Watton United F.C., founded in 1888; W1987–2000.

'Breda is the nickname of Knockbreda F.C., founded in Belfast in 1948; a short form of the parish name; Wikipedia.

Brettsiders is the nickname of Hadleigh United F.C., founded in Suffolk in 1892. The river Brett flows through the town; W1995–2013.

Brewers is a nickname for clubs in a town with a substantial brewing industry, or connected in some way to a brewing business. The clubs are:

⚽ Alton Town F.C., founded in Hampshire in 1928 as a works side for the brewery Courage & Co., renamed Bass (Alton) F.C. in 1979, and then Alton Town Bass after a merger with Alton Town in 1990. The club plays at the Bass Sports Ground; Wikipedia. See also Town.

⚽ Burton Albion F.C., from the substantial brewing industry in Burton upon Trent. Formed in Staffordshire only in 1950, it was a successor to four previous Burton teams with traditional names dating back to 1871: Burton Swifts, Town, United and Wanderers; recorded in W1979/80–2009 and SSY2004/5–12/13. See also Albion.

⚽ Mitchells and Butlers F.C., founded in West Midlands, originally as a works side for the Mitchells and Butlers brewery. The brewery was founded in 1898 and merged with Bass in 1961; production switched to Burton upon Trent in 2002; the football club is recorded on the FCHD between 1987 and 1998; the nickname appears in W1994–5. See also Albion.

⚽ Tadcaster Albion A.F.C., founded in 1892, originally as John Smith's F.C., from the famous brewery in this North Yorkshire town. The club renamed in 1923, then reverted to John Smith's in 1926, while another club set up with the Tadcaster name, and the two then merged during the Second World War; Miller & Wright 1996, W2008–13.

⊕ Watford F.C. Founded in 1881 as Watford Rovers, the club changed to West Herts in 1893, then to Watford F.C. after a merger with Watford St Mary's in 1898. The nickname is said to come from the fact that Benskins Brewery owned the land on which the home ground of Vicarage Road was built, to which the club moved in 1922. The brewery, which was a mainstay of the Watford economy, had purchased the land for the club in 1921 and rented it out for very little payment. Nevertheless, the club tradition is that the nickname was always unpopular and it competed with 'Blues' after the adoption of blue shirts in 1927. If so, its longevity requires explanation. There is perhaps a possibility that the nickname was associated with the club before 1922, because the previous ground was that of the Rose and Crown pitch, another public house association, but perhaps it simply refers to the local economy more generally, as with other trading nicknames. Recorded in G1956–76, Churchill 1958, Richards 1960, Avis 1966–70, RY1970/1 and Pickering 1994. See also Blues, Golden Boys, Hornets, Horns / 'Orns, Saints, Wasps, Yellow Army.

⊕ Wickwar Wanderers F.C., founded in Gloucestershire in 1990. The club's website records previous teams in the town with the suffixes Athletic, Rovers and United, which had the nickname 'The Brewers' in the early decades of the twentieth century, recording the brewery works of Arnold, Perret and Co.

Brewery Boys is a nickname for two clubs, which are:

⊕ Bridgend Town F.C., founded in South Wales in 1954. Here, the nickname is a recent coining based on the club's move to a ground called The Brewery Field, and was used by 'Wales Online' on December 27, 2012; Huws 2013. See also Bridge, Town.

⊕ Hook Norton F.C., founded in the village near Banbury, Oxfordshire, in 1898. Although the club is not a works side, Hook Norton Brewery dominates the village, as the building is a substantial Victorian 'tower' brewery; it makes many fine real ales; W2008. See also Hooky.

Brickies is a nickname for clubs who play near substantial brick-making industries. The clubs are:

⊕ Fletton United, before its change of name to Peterborough and Fletton United in 1923. Fletton has major brick works and is a suburb of Peterborough. See also Posh.

⊕ Sittingbourne F.C., founded in Kent in 1886. After the coming of the railway to the town in 1858, it became a major producer of bricks for the rapid expansion of London; W1979/80 and W1982/3–2013. See also Bourne.

Bricky is the nickname of Brickfield Rangers F.C., founded in Wrexham in 1976; recorded in RW2011. A friendly short form of the place-name, used on many websites, but one records that the club's home ground is also nicknamed 'The Brickie'.

Bridge is a nickname for clubs with the element *–bridge* in their place-name. Examples are:

- Ardstraw Bridge F.C., founded in Newtownstewart, Co. Tyrone in 1972. Both the nickname and an image of a bridge are on the club badge; Wikipedia.
- Bridgend Town F.C., founded in South Wales in 1954. A short form of the place-name; Wikipedia. See also Brewery Boys, Town.
- Cooksbridge F.C., founded in East Sussex in 1962; W1989–90. See also Cooks.
- Darlington Cleveland Bridge F.C., founded in Co. Durham in 1903; recorded in Barton 1984 & 1985; W1983/4–96.
- Hullbridge Sports F.C., founded in Essex in 1947, from the last element of the place-name; Wikipedia. See also Sports.
- Merlins Bridge A.F.C., founded in Pembrokeshire at an uncertain date, but the nickname appears in match reports from 1972–3 on the 'Pembrokeshiresport.co.uk' website. See also Wizards.
- Newbridge-on-Wye F.C., founded in Powys in 1920; a short form of the place-name, recorded in RW2011. Huws 2013 has it in the form 'Bridgemen'. See also Wyesiders.
- Stambridge F.C., founded in Essex in 1888. Both the year and a stylised bridge appear on the club badge. The club renamed as United in 2001; W1990 and W1992.
- Woodbridge Town F.C., founded in Suffolk in 1885; W1992–6. See also Woodpeckers.
- Worsbrough Bridge Miners Welfare and Athletic F.C., founded in South Yorkshire in 1923, originally as W.B. St James. The nickname 'Bridge' appears on Wikipedia. See also Briggers.

Bridgers is the nickname for two clubs with the element 'bridge' in their place-name. The clubs are:

- Ivybridge Town F.C., founded in Devon in 1925; Wikipedia. See also Ivies / Ivys.
- Wadebridge Town F.C., founded in Cornwall in 1894; recorded in Avis 1966–70 and W1993–2004, W2009–11.

Bridges is the nickname for Three Bridges F.C., founded in 1901. The West Sussex village near Crawley originally had three bridges, and the nickname is appropriately in the plural; W1983/4–90 and W1995–2013.

Brig is a northern dialect word for Bridge and appears in the nickname of three clubs. In the Scandinavian languages the word for 'bridge' is pronounced with a hard g, as 'brigg'. This word seems to preserve the Viking pronunciation. The Lincolnshire place-name Brigg is the same word. The clubs are:

- Bamber Bridge F.C., founded in 1974. The nickname for this village in Lancashire is 'The Brigg', and the villagers are 'The Briggers', so it is also used for the football club, though the club tradition is to have only one g; W1994–2013.
- Bonnybridge F.C., founded in Stirlingshire in 1941, folded in 2003; SFHA.
- Worsbrough Bridge Miners Welfare and Athletic F.C., see next entry.

Briggers is a nickname of Worsbrough Bridge Miners Welfare and Athletic F.C., founded in South Yorkshire in 1923, originally as W.B. St James, recorded in W2012–13. See also Bridge.

Bris is the nickname of Brislington F.C., founded in Bristol in 1957; a short form of the place-name; W1995–2013. Miller and Wright 1996 record the variant form 'Briz', which reflects its pronunciation more closely.

Britannia is a football club suffix, though a rare one. The word is the Roman name for Britain, popular for nationalistic reasons. It is recorded for Stockland Britannia in AFBC (though no record exists of this club on the internet so it is not even clear which Stockland the club came from). Two clubs called Britannia F.C. exist today at Salford and Stourbridge, and F.C. Britannia is based at Beaumont Leys, Leicestershire. A historical club was Britannia Rovers at Middlesbrough (1897, FCHD), and the earliest usage was probably Bainsford Britannia in 1880, the original name of East Stirlingshire F.C.

Broch is a nickname for Fraserburgh F.C., founded in Aberdeenshire in 1910. In Scotland, 'broch' is the name of a type of ancient Pictish tower originating in pre-Christian times, but the word can also be used for the same meaning as the English place-name element –burgh, which itself can either refer to a fortification or a town. In this case, it is simpler: there are no brochs at Fraserburgh, the nickname copies the local Scots nickname for the town. Recorded in RS1993–2012, SFHA.

Broch United is the nickname of Fraserburgh United F.C., founded in 1976; so-called to distinguish it from the club in the previous entry; Wikipedia and SFHA record the fuller form, the club's own website just uses 'The Broch'.

Broddy is the nickname of Brodsworth F.C., near Doncaster, established in 1912. The club's official name has changed from B. Main (for the colliery), B. Miners' Welfare in 1963, B. Welfare in 2006, to just Brodsworth in 2011. The friendly short form appears as 'Brody' in W1994–2000, and as 'Broddy' in W2001–11.

Brook is the nickname for three clubs, from their official name. The clubs are:
- ⚽ A.F.C. Hayes, founded in London in 1974. The nickname comes from their first name, Brook House F.C., when they were a pub team based at the pub of the same name. W2007 (for Brook House), W2008–13 (for A.F.C. Hayes).
- ⚽ Millbrook A.F.C., founded in Cornwall in 1973 (Williams) or 1896 (Wikipedia) or 1888 (club's own website); the nickname is definitely printed in W1994–2005.
- ⚽ Shirebrook Town F.C., founded in Nottinghamshire in 1985, originally as S. Colliery, renaming in 1993; Miller and Wright 1996. See also Town.

Brookies is the nickname for the Derbyshire side, Holbrook Sports F.C., founded in 1996; as a pluralised friendly short form of the place-name; W2002–5.

Brooksiders is the nickname of Letcombe F.C., founded in Berkshire in 1990. The Letcombe Brooke runs through the village of Letcombe Regis to Wantage; W2000–13.

Brotherhood is an excellent nickname for a sports side or a religious group and both are expressed in Hafod Brotherhood F.C., a football club originally formed in the 1920s by the religious movement of the same name, founded in Swansea in 1910. An article on the club appears in *South Wales* for June 26, 2010; Huws 2013.

Brox is a nickname for Broxburn Athletic F.C., founded in West Lothian in 1948; a shortened form of the place-name, recorded on both Wikipedia and the club's own website. The club badge, however, shows an image of a badger, suggesting that the nickname may be punning with 'brocks' (AFBC and club website), though the team play in red. See also Burn.

Brum is a nickname for the city of Birmingham, as a short form of the local dialect pronunciation as 'Brummagem'. The inhabitants are called Brummies. The nickname is used for Brimingham City F.C. in Avis 1954–70. See also BLose, Blues, Heathens, Smallheath.

Bryn is a nickname of Bryntirion Athletic F.C., founded in Bridgend Co. Bor., Wales, in 1956; a short form of the place-name, recorded on Wikipedia in 2011, the nickname there changed in 2012 to Tirion. See also Athletic, Tirion.

B.U.'s is the nickname of Bo'ness United F.C., founded near Falkirk in 1945; from the club's initials; Wikipedia and SFHA.

Bucketshakers is an unofficial nickname for Bury F.C., from the perspective of Rochdale (recorded on the Football Fans Census website, 2003). The nickname puns on the official nickname, The Shakers, and suggests fund-raising efforts by the shaking of buckets. See also Grave Diggers, Shakers.

Buckley Babes was an unofficial nickname for the side at Wolverhampton Wanderers put together by manager Major Frank Buckley in the 1930s; recorded in Pickering 1994. See also Dingles, Tatters, Wanderers, Wolves.

Bucks is a nickname for clubs associated in some way with a building or place called 'Buck', or it may be used as a pun on this sound in the place-name. A buck is a stag, a male deer, a common element in pub and hotel names for its visual, heraldic quality, but it also carries connotations of male athletic prowess (and Bottle may record this meaning). In Chappel 1811 it is defined as 'a gay debauchee' (!). Stags are frequently used as symbols for forests, though this extra meaning does not seem to be present in nicknames using 'Bucks' (though it is definitely there for 'Stags'). The examples are:

- A.F.C. Telford United, founded in 2004 as a successor to the old Telford United F.C.; the club play at the New Bucks Hotel ground, built in 2000 as a replacement for the old Bucks Hotel ground. The nickname was also used for Telford United (1969–2004), successor to Wellington Town; Miller & Wright 1996, W2001–4 and SSY2004/5 for the old club; W2007–13 and SSY2012/13 for the new. See also Lilywhites (for both Telford and Wellington).
- Bootle F.C., founded in 1953. The Merseyside club's home ground was Bucks Park, now the New Bucks Park Stadium, and presumably was originally named from the presence of stags; recorded in W1979/80–2003. Dobson 1973, however, records

'Bootle "Buckoes"' as a nickname for the people of the town and suggests that it derives from a word for 'tough fighting men'. The expression is unrecorded on the internet, but *buckoes* does appear as a pirate expression, presumably either a variant of bucks or even of buccaneers, and used in the same way as the more famous expression 'me hearties'. It may, of course, derive from the Anglo-Irish word *buachaill* (pronounced a bit like 'buckle', see Dolan 1998), which means lad or boy and is used in popular speech, which could easily have spread to Merseyside.

⚽ Buckland Athletic F.C., founded in Devon in 1977, a play on the place-name; W2008–13.

⚽ Buckley Town F.C., founded in Flintshire in 1978 in a merger between B. Wanderers and B. Rovers. The club has a buck's head on its badge; an adaptation of the place-name; recorded in RW 2011. See also Claymen, Trotters, Wanderers.

⚽ Buxton F.C., founded in Derbyshire in 1877; the club has a proud stag on its badge, but the nickname is from the opening syllable of the place-name; recorded in Avis 1966–70, W1979/80–2013. A programme reproduced in W2005 (p. 594) further puns with the slogan 'The Bucks Stop Here'.

⚽ Long Buckby A.F.C., founded in Northamptonshire in 1937, originally as Long Buckby Nomads, a pluralised short form of the place-name; W1982/3–2013.

Buddies is the nickname of St Mirren F.C., founded in Paisley, Renfrewshire in 1877. St Mirren is the patron saint of Paisley. The Buddies nickname is that of the residents of Paisley, so-called, apparently, for their clannishness (from the Scots word 'bodies' for people, as in English 'somebody'). The nickname presumably refers to a perceived reserve in contrast to the friendliness of Glaswegians, so a synonym might be 'The Cliques'. Recorded through RY1973/4–SSY2012/13 and in RS1993–2012. Pickering 1994 mentions the nickname as having been "coined during the years of mass emigration to Canada and elsewhere", but does not explain or date this strange comment. See also Black and White Army, Paisley Brazilians, Saints.

Budgies is an unofficial nickname for Norwich City F.C., from the perspective of Ipswich Town supporters, and recorded on the 2003 Football Fans Census website. The nickname uses the slightly derogatory nickname for budgerigars, the popular cage bird, as a satire on the official nickname, The Canaries. Budgies are astonishingly multi-coloured, but the 'canary' yellow and green colours are their natural appearance. See also Canaries, Cits / Citizens.

Buds is the nickname and part official name of Aberbargoed Buds F.C., founded in Caerphilly Co. Bor. in 1957. The club was formed after the closure of A. Town and may have taken the Buds suffix as meaning 'new growth', or renewal, but the club's own website offers an acronym as an alternative idea, with the cautionary use of the word 'supposedly': Bedwelty Urban District Sides.

Buffs is the nickname of Kilwinning Rangers F.C., founded in Ayrshire in 1899. The nickname is usually used to refer to the Royal East Kent Regiment, who accepted the nickname in 1744 and held it till the closure of the force in 1961. It referred to the 'buff' colour, yellowish, of military leather garments worn under armour. The football club's website states that the nickname is recorded in the *Irvine Herald* as early as 21 September 1900, but acknowledges the difficulty of explanation. One theory is that a soldier from the East Kents once played for the team (though one wonders if the Ross-shire Buffs (the Seaforth Highlanders), might be a more likely association); another is that the term was simply a Victorian expression for 'smashing' (compare 'bully' or 'fizzer', though this meaning of Buff is not recorded in Partridge or the OED); or that the club played in a dull yellow-coloured, 'buff' strip. The last sounds entirely convincing, except that the early newspaper report used the phrase "the so-called Buffs", implying that the club were called Buffs but weren't actually buff-coloured (or perhaps were considered unequal to the reputation of the regiments). A buff yellow is not the club colour today and the colour in 1900 is not published. There are several specialised meanings of *buff* in the Scots Dictionary but none seem relevant. It is a surprisingly difficult nickname to explain; Wikipedia, SFHA, and a centenary badge in AFBC.

Builders is the nickname of Downes Sports F.C., founded in Hinckley, Leicestershire in 1968 (W), or 1971 (Pyramid Passion website); the name was taken from the large building company of F. E. Downes and Sons; W2002–5.

Bulldogs is the nickname of Ton Pentre A.F.C., founded in 1935 in Rhondda Cynon Taf, Wales; recorded in Avis 1966–70, W1979/80, W1987, W1996 and RW1994–2011. The nickname (also recorded on the club badge with a fierce-looking stylised bulldog, AFBC) seems to be an arbitrary choice, in the same style as rugby clubs, though the qualities of the beast are entirely appropriate, suggesting determination and fearlessness, and the dog is widely used as a symbol of Britishness. See also Rhondda Bulldogs, Ton.

Bullets is the nickname of Alsager Town F.C. in Cheshire, founded in 1965, in a merger of A. Institute and A. United. The nickname refers to the Second World War, when a major armaments factory was built here and the town expanded dramatically to house the employees; W2007–13.

Bulls is a nickname for several clubs (see Huws 2013 for further Welsh examples). Four are listed here:

🐂 Becketts Sporting Club F.C., founded in Birmingham in 1980; recorded in W1993–4. The club was in the vicinity of Beckett's Farm, but there seems no specific reason for the nickname.

🐂 Builth Wells F.C., founded in Powys in 1879 or 1883; a bull appears on the club badge and is popularly associated with the town, and it is famously used for the local rugby club; Huws 2013. See also Ambers, Black and Ambers, Wyesiders.

🐂 Hereford United F.C., from the famous breed of Herefordshire cattle. Founded in 1924 as a merger (hence the United), the club tradition is that the nickname was inherited from one of the previous clubs, but it has only recently appeared in mainstream printed sources; W1998–2006 and W2013, and SSY2004/5–06/7.

See also Lilywhites, Whites, United.

☺ **Holt United F.C.**, founded in Dorset in 1966. The nickname appears on the club badge in AFBC, but there seems no specific reason for it.

Bully Wee is the nickname of the Scottish side Clyde F.C., now based in Cumbernauld, but founded on the banks of the Clyde at Barrowfield in 1877. There are four theories concerning the meaning of the nickname but only one plausible answer **(1)**, which is that 'Bully' is the standard Victorian word meaning 'good' or 'first rate' (as in 'Bully for you!' and 'Bully beef') and 'Wee' is the Scots word for small, so the name means 'The Good Little Club'. The phrase was probably 'Bully Wee Clyde' originally, which is exactly how it is phrased in Johnston 1934; the expression positively contrasts this particular Clyde-side club with the larger ones. The three absurd theories are **(2)** that the early support base was in the tough district of Bridgeton, where wee bullies predominated (but why would the words be reversed and then applied to the club?); or **(3)** that some French visitors watching a match once remarked "But il'y, oui?", said to mean "Their goal, yes?" and sounding like 'Bully wee?', but this combination of words is simply not French and would hardly have been memorable, even if it had been said, because it was in a private conversation during one match. **(4)** Finally, Pickering 1994 records the nickname but adds another preposterous story, that it derives from a celebrated side in which the players were all short in stature! The true meaning of 'Good little club' is honest enough! Recorded in Johnston 1934, G1956–76, Harvey 1959, Avis 1966–70 and RS 1993–2012 and throughout RY and SSY from 1970/1 to 2012/13.

Buntings is the nickname for Buntingford Town F.C., founded in Hertfordshire in 1897. The place-name does refer to the bunting bird (the yellowhammer is a well-known variety, Mills 1991) and the bird is a badge of the town as well as the club; AFBC.

Burgh is a nickname for Scottish clubs with the element –burgh in their place-name, meaning 'town'. The clubs are:

☺ **Edinburgh University A.F.C.**, founded in 1878, but not having a continuous existence to the present. Recorded in RS 1993–7 and 2000–1 and SFHA.

☺ **Johnstone Burgh F.C.**, founded in Renfrewshire in 1956; Wikipedia, SFHA.

☺ **Musselburgh Athletic F.C.**, founded in East Lothian in 1934; Wikipedia, SFHA.

☺ **Newburgh F.C.**, founded in Fife in 1909, originally as N. West End, renaming in 1935; Wikipedia, SFHA.

Burn is a nickname for Scottish clubs which have this element in their official name. It is the common northern English and Scots word for a small river or stream; surprisingly, all examples come from West Lothian. See also Burnie. The clubs are:

☺ **Broxburn Athletic F.C.**, founded in West Lothian in 1948; a short form of the place-name; Wikipedia and club website, SFHA. See also Brox.

☺ **Stoneyburn F.C.**, founded in West Lothian in 1983; SFHA. See also Fulshie.

Burnie is a friendly form of the previous nickname (also occurring as **Burny**). Two clubs which use this version are:

- Blackburn United F.C., founded in West Lothian in 1978; Wikipedia.
- Whitburn Junior F.C., founded in West Lothian in 1933; Wikipedia, SFHA.

Bury is the nickname of St Margaretsbury F.C., founded in Hertfordshire in 1894, originally as Stanstead Abbots. The place-name element refers to a *burh* (*byrig* dative), a fortified settlement; W1986 and W1993–2005. See also Athletic.

Busby Babes was an unofficial nickname for a group of players for Manchester United F.C. during the years of Matt Busby's management of the club. The nickname refers to the relative youth of the players, who were trained in the club rather than bought in from rival teams. They won league championships between 1955 and 1957, but were seriously affected by the tragedy of the Munich air disaster in February 1958; the expression is widely used throughout football literature and was in use before 1958. See also Coach-Builders, Fergie's Fledglings, Heathens, Man, Manure, Munichs, Outcasts, Red Devils, Reds, United.

Butchers is a nickname for Abergavenny Thursdays F.C., founded in Monmouthshire in 1927. The main industry of Abergavenny at the time was the famous cattle market and associated meat trades; Wikipedia. See also Pennies, Thursdays.

Buttercups is recorded as a nickname (as 'Bacup Buttercups') for Bacup Borough F.C. in Dobson 1973, with the explanation that "the football team play in yellow jerseys". However, because the club is also nicknamed 'The Lilywhites', for their white shirts, this must be the wrong explanation; the nickname seems more likely to be one for the locality, as a pun on the place-name, transferred to the club. The local pronunciation is 'Bay-cup', so it rhymes with the popular expression "Wake up, Buttercup", a potential stimulus to the nickname (thanks to Chris Lewis). See also Borough, Lilywhites.

Bux is the nickname of Buxted F.C, founded in East Sussex in 1918, a short form of the place-name. Nevertheless, the same ideas are present here as in Bucks (q.v.), as Buxted Park features large in Buxted and Ashdown Forest is also near (thanks to Pam Combes for local advice), and in 2008 the players even posed in the nude for a charity calendar, suggesting the 'male athleticism' idea as well; W1993–6.

Buzz was a nickname for Merstham F.C., founded in Surrey in 1892; recorded in Miller & Wright 1996. The nickname must be a play on the club colours, amber and black, which are traditionally associated with wasps or bees, which make the familiar buzzing sound; the club badge also seems to show these insects. See also Moatsiders.

Buzzards is a nickname for Leighton Town F.C., founded in Bedfordshire in 1885. The town's full name is Leighton Buzzard and although this is based on a thirteenth-century family name, Busard (Mills 1991), a buzzard bird appears on the club badge and the nickname is used in local journalism (e.g. *Leighton Buzzard Observor*, 24 September 2012). The nickname is also used for the local rugby team. A buzzard is a handsome bird of prey and makes an appropriate sporting nickname. See also Reds, Sand Dobbers, Town.

C's is recorded as the present nickname of Coulsdon Town F.C., founded in London in 1968, originally as Reedham Park, then Netherne (1992), then C. Town (2006) before a merger with Salfords in 2007 generated the new name C. United, but in 2011 the club reverted to the name of C. Town; Wikipedia. See also Tops.

CA is a nickname of Sunderland Ryhope Community Association F.C., founded in 1961, originally as Ryhope Youth Club, renaming as Ryhope Community Association F.C. in 1971 and after a series of recent mergers becoming the present club in 2006. The nickname is an initialism of Community Association; Wikipedia. See also Ryes (and under Seahorses for one of the ancestor clubs, Kennek Roker).

Cabbage seems an unlikely nickname for the Edinburgh side, Hibernian F.C., founded in 1875, but it is based on rhyming slang: 'cabbage and ribs' / Hibs; Wikipedia. See also Hibs / Hibees, Turnbull's Tornadoes.

Caber was the nickname for Caberfeidh F.C., founded in New Elgin, Moray in 1972, closed in 1988. A short form of the place-name recorded on SFHA.

Cabes is the nickname of Beith Juniors F.C., founded in 1938. The Scots word means 'The Cabinet Makers', carpentry being one of the traditional industries of this Ayrshire town (though the last manufactory closed in 1983); Wikipedia, SFHA. See also next entry and Mighty.

Cabinet Makers was the nickname for the original Beith F.C., 1888–1938. See previous entry for explanation; Historical Football Kits website.

Cables is the nickname for Prescot Cables F.C., founded in 1884, originally as Prescot F.C. and as an offshoot from P. Cricket Club. The British Insulated Cables company was founded in 1890 and is the town's major employer. Recorded in Avis 1966–70. See also Tigers.

Cae is the nickname of Penycae F.C., founded in Wrexham in 1982; a short form recorded in RW1994–2011.

Caldersiders is a nickname of Padiham F.C., founded in Lancashire in 1878, but folded in 1916, reformed in 1949; from the club's location beside the River Calder. The nickname appears today (W2010–13), but according to Wikipedia was also used for the earlier club. See also Storks.

Caledonia/n/s is a club suffix, using the Roman Latin name for the country we now call Scotland. See following entries for examples.

Caley is a friendly short form of 'Caledonia/n' and appears as a nickname for clubs with this suffix. The clubs are:

☻ Caledonian F.C., founded in Inverness in 1885, which merged with Inverness Thistle in 1994 to form Caledonian Thistle, renaming as Inverness Caledonian Thistle in 1997. A friendly short form of the official name, which is an adjective from the Latin name for the country we now call Scotland. Recorded in RS1993–4 for Caledonian, RS1995–6 for Caledonian Thistle, RS1997–2012 for Inverness Caledonian Thistle. Avis 1970 records 'Calies' as the nickname for any club having 'Caledonian' in their name. See also Blues, Caley Thistle.

⊕ Irvine Caledonia F.C., founded in Ayrshire in 1896, closed in 1898. Despite its short life and early existence, the SFHA records two nicknames for the club. See also Black and Gold Brigade.

Caley Thistle is a nickname for Inverness Caledonian Thistle F.C., founded in 1994, in a merger between I. Thistle and Caledonian; SSY2012/13. See also Caley, ICT, Jags.

Calies was the nickname of London Caledonians F.C., founded in 1886, and primarily for Scots living in London; recorded in Fabian & Green 1960, vol. I, p. 273. The club's last recorded match was in 1939. Avis 1970 records this nickname for any club having 'Caledonian' in their name.

Cambrian is the nickname of Cambrian and Clydach Vale Boys and Girls Club, founded in Rhondda Cynon Taf in 1965, originally as Cambrian United. The nickname and part official name is an adjective from Cambria, a Latin name for Wales. The club is frequently referred to as just 'Cambrian', including on the club's website. See also Sky Blues.

Camby Talbot is a nickname for Cambusnethan Talbot A.F.C., founded in North Lanarkshire in 1999. The nickname combines a friendly short form with the full suffix; Wikipedia. See also Talbot.

Camels is a nickname for two clubs with names which suggest camels, but which do not really refer to the famous desert-travelling mammal. Examples are:

⊕ Camelford F.C., founded in 1893. The Cornish place-name refers to the River Camel; W2012–13.

⊕ Cammell Laird F.C., founded in 1907, originally as the Cammell Laird Institute team. Cammell Laird is a major ship-building firm in Birkenhead, Wirral. The club badge shows both a warship and a camel; Wikipedia. See also Laird/s, Shipyarders.

Campers is an unofficial nickname for Prestatyn Town F.C., founded in Denbighshire in 1910; the nickname (as in 'holiday camp' for this popular seaside resort) has been used in the forum of the club's own website, on 19 September 2009 and 12 November 2012; Huws 2013. See also Seasiders.

Camrose Blues is a nickname for Basingstoke Town F.C., founded in Hampshire in 1896, for their blue and yellow strip and their home turf, The Camrose Ground; recorded in RNL2001–2. See also Blues, Dragons, Stoke.

Can Cans is the nickname of Forres Mechanics F.C., founded in Moray in 1884. The nickname puns on the middle sound of 'Mechanics', using the name of the famous French dance invented in 1830. It can be spelled Can Can, Can-Can or Cancan. Recorded in RS1993–2012, SFHA.

Canaries is a nickname for clubs which play in yellow shirts, but most will be so named under the influence of the famous Norwich City, itself so named for a slightly different reason. The clubs are:

⊕ Barwell F.C., founded in Leicestershire in 1992 in a merger of Barwell Athletic and Hinckley; yellow shirts and green shorts; W1994–6, W2002, W2012–13. See also

Kirkby Roaders.

☺ Caernarfon (or Carnarvon) Ironopolis F.C., founded in Gwynedd in 1895, closed 1903. The club was a works side for the De Winton iron works and were normally nicknamed 'The Nops', but a match report in the *North Wales Chronicle* for 26 January 1895 uses 'Canaries', which is evidence that the nickname was originally adapted from the town's place-name, as in the next entry (thanks to Richard Huws). See also Nops.

☺ Caernarfon Town F.C., founded in 1876; recorded in W1980/1–95, W1996–2005, RW 1994–2011, and in AFBC. The Gwynedd club plays in yellow shirts with green shorts, the same colours used by other clubs with this nickname, though here the nickname is also suggested by the place-name, and the previous entry helps confirm this.

☺ Garden Village A.F.C., founded in Swansea in 1922. The colours associated with canaries are yellow and green, which are also associated in Wales with daffodils (q.v.), but here the club plays in black and white stripes. Nevertheless, there are three small birds on the club's badge. It may be that the nickname was formed in the same way as that of Norwich, as a celebration of the locality's canary-breeding pastime (see also Linnets for Barry Island), but in this case the colours never transferred to the strip. See also Village.

☺ Hitchin Town F.C., originally founded in Hertfordshire in 1865, reformed in 1928. The club play in yellow shirts and green shorts, first adopted in the 1928 reformation. Recorded in Avis 1966–70, W1979/80–2013.

☺ Keynsham Town F.C., founded in Somerset in 1895, reformed 1945; W1982/3–91 and Miller & Wright 1996, for an all-yellow strip at the time (now black and amber); the opening syllable of the place-name must also have encouraged the nickname. See also K's.

☺ Norwich City F.C., not from their distinctive yellow and green colours (which came afterwards), but from the fame of Norfolk as a centre for canary breeding. The club was founded in 1902 and was first nicknamed The Cits or The Citizens. In 1905 the *Eastern Daily Press* interviewed new manager John Bowman, who said that he knew of the city's existence beforehand and "I have … heard of the canaries". By 1907 the change had been made. A new strip appeared in yellow and green, a canary badge was added to the shirts as early as 1908 (most unusual for the time), and the new stadium in 1908 was soon named 'The Nest'. Howard Chandler reports that *Luton News*, reviewing forthcoming fixtures on December 31st 1908, used the nickname. Striking images of canaries have appeared on the club's formal badges since 1922. It is one of the nicknames featured on the 1933 Ogden cigarette card set, the 1936 Thomson 'stamp' album, Churchill 1958, Norris 1959 and AA 1960 give the strip colour as the explanation; Avis 1954–70, G1956–76, Richards 1960, SWSCYB 1962–3, and throughout RY1970/1–SSY2012/13. See also Budgies, Cits / Citizens.

☺ Stotfold F.C., founded in Bedfordshire in 1904, originally as S. Athletic. The club is traditionally nicknamed 'The Eagles' but 'Canaries' is recorded in W1985, and the club has long played in a yellow shirt with black shorts. See also Eagles.

Candy Rock is the nickname for St Roch's F.C., founded in Provanhill, Glasgow, in 1921. The nickname is Glaswegian rhyming slang, with Rock pronounced the same way as the saint's name, and Candy is merely there to complete the phrase and confuse those who don't know; Wikipedia, SFHA.

Candystripes is the nickname of Derry City F.C., founded in 1928. The Northern Ireland club plays in the Irish Republic's leagues. The club plays in red-and-white striped shirts, which were adopted in 1934 in tribute to the strip of Sheffield United, shortly after Billie Gillespie, player for Sheffield 1913–32, became the player-manager of Derry. The red-and-white stripes are considered to be like those in various sweets, such as candy rock, hence the nickname. Recorded in RI1997, 2006.

Capitals is a nickname for Winchester City F.C., founded in Hampshire in 1884. The famous city of Alfred the Great used to be the capital of the kingdom of Wessex, then of England, before London was adopted as the capital during the reign of Edward the Confessor (1042–66); Wikipedia and W2013. See also Citizens, City.

Cards is a nickname of three clubs, either as a short form of the place-name Cardiff or of the colour 'cardinal red'. The clubs are:

☺ Cardiff Corinthians A.F.C., founded in 1898. The team plays in a maroon and amber strip: the nickname expresses 'Cardiff' rather than the colour cardinal red; Wikipedia. See also Alpha, Corinthians, Corries.

☺ Gorleston F.C., founded in Norfolk in 1887. The club adopted green colours in 1903, but the club's own website states that they were first nicknamed The Cards, from wearing cardinal red shirts with blue shorts. See also Greens.

☺ Woking F.C. (as both 'Cards' or 'Cardinals'). Founded in Surrey in 1889, the club adopted colours of cardinal red and white halves early on, and it is from the cardinal red that the nickname comes. The club's badge copies that of the town, and looks ecclesiastical because it shows the cross of Edward the Confessor, but there is no religious association in the nickname; nevertheless, one of the old enamel badges illustrated in AFBC shows an image of a cardinal. The nickname appears in full in the title of the 1997 club history by Roger Sherlock: *Cardinal Red*. Recorded in Avis 1966–70 (as Cardinals), W1979/80–90 and W1992 and Miller & Wright 1996 as Cardinals, W1991 and W1994–2013 and SSY2004/5–09/10 as Cards.

Cartoon Army is an unofficial nickname for Newcastle United F.C., from the perspective of Sunderland supporters, recorded on the 2003 Football Fans Census website. The nickname puns on the expression 'Toon Army' for supporters of the club, and the slightly derogatory word for traditional hand-drawn animated films, cartoons. See also Barcodes, Entertainers, Frenchcastle, Geordies, Magpies, Skunks, Toon, Tyneside Professors, Tynesiders.

Castle is the nickname of Newcastle Town F.C., formed in 1964 in Newcastle-under-

Lyme, Staffordshire. A short form of the place-name, recorded in W1994–2013.

Castlebar is the nickname of Castlebar Celtic F.C., founded in Co. Mayo in 1924. The place-name is cited as a nickname on Wikipedia, though the club's own website uses 'Celtic'. See also Celtic.

Castlemen is a nickname for two clubs associated in some way with medieval castles, though in the second case it is because of the place-name; Huws 2013 reports several more examples in Wales. The clubs are:

⚽ Harlech Town F.C., founded in Gwynedd in 2010. The impressive fortress of Harlech Castle overlooks the playing field; club website and Huws 2013.

⚽ Rochdale Town F.C., founded in Lancashire in 1924, originally as a church side in the town of Castleton in Rochdale borough. In 1990 they were renamed Castleton Gabriels, then Rochdale Town in 2008; Wikipedia. See also Angles, Gabs, Garrison, Guardians, Messengers.

Casuals is a football club name suffix. The name implies a certain degree of relaxed self-confidence, or indifference to rules and regulations; and also amateur status in contrast to the paid professionals. The word has also been used as a name for various football cultural movements, such as the Aberdeen Casuals. The modern Casuals United, however, is nothing to do with football, because it is a right-wing protest group. The clubs are:

⚽ Casuals F.C., founded in London in 1878, which merged with the Corinthians in 1939 to form the Corinthian Casuals. The nickname is recorded for the new club in W1982/3–5, W2006–13, Miller & Wright 1996. See also Amateurs, Corinthians, Pink and Chocolate.

⚽ Corinthian Casuals, see previous entry.

⚽ Icklesham Casuals F.C., founded in Sussex in 1937; badge in AFBC, club website.

⚽ Walton Casuals F.C., founded in Surrey in 1948; recorded in W2006–7. See also Stags.

⚽ Westminster Casuals F.C., founded by members of the Conservative Party in London in 1991. Founder Alex Aiken claims on the club's website that "Casuals seemed to sum up our chaotic approach".

⚽ Wolverhampton Casuals F.C., founded in 1899 as W. Old Church F.C., renamed Amateurs in 1914, becoming Staffordshire Casuals in 1946 and then W. Casuals in 1981; W1986–90.

⚽ Yeovil Casuals F.C., founded in Somerset in 1895 and so-called until renaming as Yeovil Town in 1907; Wikipedia. See also Glovers.

Cats was a nickname of Kilkenny City A.F.C., founded in Co. Kilkenny in 1966, originally as EMFA F.C., but dissolved in 2008. The unusual name EMFA is a composite of the first letters of the street names Emmett Street and Fatima Place. The club was renamed in 1989. The nickname used that of the natives of Kilkenny. The proverbial expression 'to fight like Kilkenny cats' refers to a notorious folk tale in which two fighting cats were tied together by their tails by soldiers in 1798 (see

Ayto & Crofton 2005, p. 611); RI1997, 2006. See also Black Cats, City.

Cattachs is the nickname of Brora Rangers F.C., founded in Sutherland (now part of Highland) in 1879. The nickname uses the local expression for anyone from the historic county of Sutherland. The word has also become a local surname; its etymology is unknown, though it seems related to 'Cataibh', the name for the Eastern area of the county which is often used to refer to the whole county. The badge of the club, however, shows a heraldic image of a Scottish wildcat (several examples in AFBC). This animal is also on the badge of neighbouring Golspie Sutherland F.C. (1877) and the animal is well-known in the area. This does not mean that the nickname has a feline etymology, but the coincidence of sounds and symbol can still generate an attractive punning association. Recorded in RS 1993–2012, SFHA.

Cauther is the nickname of West Calder United F.C., founded in West Lothian in 1950. The nickname is used for each of the towns of West, Mid and East Calder, based on local pronunciation (first recorded in 1886 according to the Scots Dictionary). The place-name Calder also occurs elsewhere and generates local variants as a nickname: Cawdor in Nairn, Cadder in Lancashire; Wikipedia, SFHA.

Cavaliers / Cavs are nicknames for two clubs, based on the nickname used by the Parliamentarians for the flamboyant royalist soldiers during the seventeenth-century Civil War. The word is related to 'cavalry', for horse-riding soldiers. The name is proverbally used to express taking advantage over rivals, all ideologies suitable for a sporting side, and it appears in many sports throughout the world:

⊕ F.C. Cavaliers, based at Carrington in Nottingham; internet records for the club starting in 2011. 'Carrington Cavaliers' is also used for a cricket club.

⊕ Nelson Cavaliers A.F.C., founded in 1972 at Nelson in the Caerphilly Co. Bor. The club folded in 1975 but was reformed in 1983; the club website uses it as a nickname; Huws 2013.

Cedars was a nickname of Leytonstone F.C., founded in Greater London in 1886, recorded in Fabian & Green 1960, vol. I, p. 269), said to be after the trees at the corner of Davies Lane, Leytonstone. The club ceased to exist in a merger with Ilford in 1979, and is now represented by Dagenham and Redbridge F.C. ('The Daggers'). See also Stones.

Cefni is a nickname of Llangefni Town F.C., founded on Anglesey in 1897. The place-name means 'church at [the river] Cefni' (Owen & Morgan 2007), so the nickname is either a reference to the river-side location or a friendly short form of the village name, but the lenited (mutated) form in the place-name (c becoming g) has been reversed, showing that the nickname was coined by Welsh speakers; Wikipedia. See also Dazzlers.

Celebrant was a nickname for Gretna F.C., founded in 1946 and closed in 2008. Gretna Green in Dumfries and Galloway was the famous centre for runaway marriages before a change in Scottish law in 1856, and the town continues to be a popular location for marriages for romantic reasons. A celebrant is the name of the official who presides over a wedding ceremony; Wikipedia. See also Anvils, Black and Whites, Borderers, Monochrome, Weddingmakers.

Celtic / Celts are nicknames for clubs with the word 'Celtic' in their official name. These clubs frequently have an Irish Roman Catholic ancestry, but may also be named under the influence of the famous Glasgow side. In this context, the word is pronounced 'Seltic'. Another 'Irish' name in use is Hibernian. Huws 2013 lists several more examples in Wales. The clubs are:

⚽ Belfast Celtic F.C., founded in 1891, closed in 1949; as 'Celts' on Wikipedia. See also Grand Old Team, Mighty Belfast Celtic.

⚽ Blantyre Celtic F.C., formed in Lanarkshire in 1914, originally as B. United but changing to Celtic in 1916. The club was dissolved in 1992; Wikipedia.

⚽ Castlebar Celtic F.C., founded in Co. Mayo in 1924. The club plays in a Celtic-like strip at the Celtic Park Ground and the suffix is used as a nickname on the club's own website. See also Castlebar.

⚽ Celtic F.C., founded in Glasgow in 1887, by Brother Walfrid, an Irish Catholic brother who was inspired by the work of the Hibernian club in Edinburgh. It was he who also coined the name 'Celtic', to convey its importance as a club for Irish immigrants. An early postcard reproduced in McCarra's *Scottish Football* (1984), shows a player in the strip of 1903–5 with a motto 'Come Away, Celts!' Recorded in BoF1905–6 (p.268), Johnston 1934, the 1936 Thomson 'stamp' album, *Stedfast* May 1963, Avis 1966–70, and SSY2012/13 (all as 'Celts'). See also Bhoys, Hoops, Lisbon Lions, Quality Street Kids, 'Tic, Tims.

⚽ Colwyn Celts F.C., a youth side recently formed in Colwyn Bay, North Wales. The nickname 'Celts' is used on internet match reports from 29 April 2012 onwards.

⚽ Cwmbrân Celtic F.C., founded in Torfaen Co. Bor. in 1925, originally as the club for the local Catholic Young Men's Society, it became Cwmbrân Catholics in the 1960s and 'Celtic' in 1972; recorded in RW2011.

⚽ Donegal Celtic F.C., founded in Belfast in 1970. The club's name, nickname and strip are in tribute to the Glasgow Celtic side. The club plays at the Donegal Celtic Park; Wikipedia. See also D.C., Wee Hoops.

⚽ Draperstown Celtic F.C., founded in Co. Londonderry in 1968. The club's name, nicknames and strip are in tribute to the Glasgow Celtic club; Wikipedia. See also D.C., Half Hoops.

⚽ Farsley Celtic A.F.C., founded in the village near Leeds in West Yorkshire in 1908, and closed in 2010. The club played in an all-blue strip despite the Celtic suffix and nickname, which normally deploys in green. The programme continued to be called *Follow the Celts* long after 'The Villagers' was adopted as a nickname. Recorded in Avis 1966–70, W1991–3 and Smith 1991/2–1994/5. See also Little Celts, Villagers, Village Lads.

⚽ Stalybridge Celtic F.C., founded in Greater Manchester in 1909. The club called itself Celtic from the outset, but it was a successor to Stalybridge Rovers. The reason for the Celtic suffix is exactly the same as that for the Glasgow club. During the nineteenth century, a great many Irish immigrants moved to the town to find work during the industrial revolution, and the name honours the Irish culture they brought with them. The famous song, 'It's a Long Way to Tipperary', was actually written in Stalybridge in 1912; Avis 1966–70, W1979/80–2013.

- West Allotment Celtic F.C., founded in Longbenton, near Newcastle-upon-Tyne, in 1928. The club has a pithead on its badge but plays in green and white hoops like the famous Glasgow side. The Roman Catholic church is prominent in the locality, which presumably had a large number of Irish or Glaswegian immigrants during the Industrial Revolution; Wikipedia. See also West.

Centurions is the nickname for Cirencester Town F.C., founded in Gloucestershire in 1889. Cirencester was the important Roman town of Corinium from the first century onwards; the club's home ground is called Corinium Stadium and a centurion's head appears on the club badge; W2003–13. For other 'Romanesque' clubs, see Gladiators, Romans. See also Ciren, Town.

Cestrians is a nickname for clubs in a town with the place-name element 'Chester', using the medieval Latinised form of this ancient Roman place-name (e.g., *Cestre* in Domesday Book, 1086). Other nicknames also use the word as part of a longer one (e.g. Gloucestrians). The clubs are:

- Chester F.C., founded in 1885, renamed City in 1883, and closed in 2010. Recorded in Pickering 1994. See also Blues, City, Ivies, Magpies, Romans, Seals.
- Chester-le-Street Town F.C. in Co. Durham, founded in 1972. The nickname is recorded in Barton 1984 & 1985, W1982/3–2013.
- Stockport County F.C., using the nickname in tribute to the county of Cheshire, recorded in Avis 1966–70. See also County, Hatters.

Chaddy is the nickname of Chadderton F.C., founded in Greater Manchester in 1947, originally as Millbrow, then Chadderton Amateurs, becoming the present name in 1957. A friendly short form of the place-name, W1990–2013.

Chairboys is the nickname of Wycombe Wanderers F.C., founded in Buckingham-shire in 1887, apparently by apprentices working in the local furniture-making industries for which High Wycombe was famous in the nineteenth century. The nickname clearly puns with the more familiar word 'choirboys', and the town still has an important role in furniture design and making. It appears in Rothmans since 1994–5, with, unusually for this series, an explanation: "after High Wycombe's tradition of furniture making". A fanzine is called *Chairboys Gas*; W1988–93 and RY1994/5–SSY2012/13. See also Blues, Wanderers.

Charterhouse was the nickname for Shepshed Charterhouse F.C., founded in Leicestershire in 1975 as a successor to Shepshed Albion (1890–1975). The club is recorded with this nickname in W1979/80. In 1991 the club reverted to its old 'Albion' suffix but folded and was succeeded by S. Dynamo in 1994. A Charterhouse is the name for a medieval house of Carthusian monks, a name often retained for the buildings after the Reformation and used for schools established in those buildings. In this case the name honours Garendon Abbey. See also Albion, Dynamo, Raiders.

Chase is a nickname for Chasetown F.C., which was founded in 1954 as Chase Terrace Old Scholars (from Chase Terrace High School in Staffordshire), so the nickname is a short form of the official name, but the word also suggests competitive running; Wikipedia. See also Scholars.

Chats is the nickname for Chatham Town F.C., founded in Kent in 1894; a short form of the place-name recorded in W1979/80–2013.

Cheaterfield is an unofficial nickname for Chesterfield F.C., from the perspective of Mansfield supporters. It is recorded on the 2003 Football Fans Census website. The nickname puns on the place-name and implies that the club won promotion through cheating, though the insult misfires when one realises that cheetahs are the fastest cats in the world. See also Blues, Spireites, Team of Surprises, Town.

Cheesemen is the nickname of Cheddar A.F.C., founded in Somerset in 1892. The club badge shows a 'friendly' cheese holding a football and the nickname is after the locality's fame as the original source of the most popular cheese in the world. Recorded in W2013 and Wikipedia.

Chelsea Headhunters is the nickname of the more hooligan branch of supporters of Chelsea F.C. The name replaces the earlier 'Chelsea Shed Boys' (1970s and '80s). 'Headhunters' implies tribal savagery, but 'Shed Boys' refers to The Shed, the end of the stadium where more vocal supporters tended to gather; Wikipedia. See also Blues, Chelski, Drake's Ducklings, Pensioners.

Chelski is an unofficial nickname for Chelsea F.C., coined by supporters of rival teams. It adopts a Russian suffix in mockery of (or perhaps tribute to) Chelsea's owner, the Russian billionaire Roman Abramovich, whose investments since 2003 have transformed the fortunes of the club. The nickname is early, it is used in the title of Harry Harris' *The Chelski Revolution* (London: Blake Publishing, 2003). See also Blues, Chelsea Headhunters, Drake's Ducklings, Pensioners.

Chemists is recorded in W1986 as the nickname for Boots Athletic F.C., a Nottinghamshire works side for the head office of Boots the Chemists. The club continued to be listed without a nickname till 1993.

Chenecks is a unique word, used only for Northampton Old Northamptonians Chenecks F.C., founded in 1946, originally as a school side called Chenecks F.C., for boys at Northampton Grammar School who wanted to play football rather than going along with the school's preferrence for rugby. The word is an artificial composite of letters from the school's 'houses': *Ch*ipseys, *Sp*encers, *Be*cketts and *St* Crispins; Wikipedia.

Cherries is a nickname for two clubs which play in red shirts. The clubs are:
- A.F.C. Bournemouth, and the earlier Bournemouth and Boscombe Athletic F.C., from the cherry-red colour of their shirts. An alternative explanation is that their

home ground, Dean Court, was built in 1910 next to a cherry orchard, though the colour is the more obvious explanation. The 1933 Ogden card gives the colour reason, but adds that the club is visually depicted as a courtier. The cartoon shows a well-dressed man of the Tudor period holding a football, perhaps suggesting that some sense of exclusivity (as in cherry-picking) is the sense. An alternative form is the Cherry Bees (Avis 1970). 'Cherries' is the nickname in G1956–76, Churchill 1958, Norris 1959, Harvey 1959, Richards 1960, Avis 1966–70, and throughout RY and SSY from 1970/1 to 2012/13. See also Seasiders.

⚽ Sturminster Newton United F.C., founded in Dorset in 1871, originally as Panthers F.C. until the 1890s, renaming as Sturminster St Mary's until 1945, then the present name. The team wears a red shirt with black shorts; Wikipedia. See also Panthers.

Cherrypickers was the nickname and part official name of Glenbuck Cherrypickers F.C., founded in the 1870s as G. Athletic, and dissolved in 1932 after the collapse of the town's coalmine. The town itself no longer exists but the club has been the subject of a printed history by M. H. Faulds and Wm. Tweedie, *The Cherrypickers. Glenback, Nursery of Footballers* (Muirkirk, 1951), which argues that the word started as a nickname, adopted as an official name in c.1900, because of a local association with the 11th Hussars during the Boer War. This regiment was nicknamed 'The Cherry Pickers' after an incident during the Peninsular War in Spain, in which the soldiers had raided a cherry orchard.

Chessey is the nickname of Chessington and Hook United F.C., founded in Surrey in a merger between C. United (1921) and Hook Youth in 1986; a friendly short form of the place-name; W2008–13. See also Blues.

Chi is a nickname for Chichester City F.C., founded in Sussex in 2000, in a merger between C. City (1893) and Portfield (1896). The nickname is a local expression for the city of Chichester. Although it is a short form of the place-name, it is pronounced with a long *i* (as in high) (thanks to Pam Combes for advice). Recorded in W2011–13. See also City, Lilywhites.

Chicken-bree Team was an unofficial nickname for Renton F.C., an early Scottish pioneering club (1872–1922) from Dumbartonshire. The expression uses a Scots word for brew, or broth, though the true sense may not be 'chicken soup' as Wikipedia records a story that it was a mixture of port wine and eggs, a special diet the players thrived on; but the nickname has another possible explanation. Johnston 1934 (p. 29) records the tradition that the large expenditure on chickens in the club's books in the 1880s actually meant 'veiled professionalism', or secret payments to the players. It is possible that both are true, the costs of the special diet hiding a further outlay in wages. Nevertheless, "for the rest of Renton's life it passed under the name of the 'Chicken-bree' team".

Chickens is a nickname for two clubs, for different reasons. The clubs are:

⚽ Bradford City F.C., where it is an unofficial nickname from the perspective of Huddersfield supporters (recorded on the Football Fans Census, 2003). The nickname mocks the official nickname of 'Bantams', but if it was intended to suggest cowardice (one meaning of 'chicken'), the nickname fails, because bantams used to be used in cock-fighting. See also Bantams, Citizens, Cocks, Gents, Paraders, Sadford.

⊛ **Chickerell United F.C.**, founded in Dorset in 1910. The nickname is here a playful pun on the place-name, and is recorded in local match reports (*Daily Echo*, 7 May 2012); a handsome chicken appears on the club badge, standing on a football.

Chicks is the nickname of Dorking F.C., founded in Surrey in 1880. The Dorking is a famous breed of chicken, and one appears on the club badge. Recorded in Avis 1966–70, W1979/80–2013.

Chinnocks is the nickname for West and Middle Chinnock F.C., founded in Somerset in 2007; a pluralised short form of the official name, recorded on the club website.

Chippy is a nickname of Chipping Norton Town F.C., founded in Oxfordshire in 1893, and recorded on the club website. See also Magpies.

Chips is the excellent nickname for Chipstead F.C., founded in Surrey in 1906; a short form of the place-name; W1989–2013.

Chocolates was a nickname for Llanfairpwll F.C., founded in Anglesey in 1899, originally as L. Rovers. The 'boys in black and white' website reports that in the 1920s the players wore a chocolate-brown shirt, inspiring this nickname, but these are not the present colours and the club does not seem to have a current nickname. In the 1860s the village became famous for the invention of the longest place-name in Europe, with 58 letters, the full version of which does appear on the club badge as well as on the famous railway station platform. The club's website announces that they have the longest football club name in the world: Clwb Pêl Droed Llanfairpwllgwyngyllgogerychwyrndrobwllllantysiliogogogoch F.C.; websites and Huws 2013.

Church is the nickname of Alvechurch F.C., founded in Worcestershire in 1929, and reformed in 1996; a short form of the place-name; W1979/80–2013.

Church / Churches is a nickname for Norwich CEYMS F.C., founded in 1988. The abbreviation in the name stands for Church of England Young Men's Society; both forms are recorded on Wikipedia.

Cider Army is another nickname of Bristol City F.C., founded in 1897. The name refers to the local cider industry of Somerset. Since 2005 the mascot has been a robin called Scrumpy (another name for cider); Wikipedia. See also Babes, City, Eighty-Twoers / 1982 Ltd, Reds, Robins, Slave Traders, Turnips, Wurzels.

Ciren is a nickname for Cirencester Town F.C., founded in Gloucestershire in 1889; a short form of the place-name; W1997–2002. See also Centurions, Town.

Citizens is a nickname for clubs representing a city, and usually having 'City' in the club official name. Where there are rival clubs in the same place (as in Manchester), the nickname may imply a sense of legitimacy, in contrast to the rivals, but this is not the primary meaning. The examples are:

☺ Clwb Pêl-Droed Dinas Bangor (Bangor City F.C.), founded in Gwynedd in 1876. The club's own website acknowledges this nickname but uses 'City' in its discussions. The Welsh language version of the nickname is *Y Dinasyddion* and is also well-established (thanks to Richard Huws); Avis 1966–70, W1986–2005, RW 1994–2011. See also City, City Slickers.

☺ Bradford City F.C., founded in West Yorkshire in 1903; Wikipedia. See also Bantams, Chickens, Cocks, Gents, Paraders, Sadford.

☺ Brechin City F.C., founded in Angus in 1906, in a merger of B. Harp and B. Hearts. Recorded in RS1993–2012 and through RY1972/3–SS2012/13. See also Hedgemen.

☺ Coventry City F.C. The nickname makes a single appearance in RY1983/4, along with other older nicknames for the club. See also Bantams, Blackbirds, Peeping Toms, Singers, Sky Blues, Wheelmen.

☺ Durham City A.F.C., founded in 1949; recorded in W1979/80–93 and Barton 1984 & 1985. See also City.

☺ Gloucester City A.F.C., founded in 1883, renamed as G. City in 1902; the nickname is said on Wikipedia to have been used in local media in the club's early history. See also City, Gloucestrians, Tigers.

☺ Leeds City F.C., founded in West Yorkshire in 2005. A much earlier club of the same name and nickname was an ancestor club for Leeds United (1904–19), also recorded on Wikipedia.

☺ Manchester City F.C., founded in 1880, reformed as City in 1894. The nickname is recorded as early as 1933 (Ogden) and in Johnston 1934, G1956–76, Churchill 1958, AA 1960, Richards 1960, RY1971/2–82/3, 1986 Panini sticker, and RY1991/2–SSY2012/13. See also Bitters / Bitter Blues, Blues, City, Council Housers, Man, Massives, Sheik City, Stockports.

☺ Norwich City F.C., see Cits / Citizens, below.

☺ Prudhoe Town F.C., founded in Northumberland in 1959 as Ovington, renaming to Prudhoe East End in 1984 and the present name in 1994. The nickname is actually rather mysterious because Prudhoe is a modest town and Citizens is usually used to represent a city; W1992–4 for East End; W1995–2009 for Town.

☺ Welwyn Garden City F.C., founded in Hertfordshire in 1921; W1993–2013.

☺ Winchester City F.C., founded in Hampshire in 1884; Wikipedia. See also Capitals, City.

Cits / Citizens were the first nicknames of Norwich City F.C., from its foundation in 1902 to 1907, when the club started to use 'The Canaries' (q.v.); Wikipedia. 'Cits' appears to be a unique form for 'Citizens'. See also Budgies, Canaries.

City is a football club name element, if the home of the team is a city. It is frequently used on its own to refer to the club. It might also be used to emphasise a sense of local legitimacy (see Citizens). As with 'Town', most clubs which have 'City' as a nickname also have other nicknames. Listed here are those which have been noticed as 'City':

⚽ Bletchley Town F.C., recorded in W2000 for the club in Milton Keynes, Buckinghamshire, which was the brief renaming of Milton Keynes F.C. in 1999. The club had previously been nicknamed Borough, and this entry as 'City' appears to be an error, caused by the confusing relationships between several clubs called Milton Keynes City and Bletchley. See also Borough.

⚽ Clwb Pêl-Droed Dinas Bangor (Bangor City F.C.), founded in Gwynedd in 1876. The club's own website acknowledges the nickname 'Citizens' but uses 'City' in its discussions; W1980/1–5 list 'City'. See also Citizens, City Slickers.

⚽ Bath City F.C., founded in 1889 (as Bath A.F.C.), recorded in Avis 1966–70 and W1979/80–93, W1999–2005. See also Romans, Stripes.

⚽ Bradford City Womens F.C., founded in West Yorkshire in 1988; Wikipedia and club's own website.

⚽ Brechin City F.C., founded in Angus in 1906; Pickering 1994. See also Hedgemen.

⚽ Canterbury City F.C., founded in Kent in 1946; recorded in Avis 1966–70, W1979/80–2002.

⚽ Chelmsford City F.C, founded in Essex in 1938; Avis 1966–70, W1979/80–2013. See also Clarets.

⚽ Chester F.C., recorded in Avis 1966–70, despite the fact that the club did not rename as Chester City till 1983; RY1994/5–2000/1, SSY2004/5–09/10. The club reformed in 2010 and the nickname is also recorded in SSY2010/11 for the new Chester F.C. See also Blues, Cestrians, Ivies, Magpies, Romans, Seals.

⚽ Chichester City F.C., founded in 2000, in a merger between C. City (1893) and Portfield (1896). Recorded for the old club in W1983/4–5. See also Chi, Lilywhites.

⚽ Cork City F.C., founded in Co. Cork in 1984; RI1997. See also Leesiders, Rebel Army.

⚽ Durham City A.F.C., founded in 1949; W1994–2013. See also Citizens.

⚽ Edinburgh City F.C., founded in 1928, reformed in 1986; RS1994–2001; SFHA (though for a club founded in 1966). See also City Slickers.

⚽ Elgin City F.C., founded in the Morayshire cathedral city in 1893; RY2000/1–SSY2012/13. See also Black and Whites.

⚽ Gloucester City A.F.C., founded in 1883; W1979/80–85. See also Citizens, Gloucestrians, Tigers.

⚽ Guildford City F.C., founded in Surrey in 1877, originally as Guildford F.C. and reformed as Guildford United in 1921. The club took the city title in 1927, but closed in 1974, reforming again as A.F.C. Guildford in 1976. The club renamed as G. City in 2006. Avis 1966–70 records the earlier club as 'City'; W2007–13 for the new club. See also Guild, Pinks, Sweeney.

⚽ Inverness City F.C., founded in 2006; Wikipedia.

⚽ Kilkenny City A.F.C., founded in Co. Kilkenny in 1966 but dissolved in 2008;

Wikipedia. See also Black Cats, Cats.

- Leeds City F.C. was a predecessor of Leeds United, founded in 1904, dissolved in 1919 and replaced by the present club; recorded in Pickering 1994.
- Leicester City F.C., founded in 1884 as Leicester Fosse, the club reformed in 1919 as the present name, which was just after Leicester was given city status. See also Filberts, Fosse / Fossites, Foxes, Ice Kings, Nuts.
- Lincoln City F.C., founded in 1884; recorded in Pickering 1994, who adds that this was the first club to adopt the City suffix, in 1892. See also Imps / Red Imps, Deranged Ferrets.
- Manchester City F.C., founded in 1880, reformed as City in 1894. Recorded early, in BoF1905–6, and in RY1970/1 and the Williams League Directories 1985–95. See also Bitters / Bitter Blues, Blues, Citizens, Council Housers, Man, Massives, Sheik City, Stockports.
- Milton Keynes City F.C., recorded in W2001–4 for the second club with this name (successor to Mercedez Benz F.C.). See also Blues.
- Oxford City F.C., founded in 1882; W1979/80–86 and W1994–2013.
- St Albans City F.C., founded in Hertfordshire in 1908; W1982/3–6. See also Saints.
- Stoke City F.C., founded in Staffordshire in 1863, originally as Stoke Ramblers F.C., reformed as Stoke in 1908, renamed as City in 1925; recorded in Pickering 1994. See also Clayheads, Jolly Green Giants, Potters, Sjoke City.
- Truro City F.C., founded in Cornwall in 1889. Recorded in Avis 1966–70 and W2010–13. See also Tinmen, White Tigers.
- Wells City F.C., founded in Somerset in 1890. The nickname has not actually been noticed in use, but none other is known for the club.
- Winchester City F.C., founded in Hampshire in 1884; W2006–10. See also Capitals, Citizens.
- Worcester City F.C., founded in 1902; Avis 1966–70, W1980/1–2013. See also Blues, Dragons, Faithfuls, Loyals, Royals.
- York City F.C., founded in 1922. The nickname is used in RY1971/2. See also Minstermen, Y-Fronts, Yorkies.

City Devils used to be the nickname of Cambridge City F.C., founded in 1908 as C. Town, changing to City in 1951. The nickname may be a playful reference to their break from the church side Cambridge St Mary's when they were founded in 1908. It is recorded in W1979/80–93, Smith 1991/2–1995/6, and Pickering 1995. See also City, Lilywhites.

City Gents, see Gents.

City Slickers was a temporary nickname for Edinburgh City F.C., recorded only in RS1993. The nickname uses an American idiomatic phrase for anyone from a town or city who is unused to rural lifestyles, suggesting the sense of 'sophisticates'. The nickname has also been recorded for Bangor City on the Seasiders Online website (23 October 2009, though Huws 2013 dates it much earlier, to journalism in the

1960s). For Edinburgh, see also City; for Bangor see also Citizens, City.

Civil is the nickname for Newport Civil Service F.C., founded in Wales in 1963; Wikipedia.

Clach is a nickname for Clachnacuddin F.C., founded in Inverness in 1885, from the first syllable of the place-name; Wikipedia. See also Lilywhites.

Clacks was the nickname of Clackmannan F.C., founded in 1961, folded in 1995. The nickname was a popular one for the small county of Clackmannanshire; SFHA.

Clan is a nickname for Easington Sports F.C., founded in 1945 in a suburb of Banbury, Oxfordshire. The name is usually associated with Scottish family networks and there seems no specific reason why the club use it, but it suggests many ideas, such as 'family', 'team', 'rivalry' and 'loyalty'. The nickname is recorded on the club's own website, with the detail that it dates from the outset of the club, but without explanation; Wikipedia, W2010–13. See also Sports.

Claret & Blues is a nickname for clubs which play in these colours. The clubs are:

- ☺ Aston Villa F.C., founded in Birmingham in 1874; recorded on Wikipedia in the singular, 'The Claret and Blue'. The 1905–6 *Book of Football* mentions 'Aston "Clarets"' on p. 26, but the Historical Football Kits website shows that the two colours have always been used together since 1886. See also Lions, Perry Bar Pets, Seals, Villa / Villans / Villains.

- ☺ Hastings United F.C., founded in 1948 and folded in 1985. This club was the subject of a history by Philip Elms in 1985, called *The Claret and Blue*, but it appears that its official nickname was The U's and this was assumed in a rebranding of Hastings Town as a new Hastings United in 2002. See also Arrows, Town, U's, United.

- ☺ West Ham United F.C., founded in London in 1895. The phrase is used as the name of a fans' website. See also Academy of Football, Cockney Boys, Eastenders, Hammers, Hamsters, ICF, Irons, Wet Sham.

Clarets is a nickname for clubs who play in claret-coloured shirts, often combined with other colours. Examples are:

- ☺ Burnley F.C., founded in Lancashire in 1882, who first adopted the claret-and-sky-blue strip for the 1910–11 season. The nickname appears in all but the first of the Rothmans series: RY and SSY from 1971/2 to 2012/13 and in G1976. See also Dingles, Gene Puddle, Moorites, Royalites, Turfites.

- ☺ Chelmsford City F.C., founded in Essex in 1938; an all-claret-coloured strip; W1994–2013. See also City.

- ☺ Horley Town F.C., founded in Surrey in 1891 as Horley F.C., and merging with Gatwick Rovers in 1908. The word 'Town' was added in 1975. The club plays in a claret and blue strip; W2008–13. See also Hammers.

- ☺ Launceston F.C., founded in Cornwall in 1891; claret shirts and socks with blue shorts; W1994–2013.

Clarkie's was the nickname for Gateshead Clarke Chapman F.C., founded on Tyneside in 1949; the club was based at the Clarke Chapman Sports Ground and was sponsored by the Clarke Chapman engineering company; recorded in W1985–8.

Class of '66 was a nickname for the famous England national side which won the World Cup in 1966. Recorded in Pickering 1994. See also Roy's Boys, Sassenachs, Sven's Men, Three Lions.

Clayheads is a derogatory unofficial nickname for Stoke City F.C., from the perspective of Crewe supporters, and recorded on the 2003 Football Fans Census website. The nickname is a play on the official nickname, 'The Potters', coined in honour of the traditional porcelain industry. See also City, Jolly Green Giants, Potters, Sjoke City.

Clayholers is a nickname for Stranraer F.C., founded in Dumfries and Galloway in 1870. The nickname uses the name for people from the old part of Stranraer, an area called 'The Clayhole'. It is pronounced 'Cl'yhole' locally; printed in SSY2012/13. See also Blues.

Claymen is a nickname for Buckley Town F.C., founded in Flintshire in 1978, in a merger between B. Wanderers and B. Rovers. The nickname looks like a pun on the sound of the last syllable in the place-name: –*kley*, but it actually records the importance of the clay industry here, used for pottery and brick-making (thanks to Richard Huws); recorded in RW2011. See also Bucks, Trotters, Wanderers.

Cleveland Cowboys was a proposed nickname for Middlesbrough F.C., and was even listed as such by Moss 1983. It was the idea of Malcolm Allison (1927–2010) during his managership of Middlesbrough in the 1980s, but it would have given the club an entirely inappropriate American style. Cleveland was the new county (1974–96), of which Middlesbrough was the capital. See also Boro, Ironsiders, Nops, Riversiders, Scabs, Smoggies, Teessiders, Washers.

Club is the nickname of three clubs, for different reasons. The clubs are:

- Fisher Athletic F.C., founded in Bermondsey on 1908. The club was refounded as Fisher F.C. in 2009. The nickname is recorded in W1982/3–90 but it seems to have started as a popular expression for the club from the outset, when it was formed without a name as a sports club for underprivileged youths by the headmaster of the Catholic Dockhead School. It was named after the martyr, St John Fisher, three weeks later, and even today 'The Club' appears as an expression on the club's own website. See also Fish.
- Sheffield F.C., founded in 1857. This club is internationally recognised as the oldest one in the world, so it is quite entitled to call itself *The* Club; W1994–2007. See 'Countrymen' for another detail. The 1905–6 *Book of Football* uses the expression 'Sheffield Club' (p.184), which perhaps suggests that the nickname is a short form of this expression. See also Dinosaurs.
- South Shields Cleadon Social Club F.C., founded in Co. Durham in the early 1960s; the nickname appears in W1995–2004. Here, the nickname emphasises the connection with a social club. Today, the club is called Cleadon Club F.C.

Clun is the nickname of Pontyclun F.C., founded in Rhondda Cynon Taf in 1896; a short form of the place-name recorded in RW 1994–6.

C.O.s is the nickname of Clapton Orient F.C., as used in Johnston 1934. The expression neatly chimes with the abbreviation for 'Commanding Officer' but was only possible when Orient had Clapton in its official name (between 1898 and 1946). See also O's, Orient.

Coach-Builders was a nickname for Newton Heath LYR F.C., founded in 1878. This is the ancestor team of Manchester United, originally a works side for the Lancashire and Yorkshire Railway employees at Newton Heath; the club renamed as Manchester United in 1902. The nickname is recorded in BoF1905–6, p. 242. See also Busby Babes, Fergie's Fledglings, Heathens, Man, Manure, Munichs, Outcasts, Red Devils, Reds, United.

Coad's Colts was a nickname for the players of the Dublin side Shamrock Rovers F.C., during the player-managership of Paddy Coad (1949–60). Under his leadership, the club had a radical youth recruitment programme; Wikipedia. See also Hoops, Rovers.

Coasters is a nickname for clubs whose home is beside the sea, at the coast. The examples are:

- A.F.C. Fylde, founded originally as Kirkham and Wesham F.C. in Lancashire in 1988, renaming in 2008; used on the club's own website and in match reports in the *Blackpool Gazette*. The old club had a badge showing a dove with an olive branch, but I have found no record of them having been nicknamed 'The Doves' (AFBC).
- Lossiemouth F.C., founded in the harbour town in Moray in 1945. The club shows a lighthouse on its badge. Recorded in RS 1993–2012; SFHA.

Cobblers is the nickname for two clubs based in shoe-making centres, a cobbler being the traditional name of a shoe-maker. A Scottish club's nickname with the same meaning is 'Souters'. The clubs are:

- Northampton Town F.C., founded in 1897. Much of the old county of Northamptonshire was involved in the shoe industry in the nineteenth century. The nickname is recorded early, in BoF1905–6, alongside 'Bootdom' as a nickname for the town, and also 'Town'. Howard Chandler reports that *Luton News*, reviewing forthcoming fixtures on December 31st 1908, used the nickname. The later mainstream sources are the 1933 Ogden card, Johnston 1934, G1956–76, Churchill 1958, Norris 1959, Avis 1954–70, Richards 1960, SWSCYB 1962–3, and throughout RY1970/1–SSY2012/13. *A Load of Cobblers* is a fanzine. Addis 1995 reprints newspaper articles of 1947 which use the nickname (pp. 23–4). See also Shoe Army, Tayn, Town.
- Street F.C., founded in Somerset in 1880, after the village's substantial shoe-making tradition. Since 1967 the club's home pitch has been The Tannery and the nickname appears on the club badge. The village now has a Shoe Museum; W2000–13.

Cobbydalers is the nickname of Silsden F.C., founded in 1904. The nickname is that of the town, which lies at the head of the Yorkshire Dales near Keighley, and which is used in many local businesses and charities, such as The Cobbydale Singers. The meaning of the *cobby* element is not clear because there are too many choices. It is a standard colloquial word variously meaning headstrong, obstinate, stout, hearty, lively, brisk or merry, so it could be derogatory or suggestive of happiness; Wikipedia.

Cobs is the nickname of Holker Old Boys F.C., founded for 'old boys' (meaning 16-year-olds) of Holker Central Secondary School in Holker Street, Barrow-in-Furness in 1936. The school has long gone, the club survives independently. The nickname is almost certainly an acronym, adapted from the school and club name. A reference to the former Barrow and Watford player Keith Eddy on the internet records that he started playing football for 'Holker C.O.B.S', a strong clue that the name means 'Holker Central Old BoyS'; W1994–2013. See also Stags.

Cock 'n' Hens is a nickname for Glentoran F.C., founded in Belfast in 1882. The club badge shows an image of a chicken (Wikipedia and AFBC). The nickname may derive from rhyming slang between the place-name and the alternative nickname: Glens / Hens. Recorded in *Stedfast* July 1963 (as 'The Cock and Hens'), Pickering 1994 (as Cock and Hens), RNI2007 (as Cock 'n' Hens). See also Glens.

Cock Robins was the nickname of Croydon Common F.C., established in 1897 and closed in 1917, from the claret shirts. The nickname is used in the title of Alan Futter's 1990 history of the club, *Who Killed the Cock Robins?* See also Robins.

Cockerels is a nickname of Croesyceiliog F.C., founded in Cwmbrân, Torfaen Co. Bor., in 1964; recorded in RW2011. The club shows a cockerel on its badge, and the place-name itself means 'the cock's cross', from the name of a tavern at a cross-roads, first recorded in 1628, but there have been other 'Cock' inns there since (see Owen & Morgan 2007). See also Croesy.

Cockney Boys is an unofficial nickname for West Ham United F.C., using the nickname for those born and bred within central London. Adrian Room argues that the word 'Cockney' derives from the Middle English word *cokeney*, 'cock's egg', meaning a small or misshapen egg, and was applied to the people of the capital of England because of their ill health, compared to the robust health enjoyed by the countryman (Room 2006); Wikipedia. See also Academy of Football, Claret and Blues, Eastenders, Hammers, Hamsters, ICF, Irons, Wet Sham.

Cocks is an unofficial nickname for Bradford City F.C., from the perspective of Huddersfield supporters (recorded on the Football Fans Census, 2003). The nickname is a play on the official nickname of 'Bantams', which are a breed of chickens which used to be used in cock-fighting. See also Bantams, Chickens, Citizens, Gents, Paraders, Sadford.

Cod Army is a nickname for Fleetwood Town F.C. Founded in 1997 (but earlier clubs go back to 1908), the nickname is a strong reminder of the importance of the fishing industry to this Lancashire coastal town. Various websites give this as a nickname for the club's supporters, but SSY2012/13–12/13 have it for the club. See also Fishermen, Reds, Trawlermen.

Codheads was a nickname for Marske United F.C., founded in North Yorkshire (Redcar and Cleveland) in 1956. The nickname is printed in W1994–6 and illustrates the 1980s and '90s popular use of expressions in *–heads* to denote single-minded behaviour, usually for mockery. In this case it refers to the town's fishing industry, though this has hardly ever been an exclusive trade in this attractive seaside resort. See also Seasiders.

Coed is a short-form nickname for two Welsh clubs which have this element (meaning 'woodland') in their place-name. The clubs are:

⚽ A.F.C. Llwydcoed, founded in 1931, reformed 1948, originally as Llwydcoed Welfare F.C., for this local mining community in Rhondda Cynon Taf; recorded in RW1994–2011.

⚽ Pencoed Athletic A.F.C., founded in Bridgend Co. Bor. at an uncertain date, but before 1999; used in a match report on 'Wales Online' on 18 October 2012.

Coedy is the nickname of Coedpoeth United F.C., founded near Wrexham in 1885; a friendly short form of the place-name, recorded in RW2011.

Cogan is the nickname for Cogan Coronation A.F.C., founded near Penarth in the Vale of Glamorgan in 1961, based at the Cogan Coronation Club. The nickname is used on the club's own website.

Colemen / Coalmen is the nickname of Coleshill Town F.C., founded in Warwickshire in 1894, a play on the first syllable of the place-name; W1986–92 has 'Colemen', W1993–2005 has 'Coalmen'. See also Coleshillites, Colts, Greens, Rabbits.

Coleshillites is an early nickname for Coleshill Town F.C., founded in Warwickshire in 1894; an abstraction from the place-name, recorded on a fans' website. See also Colemen / Coalmen, Colts, Greens, Rabbits.

College is a nickname for at least three clubs based at educational institutions. The clubs are:

⚽ Bilston Community College F.C., in West Midlands; recorded in W1998–9.

⚽ New College Academy F.C., founded in Wiltshire in 2002, originally as New College Swindon F.C.; W2012–13.

⚽ University College Dublin A.F.C., founded in 1895, originally as Catholic University Medical School F.C. The club changed its name in 1908, when the university took over the medical school. Recorded in RI2006. See also Students.

Colliers is a nickname for clubs associated with a coal-mining community or as a works side for a colliery (see also Colliery and Colls). Many also have the word 'Welfare' in their title, for the Miners Welfare Association. The Examples are:

⚽ Ashington Community A.F.C. in Northumberland, founded in this coal-mining town in 1883, and famous as the birth place of Bobby and Jackie Charlton; recorded in Barton 1984 & 1985, W1980/1–2013.

⚽ Barnsley F.C., from the coal industry in Barnsley's hinterland. The 1933 Ogden card records the name and adds "It used to be said of Barnsley that whenever they wanted a player they went to a coal pit in the district and shouted down the shaft"; also in the 1936 Thomson 'stamp' album. The nickname continues to appear quite late, in G1956–65, Churchill 1958, Harvey 1959, Sweetule 1959, Richards 1960, SWSCYB 1962–3, Avis 1966–70 (as well as Tykes) and Moss 1983. The early editions of Rothman's Year Book prefer 'Tykes' but Colliers makes a come-back, appearing as an alternative nickname in RY and SSY from 1985/6 to 2012/13. See also Battling Barnsley, Reds, Saints, Tykes.

⚽ Chirk A.A.A.F.C., founded in Wrexham Co. Bor. In 1876; recorded in RW2011 and on an old enamel badge in AFBC. The nickname records the town's coalmining industry, which was a mainstay of the local economy from the seventeenth century to the 1990s. See also Triple A's.

⚽ Denaby United F.C., founded in South Yorkshire in 1895; recorded in Avis 1966–70. See also Reds.

⚽ Fryston Community Welfare F.C., founded in West Yorkshire in 1910; W1983/4–5 (as Colliery or Colliers). The club is now called Fryston A.F.C.

⚽ Grimethorpe Miners Welfare F.C., founded in South Yorkshire in 1972; disbanded in 2000; W1986–91.

⚽ Horden Colliery Welfare A.F.C., founded in Co. Durham in 1908; recorded in Barton 1984 & 1985, W1982/3–5 and W1992–2013. See also Welfare.

⚽ Hucknall Colliery Welfare F.C., founded in Nottinghamshire in 1945, renaming as 'Town' in 1987; W1985. See also Town, Yellows.

⚽ Woolley Miners Welfare F.C., founded in South Yorkshire before 1971 (FCHD), the club seems to disappear after 1990; W1986–90.

Colliery is a nickname for any club with Colliery in the official name (see also Colliers and Colls). Examples include:

⚽ Easington Colliery F.C., founded in Co. Durham before 1920, reformed in 1964 and 1981; W1982/3–2005; Barton 1984 & 1985.

⚽ Fryston Community Welfare F.C., founded in West Yorkshire in 1910; W1983/4–5 (as Colliery or Colliers). The club is now called Fryston A.F.C.

⚽ Rossington Main F.C., founded in South Yorkshire in 1919, originally as R. Colliery; Miller & Wright 1996, W1997–2013.

⚽ Thorne Colliery F.C., founded in South Yorkshire in c.1929. The nickname appears on the club's website and in W1986.

Colls is a nickname for clubs associated with a group of collieries (see also Colliers and Colliery). The examples are:

⚽ Atherton Collieries A.F.C., founded in Lancashire in 1916; W1994–2005. See also Colts, Miners, Sooty, Welfare.

⚽ Pontefract Collieries F.C., founded in West Yorkshire in 1958; W1982/3–2013.

Colnesiders used to be one of the nicknames of Huddersfield Town A.F.C., because the Leeds Road stadium (used 1908–1994) was virtually on the banks of the River

Colne. The nickname would fit many other such riverside nicknames, but it is only mentioned on two websites and must have been rarely used. See also Scarlet Runners, Terriers, Town.

Colony is the nickname for Colony Park F.C., founded in Aberdeenshire in 1978; a short form of the club name used in internet match reports.

Colts is a common football club nickname for youth sides (from the word for young male horses), and it is also used in cross-country running, horse racing and cricket (the last for a player in his first season). Huws 2013 records its use for several Welsh teams in the Swansea area, which field both adult and youth sides. Four 'adult' clubs elsewhere which use it are:

- Atherton Collieries F.C., founded in 1916; here, the nickname may either be a pun on the second word in the official name, or it could simply be a repeated typing error in the Williams directory: W2006–13. The club has certainly not become an all-youth side. See also Colls, Miners, Sooty, Welfare.
- Castell Alun Colts F.C., founded in 1982 in Hope, Flintshire. Recorded in RW1994–5.
- Coleshill Town F.C., founded in Warwickshire in 1894, is a recent addition to the nicknames of the club since a merger with Dosthill Colts of Tamworth in 2011; Wikipedia. See also Colemen / Coalmen, Coleshillites, Greens, Rabbits.
- Cwmfelinfach Colts A.F.C., founded in Caerphilly Co. Bor. in 1978. The club expanded by acquiring Fleur-de-Lys A.F.C. in 2001, and in turn merged with Crusaders A.F.C., merging again in 2008 with Ynysddu Welfare to become the new Ynysddu Crusaders; internet history of local football dated July 2012.

Commandos was a nickname for Royal Marines F.C., founded at Lympstone in Devon in 2008, folded in 2012; W2011–12.

Common is the nickname of the Sussex side, Little Common F.C., founded in 1966, originally as Albion United, changing to Little Common Albion in 1986; W1988–90 (as Commoners) and W1994–5 (as Common).

Commoners is the nickname of Mole Valley Sutton Common Road F.C., founded in Surrey in 1978. 'Mole Valley' was added to the name in 2008; W2012–13 record 'Commoners', W2009–11 'Commers'.

Comrades is a football club name element, and a natural one for a band of warriors. It is usually, however, associated with the Comrades of the Great War Society, which set up social clubs for returning veterans throughout the UK after the First World War. It is often used as a nickname for those football clubs, and, like the clubs formed in the Miners Welfare movement, the football club may have survived long after the demise of the social initiative which founded it. Examples are:

- Ballycare Comrades F.C., founded in Co. Antrim in 1919 by returning soldiers from the 12th Royal Irish Rifles. Recorded in RI 1997, RNI 2007.
- Berkhamsted Town F.C., founded in Hertfordshire in 1919 as B. Comrades. The club renamed as Town in 1922 but retained Comrades as a nickname. It closed in

2009 and the successor club, Berkhamsted F.C., has also adopted the nickname (recorded in W2012–13). See also Berko, Lilywhites.

- Bewdley Town F.C., originally founded as Wribbenhall Victoria in Worcestershire in 1885, soon renaming as Bewdley Victoria and then as B. Comrades after the First World War. The club played as The Comrades until 1927. The club revived the Comrades official name in 1952 and used it till 1974. The club was reformed in 1978 as B. Town, but soon started to use the Comrades suffix for its youth sides. See also Town, Vics.

- Blaenau Ffestiniog Comrades of the Great War F.C., founded in Gwynedd in c.1919. The website of the present Blaenau Ffestiniog Amateurs gives a history of previous clubs in the town, back to 1882. This was the name adopted when the club reformed after the First World War, but by 1921 they were playing under the name of Blaenau Ffestiniog F.C. See also Amateurs, Quarry Men.

- Eastbourne United Association F.C., founded in 1894, originally as First Sussex Royal Engineers, then Eastbourne Royal Engineers Old Comrades in 1920, the simpler Eastbourne Old Comrades in 1922, then E. Comrades in 1928, before adopting E. United in 1951; Wikipedia, and an enamel badge in AFBC. See also U's, United.

- Eccleshall Comrades F.C., founded in Staffordshire in 1918. The club was still playing in 1926 and was reformed in 1971 as Eccleshall F.C. The club website says that the 1918 club was 'probably based at the Comrades of the Great War Society in Gas Works Lane'. See also Eagles.

- Shotton Comrades F.C., founded in Co. Durham in 1973 for older players from Shotton Juniors club. The reason for the nickname is unclear, though there is a Shotton Comrades Social Club in the town; W1985–93. See also Coms.

- Stone Comrades F.C., founded in Staffordshire in 1919. Mentioned on the website of Eccleshall F.C.

- Westerhope Comrades F.C. A badge for this club is illustrated in AFBC. The club is based at Newcastle-upon-Tyne and is no doubt associated with the Comrades social club in Westerhope. A match report from 2007 is on the internet.

Coms is a short form of Comrades and appears as the recent nickname of Shotton Comrades F.C., founded in Co. Durham in 1973; W1994–2005. See also Comrades.

Constitution (or Constitutes) is the nickname of Dergview F.C., founded at Castlederg, Co. Tyrone in 1980, in a merger of F.C. Castlederg and Mourneview Celtic F.C. The reason for the nickname is not published. The local newspaper is called *Tyrone Constitution* but no connection is known; Wikipedia. See also Derg.

Cooks is the nickname for two clubs, based on their place-name. The clubs are:

- Cogenhoe United F.C., founded in 1967. The nickname is a pun based on the local pronunciation of the Northamptonshire place-name as 'Cook-no'; W1989–2013.

- Cooksbridge F.C., founded in East Sussex in 1962; W1988. The club seems to

105

disappear after 1990. See also Bridge.

Corinthians / Corinths is a football club suffix and often also used as a nickname for clubs so called. Greek classical names were very popular in sport, even before the establishment of the new Olympic Games in 1896, and such names were also used for many leagues, many of which survive (e.g., Athenian, Corinthian, Hellenic, Isthmian and Spartan). 'Corinthian' is certainly classical because it is the name of one of the ancient Greek styles of architecture, and the ancient Isthmian Games were held on the Isthmus of Corinth. Nowadays, the word simply refers to sport with a hint of classicalism, but the word in English originally meant something else. The 1699 'Canting Crew' dictionary defines a Corinthian as "a very impudent, harden'd, brazen-fac'd Fellow" (Simpson, 2010), because of the reputation that ancient Corinth had in the Bible for lawlessness and licientiousness. Then the meaning shifted, to describe the similar behaviour of young aristocrats, shifting again to become the more neutral "phrase applied to men of fashion" (Thackeray's 1854 definition in the OED). This was the meaning of the word at the time of the foundation of Corinthian F.C. in 1882, so its first use in football is like other words in this dictionary, such as Blades, Bloods, Bucks, and Knuts. The OED records it as still meaning 'a swell' in 1890, from *The Daily Telegraph*. The success of the Corinthian club, however, meant that the word shifted in meaning again, becoming "a wealthy amateur of sport who rides his own horses, steers his own yacht, etc." (OED). To the Victorians, this was the so-called ideal, that sportsmen should be independent, non-salaried 'amateurs', and this club was considered to represent that ideal. In modern times, however, the word simply connotes sport without any value judgement or any suggestion that the players are wealthy amateurs. The suffix is also popular overseas, notably used for 'Sport Club Corinthians Paulista', founded in São Paulo, Brazil in 1910, who beat Chelsea to take the World Club Cup on 16 December 2012. 'Corries' appears as a variant of the nickname. Clubs nicknamed Corinthians are:

⚽ Cardiff Corinthians A.F.C., founded in Wales in 1898; the word is used as a nickname on the club's own website.

⚽ Corinthian F.C., founded in Hartley, Kent, in 1972, originally as a youth side; Wikipedia.

⚽ Corinthian Casuals F.C., formed in the 1939 merger between Corinthians and Casuals. See also Amateurs, Casuals, Pink and Chocolate.

⚽ Corinthians F.C., the famous club founded in London in 1882, merging with Casuals in 1930 to form the modern Corinthian Casuals. The club history by Edward Grayson (*Corinthians and Cricketers*, London: Naldrett Press, 1955) sometimes uses the nickname 'Corinth' or 'Men of Corinth'. The fame of this club almost certainly caused the shift in the meaning of the name 'Corinthian'. The club is mentioned throughout BoF1905–6 but without a nickname..

⚽ Crendon Corinthians F.C., a youth side founded at Long Crendon in

Buckinghamshire in 1999; club website.

- Islington Corinthians F.C., founded in London in 1932, closed in c.1940. An old badge of the club appears in AFBC.
- Rothwell Corinthians F.C., founded in Northamptonshire in 1932; W1996–2013.
- Swindon Corinthians F.C., founded in Wiltshire before 1910 and surviving into the 1930s. Known from two postcards in the local collection at Swindon Central Library.
- Tarleton Corinthians, founded in Lancashire in 1936. The club has a Corinthian column on its badge and the motto 'A Pillar of Strength'. The suffix might just have been suggested by the opening syllable of the name of the home ground in Carr Lane; club website.

Cormorants is the nickname of Clwb Pêl Droed Tywyn / Bryncrug F.C., formed in a merger of two clubs in Gwynedd in 1989. The bird appears on the club's badge, together with the date '1886' for one of the earlier clubs. The nickname is recorded on the 'nonleaguematters' website for a match report of 26 August 2012. Richard Huws explains it as a reference to the nearby cormorant conservation centre at Craig yr Aderyn; websites and Huws 2013.

Corn was a nickname used for Runcorn F.C. (est. 1918, closed 2006), as a short form of the place-name, recorded in Avis 1966–70. See also Linnets.

Corner is the nickname of Chimney Corner F.C., founded in Co. Antrim in 1952; a short form of the place-name. Recorded in RNI 2007.

Cornies is listed on Wikipedia as an alternative nickname of Wellingborough Town F.C., founded in 1867, reformed in 2004. The traditional nickname for the club is 'The Doughboys', but corn-milling is one of the main industries of the town. Another Wellingborough Club, Whitworths, is nicknamed 'The Flourmen' (q.v.). See also Doughboys.

Corribsiders is a nickname for Corrib Celtic F.C., founded at Annaghdown, Co. Galway, in 1980. The nickname and official name is taken from the nearby Lough Corrib.

Corries is a nickname of two Welsh clubs, which use it as an abbreviation for the word 'Corinthians' (q.v.) in their official name, though sometimes the nickname is used as a formal name. Huws 2013 includes two further Welsh examples. The clubs are:
- Brecon Corinthians A.F.C., founded in Powys in 1946; recorded in Avis 1966–70, W1987 and RW 1994–6.
- Cardiff Corinthians A.F.C., founded in 1898; recorded in RW1994–2011 and the club's own website. See also Alpha, Cards, Corinthians.

Corsetmen was the nickname of Symington's F.C., a works side for employees at the R. & W. H. Symington factory in Market Harborough, Leicestershire. Addis 1995 mentions the nickname during the 1952–3 season (p. 57), and Twydell 1989 records the club's history and nickname (1914–55, 1960–70), also reproducing a headline from *Harborough Mail* in 1955 which uses it. The company was famous for the making of corsets and other ladies' underwear between 1876 and 1997. The building today houses a corset museum, and Borough Alliance F.C., established in 2003, now play on the old Symington's Recreation Ground.

Cote is the nickname of Wilmcote F.C., founded in Warwickshire in 1971. A short form of the place-name recorded in W1993–5.

Cottagers is a nickname for two clubs with the word 'Cottage' in the name of their home ground. The examples are:

⚽ Fulham F.C., founded in London in 1879, based on the name of their home ground Craven Cottage. The stadium was built in 1896 on derelict land formerly occupied by a hunting lodge built by Baron William Craven in 1780. The original 'cottage' was destroyed by fire in 1888, but the name survived as a place-name. The nickname is recorded early, in BoF1905–6 (and with the variant 'Craven Cottagers'), and on the 1933 Ogden card set, and in Johnston 1934, the 1936 Thomson 'stamp' album, Avis 1954–7, G1956–76, Churchill 1958, Richards 1960, SWSCYB 1962–3, and throughout RY and SSY1970/1–2012/13. The cheerleaders of the team are called the Cravenettes, and the old mascot used to be a knight called Sir Craven of Cottage. See also Badgers, Lilywhites, Whites.

⚽ Wednesfield F.C., founded in West Midlands in 1961, originally as W. Social F.C. The club's home is called the Cottage Ground; W1994–2005. See also Social.

Cougars is the suffix and nickname for Cosheston Cougars F.C., founded in Pembrokeshire in 2010. 'Cougars' is used as a nickname on Twitter and on Pembrokeshiresport.co.uk (also 'Cosh Cougars' there on 23 June 2012). The North American mountain lion (the same species as pumas and panthers) makes for a splendid sporting symbol, if unexpected in Wales; Huws 2013.

Council Housers is an unofficial nickname for Manchester City F.C., coined by Manchester United supporters, who call the City stadium The Council House, because it was built by the local council. The City of Manchester Stadium (also known as Eastlands and now named Etihad Stadium) has been leased by the club since it was used in 2002 for the Commonwealth Games; recorded on several websites. See also Bitters / Bitter Blues, Blues, Citizens, City, Man, Massives, Sheik City, Stockports.

Countrymen is the nickname of Hallam F.C., founded in 1860 and the second-oldest club in the world, who play at Sandygate Road, which is the oldest football ground in the world (established 1804 as a cricket ground, football since 1860). On the 26 December 1860 the ground hosted the first-ever inter-club match, between Hallam and Sheffield F.C. (see Club). The home ground is no longer in the countryside, but the nickname was clearly made to contrast the two clubs, one for the city and one for the country, relevant at the time of the coining. The nickname is recorded in the title of the 1987 club history by John A. Steele: *The Countrymen*; and in W1994–2013.

County is a common football club name element, theoretically meaning a team which represents a county, but very few clubs do, inter-county competitions being rare. However, the Local Government Act of 1888 constituted all municipal boroughs with a population of 50,000 or more as 'county boroughs', so this is often the sense in which 'county' is used (e.g., Wigan was a county borough 1880–1974, Wigan County was a football club 1897–1900). In Scotland, some of the ancient counties were very small and had low populations; two of them have clubs which could be said to represent their shires (Ross and Nairn), and another club, Alloa Athletic, was originally called Clackmannan County when formed in another small county in 1878 (see Hornets, Wasps). A small number of Irish and Welsh clubs could also be said to represent their shire, but only in this informal sense, where they are the only 'mainstream' club in the county. Clubs who have adopted the county name, which can also be used as a nickname, are:

- Derby County F.C. founded in 1884. Here the County name follows the club's foundation as an offshoot from Derby County Cricket Club and it was called County from the outset, though Derby did become a county borough four years later in the 1888 act; Wikipedia. See also Rams, Sheep and, for Derby County Ladies, Ewes.
- Haverfordwest County A.F.C., founded in Pembrokeshire in 1899. Wikipedia records that the County suffix was adopted in 1956 after the club's promotion to the Welsh League Premier Division, so there is a sense here that the club represents the county in the mainstream of Welsh football. See also Bluebirds, West.
- Kildare County F.C., founded in 2002 and based at Newbridge, folded in 2009. The club could be said to have represented the County of Kildare in the League of Ireland, as it was the only mainstream club in the county; Wikipedia. See also Thoroughbreds.
- Nairn County F.C., founded in 1914. Here, the club can be said to represent the shire; Wikipedia. See also Wee County.
- Newport County F.C., founded in Monmouthshire in 1912. The town had become a county borough in 1891. The nickname 'County' is recorded in Avis 1966–70. See also Black and Ambers, Cromwellians, Exiles, Ironsides, Port, Wasps.
- Notts County F.C., founded in 1862. Here the club is based in Nottingham, but in an area of the city which was officially outside the city boundaries; recorded early, in BoF1905–6 (the book also uses 'Notts'), and late, in Pickering 1994. See also Lambs, Magpies.
- Ross County F.C., founded in 1929 and based at Dingwall in the small Scottish county of Ross-shire. Recorded in RS1993–2012. See also Staggies.
- Rotherham County F.C., founded in Yorkshire in 1877, originally as Thornhill, renaming as R. County in 1905. The town became a county borough in 1888, the population of the town having already passed 50,000 before 1871. In 1925 the club merged with Rotherham Town to form the present-day R. United; Wikipedia. See also Merry Millers / Millers.
- Stockport County F.C., which adopted the County name in 1890, the year the town

became a County Borough. Recorded in RY1979/80 and through RY1981/2–SSY2012/13, and W2012–13. See also Cestrians, Hatters.

☺ Wigan County F.C., established in the Wigan County Borough in 1897, closed 1900; the nickname is recorded in the Wikipedia article. For the successor club, see Athletic, Latics, Pie-Eaters / Pies.

Covies is a nickname for two clubs, each formed as friendly short forms of different words related to the clubs. The clubs are:

☺ Farnborough North End F.C., founded in Hampshire in 1967 as F. Covenanters, a church side. The present name was adopted in 1998, but Wikipedia records that during the 1980s the club adopted the official name 'Covies' to distinguish it from another church side. The expression is a friendly short form of Covenanters. See also North End.

☺ Westport United F.C., founded in Co. Mayo in 1911. Here, the nickname is that of the natives of Westport. It is a popular phrase used in local businesses and artistic productions such as the internet soap opera, *Covies*. Here, the word appears to be derived from the mainstream word 'cove' for a bay or inlet of the sea; Wikipedia.

Cowboys was the nickname for Ebbw Vale F.C., founded in Blaenau Gwent Co. Bor. in 1888, reformed in 1907. The nickname is recorded early, in Avis 1966 and 1970, and late, in W1994–9 and RW1998, but in 1998 the club was dissolved. A new Ebbw Vale Town F.C. was started in 2007 but has not assumed the old nickname. Huws 2013 records a second Welsh example as a suffix, Tirydail Cowboys F.C., founded in Ammanford, Carmarthenshire, after the Second World War. The nickname is a popular choice in American football but seems out of place here. However, although Ebbw Vale's economy was long dominated by the coal and steel industries, the local livestock industry remains prominent. The nickname does not seem to be a play on 'Western', as there is no such geographical sense in the club's location. There is, perhaps, the slight possibility that the nickname was suggested by the spelling of the place-name, or its meaning. The river name 'Ebbw' is believed to mean 'The Wild Horse' (Owen & Morgan 2007). However, it may simply be that the nickname refers generally to the popularity of American culture in the twentieth century, 'Cowboys' connoting fun, freedom and fashion.

Cowden is a nickname of Cowdenbeath F.C., founded in Fife in 1881, as a short form of the place-name. Recorded in RS1993–2012, RY1972/3–93/4 and SSY2012/13. See also Beath, Blue Brazil, Brazil, Fifers, Miners.

Crabs is a nickname for clubs at the seaside where there is a local crab industry. The examples are:

☺ Cromer Town F.C., founded in Norfolk in 1997 as a successor to Cromer Town (1898) and Madra United (an acronymic name for Mundersley And District Recreational Association). The town has a major crab-processing factory; Wikipedia.

☺ RAF Lossiemouth F.C., founded at the RAF base in Moray in 1970, but in a coastal town with a crab industry; Wikipedia.

❀ Thurso F.C., founded in Caithness (Highland) in 1998. Thurso is a major producer of crabs with several processing and distribution businesses for the industry; Wikipedia. See also Vikings.

Craigie is the nickname of two Scottish clubs, as a friendly short form of the place-name. The clubs are:

❀ Craigneuk F.C., founded in Lanarkshire in 1877, closed 1878. Recorded on SFHA.

❀ Craigroyston F.C., founded in Edinburgh in 1976. A friendly short form of the official name, recorded in RS 1993–2001.

Cranes is the nickname for two clubs with the bird (correctly) referred to in their place-names. The clubs are:

❀ Cranborne F.C., founded in Dorset in 1914. A crane appears on the club badge (AFBC) and the nickname appears on the club's website.

❀ Cranleigh F.C., founded in Surrey in 1893. A handsome crane appears on the club badge; W1994–2002.

Crazy Gang was a nickname of Wimbledon F.C. after their successful F.A. Cup win in 1988, first applied to the players for their allegedly crazy style and then to the club as a whole; the nickname is certainly used by the commentator at the end of the match against Liverpool in the final. The new A.F.C. Wimbledon club has assumed the nicknames of the old club, but Milton Keynes Dons F.C. (a renaming of Wimbledon F.C. after their move to Milton Keynes) also claims them. Recorded in RY1998/9–SS2004/5 for Wimbledon and listed in SSY2005/6–10/11 for Milton Keynes Dons. See also A.F.C., Dons, Franchise F.C., Wombles.

Creeksiders is a nickname for Faversham Town F.C., founded in 1884 in Kent. Although the club's home on Salter's Lane is not next to the famous Faversham Creek, the port is well-known for the length of this navigable tidal waterway which runs from the 'River' Swale (the channel separating the Isle of Sheppey from the mainland) into the centre of the town; Wikipedia. See also Lilywhites, Sorters, Town.

Creesiders is the nickname of Newton Stewart F.C., founded in Dumfries and Galloway in 1884. The town is on the banks of the river Cree; Wikipedia, SFHA.

Crescents is a nickname for Team Bath F.C., founded in 1999 for Bath University. The nickname is based on the famous Crescent row of Georgian architecture in the city; Wikipedia. See also Scholars, Team.

Crew was the nickname for Edinburgh Athletic F.C., founded in 1968 and originally called Manor Thistle F.C., formed by the firms of solicitors in Manor Place in Edinburgh; the club merged with Leith Athletic (estab. 1996) in 2008. The nickname is recorded in RS1993–7 for Manor Thistle, and in RS2000–1 for Edinburgh Athletic. The nickname does not seem to mean anything other than 'team', but the word comes from the military word 'recruit' (the Scots Dictionary records seventeenth-century forms as 'recroo', which provides an easy transition to 'crew'), so perhaps the nickname originally suggested either a sense of 'newcomers' or even of 'those called to service against their will'. See Athletic for the new club.

Crick is the nickname of Cricklade Town F.C., founded in Wiltshire in 1897; a short form of the place-name; W2008–13.

Cricketts was the main nickname of Oldbury United F.C., founded in West Midlands in 1958, folded in 2009. Cricketts is a surname, probably derived from the Somerset place-name of Cricket, which has a different etymology to that of the insect or the game. Here, it refers to the name of the club's home ground, which was presumably called Cricketts after an early owner; W1982/3–6 and W1993–2005. See also Blues.

Crocks is the nickname of Crockenhill F.C., founded in Kent in 1946. Although clearly a pluralised short form of the place-name, it is difficult to see which of the many meanings of the resultant word might be suggested in the nickname, if any. The original place-name element is also of an unknown meaning; W1979/80 and W1983/4–99.

Croesy is a nickname of Croesyceiliog Association F.C., founded in Cwmbrân in Torfaen Co. Bor. in 1964; a short form of the place-name, frequently used for the club on the internet and in business names in the town. See also Cockerels.

Crofters was the nickname for Burton United F.C., founded in Staffordshire in 1901 in a merger of B. Swifts (1871) and B. Wanderers (also 1871). The club folded in 1910. The nickname is recorded in BoF1905–6 (p.154) and refers to the name of the Peel Croft Ground which was taken over from B.Swifts.

Croms is the nickname of Huntingdon Town F.C., founded in 1980, originally as Montagu, renaming as Sun, before taking the present name in 1996. The town in Cambridgeshire is the birthplace of Oliver Cromwell, and the football club is affiliated with the local Cromwell Club. An outline image of the famous regicide appears on the club badge; AFBC, Wikipedia.

Cromwellians was a proposed nickname for Newport County F.C. in a competition in 1913. Apart from the obvious republican associations, the ground of Newport is on Cromwell Road, Cromwell's soldiers were nicknamed The Ironsides, and the town is dominated by the steel industry, the Ironsides being the nickname which won the competition. See also Black and Ambers, County, Exiles, Ironsides, Port, Wasps.

Cross was the nickname of two clubs, because they originally had this word in their official names. The clubs are:

⚽ Northfield Town F.C., founded in Birmingham in 1966, originally as Allens Cross, then Cross Castle United before using the Northfield place-name. The club badge displays '1966' and has a blue 'X' to represent the original name; W1983/4–96.

⚽ Tollcross United F.C., founded in Edinburgh in 1971. The club merged with Tynecastle Boys Club (established in 1928, originally as a Meccano model-making club before succumbing to the attractions of football) in 2005, to form the new

Tynecastle F.C. Recorded in RS 1993–7, 2000–1.

Crown is the nickname and part official name of Crown Scissett F.C., founded in the West Yorkshire village in 2003 and based at the Crown public house on Wakefield Road; club website.

Crows is a nickname for three clubs, each of which is in a place which has an association with the bird. The clubs are:

- Borth United F.C., founded in Ceredigion in about 1873 when the first match is recorded, though the more formal existence of the club is not known till about 1928. Bird names are popular in Wales and the club had a badge of a crow standing on a football, but no specific reason for the nickname is known. See Huws 2011.

- Crowborough Athletic F.C., founded in East Sussex in 1894. The place-name does actually mean the hill of the crows (Mills 1991), and the club has a distinctive badge of a crow within a large capital C; W1983/4–2002, W2009–13. See also Boro.

- Cwmbrân Town A.F.C., founded in Torfaen Co. Bor. in 1951. The club badge shows a crow on a football and the team plays in a black-and-white strip. The place-name is traditionally interpreted as meaning 'Valley of the Crows', but it is more likely that it means 'Valley of the [river] Brân', though the river name means crow or raven in the sense of using the bird as a symbol for darkness (see Owen & Morgan 2007; many Welsh river names are based on animals). See also Town.

- Rhosgoch Rangers F.C., founded in Powys at an uncertain date. The club's home ground is in Crow Lane; February 2013 edition of *Welsh Football*.

- Royston Town F.C., founded in 1872. The Hertfordshire town has long used a crow as a symbol, and now there is some evidence that the local crows are even a unique variety. The town coat of arms has a hooded crow, known as the Royston Crow, as a crest and the club badge features a black and white bird, though it does not look at all crow-like. There is also a local newspaper called *The Royston Crow*. W1983/4–2007 and W2012–13.

Crues is a nickname of Crusaders F.C., founded in Belfast in 1898; a short form of the club's official name. Recorded in RNI2007. See also Hatchetmen, Team with No Boots.

Crumlin Boys is a nickname for Crumlin United F.C., founded in Dublin in 1967; Wikipedia.

Crusaders is a football club name suffix and can also be used as a nickname. The word is commonly used in sport, in the sense of a team of roving warriors like other 'travel' names. It is also very popular for youth sides. Not every club so called uses it as a nickname, and in the case of Hungerford it is a nickname without appearing in the official name. See also Crues, above, as a nickname for Crusaders F.C. in Belfast. The clubs who use Crusaders as a nickname are:

- Army Crusaders F.C., founded in 1922. This club is the British Army's official officer corp football side.

- Comberton Crusaders F.C., founded in Cambridgeshire in 1988.

☉ Crusaders F.C., founded in London in 1863, closing in the 1890s. Tthe club was one of the founder members of the Football Association. Although not a nickname, this appears to be the earliest usage of the word. At this time in football history, many clubs adopted names which later became popular suffixes, but at the time were unique.

☉ Dalton Crusaders F.C., founded in West Yorkshire in 2005. The club shows a mounted knight on its badge; club website.

☉ Ely Crusaders F.C., founded in Cambridgeshire in the 1960s.

☉ Hungerford Town F.C., founded in Berkshire in 1888. W1979/80–2013; Pickering 1994 mentions the nickname as deriving from a fanzine, though it seems more likely that the nickname appeared first. No explanation for the nickname appears to have been published. Badges for the club in AFBC show the Islamic crescent and star symbol (also used by Drogheda United and Portsmouth, for local associations with King Richard the Lionheart).

☉ Potters Bar Crusaders F.C., founded in Hertfordshire in 1948. The story on the club website is that a group of boys met on the pavement of Auckland Road and formed a football club they called 'The Auks', based on the road name, but changed it a week later to Crusaders Sports Club; there does not seem to have been a specific reason for the choice of name; recorded as a nickname in W1986 and W1995.

☉ Ynysddu Crusaders F.C., founded in Caerphilly Co. Bor., originally in 1915, folded 1939. A new youth side called Crusaders A.F.C. was formed in 1963 which, through a series of mergers, and a final merger with Ynysddu Welfare A.F.C. (1947) became the present club in 2008. The club badge shows a crusader knight on horseback; internet history of local football dated July 2012, Huws 2013.

CTK is an initialism for Christ the King F.C., a Catholic church side founded by the church of that name in Coventry in 1946. The initialism is used on the club's own website and in internet match reports. The club does not seem to have any other nickname.

Cuckoos is a nickname for three clubs; two of the examples refer to a popular folktale in which the bird stands for both the advent of spring and rustic simplicity, the third refers to the meaning of the place-name. The clubs are:

☉ Marsden F.C., founded near Huddersfield in West Yorkshire in 1907. Here, the story of the Marsden cuckoo copies that told in other locations, that the villagers tried to capture a cuckoo by extending a wall, in order to prolong the spring, but the bird easily flew away. Virtually identical tales exist for Brindle and Chipping in Lancashire (see Dobson 1973). The town holds an annual cuckoo festival in April. The club nickname is recorded on many local websites and a cuckoo appears on the club badge.

☉ Risca United F.C., founded in 1946, in the Caerphilly Co. Borough. Recorded in RW1994–7. Bird names are popular as nicknames for Welsh clubs, but the nickname here refers to the local folktale of the Risca cuckoo, in which villages attempted to trap the bird by building a hedge, to keep the sun shining. The Risca version is now the subject of a children's book, *Rhys and the Cuckoo of Risca* (Lewis 1997), and the nickname is also used for the local rugby club (with thanks to Richard Huws).

⊕ Yaxley F.C., founded in Cambridgeshire in 1900 as Yaxley Rovers, reformed in 1962. The club near Peterborough has a flying cuckoo on its badge and the village crest is also a cuckoo; the place-name Yaxley means 'wood [or clearing] of the cuckoo' (Mills 1991); W2010–13.

Cuikie is the nickname of Penicuik Athletic F.C., founded in Midlothian in 1888; a friendly short form of the place-name; Wikipedia. See also Rookie Cookie.

Cully is the nickname of the Devon side, Cullompton Rangers F.C., founded in 1945; a friendly short form of the place-name, unusually preceded by 'The'; W2008–13. See also Rangers.

Culture Club was a temporary unofficial nickname for Liverpool F.C., coined in 1988 by television commentary. The nickname was in ironic contrast to the 'Crazy Gang' nickname for Wimbledon, when the Crazy Gang beat Liverpool 1-0 in the FA Cup final; the expression is used by the commentator at the match. See also Anfielders, Kop / Kopites, Liddellpool, Mariners, Merseysiders, Micky Mousers, Pool, Reds, Spice Boys.

Cumbrians is the nickname of two clubs within the county of Cumbria. The clubs are:

⊕ Carlisle United F.C. The new county of Cumbria was formed to include the whole of the Lake District in 1974, but the nickname predates this by at least 18 years: recorded in G1956–76, Churchill 1958, Harvey 1959, Richards 1960, Jeffrey 1961, Avis 1966–70, throughout RY and SSY 1970/1–2012/13, and W2005. See also Blues, Foxes.

⊕ Penrith F.C., founded in 1894. Although they are now called 'The Blues', 'Cumbrians' is the nickname recorded in W1979/80–80/1. See also Blues.

Curfews is the nickname for Chertsey Town F.C., founded in Surrey in 1890. The unique nickname refers to the famous Curfew Bell of St Peter's Church, which still marks the passing of the curfew time, for when the streets are emptied and everyone is confined to their houses, though now only ceremoniously. The nickname is recorded in W1986–2013, though W1982/3 has 'Town'; *The Curfew* is the name of the programme. The short-lived rival series of non-league annuals by Bruce Smith (1991/2–5/6) persistently printed the error of 'Curlews' for the club, and the one-off Miller & Wright 1996 produced the singular 'The Curfew'. See also Curlews, Town.

Curlews is a false nickname for Chertsey Town, persistently recorded in Smith 1991/2–5/6; and also in Pickering 1994. The correct nickname is Curfews (q.v.).

Curzon was a nickname for Curzon Ashton F.C., founded in Ashton-under-Lyne, Greater Manchester, in 1963 originally as Curzon Amateurs; W1982/3–2000; Pickering 1994 has it in the form 'The Curzons'. See also Blues, Nash.

Cutlers has been used as a nickname for Sheffield United F.C., as a variant of Blades, also in honour of the city's major cutlery-making industries; Wikipedia. See also Blades, Blunts, Laneites, Pigs, Red and White Wizards, United.

Cutters is a nickname for Daisy Hill F.C., founded in Greater Manchester in 1894. This uses the nickname of the notorious BLU–82B bomb, the Daisy Cutter, used as a weapon of mass-destruction by the Americans in the Vietnam War. The name itself is derived from a more innocent nineteenth-century baseball term for a ball which skids along the grass, cutting the daisies. Room 2010 cites its use as a cricket term, and BoF1905–6 uses it with the same sense in football (p.73); Wikipedia. See also Daisies.

D&D is the nickname of Douglas and District F.C., founded in the Isle of Man in 1996, originally as Barclays F.C., from an affiliation with the bank, but changing name in 2001. The bank's eagle symbol is still on the club badge; an initialism based on the official name; Wikipedia and club's own website.

Dabbers is the nickname for Nantwich Town F.C., founded in Cheshire in 1884. The nickname is taken from the local expression for people born and bred within the town boundaries of Nantwich, but the meaning of the word has been forgotten in Nantwich itself. A great many theories have been floated, but now just one piece of evidence has been found, remarkably in a football context, which clinches the meaning. Nantwich has three claims to fame: the number of its black-and-white ancient buildings, and its two industries of salt making (since Roman times) and leather-tanning. So, one recent theory suggests that it refers to wattle-and-daubing (this would be more convincing if the word was daubers), others that it refers to a technique called dabbing in the trades mentioned (and there are several other suggestions). The primary meaning has to be 'one who dabs' and the essential meaning of dabbing is poking, rubbing, kneading (as bread dough), touching. In traditional printing, for instance, a dabber is a pad used to apply ink to a printing plate, or the worker who does the dabbing, but none of these meanings provide a reason for applying it to the people and footballers of Nantwich ... until now. In the 1983–4 Williams *Non-League Football Yearbook*, the football club for Leighton Buzzard in Bedfordshire is nicknamed 'The Sand Dobbers'. That town's main industry has long been sand extraction, and here the expression, preserved by the town's Sand Museum, refers to those who dug the sand out of the ground and loaded it into carts. The OED confirms that words in *dab-* and *dob-* are variant spellings of the same words. So, this is what the word means for Nantwich: it refers to those who dug the salt out of the ground and *dabbed* it into carts. For Nantwich, the nickname is recorded in W1979/80–2013 and it appears in the title of a club history of 1983: Michael Chatwin's *Centenary Dabbers*.

Daffodils / Daffs / Superdaffs are nicknames for Llanidloes Town F.C., founded in Powys in 1875, originally as L. United. The club plays in yellow shirts and green shorts, the same colours of the daffodil. Daffs is the form recorded in RW1994–8 and on the club website; all three forms are on Wikipedia. The nickname raises the question why daffodils are regarded as a Welsh national symbol. The traditional explanation is that it dates only from 1911, when it was used at the investiture of the then Prince of Wales in Caernarfon, and was soon popularised by Lloyd George in preference to the leek. However, both leeks and daffodils share the same word in Welsh (*Cenhinen* and *Cenhinen Pedr*), the daffodil flowers in spring, at the time of St David's Day (1 March), and even the name in English suggests the name David (Dafydd in Welsh), all making for an easy adoption of the daffodil as a symbol of Welsh nationality. See also Town.

Daggers is the nickname of Dagenham and Redbridge F.C., formed in 1992 in a merger of Dagenham Forest and Dagenham (1949). The club history is one of mergers (Ilford, Leytonstone and Walthamstow Avenue all lie behind it). The nickname is a neat pun on the opening syllable of the place-name, and is inherited from the earlier Dagenham club, recorded in Avis 1966–70, W1979/80–92 for the old club; W1994–2007 and SSY2004/5–2012/13 for the new. See also Reds, Stones.

Dahlies was the nickname of Coltness United F.C., founded in North Lanarkshire in 1934, renaming as Newmains United Community F.C. in 2006. The nickname is recorded on SFHA (for both names of the club); the word is not in the Scots Dictionary, but it seems to be a friendly Scots form of 'Dahlias', flower names being popular amongst Scottish clubs. The nickname probably refers to the club colours, though dahlias appear in many varieties. See also United.

Daisies is a nickname of Daisy Hill F.C., founded in 1894, from the place-name in Greater Manchester, and celebrated with such a flower on the club badge. The side were briefly renamed Westhoughton Town 1989–94; Wikipedia. See also Cutters.

Dale (or Dales) is a nickname for clubs with the element 'dale' in their official names. Examples are:

- Archdale's '73 F.C., founded in Worcestershire in 1926 as a works side for the Archdale Machine Tool Co. The '73' in the name commemorates the year in which the workers bought the club for themselves; a short form of the official name, appearing in W1993–5 as 'Dales'.
- Armadale Thistle F.C., founded in West Lothian in 1936; Wikipedia, SFHA.
- Nithsdale Wanderers F.C., founded at Sanquhar, Dumfries and Galloway, in 1897, closed in 1964. A new club of the same name was founded in 2001; SFHA. See also Wanderers (for the new club).
- Rochdale A.F.C., founded in Greater Manchester in 1907 as a revival of earlier attempts to set up a Rochdale club. Recorded in Avis 1966–70, RY1974/5–SS2012/13, G1976. See also Vallians.
- Rossendale United F.C., founded in Lancashire in 1898, folded in 2011. The nickname is recorded in Avis 1966–70 as 'Dale', in W1994 as 'Dales'. See also Rossy, Stags.

⚽ Tividale F.C., founded near Dudley in the West Midlands in 1954. Recorded in W1979/80 and W1986–90. W1993 and Miller & Wright 1996 as 'Dale', and in W1994–2004 as 'Dales'.

Dalers is the nickname of Holmesdale F.C., founded in 1956, originally as a church side called Holmesdale Baptist F.C. The Baptist suffix was abandoned in 1957; the official name was taken from the club address in Holmesdale Road, South Norwood, London; Wikipedia.

Dandies is a nickname for Aberdeen F.C., founded in 1903. In Scotland, the word 'dandy' does not have the connotations of Georgian snobbery and weird effete fashions that it has in England, but is used to mean 'pleasing' or 'impressive', appropriate for a Scottish Premier League club. A variant form is 'Dandy Dons'; SSY2012/13. See also Black and Golds, Dons, Red Devils, Reds, Wasps.

Dandy Dons is a variant nickname for Aberdeen F.C., used on many websites including the club's own. See previous entry.

Danes is the nickname of Rothesay Brandane F.C., founded in 1946 on the Isle of Bute; a short form of the second name in the official name, but nevertheless suggesting the area's Viking heritage (though that would have been Norse rather than Danish). Brandane is a nickname for anyone from the Isle of Bute, and is believed to derive from the name of St Brendan of Clonfert, the sixth-century patron saint of Bute. The nickname is known in print in modern times from W. F. Skene's *Celtic Scotland* (1876, vol. II, p. 77): "The name of Brendan is preserved in the designation given to the people of Bute of 'The Brandanes'." The nickname 'Danes' appears on the club's own website.

Daniels is the nickname of Stamford A.F.C., founded in Lincolnshire in 1896. The club tradition is that the nickname is from the local celebrity Daniel Lambert, allegedly the heaviest man in England when he died in Stamford in 1809, weighing 335 k.g. (52 stone, 11 lbs), and who is buried at St Martin's Churchyard, very close to the club's home ground. Until recently, his clothes were on display at Stamford Museum. An outline picture of Daniel Lambert appears on one of the club's earlier enamel badges. Local historian Chris Hunt, however, raises the possibility that the nickname started as a reference to an early Vice-President of the club, one H. T. Daniels, who had also been mayor of Stamford in 1904, but this idea currently lacks documentation. It is not impossible that the nickname started for one reason, then shifted to a different explanation when its origin had been forgotten. Kevin Troop reports that the alternative form 'Dannies' is frequently heard at matches; W1980/1–2013. See also Town.

Darans is the official nickname of C.P.D. Llanberis, founded in Gwynedd in 1890. The club has had a variety of official names: L. United, L. Athletic and C.P.D. Locomotive Llanberis, but *Y Darans* appears to have been the main nickname for all or most of the club's history. It is the lenited (mutated) Welsh word for 'thunder': *taran*, which mutates to *daran* in most expressions. It is the name given by Jesus to

James and John, the sons of Zebedee in Mark 3, v. 17: *the Sons of Thunder*. The nickname is recorded in the title to the 1991 Welsh-language history of the club by Arwel Jones: *Y Darans: Clwb Pêl-Droed Llanberis 1890-91–1990-91*. The location in Snowdonia is a centre for Non-Conformism and Biblical names are common, but the expression in English was also widely used to describe forceful preachers in the nineteenth century; the nickname describes the club as a forceful sporting side, striking fear in the opposition. As with some of the other nicknames for Llanberis, the form – *Y Darans* – is a mixture of Welsh and English. It takes the Welsh singular 'Y' for 'The', but closes with the English pluralising –s, which is not Welsh.

There is a slight possibility that the nickname may have been reinforced, or perhaps originally suggested, by the club colours. In Weekley 1921 'thunder and lightning' is recorded as a colloquial phrase for black-and-yellow colours, and the club plays in a black-and-amber strip (see Blac and Amber for an explanation of the colours).

The variant forms recorded in RW (Darrens 1994–5, Darrans 2011) are simply typing errors, but they suggest a different Welsh word. Here, the word could be *tarren*, meaning 'rock'; the element occurs in place-names in South Wales, so the nickname could have been interpreted as that word by a South Walian, leading to the variant spelling. This would mean that the nickname was misinterpreted as meaning 'The Rocks', not inappropriate for a team from mountaneous Snowdonia. See also Beris, Blac and Amber, Llanbêr, Loco / Locomotives, Teigars.

Darians was a nickname for Aberdare Athletic F.C., founded in Rhondda Cynon Taf in 1892, folding after a failed merger with the neighbouring Aberaman club in 1928, but reformed in 1947 as Aberdare Town. The nickname is a pluralised short form of the place-name, used generally for the people and various institutions of Aberdare (see Huws 2013); the nickname is recorded on the Wikipedia page for the town and is said to have referred to the 1921–8 incarnation of the club; Huws applies it to a successor Aberdare Town that existed from 1934 to 1939. See also Aber.

Dark Blues is the main nickname for Dundee F.C., founded in a merger in 1893 between East End F.C. and Our Boys F.C. (both 1877 clubs). The club plays in very dark blue shirts with white shorts. Recorded in Johnston 1934, mentioned in the 1936 Thomson 'stamp' album, RS1993–2001, and through RY1974/5–SSY2012/13. See also Blues, Bonnets, Dee, Dens Parkers.

Darlo is a nickname for clubs whose place-name begins with the letters *Darl–*. Examples are:

☉ Darlaston Town F.C., founded in the West Midlands in 1874; Wikipedia and club's own website. See also Blues.

☉ Darlington F.C., founded in 1883. Between 2006 and 2010 the club's mascot was one Darlo the Dog, a dalmation (and the club's colours are suitably black and white). Financial difficulties have made the club refound itself in 2012 as 'Darlington 1883 F.C.'. The nickname appears on Wikipedia for both clubs. See also Eighteen-Eighty-Three (1883), Quakers.

Darreners is the nickname of Darwen F.C., founded in 1870, and reformed in 2009 as A.F.C. Darwen. The nickname is the place-name, spelled according to the local pronunciation and with *–ers* on the end to show it means people from that place. In Avis 1966–70 the nickname appears as 'Darren'. Dobson 1973 records the nickname ('Darren') for the town, but not the club, but adds 'Darren Rangers' as a nickname for an unknown football club; Wikipedia records 'Darreners' for the people of the town. See also Anchormen, Salmoners.

Darrens, see **Darans**

Darts is a nickname for two clubs with a place-name which easily puns on 'dart', coining a satisfying sporting nickname. The examples are:

☺ Dartford F.C., founded in Kent in 1888 as a branch of the Dartford Working Men's Club. Recorded in Avis 1966–70, W1979/80–2013.

☺ Dartmouth A.F.C., founded in Devon in 1999 in a merger between D. United (1908) and D. Y.M.R.C.; W2008–12.

Dazzlers is a nickname of Llangefni Town F.C., founded on Anglesey in 1897; it is recorded in RW2000–11. The nickname is the popular English word for a display so spectacular that it is blinding, and it is used elsewhere in football as a motivating name for youth sides (e.g. Littleover Dazzlers in Derbyshire, 1971, and South Wimbledon Dazzlers in London). The meaning is the same as the word popularly used in politics and the media, 'blinder', for a spectacular performance. See also Cefni.

D.C. is a nickname used by two Northern Ireland clubs which coincidentally have the same initials and take their inspiration from Glasgow's Celtic. The two clubs are:

☺ Donegal Celtic F.C., founded in Belfast in 1970. The club's name, nickname and strip are in tribute to the Glasgow Celtic side. The club plays at the Donegal Celtic Park; Wikipedia. See also Celtic, Wee Hoops.

☺ Draperstown Celtic F.C., founded in Co. Londonderry in 1968. The club's name, other nicknames and strip are in tribute to the Glasgow Celtic club; Wikipedia. See also Celtic, Half Hoops.

De Town is the nickname of Longford Town F.C., founded in Co. Longford in 1924. The spelling humorously suggests the traditional Irish pronunciation of 'The', but it is not the official form of the nickname; Wikipedia. See also Town.

Dealers is a nickname for Deal Town F.C., founded in Kent in 1908. The commercial trading centre gave its name to 'deal' imported timber, and the nickname puns with a word for traders (or even those who control the cards in a game). See also Fivers, Town.

Dean is a nickname for Gala Fairydean F.C., founded in Galashiels near Edinburgh in 1907; a short form of the official name. Recorded in W1982–3, RS1993–7, 2000–1. See also Braw Lads, Fairies, Gala.

Deans is the nickname of two clubs with the place-name element 'dean' in their official names. The clubs are:

- Horndean F.C., founded in Hampshire in 1887; W1987–8, W1995.
- Withdean F.C., founded in Sussex before 1983, originally as Westdene, renaming in 1989. The club was reformed as 'Withdean 2000' in 2000 but folded in 2004; Miller and Wright 1996.

Decies was the nickname of Rothes Decimals F.C., founded in Moray in 1969, closed 1988. The short form of the suffix is easier to explain than the suffix itself. A video posted on Youtube has a comment attached with the variant spelling 'The Dessies', which shows how the nickname was pronounced; SFHA (as 'Decies').

Dee is a nickname for two Scottish clubs with the river name 'Dee' in their place-name. The clubs are:

- Banks o'Dee F.C., founded in 1902 in Aberdeen, and adopting its present name in the 1920s. The club ground is Spain Park, on the banks of the River Dee; Wikipedia, club's own website and SFHA. See also Rechabites.
- Dundee F.C., founded in 1893. Although the Scottish place-name refers to the River Dee, the nickname is a short form of the town's name. Recorded through RY1974/5–SSY2012/13 and RS2003–12. See also Bonnets, Dark Blues.

Deesiders is the nickname for Culter F.C., founded in Aberdeen in 1891, from the River Dee location. The nickname appears in match reports on the club's own website. The nickname has also been used for Connah's Quay Nomads in Wales (*Daily Post*, Liverpool, 8 March 2004; see also Nomads, Westenders).

Demolition Squad was a nickname for Cemaes Bay F.C., founded in 1976 on Anglesey, recorded in RW1994–6. The nickname expresses both the destructive power of the club and its early association with businessman Joe Davis who was head of a Cheshire demolition company; the club was also sponsored in the 1990s by a Liverpool scaffolding company, King's (thanks to Richard Huws). See also Bay, Seasiders.

Dennyboys is the nickname of Thackley F.C., founded in 1930. The West Yorkshire side plays at the Dennyfield stadium near Bradford; W2012–13. See also Reds.

Dens Parkers was a nickname for Dundee F.C., founded in 1893. It is recorded in the first few Rothmans Yearbooks: RY1970/1–73/4, and is an adaptation of the name of the home ground since 1899, Dens Park. See also Blues, Bonnets, Dark Blues, Dee.

Dentals was the nickname of one of the earlier clubs from which the modern Barnet F.C. was formed, Alston Works A.F.C., later Barnet Alston F.C., which was made of workers from this dentures factory, hence the nickname Dentals. The club was founded in 1901, merged with Barnet Avenue in 1912 and eventually emerged as the modern Barnet F.C. in 1919; Wikipedia. See also Bees, Hillmen.

Deranged Ferrets is an unofficial nickname for Lincoln City F.C., and the name of the club's fanzine. The story is that the manager Colin Murphy (1987–90) won an award from The Plain English Society for the clarity of his writings, and he commented afterwards words to the effect "It doesn't matter what I write as long as I can get them running around like deranged ferrets for ninety minutes". The fans liked the phrase so much they named the club magazine after it. I have been told verbally that many fans now use the modified phrase 'Drain Ferrets' to describe the club, because the home ground is beside a drainage channel, and drains are a common feature of the Lincolnshire fens.

Deres is the nickname of Erith and Belvedere F.C., founded in 1922. The club is based in Welling, in the London borough of Bexley and the nickname is clearly a pluralised short form of the second name, but the club also has a deer's head on its badge; Avis 1966–70, W1982/3–2013.

Derg is the nickname of Dergview F.C., founded at Castlederg, Co. Tyrone in 1980, in a merger of F.C. Castlederg and Mourneview Celtic F.C. A short form of the place-name, recorded in RNI2007, but the internet gives 'The Constitution' (q.v.) as the preferred nickname.

Devils is the nickname and part official name of Sporting Devils F.C., founded at Crawley in Sussex in 2004; the nickname is used on the club website.

DH was the nickname for De Havilland F.C., founded in Hertfordshire in 1934; this was the works side for the De Havilland aircraft company at Hatfield Aerodrome, but the Aerodrome closed in 1994 and the club disappears from the FCHD in 1997; the initialism is recorded in W1994–6.

DHSOB is an acronymic nickname for Douglas High School Old Boys A.F.C., founded on the Isle of Man in 1926. It is so used on many websites, though it is difficult to imagine it being pronounced.

Diamonds is a nickname for two clubs. The word is used in several sports in reference to diamond shapes: in badges or strip, in areas of the playing pitch, or in formations in playing tactics. Here, the nickname refers to diamond shapes on the strip in one case, but is primarily an adaptation of 'Dynamo' in the other. The two clubs are:

⬡ Airdrie United F.C., founded in North Lanarkshire in 2002 as a successor to Airdrieonians F.C. (1878–2002). The nickname is inherited from the older club and refers to the distinctive V-shape (or diamond-shape) on the shirts, usually highlighted in red on a white shirt. The earlier club adopted this design in 1912. RS1993–2001 and RY1970/1–2002/3 for the older club, and SSY2012/13 for the new club. See also Excelsior, Onians, Waysiders.

⬡ Rushden and Diamonds F.C. Founded in Northamptonshire in 1992, in a merger between Rushden Town (1889) and Irthlingborough Diamonds (1946). The nickname was inherited from Irthlingborough and is in use as a nickname in a newspaper cutting of 1969–70 reprinted in Addis 1995 (p. 224). According to Addis 1995 (p. 200) and Ferris 2005 the Irthlingborough club adopted the Diamonds name in tribute to the famous Moscow Dynamo club, which had toured Britain in 1945. Although dynamo and diamonds seem only slightly similar in sound and not at all in meaning, the Russian name has a palatalised pronounciation, *d'ee* rather than *die*, so the opening sounds are more alike than the letters suggest, and the Moscow club have a badge displaying the letter 'D' in a diamond frame. Tragically, in 2011 the club folded in a financial meltdown, and The Diamond Centre is now used by Kettering Town, but a new club has been formed, called A.F.C. Rushden and Diamonds (as yet no nickname recorded); W1979/80–92 for Irthlingborough, W1995–2001, RY2001/2–SSY2011/12 and W2007–11 for the merged club. See also Annies, Russians.

Dick-Kerr's counts as a nickname for Preston Ladies F.C., founded during the First World War as the Dick, Kerr's Ladies F.C., based at the Dick, Kerr & Co. armaments factory in Preston, Lancashire. The side played its first match at Preston on Christmas Day 1917. The club was very successful, raising substantial amounts of money for wartime charities and raising the profile of women's football to a wide audience, but the cynics of the Football Association banned women's football from its own grounds on 5 December 1921 and did not change it policy till 1971. Nevertheless, the club continued to play till 1965 and is today universally recognised for its pioneer achievement and the excellence of its football. The club changed its name in the late 1920s, so use of the name 'Dick, Kerr Ladies' now counts as a nickname, though the club never had a formal nickname; Pickering 1994 actually calls it a nickname. The club was the subject of a history by Gail J. Newsham (*In a League of Their Own*, 1994), who also runs the commemorative website.

Dicko's was the nickname of Croxley Guild of Sport F.C., founded in Hertfordshire in 1920, reformed in 1983. A short internet essay by Phil How explains it. The Croxley Guild was the social club of the Croxley Paper Mills owned by the Dickinson family, to which the football club was originally attached. The paper mill closed in 1980, but the football club continues and during the 1990s still used the nickname for the club which it had had during the Dickinson family years; recorded in W1993–6.

Diffs / Divs are alternative nicknames for two Welsh clubs, where the nicknames are short forms of the place-name Cardiff. The two clubs are:
- Cardiff Metropolitan University F.C. founded as UWIC Inter Cardiff F.C., in a merger in 2000 between Inter Cardiff F.C. and UWIC F.C., renaming in 2012; Wikipedia. See also Inter / International, Seagulls, Sheep.
- Ely Rangers A.F.C., founded in Cardiff in 1965; Wikipedia. See also Floggers, Griffins.

Dinc / Ding was the nickname of Yeading F.C. Founded in London in 1960 (though with a late-Victorian predecessor), the club merged with Hayes in 2007 to form Hayes and Yeading United F.C. The nickname appears in two forms: as *The Dinc* in W1991–9 and as *The Ding* in W2000–7. It is clearly based on the last syllable of the place-name, but the earlier form expressed the dialect pronunciation of –*ing*, which one often hears in expressions like 'I don't know anythink'. The later version reverts to mainstream English. See also Missioners, United.

Dingles is an insulting unofficial nickname for at least three clubs, from the perspective of rival supporters. It is recorded for each of these clubs on the 2003 Football Fans Census website. The nickname refers to a family on television's soap opera *Emmerdale*, who were notorious for their bad behaviour. The clubs so called are:

☺ Blackburn Rovers F.C., from the perspective of Burnley. See also Blue and Whites, Highwaymen, Jackburn, Plastics, Riversiders, Rovers.

☺ Burnley F.C., from the perspective of Blackburn Rovers. See also Clarets, Gene Puddle, Moorites, Royalites, Turfites.

☺ Wolverhampton Wanderers, from the perspective of West Bromwich Albion supporters (see also www.baggies.com). See also Buckley Babes, Tatters, Wanderers, Wolves.

Dinno is the nickname of Dinnington Town F.C., founded in South Yorkshire in 2000; a friendly short form recorded in W2008–13.

Dinosaurs is an unofficial nickname for Sheffield F.C., founded in 1857 and widely recognised as the oldest club in the world. 'Dinosaurs' is a word which can be used perjoratively, but we salute Sheffield as the *magnificent originals*. The club also played in the very-first inter-club match, with Hallam F.C. ('The Countrymen') on 26 December 1860. In July 2011 the club achieved widespread publicity from their decision to sell their handwritten copy of the oldest football rule book in the world. Inevitably, publicity used the phrase 'Dinosaur Museum'. The nickname appears on many websites and makes for colourful headlines, e.g. 'Nuneaton out to make Dinosaurs extinct', *Coventry Telegraph*, 25 November 2011. See also Club.

Dirty Leeds was an unofficial nickname for Leeds United A.F.C. during the hard-playing years of the Don Revie management (1961–75), because of their determined style of playing. Today, the nickname is adopted with pride and appears on t-shirts, book titles and in the names of supporters' websites, but I have not been able to trace the date of its first use by journalists. See also Owls, Peacocks, United, Whites / Mighty Whites.

Div's see Diffs / Div's.

Dockers is a nickname for clubs whose home is in a port, or docks. Examples are:

☺ Erith Town F.C., founded in Kent in 1959, originally as Woolwich Town, renaming as Erith in 1997. The club has a ship on its badge and is based in Erith, in the London borough of Bexley. It is a Thameside dock location; W2001–13. In 2010 the club temporarily renamed as Erith and Dartford Town, but reverted to the old name as the new season started, nevertheless, for W2011 the nickname appears under the new name. Surprisingly, Erith and Dartford Town also become the name of a completely independent club in 2010, which in 2012 has renamed as Kent Football United F.C.

☺ Hartlepool United F.C., in honour of the town's shipbuilding and dock businesses. Founded in Co. Durham in 1908, the club had a plural –s on the end until 1968, due to there being more than one Hartlepool, e.g. the older team, West Hartlepool F.C., which ran from 1881 to 1910. The nickname is mentioned on many websites, though it does not appear in formal sources. Nevertheless, in the 1950s the club certainly had a docker mascot. See also Monkey Hangers, Pool, Pools.

🔘 Immingham Town F.C., founded in Lincolnshire in 1912, reformed in 1945, 1969; the nickname appears on a supporters' website. See also Pilgrims.

🔘 Millwall F.C., at the time of their origins in the docklands of the Isle of Dogs between 1885 and 1910. The club was founded by employees of the Dundee company J. T. Morton as Millwall Rovers, changing to Millwall Athletic in 1890 and to just Millwall in 1910. The club moved away from its dockland base in 1901 and in 1910 moved to a new purpose-built home in New Cross. The nickname is recorded as early as BoF1905–6 (p.16), and in Johnston 1934 (p. 59). Recently, the club has become proud of its dockland origins, returning to the Dundee Blue strip and in 2011 renaming the East Stand at The New Den ground as The Dockers' Stand. See also Lions, Spanners.

🔘 Newhaven F.C., founded in the international ferry port in East Sussex in 1887; W1983/4–99; club badge in AFBC.

🔘 Seaford Town F.C., founded in the port in East Sussex in 1889; Wikipedia. See also Town.

🔘 Swansea Dockers A.F.C., founded in 1947 as a works side for employees of the National Docks Labour Board, and originally called Swansea N.D.L.B. F.C., renaming in 1950. The club website records the nickname; Huws 2013.

🔘 Tilbury F.C., founded in 1900 in the Essex town famous for its deep-water docks. Recorded in Avis 1966–70, W1979/80–2013.

🔘 Woolwich Town F.C., founded in Kent in 1959 (briefly named W. Heathway in 1989); Miller & Wright 1996. This club renamed as Erith Town in 1997 (see above).

Dodgers is the nickname of Coffin Dodgers F.C., founded recently, before 2011, in the Shetland Isles. The club is intended for players in their 40s, hence the name, defying old age. As a nickname, however, 'Dodgers' has a sporting edge. The nickname is used on the club's own website.

Doggy is the nickname of North Ormesby Sports F.C., founded in Cleveland in 1993. The nickname is that of the town itself (Doggy or Doggy Town). Like many such nicknames, there are several theories to explain it, which are summarised on the 'Communigate' website devoted to Teesside dialect; these range from it having something to do with real dogs (dog-like smells, loose dogs, dog-racing), or perhaps that it came from railway workers and referred to a 'dog leg track', which has been suggested as the explanation for a similar nickname for West Cornforth in Co. Durham (though, inevitably, another website links it to the manufacture of 'dog iron', and frankly the railway tracks in neither place reveal the feature needed). Most uses of 'dog' in nicknames are originally pejorative, however. The nickname may be popular today but it might not have been polite when it was coined; W1995.

Dogs of War was an unofficial nickname for Everton F.C. during their successful FA Cup winning season in 1995; mentioned on multiple websites. See also Bitters /

Bitter Blues, Black Watch, Bluenoses, Blues, Merseysiders, Moonlight Dribblers, People's Club, School of Science, Toffees/Toffeemen.

Dokens is the nickname of Dundee North End F.C., founded in 1895. The nickname takes the Scots word for the dock plant (occurring in such phrases as "Nae worth doken", or 'not worth a dock leaf', for something of negligible value). The club's badge displays a prominent dock leaf and the nickname appears on the club's own website. However, the nickname is not Scots self-deprecating humour, but is said locally to derive from the fact that the club's North End Park ground was originally a field covered in dock leaves (West Bromwich Albion's ground is named 'The Hawthorns' for a similar reason). (Thanks to Roger Leitch and Charles M. Milne).

Dollies is the nickname for Glastonbury Town F.C., founded in Somerset in 1890, originally as G. Avalon Rovers, the club was renamed by 1901 and added the 'Town' suffix in 2003. The nickname is recorded in Avis 1966–70 and is still regularly used by local journalists. It cannot have the same explanation as the next entry (for which Dollies also exists as a variant) because the club wears red or yellow shirts. It could well be that an earlier yellow strip was associated with the golden colour of corn dollies, and so the nickname was chosen primarily as a colour metaphor, but one which chimed with Glastonbury's fame as a centre for mystical folklore. See also Killman.

Dolly Blues is the intriguing nickname for Lancaster City F.C., founded in 1905, originally as Lancaster Athletic. The team play in dark blue shirts and socks, with white shorts. The story is that the shade of blue resembled that of the Dolly Blue detergent. This brand was, however, made in Lancashire by William Edge and Sons (established in Bolton in the 1870s), so there was a local encouragement to the name. The company is now part of Reckitt and Colmans. The brand used a children's doll as a trade mark, but the word dolly was the old scraper board used to wash clothes against, in a dolly tub, before automatic washing machines became widespread. Lancaster now also has a Dolly Blue Tavern. The progress of the nickname in the directories suggests some initial uncertainty in the nickname's acceptance: Dollies in Avis 1966–70, W1979/80 and W1982/3–86 and Moss 1983; Dolly Blues in W1980/1–81/2, W1986–90; Blues in W1991–3 and Smith 1991/2–95/6 and finally settling at Dolly Blues in W1994–2013.

Dolphins is a nickname for three clubs. Two, in the south of England, are seaside locations which are frequented by the favourite sea mammal, the other is based on a Dublin place-name. The examples are:

☺ Brighton and Hove Albion F.C., before the introduction of the Seagulls nickname. According to Ferris 2005, the fans were embarrassed by the Dolphins nickname (though only Seddon 2004, p. 203, explains that this was because of 'Flipper' taunts), and in a 1975 match against Crystal Palace the supporters adopted Seagulls as a rhyming response to chants of the opponent's nickname, The Eagles. 'Dolphins' is recorded in G1976 and for three years in RY, from 1975/6 to 1977/8, suggesting that it still took two or three years for the nickname to change officially to 'Seagulls'. See also Albion, Flippers, Seagulls, Seasiders, Seaweed, Shrimps, Tesco's.

☺ Dolphin F.C., founded in Dublin in 1921; the club is recorded in Johnston 1934 and has a short Wikipedia account which uses 'Dolphins' as a nickname. The club's home ground was Dolphin Park in the Dolphin's Barn district of Dublin. The club seems to have folded after the 1936–7 season.

☺ Poole Town F.C., founded in 1890. Two dolphins are shown on the club badge, and they are regular visitors to this Dorset resort; Avis 1966–70, W1979/80–96 and W2007–13.

Doms is the nickname of Stone Dominoes F.C., so the nickname is a short form of Dominoes, but why call a football club 'Dominoes'? The club was founded in the Staffordshire town of Stone in 1987 for St Dominic's Catholic Church Scout Club Beaver Group, and the boys themselves chose Dominoes as a pun on Dominic's (though ultimately the two words have the same root). One of the gaming pieces appears on the club badge. There are sculptures of stone dominoes at the club ground and the team plays in appropriate red, black and white colours; W2007–13. (The renaming of this club as Stone Dynamoes in W2006–8 is a typing error.)

Donkey Lashers is an unofficial nickname for Blackpool F.C., from the perspective of Preston supporters (see Football Fans Census, 2003). The nickname refers to Blackpool's seaside location and the popularity of donkey rides on the beach, but with the *outrageous* suggestion that the donkeys are whipped. See also Atomic Boys, Merry Stripes, 'Pool, Seasiders, Tangerines.

Donny is an alternative nickname for Doncaster Rovers F.C., founded in South Yorkshire in 1879; which reuses a general nickname for the place. The club's current mascot is a brown dog called Donny Dog. The nickname appears on a great many websites, including Wikipedia. See also Rovers, Vikings.

Donny Belles is a nickname for Doncaster Rovers Belles Ladies F.C., founded in 1969, originally as Belle Vue Belles, renaming as Doncaster Belles in 1971. This form of the nickname neatly combines with the nickname for Doncaster; Wikipedia. See also Belles.

Dons is a nickname for clubs which have the element –*don* in their place-name (usually meaning 'hill' in English, but it can also be a Celtic river name or a personal name). However, it may also appear as a suggestion of an educational institution (as in 'Oxbridge dons', where the word is a short form of the Latin *dominus*, meaning 'lord' or 'sir', as a sign of respect: the OED records a usage with this meaning in 1907, but astonishingly the dictionary does not give a full entry for this famous word). Often, the nickname deliberately puns on both meanings. Examples are:

☺ Aberdeen F.C., founded in 1903. Modern Aberdeen is at the mouth of the River Dee, but the place-name refers to the River Don, where Old Aberdeen is located. The city is also home to one of Scotland's ancient universities, founded in 1495, so both meanings of the nickname are used here. The nickname appears to have first been used in 1913; recorded in the 1936 Thomson 'stamp' album (where it shows university dons in academic dress playing football), Harvey 1959, G1956–76, and *Stedfast* April 1963 (again a cartoon of players in academic dress), Avis 1966–70 and RS 1993–2012, and throughout RY1970/1–SSY2012/13 (except for SSY2008/9–10/11). A variant form is Dandy Dons. See also Black and Golds, Dandies, Red Devils, Reds, Wasps.

- A.F.C. Wimbledon, founded in 2002 in protest against the move of the old Wimbledon club to Milton Keynes. The nickname is the same as that of the old club; W2003–11, SSY2011–12. See also A.F.C., Crazy Gang, Wombles.
- Clandown F.C., founded in Somerset in 1875; the nickname here seems to be a pluralised short form of the place-name; W1986–90. The club seems to have closed during the 2003–4 season.
- Donington F.C., founded in the Lincolnshire fens in 1996. Here, the nickname is a play on the opening syllable of the place-name, which refers in this instance to an Anglo-Saxon personal name, Dunna, recorded in Domesday Book. The youth sides of the club are officially called 'Young Dons'.
- Hendon F.C., formed in 1908 as Christ Church Hampstead, the club became Hampstead Town in 1909, then Hampstead in 1926 and Golders Green F.C. in 1932, before changing again to Hendon in 1946. A pluralised short form of the place-name, recorded in W1979/80–2013. See also Greens.
- Milton Keynes Dons F.C. Founded in 2004 as a successor to Wimbledon F.C., the new location is the home of the Open University, so the nickname continues to additionally suggest an educational background for the club, as the first usage did. Recorded in SSY2005/6–12/13. See also Crazy Gang, Franchise F.C.
- Oxford United F.C., founded in 1893; although the primary sense here seems to be educational, the club was founded as Headington United, and the last element in that place-name was originally *dun* for hill (see Mills 1991), so again, both meanings apply. The nickname appears in RY1974/5–75/6. See also Boys from Up the Hill, U's, United, Yellows.
- Wimbledon F.C., founded in 1889 as Wimbledon Old Central F.C., from the Old Central School on Wimbledon Common that many of the players had attended as children (so, although the place-name is the main explanation, there is still a hint of the alternative meaning). The name changed to Wimbledon F.C. in 1905. In 2002 the club began a relocation to Milton Keynes and in 2004 the new club Milton Keynes Dons F.C. took the nickname in honour of its past history, and Wimbledon F.C. closed down. One of the club badges illustrated in AFBC shows the academic hat known as a mortarboard. The entirely new A.F.C. Wimbledon was founded in 2002 in protest against the move, and also claims the club's nickname heritage. Recorded through RY1977/8–SSY2004/5 and SSY2010/11–12/13. See also A.F.C., Crazy Gang, Wombles.

Doonhamers is a nickname for the Scottish club, Queen of the South F.C., founded in 1919, in a merger between Dumfries F.C. (1897), Fifth King's Own Scottish Borderers F.C. (1908) and Arrol-Johnston F.C. The nickname is a popular expression in Scots for the town of Dumfries, *Doon hame*, or 'Down home', similar in meaning to the English nickname 'Ar Tarn', or 'Our town'. The nickname was applied to the town by the Scottish poet David Dunbar during an election campaign in 1857. The club's mascot is one Doogie the Doonhamer, a border collie. The club's official name refers to another nickname for the town, contrasting it to Edinburgh which is known as Queen of the North (see Room 2006). Recorded in RY1972/3 and through RY1974/5–SSY2012/13 and in G1976 (wrongly, as Doonhammers) and RS1993–2012. See also Qos, Queens.

Dossers is an unofficial nickname for Motherwell Football and Athletic Club, founded in North Lanarkshire in 1886. The town is associated with the steel industry and the 'footballcrests.com' website suggests that the nickname refers to workers who slept during the nightshifts. The word certainly means 'sleepers' (first recorded in 1866, OED), today carrying the perjorative sense of 'sleeping on the job', but it is difficult to believe that this could refer to steelworkers generally, even if sleeping arrangements are provided sometimes for shift workers. The more likely explanation is that the club is seen as a 'sleeping giant', about to spring forth, because Motherwell has been at the top of Scottish football since 1984 but have only won one trophy since then, the Scottish Cup in 1991; Wikipedia and many other websites record the nickname, and the word is often used casually for other clubs. See also Steelmen, Well.

Doughboys is the nickname of the Northamptonshire club Wellingborough Town F.C., originally founded in 1867, reformed in 2004. The traditional explanation is that the nickname refers to a local pastry dish called *'ock 'n' dough*, using a *hock* of bacon which is a cheap cut. The dish certainly exists and is the name of a local pub. Flour milling is a mainstay of the local economy, but the nickname is more likely to refer to this specific dish because it is known to have also been a nickname for the town (Jones-Baker 1981, p. 58). so the name may simply refer to the industry rather than the specific local dish. Addis 1995 reprints a newspaper article of 1958 which uses the nickname (p. 99). Recorded in W1979/80–2013. See also Cornies.

Dow is a nickname of Irvine Meadow XI F.C., founded in North Ayrshire in 1897 and based at Meadow Park; a short form of 'Meadow', listed in SFHA. Interestingly, Wikipedia now lists the other part of the same word as the basis of the nickname. See also Medda.

Down is the nickname of Odd Down F.C., founded in Somerset in 1901 in what was then the village of that name, now a suburb of Bath; W1982/3–90 and W2011–13.

Draconians / Dracs are nicknames for Cardiff Draconians F.C., founded in 1963. The popular expression for the excessive application of rules is based on Draco, a seventh-century B.C. Athenian law scribe. The short form 'Dracs' is also used on the club website. The suffix is an unusual one, actually suggesting heartless pedantry, but it also connotes toughness, discipline, and the word clearly chimes with the popular 'Dragons'. In England, the Dragon School at Oxford have a magazine called *The Draconian*, and permission to use the name was given to the Cardiff club by the Welsh F.A., who had previously used it for a representative Welsh amateur side. The club have a Welsh dragon on their badge. The club was temporarily renamed Gabalfa Draconians between 1983 and 1999. England also has a football club called Old Draconians, formed in St Albans in 2009; club website, Huws 2013.

Dragons is an excellent nickname for a club wishing to associate itself with this magnificent legendary beast, but sometimes there may be a specific local reason for the adoption. It is very popular in Wales, where it is a national symbol (see Huws 2013 for many more Welsh examples). The nickname was used for the fictional football club Harchester United on the satellite television soap opera *Dream Team*, 1997–2007. The clubs are:

- ⚽ Baglan Red Dragons F.C., founded in Neath Port Talbot Co. Bor. in 1984, originally as Red Dragons, 'Baglan' being added to the official name in 1999. The club's own website uses the nickname, also used by Wales Online 29 March 2009. See also Evans Bevan Boys.
- ⚽ Barry Town A.F.C., founded in Vale of Glamorgan in 1912. The club used to be called 'The Linnets', but they adopted the defiant Welsh name of the Barri Dragons during an exile in Worcester in the 1992–3 season, and the new nickname soon supplanted the old; recorded in Miller & Wright 1996, W1998–2005, RW1998–2011. See also Linnets.
- ⚽ Basingstoke Town F.C., founded in Hampshire in 1896 in a merger between Aldworth United and Basingstoke Albion. There are several strong reasons why Basingstoke should have adopted a dragon as a badge and a nickname, but its origins may simply lie in an earlier nickname and mascot. First, the town's church is dedicated to St Michael, and the town arms show a traditional image of St Michael slaying a dragon. This image is also on the badge of the football club. Basingstoke is in the heart of Hampshire and the dragon is also a traditional image for the Anglo-Saxon kingdom of Wessex. Nevertheless, the nickname is recent, recorded in W2007–13; the earlier nickname is 'Stoke', a short form of the place-name which generated the mascot Stokie the Dragon, whose name puns on the stoking of fires. This seems more likely to be the origin of the nickname. See also Blues, Camrose Blues, Stoke.
- ⚽ Pontypridd Town A.F.C., founded in Rhondda Cynon Taf in 1992, in a merger with Ynysybwl F.C. The club shows two Welsh dragons on its badge. Recorded in RW1995–6. See also Ponty.
- ⚽ Wales National Football Team, which first played in 1876. The English, Scottish and Welsh national teams are the three oldest in the world. The international under-21s side is known as 'The Young Dragons'. Avis 1970 records the nickname as 'Red Dragons', the nickname now used by Wrexham.

‹ Wivenhoe Town F.C., founded in Essex in 1925, originally as Wivenhoe Rangers. The badge shows a yellow wyvern kicking a football and the idea is based on a folk etymology of the place-name, assuming that it contains a reference to wyverns. Proper dragons have four legs and two wings, a wyvern has two legs and two wings; W1988–2013. See also Town.

‹ Worcester City F.C., founded in 1902. The connection here seems to be Royal Worcester Porcelain, which in the eighteenth century had a famous Chinese dragon range, called the Worcester Dragon. Today, 'Worcester Dragons' is a name also used in other sports, such as the boating club; Wikipedia. See also Blues, City, Faithfuls, Loyals, Royals.

Drain Ferrets, see Deranged Ferrets.

Drake's Ducklings was an unofficial nickname for the side at Chelsea F.C. under the managership of Ted Drake between 1952 and 1961. The expression illustrates the remarkable tendency for nicknames of particular sides to find a word which alliterates with the manager's name, in this case also punning on the male duck being called a drake. Recorded in Pickering 1994. See also Blues, Chelsea Headhunters, Chelski, Pensioners.

Dream Team is an unofficial nickname for Berwick Rangers F.C., founded in Northumberland in 1884. The nickname probably dates from the years of the satellite television soap opera, *Dream Team* (1997–2007; see 'Dragons' for Harchester United); SSY2012/13. See also Black and Gold, Borderers, Rangers, Wee Gers, Wee Rangers.

Drogs / Super Drogs are nicknames for Drogheda United F.C., founded in Co. Louth in 1975, in a merger of D. United (1919) and D. F.C. (1962); they are pluralised short forms of the place-name. 'Drogs' is the nickname used on the club's own website; RI2006. See also Boynesiders, Turks, United.

Drove is the nickname for Parson Drove F.C., founded in Cambridgeshire in 1921; Wikipedia and club's own website.

Druids is a nickname of three clubs in Wales, where there is a natural patriotic pride in the ancient Celtic pagan priests. The word is also used in Wales as a public honour (and see Huws 2013 for further Welsh examples). The clubs are:

‹ Cefn Druids F.C., founded in 1992 in a merger between Cefn Albion and Druids United (founded in 1869, renamed Druids in 1872). The club is based at Cefn Mawr near Wrexham; Wikipedia. See also Ancients, Zebras.

‹ Maesycwmmer F.C., founded in Caerphilly Co. Bor. in 2010. There seems no obvious reason for the nickname, other than the patriotic association; Wikipedia. See also Maesy.

‹ Ruabon Druids F.C., an ancestor club of Cefn Druids, above, founded in 1869 as Plasmadoc F.C., the club merged with other Ruabon clubs in 1872 to form Ruabon Druids. This club disappeared in 1923 in a merger with Acrefair United to form Druids United, which was nicknamed 'The Ancients' or 'The Druids' (Wikipedia), which lasted till the merger of 1992. See also Ancients, Zebras.

Drum is the nickname for Drumchapel Amateur F.C., founded in Glasgow in 1950. A short form of the place-name, but which nevertheless suggests some campaigning action; Wikipedia.

Drums was a nickname for Drumcondra F.C., in Dublin, which joined the Irish leagues in 1928 but was dissolved in 1972. The nickname was a pluralised short form of the place-name. A descendent of the club survives today as D. A.F.C., playing in the Leinster Senior League; Wikipedia and a modern badge in AFBC.

Dublin Saints is a nickname for St Patrick's Athletic F.C., founded in Dublin in 1929. Recorded in RI2006. See also Pat's, Saints.

Dubs was a nickname for Dublin City F.C., founded in 1999, originally as Home Farm Fingal, in a split from Home Farm Everton (1928). The club was renamed Dublin City in 2001 but folded in 2006. A pluralised short form of the place-name, recorded in RI2006. See also Vikings.

Ducks is a nickname for two clubs for different reasons. The clubs are:

☻ Aylesbury United F.C., founded in 1897 in a merger between Night School F.C., Printing Works F.C. and Aylesbury Town F.C. The club badge features a duck and the nickname celebrates the famous Aylesbury breed of duck. In the 1990s the club invented the 'duck walk' goal celebration; recorded in Avis 1966–70, W1979/80–2013.

☻ Ballinamallard United F.C., founded in Co. Fermanagh in 1975. The place-name is *Béal Átha na Mallacht* in Irish, meaning 'Ford mouth of the Curses', the Curses being the river name, but the spelling and pronunciation have shifted to the present form under English influence (a common occurrence in the Celtic areas, where English speakers naturally twisted difficult words into familiar ones), and both alternative nicknames reflect the suggested incorrect meaning. See also Blues, Mallards.

Duds is a nickname for the West Midlands side, Dudley Town F.C., founded in 1893, from a friendly short form of the place-name; Wikipedia. See also Robins.

Dumfries F.P.'s is the nickname for Dumfries High School Former Pupils F.C., founded in 1970 in Dumfies and Galloway; RS1995–7.

Dumps is an older unofficial nickname for Dunfermline Athletic F.C., founded in 1885. The club historians Jim Paterson and Douglas Scott refer to the nickname as dating from the early 1900s and say it was coined by English sailors working at the Rosyth naval base. It puns on both the sound of the place-name and the popular insult for a place of little merit. See also Fifers, Leishman's Lions, Pars.

Duns is a nickname for clubs with the place-name element *dun*, which usually refers to a hill (it is the same word as *don*). The clubs are:

☻ Dundela F.C., founded in Belfast in 1895. Recorded in RNI2007. See also Henrun.

☻ Dundonald F.C., founded in Co. Down in 1956; Wikipedia.

Dwarfs is an unofficial nickname for Cardiff City F.C., from the perspective of Swansea City supporters. It is recorded on the 2003 Football Fans Census website. The nickname is said to mock the club's claim to be a sleeping giant. See also Bluebirds, Redbirds, Welsh Bluebirds.

Dynamo/s or Dynamoe/s is a football club suffix usually adopted in tribute to the highly successful Moscow or Kiev Dynamo sides. The word usually means an electricity generator, and it was first adopted because the Russian clubs were formed by electricity workers, but the concept of power generation soon made it an influential name. Clubs so called often also use it as a nickname. Some take the word in plural, others in singular, some add a final e, others not. Most of the 'Dynamo' clubs have a badge which displays a letter 'D' in the same style as the Moscow club's badge. A variant form is 'Mo's' or 'Moes'. The clubs are:

◉ Blackwood Dynamos F.C., founded in Dumfries in 1972, originally as Auldgarth F.C., and renaming after a change of address in 1999 to Crichton F.C. Recorded in RS1995–7 (the 1995 entry spells it 'Dynamoes').

◉ Colne Dynamoes F.C., founded in Lancashire in 1963, but folded in 1990, after heroic efforts to achieve League status. The club has a commemorative page on Wikipedia and the nickname is recorded, with the –e spelling, in W1983/4–90.

◉ Loughborough Dynamo F.C., founded in Leicestershire in 1955, and named after the Moscow side; recorded in W2008–13. See also Moes.

◉ Pentwyn and Llanedeym Dynamos F.C., founded in Cardiff in 1989 in a merger of two local clubs. The original Pentwyn side was called Dynamos, founded in 1975; Wikipedia and a badge in AFBC.

◉ Shepshed Dynamo F.C., founded in Leicestershire in 1994 as a successor to S. Charterhouse. The design of the prominent letter D on the club's badge is very similar to that of the nearby Loughborough Dynamo F.C., both being based on the Moscow design; W2001–13. See also Albion, Charterhouse, Raiders.

◉ Tralee Dynamos F.C., founded in Co. Kerry in 1961, used on the club's own website. See also Kingdom Boys.

Dyrni is the nickname of Llandyrnog United F.C., founded in Denbighshire in 1975. Recorded in RW1994–5. The nickname is a friendly short form of the place-name, which records a rare early saint's name, probably that of Tyrnog.

E's is a nickname for two clubs whose official names begin with this letter. The clubs are:

◉ Enfield 1893 F.C., formed in London in 2007 as a successor to Enfield F.C., itself founded in 1893 as Enfield Spartans. The nickname is inherited from the previous club. In 2010 the club expanded by absorbing Brimsdown Rovers (The Magpies); W1988–2007.

◉ Epsom and Ewell F.C., founded in Surrey in 1960 as a merger between Epsom Town (1917) and Ewell and Stoneleigh; W1982/3–2013, though W1979/80 uniquely records the nickname as 'EE's'.

Eagles is a popular nickname for a football club, sometimes because of a specific local reason but often for no reason whatsoever, other than the club's desire to associate itself with the athletic prowess of this magnificent predator bird. The image is also very popular in heraldry and is a national symbol in many countries. Examples are:

- ⚽ Armagh City F.C., founded in Co. Armagh in 1964, originally as Milford Everton. The club adopted the present name after Armagh achieved city status in 1988. The club has an eagle on its badge; recorded in RNI2007.
- ⚽ Arnold Town F.C., founded in 1989. The badge of the Nottinghamshire club shows a flying eagle and the place-name is believed to mean 'the valley [or 'nook of land'] of the eagles' (Mills 1991). The club's new home is called the Eagle Valley ground and the programme is *The Eagle Eye*; W1994–2013, AFBC.
- ⚽ Bedfont Sports F.C., founded in Middlesex in 2002; W2010–13.
- ⚽ Bedford Town F.C. Founded in 1908, closed 1982, reformed in 1989, the eagle is that on the arms of Bedford Borough Council, itself inspired by the design of the fifteenth-century seal of the town. The long-established use of eagles in Bedfordshire heraldry make the bird a popular choice for local businesses. The new club's home ground is called The New Eyrie, the old one was called The Eyrie. Twydell 1988 has a history of the earlier club and records that the nickname had appeared by 1911, and that 'Eaglets' was used for the reserve side; he illustrates various heraldic eagles used as the club badge. Recorded in Avis 1966–70, W1979/80–81/2, W1992–2013.
- ⚽ Crystal Palace F.C., founded in 1905, originally for employees of the famous Crystal Palace exhibition centre. According to Ferris 2005, the nickname was adopted for no particular reason by the manager Malcolm Allison in 1973, but since then a large eagle has stood astride a football on the club badge; recorded in RY and SSY from 1974/5 to 2012/13. See also Eagles, Glaziers, Palace, Team of the Eighties.
- ⚽ Eccleshall F.C., founded in Staffordshire in 1971. The club has an American-style eagle on its club badge, but the nickname is probably based on a misreading of the place-name's first element, long believed to refer to eagles but now known to mean 'church'; Wikipedia..
- ⚽ Eccleshill United F.C., founded in West Yorkshire in 1948. The club badge shows an eagle. The first element of the place-name actually means 'church' but the eagle may derive from the older belief that the name meant 'Eagle's Hill'; W1989–2013.
- ⚽ Elmore F.C., founded in Devon in 1947; the club has a magnificent flying eagle clutching a football as its badge but there seems no specific reason for the nickname, though it may stem from a similar misunderstanding of the place-name as in the previous two entries; W1986–2013.
- ⚽ Hinckley Town F.C., founded in Leicestershire in 1958 as Westfield Wanderers, renaming as H. Town in 1972 and then merging with H. Athletic to form Hinckley United in 1997; W1991 and Smith 1991/2–93/4, Pickering 1994. The modern club shows both an eagle and a robin on its club badge (AFBC). See also Knitters, Robins, Town, United.
- ⚽ Letchworth Garden City Eagles F.C., founded as a youth side in Hertfordshire in

134

1979 and with an adult team formed in 2008; Wikipedia.

☺ Neath Athletic F.C., founded in Neath Port Talbort Co. Bor. in 2005 in a merger between Neath F.C. and Skewen Athletic, but with ancestor clubs from 1922. Earlier names for the clubs include National Oil Refineries F.C. and BP Llandarcy; recorded in RW2011. The club reverted to the name of 'Neath F.C.' in 2008 but folded in 2012. The reason for the nickname may have been entirely arbitrary, but an eagle did appear on the club badge and the club's website was called 'The Eagle's Nest'; club website, Wikipedia.

☺ Stotfold F.C., originally founded as S. Athletic in 1904. The badge of the Bedfordshire club features a rather Germanic-looking eagle, and local heraldry reasons make eagles a popular choice in Bedfordshire (see Bedford, above); W1986–2013. See also Canaries.

Eaglets was the official nickname of the reserves side for Bedford Town F.C. The reserves were reformed in 1946 and played until the closure of the main club in 1982. See Twydell 1988.

Earls is a nickname for Earlswood Town F.C., founded in the West Midlands in 1968; W1993–5.

East is the nickname of East United F.C., founded in Castlepark, Galway in 2003. The locality also has a 'West' club; Wikipedia.

Eastenders is an increasingly popular unofficial nickname for West Ham United F.C., from its location in the East End of London, and its popularity as the club of choice on the BBC television soap opera, *Eastenders*. It was used by the BBC commentators during the Championship playoff match against Blackpool on 19 March 2012. See also Academy of Football, Claret and Blues, Cockney Boys, Hammers, Hamsters, ICF, Irons, Wet Sham.

Edge is the nickname and part official name of Hade Edge A.F.C., founded in West Yorkshire in 1908, reformed in 1989. The nickname is used on the club's own website.

Edinboro Darlings is recorded in Johnston 1934 as an alternative nickname for the Edinburgh side Heart of Midlothian F.C., founded in 1874. The nickname refers to the affection for the club within the city, rather than its popularity elsewhere. It perhaps dates from about 1901, when the expression 'England's Darling' was widely used for King Alfred the Great, in the national celebration of his thousand-year anniversary. The city's place-name is strangely spelt wrong ... perhaps because 'Boro' was already a popular football club nickname. See also Famous, Hearts, Jam Tarts, Jambos, Jammies, Maroons.

Eighteen-Eighty-Three / 1883 is a nickname for the new Darlington 1883 F.C., founded in 2012 as a reformation of the old club, founded in 1883. The new nickname appears on Wikipedia, but the club also uses the old nicknames. See also Darlo, Quakers.

Eighty-Twoers / 1982 Ltd are unofficial nicknames for Bristol City F.C., from the perspective of Cardiff City supporters, according to the 2003 Football Fans Census website. The taunting nicknames refer to the financial problems of the club in 1982, which resulted in bankruptcy. The new business owners of the club called themselves 'Bristol City Football Club (1982) Ltd.' See also Babes, Cider Army, City, Reds, Robins, Slave Traders, Turnips, Wurzels.

EK is an initialism for East Kilbride Thistle F.C., founded in Lanarkshire in 1968; SFHA. See also Jags.

Elyrch is the Welsh word for 'swans', and has been used as a translation of the nickname for Swansea City A.F.C., despite the false etymology of the original coining; used on many Welsh language websites. See also Jacks, Swanselona, Swans.

Emerald Greens was the nickname of Bridlington Trinity F.C., founded in 1950, folded in 1990, from the colour of their strip. Recorded in W1979/80–90 and Moss 1983.

Emeralds was the nickname for at least two, but related, clubs, for their emerald-coloured green shirts. The clubs were:

⚽ Upton Town F.C., founded in Worcestershire in 1904 and folded in 2004; W1993–6. The club was reformed in 2006, when Welland Athletic renamed itself as Upton Town, but the new club plays in red.

⚽ Worcester Athletico F.C., founded in 1996 as a renaming of Upton Town after a change of ground (discussed, but without a nickname, in Miller & Wright 1996); W1997–8. The club seems to disappear in 1998.

Emlyn is the nickname of Newcastle Emlyn A.F.C., founded in the town on the border of Ceredigion and Carmarthenshire before 1912, reformed 1967; a short form of the place-name recorded in RW2011.

End is a nickname for clubs which have this element in their official names. The clubs are:

⚽ East End F.C., founded in Aberdeen in 1887; Wikipedia, SFHA.

⚽ West End F.C., founded in 1964 at Mayhill in Swansea; recorded in RW2011.

Engineers is the nickname for Tredomen Athletic F.C., founded in 1921 in Caerphilly Co. Bor. The nickname is recorded in RW1994 and refers to the town's former major employer, the British Coal Board's Tredomen Engineering Works.

Entertainers was a nickname for Newcastle United F.C. during the Kevin Keegan management of 1992–7; the phrase was coined by Sky Sports and referred to the attacking philosophy of the club; Wikipedia. See also Barcodes, Cartoon Army, Frenchcastle, Geordies, Magpies, Skunks, Toon, Tyneside Professors, Tynesiders.

Eosiaid is the nickname of CPD Llanybydder, founded in Carmarthenshire before the 1951–2 season, when they were the county league champions. The nickname is Welsh for 'The Nightingales', and one appears on the club badge. Bird nicknames are popular in Wales, though there seems to be no particular reason for the choice of the nickname. It seems unlikely to be deliberately ironic … but the bird is known for its song, and the place-name probably means 'the church of the deaf ones' (Owen

& Morgan 2007).

EP is the nickname for East Preston F.C., founded in West Sussex in 1947, reformed 1966. The nickname appears on a Sussex football website.

Eric Cartman's Barmy Army, see Barmy Army.

Esh is an older nickname for Esh Winning F.C., founded in Co. Durham in 1967; W1985–2004. See also Stags.

ET's is a nickname for Enfield Town F.C., which was founded in London in 2001 while Enfield F.C. still existed (that team reformed in 2007 as Enfield 1893 F.C. and is nicknamed The E's). The nickname is a pluralised initialism; W2003–13. See also Towners.

Ewes is a nickname for two clubs. A ewe is a female sheep. The clubs are:

- Colchester United F.C., an unofficial nickname from the perspective of Southend supporters (Football Fans Census, 2003). The nickname cleverly puns on the sound of the official nickname, The U's, in a way which has also occurred to the Scottish club nicknamed 'The Yowes'. See also Grandad's Army, Oystermen, U's.

- Derby County Ladies F.C., founded in 1989. Here, the nickname cleverly uses the female form of the nickname used by the affiliate club, 'The Rams'; Wikipedia.

Evans Bevan Boys is the nickname for Baglan Red Dragons F.C., formed at Neath Port Talbot in 1984. The club is based at the Evans Bevan Fields in Baglan and the nickname is used on Wales Online on 29 March 2009 and in the *South Wales Evening Post* for 16 December 2008; Huws 2013. See also Dragons.

Excelsior is a football club suffix and a nickname from that. It is a Latin word meaning 'ever upward', and sometimes appears as an expression, meaning 'well done' or 'may you prosper'. It is often used as a business or club name, connoting excellence. As a football club suffix it may have first been used by Birmingham Excelsior F.C., between 1876 and 1888, soon followed in Scotland in 1878 by Excelsior F.C., which renamed as Airdrieonians in 1881. One of the ancestor clubs of Luton Town, founded in a merger in 1885, was called Excelsior. It is also popular in many other countries: the Dutch club, SBV Excelsior of Rotterdam was founded in 1902. Two English clubs which currently use the suffix are Shipston Excelsior F.C., founded in Warwickshire in 1903 (the club badge illustrated in AFBC shows a prominent 'X'), and Westerhope Excelsior, founded in Tyne and Wear in 2009. Two other early uses of the suffix, before 1889 and 1919 respectively, are Crook Excelsior (see Black and Amber) and Gornal Wood Excelsior (see Peacocks). See Huws 2013 for several Welsh examples.

Exiles is the nickname for two Welsh clubs which were obliged to play briefly in English leagues. The clubs are:

- Llanymynech F.C., reformed in Powys in 2011, and located on the English–Welsh border. The older club of this name had a badge which proudly displayed its successful wins of the Mongomeryshire Cup in 1926, 1927, 1936, 1946 and 1961, but the new club now displays 'MMXI' instead. During its first year the reformed club was obliged to play in the North Shropshire Sunday Football League, but returned to the Welsh leagues in 2012. The nickname 'Exiles' was used in the Powys *County Times* on 23 February 2012. The club's own website, and Twitter, however, use 'Llany'.

⚽ Newport County A.F.C. Founded in 1989 as a successor to the old club which went bankrupt, the club was forced to play its first season in exile in the Gloucestershire town of Moreton-in-Marsh. Since returning to Wales, the nickname has been kept and it now appears on the club's badge. A badge from a supporters' group, from 1996, uses the phrase 'Over the Bridge Exiles' with an image of the Severn Bridge (AFBC). A Welsh-language version is 'Yr Alltudion'. Recorded in RW1994–2011, W1991–2013. See also Black and Ambers, County, Cromwellians, Ironsides, Port, Wasps.

Eyes is the nickname for Peterborough Northern Star F.C., founded in 1905 as Northern Star, a works team for two brickyards known as Northern (in the village of Eye, near Peterborough) and Star (in Peterborough). In the 1950s the club was known as Eye United but took the present name in 2005; Wikipedia.

F1 is the nickname of F1 Racing F.C., founded in Dunnington near York in 1993, originally as Regional Railways North-East, renaming as Northern Spirit in 1998 and the present name in 2002. The nickname and opening of the official name is an abbreviation for 'Formula One', usually used in a motor-racing context and referring to the top rank of the range of specifications (formulas) for racing cars. The club badge shows a 'racing' chequered flag with an image of a modern train with a football and the Latin motto 'Advebo in Rail via' (meaning something like 'I will travel by railroad'). There seems to be no specific motorsport connection with the club; 'F1' is used as a nickname on the club website.

Fail is an unofficial nickname for Port Vale F.C., from the perspective of Stoke City fans, recorded on the 2003 Football Fans Census website. The nickname is a derogatory rhyming pun on the official name of the club. See also Vale, Valiants.

Fairies was once an alternative nickname for Gala Fairydean F.C., founded in Galashiels near Edinburgh in 1907; really, a short form of the official name. Recorded in W1982–3. See also Braw Lads, Dean, Gala.

Faithfuls is one of the nicknames for Worcester City F.C., founded in 1902, which records the city's association with King Charles I. The last battle in the English Civil War in 1651 took place here. The city helped the king escape. He was captured elsewhere, but Worcester was named *Fidelis Civitas*, the faithful city, for staying loyal; Wikipedia. See also Blues, City, Dragons, Loyals, Royals.

Famous is a nickname of the Edinburgh side, Heart of Midlothian F.C., founded in 1874; it seems to be a short form of a longer phrase 'The Famous Heart of Midlothian'; Wikipedia. See also Edinboro Darlings, Hearts, Jam Tarts, Jambos, Jammies, Maroons.

Famous Five was a nickname for five effective players at Hibernian F.C. who played together between 1949 and 1955: Gordon Smith, Bobby Johnstone, Lawrie Reilly, Eddie Turnbull and Willie Ormond. The nickname puns on the contemporary 'Famous Five' series of children's novels written by Enid Blyton; Wikipedia.

Farm is a nickname for two clubs with the word Farm in their official name. The clubs are:

⚽ Bristol Manor Farm F.C., founded in Avon in 1960; W1982/3–2013.

⚽ Home Farm Everton F.C., founded in Dublin in 1928, originally as Home Farm Drumcondra; recorded in RI1997. The club has a distinctive badge showing a farmer sowing seed.

Farmer's Boys is the nickname of Neilston Juniors F.C., founded in East Renfrewshire in 1945. The village has been the location of an important agricultural show for some two hundred years, and the club's anthem is the folksong 'A Farmer's Boy'; Wikipedia, SFHA.

FC, the abbreviation for football club, has become a prefix for clubs adopting the Continental style of reversing the usual order of name and suffix. Sometimes, the initialism then becomes a nickname in its own right, especially if it is used to distinguish two clubs with the same place-name. This has happened in the case of FC United of Manchester, recorded in W2006–13 as having the nickname 'FC', a politer term, but less expressive, than the entry which follows (Wikipedia offers the slight variant 'FC United'), and A.F.C. Wimbledon (see AFC).

FCUM is the nickname for F.C. United of Manchester. This famous and increasingly successful club was formed in 2005 as a rebellion against the commercial takeover of Manchester United by the Glazer brothers, and it seeks to recover the lost fan base by being a genuine expression of its supporters' dreams. The words in the club's name seem to be arranged deliberately so this acronym could be made, expressing not only total contempt and disillusionment with the cynical commercialism of football in these degenerate days, but also the confidence to go it alone: *fuck 'em*. More politely, W2006–13 records the nickname as 'FC'; 'FCUM' appears on Wikipedia. See also FC, Red Rebels.

Fed is a nickname for two clubs which used to have the word 'Federation' in their official name or history. The clubs are:

⚽ Broughty Athletic F.C., founded in Dundee in 1922, originally as Broughty Ex-Servicemen's F.C.; the name changed in 1951. The nickname derives from the initial name, in that the ex-servicemen's organisation the club was affiliated to was known as the Ex-Service Federation; Wikipedia and SFHA (for Broughty Ferry, as Feds).

⚽ Dunstan UTS F.C., founded in Northumberland in 1975, originally as Whickham Sports. The current name is from the sponsorship of the Tyneside engineering company UTS Ltd (the stadium has also been renamed), but between 1986 and 2006 the club was called Dunstan Federation Brewery F.C, from which the short-form nickname comes; W1993–2009 for the older use of the nickname, W2010–13 for the new.

Felin is the nickname for C.P.D. Y Felinheli, founded in Gwynedd in 1977 and originally known as Port Dinorwic F.C.; a short form of the place-name, which means 'The Tidal Mill' (Owen & Morgan 2007). Recorded in RW 1994–5.

Fenmen is the nickname of Wisbech Town F.C., founded in Cambridgeshire in 1920. This major fenland town is the capital of the Fenland District of the county and is often regarded as the cultural capital of the whole fenland area of Eastern England, and the club's ground is called Fenland Park. Recorded in Avis 1966–70, W1979/80–2013.

Fergie's Fledglings was a nickname for the young players at Manchester United in the late 1980s and 1990s, under the guidance of the manager Alex Ferguson. Some 24 players are considered the fledglings, and the expression first occurs in the 1988–9 season. The phrase is clearly a tribute to the similar phrase, 'The Busby Babes'; Wikipedia. See also Busby Babes, Coach-Builders, Heathens, Man, Manure, Munichs, Outcasts, Red Devils, Reds, United.

Fern was a nickname for Ferndale Athletic A.F.C., in Rhondda Cynon Taf; the club was founded in 1945, folded in 1999; it appears on the FCHD between 1961 and 1998. The club badge in AFBC shows an image of a fern leaf. Richard Huws records that the nickname is today used for a Ferndale rugby club. See also Athletic.

Ferry is the nickname of Briton Ferry Llansawel F.C., founded in a merger in the Co. Borough of Neath Port Talbot between the B.F. Athletic and Llansawel clubs in 2009. The 'Ferry' side of the club was originally founded in 1925 as B.F. Ex-Schoolboys, but renamed as 'Athletic' in 1926. The nickname is used on the club's own website; Huws 2013.

Ferrytoun/town is the nickname of Creetown/toun F.C., founded in Dumfries and Galloway in 1905, originally as the Creetown Rifle Volunteers F.C. The present name was taken in 1920. Creetown is a small seaport, which used to be called 'Ferrytown of Cree'. Recorded in RS1995–7 and SFHA with different spellings of 'town'.

FGR is a nickname for Forest Green Rovers F.C., founded in Gloucestershire in 1890. The initialism appears on the club badge and is listed on Wikipedia. See also Green, Green Army, Lawnmowers, Little Club on the Hill, Rovers.

Field is a nickname for some clubs with the place-name element –*field* in their place-name. Examples are:

⚽ Ashfield F.C., founded in Possilpark, Glasgow, in 1886; Wikipedia.

⚽ Kendal Town F.C., founded in Cumbria in 1919 as Netherfield A.F.C., renamed Netherfield Kendal in 1998 and the present name in 2000; a short form of the older name; W2001–2. See also Town.

⚽ Mangotsfield United F.C., founded in Gloucestershire in 1951; W1980/1 and W1985–2013. See also Mangos.

⚽ Netherfield A.F.C., recorded in Avis 1966–70. The club was renamed Netherfield Kendal in 1998 and then Kendal Town in 2000; W1980/1–2000. See above.

⚽ Portfield F.C., founded in West Sussex in 1896. The club merged with Chichester City in 2000 to form Chichester City; W1983/4–90 and W1994–2000.

⚽ Westfield F.C., founded in Surrey in 1953; Wikipedia. See also Yellas.

⚽ Westfield F.C., founded in Sussex in 1927; W2006, W2009–13 and in W1982/3 as Fields. See also Parishioners.

Fields is a nickname for two clubs with this word in their official names. The clubs are:

⚽ Westfields F.C. The Herefordshire club was founded in 1966 and the nickname copies the plural form of the place-name; W1985–2013.

⚽ Wigston Fields F.C., founded in Leicestershire in 1947. The club seems to disappear after 1994; W1993–4.

Fifers is a nickname for anyone from the Scottish county of Fife, and can appear as a nickname for any of the Fife clubs. The usage has been noticed for the following clubs:

⚽ Cowdenbeath F.C., recorded in Avis 1966–70. See also Beath, Blue Brazil, Brazil, Cowden, Miners.

⚽ Dunfermline Athletic F.C.; recorded in Avis 1966–70. See also Dumps, Leishman's Lions, Pars.

⚽ East Fife F.C., founded at Methil in 1903. There is now a tendency for the nickname to take the short form of the official name, as 'The Fife'. Recorded in Avis 1966–70, through RY1972/3–SSY2012/13 and RS1993–2007 as 'Fifers', RS2008–12 as 'The Fife'.

Filberts was the older nickname of Leicester City F.C., founded in 1884, originally as Leicester Fosse, reformed with the present name in 1919. The nickname is from the club's stadium in Filbert Street, to which the club moved in 1891. (Filbert Street could have been named from the surname Filbert, or because hazelnuts grew nearby, a filbert nut being a type of hazelnut, so-called because they ripened by 22 August, St Philbert's Day in the medieval calendar.) The mascot today is Filbert Fox. Recorded on the 1933 Ogden card set and in G1956–76, Churchill 1958, Norris 1959, Richards 1960, SWSCYB 1962–3, Avis 1966–70 (which also gives the variant nickname 'City'); RY1970/1–98/9. See also City, Fosse / Fossites, Foxes, Ice Kings, Nuts.

Finch is a nickname of Finchampstead F.C., founded in Berkshire in 1952. The nickname is a short form of the place-name, which does actually refer to the bird, and one appears on the club's badge. The club colours, however, are blue and white stripes, unrelated to the bird; W2001–8. See also Finches, next entry.

Finches is a nickname for two clubs, based on the place-name, which in each case does refer to the bird (see Mills 1991). The clubs are:

⚽ Finchampstead F.C. (see previous entry). The variant form The Finches is recorded in W2009–13, but both Wikipedia and the club's own website keep 'The Finch'.

⚽ Finchley F.C., founded in London in 1874; W1983/4–91. The club disappeared in a merger in 1991, to form Wingate & Finchley (see Blues).

Fingal was a nickname for Sporting Fingal F.C., founded at Fingal in Co. Dublin in 2007, but dissolved in 2011; a short form of the official name; Wikipedia. See also Ravens.

Firm is recorded as the nickname of Avon (Bradford) F.C., founded in Bradford-upon-Avon, Wiltshire, in 1920, and seems to have folded after 1988; W1983/4–8. 'The Firm' expression has long been used to refer to family businesses (including unusual ones like the royal family), and in football refers to long-standing traditional rivalries (especially Celtic–Rangers), or bands of supporters. It derives from the word *firma* in Italian and Spanish, for a common romance or endeavour, and this is the sense which lies behind its football usage.

In the case of Avon F.C., the nickname may express the idea that the club was a local enterprise which enjoyed the support of all Avon ... but it might also have been a play on the 'Avon' cosmetics company whose advertising made 'Avon Calling' into a household catchphrase in the 1960s. 'Avon Calling' was certainly a popular expression in the county: it was used as the name of a record of local rock music from Bristol in 1969. A new Bradford Town was formed in 1992 (see 'Brad').

The Glasgow usage is not recorded in the Scots Dictionary or the OED. It may reflect an early nickname for Glasgow as 'The City of Football' (used in BoF 1905–6, pp. 46, 269), in the sense that football seemed to have become the main industry of the city by the turn of the twentieth century; the expression 'Old Firm' would then describe this speciality, the more so when it was undiluted, with two Glasgow teams playing against each other. The expression is confined to Celtic–Rangers matches, however, and might always have had this specific meaning. Wikipedia acknowledges the uncertainty in the meaning but suggests a slightly different idea, that the word derives from the commercial opportunities provided to traders by these popular events. If this was the original meaning, it may derive from a Scots pronunciation of 'farm', 'the old farm' being the time of year when the traders could cash-in. The more tribal sense of 'our enterprise', however, seems a more likely meaning, describing the overwhelming enthusiasm of the city for both teams.

'Firm' is also used generally in football to describe bands of supporters, especially those with hooligan behaviour (see for example 'ICF'). This usage is recorded in Pickering 1994, and the OED records its sarcastic use for the criminal 'firm' of the Kray twins in 1969. The sense of 'roving warriors' certainly lies behind many early club names, and 'Army' is another word used for supporters; it all connotes 'loyalty'. This wider football usage possibly derives from the Glasgow phrase, however, as Celtic–Rangers matches have long been noted for violence. Pickering cites press reports from the notorious event of 1909. This sense does not seem to lie behind the Avon nickname, but all three examples could carry the primary meaning of 'our enterprise', 'what we do'.

Firs was a nickname for Chippenham United F.C., founded in Wiltshire in 1947, closed in 1962. The nickname is that of the club's home ground, 'The Firs', and is recorded in the club's history, Twydell 1988 (p. 93). After closure, the land was used for housing, but the fir trees, on three sides, were kept and the name survives as a street name. The trees are always there in team photographs. The club's first programme, however, calls the club 'The United'. See also United.

Fish is the nickname of Fisher F.C. The Bermondsey club was refounded in 2009 after the closure of Fisher Athletic F.C., founded in 1908 but going through several renamings. The name is not a place-name but comes from St John Fisher (1469–1535), a Catholic martyr. 'The Fish' is recorded in Williams for the older clubs: Fisher Athletic in W1988–93, Fisher '93 in W1994–6, Fisher Athletic (London) in W1997–2009 and for Fisher in W2010–13. See also Club.

Fish Suppers was a nickname for Maxwelltown F.C., founded in Dumfries and Galloway in 1918, closed in 1924. The nickname is recorded on SFHA but is difficult to explain. Maxwelltown is an inland location, now part of Dumfries. It is possible that the club had a tradition like that of Charlton Athletic, which generated the 'Addicks' nickname.

Fishermen is a nickname for clubs in a coastal location with a fishing industry (see also Cod Army, Mariners, Trawlermen, Trawler Boys, etc). Examples are:

- Appledore F.C., founded in Devon in 1912, but renaming 1978–98 as Appledore-B.A.A.C. after a merger with the football section of the Bideford Amateur Athletic Club. The nickname appears for that club in W1995–6.
- Eyemouth United F.C., founded in Berwickshire in 1949. Recorded in RS1993–7, 2000–1, SFHA.
- Fleetwood Town F.C., founded in Lancashire in 1908, with reformations in 1977 and 1997. The nickname is recorded in W1979/80–96 and W2007–12, but the modern club prefers 'The Trawlermen'. See also Cod Army, Reds, Trawlermen.
- Grimsby Town F.C., more recently nicknamed 'The Mariners', which almost means the same thing. 'The Fishermen' is recorded on the 1933 Ogden cigarette card set, and in SWSCYB 1962–3; both names appear in Churchill 1958, AA 1960 and Jeffrey 1961; it last appears in *Stedfast* in November 1963. See also Mariners.
- Porthleven F.C., founded in Cornwall in 1896; W1992–2005.

Fivers is a nickname for Deal Town F.C., founded in Kent in 1908, originally as Deal Cinque Ports. The name was changed to Town in 1920. The nickname refers to the five 'Cinque Ports', a medieval association for defensive and trading purposes, but Deal was one of the seven 'limb' members of the federation. The nickname puns with the slang expression for £5 notes. See also Dealers, Town.

Fizzers is the nickname for Sandhurst Town F.C., founded in Berkshire in 1910. The club's own website proposes two explanations, neither convincing. One is that it refers to the setting up in Sandhurst in 1933 of the Friendly Insurance Society (so F.I.S.'ers), but the firm does not seem to have had any particular relationship with the club. The other is that supporters would stand behind the goal of the opposing side and traditionally shout "Fizz! Fizz! Bang!" if a goal was scored, but this exuberant expression would make more sense if the club nickname already existed, or if there was at least a similar word relevant to the locality. The word is actually in standard dictionaries, and slang dictionaries. In the nineteenth century a fizzer was "anything excellent or first-rate" (OED). It seems to derive from the sound of the word 'physical'. In the military, it came to be used for army parade grounds (i.e. parading in one's best uniform in excellent formation and energetic marching) and thus it also came to be used for army punishments, because being sent out on parade, marching up and down by oneself, was a standard punishment, and in this sense the word seems to return to its origins as 'physical'. In this context the word is entirely mainstream, being used, for example, by Corporal Jones in *Dad's Army* (episode 6.7, 'The Recruit'). Sandhurst is famous, of course, for the Royal Military Academy, and so it was only natural that the word came to be used for the football club too, in the sense of excellence on show, and in tribute to the town's most famous activity, in the same way that many clubs are nicknamed from the main trade of their home; W1994–2013.

Fleet is a nickname for clubs with the element *–fleet* in their place-name. Examples are:

⚽ Ebbsfleet United F.C. The club was founded in Kent in 1946 as Gravesend and North Fleet United, as a merger between Gravesend United and North Fleet United (founded 1890, whose colours and stadium transferred to the new club), and only changed its name to Ebbsfleet in 2007. The nickname is inherited from the earlier Gravesend and North Fleet club: it is recorded in Avis 1966–70, W1979/80–2007 and SSY2004/5–06/7; and in W2008–13 and SSY2007/8–10/11 and SSY2012/13 under the new name.

⚽ Thurrock F.C. Founded in Essex in 1985, the club was called Purfleet F.C. until 2003; W1994–2003 for Purfleet; W2004–13 for Thurrock.

Fleur, see Flower

Flixs was a nickname for Flixton F.C., founded in Greater Manchester in 1960; W1994–5. The nickname is clearly a pluralised short form of the place-name. See also Lions, Valley Roaders, Valiants.

Flippers was an unofficial and taunting nickname for Brighton and Hove Albion when they were known as 'The Dolphins', from the popular 1960s children's television series and film, *Flipper*, recorded in Seddon 2004, p. 203. According to Ferris 2004, fans responded in a 1975 match against Crystal Palace by adopting 'Seagulls' as a rhyming response to chants of the opponent's nickname, 'The Eagles'. See also Albion, Dolphins, Seagulls, Seasiders, Seaweed, Shrimps, Tesco's.

Floggers is an unofficial nickname for Ely Rangers A.F.C., founded in Cardiff in 1965. The word usually refers to those who sell things, especially implying cheapness, but it can also refer to corporal punishment or extreme endeavour. The reason for the nickname is entirely obscure, but it may be intended satirically, from a rival perspective, in the sense of hopeless endeavour, as in 'flogging a dead horse'; Wikipedia.

Flourmen is the nickname of Wellingborough Whitworth F.C., founded in 1973, originally as a works side for Whitworths, the UK's leading supplier of home baking products such as flour, which has operated from the Victoria Mill in Wellingborough since 1886. Wellingborough Town has a related nickname from the same industry (The Doughboys); W2010–13.

Flower was the nickname of Fleur-de-Lys F.C., founded in Gwent at an uncertain date. The club struggled and was taken over by near-neighbour Cwmfelinfach Colts in 2001; after a series of further mergers the present Ynysddu Crusaders was formed in 2008. The nickname 'Flower' is that of the village, itself named from the French for 'flower of lily', the medieval symbol of the French monarchy; it is believed that the unusual place-name originates in a colony of Huguenot refugees. The nickname is also used by the local rugby club (see Huws 2013); internet history of local football dated July 2012. Another local club, Fleur-de-Lys Welfare A.F.C., founded in 1926, is nicknamed 'Fleur' (used on club website).

Flyers is the nickname for two clubs, for different reasons. The clubs are:

☉ Feltham F.C., founded in London in 1946, originally as Tudor Park, renaming in 1963. The nickname refers to an expression in motorsport for the Aston Martin sports cars which were made at the former Whitehead Aircraft Company's plant in Feltham between 1926 and 1956: 'Feltham Flyers'. It appears in the title of a popular print of Aston Martin cars at Goodwood in 1956; W1982/3–83/4 and Moss 1983. See also Blues, Boro.

☉ Lye Town F.C., founded in 1930, originally as Lye and Wollescote. The nickname seems to be both a pun on the place-name and a record of their position in the 'top flight' of the West Midlands Premier League. The *Malvern Gazette* ran a headline on 14 June 2007: "Malvern defeat high-flyers Lye'; W1985–2005.

Flying Blues is the nickname for Marlow United F.C., founded in Buckinghamshire in 1977. The club does play in blue, but also in orange and black. The nickname is one of exuberance, not referring to anything specific about flying; W2009–10.

Ford is the nickname of Hurlford United F.C., founded in Ayrshire in 1938; as a short form of the place-name; Wikipedia, SFHA.

Ford or Fords was the nickname of Ilford F.C., founded in London in 1881, from the second syllable of the place-name. The club survived till 1979, and then merged with Leytonstone to form Leytonstone and Ilford (1979–87), merging again with Walthamstow Forest in 1988 to form Redbridge Forest (1988–92), which merged with Dagenham in 1992 to form the new Redbridge and Dagenham ('The Daggers'). An entirely new Ilford F.C. ('The Foxes') was independently formed in 1987. Recorded in W1979/80 for Ilford and in W1981/2–9 for L. & I, varying between the plural and singular spellings, and in W1990–2 for Redbridge Forest (as 'Fords'). See also Foxes (for the new Ilford).

Forest / Foresters is a nickname for Nottingham Forest F.C., adapted from the official name. Founded in 1865, the club was called Forest from the outset from their use of the Forest Recreation Ground (1865–79). The Forest in the ground name is derived from Sherwood Forest, and the 1933 Ogden card claims that the site was forested before it was cleared to make the pitch. The nickname is recorded early: BoF1905–6 uses both 'Forest' and 'Foresters'; recorded in Johnston 1934, the 1936 Thomson 'stamp' album, G1956–65, Churchill 1958, Richards 1960 and SWSCYB 1962–3 (as Foresters), Avis 1966–70 (as Forest) and in RY1970/1–72/3 (as Forest). The nickname makes a late appearance in the Williams League Directories 1985–90 and on the 1986 Panini sticker (with a Robin Hood cartoon). The club badge features a prominent single tree with the word Forest beneath it. See also Garibaldi Reds, Pied Pipers, Reds, Robin Hoods, Tricky Trees.

Foresters is a nickname for clubs associated with ancient woodland because of their location. The clubs are:

- Cinderford Town A.F.C., founded in Gloucestershire in 1922. The club is on the fringe of the Forest of Dean, and it displays a stag and a tree on its badge; W2010–13. See also Town.
- Forest F.C., a famous amateur side of the early years of football, founded in 1859 by 'Old Harrovians' from Harrow School, and named from Epping Forest; recorded in BoF1905–6, pp. 255–6. In 1863 the club renamed as 'The Wanderers', under which name it continued to flourish until about 1880, surviving until at least 1883. See also Wanderers.
- Lyndhurst F.C., founded in Hampshire in 1885; the nickname is based on the New Forest location; Wikipedia.
- Nottingham Forest F.C., see as Forest, above.

Fort is the nickname for Fort William F.C., founded in the Highland town in 1984, as a short form of the place-name. Recorded in RS1993–2012, SFHA.

Forters is a nickname for Hythe Town F.C., founded in Kent in 1910, reforming as Hythe United in 1992, reverting to Town in 1995; the nickname is recorded on Wikipedia and refers to the club's stadium in Fort Road. See also Reds, Town.

Fosse / Fossites were nicknames for Leicester Fosse F.C., both used in BoF1905–6. The club was the ancestor of Leicester City F.C., founded with this name in 1884 and playing on a field near Fosse Road; they reformed in 1919 as the present name, which was just after Leicester was given city status. The Fosse Way is the name of the Roman road from Exeter to Leicester. See also City, Filberts, Foxes, Ice Kings, Nuts.

Fosters is the nickname of Cockfosters F.C., founded in London in 1921, originally as Cockfosters Athletic; W1986, W1994–2013. An enamel badge in AFBC, however, shows an image of a strutting cock chicken.

Foundry is the nickname of Albert Foundry F.C., founded in Belfast in 1981, but evoking the name of an earlier club of 1923–78; Wikipedia.

Foundrymen is the nickname of Stewarts and Lloyds Corby F.C., founded in 1935 as a works side for the Stewarts & Lloyds Iron & Steel Co. in the Northamptonshire town of Corby; W2005–13.

Fowlers was a nickname for Southall F.C., founded in London in 1871. The nickname refers to the club president, R. F. Fowler, and is recorded in W1986–2004. See also Hall.

Foxes is a nickname for clubs associated in some way with this popular animal, because of heraldry or because of fox-hunting or as a play on words. The clubs are:

- Brache Sparta F.C., founded in Bedfordshire in 1960. The nickname is an adaptation of the name of the club's Foxdell Sports Ground in Luton; W1998–2009. Although the nickname does not appear in Miller & Wright 1996, they record that the club was founded by engineers at the Vauxhall Motors plant on the Brache estate, with a suffix taken in tribute to the Russian side Spartak Moscow (though Wikipedia states it was the Czech side Sparta Prague). The club has a cute fox head on its badge.
- Carlisle United F.C., because the famous huntsman John Peel (c.1776–1854) lived in Cumberland, the club's home county. A fox was on the club badge by 1970. Nowadays, Carlisle is known as the Cumbrians, but the fox tradition is still reflected in the club's mascot, a fox called Olga (which is an anagram of 'goal'); Wikipedia. See also Blues, Cumbrians.
- Farleigh Rovers F.C., founded in Surrey in 1922; W2009–13. The club is based in traditional foxhunting country, a running fox appears on the club badge and Farleigh Fox is the mascot.
- Ilford F.C., founded in London in 1987. The old club called Ilford (1881–1979) used to have the same arms as the borough of Ilford, which has a fox head as a crest. The new club has also taken a fox as a crest and a nickname, and a mascot; W2006–13. See also Fords (for the old Ilford).
- Leicester City F.C. Originally founded in 1884 as Leicester Fosse F.C. (playing on a field near Fosse Road), they reformed in 1919 as the present name, which was just after Leicester was given city status. Leicestershire has a strong fox-hunting tradition, but the fox only appeared on the club's badge in 1948. The mascot is Filbert Fox (named from the Filbert Street stadium), but there is also a Vicky Vixen mascot (also used by Leeds Vixens L.F.C.). Recorded in RY1974/5–SSY2012/13. See also City, Filberts, Fosse / Fossites, Ice Kings, Nuts.
- Llanboidy F.C., founded in Carmarthenshire in 1980. The club badge shows a fox playing with a football. The nickname is used on the club website, as well as 'Llan', and Huws 2013 explains it as an association with the Carmarthenshire fox hunt.
- Stocksbridge Works F.C., founded in South Yorkshire before 1949; this club was the British Steel side, which merged in 1986 with Oxley Park Sports to form Stocksbridge Park Steels F.C. 'The Foxes' nickname is recorded in W1985–6 for Works and here it refers not to the animal but to Samuel Fox, founder of the steel works in 1842, which also bore his name. See also Steels.

Foxhunters is the nickname of Bicester Town F.C., founded in Oxfordshire in 1896 in a merger between B. Rovers and B. Harriers. The nickname records the local foxhunt pack. Despite celebrating the hunters, however, the club badge shows a cute fox with a bushy white tail; W1983/4–2011. The club folded in 2011.

France is an unofficial nickname for Arsenal F.C., coined by supporters of Tottenham Hotspur, and recorded in 2003 on the Football Fans Census website. The nickname is a reference to the French nationality of the great manager Arsène Wenger. See also Boring Arsenal, Gooners, Gunners, Invincibles, Lucky Arsenal, Reds, Royals, Woolwich.

Franchise F.C. was an unofficial nickname for Wimbledon F.C., dating from 2002 or 2003 (Football Fans Census website), from the perspective of supporters of the new A.F.C. Wimbledon, founded in 2002 after the original club had moved to Milton Keynes in that year. The nickname uses an expression from business (referring to locality, area of operations, patch) to mock the consortium which took the club away from its roots and even renamed it in 2004. See also Crazy Gang, Dons, Wombles.

Freebooters is the nickname and part official name of Freebooters A.F.C., founded in Co. Kilkenny in 1950. The club took its name from the Cork club also called Freebooters, which in turn was inspired by a great Dublin club of the name, which had closed in 1906 (the word is cited as a nickname for the old Dublin club on Wikipedia). A freebooter is a pirate, and pirate swords appear on the badge of the Kilkenny club. The name suggests both the sense of travel, used in many club names, and a splendid freedom from restraint. The 'booter' element in the word is derived from 'booty', plunder, but it makes an excellent pun with football boots. See also Team of Millionaires.

Frenchcastle is an unofficial nickname for Newcastle United F.C., spontaneously appearing after the manager Alan Perdew invested in several new players, ending up with more French-born players than Arsenal. The nickname is somehow appropriate as the castle is a French (Norman) invention, imported into England after 1066, and reaching Newcastle in 1080. The nickname seems to appear on websites by 24 January 2013, with 'French Revolution' another phrase in use. See also Barcodes, Cartoon Army, Entertainers, Geordies, Magpies, Skunks, Toon, Tyneside Professors, Tynesiders.

Frew is the nickname of Renfrew F.C., founded in 1912; as a short form of the place-name; Wikipedia, SFHA.

Friars seems to have been an unofficial nickname for Kettering Town in the 1950s. Although the club has always used 'The Poppies' as an official nickname, an ancestor club was Grey Friars F.C. which appears in league tables for 1880–1. 'The Friar' (looking like Friar Tuck) was a mascot who continued to represent Kettering as late as the 1950s and who is illustrated in several photographs in Addis 1995. He was also used as a cartoon image for the club, but it is possible that the mascot actually represented the 'Holy City' nickname for the town of Kettering. There are today some amateur clubs called Greyfriars, for whom Friars might be in use as a nickname, though, again, the usage is not recorded (Greyfriars of King's Lynn, Greyfriars Athletic of Bristol and Greyfriars Celtic, a youth side in Nottinghamshire). For Kettering see also Holy City Boys, Kets / Kettles, Poppies.

Fulshie is a nickname of Stoneyburn F.C., founded in West Lothian in 1983. The club was originally affiliated with the Foulshiels Colliery, from which the nickname comes in a friendly short form. Spoil from the works was used in the construction of their home ground; Wikipedia, club website and a badge in AFBC. See also Burn.

Furnacemen was the nickname of Kilwinning Eglinton F.C., founded in Ayrshire in 1893, closed in 1937. The nickname is recorded twice on SFHA as 'Furnaceman' but this is probably an error for '–men'. The town was once a centre for ironfounding; Eglinton Castle is famous for the extraordinary Gothic tournament held in 1839.

G's is the nickname for two clubs with the letter 'G' in their official names, and a third club where the initialism represents something else. The clubs are:

⚽ Blackheath Electromotors (or Electrodrives after 1992) F.C., founded in the West Midlands in 1920; recorded in W1994–5. Here, the nickname probably represented the General Electric Company, which had taken over the Blackheath factory in 1967.

⚽ Coventry Copsewood F.C., founded in 1922, originally as a works side for Peel Connor employees; the company was renamed G.E.C. (Coventry) in 1934 and G.P.T. (Coventry) in the 1970s, then Marconi (Coventry) in 1999 and the present name in 2005. The nickname survives from the 'G' period; W1995.

⚽ Godalming Town F.C., founded in Surrey as G. United in 1950. The club has changed its name several times and was called Godalming and Guildford F.C, 1992–2005; W2009–13, and it appears on programmes by 2008 (see W2008). See also Gees, Weys.

⚽ G.P.T. (Coventry) F.C., for which see Coventry Copsewood, above; W1995.

Gable Endies is the nickname for Montrose F.C., founded in Angus in 1879. The nickname is that of the elegant town of Montrose. During the eighteenth century the town was a centre for smuggling as well as legitimate trade and the story is that the wealthy merchants built their great houses 'gable to gable'; this architecture is not quite so obvious in the town today as the nickname suggests. The town's nickname has a slightly different form: 'The Gable-Enders'. Recorded through RY1972/3–SSY2012/13 and in RS 1993–2012; AFBC has a badge with the nickname dated 2001–2.

Gabs was the nickname of Castleton Gabriels F.C., founded in Lancashire in 1924, originally as St Gabriel's. At first, the club was a Catholic church side for St Gabriel and the Angels in the town of Castleton in Rochdale borough. In 1990 they were renamed Castleton Gabriels, and then Rochdale Town in 2008. The nickname is recorded in W1994–2008. See also Angels, Castlemen, Garrison, Guardians, Messengers.

Gala is a nickname for the Galashiels side, Gala Fairydean F.C., founded in 1907. The nickname is that of the town of Galashiels, which is also used by the local rugby club: Gala Rugby Football Club; Wikipedia. See also Braw Lads, Dean, Fairies.

Galabankies is a nickname for Annan Athletic F.C., founded in 1942. The Dumfries and Galloway side plays at the Galabank Ground in Annan. Recorded in RS2009–12 and SSY2009/10–2012/13. See also Athletic, Black and Golds.

Gambians is a recent unofficial nickname for Sutton United F.C. in Surrey. In 1999, a club was formed in Banjul, in the African country of The Gambia, who renamed themselves Sutton United F.C. after a donation from the London club. A friendship has developed between the two Suttons, hence the nickname; Wikipedia. See also U's.

Garibaldi Reds is a nickname for Nottingham Forest F.C., founded in 1865, in honour of the fact that the colour of their shirts was based on the red shirts worn by the supporters of Garibaldi, the Italian patriot who united Italy, and who was much respected in Britain after his visit in 1864. The nickname is recorded in Pickering 1994. See also Forest/Foresters, Pied Pipers, Reds, Robin Hoods, Tricky Trees.

Garrison is a nickname for Rochdale Town F.C., founded in 1924, originally as a church side in the town of Castleton in Rochdale borough. In 1990 they were renamed Castleton Gabriels, and then Rochdale Town in 2008. The word is usually used for the occupants of a fort or a castle, though neither Rochdale Castle or the town of Castleton are *garrisoned*; Wikipedia. See also Angles, Castlemen, Gabs, Guardians, Messengers.

Gas / Gasheads are unofficial nicknames for Bristol Rovers F.C. Founded in 1883 as Black Arabs F.C. (named from the Arabs rugby team and the black strip they wore), the name changed to Eastville Rovers in 1885, then to Bristol Eastville Rovers, before becoming Bristol Rovers in 1898. The Eastville ground was their home from 1897 to 1986 and this ground formerly had a prominent gasworks next door, hence the name. Originally meant as an insult but now accepted, Bristol City supporters called Bristol Rovers fans Gasheads (recorded on Football Fans Census, 2003); Wikipedia records 'Gas'. See also Arabs, Black Arabs, Pirates, Purdown Poachers, Rovers, Squatters, Tesco's.

Gasmen was the nickname of Bournemouth Gasworks Athletic F.C., founded in Dorset in 1899, originally as a works side, closed in 1973; Wikipedia. See also Lights.

Gate is a nickname for clubs with the element *–gate* in their official name. The examples are:

☉ B.S.C. (Parkgate) F.C., founded in 1969 as a works side for the British Steel Corporation site at Parkgate near Rotherham, South Yorkshire; recorded in W1982/3–6 and W1987–2007 for the successor clubs. The club became R.E.S. Parkgate in 1990, and Parkgate F.C. in 1994, but the entries in Williams frequently call the club just Parkgate after 1987. It is now nicknamed The Steelmen (q.v.).

☉ Highgate United F.C., founded in Birmingham in 1948; W1979/80–80/1 and

W1987–2013. See also Reds.

⚽ Margate F.C., founded in Kent in 1896. The club was briefly renamed Thanet United 1981–9. Recorded in Avis 1966–70, W1980/1; W1981/2–6 for Thanet United; W1990–2013 and SSY2004/5; Smith 1991/2–95/6 persistently spells the nickname 'The Gat'. 'Gat' is used on the south-east coast for a sea channel which is subject to silt from currents, but this feature is not present at Margate, neither does it reflect the local pronunciation, so it is likely to be a typing error. See also Islanders, Lilywhites, U's.

⚽ Redgate Clayton F.C., founded in Staffordshire in 1969; W1993–5.

⚽ Squire's Gate F.C., founded in Blackpool in 1948, originally as Squire's Gate British Legion; Wikipedia.

⚽ St. James's Gate F.C., founded in Dublin in 1902; RI1997.

⚽ Thanet United F.C., see under Margate, above.

Gates is the nickname of Oakengates Athletic F.C., founded at Telford in Shropshire in 1886 (original as O. Town, renaming to Athletic in 2005); here the short form copies the plural in the place-name; Wikipedia.

Gay Puritans is the older nickname of Banbury United F.C. Founded in Oxfordshire in 1931 as Spencer Villa, a works club, it became Banbury Spencer in 1934, then Banbury United in 1965. The nickname dates from before 1966 (recorded in Avis 1966 for Banbury Spencer, Avis 1970 and W1988–90, W1993 for United). The club dropped the 'Gay' prefix and became 'The Puritans' by the time of W1992 (no nickname is listed for the club in W1991). In both traditional and modern definitions, the nickname is a remarkable contradiction in terms, but other nicknames seem to carry a similar meaning: Dandy ('Dandy Dons' or 'Dandies'), Jolly ('Jolly Boys') and Merry ('Merry Millers'); 'Happy Puritans' seems the best translation. See also Puritans, United.

Gees was a nickname for Godalming and Guildford F.C., established in Surrey in 1992 in a renaming of Godalming Town (to which name the club reverted in 2005); a spelled-out version of an initialism, though probably intended to suggest 'two Gees' for the two names in the official name, W1999–2006. See also G's, Weys.

Gene Puddle is an unofficial nickname for Burnley F.C., from the perspective of Blackburn Rovers, recorded in the 2003 Football Fans Census. The nickname could have been coined for any location, as it merely suggests that the DNA of the town is so degenerate that it is best described as a gene puddle rather than the usual gene pool (an amusing idea, but scientific nonsense). See also Clarets, Dingles, Moorites, Royalites, Turfites.

Generals is the nickname for Chesham United F.C. Founded in Buckinghamshire in 1917 in a merger between C. Generals and C. Town, the original name came from a church side for the General Baptist Church (now Broadway Baptist Church) in Chesham; W1992–2013. See also United.

Gents is the nickname and part-official name of Galmpton United and Torbay

Gentlemen A.F.C., founded in Devon in a merger in 2008; used in *This is Devon*, 3 May 2010.

Gents / City Gents was an unofficial nickname for Bradford City in the 1960s. According to Ferris 2005, the 'Bantams' nickname was regarded as having "unwelcome chicken attributes", so 'City Gents' or just 'Gents' was proposed as a replacement. *City Gents* was already the name of the club's fanzine, but the idea was dropped "probably because the name suggests a men's lavatory"; the nickname is printed in G1976. See also Bantams, Chickens, Citizens, Cocks, Paraders, Sadford.

Geordies is a traditional nickname for the people of Newcastle-upon-Tyne, but it also appears as a football club nickname. The name has an uncertain origin, though all theories agree that it is an affectionate form of the personal name George, first recorded in print in 1823 (and next in a *Glossary of North Country Words* in 1829). One theory is that it recalls Newcastle support for King George II during the 1745 Jacobite rebellion; another that it refers to a miner's safety lamp invented by George Stephenson in 1815. For it to be recorded in print so early, however, the 1745 explanation seems more convincing. The clubs are:

- Hanwell Town F.C., founded in 1920 in the London borough of Ealing. The club adopted black and white stripes like the strip of Newcastle United, and were originally formed by a group of men from Newcastle; Wikipedia. See also Magpies, Town.
- Newcastle United F.C., founded in a merger in the Geordie capital in 1892. The nickname appears on the 1933 Ogden cigarette card, Shawcross 1961 and as an alternative in Avis 1966–70. See also Barcodes, Cartoon Army, Entertainers, Frenchcastle, Magpies, Skunks, Toon, Tyneside Professors, Tynesiders.
- St George's A.F.C., founded in Douglas, Isle of Man, in 1919. Here the nickname returns to its origins with the personal name George; used on the club's own website.

'Gers is an abbreviation for the football club suffix Rangers (q.v.), and is occasionally used as a nickname on its own (see also Wee 'Gers). Examples are:

- Arniston Rangers F.C., founded in Gorebridge, Midlothian in 1878; recorded on Wikipedia. See also Arnie.
- Carrick Rangers F.C., founded at Carrickfergus in Co. Antrim in 1939; Wikipedia. See also Rangers.
- Kintbury Rangers F.C., founded in Berkshire in 1890; Wikipedia. See also Rangers.
- Rangers F.C., founded in Glasgow in 1872. Recorded throughout RY1970/1– SSY2012/13 and in RS1993–2012, G1976. See also Blues, Huns, Iron Curtain, Light Blues, Rangers, Teddy Bears.

Ghosts is the spooky nickname of Fakenham Town F.C. in Norfolk, founded in 1884. The reason is not entirely clear. There is a well-known poem by Robert Bloomfield, 'The Fakenham Ghost', first published in an anthology in 1802 and then often reprinted separately as a children's pamphlet, but Bloomfield was a Suffolk poet and there is another Fakenham in Suffolk. To the south-west of the town is Raynham Hall, location of the famous 1936 *Country Life* photograph of a ghost on the staircase, but Raynham Hall is far enough away to cast some doubt on this being the origin of the nickname. Norfolk in general is associated with the classic ghost stories of M. R. James, but none are specific to Fakenham. The club badge shows an eerie black nondescript *form* on a white background (seemingly a crude old woodcut, certainly not the same shape as the Raynham Hall photograph, the ghost is apparently holding a rolling pin). The best explanation seems to be that it is a tribute to the Bloomfield poem, staking a claim that the poem is about the Norfolk Fakenham, and perhaps with an encouragement to coin the nickname after the 1936 publicity from *Country Life*. Amusing 'explanations' offered by word of mouth include (1) the team must have failed to turn up to a match one day, but somehow won it anyway; (2) the club's ground is haunted; or (3) the goal-keeper is never there and (4), typically, "If old *so-and-so* was still around, he'd know". Recorded in W1989–2013.

Gills is the nickname of three clubs with a place-name which begins with this sound. The clubs are:

❂ Gillingham F.C., founded in Kent in 1893 as New Brompton F.C., renaming in 1912. Recorded throughout RY and SSY1970/1–2012/13, G1976.

❂ Gillingham Town F.C., founded in Dorset in 1879; Wikipedia.

❂ Guilsfield F.C., founded in Powys in 1957. Recorded in RW2001. See also Guils.

Gilly is the nickname for Gillford Park F.C., founded in 2004 as G.P. Spartans, renaming in 2006 and based near Carlisle at the Gillford Park Stadium; in 2012 the club renamed as 'Celtic Nation F.C.' The club has a similar strip to the Glasgow side.

Gingerbread Men is the nickname of Market Drayton Town F.C., founded in Shropshire in 2003 as a successor team to the Little Drayton Rangers (itself a successor to an earlier club called 'Town', and probably nicknamed The Draytonians). The nickname celebrates the town's local gingerbread recipe, first recorded in 1793 and still made in the town today by a company called Image on Food; Wikipedia.

Gingerbreads is the nickname for Grantham Town F.C., founded in Lincolnshire in 1874. The famous Grantham Whetstones were the earliest recorded biscuits on public sale, and a major attraction for travellers on the Great North Road, but in 1740 a baker of the whetstones, William Egglestone, accidentally added ginger to the baking, and was delighted and astonished at the results. Henceforth, Grantham Gingerbread became famous, and the business survives today under the name of Catlins on the town's High Street. The club history by Jon Barnes (2003, p.10) states that the nickname became popular during the 1935–6 season, but was probably used by supporters before it appeared in the local newspaper. Recorded in Avis 1966–70, W1979/80–2013.

Gladiators is a nickname for two clubs which seem to have no connection with the classical combative spectator sport, but it makes a good nickname for football clubs because football is also a classical combative spectator sport, though FA rules prohibit the slaughter of the losers. The clubs are:

☻ Matlock Town F.C. Founded in Derbyshire in 1878, the club's badge shows a Roman gladiator posed for action, yet there seems no specific reason for the nickname other than the sense of classical combative spectator sport; W1979/80–2013.

☻ Milton Keynes City F.C., recorded in W1979/80–85. This is the first club called M.K.C., which was descended from Bletchley Park F.C., founded in 1956, renaming to M.K.C. in 1974, folding in 1985. There is also a modern club called Bletchley Town, founded in 2005, which has recently readopted this older nickname. There does not seem to have been a specific reason for the choice of nickname, other than associated prowess. See also Blues, City, Moles.

Glan is a nickname for Glantraeth F.C., founded on Anglesey in 1984; a short form of the place-name; Wikipedia.

Glasgow Uni is the nickname of Glasgow University F.C., founded in 1877, the earliest Scottish university team. The short form of 'University' seems to have entered English from Australian usage; used in internet match reports for this club.

Glassboys is the nickname for two clubs, for glass manufacturing reasons. The clubs are:

☻ Stourbridge F.C., founded in West Midlands in 1876 as Stourbridge Standard. 'Stourbridge Glass' was already famous in the 1600s, and by 1861 glass production here employed over 1,000 people in eleven factories; W1981/2–2013.

☻ Triplex F.C., founded in 1951 (according to W1993) or 1931 (website) in Birmingham as T. Safety Glass, renaming to Triplex in 1984. It is not entirely clear if this club is the same as the following entry. It seems to have folded when Richmond Swifts took over its ground in 1994; W1993.

Glasses (as in spectacles) is a nickname for Preston North End F.C., in British Sign Language. The remarkable nickname refers to the 1922 F.A. Cup Final in which the goalkeeper James Mitchell wore glasses. The incident is famous, but the nickname is unique to this language, and has been discovered by linguists Richard Coates and Rachel Sutton-Spence (see Coates and Sutton-Spence, 2013). See also Invincibles, Lilywhites / Whites, North End, P.N.E., Proud Preston.

Glassmen is a nickname for Pilkington XXX F.C., founded in 1931 according to Wikipedia, but this may be an error for the previous entry. The present club was called Burman Hi-Ton, a works side for a glass factory, before it renamed as Pilkington XXX in 2002; recorded in W2005. See also Pilks.

Glaziers is the older nickname of Crystal Palace F.C. Founded in 1905 by employees at the Crystal Palace, the huge glass exhibition centre destroyed by fire in 1936, the nickname obviously relates to the magnificent glass structure. It is recorded on the 1933 Ogden card, Johnston 1934, the 1936 Thomson 'stamp' album, Avis 1954–70, G1956–76, Churchill 1958, Richards 1960, Jeffrey 1961, SWSCYB 1962–3 and RY1970/1–73/4, when it was supplanted by 'The Eagles'. See also Eagles, Palace, Team of the Eighties.

Glebe is the nickname of Glebe Rangers F.C., founded at Ballymoney, Co. Antrim in 1989. The club uses this nickname on its website, though RS2007 gives Rangers. The club badge shows a Scottish saltire, presumably showing respect for the Scottish Rangers club; the expression 'Wee Glebe' has been seen (which would chime well with Scottish clubs) but does not seem to be widely used.

Glens is a nickname for Scottish and Northern Irish clubs with the place-name element Glen in their official name. The word is a Scots name for a lush wide valley. The clubs are:

⚽ Glenafton Athletic F.C., founded in Ayrshire in 1930; club's own website. See also Afton.

⚽ Glenrothes F.C., founded in Fife in 1964; Wikipedia.

⚽ Glentanar Junior F.C., founded in Aberdeen in 1978; Wikipedia.

⚽ Glentoran F.C., founded in Belfast in 1882. Recorded in RI1997, RNI2007. See also Cock 'n' Hens.

⚽ Rutherglen Glencairn F.C., founded in 1896 (here the plural form seems to record the double use of the word in the club name, the SFHA has it in the singular); Wikipedia, SFHA.

Glorious Hoops is a nickname for Queen's Park F.C., founded in Glasgow in 1867, and the oldest surviving Association Football Club in Scotland. The nickname refers to the unusually narrow black-and-white hoops first adopted by the club in 1873 and worn more or less ever since; Wikipedia. See also Amateurs, Queen's, Q.P., Spiders.

Gloucestrians was an early nickname for Gloucester City A.F.C., founded in 1883; the nickname is mentioned on Wikipedia as used in local media during the club's early years. See also Citizens, City, Tigers.

Glovers is the nickname for Yeovil Town F.C., founded in Somerset in 1895 as Y. Casuals, renaming as Town in 1907, then as Y. and Petters United in 1914, before reverting to the Town name in 1946. The nickname records the importance of Yeovil for the glove-making industry in the nineteenth century. Recorded in W1979/80–2003 and SSY2003/4–12/13. The nickname is surprisingly not used in Goodall 1982. See also Casuals.

Gnashers is the nickname of Murton A.F.C., founded in Co. Durham in 1891, originally as Murton Colliery Welfare. The nickname is not explained but it seems to refer to the famous children's cartoon character Dennis the Menace and his dog Gnasher, because the red-and-black strip of the club is very like the red-and-black top worn by Dennis. However, the Williams directories reveal the existence of another club in 1994–5 called Murton International, nicknamed 'The Nash' (q.v.). The two clubs shared the same ground and their nicknames seem related; W1994–2004.

GNG is a nickname for Guru Nanak Gravesend F.C., founded in Kent in 1965. The side was formed for Asian youth and named in honour of the founder of the Sikh religion (and it is not the only club in the world so named). The initialism appears on the club's own website. A variant nickname is "Gnu", presumably a pun on the first word but possibly an acronym suggesting Guru Nanak United (used on Kent Youth League website). See also Gurus.

Goddy is the nickname of Godmanchester Rovers F.C., founded in Cambridgeshire in 1911, a friendly short form of the official name; W2003–8. See also Goody, Rovers.

Gold and Black Army is the nickname for Torpoint Athletic F.C., founded in 1887. The Cornish side plays in black shorts and socks with a gold shirt; Wikipedia. See also Point.

Gold 'n' Blacks is the nickname for Stowmarket Town F.C., founded in Suffolk in 1883. The club plays in gold shirts with black shorts and socks; Miller & Wright 1996. See also Stow.

Golden Boys is an alternative nickname of Watford F.C., given after their adoption of a golden shirt (and black shorts) in 1959. The colour changed to yellow in 1976. See also Blues, Brewers, Hornets, Horns / 'Orns, Saints, Wasps, Yellow Army.

Golds is a nickname for two clubs which play in gold-coloured (yellow) shirts. The clubs are:

- Littlehampton Town, see under Marigolds.
- Ossett Albion A.F.C., founded in West Yorkshire in 1944. The club plays in gold-coloured shirts with black shorts and socks; Wikipedia. See also Albion, Unicorns.

Gooners is an unofficial nickname for Arsenal F.C. The nickname is a play on the official nickname, 'The Gunners'. It is said on Wikipedia that the nickname refers to Arsenal supporters, but it is often difficult to separate nicknames for club and fans, and the 1999 children's book by Patricia Borlenghi cites it as a nickname for the club. See also Boring Arsenal, France, Gunners, Invincibles, Lucky Arsenal, Reds, Royals, Woolwich.

Goody is an alternative nickname for Godmanchester Rovers F.C., founded in Cambridgeshire in 1911, a friendly short form of the official name, but clearly adapted from the variant form Goddy, appearing late, in W2009–13. See also Goddy, Rovers.

Goths was the nickname of Gothic F.C., founded in 1898 as a works team for the Norwich business of Laurence, Scott and Electromotors. The factory was called the Gothic Works, no doubt from its architectural style, and the club survived to the 1980s.

'Gow is the nickname of Lesmahagow F.C., founded in Lanarkshire in 1885; a short form of the place-name; W1982/3, SFHA.

Gowfers is the nickname of Carnoustie Panmure F.C., founded in Angus in 1936. The nickname is the Scots for golf and celebrates the association between the town and that unusual game; Wikipedia, SFHA.

Goyts is the nickname of Goytre United F.C., founded in Goytre near Port Talbot in

1963; recorded in RW1994–2011. The club website also uses the variant form The Goyt.

Grace is a nickname for Potters Bar Town F.C., founded in Hertfordshire in 1960 as Mount Grace Old Scholars F.C., for former pupils of that school, renamed Potters Bar Town in 1991; W1994–2013. See also Scholars.

Grandad's Army was a nickname for the heroic Colchester United side of 1971, for their impressive performance during the FA Cup run, and because seven of the players were aged over 30. Recorded in Pickering 1994. See also Ewes, Oystermen, U's.

Grand Old Team was a nickname for Belfast Celtic F.C., founded in 1891, closed in 1949; Wikipedia. See also Celtic / Celts, The Mighty Belfast Celtic.

Grasshoppers is an attractive suffix and nickname for youth sides, seemingly describing not only the action on the pitch but also chiming with the proverbial expression 'knee-high to a grasshopper'. However, it has also been used for adult sides, famously for Grasshopper Club Zürich in Switzerland, from 1886. Some of the present-day clubs are:

- Bridgwater Grasshoppers F.C., founded in Somerset in the early 1980s.
- Chantry Grasshoppers F.C., founded in Suffolk in 1982.
- Grasshoppers F.C., founded in Truruo, Cornwall, in 2000.
- Uckfield Grasshoppers '81 F.C., founded in Sussex in 1981.
- Wigginton Grasshoppers F.C., founded in York in 1982.

Grave Diggers is recorded on the 1933 Ogden card as a visual pun for Bury F.C., with the explanation that the club buries the hopes of rival teams, though it is more obviously connected to the place-name. See also Bucketshakers, Shakers.

Gravelmen / G-Men is a nickname for Grays Athletic F.C., founded in 1890. The club was formed near several Victorian chalk pits and landfill sites, and the nickname is based on the geology of the district, but perhaps with an encouragement from the opening letters of the club name to take this word rather than, say, Chalkies (the place-name, however, is based on a family surname). The club is now based at Corringham in Essex; Wikipedia. See also Blues, Boys from Rathbone Street, Grays.

Grays is an alternative nickname for Grays Athletic, founded in 1890; as a short form of the official name; Wikipedia. See also Blues, Boys from Rathbone Street, Gravelmen / G-Men.

Grecians is the nickname of Exeter City F.C., formed in 1904 in a merger between Exeter United (1890) and St Sidwell's United. The club's home ground of St James' Park is only a few minutes' walk from St Sidwell's parish church, and the new club soon adopted the nickname long associated with the parish and no doubt used by its early football team, but why were the St Sidwell parishioners called 'Grecians'? The tradition is ancient, possibly recorded from the seventeenth century, and derives from the sense that St Sidwell's was outside the city walls and, from the perspective of the citizens on the inside, looked threatening, like the Ancient Greeks besieging

Troy. There are three literary threads which confirm this interpretation. The earliest is an administrative document of 21 July 1669 which is preserved in the collection of anecdotes made by the poet Robert Southey, printed in *Robert Southey's Common-place Book*, fourth series: *Original Memoranda etc.* (London, 1851, p. 380). The document refers to the labour of making the river navigable by "300 Grecians (?) of the Parish of St Sidwell's...". The question mark suggests some doubt as to the reading, but if Southey had been unaware of the tradition, he would naturally have been surprised to read the word and so may have doubted it. The second source is a local satirical poem by Andrew Brice mocking the politics of the 1737 election in Exeter. This was printed later, in 1770, under the title of *The Mobiad*. Here, the 'yellow Greeks' are the Whigs, the Blues the Tories. Brice says "The yellow GREEKS with vast Huzza rush in; | And Blues look bluer at the dauntful Din." He then adds a note: "GREEKS, so we surname, I know not why, the rugged inhabitants of St. Sidwell's. The title seems to have arisen from their contending with the City at Foot-ball etc, they being called Greeks as making an Invasion, and the Townsmen perhaps Trojans in defending their Ground, etc." So, by 1770 at the very latest, the nickname is established. The final literary thread sums up the ideas well in an article called 'Exeter Sixty Years Ago' in *All the Year Round. A Weekly Journal. Conducted by Charles Dickens*, XIV (28 October 1865), 319–25, which states (p. 320), in the context of the parish traditions of 'beating the bounds': "There was a remote parish—that of St. Sidwell's—the claims of whose "boys" to the right of citizenship were doubtful. They were contumaciously called Grecians; but the parish being large, and its warriors numerous, the citizen lads were accustomed to combine against "the outer barbarians," and the battles raged furiously, and black eyes and bloody noses were left to exhibit the results of the fray. Each parish had in turns suffered the ignominy of defeat and reaped the laurels of victory. Each had its heroes and its poltroons—the leaders of the forlorn hopes and the lingerers in the rear."
Some internet sources add the story that there was a popular re-enactment of the Siege of Troy in 1726, in which St Sidwell's parishioners played the part of the Greeks, but I have not been able to confirm this detail, and others add the detail that the story of Troy was certainly known in Exeter as long ago as c.1190, when 'Joseph of Exeter' had translated Homer's *Iliad* into Latin, though it would be unreliable to argue that the St Sidwell's tradition goes that far back.

There can be no doubt that this is the right explanation for the nickname, so it seems irrelevant to list alternative theories, but they include the colourful ideas that the parish had children who were nicknamed the 'greasy 'uns'; or that the Cornish word for Exeter, *Caeresk*, has become mutated in speech to Grecians, from calling the inhabitants Caereskuns (but this would refer to the city rather than the outside parish, and in any case Oliver Padel informs that the Cornish word for Exeter was a scholarly invention of the seventeenth century); or that it referred to Greek nationals from St Sidwell's who were market traders in the city (Fabian & Green

1960 cites this idea with the words "a community of local barrow-boys who held an open-air market near to the ground" (vol. ii, p. 364). The 1933 Ogden card features the nickname and it is recorded in Johnston 1934, G1956–76, Churchill 1958, *Stedfast* January 1965 (as 'The Greeks', with a cartoon showing a goal with Grecian columns), Avis 1966–70, RY1970/1–SSY2003/4; W2004–8; SSY2004/5–12/13. See also Trojans for another nickname based on the Siege of Troy.

Green is a nickname for clubs with the element 'Green' in their place-names. The plural form is usually used for the colour, but some of these are also based on a place-name. The clubs are:

🟢 Bedfont Green F.C., established in Middlesex in 1965, renaming as Bedfont Town in 2010; from the club's official name; W2006–8. See also Peacocks.

🟢 Colletts Green F.C., founded in Malvern, Worcestershire in a renaming of Three Nuns F.C. in 1992; the club disappears from FCHD in 1999; W1995.

🟢 Forest Green Rovers F.C., founded in Gloucestershire in 1890, originally as Nailsworth & Forest Green. The club had renamed before 1894 and also had a brief period named Stroud F.C. (1989–92). The successful side has several nicknames; W1982/3–5 and Miller & Wright 1996. See also FGR, Green Army, Lawnmowers, Little Club on the Hill, Rovers.

🟢 Frimley Green F.C., founded in Surrey in 1919; the club plays in blue; W1994, W2006–13.

🟢 Leverstock Green F.C., founded in 1895 (the Hemel Hempstead side also plays in green shorts and socks with white shirts); W1994–2013.

🟢 Longwell Green Sports F.C., founded in Gloucestershire in 1966; W2010–13. See also Sports.

🟢 Slade Green F.C., founded in London in 1946, originally as S.G. Athletic, renaming in 1949. The club also plays in green shirts; W1983/4–2009.

Green and Blacks is a nickname for St Blazey A.F.C., founded in Cornwall in 1896. The club plays in green and black stripes, with green shorts and black socks; W2008–13.

Green and Reds was the nickname for Huntingdon United F.C., founded in Cambridgeshire in 1947 in a merger of the older H. Town and H. Wanderers; W1998. The club merged with 'RGE Huntingdon' to form H. United RGE in 2005. The RGE Engineering Group is a company based in nearby Godmanchester.

Green and Golds is the nickname of Vale Recreation F.C., founded on the island of Guernsey in 1932. The club plays in these colours and it is also the name of the fanzine. See also Rec.

Green and White Army is a nickname for two sides which play in these colours. The teams are:

🟢 Birtley Town F.C., founded in 1993. The club near Gateshead play in green and white hooped shirts, white shorts and green socks; Wikipedia. See also Hoops, Super Greens.

☻ Northern Ireland National Team. The Belfast-based Irish Football Association first fielded a team for the island of Ireland in 1882, but after the independence of the Republic in 1921 its responsibility was confined to the North. Nevertheless, the team from the North continued to call itself 'Ireland' until the 1970s; Wikipedia has the nickname but prefers to apply it to the fans. See also Norn Iron, Our Wee Country.

Green Army is a nickname for six clubs, for different reasons. The clubs are:

☻ Ash United F.C., founded in Surrey in 1911. The club plays in an all-green strip; W2013. See also United.

☻ Bangor University F.C., founded in Gwynedd but of uncertain date. The club plays in an all-green strip and the nickname is recorded on Wikipedia. See also Students.

☻ Battersea Ironsides F.C., founded in London before 1994. The club wears a Celtic-like green and white strip; used on the club's own website. See also Ironsiders / Ironsides.

☻ Bethnal Green United F.C., from the second word in the place-name, but also because the team play in an all-green strip; Wikipedia.

☻ Forest Green Rovers F.C., founded in Gloucestershire in 1890; recorded on Wikipedia. See also FGR, Green, Lawnmowers, Little Club on the Hill, Rovers.

☻ Plymouth Argyle F.C., from the distinctive and unusual dark green colour of their strip. The military base had been the home of the Argyll and Sutherland Highlanders before the club was set up in 1886 as Argyle F.C. (changing to Plymouth Argyle in 1903), and the early colours reflect those of the regiment: green and black 1899–1901, then green and white for most of the rest of the club's history. See also Argyle, Pilgrims.

Green Lions is the nickname of Guernsey F.C., founded in 2011 and adventurously entering the English Combined Counties League Division One (covering mainly the Surrey area). Three lions are the national symbol of the island of Guernsey, and three lion heads appear on the badge of the club, in green, the national colour of the island. The nickname is also used for the Guernsey Offical Football Team when it plays in the international Island Games (founded 1989) and the local inter-island Muratti Cup (founded 1905); W2012–13.

Green Machine is recorded in W1993–8 as the nickname for Bexhill Town F.C. in East Sussex. The club flourished in the 1950s as B. Athletic and was renamed Town in 1969. It merged with neighbouring B. A.A.C. in 2002, to form the present B. United (see United). The club played in a green and white strip. 'Machine' was a fashionable word in the computerised 1990s, but it had been used in football before, in the 1940s, for the River Plate club in Argentina. It carries a sense of unstoppable progress.

Greenbacks is the nickname of Bedworth United F.C., founded in 1895, though the current club is the fourth incarnation of Bedworth Town, and took its present name in 1968. The Warwickshire club plays in green shirts and socks with white shorts, and the nickname is a pun combining the phrases 'the shirt on your back' (meaning 'everything you have') and the well-known nickname of American paper money; W1979/80–2013.

Greens is a nickname for clubs with the word 'Green' in their official name, or which play in a green strip, or for both reasons. Examples are:

- Bromsgrove Rovers F.C., founded in 1885, for their mainly green strip; W1979/80–88 and W1994–2010. The club has now folded. See also Rovers.
- Carno F.C., founded in Powys in 1960. The club wears dark green shirts and the nickname is used on a website reviewing a match against Builth Wells on 28 October 2010; Huws 2013.
- Coleshill Town F.C., founded in Warwickshire in 1894, for the green strip, recorded on a fans' website. See also Colemen / Coalmen, Coleshillites, Colts, Rabbits.
- Gorleston F.C., founded in Norfolk in 1887. The club adopted green colours in 1903, currently playing in green and white shirts with green shorts and socks, and their home ground is called Emerald Park. Initially, however, the club was nicknamed 'The Cards', from wearing cardinal red shirts with blue shorts. Recorded in W1979/80–2005. The club's own website also uses the expression 'Green Army!' See also Cards.
- Hendon F.C. Formed in 1908 as Christ Church Hampstead, the club became Hampstead Town in 1909, then Hampstead in 1926 and Golders Green F.C. in 1932, before changing again to Hendon in 1946. They play in a distinctive all-green strip, though the nickname may also refer to the Golders Green connection. Recorded in W1979/80–2013. See also Dons.
- Holmer Green F.C., founded in 1908. The Buckinghamshire side plays in a green and white strip; Wikipedia.
- Keyworth United F.C., founded in Nottinghamshire in 1910; green shirts and black shorts; W1985.
- Kidlington F.C., founded in Oxfordshire in 1909. The club plays in an all-green strip; Wikipedia.
- Northwich Victoria F.C., founded in Cheshire in 1874, for their green and white hooped shirts; W1989–90 and W1999–2013. See also Trickies, Vics.
- Sleaford Town F.C., founded in Lincolnshire in 1968. The club plays in green shirts and socks with black shorts; Wikipedia. See also Town.
- Whitton United F.C., founded in 1926. The club plays in an all-green strip; Wikipedia. See also Boyos.

Griff is a nickname for Nuneaton Griff F.C., founded in Warwickshire in 1972, originally as N. Amateurs. Griff is a hamlet near the club, and the nickname is merely a short form of the official name; W2001–5. See also Heartlanders.

Griffins is the nickname of two clubs, for different reasons. The clubs are:

- Bloxwich United F.C., which had a brief existence in the West Midlands. Formed in a merger between Bloxwich Town and Blakenall in 2001, Blakenall later withdrew from the alliance and the club folded by 2005; the nickname is recorded in W2001. Griffins are mythical beasts combining parts of lions and eagles, so the choice here was the closest possible match between the Lions of Blakenall and the Kestrels of B. Town. For a new club called B. United, see Red Lions. For B. Town, see also Kestrels.

⚽ Ely Rangers A.F.C., founded in Cardiff in 1965. The club is based in Wenvoe, near Cardiff, near the housing estate beside the Ely river. The story goes that the old-style Barclays Bank eagle image used on the club badge in honour of the bank's sponsorship since the late 1960s, was mistaken by supporters as a griffin (the mythical beast which is a lion with an eagle's head and wings; this beast was actually used as a symbol by the Midland Bank). The story is entirely plausible, and shows how easily mythologies and trade logos can become confused, but comparison with another nickname raises the possibility of a further confusion influencing the nickname. The football club at Wivenhoe in Essex is nicknamed 'The Dragons' (q.v.). There, the club badge shows a wyvern and there is a mistaken but traditional belief that the place-name contains the word wyvern, and the nickname was generated in a confusion of wyverns and dragons. Here, the place-name Wenvoe has an uncertain etymology, but superficially looks similar to Wivenhoe. The same confusion might also have happened here: first the idea that the place-name referred to wyverns, and then a confusion that wyverns were the same as griffins. Recorded in RW2001–11. See also Diffs / Divs, Floggers.

Grove is a nickname for two clubs with the place-name element 'grove' in their official names. The clubs are:

⚽ Hengrove Athletic F.C., founded in Bristol in 1948; club website and Wikipedia. See also Hens.

⚽ Kidsgrove Athletic F.C., founded in Staffordshire in 1952; W2003–13.

Groveites was the nickname of Sheffield Wednesday F.C. at the time when their ground was Olive Grove (1887–98); Wikipedia. See also Blades, Groveites, Owls, Pigs, Wednesday, Wendys.

Guardians is a nickname for Rochdale Town F.C., founded in 1924, originally as a church side for the catholic St Gabriel and the Angels. The term obviously refers to the expression 'guardian angel'; Wikipedia. See also Angles, Castlemen, Gabs, Garrison, Messengers.

Guardsmen is a nickname for the new Windsor F.C., founded in Berkshire in 2011 after the demise of Windsor & Eton F.C. (1892). The nickname is a reference to the various guards regiments whose traditional role has included the ceremonial guarding of the royal family at Buckingham Palace and state occasions. The club is appropriately adjacent to Windsor Castle, which appears on the club's badge. The club mascot is one Scotty the Stag, but because the manager is called Keith Scott, neither the mascot nor the club nickname may necessarily refer specifically to the Scots Guards. See also Royalists, Royals.

Guild is a nickname for A.F.C. Guildford City, founded in 1877, originally as Guildford F.C. and reformed as Guildford United in 1921. The club took the city title in 1927, but closed in 1974, reforming again as A.F.C. Guildford in 1976. The name puns on the first syllable of the place-name, but also suggests 'club'. It appears on several websites though not on the club's own or Wikipedia. See also City, Pinks, Sweeney.

Guils is the nickname of Guilsfield F.C., founded in Powys in 1957; recorded in RW2011; a short form of the place-name. See also Gills.

Gulls is a nickname for clubs beside the sea, and is a variant word for Seagulls (q.v.). The clubs are:

⚽ Canvey Island F.C. Formed in Essex in 1926, the club for this seaside resort has a stylised seagull on its badge; W1982/3–2013 and SSY2005/6–6/7. See also Islanders, Yellow Army.

⚽ Keadue Rovers F.C., founded in Co. Donegal in 1896. The club badge shows two flamboyant seagulls in the club colours of green and red; Wikipedia.

⚽ Mullion F.C., founded in Cornwall in 1902; the location is a holiday resort on the Lizard peninsula; W1994–5.

⚽ Torquay United F.C., founded in Devon in 1899, merging with Ellacombe to form T. Town in 1910, reverting to the name of United in 1921 after a merger with Babbacombe F.C. From 1921 to 1954, the club wore black and white, so they were called the Magpies; the present nickname is since their adoption of predominantly yellow colours after 1954: seagulls for a seaside town. In 1968, the club introduced a badge with a striking image of two blue triangles on yellow, said to represent two seagulls in flight, and new versions of this symbol have appeared since; G1976, W2008–9 and throughout RY1970/1–SSY2012/13. See also Magpies.

Gunners is the nickname for at least three clubs, one of which is famous and probably inspired the others, but all three have a military association. The clubs are:

⚽ Arsenal F.C., founded in 1886 by workers at the Royal Arsenal in Woolwich, south-east London. The club was first called 'Dial Square' (after the building at the entrance to the armaments factory) but was renamed Royal Arsenal in the same year. In 1888, the club adopted their first crest, which featured three cannons, based on the coat of arms of the Borough of Woolwich. The nickname may have been in use since then (it is recorded in BoF1905–6, on the 1933 Ogden card, in Johnston 1934 and on the 1936 Thomson 'stamp'), but between 1893 and 1914 the club was called Woolwich Arsenal and the nickname 'Woolwich Reds' may have been the one in use before 1914. The club has always had a shade of red as its strip colour. The Gunners nickname was certainly in use by 1922, when a crest was adopted with a single cannon, because the nickname appears on the crest. Two guns originally made at the armaments factory and now on loan from the Royal Artillery Museum based in the old factory, stand guard outside the new Emirates Stadium. Arsenal supporters are known to refer to themselves as The Gooners (q.v.). Recorded in Avis 1954–70, G1956–76, Churchill 1958, Richards 1960 and SWSCYB 1962–3, and throughout RY and SSY from 1970/1 to 2012/13. See also Boring Arsenal, France, Gooners, Invincibles, Lucky Arsenal, Reds, Royals, Woolwich.

⚽ Garrison Gunners F.C., the Isles of Scilly club, so-renamed in 1984, previously The Rangers (not that they could range very far). There are only two clubs on the islands, which have the world's smallest football league; Wikipedia. See also Wanderers.

⚽ Ynys-las Gunners F.C., founded in Ceredigion in 1937, when the Royal Artillery 408 Battery Territorial Army based in the village entered a team in the district league for two seasons. Recorded in Huws 2011.

Gurus is a nickname for Guru Nanak Gravesend F.C., founded in Kent in 1965. The side was formed for Asian youth and named in honour of the founder of the Sikh religion (and it is not the only club in the world so named). The nickname is used on the club's own website. See also GNG.

Gwalch is the nickname of C.P.D. Gwalchmai, founded on Anglesey in 1946; recorded in RW2011.

Gymns is the nickname of Gymnasium F.C., founded in Douglas, Isle of Man, in 1890. The nickname is a short form of the official name, which, although based on a standard word for a sports club, is nevertheless in the 'classical' tradition because the word comes from Ancient Greece. The nickname is mentioned in W2001, p. 1025 and on Wikipedia.

Gypsies is a nickname for Bohemians F.C., founded in Dublin in 1890. The names Bohemians and Gypsies have slightly different meanings in Ireland compared to Britain and other countries. In France, where the concept of 'Bohemian' as a word for non-conventional life-styles developed, Gypsies or Romany are also called Bohemians because of the mistaken belief that they came from Bohemia in the Czech Republic. As the word 'Bohemian' became more widely used throughout the world, it developed the primary sense of artistic, creative lifestyles conducted under extreme poverty and with no fixed abode (this meaning was fixed by the time of Puccini's opera *La Bohème*, 1896). The word therefore has an overlap in meaning with the popular football name 'Wanderers', with the added suggestion of creative flair. In Ireland, the traditional Romany Gypsies are very rare and the word is used for the Irish travellers (who are very numerous). There is a popular school of thought that the Irish travellers descend from victims of the Famine or from ancestors who were expelled from their lands by British colonialists, giving Irish travellers political and cultural respectability. The Irish travellers do craft work and have a sporting side from their association with horse-dealing. So, in Ireland, 'Gypsies', like 'Bohemians', are both words which connote creativity and travel, making one a satisfying nickname for the other. (The word Gypsies was coined in the mistaken belief that the Romany came from Egypt; the name Romany is the name the Gypsies use for themselves, and is ultimately a Sanskrit word.) Recorded in RNI1997, 2006. See also Big Club, Bohs.

Habbies was a nickname for Kilbarchan Athletic F.C., founded in Renfrewshire in

1909, closed in 1923. The nickname copies that used for anyone living in Kilbarchan, after the famous sixteenth-century village piper, Habbie Simpson (1550–1620), who is also commemorated in a statue on the Town Steeple. 'Habbie' is a friendly Scots form of Herbert (Scots Dictionary, Wikipedia); recorded on SFHA.

Haddicks is the middle-form of the nickname for Charlton Athletic F.C., in its transition from Haddocks (q.v.) to Addicks (see discussion under Addicks). This middle form appears early, in *The Kentish Independent* in 1910, but continues to appear quite late: in G1956–76, Churchill 1958, Harvey 1959, Richards 1960, Avis 1966–70 and the Vernon 1970–1 pamphlet, RY1970/1–90/91 and RY1993/4, the Williams League Directory 1985–90, and Pickering 1994. See also Addicks, Haddocks, Red Army, Robins, Valiants.

Haddocks was the early form of the nickname for Charlton Athletic F.C., founded in 1905, which had mutated to Addicks by 1910 (see Addicks for discussion). However, the nickname makes a late appearance as Haddocks in SWSCYB 1962–3. See also Addicks, Haddicks, Red Army, Robins, Valiants.

Half-Halfs is an unofficial nickname of Tooting and Mitcham United F.C., which was formed in a merger in 1932 between Tooting Town (1887) and Mitcham Wanderers (1912). The nickname mocks the divided origins of the club, though mergers are entirely the norm in the history of football; Wikipedia. See also Lilywhites, Stripes, Terrors, Tooting Terrors.

Half Hoops is a nickname for Draperstown Celtic F.C., founded in Co. Londonderry in 1968. The club's name, nicknames and strip are in tribute to the Glasgow Celtic club. Here, the word 'half' records the relative size of the club, as an alternative to the use of the Scots word 'Wee' (which has been used by Donegal Celtic); Wikipedia. See also Celtic, D.C.

Hall is a nickname for clubs with the element 'hall' in their place-name. The examples are:

- Mildenhall Town F.C., founded in Suffolk in 1898; W2001–13. See also Town, Yellows.
- Southall and Ealing Borough F.C., founded in London in 1871. A short form of the place-name, recorded in W1979/80–85, W2005–6. The club is often called simply Southall F.C. See also Fowlers.

Halls is the nickname for Hall Russell United F.C., founded at Bridge of Don, Aberdeenshire, in 1968. The name and nickname record a previous club of 1915–63 which was a works side for the Hall Russell Shipyard, Wikipedia.

Ham Bappers is the nickname of Pulrose United A.F.C., founded on the Isle of Man in 1932. The story is that player Karl Kelly shouted out "We'll flog you for ham baps!" [ham sandwiches] during a match against St Mary's when a young Saints supporter crossed the pitch on his father's Kawasaki motorbike. This was probably during the 1993 match when Pulrose beat Saints 5–0. The exclamation evolved into the nickname; Wikipedia. See also Pully.

Hamlet is the nickname of Dulwich Hamlet F.C., founded in 1893. Dulwich was originally a village or a hamlet within the London borough of Southwark. Recorded in Avis 1966–70, W1979/80–2013.

Hammers is a nickname for several clubs, either because of local engineering industries or as a pun on the place-name, and often for both reasons (making it impossible to distinguish). The clubs are:

☻ Cobham F.C., founded in Surrey in 1892. The nickname is primarily a reference to their ground in Anvil Lane; W1986–8, W1997–13. Crossed hammers, however, appear on a club badge (AFBC).

☻ Cradley Town F.C., founded in 1970. The West Midlands Town was a major centre for the manufacture of iron chains and nails. The club badge shows chains, an anvil, two hammers and a football; W2005–10. See also Lukes.

☻ East Ham United F.C., founded in Essex in 1933. Here the nickname seems to be a pun on the place-name, but cannot have been uninfluenced by the West Ham usage. The club merged with Barking in 2001 to form a Barking and East Ham United, which folded in 2006. A Barking side was reformed, but not The Hammers; W1980/1–2001.

☻ Hamworthy United F.C., founded in Poole, Dorset in 1970, in a merger between H. (1926) and Trinidad Old Boys. In this case, the nickname is entirely a pun on the place-name, though the club badge shows crossed industrial hammers; Wikipedia.

☻ Horley Town F.C., founded in Surrey in 1891 as Horley F.C. The word 'Town' was added in 1975; the nickname celebrates the ancient ironstone industry of the Surrey Wealden area. The club badge shows interlocking letters HTFC in a style clearly representing wrought iron, and the crest of the Dorking and Horley Rural District Council shows a griffin holding a 'war hammer', representing the iron industry; W1982/3–83/4. See also Clarets.

☻ Norton Woodseat F.C., based in the village near the major engineering centre of Sheffield. The club joined the second division of the Yorkshire League in 1949 and renamed itself Dronfield United between 1984 and 1991. The club is recorded in volume 37 of the *Gone but Not Forgotten* series. Recorded in Avis 1966–70.

☻ Warlingham F.C., founded in Surrey in 1896. Here, the nickname appears to be based only on the *–ham* in the place-name; W2009–12. See also Wars.

☻ West Ham United F.C. Founded in 1895 as Thames Ironworks F.C., the name changed to West Ham in 1900. The crest of the club has always featured a pair of crossed rivet hammers, as used in the ironworking industry, and the club tradition is that the nickname refers to its ironworking ancestry rather than its official name, though, as with the other uses of this nickname, it is not always possible to separate one idea from another. It is recorded early, in BoF1905–6, and on the 1933 Ogden card set, the 1936 Thomson 'stamp' (with the addition that 'Hams' is used by opposing fans), and in Norris 1959 and Sweetule 1959 (the last two claiming the place-name as the source), Avis 1954–70, G1956–76, Churchill 1958, Richards

1960, AA 1960, and throughout RY1970/1–SSY2012/13. See also Academy of Football, Claret and Blues, Cockney Boys, Eastenders, Hamsters, ICF, Iron, Wet Sham.

⚽ Woodley Hammers F.C., a youth side founded in Berkshire in 1973. The club website explains that the club first played in a secondhand kit from West Ham United.

⚽ Yorkshire Amateurs A.F.C., founded in 1918 and based in Leeds. The nickname here certainly means 'Amateurs' and it appears as *Ammers* in W1999–2012, but before that, in W1982/3–6, it is recorded as 'Hammers'. See also Ammers.

Hammies / Hams are nicknames for Eaglesham Amateurs F.C., founded near Glasgow in the early twentieth century, as a friendly short form of the place-name's final element; both these forms are used on the club's own website.

Hamsters is an unofficial nickname for West Ham United F.C., from the perspective of Millwall supporters, recorded on the 2003 Football Fans Census website. The nickname is a gentle pun on the official nickname, 'The Hammers', citing instead the popular pet rodents. See also Academy of Football, Claret and Blues, Cockney Boys, Eastenders, Hammers, ICF, Irons, Wet Sham.

Happylanders was the nickname for Lochgelly United F.C., founded in Fife in 1890, closed in 1928. An area of Lochgelly is called Happy Land (or Happyland), which is mentioned in the Scottish folk song, 'The Kelty Clippie'; Wikipedia.

Harbour Rats is the nickname of Larne F.C., founded in Co. Antrim in 1889. Larne is a harbour, and has a ship on its badge, but it is difficult to find any specific reason for this amusing nickname; a harbour rat is an expression for a long-term habitual dweller of harbours, but meant respectfully (like 'Seadogs' is). Recorded in RNI2007.

Harbourmen is the nickname of Holyhead Hotspur F.C., founded on Anglesey in 1990, as a successor club to Holyhead Town. The location is the major port for trade and ferry links between Britain and Dublin. An enamel badge issued by the local Maritime Museum in 2008 commemorates football in Holyhead from 1880 and displays the nickname (AFBC), and Richard Huws confirms that the nickname was also used by the older club; Wikipedia. The nickname appears to have also been used by Colwyn Bay F.C., as another enamel badge recording just 'Harbourmen' is as identified as this club in AFBC. For Holyhead, see also Spurs; for Colwyn Bay, see also Bay, Seagulls, Seasiders.

Hares is the nickname of two clubs, both from playful adaptations of the club's place-name. The clubs are:

⚽ Harefield United F.C., founded in the London borough of Hillingdon in 1934 after a merger between Breakspear Institute F.C. and Harefield F.C. Alas, the early spellings of the place-name in Domesday Book show that the place-name does not refer to hares (see Mills 1991). Recorded in W1979/80–2013, the Smith directories record it as 'The Hare': 1991/2–1995/6.

☉ March Town United F.C., founded in 1885 as March Town. The nickname nicely puns on the Cambridgeshire place-name and the third month of the year, in which hares are proverbial for their wild antics ("as mad as a March hare"). The club also has a splendid badge showing a hare behind a football. Recorded in Avis 1966–70, W1979/80–2013. See also Railwaymen.

Harlequins, see Quins.

Harp is a Scottish football club suffix and the nickname of Lochee Harp F.C., founded in Dundee in 1904. The word refers to the harp as one of the national symbols of Ireland, and was a popular choice in the nineteenth century for Scottish clubs expressing an Irish or Catholic affiliation, as with the names Celtic or Hibernian. Other examples were Brechin Harp and Dundee Harp; Wikipedia, SFHA.

Harps is a nickname for clubs with the element 'Harp' in their official name (an early fashion for adopting one of the national symbols of Ireland as a way of displaying Celtic cultural identity), or because the word puns on the place-name. The clubs are:

☉ Finn Harps F.C., founded in Ballybofey, Co. Donegal, in 1954. The club shows an Irish harp on its badge. The river Finn flows past the town, and the club plays at the Finn Park. Recorded in RI1997, 2006.

☉ Harpenden Town F.C., founded in Hertfordshire in 1891; a pluralised short form of the place-name; Wikipedia. See also Town.

Harriers is the suffix and nickname of three clubs. The word comes from the animal kingdom where it can refer either to the hare-hunting dog, which is a bit like a foxhound, or to several species of hawks. It is the dog which usually connotes running and a dogged determination to succeed, hence its usage in the name of many athletic clubs; early, surviving, examples being Birchfield Harriers, founded in Birmingham in 1877 and Clydesdale Harriers, founded in Glasgow in 1885. Nevertheless, the football clubs adopted the bird of prey as their badge, suggesting that the meaning has shifted in favour of the more exciting visual image; the Birchfield Harriers use a running stag as their badge. The clubs are:

☉ Cwmbach Harriers F.C., founded in Rhondda Cynon Taf in 1923. The club seems to have folded during the 1930s; Huws 2013.

☉ Halesowen Harriers F.C., founded in West Midlands in 1961, closed in 2003 (Wikipedia). The club badge in AFBC shows a bird of prey. See also Lilywhites.

☉ Kidderminster Harriers F.C., founded in Hereford & Worcester in 1886. The club was founded as an offshoot from an athletics club of the same name. The club badge has long shown a harrier bird; Avis 1966–70, W1979/80–2000, RY2000/1–02/3; SSY2003/4–12/13; W2006–13; AFBC. See also Kiddy, Reds.

Harry Hill is a nickname for Harrow Hill F.C., founded in Gloucestershire in 1932; a friendly form of the place-name, simultaneously punning as a personal name; W1998–2010. See also Hill.

Harry Wragg's was an unofficial nickname for Partick Thistle F.C. The nickname is rhyming slang with 'Jags', the official nickname for the club. Harry Wragg (1902–

85) was a famous jockey and his name has also been used as rhyming slang for a cigarette (fag); Potter & Jones 2011, p. 252. See also Jags, Thistle.

Hassy is the nickname of Haslingden F.C, founded in Lancashire in 1969; a friendly short form of the place-name recorded in Miller & Wright 1996. The club folded in 1998.

Hatchetmen is the nickname of Crusaders F.C., founded in Belfast in 1898. The club shows a crusader badge rather like that used by the *Daily Express* newspaper. The club website states that the club was consciously named after the medieval knights and the nickname dates from around 1949. It also appears as 'Hatchet Men'. The crusader knights are traditionally shown holding a sword (as on the badge), rather than a hatchet (an axe), so the nickname must be taken as the colloquial expression for those who are able and willing to take on difficult but necessary tasks concerning the destruction of something, a suitable nickname for a sporting side, which should strike fear in the opposition. Recorded in RI1997, RNI2007. See also Crues, Team with No Boots.

Hatters is a nickname for two clubs associated with traditional hat-making industries in their locality. The clubs are:

- Luton Town F.C. Founded in Bedfordshire in 1885, in a merger of Excelsior and L. Town Wanderers, and at a time when the straw-plaiting, hat-making and allied trades employed over a third of the population of Luton (1871 census). The club displayed a badge showing a straw boater on its shirts from 1933 (Historical Football Kits website) and the nickname is first recorded on the 1933 Ogden cigarette card. It later appears in G1956–76, Churchill 1958, Richards 1960, SWSCYB 1962–3, Avis 1966–70, Pickering 1995, throughout RY1970/1–SSY2012/13, and W2010–13. Today, a straw boater is a crest above the club's shield. Howard Chandler reports that early issues of *Luton News*, from December 31st 1908, presented weekly cartoons showing Luton supporters wearing straw boaters, showing that the association was in peoples' minds quite early, even if does not seem to have become a nickname for the club till much later. Howard Chandler reports that a Queens Park Rovers programme for 1951 states 'welcome the Hatters', referring to the team, and 'We can expect a strong contingent of "Hatters"', referring to supporters. See also Lilywhites, Lootown, Lutonians, Reds, Straw-Hatters / Straw-Plaiters.

- Stockport County F.C., and was included in the 1933 Ogden card set, the 1936 Thomson 'stamp' album and G1956–76, Churchill 1958, RY1970/1–78/9, RY1980/1, RY1985/6–SSY2012/13, and W2012–13. Unlike Luton, they have never adopted the hat as a badge. The club has nearly always played in blue and white (the supporters are called the Blue and White Army). See also Cestrians, County.

'Haven is the nickname of two sides with the name 'haven' in their place-name. The clubs are:

- Peacehaven and Telscombe F.C., founded in Sussex in 1923; W1979/80 and

W1987–90. See also Tye.

- Whitehaven Amateur F.C., founded in Cumbia in 1994 after the closure of Marchon A.F.C. The nickname is simply the last two syllables of the place-name; Wikipedia.

Hawks is a nickname for three clubs, sometimes because the bird is slightly suggested by the place-name, otherwise simply because the magnificent bird of prey makes an appropriate symbol for a sporting club. The clubs are:

- Blidworth Welfare F.C., refounded in Nottinghamshire in 1980; in this case the choice of nickname appears to be arbitrary; W1994–9. See also Welfare.

- Harlow Town F.C., founded in Essex in 1879. The club has a prominent flying hawk as a crest on its badge. Possibly the opening letters of the place-name gave an encouragement to the choice; W1995–2013. See also Lilywhites, Owls.

- Havant and Waterlooville F.C., formed in Hampshire in 1998 in a merger of Havant (1883) and Waterlooville (1905). The nickname may have been suggested by the initials in the club's name: H&W, but a neighbouring village, Horndean, also has a football club called the Hawks, so there may be a local explanation; W2001–13. See also Borough, Magnets, Ville.

- Whitehawk F.C., founded in Sussex in 1948, originally as Whitehawk and Manor Farm Old Boys). The nickname is an adaptation of the place-name. White Hawk Hill is a place-name known at least since the sixteenth century and refers to a chalk hill overlooking what is now a suburb of Brighton. Carved into this chalk is a large hawk, called The White Hawk, but this dates only from 2001; W1983/4–2013.

- Willesden Hawkeye F.C., founded in London in 1984. The nickname is an adaptation of the suffix, which probably records an association with the long-established Hawkeye Sports World shop in Willesden. The name became mainstream after it was used for a character in James Fenimore Cooper's novel *The Last of the Mohicans* (1826). The club seems to disappear after 1996; W1994–6.

Haws is the nickname of Hill of Beath Hawthorn F.C., founded in Fife in 1975. The nickname appears on the club badge (AFBC, dated 2000) and is a pluralised short form of the suffix; Wikipedia, SFHA. For other Scottish 'flower' nicknames, see also Rose, Thistle and Violet.

Hay was the nickname of Cheslyn Hay F.C., founded in the West Midlands in 1984; a short form of the place-name; W1994–5. The club seems to have folded before 2000, when a new Cheslyn Hay Athletic was formed.

Hayes is the nickname of Heath Hayes F.C., founded in Staffordshire in 1965, originally as Heath Hayes United; Wikipedia.

Heartlanders is the nickname for Nuneaton Griff F.C., founded in Warwickshire in 1972, originally as N. Amateurs. Griff is a hamlet near the club. The nickname comes from the nickname of Nuneaton as Heartland, for the centre of England. It was also used for the local newspaper, *Heartland News*; Wikipedia. See also Griff.

Hearties is the nickname for Buchanhaven Hearts F.C., founded in 1908 at Peterhead in Aberdeenshire. At first glance, the club seems likely to have taken its suffix in tribute to the famous Heart of Midlothian side, as did many other Scottish clubs, but this time expressed as a pluralised friendly short form; the nickname does also appear in the form 'Hearts'. However, there may be a piratical pun behind the nickname and suffix. Buchanhaven neatly chimes with 'buccaneers', and 'Me Hearties' is the traditional pirate expression in popular culture. This 'different' spelling may therefore deliberately refer to this pirate meaning; Wikipedia, SFHA. See also the discussion for Bootle under 'Bucks', which may record another piratical pun.

Hearts is a nickname of the Edinburgh side, Heart of Midlothian F.C., founded in 1874, as a short form of the official name. The Heart of Midlothian was the name of the Edinburgh jail, demolished in 1817, made famous and memorable by Sir Walter Scott's novel (1818). The mosaic on the Royal Mile which records its location is also the basis of the design of the club badge, though the football club was named initially from the Heart of Midlothian Dance Hall where the original lads socialised. Recorded in Johnston 1934, Avis 1954–70, RY1991/2–SSY2012/13, AFBC. See also Edinboro Darlings, Famous, Jam Tarts, Jambos, Jammies, Maroons. There are at least four other clubs which use the nickname, presumably in tribute to the more famous and earlier side. These are:

- Buchanhaven Hearts F.C., founded in Aberdeenshire in 1908. See also Hearties.
- Buncrana Hearts F.C., founded in Co. Donegal in the 1960s; the nickname appears on the club's badge and on Wikipedia.
- Cupar Hearts A.F.C., founded in Fife. The club is of unknown age but play in the Kingdom League, which was formed in 1984. The club's own website uses the nickname.
- Kelty Hearts F.C., founded in Fife in 1950. The club took its official name from the more famous Hearts, and this version of the nickname soon followed; the club's own website cites this nickname. See also Jambos.
- Rhyl Hearts F.C., founded as a youth side in North Wales in 1970, but since 2011 also a senior club. Huws 2013 reports that the name was adopted in tribute to the Scottish-born players in Rhyl F.C.; club website.

Heath was a nickname for Haywards Heath Town F.C., founded in West Sussex in 1888, adding the 'Town' suffix to the name in 1989; the nickname is only recorded in W1988 and probably went out of fashion after the club rebranded as Haywards Heath Town. See also Bluebells.

Heathens is a nickname for clubs with the word 'Heath' in their official name; the two words may have completely different meanings but the nickname suggests a certain barbaric splendour. Examples are:

- Birmingham City F.C., founded as Small Heath Alliance F.C. in 1875, renaming in 1905. Wikipedia quotes a reference from the *Sheffield and Rotherham Independent* which uses the nickname in a match report on 1 February 1892, and it also appears in BoF1905–6. More recently, the nickname has been used for the name of a fanzine. There was also a visual pun on the name which survived the rebranding as

Birmingham. The 1933 Ogden cigarette card says that the club was always depicted as a 'negro' (presumably one who had not been 'converted', hence a heathen). In the cartoon on the card the black man inexplicably carries an open razor as well as a football, but the meaning of that detail is unknown. See also BLose, Blues, Brum, Smallheath.

☺ Cadbury Heath F.C., founded in 1894, near Bristol; Wikipedia.

☺ Cradley Heath F.C., founded in West Midlands in c.1922, folding in c.1997 (FCHD and Wikipedia).

☺ Flackwell Heath F.C., founded in Buckinghamshire in 1907; W1982/3–6 and Miller & Wright 1996. The nickname still appears on Wikipedia but it changed to Heath in W2007–13.

☺ Hampstead Heathens F.C. This early football club, founded in 1868, is famous for its part in the first FA Cup competition in 1871–2 but seems to disappear after 1872. Although Heathen here appears as a suffix, it is also clearly based on the place-name element 'Heath'. The name has been revived for a modern club founded in 1975.

☺ Newton Heath LYR F.C., founded in 1878. This is the ancestor team of Manchester United, originally a works side for the Lancashire and Yorkshire Railway employees at Newton Heath; the club renamed as Manchester United in 1902; Wikipedia. See also Busby Babes, Coach-Builders, Fergie's Fledglings, Man, Manure, Munichs, Outcasts, Red Devils, Reds, United.

Heavies is the nickname for Heavitree Social United F.C., formed in Devon in 1885, originally as H. United, merging with H. Social Club in 2004 to form the new club. The nickname is a pluralised short form of the place-name, with an intimidating double meaning; recorded in W1982/3–99 for the old club, and on the present club's website.

Hedgemen is a nickname for Brechin City F.C., founded in Angus in 1906, in a merger of B. Harp and B. Hearts; and for a unique reason: they have a major ancient beech hedge running along the whole of one side of their ground (The Hedge Side), at Glebe Park. This fantastic feature has now been under threat for three years because the inflexible jobsworths at UEFA want to see the pitch size extended by three feet to fit new regulations; SSY2012/13. Comments from 2005 on the club's website forum give the variants 'Hedge Boys' and 'Hedgies'. See also City.

Heed is a nickname for Gateshead F.C., expressing the local pronunciation of the 'head' in Gateshead; W2012–13 and SSY2010/11–12/13. See also Boro, Laides, Tynesiders.

Hemel is an earlier nickname for Hemel Hempstead Town F.C. Founded in Hertfordshire in 1885 as Apsley F.C., the name changed to the present one in 1955; W1979/80–2003. See also Tudors.

Henrun was a nickname for Dundela F.C., founded in Belfast in 1895. It is recorded in RI1997 as the club nickname; it is a re-use of the nickname (as 'The Hen Run') of Wilgar Park, the home ground since 1900; presumably the land was originally used for free-range hens ... though there may be some rhyming slang with the place-name. The club nickname is now 'The Duns' (q.v.).

Hens is a nickname for Hengrove Athletic F.C., founded in 1948 in the Bristol suburb of Whitchurch. There are several possible meanings of the place-name element *hen–*, including (but rarely) a reference to real hens, but here the nickname is a short form of the place-name; Wikipedia. See also Grove.

Herby is a nickname for Herbrandston F.C., founded in Pembrokeshire in 1970. The nickname is a friendly short form of the place-name, but may have been influenced by the series of *Herbie* films since 1968. The club website spells it 'Herby', another uses 'Herbie'; Huws 2013.

Herd was the nickname for Cirencester United F.C., founded in Gloucestershire in 1969. 'The Herd' was the club's original official name when it was founded as a youth side by the Rev. Adam Ford; the club renamed in 1990. The word is usually used for a family of cattle, and it seems here to carry the same sense as 'flock', the usual word used for a priest's following, because of the good shepherd metaphor, but the meaning remains rather difficult to pin down and slightly mysterious. The club folded in 2009; W1994–2010.

Herrings is the English language nickname for Nefyn United F.C., founded in Gwynedd in 1932, originally as Nefyn Celts. The location on the Llŷn Peninsula is important for the herring industry, and three herrings appear on the club badge. Recorded in RW1994–5. See also Penwaig.

Heys is the nickname of Prestwich Heys Amateur F.C., founded in Greater Manchester in 1938; a short form of the place-name, recorded in W1979/80 and on Wikipedia.

Hi-Bees, see under 'Hibs'.

Hi-Hi's is the nickname of Haddington Athletic F.C., founded in East Lothian in 1939. The nickname was also used by the Third Lanark Athletic Club (1872–1967), based in Glasgow (see also Redcoats, Sodgers, Thirds, Volunteers, Warriors). Although mysterious, it is believed that the Third Lanark nickname originated in an early supporters' chant, "Hi! Hi! Hi!". A crucial piece of evidence is an early postcard reproduced in Kevin McCarra's *Scottish Football* (1984). There, a Third Lanark player is shown in the strip of 1900–02 and with the Third Lanark Rifle Volunteers badge (both strip and name were changed in 1903), and a motto 'Hi, Hi, Hi!' The Scots Dictionary records its mainstream use for the Third Lanark since an appearance in *The Sporting Post* on 6 Dec. 1952, but the phrase (now as 'Hi-Hi') appeared on club programmes in the late 1940s (one seen for 3 January 1949). What does it mean? It could be the mainstream word 'High!', said three times for emphasis (as in phrases like 'Sell! Sell! Sell!'), and willing the club on to higher achievements. Another piece of evidence, however, is an unrelated Irish comic postcard of c.1900, which shows an Irish horse-and-cab driver with a gentleman in top hat and tails. The driver is saying to the customer "Hi, Hi, Sir!" This suggests that the phrase originates in an attempt to convey an Irish pronunciation for the standard expression "Aye, Aye,

Sir!", which would mean that the early Third Lanark supporters were chanting "Yes! Yes! Yes!" (or rather, "Aye! Aye! Aye!"). Why the letter H? The classic Gaelic dictionary by MacAlpine (1832) states it rather well. The single entry for the letter H reads: "H, h, this letter is not acknowledged in our Alphabet; but to keep the Gaelic in character with us, the Highlanders, who are THE BRAVEST and *most singular* people in the WHOLE WORLD, (as the SCOTS TIMES says,) it is used, not only in every word, but almost in every syllable expressed or understood." So, in nineteenth-century thought, all Gaelic expressions got an h, just to suggest Gaelic pronunciation, and *that* is why 'The Hi-Hi' came about!

For comparison, though grammatically unrelated, Celtic have a not-dissimilar chant, 'Hail, hail!' which forms the first line of the supporters' song 'Hail, hail! The Celts are here!' It simply means 'Hello, hello!' Celtic's main nickname, 'The Bhoys', also uses the 'h' fashion to suggest Irish pronunciation.

In the case of Haddington, the Scots Dictionary dates its appearance there much later, in *Linlithgow Today* on 28 Nov. 2003, also without explanation. The place-name is pronounced 'had–', though the invented spelling of a Scots version, *Haidintoun*, might suggest the same opening sound but not justify its repetition. Because Haddington is far away geographically from the Gaelic cultural area, it seems more likely to have been adopted after the closure of Third Lanark, and in tribute to the celebrated achievements of that great club; Wikipedia, SFHA.

Hibees is the nickname of Thornton Hibernian F.C., founded in Fife in 1935. The nickname is another variant short form of Hibernian; the nickname also appears for the Edinburgh Hibernian club (see next entry); Wikipedia.

Hibs is a nickname for clubs with the name 'Hibernians', formed from the Latin name for Ireland, in their official name. The famous Edinburgh club seems to have been the first to use the name. The Cork and Duntocher clubs are defunct and it is not known for certain if they used the 'Hibs' nickname:

⚽ Cardiff Hibernian F.C., founded as the 53rd Signals F.C., and entering the Cardiff Combination League in 1963, changing name in 1967 (see Combination League website). Despite the British Territorial Army origin, the Irish sympathy of the team is reflected in its name and its green playing colours, but the reason for it is not explained. 'Hibs' is often used for the club in internet commentary; Huws 2013. See also Signals.

⚽ Cork Hibernians F.C., founded in Ireland in 1957 but dissolved in 1977. In this case the club was formed for members of an Irish friendly society, the Ancient Order of Hibernians.

⚽ Duntocher Hibernian F.C. in Dunbartonshire in 1894, closed in 1980.

⚽ Galway Hibernians F.C., founded in Co. Galway in 1942. The nickname appears on Wikipedia and the club's own website.

⚽ Hibernian F.C., founded in Edinburgh in 1875. The club adopted a name based on the Roman name for Ireland because they were founded by Irish immigrants. Their name, colours and badge continue to reflect their Irish origins. A variant on the Hibs nickname is 'Hibees', or 'Hi-bees', whereas fans are called 'Hibbies'. Recorded as Hibs in G1956–76, Harvey 1959, Avis 1966–70; on the 1986 Panini sticker and in RS1993–2012 as 'Hi-bees'. The Rothmans series also has multiple spellings: Hybees (RY1970/1–71/2), Hi-Bees (RY1972/3–87/8) and Hibees (RY1988/9–SSY2012/13); Pickering 1994 has Hibs and Hibees. See also Cabbage, Turnbull's Tornadoes.

☺ Leamington Hibernian F.C., founded in Warwickshire in 1974. The reason for the Hibernian association is not recorded, but the club shield shows a thistle, a shamrock, a rose and a leek; badge in AFBC, club website uses 'Hibs'.

☺ Thornton Hibernian F.C., founded in Fife in 1935. In this club's case, the nickname has all but supplanted the suffix in the club's official name; Wikipedia, SFHA.

Highland Dynamite is a nickname for Cove Rangers F.C., founded in Aberdeen in 1922. The nickname conveys the sense that the club is an effective Highland force. It seems to have grown from a supporters' chant which is posted on the internet with a date of 2008: "We're blue! We're white! | We're Highland Dynamite! | Cove Rangers! Cove Rangers!" See also Tooners, Wee Rangers.

Highwaymen is known as a nickame for one club, and may have been used for another. The two clubs are:

☺ Blackburn Rovers F.C. The 1933 Ogden cigarette card gives the nickname 'Rovers', but adds "they are always shown as a highwayman probably to indicate how they 'hold up' their rivals both in the Cup and the League". The same occurs in *Stedfast* December 1964, where the cartoon shows a highwayman but the nickname is 'Rovers'. See also Blue and Whites, Jackburn, Plastics, Riversiders, Rovers.

☺ Morpeth Town A.F.C., founded in Northumberland in 1894 in a merger between M. United and M. F.C. The town is on the A1 (though now bypassed), the Great North Road running between London and Edinburgh, and the traditional haunt of the eighteenth-century criminals called 'highwaymen'; W2010–13.

Hill is the nickname for clubs with this element in their official name (and see also Hillians, Hillmen, Hills). The clubs are:

☺ Bellshill Athletic F.C., founded in Lanarkshire in 1897; a short form of the place-name, used in match reports on the club's own website, SFHA.

☺ Harrow Hill F.C., founded in Gloucestershire in 1932; Wikipedia. See also Harry Hill.

☺ Maryhill F.C., founded in Glasgow in 1884; Wikipedia, SFHA.

Hill Club is recorded as a nickname for Penhill F.C., founded in Wiltshire in 1970. The club renamed as Swindon Athletic in 1989 and then merged with Supermarine (see Marine) in 1992; W1989–90. See also PYC.

Hillians is the nickname for Burgess Hill Town F.C., formed in West Sussex in 1882, and based on the second word of the place-name; W1983/4–2013.

Hillmen is a nickname for three clubs, either because they are in hilly areas or because of a pun on the official name. The clubs are:

- ☺ Barnet F.C., formed in 1888, folded in 1901. They were called the Hillmen because their home was High Barnet, and this traditional location is shown on the shield of the modern Barnet F.C., which displays a rounded green hill with two flags in the black and amber colours of the modern club. See also Bees, Dentals.

- ☺ Glossop North End A.F.C., founded in 1886, renaming as G. North End in 1992. Glossop lies in a valley in the High Peak Borough of Derbyshire, a very hilly area. Recorded in W1979/80–86 for Glossop F.C., but as 'Hillsmen' in W1987–8; W1994–2013 as 'Hillmen' for the new club.

- ☺ Hillingden Borough F.C., founded in London in 1872 as Yiewsley F.C., renamed as H. Borough in 1964 before folding in 1987; reformed in 1990 when Bromley Park Rangers assumed the name. See also Blues, Boro.

Hills is the nickname of Whitehills F.C., founded in Banffshire in 2000; a short form of the place-name; Wikipedia.

Hive is the nickname for Stonehaven F.C., founded in Aberdeenshire in 1919. The club plays in blue, though the away strip is in the 'bee' colours of yellow and black. However, the nickname appears to be a reference to the earlier spelling of the town name as Stonehyve or Stonehive, shown on early printed maps, and the place-name is still pronounced that way locally; Wikipedia, SFHA.

Holwell is the nickname for Holwell Sports F.C., founded in Leicestershire in 1904, originally as Holwell Works, renaming in 1988; a short form of the club name, used in match reports.

Holy Blues is a nickname for Gainsborough Trinity F.C. Founded in Lincolnshire in 1873 as a church side for Holy Trinity church, the club was first called Trinity Recreationists and it has a blue strip, Wikipedia. See also Blues, Recreationists, Trinity.

Holy City Boys is an unofficial nickname for Kettering Town F.C. The nickname is based on a nickname for the town itself, inspired by its large number of churches and chapels, which is still used today in speech and on a supporters' website (thanks to Marilyn Wood). See also Friars, Kets / Kettles, Poppies.

Home Guard is the nickname of Whickham F.C., founded in 1944, originally as Axwell Park Colliery Welfare, in Tyne and Wear. The name changed to Whickham in 1962, but the Home Guard nickname appeared at the outset. Whickham was the location of a Home Guard Unit in the Second World War, with, presumably, many of the men appearing simultaneously in the Home Guard, the Colliery and the football team; Wikipedia and club's own website.

Honest Men is the nickname of Ayr United F.C., founded in 1910 in a merger of A. Parkhouse and Ayr F.C. The Scottish side's nickname is based on Robert Burns' poem, 'Tam o'Shanter', which contains the lines 'Auld Ayr, wham ne'er a town surpasses | For honest men and bonie lasses.' Recorded in G1965–76, Vernon 1970–1, in RS1993–2012, and throughout RY1970/1–SSY2012/13.

Hooky is the nickname of Hook Norton F.C., founded in the village near Banbury, Oxfordshire, in 1898; Wikipedia records that the nickname is also used as a nickname for the village; W2002–13. See also Brewery Boys.

Hoops is a nickname for clubs which play in hoops, which are horizontal stripes around the whole circumference of the shirt. This fashionable design is widespread but not every club has it as a nickname. All the Scottish and Irish clubs with this nickname have a green-and-white strip very like that of Celtic F.C. A much smaller number follow the blue-and-white hoops of Queens Park Rangers. The clubs are:

- Birtley Town F.C., founded in 1993. The club near Gateshead plays in Celtic-like green-and-white hooped shirts, white shorts and green socks; W2008–13. See also Green and White Army, Super Greens.
- Buckie Thistle F.C., founded in Banffshire in 1889. The club plays in a Celtic-like style of green-and-white hoops; Wikipedia. See also Jags.
- Celtic F.C., founded in Glasgow in 1887. The club adopted the famous (and very influential) design of green-and-white hoops in 1903. The nickname appears to be a late addition to the Celtic collection, as it only appears in RS since 2000, and not in the RY/SSY series till SSY2012/13. It did , however, feature on an enamel badge in the 'Hoops' anniversary year of 2003 (AFBC). See also Bhoys, Celts, Lisbon Lions, Quality Street Kids, 'Tic, Tims.
- Lewis United F.C., founded in Aberdeen in 1938 (or 1942). This club also plays in Celtic-like green-and-white hoops with white shorts; Wikipedia, SFHA.
- Lurgan Celtic F.C., founded in Co. Armagh in the 1970s, reforming an older club of 1903; for their Celtic-like strip. This is the nickname in RNI2007, but Wikipedia offers 'Bhoys' (q.v.).
- Maldon and Tiptree F.C., founded in Essex in 2009 in a merger between Tiptree United F.C. (1933) and Maldon Town (1946); blue-and-white hooped shirts; W2011–13. See also Blues, Jam Makers, Strawberries, Town.
- Queen's Park Rangers F.C. (also 'Superhoops'). Founded in 1882 as St Jude's F.C., they emerged as QPR after a merger with Christchurch Rangers in 1886. The Queen's Park is a district of London named after Queen Victoria. QPR adopted the hoops style in 1892, first in green and white and then in the now-familiar blue and white in 1924; the nickname is widely used on the internet but not in Wikipedia or in the mainstream printed sources. See also Amateurs, Q.P.R., R's, Rangers.
- Shamrock Rovers F.C., founded in Dublin in 1901. The club plays in Celtic-like green-and-white hoops, which were adopted in 1926. The club's official name uses the popular word for one of Ireland's national symbols, the three-leafed clover. Recorded in RI1997, 2006. See also Coad's Colts, Rovers.
- Tuam Celtic Athletic F.C., founded in Co. Galway in 1974; Celtic-like green-and-white hoops with white shorts; Wikipedia.

Hornets is usually a nickname for clubs which play in the 'wasp' colours of gold and black, or similar, but it can also be a pun on the club official name. The nickname is an alternative to Wasps (q.v). The clubs are:

- Alloa Athletic F.C., founded in Clackmannanshire in 1878, originally as Clackmannan County. The club's official nickname is 'The Wasps', but some fans started calling the club *Hornets* after the club adopted a new cartoon-like badge showing a muscle-bound wasp. *The Hornet* is the name of a popular children's comic; SSY2012/13. See also County, Wasps.
- Debenham Leisure Centre F.C., founded in Suffolk in 1991, originally as Debenham Angels. The club plays in yellow shirts and socks, with black shorts, the hornet colours. The original name probably refers to a connection with the Angel pub in the town; W2011–13, AFBC.
- Hebburn Town F.C., founded in Tyne and Wear in 1912, originally called Reyrolles, a works side for the A. Reyrolle and Co. engineering company. The club renamed as Hebburn Reyrolles in 1986, then the present name in 1988. The club plays in the traditional yellow-and-black striped colours of hornets; W1994–2013.
- Horsham F.C. The club was founded in West Sussex in 1871 and has a red hornet on its badge, but plays in a red-and-green strip, so the nickname must have started as a pun on the first syllable of the place-name. Recorded in W1979/80–2013.
- Lisvane-Heath Hornets F.C., founded in Cardiff in 1989 in a merger of H. Hornets (1965) and Lisvane (1979). The nickname is recorded in RW1994 but the club disappears thereafter. A club called Lisvane F.C. replaced them. In 1994 the club wore tangerine shirts with navy blue shorts (not particularly hornet-like).
- Poole Borough F.C., founded in Dorset in 1999; the club colours are black and amber stripes, but the nickname also honours the name of an earlier club from the 1880s (club's own website, and also recorded on a badge in AFBC).
- Watford F.C., after their adoption of a golden shirt and black shorts in 1959. The name was given after a popular vote amongst the fans and is recorded in Avis 1966–70, and RY1971/2–79/80, G1976 and through RY1983/4–SSY2012/13. See also Blues, Brewers, Golden Boys, Horns / 'Orns, Saints, Wasps, Yellow Army.

Horns / 'Orns is an alternative nickname of Watford F.C., but is it an abbreviation of Hornets (previous entry) or a reflection of the magnificent elk-like horns on the head of the hart (male deer) on the club's badge? I favour the deer, but it is ambiguous. The hart was chosen as a symbol because of the club's presence in Hertfordshire (Hertford meaning the ford frequented by harts or stags, see Mills 1991); Wikipedia records the nickname. See also Blues, Brewers, Golden Boys, Hornets, Saints, Wasps, Yellow Army.

Hotspurs is a football club name suffix, from the nickname of Harry Percy. As a nickname, it always seems to appear in the short form. See discussion under Spurs.

Houses is the nickname for Easthouses Lily Miners Welfare F.C., founded in Dalkeith, Midlothian in 1969; a short form of the official name, recorded in RS1993–7 and 2001, SFHA.

Humbugs is another nickname for clubs which play in black-and-white stripes, because the traditional boiled 'humbug' sweet is so coloured. The clubs are:

⊕ Congleton Town F.C., founded in Cheshire in 1901; W1986–98. See also Bears, Town.

⊕ Hayling United F.C., founded in 1884, originally as Hayling Island F.C. The Hampshire side plays in black-and-white striped shirts; Wikipedia.

Huns is an unofficial nickname for Rangers F.C., founded in Glasgow in 1872. Although there is nothing specifically offensive about the name of the wild Barbarian tribe which swept across the Roman Empire in the fifth century, taking all before it, the phrase became sinister in the United Kingdom when it was used for the Germans during the First World War. The primary reason for the nickname is entirely innocent, it being a pun on the widely-accepted nickname 'Gers, taking this as an abbreviation for Germans rather than Rangers, but it also suggests the sectarian divide of Teutonic and Protestant as opposed to Celtic and Catholic. In the sectarian context a different pun, of Hanoverians vs Jacobites, offers an alternative explanation for its origin (as a playful abbreviation for Hanoverians). Pickering 1994 records the nickname but states that it primarily refers to supporters of any Protestant team. See also Blues, 'Gers, Iron Curtain, Light Blues, Rangers, Teddy Bears.

Huntsmen was a later nickname for Market Harborough Town F.C., recorded in the club history, Twydell 1988 (p. 232) as used from about 1930. The Leicestershire club ran from 1875 to 1947. The town is at the centre of 'foxhunting country', an association also used in the county symbol. See also Linnets.

Hurlers is the nickname of Ludgvan A.F.C., founded in Cornwall before 1979 when it joined the Cornwall Combination (FCHD). The nickname refers to the sport of Cornish Hurling, an earlier form of parish football, in which a ball is thrown and carried. Hurling is recorded in many Cornish names, including that of an ancient stone circle in south-east Cornwall, and 'Ludgvan Hurlers' is a nickname for the people of the town. A club badge illustrated in AFBC records the nickname (with an image of a hurling player rather than a footballer), and it also appears in local match reports on the internet.

Hurst is the nickname of Hurstpierpoint F.C., founded in West Sussex in 1888; a short form of the place-name, which is used on the club's own website. See also Point.

Hybrid Club was a nickname for Clapham Rovers F.C., founded in 1869, folding in 1911 or soon after (the club's annual dinner is mentioned in *The Sportsman* for that year). The club was a famous amateur side, but most unusually played in both Rugby Union and Association rules on alternate weeks, hence the nickname; Wikipedia (citing a book of 1892 as the source). See also Rovers.

Ice Kings was a temporary nickname for Leicester City F.C. during their successful run of victories during the frozen winter of 1962–3; Wikipedia has a whole page on the side called the Ice Kings. See also City, Filberts, Fosse / Fossites, Foxes, Nuts.

ICF is an initialism for the Inter City Firm, a group of supporters for West Ham United

F.C. The group was founded in 1972 and is still active. It took its name from the use of InterCity trains, as members travelled from outside London. The group has its own badge in claret and blue, with the intriguing motto 'These Colours Don't Run' (Wikipedia and thanks to Richard Huws). See also Academy of Football, Claret and Blues, Cockney Boys, Eastenders, Hammers, Hamsters, Irons, Wet Sham.

ICT is an initialism for Inverness Caledonian Thistle F.C., founded in 1994, in a merger between I. Thistle and Caledonian; SSY2012/13. See also Caley Thistle, Jags.

Imperial is a football club suffix, used to suggest superior status, but it might also be because the club is associated with a pub so named. The clubs so called tend to have the nickname 'The Imps' (next entry). The suffix is strangely popular in Leicestershire.

Imps is a nickname for several clubs, for different reasons. The nickname seems to have a strange cluster of appearances in Leicestershire and Lincolnshire, but there is one Welsh example. The clubs are:

⚽ Brantham Athletic F.C., founded in Suffolk in 1887. The club plays in a blue strip, but the Imp nickname seems to be an arbitrary choice because of its playful associations; W1987–91 as 'Blue Imps'; Wikipedia as 'Imps'. See also Athletic.

⚽ Cadoxton Imps F.C., founded in Vale of Glamorgan in 1972. The club was originally a youth side and the club website states that they were called 'Imps' because the boys were 'little devils'. The *Barry and District News* on 17 September 2012, and the club website, have used the expression 'Caddy Imps'; Huws 2013.

⚽ Kegworth Imperial F.C., founded in Leicestershire in 1977. The club badge shows an imp like the Lincoln one, and 'Kegworth Imps' is often used as an official name; club website.

⚽ Lincoln City F.C. The Lincoln Imp is a medieval carving of a mischievous little devil on a pillar inside Lincoln Cathedral which is traditionally associated with the city and county of Lincoln, and about which there is a well-known folktale. The club was formed in 1886 and has long played in red shirts, so a variant of the nickname is The Red Imps. The club mascot is one Poacher the Imp, the Lincolnshire Poacher being another symbol of the county, from the folksong of that name. The nickname appears as 'Red Imps' through RY1972/3–SSY2012/13, but 'Imps' is used at first, in RY1970/1–72/3. 'The Imps' is included in the 1933 Ogden card set, in G1956–76, Churchill 1958, Harvey 1959, Norris 1959, Richards 1960, SWSCYB 1962–3 and Avis 1966–70, the Williams League Directories 1985–95 and W2012–13 (all as 'Imps'). See also City, Deranged Ferrets.

⚽ Oadby Town F.C., founded in Leicestershire in 1937 or 1939, originally as Oadby Imperial. The name changed to 'Town' in 1951. The normal nickname for this club is 'The Poachers', after a local folk hero, but 'The Imps' is recorded on a club badge illustrated in AFBC. As in the following entries, it is a pluralised short form of the Imperial suffix, but it generates the remarkable coincidence that Oadby and various Lincolnshire clubs share both the Poachers and Imps nicknames, though for different reasons. See also Poachers.

☺ Oakham Imperial F.C., which operated in Rutland between 1954 and 1960 (FCHD), though the name has recently been revived for a modern amateur side from at least 2009. Here, the nickname is a pluralised short form of the suffix (thanks to Edward Baines).

☺ Rothley Imperial F.C., founded in Leicestershire in 1911; club's own website.

☺ Whitwick Imperial F.C., founded in Leicestershire, and recorded on FCHD between 1909 and 1929. A badge is illustrated in AFBC, and the village history website records the Imps nickname during the 1920s.

Indians is the nickname for Seaside A.F.C., founded in Llanelli, Carmarthenshire, in 1957. The club's own website uses the nickname, as well as Blues for the team's blue shirts. The reference is to the native Americans of cowboy films, but the use seems simply to be one of associated prowess, also generating the 'Cowboys' and 'Braves' nicknames; club website, Huws 2013..

Inter / International are nicknames for Cardiff Metropolitan University F.C. founded as UWIC Inter Cardiff F.C., in a merger in 2000 between Inter Cardiff F.C. and UWIC F.C., renaming in 2012 (both earlier clubs began in 1990). The 'Inter' element in the names is acknowledged to have been copied from the famous Inter Milan side, and the UWIC abbreviation stood for University of Wales Institute Cardiff. See also Diffs / Div's, Seagulls, Sheep.

Invicta is a nickname for Folkestone Invicta F.C., founded in Kent in 1936; RNL2000– 01. The word is Latin for 'unconquered'. It is a popular word in Kent because of the local legends that Kent was not conquered by William the Conqueror (with various explanations for how this could be true). It appears as the name of many businesses and institutions in the county, including the name of one of the Kent football leagues. See also Seasiders.

Invincibles is primarily a nickname for Preston North End, but it has also been used by two other clubs. The clubs are:

☺ Aresenal F.C., during their successful run of victories for 38 games in the 2003–4 season; recorded on Wikipedia. See also Boring Arsenal, France, Gooners, Gunners, Lucky Arsenal, Reds, Royals, Woolwich.

☺ Bonagee United F.C., founded in Letterkenny, Co. Donegal, in 1970 (originally as Arcade Athletic). The club was renamed B. Celtic in 1973, then United in 1975. The nickname is recorded on Wikipedia but is not explained; it perhaps dates from 1995 and 1996, after the club won two trophies in succession. There was a nineteenth-century connection between Northern Ireland and Preston North End, but this was experienced by the Linfield club (see BoF1905–6, p. 198).

☺ Preston North End F.C., recorded in BoF1905–6 and on the 1933 Ogden card, which states "The ... name was given them when in 1889 they carried off both the League Championship and the Cup, a feat which has since been equalled only by Aston Villa. In winning the Cup in 1889 the North End did not lose a goal in any of their ties". The record of achievement is no longer unique. The form 'Old Invincibles' is recorded in Harvey 1959 and Pickering 1994; Churchill 1958 and Avis 1954–70 have 'Invincibles'. See also Glasses, Lilywhites /Whites, North End, P.N.E., Proud Preston.

Iron is the nickname of at least two clubs in locations associated with the iron industry. Here, the nickname appears in the singular but there is also a plural example. The clubs are:

☻ Braintree Town F.C. Founded in Essex in 1898 as Manor Works F.C., for a factory making metal window frames for the Crittall Window Co. (they made windows for the *Titanic* in 1911), the club renamed itself Crittall Athletic in 1921, and later Braintree Town in 1981. The nickname comes from the metal windows factory, but since 2005 the club has had a ladies' team, naturally calling itself 'The Iron Ladies', punning with the nickname for Margaret Thatcher; W1985–2013, SSY2012/13.

☻ Scunthorpe United F.C. Formed in North Lincolnshire in 1899, merging with North Lindsey in 1910 to form Scunthorpe and Lindsey United; the club was inevitably associated with the town's important iron-working industries from the outset. The current badge is in an unusual (for football) Soviet Realism style and shows an outstretched hand clutching an iron girder, the result of a competition in the 1994–5 season. Richards 1960 records it in the singular form, but *Stedfast* December 1963 and G1976 used the plural; Rothmans also first published it in the plural, 'The Irons', in RY1970/1–81/2, then as 'The Iron' through RY1982/3–SSY2012/13. See also Nuts, Scunny, United.

☻ West Ham United, see under Irons, below.

Iron Curtain was a nickname for the defensive line of Rangers F.C. in Glasgow in the late 1940s and early 1950s, at a time when the expression was very much in the public mind because of the post-war division of Europe between Western and Communist spheres of influence; Wikipedia. See also Blues, 'Gers, Huns, Light Blues, Rangers, Teddy Bears.

Iron Ladies / Ironesses are nicknames for Scunthorpe United W.F.C., founded before 2007. Both names play on The Iron, nickname of the men's team at Scunthorpe, but the first resonates with the nickname of former prime minister, Margaret Thatcher, and the second puns with the word 'lionesses', which it sounds like, and both suggest a powerful competitive side. 'Iron Ladies' is also used by the Braintree Town L.F.C., for the same reason.

Irons is another official nickname for West Ham United F.C., which began life in 1895 as Thames Ironworks F.C. The name is recorded on the 1933 Ogden card; but in Norris 1959, Avis 1966–70 and Pickering 1994 it appears in the singular ('The Iron'), though it usually takes the plural when used for this club; RY2001/2–SSY2012/13 (as Irons). See also Academy of Football, Claret and Blues, Cockney Boys, Eastenders, Hammers, Hamsters, ICF, Wet Sham.

Ironsiders / Ironsides are nicknames for clubs which are associated with a major iron foundry industry, or which wish to proclaim some connection or admiration for Oliver Cromwell (whose republican soldiers were nicknamed Ironsides in the seventeenth century). The clubs are:

🌑 Battersea Ironsides F.C., based in London and founded before 1994. Here the nickname is also a suffix, but the reason for the choice is not known. The club badge shows a medieval knight's helmet; used on the club's own website. See also Green Army.

🌑 Middlesbrough F.C., founded in 1876. This early nickname is recorded in the 1936 Thomson 'stamp' album (as 'Ironsiders') and survived at least into the 1960s (it was featured on a Kane confectionary card in 1956, in G1956–76, Churchill 1958, Harvey 1959, Richards 1960, Jeffrey 1961, Pickering 1994). Both forms of the word occur, with Ironsides the most used. See also Boro, Cleveland Cowboys, Nops, Riversiders, Scabs, Smoggies, Teessiders, Washers.

🌑 Newport County F.C. Founded in 1912, the club held a competition to find a nickname for its second season. The one which won records the dominance of the steelworks in the town's economy, a characteristic and name it shared with Middlesbrough (and the two towns also share the characteristic of having the only two transporter bridges in Britain), but the club's ground of Somerton Park was also in Cromwell Road. Johnston 1934 records the nickname, and also the uncertainty as to the specific reason for the choice. Also recorded in G1956–76, Churchill 1958, Harvey 1959, Richards 1960, AA 1960, Jeffrey 1961, Avis 1966–70, Moss 1983, RY1970/1–88/9, W1989 and now printed again in SSY2012/13. See also Black and Ambers, County, Cromwellians, Exiles, Port, Wasps.

Ironworkers was the original nickname of Consett A.F.C., founded in Co. Durham in 1899, originally as Consett Celtic, and in association with Consett Ironworks who provided the first ground for the club. The nickname was 'modernised' to 'Steelmen' in 1967; Wikipedia. See also Steelmen.

Islanders is a nickname for clubs which are based on islands or have the word in their official name. The examples are:

🌑 B.P. Barry F.C., founded in 1991, based at the BP Sports and Social Club ground in Sully near Barry Island. The club was previously named Dow Corning F.C., as a works side for another local industry; RW1994.

🌑 Canvey Island F.C., founded in Essex in 1926 on this island in the Thames Estuary; Wikipedia. See also Gulls, Yellow Army.

🌑 Islandmagee F.C., founded in Co. Antrim in 1955. Here, the place-name is of a peninsula rather than a true island; Wikipedia.

🌑 Sheppey United F.C., founded in 1890 on the Isle of Sheppey in Kent. Recorded in W1979/80 and W1983/4–2001. See also Ites.

🌑 Thanet United F.C., formed in Kent in a temporary renaming of Margate F.C. between 1981 and 1989. The district of Thanet is traditionally named the 'Isle of

Thanet' because it used to be a separate island before the River Wantsum silted up; W1983/4–89. See also Gate, Lilywhites, U's.

Ites is a nickname for Sheppey United F.C., founded in 1890 on the Isle of Sheppey in Kent, though briefly renamed AFC Sheppey in 2007. Recorded in W1980/1 and W1986–2001. The nickname refers to the fuller expression 'Sheppey-ites' for people from the island, which is used in many online forums, and appears on a club badge in AFBC. See also Islanders.

Ivanhoe is the nickname of Ashby Ivanhoe F.C., founded in Ashby-de-la-Zouche, Leicestershire, in 1948. The town is featured in Sir Walter Scott's novel *Ivanhoe* (1820) and the club badge in AFBC shows a medieval knight's helmet. 'Ivanhoe' is a popular name for institutions and businesses within the town. Inexplicably, the Welsh club Rogerstone F.C. (see also Rogie Aces) had a previous incarnation called Rogerstone Ivanhoes (1907–12), a sign of the widespread popularity of the novel but there seems no obvious reason for the suffix here. The novel is the only possible source of the name as it is a false place-name adapted by Scott from the Buckinghamshire place-name Ivinghoe.

Ivies / Ivys is a nickname for two clubs, one for their ivy-green strip and another as a play on the place-name. The clubs are:

⚽ Chester City F.C. during the years of their dark-green (ivy-green) shirts, between 1901 and 1920; Wikipedia (as Ivies). See also Blues, Cestrians, City, Magpies, Romans, Seals.

⚽ Ivybridge Town F.C., founded in 1925; a pun on the Devon place-name (but which does mean an ivy-covered bridge), and the club also plays in green shirts. Recorded in W2008–13 (as Ivys). See also Bridgers.

Jackburn is an unofficial nickname for Blackburn Rovers F.C., from the perspective of Bolton and Preston supporters (see Football Fans Census, 2003). The nickname refers to the former owner Jack Walker, and the idea that he was burning money needlessly, but presented as a pun on 'Blackburn'. See also Blue and Whites, Highwaymen, Plastics, Riversiders, Rovers.

Jackdaws is the nickname of Caerphilly A.F.C., founded in 2002 in what is now the Caerphilly Co. Bor. The club badge shows an image of a castle and jackdaws are very much a common sight at Caerphilly castle; the nickname as yet does not seem to have any printed or internet confirmation for this club, though it is reported for an earlier Caerphilly Town, and is widely used for the local rugby club and other institutions within Caerphilly; reported in Huws 2013 from a verbal source.

Jacks is another nickname for Swansea City A.F.C. Founded in 1912, a Swansea Jack has two possible explanations, though the second is clearly derived from the first. A Swansea Jack was a popular name for a sailor from Swansea, at a time when sailors were always nicknamed Jack; the Swansea ones are still known as Jack Tars (presumably for the River Tawe at Swansea). Another idea is that the nickname records the famous black labrador called Swansea Jack who saved the lives of as many as 27 people in rough seas during the 1930s. There is a monument to him on the seafront, and photographs survive. The name is now often used for anyone from Swansea. Jacks is listed in SSY2003/4–12/13. See also Elyrch, Swanselona, Swans.

Jaggy Bunnets is the nickname of Lugar Boswell Thistle F.C., founded in Ayrshire in 1878. The phrase is a popular one in Scotland and the subject of many websites and even one devoted to reviews of cars in Scots dialect. The meaning has to be *jagged* (like the prickly thistle in 'Jags') and *bonnets*, headware (or heads themselves), despite the different spelling. So, 'Prickly headgear' ... which suggests the crown of thorns worn by Jesus (Billy Connolly has used the phrase in that context, and this alone probably explains the widespread naughty use of the expression). Another idea is 'To be held in a head lock where the school bully rubs his knuckles across the top of your heid very hard", which begins to suggest some sporting use, even if against FA rules. But there are two good reasons for the club's use of the phrase as a nickname. One is that the words themselves are slightly suggested by the sounds in the club's official name, and the other is that it refers to the midges which swarm in their millions in the nearby lush woodlands at the Rosebank Park ground. These do indeed give you a jaggy bunnet, and the club regards them as an unofficial twelfth player; club's own website, SFHA.

Jaggy Nettles is the nickname of Scone Thistle F.C., founded in Perthshire in 1882. Like the previous entry, the nickname is a Scots expression, also used as a business name and a fashion brand. It refers to the stinging nettle, or the thistle, or (rarer) the poison ivy, and might be used to describe potentially 'prickly' clothing like some Scottish wool garments. Here, however, it seems simply to be a reference to the thistle in the official name; Wikipedia, SFHA.

Jags is a nickname for clubs in Scotland. It does not refer to the furious and fast jaguar wild cat (which would also be good) but to the jagged edges of the thistle, the prickly plant which is Scotland's national symbol, and a football club name element in its own right (see also the two 'Jaggy' variants, above). Many of these clubs also show a thistle on their badge, and are frequently also referred to as 'Thistle'. An exception is the Jaguar-Daimler club. The examples are:

- Buckie Thistle F.C., founded in Banffshire in 1889. Recorded in RS1993–2012, SFHA. See also Hoops.
- Dalkeith Thistle F.C., founded in Midlothian in 1892; used on the club's own website. See also Thistle.
- East Kilbride Thistle F.C., founded in Lanarkshire in 1968; W1982/3, SFHA. See also EK.
- Forres Thistle F.C., founded in Moray in 1906; Wikipedia, SFHA.
- Inverness Caledonian Thistle F.C., founded in 1994, in a merger between I. Thistle and Caledonian (both clubs formed in 1885, the new club renaming in 1997). The nickname was also used by I. Thistle, whereas Caledonian were nicknamed 'Caley'. Recorded in W1982/3 and RS1993–4 for Inverness Thistle, RS1995–6 for

Caledonian Thistle, RS1997–2012 for Inverness Caledonian Thistle. See also Caley.

⚽ Jaguar-Daimler F.C., founded in Coventry as a works side for the car manufacturer, and here taking the popular nickname for the Jaguar sports car; recorded in W1995. The FCHB only lists the club for 1993–5.

⚽ Larkhall Thistle F.C., founded in Lanarkshire in 1878; Wikipedia, SFHA. See also Larkie.

⚽ Meadowbank Thistle F.C., founded in 1943, originally as Ferranti Thistle for an Edinburgh electrical engineering company; the club renamed to Meadowbank Thistle and then relocated to, and renaming as, Livingston in 1995. The nickname is recorded in RY1983/4–84/5 for Meadowbank. See also Lions, Livi, Thistle, Wee Jags.

⚽ Partick Thistle F.C., founded near Glasgow in 1876. An early postcard reproduced in McCarra's *Scottish Football* (1984) shows a player in the strip of 1904–5 with the motto 'Come away, Jags!' Recorded in the 1936 Thomson 'stamp' album, G1956–76, SWSCYB 1962–3, Avis 1966–70, through RY1972/3–SS2012/13 and RS 1993–2012. See also Harry Wraggs, Thistle.

⚽ Stonehouse Thistle F.C., founded in Lanarkshire in 1966, renaming as Stonehouse Violet in 1969; SFHA for the earlier club, and for an even earlier one of the same name, 1923–61. See also Violet.

⚽ Strathspey Thistle F.C., founded in Grantown-on-Spey in 1993; club's own website. See also Strathie, Thistle.

Jam Boys is the nickname for Whitchurch United F.C., founded in Hampshire in 1903. The name commemorates the jam-making factory of J. Long Ltd., the village's major employer at the time of the club's foundation; Wikipedia.

Jam Makers was a nickname for Tiptree United F.C., founded in Essex in 1933, and merging in 2009 with Maldon Town (1946) to form Maldon and Tiptree. The nickname comes from the town's leading employer, Wilkin & Sons, makers of fine preserves since 1885. Recorded in W1985–94 and 2001–10 (the early entries vary as Jammakers or Jam Makers, the later are Jam-Makers). See also Blues, Hoops, Strawberries.

Jam Tarts is an official nickname of the Edinburgh side, Heart of Midlothian F.C., founded in 1874, from rhyming slang (Hearts / Tarts). This nickname has in turn generated the variants 'Jambos' and 'Jammies'. The nickname also appears for Kelty Hearts (see under Jambos). Recorded in RY1980/1–90/1, RS1993–2012. See also Edinboro Darlings, Famous, Hearts, Jambos, Jammies, Maroons.

Jam Town is the nickname of Carluke Rovers F.C., founded in Lanarkshire in 1887. The nickname celebrates the town's chief employer, the jam-making factory of Renshaw Scott. The nickname is mentioned on many websites, but the SFHA records the variant 'Jam Tarts'. See also Rovers.

Jambos / Jambo's is a nickname for at least two Scottish clubs called 'Hearts', based on rhyming slang: Hearts / Jam Tarts / Jambos. The clubs are:

⊛ Heart of Midlothian F.C. (see discussion under Jam Tarts, above), recorded in RY2000/1–SSY2006/7 as 'Jambo's', and in SSY2007/8–12/13 as 'Jambos'; RS 2000–01 (as Jambo's), RS2003–12 (as Jambos). The AFBC records an enamel badge of 2000 with 'The Jambos'. See also Edinboro Darlings, Famous, Hearts, Jam Tarts, Jammies, Maroons.

⊛ Kelty Hearts F.C., founded in Fife in 1950. The club took its official name from the more famous Hearts, and this version of the nickname soon followed; Wikipedia, and SFHA (which also adds 'Jam Tarts'). See also Hearts.

Jammies, like the previous entry, is an alternative nickname for Heart of Midlothian, based on rhyming slang (Hearts / Jam Tarts). This particular variant is recorded in Pickering 1994, and has the advantage of also chiming with the popular slang expression for people who have a spectacular piece of good luck. See also Edinboro Darlings, Famous, Hearts, Jam Tarts, Jambos, Maroons.

JB is an initialism for Johnstone Burgh F.C., founded in Renfrewshire in 1956; SFHA.

Jed is a nickname for Jed Legion A.F.C., founded in Jedburgh, Scottish Borders, in 1930, originally as Jed Arts. A badge of the club appears in AFBC; various websites use 'The Legion', the club's own tends to use 'Jed'. See also Legion.

Jets is the nickname and part-official nickname for Oxhey Jets F.C., founded in 1972 in South Oxhey in Watford. There seems no particular reason for the name, other than association with the speed and grace of jet aircraft, though the De Havilland aircraft company (later Rolls Royce Engines) used to have a factory at nearby Leavesden, which is now the site of a film studio; W1986, W1993–6 and W2006–13.

Jimmies is a nickname for New Bradwell St. Peter F.C., founded in the 1880s near Milton Keynes in Buckinghamshire. The nickname refers to the original name of the club as New Bradwell St James F.C., Jimmy being a friendly form of James; the club renamed to Stantonbury St James in c.1901 (after the church in Newport Road), and then to Stantonbury St Peter (after the church at Stanton Low). The club website says that the club was nicknamed 'The Jimmies' till about 1926, and then 'The Peters'. In 1946–7 a nearby club called New Bradwell Corinthians merged with the club and the present name appeared. The club badge shows the crossed keys of St Peter and gives the club's foundation date as 1902 (perhaps when Corinthians was founded?); Wikipedia. See also Peters, Saint Peters.

Jo Row was a nickname for Nestlé Rowntree F.C., founded in York before 1897 when the club joined the York Football League. The nickname is a rhyming short form of 'Joseph Rowntree', the founder of the chocolate company that the club represented. The club was renamed Rowntree Mackintosh in 1969, then the present name in 1988; Wikipedia. See also Rowntrees, Trees.

Jockeys is the appropriate nickname of Newmarket Town F.C., founded in Suffolk in 1897. The club has a horse and rider on its badge, and the town is widely regarded as the world centre and birthplace of thoroughbred horse racing, with origins going back to the twelfth century; W1985–2013.

Jolly Boys is the nickname of Glan Conwy F.C., founded in 1922, reformed 1979; recorded in RW2011. The nickname is said on Wikipedia to have been that of the older club which played at the Gala Field ground in this village in Conwy Co. Borough, though its late appearance in print shows it has continuity. The nickname would seem to be a slight play on the carnival connotations of 'gala'.

Jolly Green Giants was an unofficial nickname for Stoke City F.C., spontaneously coined by Sir Alex Ferguson on 19 October 2012, on the eve of a match against Manchester United. Sir Alex was using the popular advertising phrase and image for Green Giant sweetcorn and was referring to the relative height of the Stoke players (which included Peter Crouch): "We've got the jolly green giants coming to play against us tomorrow ... Michael [Owen] is not allowed to play unless he brings a ladder. They are the biggest team in Europe." Most newspapers reported the phrase, and the *Daily Mail* ran an analysis of some of the players' relative heights; United won 4–2. See also City, Clayheads, Potters, Sjoke City.

Junction is the nickname of Llandudno Junction F.C., founded in 1975, originally as a works side called Hotpoint F.C. The nickname is used on the club's own website. The club was renamed Llanfairfechan United in 1996, then Llandudno Junction in 1999. See also Railwaymen.

Juniors is a football club name element in Scotland, where the word has the same meaning as 'Non-League' in England. Both terms are misleading. The Scottish phrase has nothing to do with pre-eleven-year olds (which is what Junior means in England, those going to 'junior school', before 'secondary school'), and the ambiguity is further stressed with the word 'senior' being used for the opposite meaning; the English phrase has nothing to do with being outside the Football Association's League system, because *all* football clubs play in leagues and there is no such thing as a non-league club. Both expressions simply mean 'not top-flight' and it is time better words were found. Nevertheless, 'Juniors' has also been a football club nickname, for Darvel F.C., founded in Ayrshire in 1889, with the so-called 'non-league' meaning, of course (Wikipedia cites it as 'The Juniors', the nickname is rather odd because the club's league only has 'Junior' clubs in it). For this club, see also Vale.

K's is the nickname for two clubs whose official name begins with K. The clubs are:
- ⚽ Keynsham Town F.C., founded in Somerset in 1895; W1994–2013. See also Canaries.
- ⚽ Kingstonian F.C., founded in 1885 at Kingston-upon-Thames; W1979/80–2013.

Kestrels was the nickname for Bloxwich Town F.C., founded in West Midlands in 1976, originally as Peel F.C. The choice of nickname does not seem to have had a specific reason, other than associated prowess; the club merged with Blakenall to form Bloxwich United in 2001, but Blakenall later withdrew and the club folded by 2005; W1986–2001. See also Griffins.

Kets / Kettles are unofficial nicknames for Kettering Town F.C., based on the opening syllable of the place-name. The 'Soccer AM / MW' website claimed in 2009 that the Kettles nickname began spontaneously during a Setanta televised match in 2007. The nickname is not popular with Poppies fans. See also Friars, Holy City Boys, Poppies.

Khaki Chums is the nickname used on the memorial erected in 1999 at Ypres, Belgium, to commemorate the extraordinary Christmas Day football match between German and British troops in 1914. Uniquely, the nickname applies to both sides in a single, supremely significant and symbolic event. The event now has its own website: www.christmastruce.co.uk

Kiddy (or **Kiddie**) is a nickname for Kidderminster Harriers F.C., founded in Worcestershire in 1886; a friendly short form of the place-name; the nickname appears in a photo caption (as Kiddie) in W1992 (p. 65). See also Harriers, Reds.

Killie is the official nickname of Kilmarnock F.C., founded in East Ayrshire in 1869; a friendly short form of the place-name. The nickname first appears in the plural, as *Killies*, in G1956–76, Harvey 1959, Avis 1966–70 and RY1970/1–82/3. It appears as Killie through RY1983/4–SSY2012/13 and RS 1993–2012.

Killman is listed in Avis 1966 and 1970 as "a nickname once used by Glastonbury F.C." The nickname is a mystery. Killman is a family surname which does appear in Somerset, but if the family had an old connection with the club, the nickname ought to have taken a different form, such as 'Killman's Boys' or 'Killmanites'. See also Dollies.

Kingdom Boys is a nickname of Tralee Dynamos F.C., founded in 1961, and also the official name for the club's youth side. The club is based in Co. Kerry and this county is often called the 'Kingdom of Kerry', partly for its remoteness and sense of independence, but also because its name – *Ciar raige* – means 'the kingdom of Ciar', an early king. Fife in Scotland is another county which is historically called a kingdom, and see also 'Men from the Kingdom' for Fanad. The highly successful Gaelic Football Team, Kerry GAA, have 'The Kingdom' as their nickname. See also Dynamos.

Kingfishers is the nickname for two clubs which have an association with this fast, effective hunter. The clubs are:

- Monmouth Town F.C., founded in 1930, according to the club badge, which also displays a handsome image of a kingfisher; the bird is found on the local Monnow and Wye rivers. However, the nickname was only adapted in 2005. It honours a local story from 1936, when the local kingfisher population was seriously threatened by floods which were damaging the nests, but a breeding pair was found nesting in a deflated football which had floated downstream and become lodged in branches overhanging the water; Wikipedia.
- Thatcham Town F.C., founded in Berkshire in 1894. The bird is shown on the club badge, and the club ground is the Waterside Park, beside the River Kennet and the famous Thatcham Reed Beds, where real kingfishers are often seen; W2012–13.

See also Town.

Kings is a nickname for clubs with this word in their official name. The clubs are:

⚽ Arnold Kingswell F.C., founded in Nottinghamshire in 1962; W1983/4–6. The club merged with Arnold F.C. in 1988 and both have now been succeeded by Arnold Town.

⚽ Castle Vale Kings Heath F.C., founded in West Midlands in 1964, originally as a pub side called Horseshoe, and other names before this one; the club renamed again as Castle Vale in 2005; at the time of this nickname the club played in an appropriate 'old gold and black'; W1987–2003 as Kings Heath, W2004–5 as Castle Vale. The club folded in 2012. See also Spitfires.

⚽ Kings Heath F.C., see previous entry.

⚽ King's Langley F.C., founded in Hertfordshire in 1886; Wikipedia.

⚽ Kingsbury Town F.C., founded by ex-servicemen in London in 1919, merging with London Tigers in 2006 to form Kingsbury London Tigers (see 'Tigers'), renamed London Tigers in 2011. The nickname also appears on the club badge; W1995–2006. See also Mustard Pots and Town.

⚽ Meir K.A. F.C., founded in Staffordshire in 1972; Meir is a place-name and K.A. stands for 'King's Arms', a pub name, but the side has long been an independent club; W1994–2005.

Kirby is the nickname for Kirby Muxloe F.C., founded in Leicestershire in 1910; a short form of the place-name; club's own website.

Kirk is the nickname of Muirkirk F.C., founded in Ayrshire in 1937, from the second element in the place-name, which means 'church'; Wikipedia, SFHA.

Kirkby Roaders is the nickname of Barwell F.C., founded in Leicestershire in 1992 in a merger of Barwell Athletic and Hinckley F.C. The club plays at the Kirkby Road ground in Barwell, Leicestershire; W1997–2011. See also Canaries.

Kirks is a nickname for Kirkley and Pakefield F.C., founded in Suffolk in 2007 in a merger between the two clubs of these names. A pluralised short form of the first place-name, recorded in W2008–13. See also Royals.

Kirrie is a nickname of Kirriemuir Thistle F.C., founded in Angus in 1921; a short form of the place-name; Wikipedia. See also Thistle.

Knappers is the nickname for Knaphill F.C., founded in Surrey in 1924, an adaptation of the first syllable of the place-name; W2009–13.

Knights is the nickname of Ludlow Town F.C., founded in 1890, and merging with Ludlow Colts in 1995. The nickname is a celebration of the medieval history, architecture, castle and heraldry of this picturesque Shropshire town; Wikipedia.

Knitters is the nickname of Hinckley United F.C. Founded in 1997 as a merger between Hinckley Town and Hinckley Athletic, the club held a competition to decide on a nickname, and 'The Knitters' was chosen. It records the major woollen and hosiery industries in the town's industrial history. The club also has two sheep as supporters on its coat of arms; Williams does not record the nickname as such but

W2002 illustrates a programme which prints the nickname and it appears in RNL2002. See also Eagles, Robins, Town, United.

Knuts, see under **Nuts**, for Scunthorpe United.

Kop / Kopites is an unofficial nickname for Liverpool F.C. and their supporters, from the official name of one of the stands at Anfield Stadium, named The Kop, or the Spion Kop, in 1905, from a battle in the Boer War in which many Liverpool men had died in 1900. Several other Kops appeared in British stadiums, but the Liverpool one is the most famous. Many of the stands so called are named because their steep terraces were believed to resemble the steep hill of the original, from which there was a good view. 'Kops' appears in the title to a book by Peter Crill, *Tops of the Kops* (2007); 'Kopites' appears on Wikipedia. See also Anfielders, Culture Club, Liddellpool, Mariners, Merseysiders, Micky Mousers, Pool, Reds, Spice Boys.

Kopettes appears to be an unofficial nickname for A.F.C. Liverpool, founded in 2008 amongst supporters of the mainstream Liverpool club. Like them, the club plays in red, and this nickname, which appears on a placard in a photograph on the internet, means 'Small Kops', as a tribute to the *Kop* nickname of Liverpool F.C. See also Reds.

Krooners is the nickname of Camberley Town F.C., founded in Surrey in 1895, originally as St Michael's Camberley F.C., then Camberley and Yorktown, and merging with Camberley Wanderers in 1967 to form the present club. A crooner is a late nineteenth-century word for a seductive singer. The spelling in k appears to be the same word, but the nickname comes from the name of the club's home ground, Krooner Park. This was bought for the club on the proceeds of two wins by a racehorse called Krooner at Haydock Park in 1920, on the generosity of the horse's owner, Bernard W. Baker. The club immortalised the horse in the name of the stadium, which opened in 1923. W1993–2008. See also Reds, Town.

L.R. is recorded as a nickname for Atherton Laburnum Rovers F.C. in W1996–7; an initialism. See also Laburnums, Panthers, Rovers.

Laburnums is a nickname of Atherton Laburnum Rovers F.C., founded in Greater Manchester in 1956 and based at the Laburnum Playing Fields in the district of Atherton. The playing fields presumably had the colourful laburnum trees growing there; Wikipedia. See also L.R., Panthers, Rovers.

Lacemakers was the nickname of Newmilns F.C., founded in Ayrshire in 1897, closed in 1929. In 1876 Joseph Hood installed a lace curtain-making machine at Newmilns and ten years later eight more businesses had opened and the industry employed 1,500 people here. It is now much reduced in scale, but still present in the town; SFHA.

Lacemen was a nickname for Tiverton Town F.C., founded in Devon in 1913, originally as T. Athletic. The nickname refers to a mainstay of the town's economy since 1815, when the industrialist John Heathcoat began to move his lace-making operations from Loughborough to Tiverton; recorded in Miller & Wright 1996.

See also Tivvy.

Laddies, see Laides.

Lads is a nickname for many football clubs but is particularly associated with Sunderland A.F.C. It is a standard English word, though more commonly used for young men in Scotland and the north of England. The nickname is displayed as "Ha'way the Lads" on the North Stand of the Stadium of Light (built 1997). For Sunderland see also Bank of England Club, Black Cats, Light Brigade, Mackems, Miners, Rokerites / Rokermen, Sols, Sund-Ireland, Team of All the Talents, Wearsiders.

Lady Imps is the nickname for Lincoln Ladies F.C., founded in 1995, originally as Lincoln City Ladies F.C. The nickname neatly exploits the 'Imps' nickname used by Lincoln City, based on the carving in Lincoln Cathedral; Wikipedia.

Lady Villans is the nickname of Aston Villa Ladies F.C., founded originally in 1973 as Solihull F.C., affiliated with Aston Villa in 1996. The nickname adapts the main nickname used by the men's club, 'The Villans'; Wikipedia.

Laides was a nickname of a club called South Shields Adelaide Athletic, one of the ancestor teams of Gateshead F.C. It was formed in 1899 and dropped the word Adelaide in 1910, before moving to Gateshead in 1930. The nickname is a pluralised short form of Adelaide, which survived as a nickname for the Gateshead club (Johnston 1934, G1956, Churchill 1958, Harvey 1959 and Richards 1960 record it as Laides). There is an Adelaide Street in South Shields which probably had some connection with the club's foundation. The variant form 'Laddies' (Historical Football Kits website and Wikipedia) is a normal Scots and Northern English friendly form of 'Lads' and would stand as a perfectly good nickname for a northern team, but is probably best explained as an error. See also Boro, Heed, Tynesiders.

Laird/s is a nickname for Cammell Laird F.C., founded in 1907, originally as the Cammell Laird Institute team. Cammell Laird is a major ship-building firm in Birkenhead; W2007–13 (as Lairds). See also Camels, Shipyarders.

Lakesiders is the nickname of two Welsh teams which are beside large lakes. The clubs are:

⚽ Bala Town F.C., founded in Gwynedd in 1921; recorded in RW2011. The town of Bala is beside a substantial ancient lake called Bala Lake or Llyn Tegid.

⚽ Llanwddyn F.C., founded in 1949 in Powys. Here the lake is a man-made reservoir, Lake Vyrnwy, but, despite the modernity of the feature, poetic nicknames for the club include 'Lake', 'Lakesiders' and 'Lords of the Lake'. The club's ground was Wddyn Park, and 'Wddyn Boys' is another nickname. The club folded in 2009 but the *Montgomeryshire County Times* reported on 31 January 2013 that the Lords of the Lake were 'to resurface'; Wikipedia, Huws 2013.

Lambs is a nickname for three clubs associated with the name for young sheep, but for different reasons. Possible explanations include 'the Lamb of God', pub or hotel names, the local wool industry, or even the proverbial relationship between lambs and lions. The clubs are:

◉ Notts County F.C., founded in 1862; this is the original nickname for the club and is said to have been from a gang of Nottingham thugs which one of the players was allegedly involved with (thus sarcastic use, thugs not being lamb-like), though the 1933 Ogden card claims it was because of the fame of the local sheep industry. The club's use of 'County' reflects the fact that much of the city of Nottingham is in the county rather than the city's official boundaries. In 1890 the club adopted the black-and-white strip which soon earned them the nickname of 'The Magpies', though 'Lambs' is still recorded in G1956–65, Churchill 1958, Richards 1960, AA 1960, Avis 1966–70 and as late as Moss 1983. See also Magpies.

◉ Stokenchurch F.C., founded in Buckinghamshire in 1886; the evidence for the nickname is its appearance on the club badge illustrated in AFBC, with an image of a lamb. The club appears in FCHD between 1953 and 1995, and disappears from the Williams directories after 1995. There is no doubting the nickname, but the reason for it is not recorded.

◉ Tamworth F.C., founded in Staffordshire in 1933 after the closure of Tamworth Castle F.C. The club first played at The Jolly Sailor ground, next to the pub of that name, before moving to The Lamb Ground in 1934, from which the nickname comes. The ground itself was named from the nearby Lamb Inn, at which players used to change; W1981/2–2013 and SSY2004/5–07/8 and SSY2010/11–12/13. See also Reds, Town.

◉ Tavistock A.F.C., founded in Devon in 1888. The town coat of arms records the local wool trade with a traditional image of a fleece on its shield, adopted as badge and nickname by the club; W1994–2013. See also Tavy.

Lancers is the nickname for Lancing F.C., founded in 1941, originally as L. Athletic. The nickname is a pun on the Sussex place-name, but uses the traditional name for a group of mounted lance-carrying soldiers (nowadays only a ceremonial dress), so suggesting a proud display; W2003–9. See also Yellows.

Landlords is a Glaswegian nickname sometimes used by supporters for their local club, as evidenced by two correspondents in an internet forum for Yoker Athletic (see 'Whe Ho') in 2012. The nickname derives from rhyming slang: club / pub, but also neatly suggests a sense of feudal loyalty.

Lane is a nickname for three clubs with this place-name element in their official name. The clubs are:

◉ Friar Lane and Epworth F.C., founded in 2004 in Aylestone, Leicester; W2011.

◉ Holly Lane '92 F.C., founded in Holly Lane, Birmingham, in 1992 (previously Holly Lane Sports and Social); W1995.

◉ Rayners Lane F.C., founded in 1933 in the London borough of Harrow; W1983/4–96 and W2001–13.

Laneites has been an occasional nickname for Sheffield United F.C. Founded in 1889, the nickname is from the home ground of Bramall Lane, and distinguishes the club from the Groveites (for Sheffield Wednesday); Wikipedia. See also Blades, Blunts,

Cutlers, Pigs, Red and White Wizards, United.

Lang is a nickname of Cambuslang Rangers F.C., founded in Lanarkshire in 1899; a short form of the place-name; Wikipedia, SFHA. See also Wee 'Gers.

Lankies is the nickname for the Northamptonshire side, Rushden and Higham United F.C., founded in 2007 in a merger between Higham Town (1876) and Rushden Rangers (1978). The nickname was that of Higham Town and is a pun on the place-name, lanky meaning tall and slim ('high'). Addis 1995 reprints a newspaper article of 1949 which uses the nickname (p. 34); W1995–2007 for Higham Town.

Larkie is a nickname of Larkhall Thistle F.C., founded in Lanarkshire in 1878; a friendly short form of the place-name, and one which also suggests 'fun'; it is recorded on Wikipedia as 'Larkie', on the club's own website as 'Larky'. See also Jags.

Larks is the nickname of two clubs, for different reasons. The clubs are:

☺ Larkhall Athletic F.C., founded in 1914. The club has an appropriate bird on its badge and the nickname puns with the place-name (though the element means the same); W1982/3–2013.

☺ Nuthall F.C., founded in the village near Nottingham in 1976; the nickname is not explained but the playing fields are close to Larkfield Road on which there is a pub called 'The Lark's Nest'. The folding of the club in 1997 was mentioned in W1998, p. 379; the nickname was recorded in W1994–7.

Latics is the nickname of three Northern clubs with the suffix 'Athletic'. The nickname is a play on 'Athletic', but shortened and rendered with an 'a' to express local pronunciation. See also Addicks for another discussion of athletic mutation. The clubs are:

☺ Ferryhill Athletic F.C., founded in Co. Durham in 1921 and closed in 2006. W1979/80 had this in the form 'Lactics', but this is a typesetting error, corrected when the nickname reappeared in W1980/1 and W1994–7.

☺ Oldham Athletic, founded in 1895 as Pine Villa F.C., apparently named from a local Pine Cotton Mill, but in 1899 another local team, Oldham County F.C., folded and 'Pine' moved to their ground, The Athletic Grounds on Sheepfoot Lane, and changed their name to Oldham Athletic as a result. It is recorded on the 1933 Ogden card, with a cartoon of an old ham; G1956–76, Churchill 1958, Richards 1960, AA 1960, Avis 1966–70 and throughout RY1970/1–SSY2012/13.

☺ Wigan Athletic F.C., founded in 1932, the club was the fifth attempt to establish a viable club in Wigan, the previous being Wigan County, W. Town, W. United and W. Borough. The first team was nicknamed 'County' (q.v.); Avis 1966–70, and through RY1978/9–SS2012/13. See also Athletic, Latics, Pie-Eaters / Pies, T'Colliers or T'Pitmen.

Lavvy is the nickname of Laverstock and Ford F.C., founded in Wiltshire in 1956; a friendly short form of the place-name; Wikipedia. The club badge presents the motto "The future's bright | it's green and white", suggesting that the club colours are another nickname.

Lawmen is the nickname for Lex XI F.C., based in Wrexham, Flintshire. The club was formed in 1965 by a group of solicitors who wanted to play football. The official name takes the Latin word for 'law' and the nickname honours the profession of the founding players. The 'XI' is the number eleven in Roman numerals. RW lists the club but always without a nickname; Wikipedia.

Lawnmowers is an unofficial nickname for Forest Green Rovers F.C., founded in Gloucestershire in 1890. The nickname is recorded on Wikipedia and plays on the name of the club's ground, called The Lawn in 1926, the New Lawn since 2006. See also FGR, Green, Green Army, Little Club on the Hill, Rovers.

Lawyers is the nickname of the Co. Durham club Tow Law Town A.F.C., founded in 1890. The nickname appears on the club badge, which also displays a pithead. The nickname is a pun on the Law element in the place-name, an Old English word for a mound (the town is on a plateau). Perhaps in ironic contrast to the Lawyers, the club supporters are nicknamed 'The Misfits'; Barton 1984 & 1985, W1979/80– 2013.

Lea is the nickname of Montrose Roselea F.C., founded in Angus in 1930; as a short form of the place-name; Wikipedia; SFHA records the nickname and calls the club 'Montrose Lea'.

Leafe is the nickname for Whyteleafe F.C., founded in Surrey in 1946 as a successor to Whyteleafe Albion. The nickname is a short form of the place-name, though the club also plays in leaf-green shirts with white shorts and socks, and their badge shows a white leaf on a green background, superimposed on a football. The place-name itself is recent, 1839, believed to have been named from the White Leaf Field, so-called because of the aspen trees which grew there, but given a 'medievalist' spelling (Mills 1991); W1982/3–2013.

Leaves was the nickname of Leavesden Hospital F.C., founded in Hertfordshire in 1908 according to a commemorative website. The Hospital itself was closed in 1992; the short-form nickname is recorded in W1986.

Leesiders is a nickname for Cork City F.C., founded in Co. Cork in 1984. The city is built on the river Lee; Wikipedia. See also City, Rebel Army.

Leghorns is an occasional unofficial nickname for Staines Town F.C. in Surrey. A leghorn is a breed of chicken, from Livonia in Italy, a town called Leghorn in English, but there seems no connection with the club here. The word is probably a pun on *Lago*nda, another nickname for the club from Lagonda Cars, and Spelt*horne* Borough (in which Staines lies); Wikipedia. See also Linos, Massive, Old Lagonda, Swans, Town.

Legion is a nickname for clubs affiliated to the Royal British legion social clubs. Two clubs are:

◉ Jed Legion A.F.C., founded in Jedburgh, Scottish Borders, in 1930, originally as Jed Arts. A badge of the club appears in AFBC; various websites use 'The Legion', the club's own tends to use 'Jed'. See also Jed.

☺ Llay Royal British Legion F.C., founded in Wrexham Co. Bor. in 1972. The nickname is recorded in RW1994–5.

Legionnaires is the nickname for Mickleover Royal British Legion F.C., founded in Derbyshire in 1945; recorded in W1997.

Leishman's Lions was an unofficial nickname for Dunfermline Athletic F.C., during the managership of Jim Leishman (1982–90), especially for the 1985–7 seasons. The nickname is recorded in the title of the contemporary book by Robert Fraser, *Leishman's Lions. The Roaring Success Story* (Dunfermline, 1987). See also Dumps, Fifers, Pars.

Levers is a nickname for Warrington Town F.C., founded in Cheshire in 1949, originally as Stockton Heath Albion, renamed Warrington in 1961. The nickname is a pluralised short form of the club's ground name: Cantilever Park, named from the adjacent Cantilever Bridge; Wikipedia in 2011 (2012 version no longer includes this nickname). See also Town, Warriors, Wire/s, Yellows.

Leythers was the nickname of Leigh Genesis F.C., founded in Greater Manchester in 2008 in a renaming of Leigh R.M.I. F.C. The initials stood for Railway Mechanics Institute. The name Genesis was used simply to imply a new beginning, but the club folded in 2011. A Leyther is a local expression for anyone from the town of Leigh, and is recorded in Dobson 1973; Wikipedia. See also Locos, Railwaymen.

Libs is a common nickname for 'Liberals', the political party or the clubs affiliated to it, and is the nickname of Canton Liberals F.C., founded in 2006 in Cardiff. The club website uses 'Canton Libs' as a nickname; Huws 2013.

Liddellpool was a nickname for Liverpool during the 1940s and '50s when the famous Billy Liddell was the club's star striker; recorded in Pickering 1994. See also Anfielders, Culture Club, Kop / Kopites, Mariners, Merseysiders, Micky Mousers, Pool, Reds, Spice Boys.

Lidos is the nickname for Afan Lido F.C., founded in the Co. Bor. of Neath Port Talbot at Aberavon in 1967. Here, the popular word for an open-air swimming pool became the name of the Lido Sports Centre before becoming the club's official name and then nickname; recorded in W1994–6 in the form 'The Lido'. See also Seasiders.

'Lie is the nickname of Arthurlie F.C., founded at Barrhead in Renfrewshire in 1874, as a short form of the place-name; Wikipedia, SFHA.

Light Blues is a nickname for clubs which play in this colour. The clubs are:

☺ Ballymena United F.C., founded in Co. Antrim in 1928, reformed as United in 1934. The club's nickname and strip (light-blue shirts and socks, white shorts) are in tribute to the famous Glasgow side; Wikipedia. See also Braidmen, Sky Blues, United.

☺ Rangers F.C., founded in Glasgow in 1872, from the light-blue strip they have worn since 1879. An early postcard reproduced in McCarra's *Scottish Football* (1984) shows a player in the strip of 1899–1904 with the motto 'Good Old Light Blues'. Fans of the club are nicknamed 'Bluenoses'. Recorded in BoF1905–6, Johnston 1934, p. 30; the 1936 Thomson 'stamp' album, G1956, RS1993–2012. See also Blues, 'Gers, Huns, Iron Curtain, Rangers, Teddy Bears.

Light Brigade was a proposed nickname for Sunderland A.F.C. since their move to the new Stadium of Light in 1997, and was one on the shortlist of nicknames voted for in that year; Wikipedia. See also Bank of England Club, Black Cats, Lads, Mackems, Miners, Rokerites / Rokermen, Sols, Sund-Ireland, Team of All the Talents.

Lights was a nickname for Bournemouth Gasworks Athletic F.C., founded in Dorset in 1899, originally as a works side, closed in 1973; Wikipedia and on an enamel badge recorded in AFBC. Gas-powered street lighting is the original application of the gas industry. See also Gasmen.

Lilies / Lillies is a nickname for two clubs which play in colours associated with this flower. The clubs are:

⚽ Chatteris Town F.C., founded in Cambridgeshire in 1920. The club plays distinctive pale-blue strip, and some varieties of lilly are in this colour, but the stylish club badge shows one with white petals; W1985–2001.

⚽ Leyton F.C., founded in Essex in 1997 in a reformation of the older club of 1868. The club is normally called 'The Lilywhites' but this alternative nickname is recorded on Wikipedia, also referring to white shirts. See also Lilywhites, Swifts.

⚽ Liverton United F.C., founded in Ilsington, Devon in 1902. The nickname is used in journalism (*This is Devon*, May 3, 2010) as 'The Lilies', but it appears in W2013 as 'Lilly's'. Nevertheless, the team plays in blue, so the nickname may refer to an older white (or pale-blue) strip or it may have been formed as a slight play on the two place-names.

⚽ Rhyl F.C., founded in Clwyd in 1878, from an originally all-white strip (now with black shorts). The club had switched to the nickname 'The Lilywhites' by the time of W1979/80–80/1. This earlier nickname is recorded in Avis 1966–70. See also Beavers, Lilywhites, Seagulls.

Lily is the nickname of Easthouses Lily Miners Welfare F.C., founded in Midlothian in 1950, originally as a side for the Easthouses Colliery, and taking the present name in 1969. The word in the official name is that of the white flower, and the club does play in an all-white strip. The flower appears on the club badge. Recorded in RS2000–1. See also Houses.

Lilywhites / Lillywhites / Lily Whites is a common nickname for clubs who play in lily-white shirts, or sometimes in an all-white strip. The word has long had an association with sport because of the Lilywhite (or Lillywhite, both spellings occur) business of sports outfitters and the editorship of Victorian sporting publications by members of the same family, but it is the shirt colour to which the nickname refers. The three spellings seem to occur at random and are not significant. Examples are:

⚽ A.F.C. Telford United, from their white shirts, refounded in Shropshire in 2004. The nickname was inherited from the older club of the same name, originally founded in 1872, renaming as Wellington Town in 1879 and as Telford United in 1969, closing in 2004; W1979/80–2000 for the earlier club; SSY2012/13 for the new. See Wellington Town, below, and see also Bucks.

⚽ A.F.C. St Austell, founded in Cornwall in 1890; Avis 1966–70, Miller & Wright 1996, W2011–13.

⚽ Bacup Borough F.C., in Lancashire, recorded in Avis 1966–70. See also Borough, Buttercups.

⚽ Barry Town F.C., in Vale of Glamorgan, recorded in Avis 1966–70. See also Dragons, Linnets.

⚽ Berkhamstead F.C. and its predecessor club B. Town, founded in Hertfordshire in 1919, originally as B. Comrades; from the white shirts. Recorded in Avis 1966–70 (as Lily Whites), W1983/4–2008. See also Berko, Comrades.

⚽ Brimscombe and Thrupp F.C., founded in Gloucestershire in 1968, when Brimscombe A.F.C. (1886) merged with Thrupp. The club plays in white shirts; W2012–13.

⚽ Bromley F.C., founded in Kent in 1892, from their white shirts. Recorded in Avis 1966–70, W1980/1–2013. See also Ravens.

⚽ Calne Town F.C., founded in 1886. The Wiltshire side plays in white shirts with blue shorts and socks; W1994–2013.

⚽ Cambridge City F.C. Founded as 'Town' in 1908, Cambridge took city status in 1951; white shirts; Avis 1966–70, W1994–2013. See also City, City Devils, Town.

⚽ Chichester City F.C., founded in Sussex in 2000, in a merger between C. City (1893) and Portfield (1896). The club plays in white shirts. Recorded for both new and old clubs in W1980/81 and W1986–2005. See also Chi, City.

⚽ Clachnacuddin F.C., founded in Inverness in 1885. The club plays in white shirts and this must be the most northern occurrence of the nickname. Recorded in W1982/3, RS1993–2012, SFHA, AFBC. See also Clach.

⚽ Clacton Town F.C., founded in Essex in 1892, now renamed F.C. Clacton; white shirts. Recorded in Avis 1966–70. See also Seasiders.

⚽ Coleraine F.C., founded in Co. Londonderry in 1927, in a merger between C. Olympic and C. Alexandra. The nickname is early, and referred to the club's all-white strip, but is no longer used; Wikipedia. See also Bannsiders.

⚽ Dover F.C., founded in Kent in 1891, folded and replaced by the new Dover Athletic in 1983; recorded in Avis 1966–70 and W1979/80–99. For Dover Athletic, see Whites.

⚽ Dundalk F.C., founded in Co. Louth in 1903 as Dundalk GNR, as a works side for the Great Northern Railway A.F.C. The club plays in white shirts. Recorded in RI1997, 2006.

⚽ Faversham Town F.C., founded in Kent in 1884; plain white shirts with black shorts.

Recorded in W1979/80 and W2007–13 (Town is the usual nickname given in W). See also Creeksiders, Sorters, Town.

⚽ Fulham F.C. In 1903 the team adopted an all-white strip, to which the name refers (though nowadays the shorts are black); Wikipedia. See also Badgers, Cottagers, Whites.

⚽ Halesowen Harriers F.C., founded in West Midlands in 1961; the club was dissolved in 2003; W1994–6. See also Harriers.

⚽ Harlow Town F.C., founded in Essex in 1879; recorded in Avis 1966–70. See also Hawks, Owls.

⚽ Henley Town F.C., founded in Oxfordshire in 1871. The team wears white shirts and black shorts; W2001–6 and W2012–13. See also Town.

⚽ Hereford United F.C., from the all-white strip adopted from their foundation in 1924, though in 1946 black shorts were introduced (said to have been made from recycled black-out curtains) and the colours have usually had a mixture of black and white since. Recorded in Avis 1966–70. See also Bulls, Whites, United.

⚽ Hoddesdon Town F.C., founded in Hertfordshire in 1879; white shirts; W1980/1–2013. See also Lowfielders.

⚽ King's Lynn Town F.C., founded in Norfolk in 1879, folded in 2009; recorded in Avis 1966–70 as an alternative to 'The Linnets' (q.v.).

⚽ Leyton F.C., founded in 1868 in Essex, recorded in Avis 1966–70. This club is legally recognised as the ancestor of the present Leyton F.C., reformed in 1997 and also nicknamed The Lilywhites; W2000–3 records the nickname as 'The Lilywhite' (singular), then W2004–11 has the plural form. See also Lillies, Swifts.

⚽ Leyton Pennant F.C., founded in Essex in 1995 in a merger between Walthamstow Pennant and a Leyton club which had some relationship with the previous and following entries, though it is not easy to reconcile the contradictory evidence in the printed and internet and legal sources as to what actually happened. In Williams *both* clubs appear between 2000 and 2003; Leyton Pennant has the Lilywhites nickname in W1996–2003. The club then renamed as Waltham Forest (see below). See also Pennant, Stags.

⚽ Leyton-Wingate F.C., founded in a merger in 1975 between Wingate (1946) and a club called Leyton, but previously Matlock Swifts (1895). Leyton-Wingate ran from 1975 to 1992, when it renamed as Leyton, before it merged with Walthamstow Pennant in 1995. The nickname appears for the various versions of the club in W1980/1 and W1994–5.

⚽ Luton Town F.C., for the period when the club played in white shirts and black shorts (Historical Football Kits gives this period as 1920–73). The nickname is recorded in an advertisement for Lillywhites, a timber merchant, in the 1948–9 *Luton News Football Yearbook*: "It's funny how a name sticks! 'Up the Lillywhites' they say – referring, of course, to Luton Town Football Club. Down to Lillywhites for Timber"; and in a song, reported from the 1940s, to the tune of 'We're forever blowing bubbles': 'They're forever winning matches, are those good old Lillywhites' (thanks to Howard Chandler). See also Hatters, Lootown, Lutonians, Reds, Straw-Hatters / Straw-Plaiters.

⚽ Margate F.C., founded in Kent in 1896. The nickname was used during the 1920s when the club played in plain white shirts. The club was temporarily renamed Thanet United 1981–9; Wikipedia. See also Gate, Islanders, U's.

⚽ Marine A.F.C., founded in Crosby, Merseyside, in 1894; white shirts. Recorded in Avis 1966–70, W1991–2 and W2004–5. See also Mariners.

⚽ Moreton Town F.C., founded in Gloucestershire in 1908; white shirts; the club disappears after 1995, though there is a youth side in the town today called Moreton Rangers; W1979/80–95.

⚽ Mossley A.F.C., founded in Lancashire in 1903, originally as Villa Park. The club plays in white shirts. Recorded in Avis 1966–70, W1979/80–2013.

⚽ Preston North End F.C., founded in 1880, the club first adopted the white shirts (and blue shorts), from which the nickname comes, in 1888. The shorter form 'The Whites' is also used. Recorded in G1956–76, Churchill 1958, Richards 1960, Avis 1966–70, and throughout RY1970/1–SSY2012/13. See also Glasses, Invincibles, North End, P.N.E., Proud Preston.

⚽ Rhyl F.C., founded in Clwyd in 1878, from an originally all-white strip (now with black shorts). Today, the club has an impressive badge showing a stylish white lily. Recorded in W1979/80–80/1, Goodall 1982, W1987–92, W1995–2005 and RW 1994–2011. An older badge, recorded in AFBC, has the nickname in the singular ('The Lilywhite'). See also Beavers, Lilies / Lillies, Seagulls.

⚽ Salisbury F.C. (renamed Salisbury City 1993), founded in Wiltshire in 1947, recorded in Avis 1966–70. See also Whites.

⚽ Skegness Town A.F.C., founded in Lincolnshire in 1946; all-white strip; Avis 1966–70, W1979/80–82/3.

⚽ Technogroup Welshpool Town F.C., founded in Powys in 1878, originally as Welshpool Town; the present official name dates from 2008. The club plays in white shirts and black shorts. Recorded in RW2011. See also Maes y Dre, Seasiders.

⚽ Tooting and Mitcham United F.C., founded in London in 1932, from the black-and-white striped shirts which they adopted in 1956. The nickname is rare for this club, but appears in Goodall 1982. See also Half-Halfs, Stripes, Terrors, Tooting Terrors.

⚽ Tottenham Hotspur F.C., founded in 1882. Since 1899 onwards, the team has played in white shirts and blue shorts; Wikipedia. See also Spurs, Super Spurs, Yids / Yid Army.

⚽ Treharris Athletic Western F.C., founded in 1889, originally as Treharris Athletic; based in the Co. Bor. of Merthyr Tydfil. In recent years the club has played in blue-and-white hoops with blue shorts, so presumably the nickname was coined at an earlier time when they played in white shirts (today, the club fields four teams, none of which play in white). The village itself was a new settlement, formed in 1873 to exploit a new coal seam, and the football club was founded some seven years before the village had a parish church. Recorded in RW1994–2011. Huws 2013 adds that the club has also been called the 'All Whites'. See also Western.

◈ Waltham Forest F.C., founded in the London borough in 2003 in a renaming of the club called Leyton Pennant. The club continued 'The Lilywhites' nickname in W2004–7 before adopting 'The Stags' nickname. See also Pennant, Stags.

◈ Wellington Town F.C., founded as Parish Church Institute F.C. in Shropshire in 1872, renamed Wellington Town in 1879; recorded in Avis 1966–70, but in 1969 the club was renamed Telford United. It survived till 2004 and was reformed as A.F.C. Telford United. See also Bucks.

◈ Welshpool Town F.C., founded in Powys in 1878. The club renamed as Technogroup Welshpool Town in 2008. The nickname is recorded in RW2002/3. The club has long played in white shirts and black shorts. See also Maes y Dre, Seasiders.

Lims is a nickname for two clubs, as a pluralised short form of the place-name. The clubs are:

◈ Limavady United F.C., founded in Co. Londonderry in 1884. Recorded in RNI2007, with 'United' as an alternative. See also Roesiders, United.

◈ Limerick F.C., founded in Co. Limerick in 1937; Wikipedia. See also Blades, Blues.

Linnets is a nickname for several clubs. In the case of King's Lynn the nickname appears to be a pun on the place-name, 'Lynn' being the local expression (though it could also be a response to the popularity of the Norwich Canaries), but in the other instances the reason is obscure. The bird is brown and slightly red-breasted, but there are no common colours amongst the clubs so nicknamed; in folksongs the linnet may be a green variety (the greenfinch is even known as a green linnet). The linnet is a songbird of the finch family and used to be caged and domesticated far more than it is nowadays, appearing in folklore and popular songs. The nickname seems to reflect this popularity, appearing for clubs associated with places where linnet-breeding was popular, just as canary-breeding was the reason for the Norwich nickname. Twydell 1988 may have put his finger on the reason for the nickname when he states that Market Harborough Town were 'on song': the linnet proverbially gives a good performance despite its lack-lustre colours. The common linnet is widely found in Britain, however, and the variant tradition recorded for Runcorn, below, suggests that the nickname may sometimes simply reflect the bird's distribution. The clubs are:

◈ Barry Town A.F.C., founded in Vale of Glamorgan in 1912. In 1992 the club had a temporary exile in Worcester under the new name of Barri Dragons, returning home in 1993. After that 'The Linnets' nickname was slowly dropped. Recorded in Avis 1966–70, W1979/80–81/2, W1991–2 and W1995–97 and RW1994–7; AFBC has it on an old enamel badge. See also Dragons, Lilywhites.

☻ Burscough F.C., founded in Lancashire in 1905, originally as Burscough Rangers (folded 1935, reformed 1946). The earlier club was also nicknamed 'The Linnets'. The club plays in green, the colour of the linnet in some folksongs, but this does not seem to be significant; W1979/80–2013.

☻ King's Lynn Town F.C., the 2010 successor club to the bankrupt King's Lynn F.C. which folded in 2009 (founded 1879). The new club has taken the nickname, badge, ground and colours of the old club. Here, the nickname is a neat pun on the place-name; Avis 1966–70, W1979/80–2013. See also Lilywhites.

☻ Lymington and New Milton F.C. The club was formed in Hampshire in a merger in 1998 between Lymington Town and New Milton, and both clubs had been nicknamed 'The Linnets'. Meanwhile, a breakaway Lymington Town also reformed in 1998 and is nicknamed 'Town', and in 2007 the merged club changed its name to New Milton Town and continued 'The Linnets' nickname. In the case of Lymington the nickname may have been encouraged as a slight pun on the place-name; W1990–98 for Lymington; W1999–2007 for the merged club; for New Milton see below. See also Town.

☻ Market Harborough Town F.C., recorded in the club history, Twydell 1988. The Leicestershire club ran from 1875 to 1947. Twydell states (p. 226) "They had adopted the nickname of 'The Linnets' [by c.1913], and were certainly 'on song' in the Final of the ... Charity Cup". See also Huntsmen.

☻ New Milton Town F.C., formed in Hampshire in the 1998 merger of Lymington Town and New Milton, the merged club then renamed in 2007 to N.M.T. 'The Linnets' nickname runs from the old New Milton to the new but it is not recorded for the old club in Williams; W2010–13.

☻ Runcorn Linnets F.C., founded in Cheshire in 2002 after the closure of Runcorn (1918–2001), as Runcorn F.C. Halton, renaming as Runcorn Linnets in 2006. The earlier clubs were nicknamed 'The Linnets' (W1979/80–2005). Pickering 1994 states that in this case the nickname is because the birds were often seen in the vicinity of the club ground; W2010–13. See also Corn.

Linos is an occasional unofficial nickname for Staines Town F.C. It derives from the association between the town and linoleum. The Linoleum Manufacturing Company was set up here in 1864 and 'Staines Lino' became world-famous before the factory closed in 1970. The factory had its own club as well, so the nickname is part transfer, part association, and perhaps part media search for colourful language; Wikipedia. See also Leghorns, Massive, Old Lagonda, Swans, Town.

Lionesses is the nickname for Millwall Lionesses L.F.C., one of the earliest women's football clubs, founded in 1972. The club is affiliated to Millwall F.C., and uses the female form of Millwall's Lions nickname; Wikipedia.

Lions is a nickname for several clubs, and a natural symbol for an English or Scottish club, as the lion is a national symbol in both countries. As 'king of the jungle', there need, perhaps, be no particular reason why the lion should be adopted as a nickname, but in many cases there is the suggestion of a reason. The examples are:

- Albion Sports F.C., founded in Bradford, West Yorkshire, in 1974; the club has a roaring lion's head on its badge, and the 'British lion' perhaps reflects the choice of 'Albion' as the official name; W2012–13.

- Andover F.C., founded in Hampshire in 1883, folded in 2011. The club sported a lion on its badge since the 1950s. The red lion mirrors that in the town coat of arms, based on a seventeenth-century seal of the town, and which was ultimately taken from the heraldry of Viscount Andover; recorded in W1979/80–2011. A new club, Andover Lions F.C., preserves the nickname.

- Aston Villa F.C., founded in Birmingham in 1874. The Lions nickname is based on the club's crest which has a heraldic lion rampant; Wikipedia. See also Claret and Blues, Perry Bar Pets, Seals, Villa / Villans / Villains.

- Benfield Park F.C., see under Newcastle Benfield, below.

- Blakenall F.C., founded in the West Midlands in 1946. The club used to play at the Red Lion ground in Somerfield Road, Leamore; recorded in W1995–7. The club disappeared in a merger with Bloxwich Town in 2001. See also Nall.

- Bookham F.C., founded in Great Bookham in Surrey in 1921. The reason for the nickname unknown, but the club has a lion on its badge. Before 1914 the club was known as the Bookham Blues; Wikipedia.

- Brierley Hill Alliance F.C., founded in West Midlands in 1887 in a merger between Brockmoor Harriers and Brockmoor Pickwicks, folded 1981; in 1993 Oldswinford F.C. (1955) renamed as Brierley Hill Town, renaming again as Brierley and Hagley Alliance in 2001 and took the Lions nickname; the club made a final merger with Withymoor Colts and renamed as B.H. & Withymoor in 2007 before folding in 2008; recorded in Avis 1966–70 and W1979/80–80/81 for the older club; W1994–2005. The nickname is strongly suggested by the middle sound of 'Alliance'. See also Swinford.

- Croydon Munipical F.C., founded in London in 2009 with reserve players from Croydon F.C., closed in 2010; W2010.

- Flixton F.C., founded in Greater Manchester in 1960; the nickname is given in the Wikipedia article on the club. The club badge is an impressive lion rampant in blue but it is not clear if the badge is the source of the nickname. Since 2004 the Williams directories have given 'Valiants' as the nickname, after the Valley Road ground, and the association between lions and valiance may have led to 'Lions' being adopted, or 'Valiants' may even have started as a play on 'Valley Lions'. See also Flixs, Valley Roaders, Valiants.

- Guiseley A.F.C. Founded in 1909, the lion nickname seems to have no specific explanation; the nickname appears late in Williams, W2011–13, but W1998 reproduced a programme which displayed the nickname in 1997.

- Heanor Town F.C., founded in Derbyshire in 1883; a red lion appears on the club badge but the source of the nickname does not appear to be local heraldry. The town has long had a Red Lion pub, but this may be coincidence; W1979/80–6, W2001–5, W2013.

☺ Livingston F.C., founded in 1943, originally as Ferranti Thistle, a works side for the Edinburgh electrical engineering firm. The club transferred to the Livingston new town in 1995. A variant form is 'The Livi Lions' (see under Livi). The reason for the Lions nickname is not known; it is just possible it is based on the opening and closing letters of the place-name, but a heraldic lion is one of the Scottish national symbols, so no special explanation need be necessary. Lions is recorded as the only nickname in RS since 1998. The supporters have their own side, which is called Olympique Lions F.C. See also Livi, Thistle, Wee Jags.

☺ London Maccabi Lions, founded in 1995. The Barnet side was originally named MALEX F.C., from the Maccabi Association London, and adopted the current name in 1999. There seems no particular reason for the lion association other than the qualities of the beast, reflected in the proud lion on the badge of the club; Wikipedia.

☺ Louth United F.C., founded in Lincolnshire in 1947, folded in 2007. The reason for the nickname is not known, but it may have been suggested by letters in the official name: L'un. Miller & Wright 1996, W1997–2004.

☺ Marchwiel Villa F.C., founded in 1984 in Wrexham. Recorded in RW 1994. The club merged with Overton in 1993 and took the nickname to the new club (see below).

☺ Millwall F.C., apparently because they were referred to as 'The Lions' during their heroic 1900 F.A. Cup campaign, though other, uncovincing explanations have been suggested. The 1933 Ogden card says that it derives from the club's lion crest; the 1936 Thomson 'stamp' album, Churchill 1958, 1959 (Sweetule) and Jeffrey 1961 suggest it is a pun on the name of the ground, The Den; but both badge and ground must have followed the nickname. Delahunty 2003, uniquely, suggests that it derives from the lion on the Scottish royal standard, because many of the early players were Scottish, but the traditional idea that it simply refers to the club's prowess in 1900 seems clear enough. Recorded in G1956–76, Richards 1960, SWSCYB 1962–3, Avis 1954–70, and throughout RY and SSY from RY1970/1 to SSY2012/13. The 1970–1 Vernon pamphlet offers the following story: "... a Cockney docker with an extremely loud voice who used to attend the matches in the early days. Whenever Millwall was putting on the pressure, he could be heard shouting, 'Come on, Millwall—eat 'em'. One day another fan got annoyed by this and shouted 'Keep quiet—they're not lions'. But the crowd disagreed..." Earlier, their nickname was The Dockers, but they had to leave their Isle of Dogs home in 1901. In 1910 the club moved to a new purpose-built ground in New Cross which they called The Den at the outset (confirming that by then they had accepted the new nickname). In 1956 the badge took the form of two lions rampant but since 1979 it has featured a single roaring leaping lion. The club's mascot is Zampa the Lion, named from Zampa Road on which the home stadium, The New Den sits. It may be a pure coincidence, but both dragons and lions live in dens, and businessman Theo Paphitis (he of the BBC's *Dragons' Den*) is now chairman of the club. See also Dockers, Lions, Spanners.

☺ Newcastle Benfield F.C., founded in 1988, originally as Brunswick Village F.C. and going through some name changes and a merger with North Shields St Columbas before settling on the present name in 2007. The club's impressive coat of arms has lion supporters but there seems no specific reason for the adoption of the nickname, other than association with the proud lion characteristics. A programme reproduced in W2005 (p.576) records the club as Newcastle Benfield Saints. Presumably 'Saints' was used as a nickname at the time; W2008–13; AFBC (for Benfield Park). See also Saints.

☺ Overton Marchwiel F.C., founded in 1993 in Clwyd, in a union of M. Villa and O. Athletic. The reason is unknown but the nickname came from M. Villa. Recorded in RW1995. In 1998 Overton Recreational F.C. was founded as a successor. See also O's.

☺ Pagham F.C., founded in Sussex in 1903. The town has a pub called 'The Lion', immediately opposite the club ground on Nyetimber Lane, though it is not clear if that is the specific reason for the nickname; W1995–2013.

☺ Penrhyncoch F.C., founded in Ceredigion in 1965. The nickname refers to the club badge, the 'Black Lion of Gogerddan', adapted from the heraldry of local aristocracy and also referred to in local hotel and pub names. The nickname was reported by Richard Huws, who found it in match reports of the 1990s in the *Montgomeryshire County Times*. See also Penrhyn, Roosters.

☺ Wembley F.C., founded in 1946. The club is based in the vicinity of the famous national stadium at Wembley, and adopted the lion as both a nickname and a badge because it is the national symbol of England. The animal is also in the coat of arms of the old Borough of Wembley, and the club colours are also the nationalistic red and white of England; W1982/3–2013.

Lisbon Lions was a nickname for the successful side of Celtic F.C. when they won the European cup at Lisbon, Portugal, on 25 May 1967. Recorded in Pickering 1994. See also Bhoys, Celts, Hoops, Quality Street Kids, 'Tic, Tims.

Little Brazil is a nickname for Clydebank Rovers F.C., formed in 2004, near Glasgow, as a breakaway from Clydebank United. The club plays in yellow and blue colours, like the Brazilian national side; Wikipedia. See also Rovers.

Little Celts was a nickname for Farsley Celtic F.C., founded in West Yorkshire in 1908, refounded in 2010 as Farsley A.F.C.. Despite the Celtic association, the Farsley sides played and play in all-blue colours, though this nickname clearly contrasts with the mighty Glasgow side; SSY2008/9. See also Celts, Village Lads, Villagers.

Little Club on the Hill is an unofficial nickname for Forest Green Rovers F.C., founded in 1890, whose first ground, The Lawn, was at the top of a steep hill in the tiny hamlet of Forest Green in Gloucestershire; Wikipedia. See also FGR, Green,

Green Army, Lawnmowers, Rovers.

Livi is the main nickname of two clubs in Livingston, West Lothian. The clubs are:

⊛ Livingston F.C., founded in 1943, originally as Ferranti Thistle, a works side for the Edinburgh electrical engineering firm. The club transferred to the Livingston new town in 1995, from which the nickname comes. This club seems to prefer the form 'Livy Lions', which is used in RY1997/8–2000/1 (as 'Livvy Lions') and through RY2001/2–SSY2012/13 (as 'Livy Lions'). See also Lions, Thistle, Wee Jags.

⊛ Livingston United F.C., founded in 1970. The nickname is rare, but has been used by journalists in match reports (e.g. 18 May 2012), SFHA records 'Livvy' for a club of this name founded in 1934. See also New Towners.

Lizards is the nickname of Lliswerry Athletic F.C., founded in the city of Newport in 1926, reformed 1977. The nickname is adapted from the first syllable of the place-name and is printed in the February 2013 editon of *Welsh Football*; Huws 2013.

Llanbêr is a nickname of Llanberis F.C., founded in Gwynedd in 1890; as a short form of the place-name, also used as a nickname for the place, and recorded on the club's own website. See also Blac and Amber, Darans, Loco / Locomotives, Teigars.

Llani Ladies is the nickname of Llanidloes Ladies F.C., founded in Powys in 2000. The club is an independent women's club and has a nickname which adapts a friendly short form of the place-name. There is a reserve side, Llani Reserves; Wikipedia.

Llay is the current nickname of Llay Welfare F.C., founded near Wrexham in 1930 and originally called Llay Miners Welfare F.C.; recorded in RW2011. See also Welfare.

Lobsters is the nickname of Redhill F.C., founded in 1894. The Surrey place-name would naturally lead to the use of red colours, which the club has always worn, usually in red-and-white stripes. The nickname is the result of a competition in 1994. It re-uses, however, an older nickname which is recorded in the 1928 club handbook. The club tradition is that a more lobster-like pink colouring appeared in the shirts and shorts after they had been washed several times, colour-fast dyes not being as developed a hundred years ago as they are today; W1995–2013. See also Reds.

Loc's / Locies / Locos are variant forms of the nickname for the Inverurie Loco Works F.C., founded in Aberdeenshire in 1903. The club was originally a works side for the Great North of Scotland Railway Co. works in Inverurie, but these closed in 1969. The nickname is more of a friendly short form of the word in the official name, rather than being a direct equivalent of English clubs nicknamed 'Locomotives' or 'Railwaymen'. Recorded in RS 2003–12 and SFHA as Locos; Wikipedia has Loc's and Locies.

Locals was a nickname for Rossington F.C., founded in South Yorkshire in 1990, in a merger between Station F.C. (1973) and Haslam Sports. The nickname certainly implies local pride, and possibly was meant to suggest that the club was more representative of the locality than the neighbouring colliery club, Rossington Main (see 'Colliery'), but the two clubs merged in 1998; W1994–6.

Lochgelly Sodgers was the nickname of Lochgelly DDSS F.C., founded in Fife in 1919, closed in 1920. The club was a temporary one for 'Discharged and Demobilised Soldiers and Sailors' and the nickname takes the old Scots word for 'soldiers', known also as a nickname for the Third Lanark club; SFHA.

Lockmen is a nickname for Willenhall Town F.C., founded in 1953 in a merger between Aston Road Villa and R.A.F. Association. The West Midlands town is historically famous for the manufacture of locks and keys (no fewer than 148 locksmiths were there in 1770). There is a lock museum in the town, and keys are on the club and town badge; W2008–13. See also Reds.

Loco / Locomotives were nicknames of Llanberis F.C., founded in Gwynedd in 1890. The club was renamed Clwb Pêl-Droed Locomotive Llanberis at the time of a sponsorship by the Snowdon Mountain Railway between 1980 and 2004, and the nicknames belong to this period though they may still appear in football literature and journalism. Both forms are recorded on the club's own website. See also Beris, Blac and Amber, Darans, Llanbêr, Teigars.

Locomotives is a nickname for Harrogate Railway Athletic F.C., founded in 1935 as a works side for the Starbreck LNER Locomotive Shed; Wikipedia. See also Rail.

Locos was a nickname for Horwich R.M.I. F.C., founded in Lancashire in 1896. The club was originally a works side, the initials standing for Railway Mechanics Institute. The nickname is so recorded in Dobson 1973. See also Leythers, Locos, Railwaymen.

Lodge is the nickname of Morpeth Riverside Lodge F.C., based in Northumberland at the Riverside Lodge public house.

Lo'hore is the nickname of Lochore Welfare Junior Football and Athletic Club, founded in Crosshill, Fife in 1934; a short form of the name. The club was founded as a miners' side and originally had the word 'Miners' in its name; SFHA.

'Lok is the nickname of Pollok F.C., founded in Newlands, Glasgow, in 1908; a short form of the place-name; W1982/3, SFHA.

Loons is the nickname for Forfar Athletic F.C., founded in 1885. The nickname uses the Aberdeenshire and Banffshire word for young men, or lads, and also refers to the origins of the club as a secondary, younger side of Angus Athletic, from which the Loons broke loose to form their own club in 1885. Simon Taylor confirms that this is one of the defining words for identifying texts in this dialect, along with the expression 'Fit like?', for 'How's it going?' Recorded in AA 1960, G1976, RY1972/3–83/4 and through RY1993/4–SSY2012/13, RS1993–2012, SFHA. See also Sky Blues.

Lootown is a derogatory unofficial nickname for Luton Town F.C., recorded on the Football Fans Census website for 2003 from the perspective of Watford supporters. The nickname merely puns on the sound of the place-name, using the colloquial expression for a toilet. See also Hatters, Lilywhites, Lutonians, Reds, Straw-Hatters

/ Straw-Plaiters.

Lords is the nickname of Lordswood F.C., founded in Chatham, Kent, in 1968. A short form of the place-name, in W1998–2013.

Lords of the Lake, see Lakesiders.

LOSC was the nickname for the Left Overs Sports Club F.C., founded in East Grinstead, Sussex, in 1967; presumably it was a club formed from reserve players, though 'Remnants' has also appeared in football, for a club formed by former school boys. The initialism is recorded in W1988–90.

Lowfielders is a nickname for Hoddesdon Town F.C., founded in Hertfordshire in 1879; the nickname is based on the ground name, Lowfield; W1994–2001. See also Lilywhites.

Loyals is one of the nicknames for Worcester City F.C., founded in 1902, which records their association with King Charles I. The city was the location of the last battle in the English Civil War in 1651. The city helped the king escape. He was captured elsewhere, but Worcester was nicknamed *Fidelis Civitas*, the faithful city, for staying loyal; Wikipedia. See also Blues, City, Dragons, Faithfuls, Royals.

Lucky Arsenal was a nickname for Arsenal F.C., during their spectacular years in the 1930s under the managership of Herbert Chapman (1925–34). Tragically, Chapman died of pneumonia while in office. Recorded in Pickering 1994. See also Boring Arsenal, France, Gooners, Gunners, Invincibles, Reds, Royals, Woolwich.

Luffs is the nickname for Loughborough F.C., founded in Leicestershire in 2001, when a club called L. Athletic changed its name (FCHD). The nickname is based on the pronunciation of the first element in the place-name and is recorded on the club badge, illustrated in AFBC.

Lukes is a nickname for Cradley Town F.C., founded in 1970, originally as Albion Haden United, in a merger between H. Rangers and A. Rovers. The club changed to the present name in 1975. St Luke is the dedication of the Anglican parish church in this West Midlands town; W1994–2004 and AFBC (where the badge claims an early foundation, 1948). See also Hammers.

Lurgan Blues is the nickname of Glenavon F.C., founded at Lurgan in Co. Armagh in 1889. The club plays in blue shirts and white shorts; RI1997, RNI2007.

Lutonians was an early nickname for Luton Town F.C. The nickname is recorded in *Luton News* on December 31st, 1908 (thanks to Howard Chandler) and also in BoF1905–6. See also Hatters, Lilywhites, Lootown, Reds, Straw-Hatters / Straw-Plaiters.

Mackems is an unofficial nickname for Sunderland A.F.C., copying a nickname for the people of Sunderland. The word is considered to derive from the verb 'to make' (which in Sunderland is pronounced 'mack'). The OED only dates it from 1980–1, in a Newcastle United fanzine, but other sources give the apparent earliest record as 1973 in a phrase "we still tak 'em and mak 'em". The most accepted theory is that it refers to Tyneside and Wearside shipyard workers in the nineteenth century, where the 'Mackems' would 'make' the ship and the Geordies would 'take' them for fitting out, but this may be an entirely false etymology. A different idea comes from Teesside, where the brewers Vaux made a bottled beer called Double Maxim, and Sunderlanders would pronounce this as 'Mackem' when ordering one. This is highly implausible, but not impossible. Anyway, the term has come to represent anyone from Sunderland, and so became an unofficial nickname for the club. The earliest use of it as a club nickname by the club itself appears to be in the fanzine *A Love Supreme* in 1989; Wikipedia. See also Bank of England Club, Black Cats, Lads, Light Brigade, Miners, Rokerites / Rokermen, Sols, Sund-Ireland, Team of All the Talents, Wearsiders.

Mackerel Men is the nickname for New Quay F.C., founded in Ceredigion at an uncertain date, but references on the internet appear from 1982. The nickname is used for the club on the Llanboidy F.C. website, for a match report from 13 March 2010, and it refers to a traditional industry in this seaside town; Huws 2013.

Mad Lions is a nickname for the Sark National Football Team. The semi-independent island in the Channel Islands has only six hundred inhabitants but heroically assembled a team to play against other island nations in the international Island Games in 2003. The team played four times, scored no goals but had 70 scored against them. The nickname puns on the team's performance and the use of the lion as a national symbol in neighbouring Guernsey (see Green Lions for Guernsey); the nickname first appears as 'Bad Lions' but has now changed to 'Mad Lions' on Wikipedia. See also Bad Lions, Wasps.

Maes y Dre is recorded as a nickname for Welshpool Town F.C., founded in Powys in 1878, in RW1994–2000/1. Despite its long-term repetition, the nickname is an error: the ground name is Maesydre and this simply means 'town field' in Welsh. See also Lilywhites, Seasiders.

Maesy is a nickname for Maesycwmmer F.C., founded in Caerphilly Co. Bor. in 2010. The nickname is a general one for the town, and is used on the club's own website. See also Druids.

Magic Mons / Mons are nicknames for Monaghan United F.C., founded in Co. Monaghan in 1979; a short form of the place-name. The club withdrew from the Irish Premier League in 2012 but survives; RI2006, as 'The Mons'; Wikipedia and an enamel badge in AFBC has 'Magic Mons'. See also Trojans.

Maglonians is the nickname of Machynlleth Town F.C., founded in Powys in 1885. The nickname appears in the title to David W. Davies's 1985 history of the club: *The Maglonians: One Hundred Years of Football in Machynlleth, 1885–1985* and also appears in RW1994. The nickname arises from the long-standing, but mistaken, belief that the Roman fort of *Maglona* was at Machynlleth and that this name lies behind the modern place-name. The fort is unidentified but may have been at Carlisle (Rivet and Smith 1979), and the Welsh place-name is unrelated, meaning 'the plain of Cynllaith' (Owen and Morgan 2007).

Magnets has been a nickname for two clubs, probably from association with magnet industries. The clubs are:

☺ Havant and Waterlooville F.C., founded in a merger in 1998, recorded only in W2000. The local economy does feature a major electromagnet maufacturer, Tesla Engineering Ltd., so the nickname may have been the result of a sponsorship deal, though this is not recorded elsewhere. By 2001 the club had settled on the nickname 'Hawks'. See also Borough, Hawks, Ville.

☺ Ripon City Magnets A.F.C., founded in North Yorkshire in 1919 in a merger of R. United and R. City, the club merged with a local works side R. Yorkshire Magnets in 1990 and added Magnets to its official name in 1991. Magnets appears as a nickname for the club on the Pyramid Passion website, but the club's own website now refers to the club as 'Ripon City A.F.C.'

Magpies is a common nickname for clubs who play in black-and-white striped shirts, often with black-and-white shorts and socks also. The nickname was made famous and influential by its use for Notts County and Newcastle United. In Europe, such design usually carries the nickname 'Zebras' (q.v.); other variants for the same strip design are Badgers, Barcodes, Humbugs, Penguins and Skunks. The magpie is a handsome black-and-white bird, though it is not actually striped. Examples are:

☺ Alresford Town F.C., founded in Hampshire in 1898, reformed 1987; black-and-white stripes; Wikipedia.

☺ Amersham Town F.C., founded in Buckinghamshire in 1890; black-and-white stripes; W1994–2003.

☺ Barmouth and Dyffryn United F.C., founded in 1864 in a merger between B. F.C. and Duffryn Ardudwy. The club plays in the tradional 'magpie' kit of black-and-white stripes with black shorts; recorded in RW2011.

☺ Bow Street F.C., founded in Ceredigion in about 1920; recorded in RW2011 and on a badge in AFBC. Traditionally, the team played in black-and-white stripes with black shorts but have recently played in red and white; the club's home ground is called *Cae Piod*, using the Welsh word for magpies. See also Piod.

☺ Brimsdown Rovers F.C., founded in Middlesex in 1947; the club was formed by a group of exiled Geordies from Newcastle, who adopted a Newcastle-like strip and the same nickname, recorded in Miller and Wright 1996. In 2010 the club was absorbed by Enfield 1893 (The E's).

☺ Chester F.C, temporarily between 1920 and 1930 when they wore a black-and-white striped shirt, changing to blue-and-white stripes in 1930 (see Historical Football Kits website). See also Blues, Cestrians, City, Ivies, Seals.

☺ Chipping Norton Town F.C., founded in Oxfordshire in 1893, black-and-white stripes; W1979/80, W1983/4 and W1987–93, W2002–7. See also Chippy.

☺ Chorley F.C., founded in Lancashire in 1875. The nickname is recorded in the title of an early club history by T. C. Gillet: *Magpie Parade* (1946); also Avis 1966–70, W1979/80–2013; black-and-white stripes. Dobson 1973 adds that 'Chorley

'Magpies' is also now used as a general nickname for people from Chorley.

۞ Colney Heath F.C., founded in Hertfordshire in 1907, for their black-and-white stripes with black shorts and socks; W1993–5, W2010–13.

۞ Dereham Town F.C., founded in Norfolk in 1884. The team plays in black-and-white stripes with black shorts and socks. W2001–13.

۞ Dorchester Town F.C. Founded in Dorset in 1880, the club has nearly always played in black-and-white and usually in stripes; recorded in Avis 1966–70, W1979/80–2013.

۞ Hanwell Town F.C., founded in 1920 in the London borough of Ealing. The club adopted black-and-white stripes like the strip of Newcastle United, and were originally formed by a group of men from Newcastle; W2007–13. See also Geordies, Town.

۞ Holsworthy A.F.C., founded in Devon in 1891; black-and-white stripes; W1992–2010.

۞ Long Sutton Athletic F.C., founded in Lincolnshire in 1983 (though there was an earlier Long Sutton Town); black-and-white stripes, and a handsome magpie on the club badge; W1992–5.

۞ Loxwood F.C., founded in 1920. The Sussex side plays in the usual black-and-white stripes with black shorts and socks; Wikipedia.

۞ Maidenhead United F.C., founded in Berkshire in 1870, in a merger of M. Town with M. Norfolkians in 1919, renaming as United in 1920 and adopting the black-and-white strip at the same time. A handsome magpie appears on the club badge; W1980/1–2013. See also Tanners, United.

۞ Newcastle United F.C., founded in 1892; the club adopted the striped shirts in 1894. The nickname is recorded on the 1933 Ogden and 1959 Sweetule cards, and in Avis 1954–70, G1956–76, Churchill 1958, Norris 1959, Richards 1960, SWSCYB 1962–3, and throughout RY1970/1 to SSY2012/13. The magpie featured on the crest of the club from 1976 to 1988. The word 'United' in the name commemorates the merger of two teams to form the club in 1892: Newcastle East End (1881) and Newcastle West End (1882). See also Barcodes, Cartoon Army, Entertainers, Frenchcastle, Geordies, Skunks, Toon, Tyneside Professors, Tynesiders.

۞ Notts County F.C. Founded in 1862, the first nickname was The Lambs (q.v.), but in 1890 they adopted the black-and-white strip which they still use, and the Magpie nickname soon followed. It is recorded as the main official nickname on the 1933 Ogden cigarette card, and in the 1936 Thomson 'stamp' album; Avis 1954–70, Norris 1959, SWSCYB 1962–3, G1976 and throughout RY1970/1–SSY2012/13. See also County, Lambs.

۞ Pembroke Borough F.C., founded in 1906, originally as Dock Stars F.C., for the dock industries of this locality; recorded in Avis 1966–70, RW 1994–5. Black, white and blue shirts and black shorts. The club left the Welsh league in 1995

(FCHD). See also Borough, Stars.

☺ Penzance A.F.C., founded in Cornwall in 1888, black-and-white stripes. Recorded in Avis 1966–70; W1992–2005 and W2010–13.

☺ Sholing Sports F.C. Founded as Sholing Athletic in Southampton in 1894, reformed after the War as S. Sports, which folded in 1994 and was revived as the modern club in 2005, the club played in black-and-white stripes, but also folded in 2011; Wikipedia.

☺ Snowdown Colliery Welfare F.C., founded in Kent in 1907, the club plays in black-and-white stripes; W1983/4–5.

☺ Stonehouse Town F.C., founded in Gloucestershire in 1898, they were also known as S. Freeway till 2007. The club plays in black-and-white stripes at The Magpies Ground; W1979/80.

☺ Torquay United F.C., between 1921 and 1954, when they wore a black-and-white strip. Recorded in Adrian 1943, Avis 1954–70. See also Gulls.

☺ Wakehurst F.C., founded in Ballymena, Co. Antrim in 1969. The club plays in black-and-white stripes with black shorts and socks; Wikipedia.

☺ Wimborne Town F.C., founded in Dorset in 1878. The club plays in black-and-white stripes and have a magpie on their badge; W1982/3, W1987–8 and W1994–2013.

☺ Woodbridge Athletic F.C., founded in Suffolk in 1995. The club plays in black-and-white stripes. The nickname appears on a badge illustrated in AFBC.

Main is the nickname of at least two Yorkshire colliery sides. The word is often used in the north of England, and Scotland, for the dominant seam of a colliery, often appearing in the colliery official name, and here transferred from that to the football club and nickname. The clubs are:

☺ Hatfield Main F.C., founded in South Yorkshire in 1936. The Hatfield Main Colliery Company was formed in 1910 and the site still produces; W1994–2003.

☺ Yorkshire Main Colliery F.C., founded in the 1920s at Edlington, South Yorkshire. The club was originally called Edlington Rangers, renamed in 1979. The mine was closed in 1985 but the club thrives. The word is used as a nickname in W1983/4–6.

Mallards is a nickname for Ballinamallard United F.C., founded in Co. Fermanagh in 1975. The place-name is *Béal Átha na Mallacht* in Irish, meaning 'Ford mouth of the Curses' (Flanagan & Flanagan 1994), but the spelling and pronunciation have shifted to the present form under English influence, and both alternative nicknames reflect the suggested incorrect meaning. Recorded in RI1997, RNI2007. See also Blues, Ducks.

Man City / Man U are unofficial nicknames for these mighty Manchester clubs, as short forms of the official names, frequently used in journalism and conversation. For City, see also see also Bitters / Bitter Blues, Blues, Citizens, City, Council Housers, Massives, Sheik City, Stockports. For United, see also Busby Babes, Fergie's

Fledglings, Heathens, Manure, Munichs, Outcasts, Red Devils, Reds, United.

Mangos is a nickname for Mangotsfield United F.C., founded in Gloucestershire in 1951. The nickname is a pluralised short form of the place-name, but chimes well with the delicious fruit; Wikipedia. See also Field.

Manor is a nickname for clubs with the element 'manor' in their place-name. The clubs are:

- Eton Manor F.C., founded in Essex in 1901; W1989–2013. The club's suffix has inspired the use of it by Southend Manor (see below). See also Braves.
- Ruislip Manor F.C., founded in London in 1938, renaming as Tokyngton Manor (see below) in 2008. Recorded in W1979/80–2009.
- Southend Manor F.C., founded in 1955. The Manor suffix is not original to Southend but was taken from the name of the Eton Manor club (see above), for whom the founder Gil Metcalf used to play; W1987–2013.
- Tokyngton Manor F.C., founded in London in 1938, originally as Ruislip Manor, then changing name in 2008; Wikipedia.

Manure is an unofficial and insulting nickname for Manchester United F.C., from the perspective of Liverpool supporters, as recorded on the 2003 Football Fans Census website. The nickname plays on the sound of 'Man U', to suggest the well-known word for animal excrement when it is used as farming fertiliser. See also Busby Babes, Coach-Builders, Fergie's Fledglings, Heathens, Man, Munichs, Outcasts, Red Devils, Reds, United.

Marigolds is the nickname of Littlehampton Town F.C., founded in 1896. The Sussex side plays in yellow shirts and socks, with black shorts, marigold being an alternative word for yellow, from the yellow plant of this name; W1983/4–2009. In W2013 appeared the shorter form 'Golds'.

Marine is the nickname of Swindon Supermarine F.C., founded in Wiltshire in 1992 in a merger between Supermarine F.C. (1946) and Swindon Athletic F.C. (formerly Penhill, 1970); the nickname and suffix come from the Swindon factory of the Supermarine Aircraft Co. (part of Vickers Armstrong since 1928), which originally made seaplanes (hence 'Super-marine', over the sea) and then the famous Spitfire aircraft. 'Supermarine' is also the name of the town's rugby club. The nickname is recorded in W1988–90 for Supermarine, and in W2001–13 for the present club. For Swindon Athletic, see Hill Club, PYC.

Mariners is a nickname for clubs in coastal towns with a sea-faring tradition. Examples are:

- Camelon Juniors F.C., founded near Falkirk in 1920. The club is actually based inland, but at the location of a major flight of locks joining the Union Canal with the Forth and Clyde Canal, which was replaced in 2002 by a rotating boat lift. The club has a splendid badge showing an ancient ship; Wikipedia, SFHA.
- Grimsby Town F.C. Founded in North Lincolnshire in 1878, the club was originally nicknamed The Fishermen. Grimsby is one of the leading bases for North Sea

trawling, and the industry is further recorded with images of a trawler and fish on the club's badge. The mascot is currently one Mighty Mariner, who recently had a companion called Mini Mariner, and who succeeded a retired famous mascot called Harry Haddock. Recorded in G1956–76, Churchill 1958, Harvey 1959, Richards 1960, AA 1960, Avis 1966–70; and throughout RY and SSY1970/1–2012/13 (with the exception of the mistake of 'Marines' in RY1971/2), and W2011–13. See also Fishermen.

☻ Liverpool F.C., from the city's great importance as one of the leading ports of England. The nickname is recorded on the 1933 Ogden card set. See also Anfielders, Culture Club, Kop / Kopites, Liddellpool, Merseysiders, Micky Mousers, Pool, Reds, Spice Boys.

☻ Marine A.F.C. Founded in 1894, the club is based on the coast at Crosby, Merseyside, but the nickname seems to pun with the club name rather than expressing seafaring. Recorded in Avis 1966–70 (as 'Mariners or Lilywhites'); W1979/80 as 'The Marines or Lilywhites' but this variant appears to be a one-off typing error: Mariners appears in W1980/1–90 and W1993–2013. David Wotherspoon's 1997 club history is called *The Mighty Mariners*. See also Lilywhites.

☻ South Shields F.C. The current version of this Co. Durham club was formed in 1974 but there are predecessors back to 1889, one of which was South Shields Adelaide (1899–1905), nicknamed the Laides (q.v.), which was taken over by Gateshead. An earlier club of the same name played from 1936 to 1974 and was also nicknamed The Mariners. The nickname honours the industrial port of South Shields; the club badge displays both a boat and an anchor. Recorded for the two recent clubs in Avis 1966–70, Barton 1984 & 1985, W1982/3–6 and W1994–2013.

Marines was the nickname and part-official name for Royal Marines A.F.C., founded in 2008 and based at Lympstone near Exmouth, Devon; the club folded in 2012; Wikipedia. 'Marines' appears once, probably in error, as a nickname for Marine F.C., normally The Mariners, q.v. and also once, in error, for Grimsby Town, also normally called The Mariners. See also Commandos.

Mark is the nickname of Craigmark Burntonians F.C., founded in 1946 in Dalmellington, Ayrshire; a short form of the place-name; Wikipedia.

Marketmen is the nickname for Needham Market F.C., founded in Suffolk in 1919, adapted from the place-name; Wikipedia and W2013.

Maroon Army is a nickname for Galway United F.C., founded in 1937. The club plays in maroon shirts with white shorts, and the same two colours are also used on the city's flag; Wikipedia. See also Tribesmen / Tribal Army.

Maroons is a nickname for clubs which play in this colour. The examples are:

☻ Heart of Midlothian F.C., founded in Edinburgh in 1874, from the club colours of maroon and white which they have worn since 1877 (this is the earliest nickname for the club). Recorded in SWSCYB 1962–3 and on the 1986 Panini sticker. See also Edinboro Darlings, Famous, Hearts, Jam Tarts, Jambos, Jammies, Maroons.

☻ Keith F.C., founded in Banffshire in 1919, who play in maroon shirts and shorts. Recorded in W1982/3, RS 1993–2012, SFHA.

☻ Whithorn A.F.C., founded in Dumfries and Galloway in 2000. The nickname appears on a club badge recorded in AFBC.

Martyrs is the nickname of Merthyr Town F.C., founded in 2010 as a successor to M. Town A.F.C. (1909–34) and Merthyr Tydfil F.C. (1945–2010). The previous teams also took the nickname, which is a translation of the Welsh place-name *Merthyr*, meaning 'martyr' or 'saint's resting place'. The club badge is the same as that of the borough council and shows the martyred St Tydfil. The club plays in the English leagues. Recorded in Moss 1983, RW 1994–8, W1980/1–2010, W2012–13 and on several badges in AFBC. See also Red and Greens, Romans.

Massive is the official nickname for supporters of Staines Town F.C. (Surrey, 1892) The club and fans were made famous by the fictional comic character Ali G., and the word reflects his language. It carries the same sense of overwhelming support that the more common word 'army' has. See also Leghorns, Linos, Old Lagonda, Swans, Town.

Massives is an unofficial nickname for Manchester City F.C., coined by Manchester United Supporters, in sarcastic mockery for an allegedly smaller fan base; recorded on the 2003 Football Fans Census website. See also Bitters / Bitter Blues, Blues, Citizens, City, Council Housers, Man, Sheik City, Stockports.

Mavericks is the nickname for Worthing United F.C., founded in Sussex in 1988. The nickname seems to chime with that of the other Worthing club, The Rebels (q.v.), in that it also suggests a club which goes against the norm. Worthing is an affluent conservative town, so perhaps both clubs adopted these nicknames to suggest 'something different', and in contrast to the sense of 'worthy' suggested by the place-name; Wikipedia. See also United.

Maze is a nickname for Lower Maze F.C., founded in Maze, Co. Down in 1960, as a short form of the place-name (which means 'Plain', Flanagan & Flanagan 1994); Wikipedia. See also Black and Red Army, Mills.

Mead is the nickname for Thamesmead Town F.C., formed in London in 1969. The 'Town' suffix was added in 1985. The club mascot is one Tommy the Thamesmead Toad; W1992–2013. The nickname is in the singular, a short form of the official name, but Miller & Wright 1996 list it as 'The Meads'.

Meadow Men is the nickname of Bridgnorth Town F.C., founded in Shropshire in 1949. The club plays at the Crown Meadow Ground; Wikipedia. See also Town.

Mechanics is the nickname of Washington F.C., founded in Co. Durham in 1947, originally as the Washington Colliery Mechanics F.C. The present name came in 1965. The club was briefly renamed Washington Ikeda Hoover F.C. in 1999–2003. Barton records the nickname in 1984 & 1985; W1982/3–2013.

Mechs / Mechanics is the nickname of A.F.C. Blackpool, founded in Lancashire in 1947, originally as Blackpool Metal Mechanics, a works side, changing to the present name only in 2008. 'The Mechanics' is also the name of the club's ground. Like 'The Tangerines', the club uses an orange strip. Recorded as 'Mechs' for A.F.C. in W2012–13, the same nickname for the older club in W1994–2008.

Medda is the nickname of Irvine Meadow XI F.C., founded in North Ayrshire in 1897 and based at Meadow Park; a friendly short form of 'Meadow'; Wikipedia. See also Dow.

Melton is the nickname for Mowbray Rangers F.C., founded in Melton Mowbray, Leicestershire, in 1983. The nickname takes the short form of the place-name, which is how the town is usually referred to locally; club website.

Men from the Kingdom is the main nickname for Fanad United F.C., founded in Co. Donegal in 1975. The nickname refers to a traditional expression for people from the peninsula of Fanad, the northernmost part of the island of Ireland, which in the eighth century was briefly a separate kingdom. The nickname appears on an enamel badge of the club (AFBC) and is used in local match reports (e.g. *Donegal Now*, 6.11.2011). See also United.

Mental Hospital used to be the nickname in the 1920s of St Francis Hospital F.C., based at the asylum in Haywards Heath, Sussex (1857–1995). The nickname is recorded on the club's own website. The club merged in 2002 with Ansty Rangers to form St Francis Rangers. See also Rangers, Saints.

Merry Millers / Millers is the nickname of Rotherham United F.C. Founded in a merger (hence United) in 1925, there was a long history of previous clubs behind the last two, dating back to the 1870s: Rotherham Casuals, R. County, R. Swifts, R. Town, Lunar Rovers (so named for playing by moonlight) and Thornhill. In 1907, Rotherham County took up residence at the Millmoor ground, from which the nickname comes, and this stadium was the home of the club until 2008. The nickname is recorded in G1956–76, Avis 1966–70 as 'Millers' and in Churchill 1958, Richards 1960 and throughout RY1970/1–SSY2012/13 as 'Merry Millers'. See also County.

Merry Stripes is the old nickname for Blackpool F.C. in the 1890s when they had a blue-and-white striped strip, before their adoption of the famous tangerine colours in 1923; Wikipedia. See also Atomic Boys, Donkey Lashers, 'Pool, Seasiders, Tangerines.

Merseysiders has been an alternative nickname for Everton F.C., from its location on Merseyside, recorded in Avis 1970. Johnston 1934, however, uses the nickname for Liverpool. For Everton, see also Bitters / Bitter Blues, Black Watch, Bluenoses, Blues, Dogs of War, Moonlight Dribblers, People's Club, School of Science, Toffees/Toffeemen. For Liverpool, see also Anfielders, Culture Club, Kop / Kopites, Liddellpool, Mariners, Micky Mousers, Pool, Reds, Spice Boys.

Messengers is a nickname for Rochdale Town F.C., founded in 1924, originally as a church side for the Catholic St Gabriel and the Angels in the town of Castleton. In 1990 they were renamed Castleton Gabriels, and then Rochdale Town in 2008.

The nickname refers to the traditional role of St Gabriel as the messenger of the Lord. In the New Testament he announces to Mary that she is with child; Wikipedia. See also Angles, Castlemen, Gabs, Garrison, Guardians.

Met is the main nickname for the Metropolitan Police F.C., founded in 1919. The nickname merely copies the traditional nickname for the Metropolitan Police Force, using the opening syllable of the first word; Wikipedia. See also Blues.

Methodists was used as an early nickname for Quorn F.C., founded in Leicestershire in 1924, originally as Quorn Methodists, changing name in 1952. The club today is nicknamed 'The Reds', but its badge shows a foxhunt in full swing, suggesting that it may occasionally have been called 'The Huntsmen', a nickname adopted by Market Harborough Town. See also Reds.

Micky Mousers is a derogatory unofficial nickname for Liverpool F.C., recorded on the Football Fans Census website for 2003, from the perspective of Manchester United supporters. The nickname is rhyming slang with Scousers, the traditional nickname for anyone from Liverpool (which inexplicably never seems to be used as a football club nickname). The stock character of American cartoon comedy, when used as an insult, usually connotes smallness and artificiality (neither of which are true for this great club). See also Anfielders, Culture Club, Kop / Kopites, Liddellpool, Mariners, Merseysiders, Pool, Reds, Spice Boys.

Mids is the nickname of Mid-Annandale F.C., founded in Lockerbie, Dumfries and Galloway, in 1959 (and a refoundation of earlier clubs with the same name, 1877–94, c.1919–26); a short form of the uncommon place-name prefix; Wikipedia, SFHA (for old and new clubs).

Mighty is a nickname of Beith Juniors F.C., founded in 1938 as a successor to Beith F.C., a mainstream Scottish senior side. The word is a standard expression of admiration for the club's achievements; club website. See also Cabes, Cabinet Makers.

Mighty Belfast Celtic was a nickname for Belfast Celtic F.C., founded in 1891, closed in 1949; Wikipedia. See also Celtic / Celts, Grand Old Team.

Mighty Blues is the nickname of Scissett A.F.C., founded in West Yorkshire in 1902, from their blue strip; used on the club's website.

Mighty Del is the nickname for Inverness Citadel F.C., founded in 2008 and reviving the name of a club of 1883–1937. The nickname appears on the club badge. The first word is laudatory, the second is a short form of Citadel. The original club presumably was so named because it was associated with a chapel building called The Citadel; club website.

Mighty K's is a nickname for Knebworth F.C., founded in Hertfordshire in 1901, folded 1995, reformed 1999; Wikipedia and club website. See also Orange Army.

Mighty Moor / Moor is the nickname of Highmoor-Ibis F.C., founded in 2001 in a merger between the Berkshire village sides Highmoor F.C. and Ibis F.C. A short form of the Highmoor place-name; W2012–13 have 'Mighty Moor', which chimes well with the 'High' in the place-name, Wikipedia just Moor.

Mighty O's is the nickname for Onchan A.F.C., founded on the Isle of Man in 1912; Wikipedia.

Mighty Whites is an alternative nickname for Corinthians A.F.C., founded in Douglas, Isle of Man, in 1930; club website. See also Whites.

Mighty Willow is the nickname of Willow Wanderers F.C., founded in 2005. The Berkshire club has a willow tree on its badge, but seems to have no home ground, so the origin of the nickname is not clear; club website.

Mikes is the nickname of Boldmere St Michaels F.C., founded in 1883 in Sutton Coldfield, West Midlands; a pluralised short form of Michael; W1983/4–2013.

Milkmen is a nickname for Felinfach A.F.C., founded in Ceredigion at an uncertain date, but before 1986 (the earliest team photograph on the internet). The nickname is used on the BBC Wales website and refers to the former presence of a large creamery in the village; Huws 2013.

Mill was the nickname of Hurley Daw Mill Miners Welfare F.C., founded in Warwickshire in 1972 The nickname is recorded in W1985–6 and on the FCHD between 1974 and 1986, when the club disbanded.

Millers is a nickname for clubs connected in some way with a mill or a place-name containing the word (see also Mills, below). The clubs are:

- Aveley F.C., founded in Essex in 1927. The club website records that the nickname dates from the 1951–2 season when they moved to the Mill Field Ground "and were promptly nicknamed The Millers"; W1991–4, 2006–13. See also Blues.
- Carlton Town F.C., founded in 1903, originally as Sneinton F.C.m changing name in 2002. Although this area of Nottingham is industrial, the nickname almost certainly refers to the famous Green Windmill at Sneinton; Wikipedia and club's own website. See also Town.
- Feckenham F.C., founded in Worcestershire in 1881. The club's home is The Old Mill House on Mill Lane; W2005.
- New Mills A.F.C., founded in Derbyshire in 1912. Recorded in W1979/80–82/3 and W2009–13, and in a club history of 1974: M. Doughty's *The Story of the Millers*.
- Northampton Spencer F.C., originally founded in 1936 for Spencer School Old Boys. The home ground is called Kingsthorpe Mill; W1991–2013.
- North Leigh F.C., founded in Oxfordshire in 1908. The club has an attractive badge of a windmill and there is a famous windmill in the centre of the town; W2010–13 and club's own website. See also Nor Lye, Windmill Army, Yellows.
- Rocester F.C., founded in Staffordshire in 1876. The nickname appears to have been an adaptation of the ground address in Mill Street; W1989–90. See also Romans.
- Rotherham United F.C., so recorded in Avis 1966–70, but see under Merry Millers, above.
- Totton and Eling F.C., founded in Hampshire in 1925, originally as Bramtoco F.C.

(a works club for the British and American Tobacco Company). In 1971 the club was renamed B.A.T. Sports, then the present name in 2007. The nickname is from the famous Eling Tide Mill; Wikipedia.

☺ Union Mills F.C., founded in the village of Union Mills, Braddan, Isle of Man, in 1920; Wikipedia.

Mills is a nickname for some works sides connected to a mill (see also Millers, above). The clubs are:

☺ Cray Valley Paper Mills F.C., founded in 1922 and reformed in 1981. The club is a works side based in Eltham, Greenwich; Wikipedia.

☺ Drumaness Mills F.C., founded in Co. Down in 1929. The name and nickname records the town's former leading employer, the William Davidson flax spinning mill of 1850–1985; Wikipedia.

☺ Lower Maze F.C., founded in Maze, Co. Down in 1960, originally as Lisburn Mills F.C. The name changed in 1996 but the old nickname has stuck; Wikipedia. See also Black and Red Army, Maze.

Miltonians is the nickname for Milton United F.C., founded in Oxfordshire in 1909, taken from the name of the village in which it is based; W2009–13. See also United.

Miners is a nickname for clubs which were initially associated with a mine as a works side, or associated with a Miners' Welfare Club (see Welfare), or whose home is in a mining community. Examples are:

☺ Atherton Collieries A.F.C., founded in 1916. The Greater Manchester side was originally associated with six local mines. A pithead is on the club's badge; Wikipedia. See also Colls, Colts, Sooty, Welfare.

☺ Blackwell Miners Welfare F.C., founded in Derbyshire in 1890; Wikipedia.

☺ Cowdenbeath F.C., founded in Fife in 1881, in a merger of C. Rangers and C. Thistle. Cowdenbeath itself is nicknamed The Chicago of Fife, due to its allegedly high level of industry. The town developed in extensive local coalfields; RY1974/5–75/6 and SSY2012/13; AFBC. See also Beath, Blue Brazil, Brazil, Cowden, Fifers.

☺ Garforth Town A.F.C., founded in West Yorkshire in 1964 as a pub team called Miners Arms F.C., but in a mining community. The club changed its name to Garforth Miners in 1978 and to G. Town in 1985, and it sports a pit wheel on its badge; W1982/3–5 for G. Miners; W1994–2013 for Town. See also Town.

☺ Gedling Miners Welfare F.C., founded in Nottinghamshire in 1919, originally as G. Colliery W., renaming in 1993. The nickname is used in match reports on the club's own website.

☺ Laxey A.F.C., founded on the Isle of Man in 1910. Laxey was a centre for the mining of lead and zinc until 1929; Wikipedia.

☺ Maltby Main F.C., founded in South Yorkshire in 1916 (closed 1965, reformed in 1970 as M. Miners Welfare, renamed Main in 1996). The name is taken from the Maltby Main Colliery and the club badge shows a miner's lamp; W1994–2013.

☺ Radstock Town F.C., founded in 1895 in the Somerset town whose main industry was coalmining from 1763 to 1973. The club badge shows a pithead and other industrial symbols, with two footballers as supporters; Wikipedia. See also Rads, Reds, Town.

⚽ **Sunderland A.F.C.**, an unofficial nickname based on the prominence of the mining industry in the area. A miners' Davy Lamp is a sculpture outside the new Stadium of Light; Wikipedia. See also Bank of England Club, Black Cats, Lads, Light Brigade, Mackems, Rokerites / Rokermen, Sols, Sund-Ireland, Team of All the Talents, Wearsiders.

Minnows is a common unofficial football club nickname in the context of a larger club playing a smaller club, used by journalists. The minnow is a proverbially small fish and the expression is derogatory. Nevertheless, another common football expression is 'giant killing', when the smaller club defeats the larger.

Minstermen is the official nickname for York City F.C. Founded in 1922 as a successor to previous amateur clubs, the name is taken from the largest, most magnificent, cathedral church in the world, York Minster. No nickname is recorded in Harvey 1959. The nickname is first recorded in Rothmans as 'Minster Men': RY1972–3–82/3 and then as 'Minstermen' through RY1982/3–SSY2004/5 and in W2006–12. Since the club's relegation to the Conference, however, SSY2005/6– 11/12 inexplicably printed the nickname as 'Minster Men', restoring it to 'Minstermen', after promotion, in SSY2012/13. The two-word form also appears in the Williams League Directories 1986–95. It cannot be coincidence that the popular *Mr. Men* series of children's books by Roger Hargreaves began publication just before the nickname appears, in 1971. Moss 1983 gives a unique variant, 'The Minster'. See also City, Y-fronts, Yorkies.

Missioners was the nickname of Hayes F.C., from the name of its first foundation in London in 1909 as Botwell Mission F.C. The small mission church the players attended was also used for changing and storing their kit. The club merged with Yeading in 2007 to form Hayes and Yeading United F.C.; W1980/1–2007. See also Dinc / Ding, United.

Mitchell's is a nickname for Irlam F.C., founded near Salford in 1969, originally as a works side for employees of the engineering firm Mitchell, Shackleton & Co.; Wikipedia See also Shack.

MK Wolves was the nickname of Milton Keynes Wolverton Town F.C., a brief renaming of Wolverton Town F.C., founded in Buckinghamshire in 1887. In their centenary year they renamed as 'Wolverton Town (Milton Keynes)', then 'Milton Keynes Wolverton Town' in 1988, then AFC Wolverton before folding in 1992; W1990. In 2004, W. Town was reborn. See also Railwaymen, Wolves.

Moatmen is the nickname of Gresley Rovers F.C., founded in Derbyshire in 1882. Since 1909 the club has played at The Moat Ground in Church Gresley; W1982/3– 2009. The club reformed as Gresley F.C. in 2009. See also Rovers.

Moatsiders is the nickname of Merstham F.C., founded in 1892. The club plays at the

Moatside Stadium in Merstham, Surrey; W2011–13. See also Buzz.

Mo's is a short-form nickname for Dynamo Star A.F.C., founded in Dumfries in about 1990. The nickname appears on one of the club's older websites. The club badge appears in AFBC.

Moes is the nickname of Loughborough Dynamo F.C., founded in 1955; it is a pluralised short form of the suffix. The story is that the club was founded by schoolboys at Loughborough Grammar School who rebelled against the poncy 'rugby-only' rules of the school and held their early meetings in secret. At the time, the famous Moscow Dynamo club was visiting England to play a friendly against Wolverhampton Wanderers, so the Moes took the name from Moscow and the kit colours from Wolves, and the rest is football history; W2003–7. See also Dynamo.

Moles is the nickname of four clubs, for different reasons. The clubs are:

☺ Aylesbury F.C., founded in 1930, as a works side and named as Stocklake F.C. after the company's move to the Stocklake Industrial Estate in Aylesbury in 1949. Then they became Hayward United, then Aylesbury Vale, then Belgrave F.C. in 1983 (from the base in Belgrave Road) before taking the current name in 2009. The nickname comes from circumstances at the home ground of Haywood Way, which for many years suffered from a large number of moles living under the pitch, and which proved so stubborn in their resistance to attempts to remove them that they became commemorated in the nickname; W2006–13.

☺ Binfield F.C., founded in Berkshire in 1892, presumably for a similar reason as in the case of Aylesbury. The club website says that it was "a massive task" to convert the field at Hill Farm Lane to a new football pitch, taking members three years to accomplish from purchase of the land in 1980; W2001–13. The club badge in AFBC shows two moles holding a football.

☺ Bletchley Town F.C., founded in Milton Keynes, Buckinghamshire in 2005. The various clubs called Bletchley and Milton Keynes are a source of great confusion, but this club is a completely new beginning and the only one to have the nickname 'The Moles'. The club website states that it was the choice of the founder, John Snead, in 2005, but the club has since also started re-using 'The Gladiators' nickname from the earlier club. The nickname appears to be in honour of the famous Second World War intelligence centre at nearby Bletchley Park, as 'mole' is a popular expression for a spy. See also Gladiators.

☺ Molesey F.C., founded in Surrey in 1953; in this case the nickname is a play on the place-name; W1980/1–2013. See also Whites.

Money Men is a nickname for Mount Merrion YMCA F.C., founded in Dublin in 1981. The nickname appears to be based on a slurred pronunciation, or rhyming slang, rendering of the official name, rather than because of excessive affluence; Wikipedia. See also Blues.

Moneys is the nickname of Moneyfields F.C., founded in 1987, originally as Portsmouth Civil Service F.C., renaming in 1994. The nickname is a pun on the official name, which itself is because the club plays at the Moneyfields Sports Ground in Moneyfields Avenue, Portsmouth; W2002–13.

Monkey Hangers is now an accepted nickname for Hartlepool United F.C. The name refers to a notorious piece of local folklore that during the Napoleonic wars a shipwreck near the town was survived only by a monkey, which was interrogated and then hung in the belief that it was a Frenchman. Whatever the truth of the original tale, it is definitely the reason for the nickname. The club's mascot is one H'Angus the Monkey (who in 2002 was elected mayor of Hartlepool), and there is also a fanzine called *Monkey Business*. Recorded on the Football Fans Census website for 2003, from the perspective of Darlington and Carlisle fans, but the nickname is well-known. See also Dockers, Pool, Pools.

Monochrome was a nickname for Gretna F.C., founded in 1946 and closed in 2008. The Dumfriesshire side played in a black and white strip and although monochrome means 'one colour' it is a common expression for black-and-white pictures; Wikipedia. See also Anvils, Black and Whites, Borderers, Celebrant, Wedding-makers.

Mons is a nickname for Bedmond Sports and Social F.C., founded in Hertfordshire before 1913; a pluralised short form of –*mond*, recorded in W1993–6.

Moonlight Dribblers was an unofficial nickname for Everton F.C., recorded in Pickering 1994, who states that the nickname appeared early in their history and referred to their reputation for training after dark. See also Bitters / Bitter Blues, Black Watch, Bluenoses, Blues, Dogs of War, Merseysiders, People's Club, School of Science, Toffees/Toffeemen.

Moonlighters is the nickname of Colby A.F.C., founded in the Isle of Man village of Colby in 1919. The nickname is said to date from before 1920, when the club joined the Isle of Man League, because friendly fixtures were often extended into dusk because of the players' work commitments. The expression is more commonly used today for employees who have a second job in the evenings; Wikipedia.

Moonrakers is a nickname for people from Wiltshire, and has been used as a nickname for Swindon Town F.C. The story is first recorded in 1787 and relates how two Wiltshire contraband smugglers hid their barrels of brandy in a village pond. Caught by excise men when they were trying to rake them out at night, they replied that they were raking for cheese, pointing to the reflection of the moon in the water, and the excise men laughed and left them to it. There was in Wiltshire a Moon F.C., which merged into Bemerton Heath Harlequins in 1989. Recorded in G1956, Churchill 1958, Harvey 1959, AA 1960 and a great many websites connect the nickname to the club. See also Railwaymen, Robins, Shunters, Spartans, Swindle.

Moorites was an early nickname for Burnley F.C. at about the time of their entry into the English League in 1888–9. It comes from the name of their home ground, Turf Moor, which they moved to in 1883; Wikipedia. See also Clarets, Dingles, Gene

Puddle, Moorites, Royalites, Turfites.

Moorlanders is the nickname for Bovey Tracey A.F.C., founded in 1950. The Devon side is located on the edge of Dartmoor; W2010–13.

Moors is a nickname for clubs with the place-name element 'moor' in their official name. The examples are:

⚽ Lincoln Moorlands Railway F.C., founded in a merger in 2007 between L. Moorlands (1989) and L. Railway F.C. The name is from the Moorland Sports and Social Club, which was also the base of the earlier club; recorded for both clubs in W2002–13.

⚽ Moor Green F.C., founded in Birmingham in 1901, closed in a merger with Solihull Borough to form Solihull Moors in 2007; W1979/80 and W1983/4–2007.

⚽ Solihull Moors F.C., founded in West Midlands in 2007 in a merger of Moor Green (1901) and Solihull Borough (1953); Wikipedia. See Boro for the earlier club.

⚽ Spennymoor Town F.C., founded in 2005 as a rescue of Spennymoor United (1901) and Evenwood Town (1931). The Co. Durham club has twice tried to restore the S. United name but "The F.A. says no". Moors was also the nickname of the old club: Avis 1966–70, Barton 1984 & 1985 and W1979/80–2005, and W2010–13 for the new.

Mosquitoes was the surprising name for an early London club founded in 1870, but which seems to disappear after 1880. Today, the name is used by Manchester Mosquitoes, an Australian-Rules football team formed in 2005 and nicknamed 'The Mozzies'.

Moss was the nickname for Mugiemoss F.C., founded in Aberdeenshire in 1887; as a short form of the place-name. The club merged with Rosslyn Sport F.C. (founded in 1923 as Rosemount) in 1989, to form Dyce Juniors F.C., which does not appear to have a nickname; 'Moss' appears on several websites and SFHA.

Motormen is a nickname for at least four clubs in places associated with car manufacturing. The clubs are:

⚽ Daventry United F.C., founded in 1968, originally as Ford Sports Daventry (W1995–2007). The Northamptonshire town was a major car-making centre, W2008–12.

⚽ Leyland Motors F.C., founded at Leyland in Lancashire in 1920. The club's ground was next door to the factory, which is today the British Commercial Vehicle Museum. The company became British Leyland in 1968, but the club survived separately, renaming as Leyland DAF–SGL in 1990 and Leyland Motors Athletic in 1993. It appears to disappear after 2001 (FCHD records it till then). An internet forum reveals that it floundered due to lack of sponsorship after the Station Garage Ltd (SGL) withdrew support; the nickname uniquely appears in W1980/1 as 'Motors Men', and as 'Motormen' in W1986. See also Tigers.

⚽ Redbridge F.C., founded in London in 1959 as Ford United, the club renamed in 2004. The club was originally a works side for employees in the Ford motor factory in Dagenham. The United suffix comes from the union in 1959 of Ford Sports of Dagenham and Briggs Sports (itself formed in 1934 as a works side for Briggs Motor Bodies workshops). W1982/3–2004 for Ford United; W2005–13 for Redbridge. See also Reds.

- Sunderland Nissan F.C., founded in Co. Durham in 1988, originally as Washington Nissan. The club closed in 2009, after the car manufacturer withdrew financial support; W2008–9.
- Vauxhall Motors F.C., founded in 1963 for workers at the Vauxhall Motors car plant in Ellesmere Port, Cheshire; the club badge is the same as that of the parent car company. Recorded in Avis 1966–70, W1990, Miller & Wright 1996 and W2001–13. See also Motors for the club at the sister plant in Luton.

Motors is a nickname for two clubs attached to the car industry. The clubs are:

- Ford Motors F.C., founded in 1967 as a works side for the Ford Motors plant in Liverpool. Recorded in W1982/3–86.
- Morris Motors F.C., formed in 1920 at Cowley, Oxford, where the motor car factory was established in 1913 (the site was sold for redevelopment in 1992); W1983/4–88.
- Vauxhall Motors (Luton) F.C., based at the company's plant in Bedfordshire. It is not clear when the club was formed, as entries give 1907, which was the year the plant was established; W1988–91. See also Motormen for the sister club at the Ellesmere Port site.

Mountain Men is the nickname for Flint Mountain F.C., founded in Flintshire in 2009. The nickname is used on the website of the Clwyd East Football league; Huws 2013.

Mullets is the nickname of Arundel F.C., founded in 1889. The Sussex town is famous for its mullet fisheries in the River Arun. Despite the nickname, the club has a red swift-like bird on its badge; W1983/4–2013.

Munichs is an unofficial, and bad taste, nickname for Manchester United F.C., coined by supporters of rivals Manchester City. It refers to the tragic Munich air crash of 1958 which claimed the lives of 23 people, including football coaches and 8 of the club's promising young players. The nickname is mentioned on hundreds of websites and often appears with a sensitive disclaimer. See also Busby Babes, Coach-Builders, Fergie's Fledglings, Heathens, Man, Manure, Outcasts, Red Devils, Reds, United.

Mushrooms / Mush were the nicknames of Mid Rhondda F.C., founded in Tonypandy, Rhondda Cynon Taf, in 1912, reformed in 1922 as Mid Rhondda United, folded in 1928. The nickname refers to the club's rapid rise as a successful side (mushrooms proverbially grow quickly). Both this and the variant form are recorded on Wikipedia. The second term may simply be a short form of Mushrooms, but the traditional expression used by the driver of a dog sled team is 'Mush!', which might actually be the word because it also connotes speed. There is an account of the club in Martin Johnes, 'Mushrooms, Scandal and Bankruptcy: the

Short Life of Mid Rhondda Football Club', *Local Historian* 32 (2002), 41–53.

Musselmen is a nickname for clubs which are in the vicinity of major mussel-producing industries. The clubs are:

🙂 Conwy United F.C., founded in 1977; recorded in RW1994–2011 and W1994–2000. The club is located near the major mussel industry of the sea between Anglesey and the Welsh mainland. The town has a mussel museum.

🙂 Shoreham F.C., founded in Sussex in 1892; W1994–2013.

Mustard Pots was a nickname for Kingsbury Town F.C., founded by ex-servicemen in London in 1919, merging with London Tigers in 2006 to form Kingsbury London Tigers (see Tigers), renamed London Tigers in 2011. The nickname seems to refer to the club colours, usually blue but with a mustardy-yellow shirt and red shorts change strip, but in W1988 the yellow shirts were listed as the main colour and the nickname appears in W1989–90. Yellow and red are certainly the colours on the traditional Colmans Mustard packaging. See also Kings and Town.

Nailers is the nickname of Belper Town F.C., founded in 1883. The town of Belper has exploited its reserves of ironstone since the thirteenth century and by 1800 had become a major manufacturer of iron and steel nails, with as many as 500 workshops in the town making them. The word has a satisfying double meaning, in *nailing* the opposition; W1979/80 and W1982/3–86 and W1993–2013.

Nall was the nickname of Blakenall F.C., founded in Walsall, West Midlands, in 1946. A short form of the official name, recorded in W1983/4–7, W1998–2001 and Miller and Wright 1996. The club disappeared in a merger with Bloxwich Town in 2001. See also Lions.

Nash is a nickname for two clubs, for different punning reasons. The clubs are:

🙂 Curzon Ashton F.C., founded in 1963 as Curzon Amateurs, in a merger between Curzon Road F.C. and Ashton Amateurs. The pun takes the last letter of Curzon and combines it with the first three letters of Ashton; Wikipedia. See also Blues.

🙂 Murton International F.C., founded in Co. Durham in 1992. Here the nickname is clearly based on the middle sound of 'International' (and the claim by this village to be an international side is most amusing), but this and Murton A.F.C. shared the same ground. Murton A.F.C. has the nickname 'The Gnashers' and the two nicknames seem related. The 'Nash' club disappeared after 1995; W1994–5.

Natives is a nickname for Whitstable Town F.C., founded in Kent in 1886. The nickname refers to the 'Native Oyster', the southern English species of oyster which has been collected here since Roman times; W1992–2013 (thanks to Paul Cullen). See also Oystermen, Reds.

Needles was the nickname for Studley Sporting F.C., founded in Warwickshire in 1920, reformed 1970. The nickname refers to the fame of the village since late Elizabethan times as a centre for the manufacture of high-quality sewing needles and surgical needles. In the nineteenth century the industry here employed 3,000 people; W1987–8. The club seems to disappear after 1987.

Nettles is the nickname for Nettleham F.C., founded in Lincolnshire in about 1905; a pluralised short form of the place-name; Miller & Wright 1996.

New Robins, see North Shields F.C. under Robins.

New Towners is a nickname for Livingston United F.C., founded in the West Lothian new town in 1970; used on many websites. See also Livi.

Newtowners was the nickname for Peterlee Newtown F.C., founded in 1976 in the Co. Durham new town. The club changed its name to Peterlee Town in 2006; Barton 1984 & 1985; W1983/4–7 and W1992–2006.

Nigger Minstrels was once an unofficial nickname for West Bromwich Albion F.C., coined by supporters themselves in 1889 when the club adopted a particularly colourful strip: red-and-blue stripes, black-and-red shorts. The name came from a form of music hall entertainment in which white singers would blacken up and pretend to be black (as on the BBC's now-notorious *Black and White Minstrel Show*, 1959–78), though it is difficult to see why, nowadays, the fans found the colours unacceptable. Thereafter, the club's blue-and-white stripes became the norm (see Historical Football Kits website). See also Albion, Baggies, Bennies, Boing!, Sandwell Town, Stripes, Strollers, Tatters (for a possible connection), Team of Boys, Tesco's, Throstles, W.B.A.

Niseachs is the nickname of Ness F.C., founded in 1937 on the Isle of Lewis. The nickname is a Gaelic word for those who live in Ness, simply meaning 'Nessians', but is is more widely known as the name of the traditional Hebridean fishing boat, mainly made in Ness, the *Sgoth Niseach*, or 'Ness-type skiff'; Wikipedia.

Nitten is a nickname for Newtongrange Star F.C., founded in Midlothian in 1890. The nickname reflects the local pronunciation of the 'Newton' part of the place-name; Wikipedia. See also Star.

Noblot / Notlob are unofficial nicknames for Bolton Wanderers F.C., from the perspective of Wigan Athletic and Blackburn Rovers supporters respectively. The nicknames are anagrams of Bolton and are recorded on the 2003 Football Fans Census. See also Reds, Savage Six, Spots, Trotters, Wanderers, Whites / Whitemen..

Nock is the nickname of Cumnock Juniors F.C., founded in Ayrshire in 1912; as a short form of the place-name; Wikipedia, SFHA.

Nomads is a football club suffix and usually doubles as a nickname for clubs so called. It may originate as a name for clubs which did not have their own home ground (as recorded in the case of Northern Nomads), but travel names were common and it might be used with the same loose meaning as Rovers, Strollers, Wanderers etc., a poetic metaphor for a band of roving warriors. Examples are:

☻ Anstey Nomads F.C., founded in 1957 in Leicestershire; W2003–5.

☻ Bavaria Nomads F.C., a club based in Alderney, originally called Aurigny Nomads, founded before 1991, which plays on the island of Guernsey; certainly used as a nickname in local journalism. 'Bavaria' refers to commercial sponsorship from the international brewery, based in the Netherlands.

☺ **Gap Connah's Quay F.C.**, founded in Flintshire 1946 as C.Q. Juniors, changing to C.Q. Nomads in 1951. The club does not seem to have ever been a homeless side, but the place itself is a port and the club badge shows a medieval ship. There was an earlier club of the name founded in 1890. The name seems to have been adapted in celebration of international travel, suitable enough for a port; prominently displayed on the club's badge; Wikipedia. See also Deesiders, Westenders.

☺ **Kings Norton Town F.C.**, founded in West Midlands in 1997 in a merger of Richmond Swifts (established 1979 as Swift Personalised Products F.C., renaming in 1994) and Richmond Amateurs; W1998–2000; the club folded in 2000. The club was also nicknamed The Nomads when it was Richmond Swifts: W1995–6. The Swift element will have been a business personal name at the outset, but the bird swift is also very much nomadic, wintering in the Tropics, so the nickname may have been a play on the surname, or perhaps even a radical adaptation from –mond in Richmond.

☺ **Neyland A.F.C.**, founded in Pembrokeshire in 1899. The club website gives the nickname and states "The Neyland United team of the 40's and 50's soon acquired the nickname of the 'Nomads' which reflected their irregular but frequent necessity to find new pitches…" A permanent home was found in 1982; Huws 2013.

☺ **Northern Nomads**, said to be because they never had their own ground; founded in Greater Manchester in c.1862, closed 1984, they shared grounds with Stalybridge and Glossop North End; Wikipedia. See also Roaming Brigade.

☺ **Oxford City Nomads**, founded in 1882, originally as Oxford Quarry Nomads. The club only added 'City' in 2007; W2008–13.

☺ **Richmond Swifts**, see under Kings Norton Town, above.

Nops is a nickname for three clubs and is a pluralised short form of the word 'Ironopolis', a fictional place-name in tribute to an area's iron and steel industry (compare Copperopolis for Swansea, Cottonopolis for Manchester). The clubs are:

☺ **Caernarfon (or Carnarvon) Ironopolis F.C.**, founded in Gwynedd in 1895, closed in 1903. The club was a works side for the De Winton & Co. Iron Works (thanks to Richard Huws). See also Canaries.

☺ **Ironopolis F.C.**, formed as a professional (i.e. salaried) rival to Middlesbrough in 1889, folding in 1894. The name Ironopolis survives in Middlesbrough for an engineering firm and a film company; recorded early, in BoF1905–6 (p.203), and in Appleton 1960, pp. 82–3 and Wikipedia. See also Boro, Cleveland Cowboys, Ironsiders, Riversiders, Scabs, Smoggies, Teessiders, Washers.

☺ **Stanley United F.C.**, founded in Co. Durham in 1880, originally as Stanley Nops, renaming in 1890. Stanley has traditionally been a colliery town but it is very close to the iron and steel centre of Consett (see 'The Steelmen'). The club folded in 2003; W1994–2003.

Nor Lye is a nickname for North Leigh F.C., founded in Oxfordshire in 1908, and formed from the local pronunciation of the two words in the place-name; Wikipedia. See also Millers, Windmill Army, Yellows.

Norn Iron is a nickname for the Northern Ireland national team, based on the local pronunciation of the country name. Wikipedia records the nickname both for the team and the country and describes it is as 'affectionate'. See also Green and White Army, Our Wee Country.

North is the nickname of Trafford F.C., which lies to the west of Manchester, but it was first founded in 1990 as North Trafford F.C., as a break-away team from Flixton F.C. The club also plays in the 'Northern Premier League Division One North', but the 1990 club name is the source of the nickname; W1994 for North Trafford and in W1995–2013 for Trafford.

North End is a nickname for two clubs with this expression in their official name. The clubs are:

⚽ Farnborough North End F.C., founded in Hampshire in 1967 as a church side called F. Covenanters. The present name was adopted in 1998; W2011. See also Covies.

⚽ Preston North End F.C. This nickname appears as an alternative to Lilywhites in RY1977/8–SSY2012/13 and appears much earlier, in BoF1905–6 (p.237). See also Glasses, Invincibles, Lilywhites / Whites, P.N.E., Proud Preston.

Noull is the nickname of Kinnoull Juniors F.C., founded in Perth in 1943; a short form of the official name; club website, SFHA.

Nuns was a nickname for Nuneaton Town F.C. between 1894 and 1937. It was founded in 1889 as Nuneaton St Nicholas, but renamed 'Town' in 1894, and was replaced by Nuneaton Borough F.C. in 1937, which was replaced in 2008 by the new Nuneaton Town; pluralised short form, Wikipedia. See also Boro, Saints, Townies.

'Nure is the nickname of Terenure College A.F.C., founded at the college in Dublin in 1972; a short form of the official name recorded on Wikipedia.

Nurserymen is a nickname for Olney Town F.C., founded in Buckinghamshire in 1903. The town still has several garden nurseries, and local historian Elizabeth Knight reports that the name refers to the Recreation Ground being built on the site of a former nursery field; the nickname appears on the club's badge, printed in Miller & Wright 1996, and Wikipedia.

Nuts has been a nickname of two clubs for slightly different but not unrelated reasons. The clubs are:

⚽ Leicester City F.C., recorded as an alternative to 'Filberts' on the 1933 Ogden cigarette card set. A filbert is a species of hazelnut, and these nuts were so called from medieval times because they ripened by 22 August, St Philbert's Day. See the next entry, however, for an illustration of how popular 'Filbert' was in 'nutty' expressions at the time of its use as a nickname for this club. See also City, Filberts, Fosse / Fossites, Foxes, Ice Kings.

⚽ Scunthorpe United F.C. (as 'Knuts'). The story is that a Rev. Thomas Cyprian Rust once described the team as 'a tough nut to crack' when awarding a trophy (but this rarely-stated story is probably entirely apocryphal). The nickname referred to a popular phrase in the second decade of the twentieth century where 'knuts' meant a fashionable, showy young man, a dandy, which is discussed in great detail in a Great War internet forum. The OED lists its first appearance in 1911, then in 1915 it was further popularised with a music hall song 'Gilbert the Filbert' ('The nut with a K ... Colonel of the Knuts'), which became a First World War marching song. It appears in a letter to *The Times* on 22 February 1916 (in the showy, fashionable sense) and was used by Sharpe's Toffee in the 1930s in an advertising mascot of a swanky character called 'Sir Kreemy Knut'. Another correspondent states that it started to be used for the football club by *The Grimsby News* during the First World War. By this time, the club had entered the Midland League and was flourishing. The 'K' spelling is interesting because it illustrates the early twentieth-century convention that you could get away with saying anything so long as there was a double meaning (hence all those *double-entendre* Edwardian postcards). Without doubt, the spelling is there to hide the word 'nuts', which had already appeared in slang in the nineteenth century with both eccentric and *risqué*, sexual meanings (see Green 2005). As a football club nickname, it could simply refer to the team as dandies or fun-loving young men, but it seems extremely likely that the nickname was originally inspired by the potentially rude first five letters of the place-name, which, so long as the 'K' spelling was used, one could get away with suggesting, even in print. 'Knut' is a common alternative spelling to the Viking personal name 'Cnut' or Canute. A Viking personal name does actually lie behind the first element, but it is *Skúma* (Mills 1991). The nickname is recorded on the Historical Football Kits website and others. See also Iron, Scunny, United.

Nuts and Bolts was the nickname of the Kent side Ashford Town F.C., founded in 1930, closing in 2010. The nickname is said to have come from the local railway works where most of the players worked as engineers in the early years. It certainly suggests mechanics of some sort. Green 2005 records the expression as originally meaning 'crazy' in the 1930s, shifting to 'the basics' in the 1960s, so it is perhaps best understood as a pun with more than one meaning. W1980/1–2010. A new Ashford United was formed in 2011, re-using the name of an earlier club, from 1891, and has assumed the distinctive nickname: W2013.

O's is a nickname for clubs with an 'O' in their official name. These are:

⚽ Leyton Orient F.C., originating not just as an obvious abbreviation of the second word in their name but because of the prominent white O displayed on the backs of the blue shirts they wore 1899–1905. The use of the name Orient is more difficult to explain. Founded as Orient F.C. in 1888 as an offshoot from the Eagle Cricket Club, the story is that they took the name on the suggestion of player Jack Dearing, who was an employee of the famous Orient Steamship Navigation Company, not necessarily because the word implied 'Eastern' (the club does have an East London location), but because it was exotic. After renaming as Clapton Orient in 1898, they moved to Leyton in 1936 and finally adopted Leyton in the name when the club reopened after the Second World War. Between 1966 and 1987 the name reverted to Orient F.C. The club coat of arms has featured wyverns as supporters since 1976, and the club mascot is one Theo (i.e. 'The O') the Wyvern. The 1933 Ogden card uses 'Eastern' as the explanation but shows a cartoon of a man in Ottoman dress. Johnston 1934 uses 'The C.O.s'. Recorded in Avis 1954–70, G1956–65 and G1976 (as Os), Churchill 1958, Richards 1960, and under the two club names throughout RY1970/1–SSY2012/13. See also CO's, Orient.

⚽ Oldland Abbotonians F.C., founded in 1910 at Oldland Common near Bristol; W2011–13.

⚽ Orpington F.C., founded in Kent in 1939; Wikipedia.

⚽ Overton Recreation F.C., founded in 1998 near Wrexham, Flintshire, as a successor to Overton Marchwiel (1933); Wikipedia. See also Lions.

O.D.'s is the nickname for A.F.C. Dunstable, founded in 1981, originally as the Old Dunstablians. The old grammar school has closed, the club renamed in 2004. Recorded in W2012–13 as 'The Od's', on Wikipedia as 'The ODs'.

Oak is a nickname for two clubs with the word 'Oak' in their official name. Both clubs also appear as 'Oaks'. The clubs are:

⚽ Mile Oak F.C., founded in 1960, from the Sussex place-name; recorded as The Oak in WW1993–2013, though earlier it appears as 'The Oaks', in W1988–90.

⚽ Mile Oak Rovers and Youth F.C., founded in 1958 at Tamworth, Staffordshire, based at the Mile Oak Hotel there; W1983/4–6 has 'Oak'; W1993–4 has 'Oaks'.

Oakey was a nickname for Wokingham Town F.C., founded in Berkshire in 1875. Recorded in Avis 1966–70 with the explanation "after the town crest, The Oakapple", though it seems more likely that both the crest and the nickname are independently coined as puns on the place-name (which does not refer to oaks but is more likely to refer to a personal name, a man called Wocca, see Mills 1991). The club merged with Emmbrook in 2004. See also Oakey, Satsumas, Town.

Oakmen is the nickname of Uckfield Town F.C. See next entry.

Oaks is the nickname for several clubs, often because of the same or similar letters appearing in the place-name. The clubs are:

⚽ A.F.C. Uckfield, founded in 1988, originally as Wealden F.C. The Sussex town has a place-name which has sometimes been interpreted as meaning 'the Oak Field', and this idea, right or wrong, lies behind the town crest and the club's nickname. For the same reason, Sussex League Division Three side, Uckfield Town F.C., is nicknamed The Oakmen, and have a 'Hearts of Oak' motto.

⚽ Caddington F.C., founded in Bedfordshire in 1971, originally as Five Oaks, from the Five Oaks School and Youth Club to which it was attached; Five Oaks is a local street name; W1994–2000.

⚽ Mile Oak F.C., see above under Oak.

⊕ Mile Oak Rovers and Youth, see above under Oak.

⊕ Oakwood F.C., founded in 1962, from the Sussex place-name; W1989–2009.

⊕ Sevenoaks Town F.C., founded in 1883. The badge of the Kent club appropriately shows seven acorns; Wikipedia. See also Town.

Oilers is the nickname of Fawley A.F.C., founded in 1923, originally as A.G.W.I. United, an oil refinery team. In 1948 it became Esso Fawley, then the current name in 2002; Wikipedia.

Oilers / Oilmen are nicknames for BP Llandarcy F.C., founded in 1922 in Neath, and now renamed Neath F.C. The nickname comes from the oil industry that the club was a work's side for, recorded in RW1994 as Oilers; RW1995–2001 as Oilmen.

Old Boys is the nickname for the Staffordshire side, Leek County School Old Boys F.C., founded in 1945; Wikipedia.

Old Firm see Firm.

Old Gold is a nickname for Carmarthen Town A.F.C., founded in South Wales in 1948. The club plays in gold shirts with black shorts and the nickname is a popular expression for darker shades of yellow; Wikipedia. See also Town.

Old Invincibles, see Invincibles.

Old Lagonda is an unofficial nickname for Staines Town F.C., founded in Surrey in 1892. The Lagonda luxury car company was set up in Staines in 1906 but sold to Aston Martin in 1947. A previous club in the town was known as 'Staines Lagonda F.C.', so the nickname is part transfer, part local history; Wikipedia. See also Leghorns, Linos, Massive, Swans, Town.

Old Lions is the nickname of Hollington United F.C., founded in East Sussex in 1893. The club badge in AFBC records the nickname with a heraldic lion. The nickname appears to be a punning adaptation of sounds in the place-name, referring also to the longevity of the club.

Old Reds, see Aul Reds (Shelbourne), Owd Reds (Accrington Stanley).

Old 'Uns was the nickname of Wednesbury Old Athletic F.C., founded in West Midlands in 1874, closed in 1893. The nickname is preserved in the title of the 1994 club history by Steve Carr: *The Old 'Uns*, and is clearly a pun on the club's official name. There were two successor clubs which also used the nickname to 1924, recorded in the author's sequel, *The Old Uns Revisited*. The clubs and nickname are also recorded on Wikipedia. The 1905–6 *Book of Football* mentions the club and once uses 'the Old Athletic' as a nickname for it (p.137).

Olympic is a football club name suffix, inevitably suggesting athletic prowess and an association with the ancient Olympic Games (named from the plain of Olympia in southern Greece). The earliest uses appear to be those by the surviving club Radcliffe Olympic F.C. (Nottinghamshire, 1876), and the famous Blackburn Olympic F.C. (1878–89); so the suffix appears long before the advent of the modern Olympic Games in 1896, but alongside many other 'classical' names like Corinthian. It can be used as a nickname for clubs with this suffix. Examples are Radcliffe Olympic and

Cookstown Olympic F.C. (founded in Co. Tyrone in 1996, originally as Sperrin Olympic, renaming in 2005), both of which use it as a nickname on their own websites. There is also the short form 'Pics' (used for Rushall Olympic). There have been a great many clubs with the Olympic suffix, but most of them have later renamed as something else, so the name is rarer today than the word's mainstream popularity would suggest. Clubs which have the suffix today are A.F.C. Worcester O. (2012); Coleraine O. (refounded 1986); Cookstown O. (Co. Tyrone 1996); Doddinghurst O. (Essex 1978); Kingsley O. (West Midlands); Morriston O. (Swansea 1988); Newpark O. (Co. Antrim 2011); Radcliffe O. (Nottinghamshire 1876); Rushall O. (Kent 1893); and Wombourne O. (Stourbridge 1991). Finally, one of the ancestor clubs of Wrexham F.C. was called Wrexham Olympic between 1883 and 1886.

Onians was a nickname for the Airdrieonians F.C., and is recorded in the Rothmans Football Yearbooks for 1972–3 and 1973–4; clearly a short form of the official name. See also Diamonds, Excelsior, Waysiders.

Orange Army is a nickname for Knebworth F.C., founded in Hertfordshire in 1901, folded 1995, reformed 1999. The club plays in an all-orange strip and the colour is adopted throughout the club's website; Wikipedia. See also Mighty K's.

Orchard is the nickname of Cherry Orchard F.C. founded in this part of Dublin in 1957; a short form of the place-name; Wikipedia.

Orchardmen was the nickname of Bedfont F.C., founded in Middlesex in 1900. The club was based at The Orchard Ground; W2008–10. The club folded in 2010.

Orient appears as a nickname for Leyton Orient F.C. in Avis 1966–70 (which also gives the variant O's). See also CO's, O's.

'Orns. See Horns.

Otters is the nickname for two clubs, for different reasons. The clubs are:

- ☺ Ottery St Mary F.C., founded in 1911. Although a pun on the Devon place-name, the town is named from the River Otter, which does actually mean a river frequented by otters (Mills 1991); W1982/3–99.
- ☺ Rustington Otters F.C., a club with several youth sides, founded in West Sussex in 1959. The nickname is used on the club's own website, but there seems to have been no particular reason for the choice of name, other than association with the playful characteristics of this popular animal. A badge appears in AFBC.

Our Wee Country is a nickname for the Northern Ireland national team, based on the small size of Northern Ireland and employing the local word for small, which Ulster has inherited from Scots. The nickname appears in the title of a fanzine for the side. See also Green and White Army, Norn Iron.

Outcasts was a temporary nickname for Manchester United F.C. in 1909. Four months after winning the F.A. Cup, the club was the only one to refuse to leave the new Players Union (established 1907), which the F.A. had banned, and were threatened with suspension. The club itself adopted the nickname 'The Outcasts', but a settlement was reached in August, in time for the 1909–10 season. Today, the Union is called The Professional Footballers' Association; Wikipedia. See also Busby Babes, Coach-Builders, Fergie's Fledglings, Heathens, Man, Manure, Munichs, Red Devils, Reds, United.

Over the Bridge was the nickname for Abingdon Town F.C., founded in Oxfordshire in 1870; as recorded in W1991–9, club programmes for 1991–93, and Pickering 1994. The name refers to the location of the football ground over the' River Thames, from Abingdon itself (not Abingdon as seen from Oxford); thanks to Edmund Bennett. See also Abbots.

Owd Reds, Th' was and is the nickname of the old and the new Accrington Stanley F.C.s There are four teams in this history: Accrington (1878–96), Stanley Villa (which evolved into Accrington Stanley I, 1891–1966) and Accrington Stanley II (1968–). All four wear / wore red shirts. Stanley Villa were named from their home in Stanley St, Accrington, and had already added Accrington to their name before the closure of the first Accrington. Pickering 1994 records the nickname as 'Old Reds', but W1987–2006 and SSY2006/7–12/13 have 'Reds'; Wikipedia uses the Owd spelling. See also Stanley / Stanleyites.

Owls is a nickname for clubs in some way associated with owls. The clubs and variant reasons are:

- Bartley Green F.C., founded in Birmingham in 1949. The association is not explained, but it may be connected with the nearby Bartley Reservoir nature reserve and bird sanctuary, or an adaptation of the local ward name, Weoley. The club's badge has a magnificent image of a flying owl.
- Bromham F.C., founded in Wiltshire in 1897. The club badge (AFBC and club website) shows a stylised owl and the nickname is used in local press reports, but the reason for it is not known.
- Cleethorpes Town F.C., founded in North Lincolnshire in 1998, originally as Lincolnshire Soccer School F.C. The nickname clearly represents the club's original base as a school ('wise owls'); Wikipedia.
- Harlow Town F.C., founded in Essex in 1879. The club is now nicknamed The Hawks but is listed as The Owls in W1979/80–93, and Smith 1991/2–95/6. The last three letters of the place-name may have encouraged the nickname, just as the first letters seem to have encouraged the new nickname. See also Hawks, Lilywhites.
- Leeds United F.C., as an occasional unofficial nickname, from the magnificent owl supporters on the club's coat of arms. Between 1964 and 1972 an owl was on the club's badge; widespread use in journalism. See also Dirty Leeds, Peacocks, United, Whites / Mighty Whites.
- Sheffield Wednesday F.C. Founded in 1867, the club was first called 'The Wednesday', because they were an offshoot of The Wednesday Cricket Club, and that was the day on which they played, a half-day for local traders. The name changed to Sheffield Wednesday in 1929 and the nickname is in the 1933 Ogden cigarette

card set, G1956–76, Churchill 1958, Norris 1959, Avis 1954–70, Richards 1960, the 1959 Sweetule card set, Shawcross 1961 and throughout RY1970/1– SSY2012/13. The nickname comes from their new ground, purchased in 1899 at Owlerton, a village on the outskirts of Sheffield; the site was renamed the Hillsborough Stadium after a constituency boundary change in 1914. The name is a pun on the spelling (though not the pronunciation) of the first element of the place-name, but unfortunately it is a mistake, because it does not mean 'owl'. Nevertheless, a crest of an owl appeared on the club's badge in 1956 and various owls have been the club mascot, the current one being Barney the Owl since 2006. See also Blades, Groveites, Pigs, Wednesday, Wendys.

Oystermen is a nickname for clubs with a seaside location and a local oyster industry. See also 'Natives' for another nickname based on oysters. The clubs are:

⚽ Brightlingsea United F.C., founded in Essex in 1928, in a merger between B. Town (1919) and B. Athletic (1908); the club merged with Regent Park Rangers in 2005 to form B. Regent; this nickname appears in W1992–2003. See also Seasiders, Tics, United.

⚽ Colchester Town F.C. Founded in 1867 it was dissolved in 1937 to make way for Colchester United F.C., founded in Essex in 1937. The town of Colchester has been prominent in oyster production since Roman times. The nickname is recorded for Colchester United in Richards 1960, but it has now been replaced by U's. See also Ewes, Grandad's Army, U's.

⚽ Whitstable Town F.C., founded in 1886. The Kentish town is famous for oysters, which have been collected there since Roman times; W1982/3–2013. See also Natives, Reds.

P's is a nickname for Paget Rangers F.C., founded in Paget Road, Birmingham in 1938, but now based in Sutton Coldfield; W1983/4–90 and W1995–7. See also Bears.

Pace is the nickname of Dunipace Juniors F.C., founded in Denny, Stirlingshire, in 1888. Although simply a short form of the place-name, the nickname satisfyingly suggests a pace-setting club; Wikipedia and internet match reports.

Paintmen was the nickname of Manders F.C., founded in West Midlands in 1935, reformed 1988; the club was a works side for the major ink, paint and varnish works of Mander Brothers Ltd at Wolverhampton; the football club seems to have discontinued after 1996; W1994–5.

Paisley Brazilians is a nickname of St Mirren F.C., founded in 1877 in Paisley, Renfrewshire. The nickname favourably compares the playing of the club with that of the famous South American national side, and similar expressions appear in football nicknames all over the world (e.g. Cameroon, the Brazil of Africa); but there is also a special connection between Paisley and Brazil. Archie McLean (1894–1871) was born in Paisley and emigrated to Brazil to play football for São Paulo in 1912. He stayed in the country for forty years, eventually teaching the national side and he is known as the 'Father of Brazilian Football'. So, Brazil really did get it from

Paisley. The nickname appears widely in internet journalism between 2003 and the present. A variant form, halfway between this and Saints, is 'Paisley Saints', which appears in RY1988/9–89/90 and in *Panini's Football Yearbook 1988/89–89/90*. See also Black and White Army, Buddies, Saints.

Palace is an unofficial nickname for Crystal Palace F.C. It is cited in Jeffrey 1961, alongside the more familiar Glaziers, and used in Goodall 1982 (p. 244). See also Eagles, Glaziers, Team of the Eighties.

Panners is the nickname of Preston Athletic F.C., founded in the East Lothian town of Prestonpans in 1945; a pun on the last syllable of the town name. Recorded in RS 1995–7, 2000–1, SFHA.

Pansies is the nickname of Dundee Violet F.C., founded in 1883. The club plays in royal blue, not violet, but the nickname is that of a popular violet-coloured flower. Presumably the club played in the violet colour in its early days, though violet is also the colour and name of one type of Scottish thistle; Wikipedia.

Panthers is a nickname for clubs wishing to associate themselves with these beautiful, sleek, athletic predators, which are often the alleged source of 'big cat' sightings. The clubs are:

- Atherton Laburnum Rovers F.C., founded in Greater Manchester in 1956. There seems no particular reason for the name other than the desired association; W1998–2013. See also L.R., Laburnums, Rovers.
- Hamilton Panthers F.C., founded in York in 1988; club's own website.
- Pentland Panthers F.C., a club which merged with Edinburgh United in 1985, but which survives as the name of their youth development teams. Apart from the attractive alliteration and the club badge (which shows a growling panther head), it is said that the club was named after the semi-legendary big cats of the Pentland Hills; club's own website. See also United.
- Sturminster Newton United F.C., founded in Dorset in 1871, originally as Panthers F.C. until the 1890s, renaming as Sturminster St Mary's until 1945, then the present name. As Panthers they were a pioneer and successful club; club website and Wikipedia. See also Cherries.
- Swansea Panthers A.F.C., established in 2010; Huws 2013.

Paraders was an older nickname for Bradford City F.C., from their home ground, Valley Parade (1886). Formed in 1903, the club used the ground from the outset and the club tradition is that they had the nickname from about the same time. Recorded in the 1936 Thomson 'stamp' album, G1956–76, Churchill 1958, Harvey 1959, Richards 1960 and Avis 1966–70 and in RY1970/1–81/2. See also Bantams, Chickens, Citizens, Cocks, Gents, Sadford.

Parishioners is the nickname of Westfield F.C., founded in 1927. The Sussex side plays at the Parish Field ground in Westfield; W2007–9. See also Field/s.

Park is a nickname for clubs which have the word Park in their official name. The clubs are:

- Aylestone Park F.C., founded in Leicestershire in 1968; W2000–1.
- Kiveton Park F.C., founded near Sheffield in 1892, originally as a works side for the Kiveton Park Colliery; the club wears a distinctive all-black strip; W1982/3–90.
- Langley Park Welfare F.C., founded in Co. Durham in the 1920s, reformed 1973; W1987.
- Maesteg Park Athletic F.C., founded in 1945; recorded in W1987 and W1994–5, RW1994–2002. An old badge of the club in AFBC shows a stag, but there is no certainty that 'Stags' was ever a nickname for the club.
- Moyola Park F.C., founded in Castledown, Co. Londonderry in 1880. Recorded in RI1997–2007.
- Phoenix Park (Bradford) F.C., founded in West Yorkshire before 1981, the club folded after 1985 and their ground was taken over by Eccleshill (The Eagles); W1982/3–5.
- Worcester Park F.C., founded in London in 1921; Wikipedia. See also Skinners.

Parkies was the nickname for two short-lived Scottish clubs, which are:

- Ayr Parkhouse F.C., founded in 1886, which merged with Ayr F.C. to form Ayr United in 1910. Wikipedia records the nickname and explains the suffix as a reference to the Parkhouse farmhouse where the team trained.
- Parkhead Thistle F.C., founded in Dumfries in 1896, closed in 1899; a friendly short-form recorded in SFHA.

Parkies / Parkway are nicknames of Plymouth Parkway F.C., founded in 1988, originally as Ex-Air Flyers Plymouth, changing to the present name in 1993; Parkies appears in W1994–6; Parkway appears in W2008–13.

Parras is the nickname of Worksop Parramore F.C., founded in Nottinghamshire in 1936, originally as a works side for the F. Parramore & Sons iron foundry; a short form of the second name, which puns with the famous nickname of the Parachute Regiment; widely used in internet journalism.

Pars is the nickname of Dunfermline Athletic F.C., founded in Fife in 1885. The nickname is said to date from just after the First World War and is not explained, but there are seven current theories. It seems extremely likely, however, that the word is the same as that used in golf. The theories from various internet sites are: (1) It derives from the *parallel* lines on the club's shirts, which have been black-and-white stripes since 1909; though this would indeed be a unique response to stripes, which are everywhere in football. (2) It has also been suggested that the stripes resemble those on a parr fish (a young salmon), but they do not particularly resemble them and the spelling is different. (3) The club's players were noted to be heavy drinkers and so were nicknamed paralytics … as a slang expression, however, Partridge (Beale 1989) tells us that 'paralytic', for drunk, only dates from c.1910, so there would only be a decade for it to become sufficiently established to form the nickname, and that in the days before radio. (4) The same word has also been used to describe the team's performance on the field; Adrian Room (2010) suggested that this may be in a mocking alteration of 'Athletic', the club's official suffix, though the same short time-span makes this difficult to accept, and both ideas are also compromised by the nickname not being 'The Paras', which would be a more natural, and easier pronunciation, for a name formed from 'Paralytics'. **(5)** English sailors visiting the Rosyth naval establishment were Plymouth Argyle supporters and unfurled a banner at a match stating 'Plymouth Argyle (Rosyth) Supporters' and the initials caught on (this is remarkably implausible but the suggestion is liked by many; this would have to have happened before the appearance of the nickname, otherwise the banner would have been in tribute to it). **(6)** The phrase 'on a par' was used during a 1913 legal contest with the Cowdenbeath club, for the comparable status of the two clubs, and the phrase caught on. This explanation is apparently well-liked in Cowdenbeath, who were claiming to be 'higher up' than Dunfermline. Finally **(7)**, a variant of this idea is that Dunfermline was 'on a par' with other clubs once they had joined the Scottish League, which was about the right time for the nickname, in 1921.

'Par' is already known in sport as a golfing expression, for the average number of shots to achieve a particular hole, and this is the word which lies behind the sensible theories 6 and 7, above. The other ideas are *remarkably* unconvincing, though 3 and 4 do contain the idea that the nickname came from the club's own disappointed fans, which seems significant. The essential meaning does seem to be 'The Equals' or 'The Averages'. It would, of course, be entirely natural for a golfing expression to transfer to football in Fife, where golf has long been important. The politics of Dunfermline's 1921 League entry, in which the club and the new Central League were persuaded to join the Scottish League in a manner which compromised their own ambitions (see Fabian & Green 1960, iv, pp. 61–2), gives some support to theory 7, but it would make more sense if it was coined by supporters of other clubs (mockingly, on the lines of "Forget your big ideas, you're on a par with us now"), and this would play against it being accepted as an official nickname.

There is one remarkable fact, however, which makes the nickname entirely explicable: after their entry to the Scottish League Division 2, the club's performance was mediocre, frequently finishing at the end of each season in 'par position', in the middle of the league table. Between 1921 and 1925, the final places are 8/20, 13/20, 7/20 and 13/20. Promotion to the First Division followed in 1926, relegation followed in 1928, and then again the club usually finished in average place: 11/20, 10/20, 3/20, 10/20. This seems far too big a coincidence to be dismissed. Mathematically, it is virtually perfect. It seems extremely likely that the fans themselves called their club 'The Pars' because they were always in 'par position' – rarely 'above par', often 'below par', they were just 'par'. This, of course, was a long time ago and the club has flourished since. Today's supporters can now take pride in the fact that 'par' also means 'the standard'.

The nickname may be later than the supporter's claim, as it does not appear in the mainstream sources from the 1930s and no documentation for an early appearance is ever cited. It does not appear on early programmes, but it would be natural for a nickname which was slightly derogatory to take some time before it appeared in print. Recorded throughout RY and SSY from 1970/1 to 2012/13 and in RS 1993–2012. See also Dumps, Fifers, Leishman's Lions.

Pat's is a nickname for St Patrick's Athletic F.C., founded in Dublin in 1929, using the traditional short form of Patrick. Recorded in RI2006. See also Dublin Saints, Saints.

Peaceful Warriors is the nickname for Newark Town F.C., founded in Nottinghamshire in 1868 (folded 1930s, reformed 1994). The nickname is recorded on a club badge illustrated in AFBC, and on Wikipedia and several other websites, but always without an explanation. The badge shows an image of the ruined Newark Castle, destroyed in the Civil War, but this is often used as an image of the town and does not seem to be relevant to the unusual nickname. It may mean something like 'sleeping giants', warriors with great potential who are about to spring into action.

Peacocks is a nickname for several clubs, but not always because of the colours. The clubs are:

🔅 Bedfont Town F.C., founded in Middlesex in 1965, originally as Bedfont Green, changing to the present name in 2010. The nickname is based on the village's most famous feature: at the entrance to St Mary's Church, two yew trees have been shaped into enormous topiary peacocks sitting on piles of cushions. The topiary is ancient, and believed to have been cut as long ago as 1704. The design was fully restored in 1990; W2009–10 for Green, W2011–12 for Town.

🔅 Corsham Town F.C., founded in 1884. At the centre of this Wiltshire town is the stately home called Corsham Court, whose peacocks are famous for wandering the streets; Wikipedia. See also Reds, Southbankers.

🔅 Gornal Athletic F.C., founded in West Midlands in 1919, originally as Lower Gornal Athletic and as a successor to a club called Gornal Wood Excelsior. The present name was taken in 1972. The club badge shows a multi-coloured stylised peacock, but the reason for the nickname is not known: colours may be the explanation, but recently the club has played in pale blue; W1993–2003.

🔅 Leeds United A.F.C. Founded in 1919 after the closure of the Leeds City club (1904–19), United took over the ground at Elland Road which is still their base. Both Leeds City and United were nicknamed The Peacocks because opposite the stadium is the Old Peacock pub, the ground itself also being nicknamed the Old Peacock Ground. In 1967, however, Jeffrey assumed the name came from the blue-and-gold strip which Leeds United wore from 1934 to 1961, as did Easterbrooke 1969. The amusing Vernon 1970–1 pamphlet says it "appears to have nothing to do with pride, strutting, or colours. Instead it comes from the name of a pub..." Recorded in the 1936 Thomson 'stamp' album, and in Avis 1954–70, G1956–76, Churchill 1958, Richards 1960, AA 1960, SWSCYB 1962–3, RY1970/1–73/4 and RY1983/4–85/6 and Moss 1983 (in RY1974/5–82/3 no nickname is listed for the club). In 1981 a stylised peacock appeared on the club's badge. See also Dirty Leeds, Owls, United, Whites / Mighty Whites.

Taunton Town F.C., founded in Somerset in 1947. The club plays in the peacock colours of purple and pale blue; W1979/80–2013.

Peas is the nickname for Peamount United F.C., founded at Greenogue Newcastle in Co. Dublin in 1983. A short form of the official name; the club also plays in distinctive pea-green shirts. The club has several sides, but is particularly famous for the success of its women's team; Wikipedia.

Peasy is the nickname of Petershill F.C., founded in Springburn, Glasgow, in 1897. The nickname clearly suggests a slurred local pronunciation of the place-name, but also chimes with the rhyming phrase 'easy-peasy', suggesting a confident stress-free side; Wikipedia, SFHA.

Pedlars is the nickname of Swaffham Town F.C., founded in 1892. The Norfolk town boasts a traditional folktale about a pedlar who found a fortune in buried treasure by following the instructions in a dream, and who used it for rebuilding the parish church. The story features on the club badge and an impressive carved image of the pedlar makes the town sign; W1991–2013.

Peelites is a nickname for Peel A.F.C., founded on the Isle of Man in 1888. The nickname is one of those for the city of Peel, often used for the club in journalism. See also Sunset City.

Peeping Toms is an unofficial nickname for Coventry City, as listed by Churchill 1958, Easterbrooke 1969 and Vernon 1970–1. The phrase is now mainstream English, but it relates to the story of Lady Godiva of Coventry in the eleventh century, who negotiated a reduction in taxation for the city if she would ride naked through the streets. A deal was arranged for nobody to look while she did so, but Tom had a peep and was struck blind. The name has also been used for a club fanzine. See also Bantams, Blackbirds, Citizens, Singers, Sky Blues, Wheelmen.

Pegasus was the official name and nickname of the combined university team Pegasus A.F.C., founded in 1948, folded in 1963. The club was formed using players from Oxford University Centaurs A.F.C. and Cambridge University Falcons A.F.C. As Fabian and Green say (1960, I, p. 398), "... Pegasus, the winged horse of the classics; to the founders Pegasus meant the combination of the Centaur, the man-headed horse, with the Falcon, a bird." A short history of the club appears in Twydell 1988. The name is also used today for several youth clubs, such as Welwyn Pegasus F.C., founded in 1970; this club took its name from the badge of a local airborne army squadron who had supported the club with donations, but the usual sense of the nickname is of youth talent 'taking flight', making Pegasus a perfect name and nickname, though one that is rarely used.

Pelican is the nickname of Bilborough Pelican F.C., founded in Nottinghamshire in 2005, in a merger of Bilborough (c.2000) and Pelican (1984); badge in AFBC. The club's own website gives a detailed history of the club. The name seems to have been taken from the Pelican pub in Bilborough.

Penguins is the nickname of Athersley Recreation F.C., founded in South Yorkshire in 1979, originally as A. North Juniors. The club plays in a black and white strip and the nickname is a welcome variant on the more common 'Magpies' for such colours. Recorded in W2013.

Penn is the nickname of Penn and Tylers Green F.C., founded in 1890, from the village of Penn in Buckinghamshire; Wikipedia.

Pennant was a nickname for the club called Leyton Pennant F.C., originating in a merger between Walthamstow Pennant and a club called Leyton in 1995. Walthamstow P. itself was a renaming in 1988 of a club called Pennant F.C., founded in 1964. In 2003 the club renamed as Waltham Forest. The word means a long triangular flag, similar to a pennon. It is used in American baseball as a trophy, and a flying pennant appears as a crest on the club badges of Leyton P. and the present club, and two smaller pennants appeared on the shield of Walthamstow P. Nevertheless, it remains slightly mysterious why a type of flag should have been used as the original club name; recorded as a nickname in Smith 1995/6. See also Lilywhites, Stags.

Pennies is a nickname for Abergavenny Thursdays F.C., founded in Monmouthshire in 1927. The club plays at the Pen-y-Pound ground. The place-name predates the ground name and is a Welsh formation adapting the English word 'pound' for a fenced place containing animals, so it means 'the pound at the end, or top, of the village'. There are several such names in Wales, but the one in Abergavenny is the earliest recorded, appearing as *Pen y pounde* in 1599. The ground would have been built on or close to this location for the name to transfer. The nickname then puns on the ground name as a short form, but its development was no doubt influenced by English pronunciation and spelling. The confident expression of commitment, 'In for a penny, in for a pound', and the Cockney rhyming slang word for 'penny', which happens to be 'Abergavenny', appear to be entirely coincidental developments (thanks to Hywel Wyn Owen and Richard Morgan for advice); Wikipedia. See also Butchers, Thursdays.

Penrhyn is a short-form nickname for two Welsh clubs whose place-name begins with this element. The clubs are:

⊛ Penrhyncoch F.C., founded in Ceredigion in 1965; recorded in RW1995–2011. See also Lions, Roosters.

⊛ Penrhyndeudraeth F.C., founded in Gwynedd in 1930. The nickname is used in historical match reports from the 1980s on the club's website. The village itself also has a nickname, 'Cockle Town', from the local cockle industry (Wikipedia), though this does not seem to have ever been used by the club.

Pens is the nickname for Penryn Athletic F.C., founded in Cornwall in 1963. A short form of the place-name, though the Cornish element 'pen' usefully means 'chief' or 'top'; recorded on the 'Goalrun' website. See also Borough.

Pensioners is the traditional nickname of Chelsea F.C., after the famous Chelsea Pensioners institution for retired service personnel. The club was founded in 1905 and adopted a Chelsea Pensioner image for their logo from the outset, which was only replaced by a succession of designs based on a heraldic lion after 1952. The nickname is recorded on the 1933 Ogden card and Churchill 1958, Norris 1959, Sweetule 1959, Richards 1960, AA 1960, SWSCYB 1962–3, Avis 1954–70 but in Moss 1983 it is described as 'formerly'. Nevertheless, it makes a late appearance on the 1986 Panini sticker. It is a club tradition that inmates of the Royal Hospital are given free entry to the matches. See also Blues, Chelsea Headhunters, Chelski, Drake's Ducklings.

Penwaig is the nickname of Nefyn United F.C., founded in 1932; recorded in RW2011. The nickname is the Welsh word for herrings, and it appears in English as well. The location on the Llŷn Peninsula is important for the herring industry. See also Herrings.

People's Club is a recent nickname for Everton F.C., coined by David Moyes (manager since 2002); Wikipedia. See also Bitters / Bitter Blues, Black Watch, Bluenoses, Blues, Dogs of War, Merseysiders, Moonlight Dribblers, School of Science, Toffees/Toffeemen.

Peppermints is the nickname for Newquay A.F.C., founded in Cornwall in 1890, reformed 1946. The club plays in red-and-white stripes, the colours of the traditional peppermint boiled sweet. The nickname appears in the title of the club history, Sandra Biggin's *A Mixed Bag of Peppermints* (the club, 1989), which records that the nickname dates from 1906. The crest on the shield of the club shows the famous Cornish black bird, the chough, though this never appears to have been used as a nickname for the club; Avis 1966–70, W1992–2005 and W2013.

Pepps is the nickname for Peppard F.C., founded in Rotherfield Peppard in South Oxfordshire in 1903. The club merged with Sonning Common in 1984, but reverted to its original name in 1990; a pluralised short form of the place-name; the club seems to disappear after 2002; W1995–6.

Perry Bar Pets is recorded in Avis 1966–70 as an old nickname for Aston Villa. The nickname was also (perhaps primarily?) used as the name of a fanzine, first published in 1897 (a retyped copy is on the internet). Perry Bar is the district of Birmingham which was the club's home. The 'Pets' suffix is a more mysterious part of the nickname, but if the expression is primarily that of a fanzine, it could be used in the sense of 'pet-topics'. See also Claret and Blues, Lions, Seals, Villa / Villans / Villains.

Pesda is the nickname of Bethesda Athletic F.C., founded in Gwynedd in 1946; recorded in RW2011. Richard Huws informs that "Pesda is a popular abbreviation for Bethesda – the famous rock festival which was held in the village was known as Pesta Roc, and people from Bethesda are often referred to as Pobl Pesda".

Peters is a nickname for New Bradwell St. Peter F.C., founded in the 1880s near

Milton Keynes in Buckinghamshire, originally as New Bradwell St James. The club later renamed as Stantonbury St Peter, and as the present name in 1946–7 after a merger with New Bradwell Corinthians. The club website suggests that Peters became the nickname after 1926. The club badge shows the crossed keys of St Peter and gives the club's foundation date as 1902 (perhaps when Corinthians was founded?); W1983/4 and W1994–2013 and club's own website. See also Jimmies, Saint Peters.

Pewits was the nickname of the old Emley A.F.C., founded in West Yorkshire in 1903, and has been resumed by the new A.F.C. Emley, reformed in 2005, together with the club's old badge featuring a coal-mining pit wheel and an image of a pewit bird. The nickname appears in W1999–2002 and in W2008–13 for the new club. Between 2002 and 2004, the club was merged with Wakefield and the same nickname appears for this club in W2003–6. Pewits, or peewits, are also called lapwings, the northern variety being a migratory visitor to Britain. The bird has been used in place-names as a metaphor for moorland places, and the OED records 'pee-wit-land' as a dialect expression for poor or undrained land, which is entirely correct for the distinctive upland location of Emley, but the adoption of the shorter spelling suggests that there is also here a pun on 'pit'. The West Riding tendency to slurr words in speech could easily blur the distinction between the two. See also Bears.

Pheasants is the nickname of the Nottingham side, Radford F.C., founded in 1964, originally as a works side for the engineering firm of Manlove & Alliots, then renaming as R. Olympic in 1977, present name in 1987. The nickname seems to be from some association with the Pheasant Inn in Prospect Street, Radford; a pheasant also appears on the club badge.

Phoenix is a common football suffix and is usually used for a club emerging from a painful reformation. The phoenix is a classical mythical bird which is reborn in fire. A great many clubs use the Phoenix name but only one use of the word as a nickname has been seen: for Bramley Phoenix F.C., founded in Leeds in 1999, on their website. An early club called Phoenix Bessemer competed in the FA Cup in 1882–3 and may be the earliest use of the name.

Picks was a nickname for Willenhall Pickwicks F.C., founded in West Midlands in 1884 and closed in a merger with W. Swifts in 1916. The use of 'Pickwicks' as a club name must derive from the popularity of Charles Dickens' novel, *The Posthumous Papers of the Pickwick Club* (1836–7). The nickname is given in the title of Horace & Peter Davis' *The Picks. The Story of Willenhall Pickwicks Football Club* (Willenhall, 1994). Another football club called Pickwicks was Brockmoor P., which became Brierley Hill Alliance in 1887 (see under Lions).

Pics is the nickname for Rushall Olympic F.C., founded in Kent in 1893 and reformed in 1951. The badge shows an Olympic flame, and the nickname is a pluralised short form of the suffix. The club adopted the name before the advent of the modern

Olympic Games in 1896 (planned from 1894, but there had been earlier, less international revivals), but perhaps the success of the 1948 London games helped encourage the reforming of the club; W1982/3–2013. See also Olympic.

Pie Eaters / Pies is a nickname of the borough of Wigan, and thus also of supporters of Wigan Athletic. Although the club was only formed in 1932, the nickname is said to date from the General Strike in 1926, when Wigan miners were forced to eat 'humble pie' and return to work before miners from other regions. The nickname is further celebrated today with the World Pie-Eating Championship which Wigan has hosted since 1992; Wikipedia. See also Athletic, County, Latics, T'Colliers or T'Pitmen.

Pie Men was an early nickname of Dudley Sports F.C., founded in the West Midlands in 1978. The club had been a works side for employees of Marsh & Baxter in Brierley Hill, a major meat-processing plant, and makers of pork pies, which closed in that year, but the football club was refounded independently, and the nickname is still heard; W1994–5.

Pied Pipers was an unofficial nickname for Nottingham Forest F.C. during the successful Brian Clough years (1975–93). This was because Brian himself had the nickname The Pied Piper, because he drew the youth out of their houses to watch the matches. See also Forest/Foresters, Garibaldi Reds, Reds, Robin Hoods, Tricky Trees.

Pier is the nickname of Amble Pier 81 F.C., founded in Northumberland, presumably in 1981. The nickname appears in on-line match reports from *The Morpeth Herald* (e.g. 21 April 2011).

Pigs has been simultaneously the unofficial nicknames of both Sheffield Wednesday and Sheffield United football clubs, aimed at each other, and recorded on the 2003 Football Fans Census website (but the nicknames are older). Oddly, the two clubs have also shared the nickname 'The Blades' in the past. Since 1899 the ground of The Wednesday was believed to have been built on the site of a former slaughterhouse, and their strip of blue-and-white stripes is considered to resemble a butcher's apron, hence the insult from United; but Wednesday reply with the claim that United's red and white strip reminds them of bacon rashers... The variant forms Piggies and Bacon Slices also appear. For both Sheffield clubs, see also Blades, Blunts, Cutlers, Groveites, Laneites, Owls, Red and White Wizards, United, Wednesday, Wendys.

Pikes is the nickname of Pickering Town F.C., founded in North Yorkshire in 1888. The nickname appears on the club badge, which also shows two pike fish apparently kissing a football. Although the original place-name is nothing to do with the fish, the nickname associates the club with a successful predator; W1983/4–6, W1992–2013.

Pilgrims is the nickname for three clubs associated with the 'Pilgrim Fathers', who sailed from Lincolnshire in 1608, first staying in Holland before eventually returning to England and sailing from Plymouth to the New World in 1620, but the name also appears as a suffix for other clubs where the sense appears to be only of one travel. The clubs are:

⚽ Boston United F.C., founded in Lincolnshire in 1933. The Pilgrim Fathers departed from Boston for Holland before returning later to southern England and sailing from Plymouth to America. As with Plymouth, the *Mayflower* ship appears on the club badge; recorded in W1979/80–2002, W2008–13, RY2002/3 and SSY2003/4–7/8. See also Stumpites, United.

⚽ Immingham Town F.C., founded in Lincolnshire in 1912, reformed in 1945, 1969; it is from Immingham that the Pilgrim Fathers first set sale, on their way to Boston; W1995–6. See also Dockers.

⚽ Pilgrim F.C., a famous amateur side of the 1870s and '80s, based in East London. The club is mentioned in BoF1905–6, pp. 125, 257, and in Fabian and Green 1960, iv, p. 331, recording a tour of the USA by the club in 1905. If the official name of the club was 'Pilgrim' then the plural form is a nickname. The FCHD records the club between 1873 and 1882. 'Pilgrims F.C.' is used today for a youth side in Kent, founded at Challock in 2007 and it appears as a suffix in the names of several modern amateur sides.

⚽ Plymouth Argyle F.C., founded in Devon in 1886, originally as Argyle F.C., changing to the present name in 1903. The nickname commemorates the departure of the Pilgrim Fathers for the New World from Plymouth in 1620. It is recorded on the 1933 Ogden card and in G1956–76, Churchill 1958, Richards 1960, SWSCYB 1962–3, Avis 1966–70, W1987–90, and throughout RY1970/1–SSY2012/13. The club's badge features the *Mayflower* ship. Much more difficult to explain is the Argyle element in the club's official name, but Plymouth in the 1880s had an admiration for the Scots. The city's church was dedicated to St Andrew and the Scottish saltire is on the local coat of arms. The club's initial committee meetings were in the Argyle Hotel on Argyle Street, and the military base had recently been the home of the Argyll and Sutherland Highlanders, whose football skills were much admired, so there are a multiple number of possible reasons for the suffix, within a general Scotophile context. See also Argyle, Green Army.

Pilks is the nickname for Pilkington XXX F.C., based in Birmingham, originally named Burman Hi-Ton F.C. in the 1990s, before the present name was taken in 2002. The nickname Glassmen is recorded in W2005 for this club, with Pilks recorded in W1982/3–9 for an earlier club called Pilkington Recreation based at Doncaster, appearing in the FCHD between 1976 and 1991. Wikipedia applies Pilks to the present P.XXX club. See also Glassmen.

Pink and Chocolate is a nickname of Corinthian Casuals F.C. Based in Tolworth near Kingston-upon-Thames, the club was formed in 1939 as a merger between Corinthian (1882) and Casuals (1878). The nickname refers to the pink and chocolate-coloured halves the club plays in, combined with dark blue shorts; Wikipedia. See also Amateurs, Casuals, Corinthians.

Pinks was a popular colour in the Victorian period and is recorded as the nickname of two clubs, based on strip colours. The clubs are:

⚽ Guildford F.C., founded in 1877, reformed as Guildford United in 1921. The nickname is preserved in Twydell 1988 and was last used in press reports of a match against Brentford in October 1920. The club played in pink-and-claret quartered shirts. The public interest shown in the match against Brentford led to demand for a new club with professional status, which was agreed by December 1920 and Guildford United was born, playing in green-and-white stripes. See also City, Guild, Sweeney.

⚽ Westminster School F.C. The school's colours, used in several sports, notably rowing, are pink and the nickname is recorded for the school football side in BoF1905–6 (p.122). The school was an important influence on the foundation of Association Football as some of the playing rules were first developed here.

PJs was the initialism for Polkemmet Juniors F.C., founded in Harthill, West Lothian, in 1974, closed 1988; SFHA.

Piod is the Welsh-language nickname of Bow Street F.C., founded in Ceredigion in about 1920. The nickname is the Welsh word for Magpies (q.v.).

Pirates is a nickname for Bristol Rovers F.C., in honour of the city's maritime heritage, though the concept seems a little contradictory as pirates must have worked against Bristol's trade. The club was founded as the Black Arabs, a name they used only for the first season of 1883–4, but which also suggests piracy because Arab pirates were once even more of a danger to the Atlantic trade than the 'Caribbean' style of pirate who is familiar today (there is no evidence that Black Arabs was ever used as a nickname for the club, it was briefly the club's official name, though it has also been the name of a fanzine). A pirate features on the club's badge, and is recorded as a visual symbol for the team on the 1933 Ogden card. 'Pirates' is a superb nickname for a sporting team, recorded in Harvey 1959, G1965–76, Avis 1966–70, and throughout RY and SSY from 1970/1 to 2012/13. One branch of supporters is nicknamed Blackthorn Buccaneers (after Blackthorn End, one of the terraces of the home ground, with Buccaneers an alternative word for pirates). The club mascots have always been pirates, with names like Captain Gas and Captain Black Arab. See also Arabs, Black Arabs, Gas / Gasheads, Purdown Poachers, Rovers, Squatters, Tesco's.

Pitmen is a nickname for two clubs, one from a mining community and another from the ground name. The clubs are:

⚽ Hednesford Town F.C., founded in 1880 in a Staffordshire coal-mining community. Recorded in W1979/80–2013. See also Whites.

⚽ Trefonen F.C., founded in Shropshire in 2008. The ground name is The Pit, recording the existence of a nearby former coal mine, and the nickname is based on this rather than the general sense of a team from a mining community; Wikipedia. See also Yellows.

Plain was the nickname of Annfield Plain F.C., founded in Co. Durham in 1890, originally as Annfield Plain Celtic F.C. Recorded in Barton 1984 & 1985, W1982/3—5. A badge in AFBC records the chant 'Howay the Plain'.

Planemakers is the nickname of two clubs which are based at aircraft factories. The clubs are:

⚽ Airbus UK Broughton F.C., founded as a works side for the Vickers Armstrong aircraft factory in Flintshire in 1946. The club now has a badge with a modern Airbus flying over a football, and the club ground is called 'The Airfield'. Recorded in RW2000–03. See also Wingmakers.

⚽ G. E. Hamble F.C., founded in 1935. The club has always been a works side for an aircraft factory, originally Folland Aircraft F.C., renamed Folland Sports after the War, then Aerostructures S&S in 1990. The current name was taken in 2011; Wikipedia.

Planemen was the nickname of BAe Weybridge F.C., in Surrey; recorded in W1986–90. According to the Football Club History Database, the club was a successor to BAC Weybridge, recorded from 1972, changing name in 1977, and changing again to Weybridge Town in 1989. After 1990 the club seems to disappear.

Planters is the nickname of Norwich United F.C., founded in 1903. The club play at Plantation Park, Blofield, outside Norwich and the motto also appears on the club badge; an adaptation of the ground name, recorded in W1992–2013.

Plastics is an unofficial nickname for Blackburn Rovers F.C., from the perspective of Burnley and Preston supporters (see Football Fans Census, 2003). The nickname refers to the money invested by the owner Jack Walker, with the two suggestions, that it was all done on a credit card and the results were artificially manufactured (i.e., man-made like plastic). See also Blue and Whites, Highwaymen, Jackburn, Riversiders, Rovers.

P.N.E. is an initialism, frequently used for Preston North End F.C. Recorded in Avis 1966–70. See also Glasses, Invincibles, Lilywhites, Proud Preston.

Poachers is a nickname for three clubs, each of them associated with a folklore tradition of poaching. See also Purdown Poachers for the slightly different meaning of 'poaching' players. The clubs are:

⚽ Boston Town F.C., formed in 1964 during a breakaway from Boston United ('the Pilgrims'). The nickname refers to the 'Lincolnshire Poacher', a popular folksong and an expression of the county's anti-establishment, but traditional, culture; W1980/1–86 and W1992–2013.

⚽ Bottesford Town F.C., established in North Lincolnshire in 1974, for the same county cultural reason as the above; W2008–13.

⚽ Oadby Town F.C., founded in Leicestershire in 1937 or 1939, originally as Oadby Imperial. The name changed to 'Town' in 1951. The nickname is a salute to the local folk hero, poacher James Hawker (c.1836–1921). His fame has spread in modern times with the publication of his diaries in 1961 and the performance of a biographical play in 1980, after which a collection raised money for a commemorative tombstone, on which is inscribed his motto "I will poach till I die"; W2008–13. See also Imps.

Pockets was briefly a nickname for Mexborough Town Athletic F.C., between 2008 and 2010, when they rebranded themselves as M. Pocket due to a sponsorship deal with the Corner Pocket Club in the town. The South Yorkshire club was founded before 1885 and has gone through many name changes. After 'Pocket' it became A.F.C. Sportsman Rovers but reverted to M.T.A. in 2012; Wikipedia. See also Athletic, Boro, Town.

Point is the nickname for three clubs with the word *point* in their official names. The clubs are:

- Hurstpierpoint F.C., founded in West Sussex in 1888; W1989–96. See also Hurst.
- Torpoint Athletic F.C., founded in Cornwall in 1887; W2008–13. See also Gold and Black Army.
- Warrenpoint Town F.C., founded in Co. Down in 1987. The nickname is also used for the town itself; Wikipedia.

Poles was the nickname of Polesworth North Warwick F.C., founded in Warwickshire in 1966. The 'North Warwick' part of the name referred to the North Warwick Sports Ground in Polesworth, which lies on the extreme northern tip of the county along the Staffordshire border; W1993–5.

Police is the nickname of PSNI F.C., the new name (since 2002) of the RUC F.C., founded in Belfast in 1928. The Royal Ulster Constabulary became the Police Service of Northern Ireland during the recent political changes in the country. Recorded in RW 2007 (RW 1997 has the nickname for the older club).

Poly is a nickname for at least two clubs which were sides for former polytechnic colleges. The clubs are:

- Thames Polytechnic F.C. The Woolwich Polytechnic was founded in 1890, renamed Thames in 1970 and became the University of Greenwich in 1992. The football club seems to have disappeared after 1992, though it is listed without a nickname in W1993; W1988–92.
- University of Ulster at Jordonstown F.C., founded in Newtownabbey, Co. Antrim in 1972. The Ulster Polytechnic became a university in 1984; Wikipedia. See also U.U.J.

Pompey is the nickname of Portsmouth F.C. The process by which the nickname became attached to the naval base and city of Portsmouth is a mystery recently reviewed by the linguist Professor Richard Coates in the academic journal *Nomina*, 32 (2011), 59–73. Pompey is an ancient Roman personal name (the Roman place-name *Pompeii* means 'Pompey's town'). Coates demonstrates that the earliest recorded use of the nickname relating to Portsmouth is actually in a football context, and as late as 1899, making all the traditional theories highly unlikely because they would require that the nickname had existed 'underground' for a hundred years before it enters the media. Its first known appearance in print is in the *Evening News* for 9 December 1899: "Wilkie, amid tremendous cheering from the Pompey lads, won the toss ...". Coates then provides ample evidence for the early use of Pompey as a name for pet dogs in eighteenth-century England and for slaves in nineteenth-century America. From the slave name came the use of Pompey as a stock character in a great many nineteenth-century American comic songs, and it is known that songs like these were brought to Portsmouth by sailors who had heard them in America. When the Royal Artillery football team was set up in Portsmouth in 1895, a supporters' song was written called 'The Pompey Chimes', in the style of these American songs, but to the tune of the chimes on the Portsmouth Guildhall clock. When the Royal Artillery team folded in 1899, support and song and nickname were transferred to the new Portsmouth F.C., which had only been established the year before. And from there it spread to the naval base and the city (a transfer it seems to have achieved as early as 1904 because it is mentioned in Rudyard Kipling's *Traffics and Discoveries*). Coates suggests that the alliteration of Pompey and Portsmouth, though sharing only the first two letters, may have helped with the adoption of the nickname. Certainly, many other club nicknames derive from only slight similarities in spelling or rhymes.

Although, as Coates admits, direct evidence for the processes of transfer is lacking, this theory provides an extremely plausible context for how the nickname could have originated, and it fits with the known chronological evidence.

Coates reviews nine other theories for the nickname (pp. 60–5), with critical comments. The theories are: (1) Roman ruins at Portchester reminded someone of the ruins of Pompeii (but Portchester is not Portsmouth!). (2) Pompey refers to the 'pomp' of the Royal Navy (linguistically possible but doubtful because the nickname is not spelled 'pompy'). (3) It refers to volunteer firemen called *pompiers* (but this is a French word with no evidence of it ever having been used by English firemen, for whom 'firemen' has been used since 1714). (4) A temperance campaigner was giving a lecture on alcohol abuse and mentioned the murder of Pompey the Great, a drunken sailor woke up and shouted out 'Poor old Pompey!' (Coates regards this as 'a projection back in time' of later football chants from rival supporters). (5) Pompey is a drunkard's slurred pronunciation of 'Portsmouth Point' (Coates states that, linguistically, this is not a convincing alcohol-induced pronunciation). (6) Pompey comes from the Indian place-name Bombay, because Portuguese sailors thought the two places looked alike (Coates provides a linguistic dismissal of this impossible idea). (7) In 1781 sailors from Portsmouth scaled the column near Alexandria in Egypt which is called Pompey's Pillar and so became known as 'The Pompey Boys' (Coates reports that scaling this column was a common tourist activity, making the feat insignificant, and the date seems implausible; it is merely a coincidence of the two names being the same). (8) The nickname comes from the *Pompée*, a French warship which was taken over by the

Royal Navy in 1793 and later became a prison ship based at Portsmouth (Coates says that it is not impossible that a phrase 'in Pompey' was taken to mean 'in prison' and then assumed to mean 'in Portsmouth', but there is no evidence that this actually happened, though the ship's existence is certainly true). And finally **(9)**, naval officers entering the harbour used to write 'Pom. P.' for Portsmouth Point in their logs (Coates says this has a vague possibility but also lacks any evidence; like the story of Posh (q.v.) being a nautical acronym, it lacks a single example in any of the thousands of surviving ships' logs).

The nickname is not on the 1933 Ogden card, but it appears in the mainstream sources of Johnston 1934, Avis 1954-70, G1956–76, Churchill 1958, the 1959 Sweetule card, Richards 1960, *Stedfast* December 1964 and throughout RY1970/1– SSY2012/13. See also Blues / Blue Army, Sailors, Skates.

Pompey Ladies is the nickname for Portsmouth L.F.C. The club is one of the earliest and most successful women's football clubs, but the date of foundation is difficult to find. The nickname adapts the nickname used by the men's club; Wikipedia.

Ponty is a nickname for two Welsh clubs which have a place-name starting with *Pont–*. The Clubs are:

- Pontardawe Town F.C., founded in 1947 in the Co. Bor. of Neath Port Talbot, originally as P. Athletic, renamed 'Town' in 1998; a friendly short form of the place-name; recorded in RW2001–11.
- Pontypridd Town A.F.C., founded in Rhondda Cynon Taf in 1992, in a merger with Ynysybwl F.C. The nickname is used on the club's own website. See also Dragons.

'Pool is a nickname for three northern clubs with this element in their place-name. The clubs are:

- Blackpool F.C., as a short form of the place-name. The nickname is used in Johnston 1934. See also Atomic Boys, Donkey Lashers, Merry Stripes, Seasiders, Tangerines.
- Hartlepool United F.C., founded in Co. Durham in 1908. The club's nickname used to appear in the plural because 'Hartlepool' has several settlements and the club represented them all and called itself 'Hartlepools', but the singular form has been used since 1968. The singular form occurs in G1976, Moss 1983, Barton 1984 & 1985. W1985–7 and throughout RY1970/1–SS2012/13. See also Dockers, Monkey Hangers, Pools.
- Liverpool F.C., as a short form of the place-name; recorded throughout RY1970/1– SSY2012/13. See also Anfielders, Culture Club, Kop / Kopites, Liddellpool, Mariners, Merseysiders, Micky Mousers, Reds, Spice Boys.

Pools was the nickname of Hartlepools United F.C. Founded in 1908, the club had a plural –s on the end until 1968, due to there being more than one Hartlepool, both in place-names and clubs. G1956–65, Churchill 1958, Harvey 1959 and Richards 1960 record the plural form. See also Dockers, Monkey Hangers, Pool.

Poppies is a nickname for clubs which play in poppy-red colours. The clubs are:

☉ Bournemouth F.C., founded in Dorset in 1875, originally as B. Rovers, then B. Wanderers, are nowadays often referred to as B. Poppies. The club tradition is that they adopted the poppy-red colours and the nickname in 1895. Recorded in W1992 as Bournemouth Poppies, in W1993–2013 as Poppies.

☉ Kettering Town F.C., founded in Northamptonshire in 1872, plays in red and has a badge with three stylish poppies on it; recorded in Avis 1966–70, W1979/80– 2013 and SSY2009/10–12/13. Addis 1995 reprints a newspaper article of 1946 and a programme of 1947 which use the nickname (pp. 4, 7). See also Friars, Holy City Boys, Kets / Kettles.

Porchey is the nickname of the Hampshire side, A.F.C. Portchester, founded in 1971, originally as Loyds Sports, then Colourvision Rangers in 1973 and Wicor Mill in 1976 and the present name in 1999; Wikipedia. See also Royals.

Port is a nickname for clubs with the place-name element 'port' in their place-name. The clubs are:

☉ Ellesmere Port Town F.C., founded in Cheshire in 1948, folded 1978, refounded in 1992, folded again in 1994; W1994. See also Town.

☉ Newport County F.C., founded in Monmouthshire in 1912, and refounded in 1989 as Newport A.F.C. See also Black and Ambers, County, Cromwellians, Exiles, Ironsides, Wasps.

☉ Newport (I.O.W.) F.C., founded on the Isle of Wight in 1888; W1980/1 and W1994–2013.

☉ Porthmadog F.C., founded in Gwynedd in 1884. The club shows a ship on its badge, but primarily the nickname is a short form of the place-name; recorded in RW1994– 2011. See also Porth.

☉ Southport F.C., founded in Lancashire in 1881, originally as Southport Central; Wikipedia. See also Sandgrounders, Yellows.

☉ Tayport F.C., founded in Fife in 1947; Wikipedia, SFHA.

Porth is a variant nickname for Porthmadog F.C., founded in Gwynedd in 1884. A short form of the place-name; recorded in W1994–9 and 2004–5. Richard Huws, however, reports that this spelling must be an error, as 'Port' is the form the nickname always takes in Wales. See also Port.

Portites was a nickame for Ellesmere Port and Neston F.C., founded sometime between the demise of E.Port (1978) and 1981 when it appears in the Chreshire League Division 2 tables; the club is listed in Williams from 1982/3 to 1989, but the nickname only appears in W1986. The nickname in –*ites* is a rather old fashioned abstraction from the place-name, but perhaps the expression had originally been used for the earlier clubs in Ellesmere.

Ports is the nickname of Portadown F.C., founded in Co. Armagh in 1924; a pluralised short form of the place-name. Recorded in RI1997, RNI2007.

Posh is the nickname of Peterborough United F.C. The long-standing official explanation is that in 1921 Pat Tirrel, player and manager of Fletton United, announced he was "Looking for posh players for a posh new team". This new team was Fletton and Peterborough United, which he set up in 1923 (it was really just a change of name to widen the support base). The nickname 'Posh' began to be used for this team, encouraged by sarcastic usage of the name in the press, and the club went bankrupt in October 1932. There can be little doubt that the meaning of the word as used by the club has the mainstream 'superior' sense, but if the press usage was sarcastic, the journalists may have had a different meaning in mind. There is a local farming expression, 'posh rotten', which means a crop which is rotten on the inside but looks fine on the outside (especially apples or potatoes). One dialect dictionary says that this originates in 'push rotten' and means "Bad enough to give way at a touch" (Sims-Kimbrey, 1995), so the term is perfect for mocking pretentious claims which are only skin-deep.

Nevertheless, in 1934 the new Peterborough United F.C. was founded, and consciously re-adopted the nickname. It is claimed that at the first match on 1 September 1934, against Gainsborough Trinity, the chant "Up the Posh!" was heard in the crowd. There is absolutely no reason to doubt the official account, especially with the local dialect adding an extra dimension, but three entirely different traditions were given the author by word-of-mouth: (1) the players were given expensive overcoats, either as part of their contract or as a reward for performance, earning them the comment "There's posh!" when seen in public; (2) or that the manager or owner of the club always turned up wearing a top hat and tails; or (3) the crowd liked the new club's new strip when they first turned out in it, commenting "There's posh!". These three explanations are clearly retrospective ideas, illustrating that even fans do not necessarily understand a long-established nickname. Early newspaper cuttings reproduced in Addis 1995 show that the nickname was well-established by 1946 (p. 11) and a cutting of c.1952 (p. 51) adds "How they came by the name I don't know. Nor apparently does anyone else. But I'm thinking it could be something to do with the quality of their football". Addis 1995 has another cutting, and a photograph, from 1953 (pp. 61–2) recording that the club had a mascot called 'Mr Posh', played by Tom Keeble, who wore a top hat, monocle and silver knobbed cane: clearly adopted after the advent of the nickname but probably the source of theory 2, above.

Peterborough has a mocking nickname of it's own, like Preston in Lancashire it is 'Proud Peterborough' ("of ancient repute for self-esteem and a surfeit of clerics", Jones-Baker 1981, p. 58). It is entirely possible that this was the main source of inspiration for the nickname: the 1933 Ogden card for Preston illustrates 'Proud Preston' with an image like that of 'Mr Posh'.

There is absolutely no truth in the myth that P.O.S.H. is a nautical acronym for 'Port Out and Starboard Home' (though that is now part of folklore and it appears as a Peterborough pub name), and even in its 'superior' sense, the word was already regarded as unsuitable for 'polite' conversation by about 1930 (Quinion 2004, Beale,

1989), lending further support to the idea that press usage was initially mocking. Needless to say, the club's successful performance in later years meant that any original sarcasm in the nickname was soon forgotten. Posh, of course, is also the nickname of one Victoria Beckham, who tried to oppose the club's use of the name in 2002, but dropped the confrontation in January 2003. Recorded in Avis 1966–70, G1976, and throughout RY1970/1–SSY2012/13. See also Brickies.

Posset is the nickname for Portishead Town F.C., founded in Somerset in 1912, originally as St Peter's Portishead before renaming in 1948. The nickname is a local nickname for the town and port of Portishead, near Bristol, from a slurred pronunciation of the place-name. Locally, it is pronounced 'Pozzet' (thanks to Brian Crabb); W2006–13.

Potters is the nickname for two clubs based in the Stoke-on-Trent 'Potteries' industrial area of Staffordshire. The clubs are:

- Eastwood Hanley F.C., founded in Hanley, Stoke-on-Trent, Staffordshire in 1946. The club folded in 1997; W1982/3–6. See also Blues.
- Stoke City F.C., recording the major potteries industry in the city, and the general name for the district, The Potteries. Founded in 1863 as Stoke Ramblers F.C., the club adopted its distinctive red-and-white striped shirts in 1878. The name is included in the 1933 Ogden cigarette card set, the 1936 Thomson 'stamp' album and in Avis 1954–70, G1956–76, Churchill 1958, Richards 1960, and throughout RY1970/1–SSY2012/13. The club's hippopotamus mascot is called Pottermus. See also City, Clayheads, Jolly Green Giants, Sjoke City.

Powermen was the nickname of Hams Hall F.C., founded in Warwickshire in 1930 as a works side for the Hams Hall Generating Station in Sutton Coldfield. By 1993 the station was no more but the club maintained an independent existence till about 2001 (FCHD); W1993–5.

Press is the nickname of Cambridge University Press F.C., founded in 1893. The club, whose membership is no longer confined to employees of the press, competes in the local leagues and uses the same badge as the publisher. Their nickname, and part official name, is a general word for all publishers and printers; Wikipedia.

Pride of the Clyde is a nickname for Greenock Morton F.C., founded in 1874. Greenock has long been a major shipbuilding centre and port, near Glasgow, on the River Clyde; Wikipedia. See also 'Ton.

Prims is a nickname for clubs with the word 'Primitive' in their official name, or history, from an affiliation with the Primitive Methodist Church. Examples are:

- Graham Street Prims F.C., founded in Derby in 1904, reformed 1953; W1982/3–6 and W2013.
- Walsall Wood F.C., founded in c.1915 in the West Midlands, originally as Walsall Wood Ebenezer Primitive Methodist F.C.. The club merged in 1982 with Walsall Sports, to form Walsall Borough F.C., renamed to the present name in 1986; Wikipedia. See also Wood.

Printers was a nickname for two clubs which were works sides for major printing businesses. The clubs were:

- Hazells (Aylesbury) F.C., a works side for the printing works of Hazell, Watson and Viney Ltd. The company ran from 1709 to 1989, when a management buy-out reduced it in size. The football club appears in the FCHD between 1957 and 1994, and the nickname in W1986–7.
- Waterlows F.C., founded in Dunstable, Buckinghamshire for Waterlow & Sons Ltd. The FCHD records the club from 1922 to 1985. In 1961, the company was acquired by Purnell & Sons and its last remnant was closed in 2009, but the football club disappears after 1985; W1983/4.

Priory is the nickname of at least two clubs, in locations with a medieval priory or monastery. The clubs are:

- Christchurch F.C., founded in the ancient Dorset monastic city in 1885; W1992–2013.
- Reigate Priory F.C., founded in Surrey in 1870; Wikipedia.

Priorymen is the nickname of Guisborough Town F.C., founded in North Yorkshire in 1973. The image on the club badge and the nickname commemorate the medieval monastery, Guisborough Priory. Recorded in Barton 1985; W1980/1–2013.

Prog was the nickname of Cannock Chase F.C., founded in Staffordshire in 1968. What appears to be an extraordinary nickname is simply a short form of the club's first suffix: Hednesford Progressive. The FCHD records the name change in 1987, and the entries terminate in 2000; W1994–5.

Proud Preston is a nickname for Preston North End F.C.. The club tradition is that this dates from their record-breaking double win in 1889, but it was already a nickname for the town by the early eighteenth century. Room 2006 quotes the entry from Daniel Defoe's *Tour Thro' the Whole Island of Great Britain*, of 1724–6: "The town … is full of gentlemen, Attorneys, Proctors, and Notaries … The people are gay here, though not perhaps the richer for that; but it has on this Account obtained the name of Proud Preston". However, the nickname would naturally also be associated with the football club itself after their heroic achievement. The club badge of a Lamb of God appeared on the shirts 1933–95, and had the letters PP below the symbol. This actually stands for 'Prince of Peace' in Latin, not 'Proud Preston', but the double meaning does no harm. 'Proud Preston' is recorded in BoF1905–6 (also as 'Prestonians'), on the 1933 Ogden card and Avis 1954–70, Churchill 1958 and AA 1960. See also Glasses, Invincibles, Lilywhites / Whites, North End, P.N.E.

Pully was the nickname of Pulrose United A.F.C., founded in 1932 on the Isle of Man. A friendly short form of the place-name, it is recorded in newspaper match reports posted on the website of Onchan A.F.C. See also Ham Bappers.

Pumas is a football suffix and nickname for several clubs, especially youth sides. Two clubs with senior sides are:

- Lightwater Pumas F.C., founded in Surrey in 2012; club website.

☺ Pontprennau Pumas A.F.C., established in 2002 in Cardiff. The nickname is used on the club's own website. The club plays in yellow, which is not unlike the golden brown of the big cat's fur; Huws 2013.

Pumphy is the nickname of Pumpherston F.C., founded in West Lothian in 1990 (reforming an older club of 1896); a friendly short form of the place-name; Wikipedia, SFHA. See also Ston.

Purdown Poachers was an unofficial nickname for Bristol Rovers F,C, in their early years. The club was founded in 1883 as Black Arabs F.C. (named from the Arabs rugby team and the black strip they wore) and originally played at Purdown, a district of Bristol; the team moved to Eastville only a year later and renamed as Eastville Rovers in 1885, then Bristol Eastville Rovers, before becoming Bristol Rovers in 1898. The nickname refers to their original home ground at Purdown and the club's reputation for poaching players from other clubs, at a time when this was controversial. The nickname is recorded on the Historical Football Kits website with this explanation. See also Arabs, Black Arabs, Gas / Gasheads, Pirates, Rovers, Squatters, Tesco's.

Puritans is the nickname of Banbury United F.C. Founded in Oxfordshire in 1931 as Spencer Villa, a works club, it became Banbury Spencer in 1934, then Banbury United in 1965. The town has a strong puritan tradition, and was a major centre of operations for the Puritan (Parliamentary) cause during the Civil War. The club badge has an image of a Puritan in traditional dress. In the '60s, '70s and '80s the club was nicknamed 'The Gay Puritans', but the simpler form was adopted in either 1991 or 1992 (the club was listed in W1991 without a nickname and the Gay prefix last appears in W1993); W1992, W1994–2013. See also Gay Puritans, United.

PYC is recorded as a nickname for Penhill F.C., founded in Swindon, Wiltshire, in 1970, in W1986–8. The initialism almost certainly stood for Penhill Youth Club. The club renamed as Swindon Athletic in 1989 and then merged with Supermarine in 1992 to form Swindon Supermarine. No nickname is recorded for Swindon Athletic but the merged club today is nicknamed 'Marine'. See also Hill Club.

QoS is an initialism for the Dumfries side, Queen of the South F.C., founded in 1919. Recorded in Avis 1970. See also Doonhamers, Queens.

Q.P. is an initialism, for the Scottish club Queen's Park F.C. Recorded in Avis 1966–70. See also Amateurs, Glorious Hoops, Queen's, Spiders.

Q.P.R. is an initialism for Queen's Park Rangers F.C., and counts as a nickname because it is so used. Recorded in Avis 1954–70. See also Hoops / Superhoops, R's, Rangers.

Quakers is the nickname of Darlington F.C. (and the refounded club in 2012), from the Religious Society of Friends, or Quakers, who, through the Pease family, were hugely influential in the industrial history of Darlington and its region. Founded in 1883, the nickname is given in the 1933 Ogden cigarette card, with a cartoon of a friendly Quaker playing football; also in G1956–76, Churchill 1958, Richards 1960,

SWSCYB 1962–3, Avis 1966–70, Barton 1985, W1985–6, W1990 and in RY and SSY from 1970/1 to 2012/13. The shield adopted in 1987 shows amongst other symbols a traditional Quaker hat and the slogan "The Friendly Club" is added below the badge on the team's shirts; W2013 for the new club. See also Darlo, Eighteen-Eighty-Three (1883).

Quality Street Kids (or Gang) was a nickname for the home-grown young players who emerged from Celtic F.C., of Glasgow, in the late 1960s, under the management of Jock Stein. Stein managed the reserve side 1957–60, and the whole club 1965–78, but the nickname refers to his players in the later period. Nobody seems to remember why the group was so nicknamed, but it almost certainly relates to the gangs of children who appeared in television advertisements for Quality Street chocolates. Recorded in Pickering 1994 as 'Kids', as 'Gang' on the club's own website. See also Bhoys, Celts, Hoops, Lisbon Lions, 'Tic, Tims.

Quarry Men is the nickname of Blaenau Festiniog Amateurs F.C., founded in Gwynedd in 1980 (with ancestor clubs going back to 1882). The town grew around a major slate industry since the eighteenth century. The form 'Quarrymen' also appears; Wikipedia. See also Amateurs, Comrades.

Quarterboys is a nickname of Rye United F.C., founded in East Sussex in 1938 in a merger of R. F.C. and R. Old Boys F.C. The club merged with Iden (1965) in 2001 but restored the old name in 2006. The nickname was adopted in 2006. The club plays in quartered red-and-black shirts, but it actually refers to the two cherubs on the medieval church clock of St Mary's in Rye, who strike their bells every quarter. The town itself has the nicknames 'Ryers' and 'Mud Heads', the latter because of its situation on coastal mud flats; Wikipedia. See also United.

Queen's is a nickname for Queen's Park F.C., founded in Glasgow in 1867, and the oldest surviving Association Football Club in Scotland. The nickname is used on the club's own website and is a short form of the official name. See also Amateurs, Glorious Hoops, Q.P., Spiders.

Queens is a nickname for clubs with the word 'Queen' in their official name. The clubs are:

⚽ Queen of the South F.C., founded in Dumfries in 1919. The club's official name refers to a nickname for the town of Dumfries, contrasting it to Edinburgh, which is known as Queen of the North (see Room 2006). The nickname may originate in the phrase in the King James Bible, where 'Queen of the South' refers to the Queen of Sheba in Matthew 12.42. The nickname 'Queens' is used in Johnston 1934 and recorded in RY1973/4–87/8. See also Doonhamers, Qos.

⚽ Queen's University Belfast A.F.C., founded at the university in 1908; RNI2007.

Quins is the nickname for two clubs with the word 'Harlequins' in their official name; a short form of the word derived from pantomime use, for the clown character called Harlequin. Although there is some uncertainty as to the etymology of his name, in the wider world the name is used to refer to anything of mixed colours (or other mixed characteristics), from Harlequin's multi-coloured traditional coat. So, in sport the name might refer to a multi-coloured strip, or a club formed from many mergers. There are more examples of the name in rugby. The clubs are:

☻ Bemerton Heath Harlequins F.C., founded in Wiltshire in 1989, in a merger of B. Athletic, Moon F.C. and B. Boys. The club plays in a mixture of black and white; W1994–2013.

☻ Grange Harlequins F.C., founded in Cardiff in 1935. Recorded in RW1995–8. The club tradition is that the nickname refers to its strip in quartered colours.

R's is a nickname for Queen's Park Rangers F.C., as an abbreviation of the suffix. The initialism has a long history, recorded in G1956–76, Churchill 1958, Harvey 1959, Richards 1960, Avis 1966–70 and RY1973/4–SSY2012/13. See also Hoops / Superhoops, Q.P.R., Rangers.

R.A. is a nickname of Darlington Railway Athletic F.C., founded in 1919, reformed in 1993. The initials suggest the Royal Academy rather than Railway Athletic, but that's football; Wikipedia. See also Railwaymen.

Rabbits was a nickname for two clubs, possibly for different reasons. The clubs are:

☻ Coleshill Town F.C., founded in Warwickshire in 1894. The fans' website records the nickname and explains it "as Coleshill's hospitality became famous for its delicious rabbit pies". See also Colemen / Coalmen, Coleshillites, Colts, Greens.

☻ Dalbeattie Star F.C., founded in Dumfries and Galloway in 1900, folded 1948, reformed 1976. It is recorded in RS1995, but RS1996–7 use 'Star'. The explanation for the nickname is not known, but almost certainly refers to a ground infestation (similar to the usage of 'Moles' for Aylesbury). See also Star.

Rabs is a nickname for Kirkintilloch Rob Roy F.C., founded in Dunbartonshire in 1878. The club's name is in honour of the famous Scottish warrior, Rob Roy, or Robert Roy MacGregor (1671–1735), the subject of Scott's best-selling historical novel of 1817; as a pluralised short form of the club name but using the local pronunciation; W1982/3, SFHA. See also Roy.

Racers / Racing is the nickname of Racing Club Warwick F.C., founded in 1919, originally as Saltisford Rovers. The club adopted the present name in 1970 and their home ground is adjacent to Warwick Racecourse; W1999–2013 has 'The Racers'; W1987–98 has 'The Racing'.

Radicals was the nickname and suffix for Llanelli Radicals F.C. Founded in Carmarthenshire in 1986 as Nuffield Rangers, the club was renamed L. Radiators after a sponsorship deal in 1987. When the Llanelli Radiators Company was taken over in 1994 by the Calsonic Kansei Corporation the club was renamed Calsonic Juniors F.C. In 2002 the senior side Llanelli Radicals was set up and took 'Radicals' for its suffix because the word could be made from the first few letters of both Radiators and Calsonic. The senior side seems to have now folded but youth sides still play under the name; club website; Huws 2013.

Radnor Robins is a nickname for Knighton Town F.C., founded in Powys in 1887;

the club plays in red shirts with white shorts and Knighton is in the historic former county of Radnorshire; Wikipedia, and a badge in AFBC shows a robin. See also Borderers, Town.

Rads is a nickname for two clubs, for different reasons. The clubs are:

☺ Morriston Olympic F.C., founded in Swansea in 1988. The nickname appears on the club's website but is not explained there. However, Morriston Library reports (Huws 2013) that the club was set up and sponsored by Olympic Radiators, based in Carmarthen, hence its suffix and nickname. See also Olympic.

☺ Radstock Town F.C., founded in Somerset in 1895. The nickname is a pluralised short form of the place-name, W1994–5. See also Miners. Reds, Town.

Rags and Berties, see discussion under 'Bitters / Bitter Blues'.

Raiders was a nickname for Shepshed Albion F.C., founded in Leicestershire originally in 1890 or 1891, but this earlier club was reformed as S. Charterhouse in 1975. The nickname appears under three different names of the club: in W1989–91 for Charterhouse. The club then re-adopted the name of S. Albion, which appears with the nickname 'Raiders' in W1993–4, in Smith 1991/2–1992/3, and in Pickering 1994). The club folded, however, and the new S. Dynamo was formed, nicknamed 'Dynamo' in W2001–12, but in W1995–9 also listed as 'Raiders'. The nickname is unique, but is very much in the same tradition as Rangers, Rovers, Vikings etc., suitable for a band of roving warriors; and as the nickname was persistent through the various late changes in the club, it probably had an ancestry going back to the first club called Albion. See also Albion, Charterhouse, Dynamo.

Rail is the nickname for Harrogate Railway Athletic F.C., founded in 1935 as a works side for the Starbreck LNER Locomotive Shed. A programme reproduced in W2005 (p. 594) is called *Track Record*; W1982/3–2013. See also Locomotives.

Railwaymen is a nickname for clubs in towns with a major railway industry. The nickname might appear as two words. The clubs are:

☺ Crewe Alexandra F.C., for the town being an important centre for railways. The nickname is recorded throughout RY and SSY from 1970/1 to 2012/13, and earlier in the 1936 Thomson 'stamp' album, G1956–65, Churchill 1958, Richards 1960, Jeffrey 1961 and Avis 1966–70. See also Alex, Robins.

☺ Darlington Railway Athletic F.C., founded in 1919 and reformed after closure in 1993. Darlington is not only a major centre for railways, it is the origin of them. Stevenson's Rocket is on display at Darlington Station; Wikipedia.

☺ Didcot Town F.C., founded in Oxfordshire in 1907. Didcot has been a major junction of railways since 1839, and until 1999 the club's ground was on Station Road. The club badge displays a locomotive wheel; W1987–2013.

☺ Horwich R.M.I. F.C., founded in Lancashire in 1896. The club was originally a works side, the intials standing for Railway Mechanics Institute. In 1995 the club moved to Leigh and was renamed Leigh R.M.I. F.C. (also nicknamed 'The Railwaymen'). In 2008 it was reformed as Leigh Genesis F.C. The name Genesis was used simply to imply a new beginning, but the club folded in 2011. Recorded in Avis 1966–70, W1979/80–95 for Horwich; W1996–2008 and SSY2004/5–5/6 for Leigh and W2009–11 for Genesis. See also Leythers, Locos.

⚽ Leigh Genesis F.C., see previous entry.

⚽ Leigh R.M.I. F.C., see Horwich, above.

⚽ Llandudno Junction F.C., founded in Conwy Co. Bor. in 1999; recorded in RW2011. See also Junction.

⚽ March Town United F.C. Before the Second World War there were two clubs in March, Cambridgeshire: 'Town' (1885) and March GER United F.C. (1911) for employees of the Great Eastern Railway. March is a major railway junction. After 1945, however, the GER side failed to reform and Town took over their ground, still called 'The GER Sports Ground' today; the club adopted the 'United' suffix in 1950. The Railwaymen nickname was used by the GER side; Pyramid Passion website. See also Hares.

⚽ Shildon A.F.C., founded in 1890, originally as S. Athletic. The Co. Durham town of Shildon was a major centre for the building of railway wagons from 1825 to 1983. Since 2004 there has been a Locomotive Museum in the town. The nickname is recorded in W1979/80–87 and W1994–2013, Barton 1984 & 1985; Stevenson's Rocket appears on the club badge. See also Shells.

⚽ Swindon Town F.C., due to the town being a major centre for the Great Western Railway. It is recorded on the 1933 Ogden card and in Churchill 1958, AA 1960, G1965, Avis 1966–70, the first Rothmans: RY1970/1; and Moss 1983 (the last described as 'among old supporters'). See also Moonrakers, Robins, Shunters, Spartans, Swindle.

⚽ Wolverton Town F.C., founded in Buckinghamshire near Milton Keynes in 1887, originally as a railway works side, W. L & NWR F.C., renaming as 'W. British Rail' 1948–81, and W. Town again 1981–7; Wikipedia. See also MK Wolves, Wolves.

Rakers was the nickname of New Brighton F.C., in Wallasey, Merseyside. It is recorded on the 1933 Ogden cigarette card and explained as deriving from Rake Lane, the location of the home ground. The club was a refoundation in 1923 of an older one which had closed in 1901. The new club closed in 1983 but was again reborn in 1993; Wikipedia records that both this and 'The Towerites' nickname are sometimes used for the modern club. Recorded in Johnston 1934, the 1936 Thomson 'stamp' album, Avis 1966–70, W1979/80–80/1. See also Towerites.

Ramblers is a football club name element, suggesting travel like many other suffixes, and it can also be a nickname for the clubs so called. Clubs which take this as a nickname as well are:

⚽ Burnham Ramblers F.C., founded in Essex in 1900; W1987–2013.

⚽ Cobh Ramblers F.C., founded in Co. Cork in 1922. Recorded in RI1997, 2006. See also Rams.

Rams is a nickname for several clubs associated in some way with rams, either as heraldry or as a pun on the place-name. The clubs are:

- Beaconsfield SYCOB F.C., founded in Buckinghamshire in 1994 in a merger of Beaconsfield United (founded 1921) and Slough YCOB; W1983/4–5 (for B. United), W2003–13; Miller & Wright 1996. 'The Rams' nickname was inherited from United and a ram's head appears on the club badge. The SYCOB of the name stands for Slough Youth Centre Old Boys, which has become an alternative nickname for the club. See also SYCOB.

- Cobh Ramblers F.C., founded in Co. Cork in 1922. Here the nickname is a short form of Ramblers. Recorded in RI1997, 2006. See also Ramblers.

- Croydon Athletic F.C., founded in Surrey in 1986, originally as Wandsworth and Norwood. The club adopted the present name in 1990 and has a ram's head as its badge; W1994–7, W2007–13.

- Derby County F.C. Founded in 1884 as an offshoot from Derbyshire County Cricket Club (hence 'County' in the name), they adopted the black-and-white colours in the 1890s and their nickname around the same time. This was also used by the First Regiment of Derby Militia, since 1855, but is based on a traditional Derbyshire folksong, 'The Derby Ram'. A ram's head first appeared on the club badge in 1924, and a stylish full ram in 1971. The club mascot is a ram called Rammie, and until 2003 the club's academy was called Ram-Arena. The nickname appears in BoF1905– 6 (p.17), the 1933 Ogden card (but with the slight explanation that it celebrates the county's agricultural pursuits), Johnston 1934, the 1936 Thomson stamp, G1956–76, Churchill 1958; the 1959 Sweetule card and Norris 1959 refer to the folksong; Richards 1960, AA 1960, SWSCYB 1962–3, Avis 1966–70, and throughout RY and SSY from 1970/1 to 2012/13. See also Sheep.

- Emberton F.C., founded in Buckinghamshire in 1968. The club has long-since disappeared (Emberton Athletic is a modern youth side there) and no specific reason for the nickname is recorded; W1994–7.

- Ramsbottom United F.C., founded in 1966. The first element of this Greater Manchester place-name does carry the same meaning (but the second element means a broad valley). A ram's *head* appears on the club's badge. Dobson 1973 records 'Ramsbottom Rams' as a nickname for the people of the town, not the club; W2009–13.

- Ramsgate F.C., founded in Kent in 1945 as Ramsgate Athletic, renaming in 1972; the meaning of the place-name is uncertain but it cannot be the male sheep. Nevertheless, the club has a magnificent leaping ram on its badge, plus the nickname in inverted commas. Recorded in Avis 1966–70, W1979/80–2013.

- Ramsey Town F.C., founded in Cambridgeshire in 1880 (the place-name probably refers to wild garlic rather than sheep, see Mills 1991); ram on the club badge; W1995–7.

Rangers is a football club suffix with the sense of travelling, roving, wandering, found in other such words, and it often forms a nickname on its own for the club so named.

The mainstream clubs Rangers F.C. in Glasgow and Queens Park Rangers in London ensured the suffix greater popularity. A short form, 'Gers, appears as a popular alternative. Huws 2013 reports several more examples in Wales. 'Rangers' clubs are:

- Ansty Rangers, see below under St Francis Rangers.
- Ards Rangers D.C., founded in 1949 in Co. Down; Wikipedia.
- Berwick Rangers F.C., founded in Northumberland in 1884; RY1973/4–74/5. See also Black and Gold, Borderers, Dream Team, Wee Gers, Wee Rangers.
- Black Country Rangers F.C., founded at Rowley Regis in West Midlands in 1996; club's own website.
- Bradley Rangers F.C., founded in West Yorkshire in 1946; W1982/3–1989. The club folded after 1993.
- Bushey Rangers F.C., founded in Hertfordshire by 1971 (FCHD); W1993–6.
- Carrick Rangers F.C., founded in Co. Antrim in 1939. Recorded in RI1997, RNI2007.
- Concord Rangers F.C., founded in 1967 on Canvey Island in the Thames Estuary; W2010–12. See also Beach Boys.
- Cullompton Rangers F.C., founded in Devon in 1945; W1994–9. See also Cully.
- Deeping Rangers F.C., founded in Lincolnshire in 1966. The club programme is called *Claret & Blue*, suggesting that the colours are an alternative nickname; W2000–13.
- Ellesmere Rangers F.C., founded in Shropshire in 1969. The nickname also appears as a motto on the club's badge; Wikipedia.
- Guernsey Rangers Football and Athletic Club, founded in 1893; Wikipedia.
- Hall Road Rangers F.C., founded in East Yorkshire in 1959, W1982/3–6 and W1994–2013. See also Blues.
- Hawarden Rangers F.C., founded in Clwyd in 1974; Wikipedia.
- Hertfordshire Rangers F.C., founded at Watford in 1865, folding in 1882. The club is commemorated as an impressive amateur side in BoF1905–6. A modern club of the same name was founded in 2008, based at Harlow in Essex (on the county border), and the club website cites 'Rangers' as a nickname.
- Killymoon Rangers F.C., founded in 1971 in Cookstown, Co. Tyrone; Wikipedia.
- Kintbury Rangers F.C., founded in Berkshire in 1890; W1983/4–99. See also 'Gers.
- Lindfield Rangers, see below under St Francis Rangers.
- Northampton Sileby Rangers F.C., founded in Northampton in 1968, originally as a works side for the Sileby Engineering Co., rcorded as Rangers on Wikipedia. See also Sileby, Vans.
- Penrhiwceiber Rangers F.C., founded in Rhondda Cynon Taf in 1961, originally as P. Welfare. Recorded in RW1996–2011.
- Queen's Park Rangers F.C., founded in London in 1885. The word is used as a

nickname for the club in BoF1905–6, Johnston 1934, and in all but the first volume of Rothmans: RY1971/2–SS2012/13. The 1986 Panini sticker has it, with a cartoon suggesting a cowboy meaning). See also Hoops / Superhoops, Q.P.R., R's.

⚽ Rangers F.C., founded in Glasgow in 1872. The suffix is used as a nickname in BoF1905–6. See also Blues, 'Gers, Huns, Iron Curtain, Light Blues, Teddy Bears.

⚽ Rathfern Rangers F.C., founded in 1974 in Belfast; Wikipedia.

⚽ Soham Town Rangers F.C., founded in Cambridgeshire in 1947, in the merger of S. Town and S. Rangers; W1988–2013. See also Town.

⚽ Stafford Rangers F.C., founded in Staffordshire in 1876; Goodall 1982, W2007–13. See also Boro.

⚽ St Francis Rangers F.C., founded at Haywards Heath in Sussex in 2002, in a merger between Ansty R. and St Francis. Ansty were called Lindfield Rangers until 1996; W2009–13. See also Mental Hospital, Saints.

⚽ Winterton Rangers F.C., founded in North Lincolnshire in 1934, recorded in W1979/80–83/4 and W1994–2007 and W2012–13. See also Reds.

Ravens is a nickname for five clubs, for metaphorical reasons. The clubs are:

⚽ Brereton Town F.C., founded in Staffordshire in 1964. Two ravens appear on the club badge (AFBC and club website), and the nickname appears to be adapted from the full name of the parish, which is Brereton and Ravenhill.

⚽ Bromley F.C., founded in London in 1892. The club badge copies the old shield of the Borough of Bromley, which features three ravens across the centre. These refer to the River Ravensbourne in the borough, and local tradition which records the story of how a raven showed Roman soldiers the site of a spring (regretably, though, the early forms of the river name show that the first element really means 'boundary', see Mills 1991). The club programme is called *Ravens Review*; Wikipedia. See also Lilywhites.

⚽ Chaddesley Corbett F.C., founded in Worcestershire in 1906. A raven is the badge of the village, from its medieval heraldic use for the Corbet family. An enamel badge showing the bird appears in AFBC and the club website uses the expression 'the Ravens of Longmore' (the club's home ground is in the hamlet of Longmore).

⚽ Coalville Town F.C., founded in Leicestershire in 1926, originally as Ravenstone Miners Athletic, from the village of Ravenstone (though the Domesday Book form of the name shows it originally meant 'the village of a man called Hrafn', see Mills 1991). The club sports a raven on its badge and plays in black-and-white colours. The raven, however, is commonly used as a metaphor for things which are black, so here the nickname satisfactorily records not only an original place-name, but a metaphor for the 'coal' in Coalville, the club's history as a miners' side, and the fact that the club plays in black shirts; W2003–13.

⚽ Dinas Powys F.C., founded in Eastbrook, vale of Glamorgan, in 1954, originally as Swan Stars. It is not clear at what point the club took the present name. A handsome raven appears on the club badge and supporters once published a fanzine called *Raven*

Loonies; club website and Huws 2013. See also Stars.

⚽ **Sporting Fingal F.C.**, founded at Fingal in Co. Dublin in 2007, but dissolved in 2011; here the bird is a popular symbol of the town, reflecting the club colours of black and white, and also used for the Fingal Ravens Gaelic football club; Wikipedia. See also Fingal.

Real Reds is a nickname for Shelbourne F.C., founded in Dublin in 1895; the club plays in red shirts and socks with white shorts. The nickname is recorded on Wikipedia and clearly distinguishes the club from others calling themselves 'The Reds'; Wikipedia. See also Aul Reds, Reds, Shels.

Rebel Army is a nickname for Cork City F.C., founded in Co. Cork in 1984. The city itself is known as the Rebel City (and Cork the Rebel County), probably because of its role in the Irish War of Independence (1919–21), but the city had a much earlier involvement in a rebellion, that of Perkin Warbeck against Henry VII (1491), which resulted in the execution of the mayor of Cork in 1499; Wikipedia. See also City, Leesiders.

Rebels is a nickname for two clubs, one for a club history reason and the other for local history. The clubs are:

⚽ **Slough Town F.C.**, formed in Berkshire in 1893 in a merger of Slough Swifts, Slough Albion and Slough Young Men's Friendly Society. After the Second World War, the club was reluctant to rejoin the Spartan League it had played in since 1921 and led a rebellion to set up a new league, which became called the Corinthian League, hence the nickname. Recorded in Avis 1966–70, W1979/80–2013. See also Wasps.

⚽ **Worthing F.C.**, where the nickname appears at odds with the affluent conservative district of Sussex the club lives in. Founded in 1886 (originally as W. A.F.C.), the club plays in an all-red strip (with a white collar) and are also known as 'The Red Army'. The most likely explanation for the nickname seems to be the Bonfire Night Riots for which Worthing used to be notorious. These were common in the nineteenth century (the 1884 riot had to be quelled by the Army), but also flared up in 1956, '57 and '58, when the situation amounted to open rebellion. The rioters were known as 'Bonfire Boys'. Another Worthing side, W. United, however, took the nickname 'Mavericks' in 1988. Perhaps both clubs merely wished to suggest they were 'something different' to the present-day comfortable norm of the town, and adopted nicknames which clashed with the word 'worthy' suggested by the place-name. Recorded in Avis 1966–70, W1979/80–2013. See also Red Army.

Rec is a common short form for 'Recreation', often used for public Recreation Grounds, and sometimes used as an official suffix for clubs which play on those grounds. Clubs who have this as a nickname are:

⚽ **Comber Recreation F.C.**, founded in Co. Down in 1950, originally as C. Youth Club; Wikipedia records it as 'Comber Rec'.

⚽ **Kilmore Recreation F.C.**, founded at Crossgar in Co. Down in 1967, originally as Kilmore United; Wikipedia.

❖ Rosyth F.C., founded in Fife in 1992 when the homeless club Dunfermline Jubilee Athletic (1967) relocated to Rosyth and renamed itself. The nickname is taken from the club's home ground, Recreation Park on Admiralty Road, but it reuses the name and nickname of earlier Rosyth clubs called Rosyth Recreation (1916–26 and 1946–57); Wikipedia.

❖ Vale Recreation F.C., founded on the island of Guernsey in 1932; Wikipedia and club's own website. See also Green and Golds.

Rechabites is a nickname for Banks O'Dee F.C., founded in Aberdeen in 1902. The nickname refers to the Independent Order of Rechabites, or Rechabites Friendly Society, which was a temperance movement established in 1835 (taking its name from the Biblical tribe, descendents of Rechab). The Aberdeen branch (or 'Tent') opened in 1905. The club's website states that the club was first called Rechabites F.C., changing its name to the present form in the 1920s. Although founded three years before the local Tent, this shows that both the club and the Tent were formed in an atmosphere of leanings towards teetotalism in Aberdeen at the turn of the twentieth century; Wikipedia, SFHA. See also Dee.

Recreationists is a nickname for Lincolnshire's Gainsborough Trinity F.C., from its first name in 1873 as a church side called Trinity Recreationists; Wikipedia. See also Blues, Holy Blues, Trinity.

Red and Blacks is the nickname of Warminster Town F.C., founded in Wiltshire in 1885. The club plays in red-and-black stripes with black shorts and red socks; W1994–2002. See also Town.

Red and Blues is the nickname of Ards F.C., founded at Newtownards, Co. Down, in 1900 (on the Ards Peninsula). The club plays in red-and-blue stripes with blue shorts and socks; RI1997, RNI2007.

Red and Greens is the nickname of Merthyr Town F.C., founded in 2010 as a successor to M. Town A.F.C. (1909–34) and Merthyr Tydfil F.C. (1945–2010). The team plays in red shirts and shorts with green socks, the background colours on the Welsh flag; Wikipedia; the Historical Football Kits website also applies it to the club of 1909 to 1934. See also Martyrs, Romans.

Red and White Wizards is an unofficial nickname for Sheffield United F.C., from their famous red-and-white striped shirts, and the fame of their 'magical' performance; Wikipedia, which also records 'Red and White Army'. See also Blades, Blunts, Cutlers, Laneites, Pigs, United.

Red Army is a nickname for Worthing F.C. and several other clubs. Worthing plays in an all-red strip (with white collars). The nickname is not an unusual one in football, where colours and 'Army' are often combined, but it also suggests the nickname of the communist armed forces, perhaps with a touch of irony in this conservative town. Pickering 1994 cites the nickname as common to many clubs, including Liverpool and Manchester United. It also appears on Wikipedia for Charlton Athletic and Wrexham. See also Rebels.

Red Devils is the nickname of at least three clubs who wear red shirts and who wish, strangely, to portray themselves as in some way demonic. The clubs are:

☻ Aberdeen F.C., founded in 1903, recorded in Vernon 1970–1 as 'The Red Devils', though 'The Reds' is a normal nickname for the club. See also Black and Golds, Dandies, Dons, Reds, Wasps.

☻ Crawley Town F.C., from their bright-red shirts, worn from the time of their foundation in West Sussex in 1896, though there seems no particular reason for this club to have the demonic label. Nevertheless, the nickname appears on the club badge. The club had a famous FA Cup match against Manchester United on 19 February 2011, where the Red Devils played against the Red Devils; W1995–7, W2004–11 and SSY2012/13. See also Reds, Town.

☻ Manchester United F.C. Founded in 1878 as the Newton Heath Lancashire and Yorkshire Railway F.C., it changed to Manchester United in 1902. At the same time the club adopted the traditional strip of a red shirt and white shorts (the previous team played in green-and-gold colours borrowed from the railway company). The club has never been one for nicknames, one is not offered in Harvey 1959, but the 1959 Sweetule card has a cartoon of red devils and describes the team as "fiery, fast moving red shirted"; also in Avis 1966–70 as an alternative to 'Reds'. The nickname Red Devils is based on the strip and their successful performance, and is also allegedly borrowed from the nickname of the Salford Rugby League team. According to Ferris 2005, the rugby side was so nicknamed by French journalists during a successful tour in 1934, and it was adopted by the football club after the Second World War; however, an even earlier source of inspiration could be the Belgian national football team, nicknamed the Red Devils since an international against the Netherlands in 1906. In 1970 the devil was incorporated into the club crest. Recorded in RY1975/6–SSY2012/13. See also Busby Babes, Coach-Builders, Fergie's Fledglings, Heathens, Man, Manure, Munichs, Outcasts, Reds, United.

Red Dragons is the nickname for Wrexham F.C. Founded in 1872 (reformed in 1883), the club has worn a strong red shirt since 1939. In 1973 the club adopted a new coat of arms with Welsh dragons as supporters, though the nickname was 'The Robins' until the 2002–3 season. The Welsh red dragon now appears on the badge of Cardiff City, but they do not, as yet, appear to have adopted it as a nickname. Recorded in RY2002/3–SSY2012/13; RW 2002–11; Wikipedia lists the nickname simply as 'Dragons'. Avis 1970 records this nickname for the Welsh national team, and in 2012 Phil Stead used it as the title of his general history of Welsh football: *Red Dragons*. See also Red Army, Robins, Town.

Red Imps, see Imps.

Red Kites is the nickname for Rhayader Town F.C., founded in Powys in 1884, folding in 2006, reformed in 2007. The Red Kite is a handsome bird of prey and the town has a feeding station and rehabilitation centre dedicated to its care, and it features on the club badge. The nickname was used by *The Leader* on 22 December

2011; Huws 2013. See also Thin Red Line.

Red Lichties is the main nickname for Arbroath F.C., founded in Angus in 1878. The nickname refers to the red lights used to aid the navigation of the fishing vessels in this important fishing community, though it is not quite clear whether the red lights were mounted on the ships or the harbour walls, or both, as both explanations are given on the internet. The club has worn a distinctive maroon colour since 1882, not quite 'red' enough to be an extra meaning in the nickname. The nickname is a very expressive one, suggesting 'homecoming from danger' and the relationship between the town and its travelling heroes. Recorded in *Stedfast* January 1964, Avis 1970, Vernon 1970–1, RS 1993–2012, RY1972/3–SSY2012/13. See also Smokies.

Red Lions is the nickname of the West Midlands side, Bloxwich United A.F.C., founded in 2006, originally as Birchills United, renaming in 2008. The club has a red lion on its badge and plays at the the Old Red Lion Ground in Bloxwich; Wikipedia.

Red Rebels is a nickname for two clubs:

- Abbey Hey F.C., founded in Manchester in 1902, originally as Abbey Hey Working Men's Club. The club plays in red shirts but the rebel part of the nickname is not explained; Wikipedia.
- F.C. United of Manchester, formed in 2005 in protest against the commercial takeover of Manchester United by the Glazer brothers. Its name neatly chimes with the nickname 'Red Devils' (q.v.). See also FCUM.

Redbirds is an unofficial nickname for Cardiff City F.C., and has appeared many times in journalism and internet forums since September 2012. The nickname is a slightly mocking allusion to the rebranding of the club as red rather than blue to suit the tastes of the club's Malaysian owners. See also Bluebirds, Dwarfs, Welsh Bluebirds

Redcoats was a nickname for the Third Lanark Athletic Club, founded in Glasgow in 1872, closed in 1967. Throughout their history, the famous side played in striking red shirts, with white shorts and socks. The club had its origins in the Third Lanarkshire Rifle Volunteers force, which also wore red tunics, so the nickname successfully puns on the nickname for the British Army since the time of Oliver Cromwell; Wikipedia. See also Hi-Hi's, Sodgers, Thirds, Volunteers, Warriors.

Redmen is the nickname for Pegasus Juniors F.C., founded in Hereford in 1955. The club wears an all-red strip and took its official name in tribute to the successful Oxford Pegasus A.F.C. (1948–63). Although formed by former schoolboys who wished to continue playing, 'Juniors' does not necessarily imply youth in football, and it was probably intended as a further tribute to the Oxford club, implying successor status. The club has a handsome red badge showing a pegasus in flight; W2007–13. See also Reds.

Reds is a common nickname for clubs who play in red shirts, or an all-red strip. There are nearly sixty clubs so-nicknamed listed here. The clubs are:

- Aberdeen F.C., founded in 1903. The club first played in black-and-gold stripes before changing to a red-and-white strip in 1966. The supporters are known as The

Red Army; SSY2012/13. See also Black and Golds, Dandies, Dons, Red Devils, Wasps.

⚽ Accrington Stanley, see Owd Reds.

⚽ A.F.C. Liverpool, founded in 2008 amongst supporters of the mainstream Liverpool club. Like them, the club plays in red; recorded in W2013. See also Kopettes.

⚽ Alfreton Town F.C. Formed in 1959 after a merger between Alfreton Miners Welfare and Alfreton United, the team plays in an all-red strip; W1982/3–86, W1991–2013, SSY2012/13. See also Town.

⚽ Arsenal F.C., from their red shirts, recorded as a nickname in BoF1905–6, Avis 1966–70 and Moss 1983. See also Boring Arsenal, France, Gooners, Gunners, Invincibles, Lucky Arsenal, Royals, Woolwich.

⚽ Backwell United F.C., founded in Avon in 1911; the club merged with Ashton Boys F.C. in 2010 to form Ashton and Backwell United; W1985–97. See also Stags.

⚽ Baldock Town F.C., founded in Hertfordshire in 1905. The club played in an all-red strip but folded in 2001; W1983/4–2001. See Town for the new club of the same name.

⚽ Barnsley F.C. Founded in 1887, they first adopted the famous red shirts in 1901; RY and SSY from 1983/4 to 2012/13. See also Battling Barnsley, Colliers, Saints, Tykes.

⚽ Beckenham Town F.C., founded in 1971. The Kent club plays in a nearly-all-red strip; W1994–2013. See also Becks, Town.

⚽ Bolton Wanderers F.C., as an early nickname. Pickering 1994 records this "in the days when the team wore red-and-white quartered shirts", but the Historical Football Kits website shows full-red shirts for the club in 1874 and 1880, and red-and-white halves in 1890–1. See also Noblot / Notlob, Savage Six, Spots, Trotters, Wanderers, Whites / Whitemen.

⚽ Bristol City F.C. Founded in 1897, the club adopted red shirts in the same decade; Wikipedia. See also Babes, Cider Army, City, Eighty-Twoers / 1982 Ltd, Robins, Slave Traders, Turnips, Wurzels.

⚽ Camberley Town F.C., founded in Surrey in 1895, originally as St Michael's Camberley F.C., then Camberley and Yorktown, and merging with Camberley Wanderers in 1967 to form the present club; red and white strip; W1980/1–83/4 and W1994–2013. See also Krooners, Town.

⚽ Cliftonville Football and Athletic Club, founded in Belfast in 1879. The club plays in red shirts and socks with white shorts. Recorded in *Stedfast* October 1963, Pickering 1994, RI 1997, RNI 2007.

⚽ Colne F.C., founded in Lancashire in 1996. The club plays in red shirts and shorts and is a successor team to Colne Dynamoes which folded in 1990; Wikipedia.

⚽ Corsham Town F.C., founded in Wiltshire in 1884; all-red strip; Wikipedia. See also Peacocks, Southbankers.

⚽ Corwen Amateurs F.C., founded in Clwyd in 1921. The nickname is recorded in

RW1994–6, and the club plays in red-and-white shirts with red shorts.

⚽ Crawley Town F.C., from their bright red shirts, worn from the time of their foundation in West Sussex in 1896; W1986–2003 and SSY2005/6–11/12. See also Red Devils, Town.

⚽ Dagenham & Redbridge F.C., established in the merger of Dagenham and Redbridge Forest in 1992; W1993–8. See also Daggers, Stones.

⚽ Denaby United F.C., founded in South Yorkshire in 1895; W2000–02. See also Colliers.

⚽ Fleetwood F.C., one of the ancestor clubs of the present-day Fleetwood Town, founded in Lancashire in 1997 but with roots going back to 1908; recorded in Avis 1966–70. See also Cod Army, Fishermen, Trawlermen.

⚽ Harrow Borough F.C., founded in London in 1933, originally as Roxonian; the club plays in an all-red strip; Wikipedia. See also Boro.

⚽ Harworth Colliery Institute F.C., founded South Yorkshire in 1931; all-red strip; W1982/3–97.

⚽ Haverhill Rovers F.C., founded in Suffolk in 1886; all-red strip; Wikipedia. See also Rovers.

⚽ Highgate United F.C., founded in Birmingham in 1948; W2009–13 (though consistently appearing here as 'Red'). See also Gate.

⚽ Hythe Town F.C., founded in Kent in 1910, reforming as Hythe United in 1992, reverting to Town in 1995; Wikipedia. See also Forters, Town.

⚽ Kidderminster Harriers F.C., founded in Worcestershire in 1886, from the red shirts which they have worn for most of the club's history. See also Harriers, Kiddy.

⚽ Knowsley United F.C., founded at Huyton in Merseyside in 1984, originally as Kirkby Town, renaming in 1988 after a change of location; W1992–7. See also United.

⚽ Langford F.C., founded in 1908. The Bedfordshire side plays in an all-red strip; W1983/4 and W1994–2013.

⚽ Leighton Town F.C., founded in Bedfordshire in 1885. The club plays in red-and-white stripes with red shorts and socks; W1994–2013. See also Buzzards, Sand Dobbers, Town.

⚽ Liverpool F.C., founded in 1892; the team first had a blue-and-white strip but adopted the red shirt and white shorts in 1894. In 1964 the manager, Bill Shankly, made the decision to go for an all-red strip. This was recalled by player Ian St John: "He thought the colour scheme would carry psychological impact—red for danger, red for power. He came into the dressing room one day and threw a pair of red shorts to Ronnie Yeats. "Get into those shorts and let's see how you look," he said. "Christ, Ronnie, you look awesome, terrifying. You look 7ft tall." "Why not go the whole hog, boss?" I suggested. "Why not wear red socks? Let's go out all in red." Shankly approved and an iconic kit was born." (Ian St John, serialised in *The Sunday Times on-line* October 9, 2005, p. 2.). The nickname is recorded early, in BoF1905–

6; the 1933 Ogden card set, mentioned in the 1936 Thomson 'stamp' album, G1956–65, Churchill 1958, Richards 1960 and Avis 1966–70, and throughout RY1970/1–SSY2012/13. See also Anfielders, Culture Club, Kop / Kopites, Liddellpool, Mariners, Merseysiders, Micky Mousers, Pool, Spice Boys.

☉ Llanelli A.F.C., founded in Carmarthenshire in 1896. The club plays in an all-red strip; recorded in Avis 1966–70, RW1994–2011, W1994–6 and W2002–5.

☉ Luton Town F.C., founded in Bedfordshire in 1885. Between 1889 and 1899 the club's colours were a dark red known as 'cochineal'. The nickname is recorded, in the past tense, in BoF1905–6. The Historical Football Kits website illustrates the kit. See also Hatters, Lilywhites, Lootown, Lutonians, Straw-Hatters / Straw-Plaiters.

☉ Manchester United F.C., as an alternative to the 'Red Devils' nickname; recorded in Avis 1966–70, RY1970/1–74/5. See also Busby Babes, Coach-Builders, Fergie's Fledglings, Heathens, Man, Manure, Munichs, Outcasts, Red Devils, United.

☉ Newton Abbot A.F.C., founded in Devon in 1964 as N.A. Dynamos, folded in 2009; W2009.

☉ Nottingham Forest F.C. Founded in 1865, the club adopted the red shirt from the outset in honour of the Italian patriot Garibaldi, whose supporters wore the shade soon called 'Garibaldi Red'. Garibaldi was then in the middle of his campaign to unite Italy and was widely admired in England, which he had visited in 1864. He was known for daring tactics, appropriate for a football club. The nickname is recorded early, in BoF1905–6. Howard Chandler reports that the 1959 FA Cup Final programme states that Forest are 'Known by their supporters as "The Reds".' Recorded in Avis 1966–70, G1976 and throughout RY1970/1–SSY2012/13. See also Forest/Foresters, Garibaldi Reds, Pied Pipers, Robin Hoods, Tricky Trees.

☉ Pegasus Juniors F.C., founded in Hereford in 1955. The club wears an all-red strip but is now nicknamed The Redmen; W1982/3–90. See also Redmen.

☉ Petersfield United F.C., founded in Hampshire in 1889, folding in 1993 and replaced by P. Town. Both the old and new clubs wear red-and-black shirts; W1986–93. See also Town, United.

☉ Plymstock United F.C., founded in Devon in 1946; red shirts; W1994–9.

☉ Purton F.C., founded in Wiltshire in 1924; all-red strip; W1998–2013.

☉ Quorn F.C., founded in Leicestershire in 1924, originally as Quorn Methodists; all-red strip; W2008–13. See also Methodists.

☉ Radstock Town F.C., founded in Somerset in 1895. The club wears a red strip; W1987–90. See also Miners, Rads, Town.

☉ Rainham Town F.C., founded in Essex in 1945; all-red strip. Recorded in W1979/80–94 (but with an error in W1991). The club closed in 1994. See also Zebras.

☉ Redditch United F.C., founded in Worcestershire in 1891, as R. Town. The nickname simultaneously puns on the place-name; W1979/80–13. See also Reds and Egore.

❂ Redhill F.C., founded in Surrey in 1894. The club has always worn red-and-white stripes; recorded in Avis 1966–70, W1982/3–93/4, W1989–90 and W1993–2013, and used in the title of the centenary history by Brian Thomas: *Up the Reds* (1995), See also Lobsters.

❂ Ryde Sports F.C., founded on the Isle of Wight in 1888, for their red shirts. The club folded in 1997; a replacement club, Ryde '98, struggled on till 2004; W1992–8.

❂ Shelbourne F.C., founded in Dublin in 1895; the club plays in red shirts and socks with white shorts. Recorded in RI1997. See also Aul Reds, Real Reds, Shels.

❂ Shifnal Town F.C., founded in 1964. The Shropshire side plays in red-and-white striped shirts with red socks, and black shorts; Wikipedia. See also Town.

❂ Stafford Town F.C., founded in Staffordshire in 1976; an all-red strip; W1995–2004. See also Town.

❂ Steyning Town F.C., founded in 1898. The Sussex side plays in an all-red strip; Miller & Wright 1996.

❂ Tamworth F.C., founded in Staffordshire in 1933, from their mainly-all-red strip; Wikipedia. See also Lambs, Town.

❂ Thackley F.C., founded in West Yorkshire in 1930, for their red shirts; W2008–11. See also Dennyboys.

❂ Tobermore United F.C., founded in Co. Londonderry in 1965. The club plays in red shirts with black shorts and socks; Wikipedia. See also United.

❂ Uxbridge F.C., founded in London in 1871. The club plays in red shirts and socks with white shorts. Recorded in Avis 1966–70, W1979/80–2013.

❂ Welling United F.C., founded in London in 1963, for the club's red shirts; W1980/1–81/2. See also Wings.

❂ Whitstable Town F.C., founded in Kent in 1886; red shirts, W1983/4–2005. See also Natives, Oystermen.

❂ Willenhall Town F.C., founded in 1953 in a merger between Aston Road Villa and R.A.F. Association. The West Midlands club plays in an all-red strip. Recorded in W1979/80–2005, and also on a badge illustrated in AFBC. See also Lockmen.

❂ Winterton Rangers F.C., founded in North Lincolnshire in 1934. This nickname is recorded in W2008–11; it is, however, unexpected because the club wears an all-blue strip with all-red only as an away strip. See also Rangers.

❂ Woodford United F.C., founded in Northamptonshire in 1946 as a successor to a pre-war club called Woodford Central. The club plays in an all-red strip; W2007–13. See also United.

❂ Workington A.F.C. Founded in 1921 as a successor to a previous club (1884–1911), the team plays in red shirts and white shorts. A badge illustrated in AFBC records the variant form 'The Redz'. Recorded in G1956–76, Churchill 1958, Richards 1960, Avis 1966–70, RY1970/1–77/8, W1979/80–2013.

Reds and Egore was an extraordinary nickname for Redditch United F.C., founded in Worcestershire in 1891, as R. Town, recorded in W1988–90. The normal nickname for the club is 'The Reds' but this alternative appears in print for those years. It has not been possible to explain it, and an enquiry to the club was unanswered. It looks as though Egore might have been a nickname for a particular manager or sponsor or chairman or even another club in partnership, but this has not been confirmed. The club badge copies the town heraldry and has a kingfisher as a crest: perhaps Egore was a nickname for the kingfisher. See also Reds.

Refounders, for Polegate Town, see under Town.

Remnants is a football club suffix, used for a famous amateur side in the 1870s. The Historical Football Kits website mentions the club for a match against Darwen in in 1878 and mentions that the club was formed by former public school boys. The unusual name seems to have meant the same as 'Old Boys'. 'Left Overs' is also used as the name of the football club (see 'LOSC'). BoF1905–6, p.256, mentions the club and suggests that it was 'of Eton growth'.

Rent Boys is a mocking unofficial nickname for any team which rents its ground rather than owns it. Superficially, the phrase is comparable to 'Squatters' and 'Council Housers', but with an added sexual defamation. The nickname appears in a great many internet football forums, and is used for several clubs.

Rhiewsiders is the nickname of Berriew F.C., founded in Powys at an uncertain date: the club website acknowledges that there is some evidence for 1872, 1883 and 1900, but no certainty till 1934. The place-name itself records the location at the mouth of the river Rhiew; Wikipedia.

Rhiw was the nickname of Troed-y-Rhiw (often Troedyrhiw) F.C., founded at Merthyr Tydfil before 1908, when the club won the South Wales Amateur Cup, originally as T. Stars and apparently originally nicknamed The Stars. The club was reformed as T. F.C., after the First World War, and again reformed in 1993. The nickname is a short form of the place-name. Tragically, the club folded in 2012; the nickname appears in on-line forums. See also Stars.

Rhondda Bulldogs is a variant nickname for Ton Pentre F.C., founded in the Rhondda valley in 1935. The nickname appears on the club's own website and has also been a club badge (AFBC). See also Bulldogs, Ton.

Rhos is the nickname of Rhos Aelwyd F.C., founded in 1943 at Rhosllanerchrugog in Wrexham Co. Bor.; recorded in RW2011. See also Aelwyd.

Ricay is the nickname of Billericay Town F.C., founded in Essex in 1890, from the last two syllables of the place-name; Wikipedia. See also Blues, Town.

Ridge is a nickname for Sandridge Rovers F.C., founded in Hertfordshire in 1896; a short form of the place-name listed on Wikipedia. See also Rovers.

Rifles is the nickname and part-official name for Heaton Rifles F.C., founded near Newcastle upon Tyne in 2007, after the closure of the club called 'Newcastle It's Just Like Watching Brazil F.C.' (see 'Brazil'). The club is not associated with a rifle club: the word is used for its general sporting connotations, not least for the appropriate word 'shoot', and the club badge displays two crossed rifles; used in internet match reports in 2012.

River Boys is a nickname for Bitton A.F.C., founded in 1892. The Gloucestershire River Boyd runs alongside the ground, but the nickname comes from an incident in 1934 when the chairman Jonathan Crowe said he would jump in the river if the team were to win the first match in their new red-and-white colours. They did, and so he fulfilled his promise in front of the supporters; Wikipedia. See also Boyds, Ton.

Riverboaters is the nickname for Caerau F.C., founded in Bridgend Co. Bor. in 1901. The nickname was used in the *Glamorgan Gazette* in 31 January 2013 and refers to the name of the club's social club, The Riverboat; Huws 2013. See also Athletic.

Riversiders is a nickname for clubs which have a stadium alongside a river, often because the ground itself is called 'The Riverside'. Examples are:

- Barrow Town F.C., founded in Leicestershire in 1901, originally as Barrow Old Boys, in the riverside location of Barrow-upon-Soar; W2002–5
- Blackburn Rovers, from the name of the famous stand at their home stadium of Ewood Park, on the banks of the river Darwen; Wikipedia. See also Blue and Whites, Highwaymen, Jackburn, Plastics, Rovers.
- Launton Sports F.C., founded near Bicester in Oxfordshire in 1980. The river here is the Cherwell; Wikipedia.
- Middlesbrough F.C., from the name of the Riverside Stadium, to which the club moved in 1995. The nickname is frequently used by journalists in match reports. The river here is the Tees. See also Boro, Cleveland Cowboys, Ironsiders, Nops, Scabs, Smoggies, Teessiders, Washers
- Ross Town F.C., founded in Herefordshire in 1993 in a merger of R. United and Woodville. The club folded in 2009. The river in the nickname is the Wye; W1997–2007.

RN is the nickname of United Services Portsmouth F.C., founded in Hampshire in 1962, originally as Portsmouth Royal Navy F.C. The initialism is often used for the Royal Navy; Wikipedia.

Road is the nickname of Maine Road F.C., based at Chorlton-cum-Hardy, Manchester, founded in 1955 as 'City Supporters Rusholme'. In the 1960s the club, formed amongst supporters of Manchester City F.C., moved their headquarters to the Maine Road Social Club and adopted the new name. Like City, the club plays in a pale blue strip; Wikipedia. See also Blues.

Roaders was a nickname for Stafford Road F.C., a works side for the local Great Western locomotive works in Wolverhampton, founded in 1876, and surviving into the 1920s. The nickname is recorded in BoF1905–6 (p.193), the dates from Wikipedia.

Roaming Brigade was a nickname of the defunct football team Northern Nomads, so called because they never had their own ground (though travel names were common). Founded in Greater Manchester in c.1862, closed in 1984, they shared grounds with Stalybridge and Glossop North End; Wikipedia. See also Nomads.

Robin Hoods was a nickname occasionally used for Nottingham Forest F.C., as recorded in Avis 1966–70. The club is based on the edge of Sherwood Forest, the legendary outlaw's home turf. The name of Robin Hood is today used as an official name by three smaller clubs: Robin Hood Colts (at Edwinstowe in Sherwood Forest), Robin Hood (Bradford) F.C., and Robin Hood Athletic F.C. ('The Hood'), both in West Yorkshire. See also Forest/Foresters, Garibaldi Reds, Pied Pipers, Reds, Tricky Trees

Robins is a nickname for clubs who play in red shirts, or in an all-red strip, from the popular red-breasted bird. There are forty examples of the nickname here:

- Altrincham F.C. Founded in Greater Manchester in 1891 as Blackheath, the club changed its name to Altrincham in 1903 and wears a red shirt (currently black-and-red stripes); recorded in Avis 1966–70, W1979/80–2013 and SSY2006/7–11/12.
- Ashton United F.C., founded in Ashton-under-Lyne, Cheshire, in 1878, originally as Hurst F.C. (the club base is in the Hurst Cross district), renaming in 1947; the club plays in red shirts; W1982/3–2013. Avis 1966–70 records 'The Robins' nickname earlier but calls the club 'Ashton-under-Lyne F.C.'. See also United.
- Bideford A.F.C., founded in Devon in 1946, and who play in an all-red strip; the club also has the nickname, and a robin, on its badge; recorded in Avis 1966–70, W1979/80–2013.
- Bosham F.C., founded in West Sussex in 1901; all-red strip with a little white; W1988–1997.
- Bracknell Town F.C., founded in Berkshire in 1896, originally as B. Wanderers. The club plays in red-and-white hooped shirts, with red shorts and socks. The nickname appears in the title of a 1996 club history by Jack Elliot: *The Robins*, and in W1986–2013. See also Town.
- Bridgwater Town 1984 F.C., founded in Somerset in 1984 as a successor to an older club from 1898. The club plays in an almost-all-red strip; recorded in Avis 1966–70, W1979/80–1983/4 for the older club; W1997–2013 for the new.
- Bristol City F.C., founded in 1897; the club adopted red shirts in the same decade. The nickname appears on the 1933 Ogden card, Avis 1954–70, G1956–76, Churchill 1958, Norris 1959, Richards 1960, and SWSCYB 1962–3, and throughout RY and SSY from 1970/1 to 2012/13. According to Ferris 2005, the nickname was adopted in 1926 when the Harry Woods song 'When the red, red robin goes bob, bob, bobbing along' was popular. A robin featured on the club's badge from 1976 to 1994, and since 2005 the mascot has been one Scrumpy the Robin. See also Babes, Cider Army, City, Eighty-Twoers / 1982 Ltd, Reds, Slave Traders, Turnips, Wurzels.
- Buckingham Town F.C., founded in 1883; all-red strip. W1982/3–2013.
- Budleigh Salterton F.C., founded in Devon in 1908. The club plays in an all-red strip; Wikipedia, AFBC.

- Carshalton Athletic F.C., founded in London in 1905; Avis 1966–70, W1979/80–2013. The club has a stylish robin badge.
- Chard Town F.C., founded in Somerset in 1920; red shirts and socks, white shorts; W1987–2013.
- Charlton Athletic F.C., founded in London in 1905. From the outset, the team played in distinctive red shirts and were certainly nicknamed the Robins by 1931. In 1946, for the F.A. Cup final, a beautiful badge of a robin sitting on a football was adopted and sewn on the shirts. The 1959 Sweetule card has this nickname, not the others used for the club, and it is also recorded in Avis 1966–70, RY1970/1–93/4, and Pickering 1994. Wikipedia lists the variant 'Red Robins'. See also Addicks, Haddicks, Haddocks, Red Army, Valiants.
- Cheltenham Town F.C., founded in Gloucestershire in 1887, because of their red shirts. The earlier strips were a bright red, hence Rubies as a nickname, but red with white started to appear after 1932 and Robins became more fashionable. Recorded in Avis 1966–70, W1979/80–99 and RY1999/2000–2002/3 and SSY2003/4–12/13. See also Rubies.
- Clanfield F.C., founded in 1895. The Oxfordshire club plays in an all-red strip; W1983/4–2013.
- Crewe Alexandra F.C., recorded thus in Avis 1954–70, Pickering 1994. See also Railwaymen.
- Croydon Common F.C., the London (Surrey) club of 1897–1917; the club played in claret shirts. A variant nickname was 'The Cock Robins'; Wikipedia.
- Downton F.C., founded near Salisbury, Wiltshire, in 1905. The club plays in red shirts and socks with white shorts; Miller & Wright 1996, W1997–2013, AFBC.
- Dudley Town F.C., founded in West Midlands in 1893, from the red shirts. Recorded in W1979/80 and W1982/3–2005. See also Duds.
- Ely City F.C., founded in Cambridgeshire in 1885 by members of St Etheldreda Football and Cricket Club. The club plays in an all-red strip and has a robin on its badge; W1985–2013.
- Evesham United F.C. Founded in Worcestershire in 1945, the club currently play in red-and-white striped shirts; W1987–2013.
- Fareham Town, founded in Hampshire in 1946; red shirts; W2009–13. See also Town.
- Frome Town F.C. Founded in Somerset in 1904, the club plays in red shirts and shorts. Recorded in Avis 1966–70, W1979/80–2013.
- Great Harwood Town F.C., founded in Lancashire in 1966, originally as Harwood Wellington (after the Duke of Wellington pub), but renaming to G.H.Town in 1978. The nickname is recorded in W1994–2006, after which the club folded. The commemorative website records the club's robin badge and pictures of players in red shirts. See also Arrad, Wellie.
- Hassocks F.C., founded in 1902. The Sussex side plays in an all-red strip;

W1983/4–2013.

- Hinckley Athletic F.C., founded in Leicestershire in 1946 in a renaming of an earlier H. United from c.1905; red shirts; this club then merged with an independent H. Town (Westfield Wanderers, 1958, renamed H. Town in 1972), to form H. United in 1997; Avis 1966–70, W1979/80–97 for Athletic. The modern club shows both an eagle and a robin on its club badge (AFBC). See also Eagles, Knitters, Town, United.

- Ilkeston Town F.C., founded in Derbyshire in 1894, reformed in 2011 as Ilkeston F.C.; nearly-all-red strip; W1982/3–2013. The programme is called *Ilson Review*, 'Ilson' being a local pronunciation of the place-name.

- Knowle F.C., founded in the West Midlands in 1926; from red shirts; W1993–7. See also Star.

- Knutsford F.C., founded in Cheshire in 1888, from the red shirts; Wikipedia.

- Milford United F.C., founded at Milford Haven in Pembrokeshire in 1885; the club plays in red shirts and the nickname appears in Avis 1966–70, W1987, RW1994–6.

- Newtown A.F.C., founded in Powys in 1875, originally as Newtown Whitestars. The club plays in an all-red strip; recorded in W1991–2005, RW1994–2011, and a badge in AFBC. See also Batmans, Stars.

- North Shields F.C., founded in Co. Durham in 1896, originally as N.S. Athletic, reformed in 1992. The club plays in an all-red strip; recorded in W1979/80–93, Barton 1984 & 1985 and W2004–13. The club was nicknamed the New Robins in W1995–2003, after its bankruptcy and reformation.

- Paulton Rovers, founded in Bristol in 1881. The club has an all-dark-red strip; W2010–13. See also Rovers.

- Redbridge F.C., founded in London in 1959 as Ford United, renaming in 2004; red shirts and black shorts, the nickname also puns with the place-name; Wikipedia. See also Motormen.

- Sawbridgeworth Town F.C., founded in Hertfordshire in 1897. The club plays in red shirts with black shorts; W1982/3–2013.

- Selby Town F.C., founded in 1919. The North Yorkshire side plays in an all-red strip; Avis 1966–70; W1982/3–6 and W1991–2013.

- Stockbridge F.C., founded in 1894. The Hampshire side plays in an all-red strip, a robin and the nickname appears on the club's badge; Wikipedia.

- Swindon Town F.C., founded in 1879 or thereabouts (Swindon Town as a name seems to date from 1883), the club tried many different colours before settling on red shirts for the 1904–5 season (see Historical Football Kits website). A robin crest was adopted in 1961. Recorded in G1956 and G1976, Churchill 1958, Norris 1959, Avis 1954–70, Richards 1960, AA 1960, and through all but the first Rothmans: RY1971/2–SSY2012/13. See also Moonrakers, Railwaymen, Shunters, Spartans, Swindle.

⚽ (A.F.C.) Tondu founded in Bridgend Co. Bor. in 1898. The club plays in red shirts and were formerly called The Tondu Robins, changing name in 1990 (FCHD). Recorded in RW1994–6.

⚽ Wigan Robin Park F.C., founded in Greater Manchester in 2005. In this case, the club not only plays in a red strip, but the club itself is named from the Robin Park Arena stadium; Wikipedia.

⚽ Wormley Rovers F.C., founded in Middlesex in 1921, reforming in 1947, for the club's red shirts; W1993–6.

⚽ Wrexham F.C., founded in Wales in 1873; the club adopted bright red shirts in 1939. Stead 2012 (p.75), however, cites a different theory, that the nickname is adapted from the name of Ted Robinson, a former player who was manager of the club 1912–24. This is entirely possible, but the dates of the red strip do not align with Robinson's dates. Historical Football Kits shows red was adopted briefly in 1919–22 and then only permanently in 1939, but which would not have been used regularly until after the War, in 1945. It seems unlikely that the club would have been called 'The Robins' while wearing blue, and the late appearance of the nickname also casts doubt on the manager origin. The nickname does not seem to appear on early programmes: it is recorded in Avis 1954–70, G1976, RW1994–2001, RY1970/1–2001/2, W2009–13. See also Red Army, Red Dragons, Town.

Rockies is the nickname of Shaftesbury F.C., founded in 1888. The Dorset town is famous for its elevated position at 718 feet above sea level, the nickname presumably arising from the expression 'rocky heights'; Wikipedia.

Rocks is the nickname for three clubs, for different reasons. The clubs are:

⚽ Bognor Regis Town F.C. Founded in 1883, the club added 'Regis' in 1929 when the town was given this suffix by King George V, and 'Town' was added in 1949. The nickname is actually difficult to explain, but seems to be a simple variant on other seaside nicknames (Beach Boys, Sandgrounders, Seagulls etc.), based on the confectionary known as seaside rock. There is an offshore, underwater reef called Bognor Rocks, but that hardly seems sufficiently representative of the town itself. The beach there is pebble-strewn but does not have actual rocks or rock pools. There is even an annual music festival called Bognor Rox (punning on Rex/Regis and rock and roll music), suggesting that the place-name suffix might also lie behind the nickname, but the general seaside connotation seems to be the essential explanation; recorded in W1979/80–2013.

⚽ East Thurrock United F.C., founded in Essex in 1969. The nickname is clearly a short form of Thurrock, though the place-name actually means 'place where filthy water collects' (Mills 1991). The nickname is recorded in Avis 1966–70 for an earlier club, West Thurrock F.C., which must have closed when ET was founded; W1982/3 and W1987–2013.

⚽ Tytherington Rocks F.C., founded in 1932. The second word of the Gloucestershire place-name records the existence of a major quarry in the village. In 1947 the club formed a youth team which was named 'The Pebbles'; W2008–13.

Roesiders is the nickname for Limavady United F.C., founded in Co. Londonderry in 1884. The club lies on the river Roe; Wikipedia, AFBC. See also Lims, United.

Rogie Aces is a nickname for Rogerstone F.C., founded in Gwent in about 1960, originally as R. United; football in the locality goes back to 1889. The nickname is recorded on the club website and refers to a supporters' song sung to the tune of the popular Northern English folksong, 'The Blaydon Races', where 'To see the Rogie Aces' forms the last line: Huws 2013 cites the whole verse from an oral source. See also Ivanhoe.

Rokerites / Rokermen is a nickname for Sunderland A.F.C., based on the name of the club's old stadium, Roker Park. The club was founded in 1879 and was based there from 1897 to 1997. This nickname (as Rokerites) and none other is recorded on the 1933 Ogden card and in the 1936 Thomson 'stamp' album, G1956–76, Churchill 1958, Richards 1960, Barton 1984 & 1985. It also appears throughout RY1970/1–88/9 as Rokerites before switching to Rokermen through RY1989/90–96/7. 'Rokerites' makes a last appearance in the Williams League Directories 1985–95. See also Bank of England Club, Black Cats, Lads, Light Brigade, Mackems, Miners, Sols, Sund-Ireland, Team of All the Talents, Wearsiders.

Rollers was the nickname of Rolls Royce Engines F.C., founded in c.1948, originally as De Havilland (Leavesden), later Bristol Siddeley Engines (1962–8), Rolls Royce 1968–91 (last appears in FCHD and Williams in that year). The nickname is the standard one used for Rolls Royce cars, here adapted for the works side at Leavesden Aerodrome in Hertfordshire; W1986.

Romans is a nickname for several clubs whose home ground is located on or near Roman archaeology. For other 'Romanesque' names, see Centurions, Gladiators and Roms. Examples are:

🌣 Bath City F.C., founded in 1889 (as Bath A.F.C.), the city is obviously proud of its Roman heritage, but the club's mascot is Bladud the Pig (from Geoffrey of Monmouth's story about the pre-Roman mythical king of Bath); W1994–2013 and SSY20012/13. See also City, Stripes.

🌣 Brading Town F.C., founded on the Isle of Wight in 1871. The town is built on the site of a Roman villa; Wikipedia.

🌣 Caerleon A.F.C., founded in 1868 in Newport Co. Bor. The club has a Roman military head as its badge and Caerleon is the site of an important Roman fortress called Isca Augusta; W1987 and Wikipedia.

🌣 Chester City F.C., for another ancient Roman city. It is recorded in Jeffrey 1961. See also Blues, Cestrians, City, Ivies, Magpies, Seals.

🌣 Irchester United F.C., founded in Northamptonshire in 1883. Archaeology has shown that Irchester is on the site of a major Roman town, but one of unknown name; Wikipedia.

🌣 Merthyr Town F.C., founded in 2010 as a successor to M. Town A.F.C. (1909–34) and Merthyr Tydfil F.C. (1945–2010). The Welsh town is named in honour of a late-Roman martyr, St Tydfil, and the club's Penydarren Park is on the site of a Roman fort; Wikipedia has the nickname for the new club but not for the old, but the Historical Football Kits website applies it to the club of 1909 to 1934. See also Martyrs, Red and Greens.

🌐 Rocester F.C., founded in 1876. The Staffordshire club is located on the site of a Roman fort near the Roman city of Uttoxeter, and a military Roman head appears on the club's badge; W1989–2013. See also Millers.

🌐 Roman Glass St George F.C., founded in a merger in Bristol in 1995 between Bristol St George (1872) and Roman Glass (1960, originally Wyndham Wanderers, renamed 1980); nickname appears on club's own website.

Roms is the nickname for Romulus F.C., founded at Sutton Coldfield in 1979. The name refers to the mythical founder of Ancient Rome, Romulus, and he appears on the club badge. Why the club called itself Romulus is another question, but it is all part of the classical names sporting tradition; W2008–13.

Roofing is the nickname of Jarrow Roofing Boldon Community Association F.C., founded in 1987. The club is based at Boldon Colliery, Tyne and Wear and was founded by Ritchie McLoughlin, who used his own Jarrow Roofing Company to build the club's stadium. The club's programme (reproduced in W2003, p. 444) records the supporters' chant 'Haway the Roofers', recording both a variant of 'Away' and also suggesting an alternative nickname for the club, The Roofers, but 'Roofing' is the form recorded in W1994–2013.

Rookettes is the nickname of Lewes Ladies, a side of Lewes F.C. which began in 2002, adapting the 'Rooks' nickname of the affiliated club; club's own website.

Rookie Cookie is a nickname of Penicuik Athletic F.C., founded in Midlothian in 1888. The nickname appears on Wikipedia and is a rhyming phrase adapted from the friendly short form of the place-name, Cuikie. 'Rooky' usually means 'dodgy', suggesting that the club is a fearsome side. See also Cuikie.

Rooks is the nickname for two clubs, both having some association with this popular black bird. The clubs are:

🌐 Carew F.C., founded in Pembrokeshire at an uncertain date; the traditional explanation here is that the nickname refers to the rooks which use Carew Castle as a rookery (Huws 2013). The nickname is also used for the Carew Hockey Club.

🌐 Lewes F.C. Founded in 1885, the club have a badge featuring a medieval castle tower with two rooks flying beside it. The club has a tradition to explain the nickname, but there is an alternative explanation. The club tradition is that the club's Dripping Pan Stadium is much-frequented by rooks, and there is a local legend that if the birds leave the ground, the football club will fold. Lewes and London both have early Norman castles, and an identical story is told about the ravens at the Tower of London. The image of the tower on the badge is not taken from Lewes Castle but is a stylised shape like the castle chesspiece, which happens also to be called a rook, adding an extra meaning to the nickname. However, there is evidence that Lewes itself was nicknamed 'The Rookery' in the nineteenth century because a large number of clergy lived there who, wearing black, made the town look like a rookery. This delightful metaphor is recorded in the *Recollections of a Sussex Parson* by Edward Boys Ellman (d. 1906, published posthumously, London: Skeffington & Son, 1912). On page 56 appears: "At that time, very few of the clergy were resident in their parishes—most of them were pluralists—and Lewes was spoken of as "The Rookery," from the number that rode out of Lewes in black coats to their various duties each Sunday." This is strong evidence that the club nickname rests on an earlier nickname for the town itself (thanks to Fiona Marsden and Pam Combes). In 2006 the club added The Rookery stand to the stadium. Recorded in W1979/80–2013 and SSY2009/10.

Roosters is a nickname for two clubs in Wales, as a pun on their place-names. The clubs are:

- ☉ Llanrwst United F.C., founded in 1983, in a merger of L. Town and L. Athletic. The nickname is now recorded as 'Rwsters' but it appears in RW1994–5 as Roosters. Here the pun marks the sound of the final syllable of the place-name, 'roost'. See also Rwsters.

- ☉ Penrhyncoch F.C., founded in Ceredigion in 1965; recorded in RW1998–2011. Here, the final element, *–coch*, means 'red'. To English outsiders this would appear to be the origin of the nickname, but the pronunciation is like Scottish 'loch' rather than 'cock', the alternative word for a rooster, a male chicken, and Richard Huws reports that this explanation is not accepted locally, and was unknown during the early years of the club. Nevertheless, it may still be the source of the nickname. The fictional cowboy character, Rooster Cogburn (in a novel of 1968, and the John Wayne films of 1969 and 1975), has a nickname which seems to have been adapted from the even-less-specific sound 'cog' in his surname, so a pun on the place-name remains plausible: such puns only need a slight suggestion. Alternatively, Richard Huws suggests that the club badge, a lion rampant called the 'Black Lion of Gogerddan', does look a little like a cockerel (it does!); and even the word *Gogerddan* (here referring to the heraldry of local aristocracy) might itself have been the origin of a similar play on words; Huws 2013. See also Lions, Penrhyn.

Rose is a nickname for Scottish clubs with the element 'Rose' in their official name. It is fashionable for Scottish clubs to choose flowers as their symbols and nicknames (Bluebell, Hawthorn, Primrose, Thistle and Violet also occur). The Rose clubs are:

- ☉ Bonnyrigg Rose Athletic F.C., founded in 1890; W1982/3, SFHA.

- ☉ Crossgates Primrose Junior F.C., founded near Dunfermline, Fife, in 1926. The club shows a primrose on its badge; Wikipedia, SFHA.

- ☉ Linlithgow Rose F.C., founded in West Lothian in 1889. A variant of this is 'Rosey Posey', a rhyming slang affectation. A single rose appears on the club badge, not a posey of them (both nicknames on Wikipedia, SFHA offers 'Rosie Posie').

Rossy was a nickname for Rossendale United F.C., founded in Lancashire in 1898, folded in 2011. The friendly short form is recorded in W1997–9. See also Dale, Stags.

Rouslers is the nickname of Bromsgrove Sporting F.C., founded in Worcestershire in 2009. The popular Worcestershire word 'to rousle' means 'to wake up' and it appears in several local business names, including that of an annual magazine, *The Bromsgrove Rousler*. W2013, club's own website, and also on the club badge.

Rovers is a common football club name element, which is frequently used as a nickname on its own (44 examples are listed here). The word suggests a team of roving warriors, as in groups of Vikings, and is similar to other 'travel' suffixes (Nomads, Rangers, Strollers, Wanderers etc). Examples are:

⚽ Atherton Laburnum Rovers F.C., founded in Greater Manchester in 1956; W1995. See also L.R., Laburnums, Panthers.

⚽ Ballingry Rovers F.C., founded in Glen Craig, Fife, in 1952; Wikipedia.

⚽ Barton Rovers F.C., founded in 1898 in the village of Barton-le-Clay in Bedfordshire; W1980/1–2013.

⚽ Blackburn Rovers F.C., founded in Lancashire in 1875. Recorded in BoF1905–6, *Stedfast* December 1964, Avis 1966–70. The suffix has now become the official nickname, with 'Blue and Whites' no longer promoted. In RY the switch is made to 'Rovers' in RY1992/3 (continuing to SSY2012/13) but the Williams League Directories use it from 1985. See also Blue and Whites, Highwaymen, Jackburn, Plastics, Riversiders.

⚽ Bristol Rovers F.C. Recorded in BoF1905–6, Richards 1960 and also appearing as the nickname in the Williams League Directories for 1985–6. See also See also Arabs, Black Arabs, Gas / Gasheads, Pirates, Purdown Poachers, Squatters, Tesco's.

⚽ Bromsgrove Rovers F.C., founded in Worcestershire in 1885. Avis 1966–70 records the nickname as Rovers, also W1986–2010. The club has now folded. See also Greens.

⚽ Buckie Rovers F.C., founded in Moray in 1889; Wikipedia, SFHA.

⚽ Carluke Rovers F.C., founded in Lanarkshire in 1887; Wikipedia, SFHA. See also Jam Town.

⚽ Clapham Rovers F.C., founded in 1869, folding in 1911 or soon after. The club was a famous amateur side, which won the FA Cup in 1880; recorded on Wikipedia and in BoF1905–6, p. 256. A modern club of the same name appears in internet records from 2009. See also Hybrid Club.

⚽ Clydebank Rovers F.C., formed in 2004, near Glasgow, as a breakaway from Clydebank United; Wikipedia. See also Little Brazil.

⚽ Clyst Rovers F.C., founded in Devon in 1926, reformed 1951, folded in 2010; W1994–2010.

⚽ Crescent Rovers F.C., founded in Wallington, Greater London, in 1947; Wikipedia.

⚽ Doncaster Rovers F.C. Founded in South Yorkshire in 1879, the club went professional in 1885 and appears to have been called Rovers from the outset, but it only adopted the Viking logo as its badge in 1972. Recorded in Avis 1966–70, RY1970/1–1997/8, W1999–2003 and SSY2003/4–2012/13. See also Donny, Vikings.

- ⚽ Englefield Green Rovers F.C., founded in Surrey in 1927, folded in 2009; W2001–9.
- ⚽ Eynesbury Rovers, founded in Cambridgeshire in 1897; Avis 1966–70, W1987–2013.
- ⚽ Forest Green Rovers F.C., founded in Gloucestershire in 1890, originally as Nailsworth & Forest Green. The club had renamed before 1894 and also had a brief period named Stroud F.C. (1989–92); W1986–9 and W1990–2 for Stroud; W1993–2013 and SSY2004/5–12/13. See also FGR, Green, Green Army, Lawnmowers, Little Club on the Hill.
- ⚽ Godmanchester Rovers F.C., founded in Cambridgeshire in 1911; W2003–13. See also Goddy, Goody.
- ⚽ Great Wakering Rovers F.C., founded in Essex in 1919. W1993–2013.
- ⚽ Gresley Rovers F.C., founded in Derbyshire in 1882; W1993, Smith 1992/2–1995/6; the club reformed as Gresley F.C. in 2009. See also Moatmen.
- ⚽ Guernsey Rovers A.F.C., founded in Port Soif, Guernsey, in 1932; used on the club's own website.
- ⚽ Harrow Hill Rovers F.C., founded in London in 1987, renaming as Hounslow Borough in 2001, dissolved 2007; W2001. See also Borough,
- ⚽ Haverhill Rovers F.C., founded in Suffolk in 1886; W1979/80–2013. See also Reds.
- ⚽ Heston Rovers F.C., founded in Dumfries in 1978. The club's website records that the first sponsor of the club had a boat called *Heston Rover*, and suggested it as a name for the new club, which began as a youth side but added adult football after a merger with Dumfries F.C. in 2008; Wikipedia.
- ⚽ Kello Rovers F.C., founded at Kirkconnel in Dumfries and Galloway in 1903; SFHA. See also Super K.
- ⚽ Kimpton Rovers F.C., founded in Hertfordshire in 1943; W1993–6.
- ⚽ Kirkwall Rovers F.C., founded in Orkney in 1912; the club also uses a Viking head as a badge and the club's own website uses the nickname.
- ⚽ Letterkenny Rovers F.C., founded in Co. Donegal in 1936; Wikipedia.
- ⚽ Muir of Ord Rovers F.C., founded in Highland before 1983 (when they won the North Caledonian League cup); Wikipedia.
- ⚽ Paulton Rovers, founded in Bristol in 1881; W1979/80–2013. See also Robins.
- ⚽ Peebles Rovers F.C., founded in Peeblesshire in 1894, reformed 2010. Recorded in RS1993–7, 2000–1.
- ⚽ Raith Rovers F.C., founded in the Fife town of Kirkcaldy in 1883. Recorded in RY1988/7–SS2012/13 and in RS1993–2012. See also Wee Rovers for a comment.

✪ Sandridge Rovers F.C., founded in Hertfordshire in 1896; W1986 and W1993–6. See also Ridge.

✪ Shamrock Rovers F.C., founded in Dublin in 1901; recorded in RI2006. See also Coad's Colts, Hoops.

✪ Sligo Rovers F.C., founded in Co. Sligo in 1928; recorded in RI1997. See also Bit o'Red.

✪ Stanway Rovers F.C., founded in Essex in 1956; W1993–2013.

✪ Talgarth Rovers F.C., founded in Powys in 2009; club website.

✪ Tandragee Rovers F.C., founded in Co. Armagh in 1909; Wikipedia.

✪ Tarff Rovers F.C., founded at Kirkcowan in Wigtownshire in 1874, closed in 2003. Recorded in RS1995–7.

✪ Threave Rovers, founded at Castle Douglas, Dumfries and Galloway, in 1953. Recorded in RS1995–7, 2000–1, SFHA.

✪ Toddington Rovers f.C., founded in Bedfordshire in 1894; W1994–9.

✪ Tolka Rovers A.F.C., founded at Glasnevin, Dublin, in 1922; Wikipedia.

✪ Tranmere Rovers, founded in Birkenhead, Wirral, in 1884, originally as Belmont F.C. but changing to Tranmere Rovers by the start of the 1885 season. Recorded in Richards 1960, and throughout RY1970/1–SSY2012/13. See also Super Whites.

✪ Tuffley Rovers F.C., founded in Gloucestershire in 1929; W1997–2006. See also Tuffs.

✪ Waterloo Rovers F.C., founded in 1978 at Welshpool in Powys; recorded in RW2011.

✪ Welton Rovers F.C., founded in Somerset in 1887; W1987–90, W1994–2013.

✪ Wigan Rovers F.C., founded in Greater Manchester in 1959; recorded in Avis 1966–70.

✪ Willand Rovers, founded near Exeter in c.1907, as W. A.F.C., then W. Wandererers for a while before being reformed in 1946 with the present name; W1994–9 and W2007–13.

Row is the nickname of two clubs, apparently both for place-name reasons. The clubs are:

✪ Collier Row F.C., founded in Essex in 1929. The club merged with Romford in 1996 and took the new nickname 'Boro'; W1983/4–97. See also Boro.

✪ Hartley Wintney F.C., founded in 1897. The club has a small deer on its badge, it plays in the Hart district of North-East Hampshire, and a deer park nearby was used for six hundred years by royal huntsmen, all suggesting that the nickname is the same word as 'roe', a small deer (the variant spelling is possible); but it may have come from the former hamlet of Hartley Row, now absorbed by Hartley Wintney; W1986–2013.

Rowntrees is a nickname for Nestlé Rowntree F.C., founded in York before 1897 when the club joined the York Football League. The club represents the famous chocolate factory and was originally called Rowntrees F.C. before renaming as

Rowntree Mackintosh in 1969, then the present name in 1988; Wikipedia. See also Jo Row, Trees.

Roy is a nickname for Kirkintillock Rob Roy F.C., founded in Dunbartonshire in 1878. The club's name is in honour of the famous Scottish warrior, Rob Roy, or Robert Roy MacGregor (1671–1735), as a short form of the club name; Wikipedia, SFHA. See also Rabs.

Roy's Boys is now being used by journalists as a nickname for the England national team, from Roy Hodgson who assumed his duties as England manager on 14 May 2012. An early usage is that in the on-line journal *The Huffington Post* on 25 May 2012, though the expression occurs earlier for Hodgson's sides at Liverpool and West Bromwich Albion. See also Class of '66, Sassenachs, Sven's Men, Three Lions.

Royal Stones is a nickname for Wealdstone F.C., founded in Middlesex in 1899. The team plays in royal-blue shirts and shorts and are also known as 'The Royals' and 'The Stones'. This combined form of the nickname is recorded in W1979/80–87. See also Royals, Stones.

Royalists is a nickname for two clubs with a slight royalist connection. These are:
* Hawick Royal Albert F.C., founded in Roxburghshire in 1947. The club plays at Albert Park, though only since 1963. The 'Royal Albert' phrase in the name is actually borrowed from another club, Royal Albert F.C. (1878), because a founder member came from Larkhall. The earlier club took it from their founding patron, a mine owner whose private yacht was called *The Royal Albert*; Wikipedia, SFHA. See also Albert, Sleeping Giants.
* Windsor and Eton F.C., founded in 1892 and earning royal patronage as well as association from their location next to Windsor Castle. Although playing well, they were expelled from their league for being in debt and folded in 2011. A successor club was formed as Windsor F.C. in 2011, assuming the old nickname and a badge showing Windsor castle, and adding a new nickname too, 'The Guardsmen'. Recorded in W1979/80–2013. See also Guardsmen, Royals.

Royalites was an early nickname for Burnley F.C. at about the time of their entry into the English League in 1888–9. It was a popular expression after the visit of Prince Albert (son of Victoria and Albert) to Turf Moor in 1886, which Pickering (1994–8) regards as probably the first visit by a member of the royal family to any football ground. See also Clarets, Dingles, Gene Puddle, Moorites, Royalites, Turfites.

Royals is a nickname for clubs with some connection to the royal family, even if only in name (see also Royalists etc), or who play in the shade of blue called 'royal blue' (or for both reasons). The clubs are:
* Arsenal F.C., a former nickname recorded by Moss 1983. Arsenal started out as the works side for the Royal Arsenal factory in Woolwich, London, in 1886. See also Boring Arsenal, France, Gooners, Gunners, Invincibles, Lucky Arsenal, Reds, Woolwich.

- Blandford United F.C., founded in Dorset in c.1893. The club plays in a royal blue strip and the nickname appears on the club badge in AFBC and on Wikipedia.

- Harthill Royal F.C., founded in West Lothian in 1992. The club plays in royal blue, as well as having 'Royal' in the official name. The club was originally called H. Royal Bar; Wikipedia.

- Kirkley and Pakefield F.C., founded in Suffolk in 2007 in a merger between the two clubs of these names. The club plays in an all-royal-blue strip; Wikipedia. See also Kirks.

- (A.F.C.) Portchester, founded in 1976 in a merger of Loyds Sports and Colourvision Rangers, and originally called Wicor Mill F.C. In 2002 the club, now called Portchester, merged with a local youth side called Castle Royals, from which the nickname comes; Wikipedia and club's own website. See also Porcheys.

- Potton United F.C., founded in Bedfordshire in 1943. The club plays in an all-royal-blue strip, though it also has a large crown as the crest on its club badge; W1992–2013.

- Reading F.C., founded in Berkshire in 1871. After the closure of the Huntley & Palmers biscuit factory in 1976, a new nickname was sought in a public competition and The Royals was the winning entry. It comes from Reading's status as the capital of the Royal County of Berkshire (the county includes Windsor Castle); recorded in RY1977/8–SSY2012/13. See also Biscuitmen.

- Sutton Coldfield Town F.C., founded in West Midlands in 1879. The club not only plays in an all-royal-blue strip, but Sutton Coldfield has enjoyed the title of 'Royal Town' since it was given a charter by Henry VIII in 1528. The badge of the club features a Tudor rose; W1988–2013.

- Wealdstone F.C. Founded in Middlesex in 1899, the team play in royal-blue shirts and shorts. Pickering 1994 uses this nickname. See also Royal Stones, Stones.

- Windsor and Eton F.C., founded in Berkshire in 1892 but folded in 2011. The successor club is Windsor F.C. Although the nickname is normally 'The Royalists', Smith 1993/4–95/6 records it as 'Royals'. See also Guardsmen, Royalists.

- Worcester City F.C., founded in 1902. It may record the city's association with King Charles I (see under Faithfuls, Loyals), or, more likely, it refers to the 1788 royal warrant which George III gave to Worcester Porcelain, which then was called 'Royal Worcester'; Wikipedia. See also Blues, City, Dragons, Faithfuls, Loyals.

Rubies was the original nickname of Cheltenham Town F.C., from the bright red shirts worn since their initial foundation (now regarded as 1887). Although a paler red with white started to be worn around 1932, and Robins became the more normal nickname, Rubies is still very much associated with the club in journalism and amongst fans. On March 15 2011 'This is Gloucestershire' reported that the club will be returning to a ruby-red strip 'next season' to mark the club's 125th anniversary, and the article recorded that the club had initially switched from a ruby-red to a 'Robin' red in 1903. See also Robins.

Russians was the nickname for Rushden Town F.C. before its merger in 1992 with Irthlingborough Diamonds to form Rushden and Diamonds F.C. Founded in 1889, the club wore a red shirt, which would have been entirely appropriate to the nickname after 1917. The similarity of the sounds of Rushden and Russians (Rush'ens), however, is more than sufficient explanation for the nickname. A newspaper cutting of 1946 (printed in Addis 1995, p. 14) shows that the nickname was in use by then. W1982/3–92 for the old club; W1993–4 and Pickering 1994 record the nickname for the new club but Diamonds soon became the main nickname. See also Diamonds.

Ruths / The Ruthless are nicknames for Ruthin Town F.C., founded in Denbighshire in about 1870, reformed 1951; as a pun on the place-name, but suggesting a team of merciless competitive spirit. The nicknames were on Wikipedia in 2011, from where they have spread to other websites, but they were no longer listed on the club's Wikipedia page in September 2012. See also Blues, Town.

Rwsters is the nickname of Llanrwst United F.C., founded in Conwy Co. Bor. in 1983, in a merger of L. Town and L. Athletic; recorded in RW 2011. The nickname is a pun on the sound of the last syllable of the place-name, 'roost' / 'roosters'. It appears as Roosters in RW1994.

Ryes is a nickname of Sunderland Ryhope Community Association F.C., founded in 1961, originally as Ryhope Youth Club, renaming as Ryhope Community Association F.C. in 1971 and after a series of recent mergers becoming the present club in 2006. The nickname is a pluralised short form of Ryhope, recorded in W1994–7. See also CA.

Saddlers is the nickname of Walsall F.C., and refers to the importance of the saddle-making industry in this West Midlands town in the nineteenth century. Founded in 1888 as Walsall Town Swifts, the present name was adopted in 1896, but the swift continues to be used on the club's badges. Recorded in G1956–76, Churchill 1958, Harvey 1959, Richards 1960, Avis 1966–70, and throughout RY1970/1–SSY2012/13. See also Swifts.

Sadford is an unofficial nickname for Bradford City F.C., from the perspective of Huddersfield supporters (recorded on the Football Fans Census, 2003). The nickname makes a pun on the place-name. See also Bantams, Chickens, Citizens, Cocks, Gents, Paraders.

Saffron is a nickname for Saffron Walden Town F.C., founded in Essex in 1872, from the first word in the place-name, which refers to the cultivation of the saffron plant here from at least the sixteenth century (Mills 1991). Saffron is yellow and used in dyes, but the club plays in red shirts with black shorts and socks; Wikipedia. See also Bloods, Wardens.

Sailors is a nickname for two clubs in Portsmouth, Hampshire, because of the Royal Navy base there. The clubs are:

☻ Portsmouth F.C., recorded on the 1933 Ogden cigarette card and in SWSCYB

1962–3, from the long-standing association between the city and the Royal Navy. Neither of these sources mention Pompey. See also Blues, Pompey, Skates.

◉ Portsmouth Royal Navy F.C., founded in 1962; W1995–2001.

Saint Peters is a nickname for New Bradwell St. Peter F.C., founded in the 1880s near Milton Keynes in Buckinghamshire; listed on Wikipedia. See also Jimmies, Peters.

Saints is a nickname for clubs which are in some way connected to a saint, because of the place-name (as St Albans), or an early association with a church club (as Southampton – St Mary's), or because the word is in the place-name. Examples are:

◉ Arnold F.C., founded in Nottinghamshire in 1928, folded and replaced by Arnold Town in 1992; an earlier name for the club was Arnold St Mary's; W1982/3—6.

◉ Banchory St Ternan F.C., founded in Aberdeenshire in 1992, in a merger of B. Amateurs and St. Ternan Amateurs; Wikipedia, SFHA.

◉ Barlestone St Giles F.C., established in Leicestershire by at least 1983; W1993.

◉ Barnsley F.C., founded in Yorkshire in 1887, originally as St Peter's F.C., changing name to Barnsley in 1899; recorded in BoF1905–6 and Johnston 1934, both for the earlier club. See also Battling Barnsley, Colliers, Reds, Tykes.

◉ Brackley Town F.C., founded in Northamptonshire in 1890, the club's home ground is St James Park; W1985–2013.

◉ Cardiff Civil Service F.C., founded in 1963, originally as St Clair's F.C. Recorded in RW 1994–2002.

◉ Chalfont St Peter A.F.C., founded in Buckinghamshire in 1926; recorded in W1979/80–2013.

◉ Downham Town F.C., founded in 1881. The club, based in Downham Market in Norfolk, is associated with the crown and arrows of St Edmund on both the club badge and the town sign, but 'Town' has now supplanted the nickname. The nickname is not recorded in Williams but it is labelled 'previously' in Miller & Wright 1996. See also Town.

◉ Hay St Mary's F.C., founded in Hay-on-Wye, Powys, in about 1889. The parish church of the famous 'book town' is St Mary's; Wikipedia.

◉ Heather St Johns F.C., founded in 1949, originally as Heather Athletic. The Leicestershire club changed its name to the present form in 2007, and St John is the patron saint of the parish church; Wikipedia.

◉ Llansantffraid F.C. (old club, 1959–96), see below under The New Saints.

◉ Llansantffraid Village F.C., founded in Powys in 2007; recorded in RW 2011. The new village team takes the traditional nickname for the older Llansantffraid club, which moved to Oswestry after a merger in 2004 and is now known as The New Saints (see below); Wikipedia.

◉ Nairn St Ninian F.C., founded in Highland (Nairnshire) in 1968; Wikipedia, SFHA.

◉ Newcastle Benfield Saints F.C., founded in 1988, originally as Brunswick Village F.C. and going through some name changes and a merger with North Shields St

Columbas before adopting the simpler 'Newcastle Benfield' name in 2007. The club is now nicknamed 'The Lions', but a programme reproduced in W2005 (p. 576) records the club as Newcastle Benfield Saints, which strongly suggests 'Saints' was used as a nickname at the time. See also Lions.

⚽ Newton St Cyres F.C., founded in Devon in 1956; W1994–9.

⚽ Nuneaton Town F.C., founded in 1889 as Nuneaton St Nicholas, but renamed to 'Town' in 1894; Wikipedia. See also Boro, Nuns, Townies.

⚽ Oban Saints A.F.C., founded in Argyll in 1960; club's own website.

⚽ Presteigne St Andrews F.C., founded in Powys in 1897. The town's parish church is dedicated to St Andrew (and the Welsh place-name for the location is Llanandras). Recorded in RW1994. See also Stripes.

⚽ Saintfield United F.C., founded in Co. Down in 1982; from the place-name; Wikipedia.

⚽ Sandiacre Town F.C., founded in Nottinghamshire in 1978. The nickname refers to the club's home ground at St Giles Park; W1994–2005.

⚽ Southam United F.C., founded in Warwickshire in 1905. The nickname is not explained in any of the club sources. The town has a Holy Well but it does not seem to be associated with any particular saint. The nickname is represented on the club badge by matchstick girl and boy saints; W1986–8 and W1993–7.

⚽ Southampton F.C., from its origins as an Anglican church-based club. Founded in 1885 as St Mary's Young Men's A.F.C., the name changed to St Mary's F.C. in 1887, then to Southampton St Mary's in 1894 and finally to just Southampton in 1896. The nickname is recorded in BoF1905–6, the 1933 Ogden card, Johnston 1934, and the 1936 Thomson 'stamp' album. It is today represented by the halo above a football on the club's badge, and the name of the current stadium, St Mary's. Recorded in Avis 1954–70, G1956–76, Churchill 1958, Norris 1959, Richards 1960, AA 1960, *Stedfast* April 1965 and throughout RY1970/1–SSY2012/13. See also Ale House Brawlers, Scummers.

⚽ St Albans City F.C., from the saint in the place-name. The Hertfordshire club was founded in 1908. Recorded in Avis 1966–70, W1979/80–2013, SSY2007/8. See also City.

⚽ St Andrews F.C, founded in Aylestone, Leicestershire, in 1973; the club's badge shows the Scottish saltire, or St Andrew's cross; Wikipedia.

⚽ St Andrews United F.C., founded in Fife in 1920 (though there were also previous clubs in the city); Wikipedia, SFHA. See also Ancients, United.

⚽ St Asaph City F.C., founded in 1965 in Clwyd. Recorded in RW1995.

⚽ St Bernards F.C., founded in Edinburgh in 1874 as the Third Edinburgh Rifle Volunteers, renaming in 1878, using the name of the nearby St Bernard's Well. The club was an important side in early Scottish football and survived until 1943. Although the Wikipedia website gives 'St Bernard' as a nickname for this club, the club had a temporary renaming in 1890 as 'Edinburgh Saints', strongly suggesting that if they had a nickname at all it was 'Saints'. The club's assets were donated for charitable use in youth football and the St Bernard's Boys Club, founded in 1949, counts as a successor to the older side.

- St Blazey F.C., founded in Cornwall in 1896; W1992–2005. See also Green and Blacks.
- St Clears A.F.C., refounded in Carmarthenshire in 1965. The nickname appears in match reports from 1972–3 on the 'Pembrokeshiresport.co.uk' website.
- St Cuthbert Wanderers F.C., founded in 1879 in Kirkcudbright, Dumfries and Galloway. The place-name Kirkcudbright means the 'Church of St Cuthbert'. After the Viking attack on Lindisfarne in 875, the monks carried Cuthbert's mortal remains to several places, including Kirkcudbright, before taking them to Chester-le-Street in 995, so it is possible that the 'Wandering' suffix has the same inspiration behind it. The club formed as a church side for the local catholic St Cuthbert's church. Recorded in RS1997, SFHA. See also Wanderers.
- St Duthus F.C., founded in Tain, Highland, in the late nineteenth century, folded in 2005. The Tain Thistle website mentions this older club and its nickname. St Duthus is the eleventh-century patron saint of the town.
- St Francis Hospital F.C., founded in 1890, based at the St Francis Asylum in Haywards Heath, West Sussex. The club dropped the word 'Hospital' from its name in 2000, before merging with Ansty Rangers in 2002 (see next entry); W1994–6. See also Mental Hospital.
- St Francis Rangers F.C., founded in a merger between St Francis and Ansty Rangers in West Sussex in 2002; W2009–13. See also Rangers.
- St Helen's Town A.F.C.; the Lancashire club was originally founded in 1903 but reformed in 1946. Dobson 1973 records the nickname as used for the town, and based on the St Helen's rugby team rather than the football club. Nevertheless, both football and rugby clubs exist and both are nicknamed 'The Saints'; Wikipedia. See also Town.
- St Ippolyts F.C., founded in Hertfordshire in 1908; W1993–6.
- St Ives Town F.C., founded in Cambridgeshire in 1887; W1995–2013.
- St Johnstone F.C., founded in Perth in 1884. The town of Perth is known as 'St John's Toun' (from their patron saint, John the Baptist). Recorded in *Stedfast* April 1964, Avis 1966–70, throughout RY1970/1–SSY2012/13 and RS 1993–2012. Many websites gives the variant 'The Saintees', a pluralised friendly form.
- St Leonards F.C., founded in East Sussex in 1971, originally as STAMCO F.C., as they were a works side for the Sussex Turnery And Moulding Company, renamed 1998, folded in 2003; W1999–2004. See also Blues.
- St Mary's A.F.C., founded in Douglas, Isle of Man, in 1893; the nickname is used in journalists' match reports.
- St Mary's A.F.C., founded in Co. Cork in 1923, reformed 1948; club's own website.

❂ St Mary's F.C., founded at Watford in c.1891 and an ancestor club of Watford, named from the merger between West Herts and St Mary's in 1898. The 1905–6 *Book of Football* records 'Saints' as the nickname for this club. See also Blues, Brewers, Golden Boys, Hornets, Horns / 'Orns, Wasps, Yellow Army.

❂ St Mirren F.C., founded in Paisley, Renfrewshire in 1877. St Mirren is the patron saint of Paisley. Recorded in Johnston 1934, G1956–76, Harvey 1959, the 1959 Sweetule card, Avis 1966–70, RY1970/1–72/3 and in RS 1993–2012. A variant form, halfway between Saints and Paisley Brazilians, is 'Paisley Saints', which appears in RY1989/90–90/1 and in *Panini's Football Yearbook 1988/89–89/90*. See also Black and White Army, Buddies, Paisley Brazilians.

❂ St Neots Town F.C., founded in Cambridgeshire in 1879; W1979/80–89 and W1995–2013.

❂ St Osyth F.C., founded in Essex in 1951; W1988. See also Toosey.

❂ St Patrick's Athletic F.C., founded in Dublin in 1929. There are also the variant forms Dublin Saints and Super Saints. Recorded in RI1997. See also Dublin Saints, Pat's.

❂ St Peters (St Albans) F.C., founded in Hertfordshire in 1902 (date on the club badge); W1993–6.

❂ Shardlow St James F.C., founded in Derbyshire in 1880 (date on the club badge); W1994–7.

❂ The New Saints F.C., founded in 2004 in a merger between Oswestry Town F.C. (Shropshire) and Total Network Solutions F.C. Total Network Solutions was a communications business, based in Oswestry, which in 1996 approached the Welsh club Llansantffraid F.C. (nicknamed 'The Saints', founded in 1959 at the Powys border town of Llansantffraid-ym-Mechain), offering sponsorship if the club would rename itself. This is claimed to be the first time in the UK that a club was actually *renamed* after the sponsors. In 2006 British Telecom took over Total Network Solutions and the deal lapsed. The club decided on a new name which preserved the original nickname (which also honoured Oswestry, named for Saint Oswald) and also preserved the same initials. Recorded in RW1994–7 and W1996–7 and a badge in AFBC for Llansantffraid; RW1998–2002 and W1998–2005 for Total Network Solutions and in RW2011 for the present club. See also Blues, TNS.

❂ Total Network Solutions F.C., see discussion under The New Saints, above.

Salamanders was the nickname of Park Rangers F.C., founded in Tividale, West Midlands in 1968, which seems to disappear after its entries in W1992–5. The nickname is recorded in W1994–5. The salamander amphibian is frequently found in distinct black-and-yellow colours, and the away strip of the club is recorded as yellow shirts, black shorts and socks, which is the likely explanation.

Salmoners is a nickname of Darwen F.C., founded in 1870, and reformed in 2009 as A.F.C. Darwen. According to the club's website, the club was forced to change its colours in 1891 when it joined the same league as Notts County, who wore

288

similar black-and-white stripes. The club chose a salmon-pink shirt which they only wore for two seasons, but the nickname stuck. Dobson 1973, however, records 'Darren Salmon' as a local ironic phrase for herring, so there was almost certainly extra encouragement to the nickname in the local culture; W1987. See also Anchormen, Darreners.

Salop is another nickname for Shrewsbury Town F.C., though Salop is usually an alternative name for the county of Shropshire, based on a Norman scribal abbreviation, rather than the town. Nevertheless, Shropshire County was one of the ancestor clubs of Shrewsbury Town, and Salop was adopted as the official county name from 1974 to 1997, although the nickname use predates this, recorded in Avis 1966–70 and G1976. The nickname is not recorded in Rothmans until 1999 (and then through RY1999/2000–SSY2012/13), but with the slightly-wrong explanation "The name 'Salop' is a colloquialism for the county of Shropshire. Since Shrewsbury is the only club in Shropshire [!], cries of 'Come on Salop' are frequently heard!" This at least gives what will be the club's own explanation. See also Blues, Shrews, Town.

Salts was the nickname for Salts (Saltaire) F.C. The club appears in FCHD for 1955–65, but the nickname is recorded in Avis 1966–70. The nickname is today used for the amateur club Saltaire F.C. The model village of Saltaire, within the boundaries of Bradford, West Yorkshire, was founded by the industrialist Sir Titus Salt in 1851.

Sand Dobbers is a nickname for Leighton Town F.C., founded in Bedfordshire in 1885. The nickname is recorded in W1983–4 (and only in that edition). The chief industry of Leighton Buzzard in Bedfordshire has long been sand extraction, and the town today has a Sand Museum. The Museum's website records that the local expression for those who dug the sand out of the ground and loaded it into carts was 'Sand Dobbers'. The expression is very significant because it also explains the mysterious 'Dabbers' (q.v.) used for Nantwich Town. See also Buzzards, Reds, Town.

Sandgrounders is the nickname of Southport F.C., founded in Lancashire in 1881, originally as Southport Central. The nickname uses that of anyone who lives in this seaside town. Two explanations are suggested: either because the location is one of sandy ground or because sandgrounding is what shrimp nets do when they rub across the sand at the bottom of the sea, but most sources prefer an interpretation based on the sandy ground of the town, as a way of saying a man from Southport is a 'Son of the Soil'. Dobson 1973 records the nickname for the town and quotes a source from 1903 with this interpretation. Recorded for the club in G1956–65, Churchill 1958, Harvey 1959, Richards 1960, Avis 1966–70, RY1970/1–78/9, W1979/80–2013 and SSY2006/7–07/8 and SSY2012/13. See also Port, Yellows.

Sandwell Town is an unofficial nickname for West Bromwich Albion F.C., from the perspective of Wolverhampton Wanderers supporters, as recorded on the 2003 Football Fans Census. The nickname refers to the original home of the club, with the suggestion that the modern club perhaps has a small support base. See also Albion,

Baggies, Bennies, Boing!, Nigger Minstrels, Stripes, Strollers, Tatters (for a possible connection), Team of Boys, Tesco's, Throstles, W.B.A.

Sappers is the nickname for the football club of the Royal Engineers, using the popular nickname for members of the Corps. The Corps was founded in 1862 and the football club dates from 1863, and was a very successful side in Victorian football. 'Sapper' is an ancient word for 'one who saps', derived from an old French word for 'spade', and has long been applied to those who did the spade work for military engineering projects. Recorded in BoF1905–6 (p.288).

Saras is the nickname for Cheltenham Saracens F.C., founded in Gloucestershire in 1964, a short form of the suffix. The club operates from a multi-sports club called Saracens, and shows two crossed oriental swords on its badge. Saracens is the name for the tough Islamic fighters who confronted the Christian Crusaders (q.v.) in the Middle Ages, and it has been a popular word for businesses, clubs and public houses since the nineteenth century; W1987–2013.

Sarnies is the nickname of Egham Town F.C., founded in Surrey in 1963 as the late reformation of an old club, the Runnymead Rovers (1877–1939). A sarny is a sandwich (Phythian 1955), and the name is a pun on the place-name: egg and ham (!); some even combine the Runnymead place-name in the phrase 'runny eggs and ham'. The nickname is recent, recorded in W1994–2013 and Pickering 1994. See also Swans, Town.

Sassenachs is an unofficial nickname for the England National Football Team, from a Scottish perspective, but it might also appear in press coverage of any Scottish club playing against any English one (for example, Addis 1995, p. 29 reprints a newspaper cartoon of 1949 which uses the nickname for a match between Corby and Peterborough, the Corby steelworks employing a great many Scottish workers). The word is first recorded in 1706 in a letter quoted by the Scots Dictionary: "We call them *Sassanich*, in Latin *Saxi* or *Saxonia*." It derives from the Scottish Gaelic *Sasunnach*, meaning 'Saxons'. Within Scotland, it might also be used for Scottish Lowlanders, from a Highland perspective (thanks to Andrew Eadie). See also Class of '66, Roy's Boys, Sven's Men, Three Lions.

Satsumas is the nickname of Wokingham and Emmbrook F.C., founded in Berkshire in a merger in 2004. The club plays in orange shirts with black shorts and socks, and the nickname is a variant on Tangerines; W2009–13. For the earlier Wokingham Town, see Oakey, Town.

Sauchie is a nickname for Sauchie Juniors F.C., founded in Clackmannanshire in 1960. Earlier, in the 1950s, the club was known as S. Juveniles (actually intended for adult players). 'Sauchie' is used as a nickname on Wikipedia and the club's own website.

Savage Six is a nickname recorded in Pickering 1994 for a notorious aggressive side at Bolton Wanderers in the 1950s. See also Noblot / Notlob, Reds, Spots, Trotters, Wanderers, Whites / Whitemen.

SAVE F.C. was an acronymic nickname for Somersett Ambury Victoria and Elm F.C.

between 1991 and 2002, when the club renamed as Broxbourne Borough Victoria and Elm F.C., with the nickname of Boro. Originally founded in Hertfordshire in 1959 by boys from Chace Boys School, Enfield, the club joined the Victoria and Elm Youth Club Centre in 1975, merged with Cheshunt Rangers in 1982 and finally merged with Ambury in 1991; Wikipedia. See also Boro.

Saxons is one of the national names of the ancient English and is a nickname for one club and the suffix for several others. The Welsh and Scottish Gaelic languages refer to the English as Saxons (Saeson, or Sassenachs, q.v.). The clubs are:

- Axbridge Saxon F.C., a Somerset youth side formed in 1998.
- Ewell Saxons F.C., a youth side founded in Surrey in about 2011.
- Salisbury Saxons F.C., a youth side formed in Wiltshire before 2009.
- Saxons F.C., a pioneer London club formed in 1874, but dissolved at an early date.
- Stockport Sports F.C., founded in Greater Manchester in 1970, originally as Woodley Athletic, then named W. Sports until 2012. The nickname appears for the first time in W2013. Apart from an obvious nationalist association, the nickname may just possibly have been suggested by the letters in the postcode of the club's ground: SK6 1QX. The new name and nickname is already the subject of a major 'branding' of the club, and the mascot is Storm the Saxon. For the earlier club, see Sports, Steelmen.
- Wellingborough Saxon F.C., founded in Northamptonshire in 1974.

Scabs is a nickname for workers who break solidarity with their mates by working through a strike. The word became well-known in the late nineteenth century (the OED even has this usage as early as 1777) and in the 1890s it was a nickname for Middlesbrough F.C. from supporters of the rival Ironopolis club, because Middlesbrough broke an agreement to form a merger. See Appleton 1960, p. 83. See also Boro, Cleveland Cowboys, Ironsiders, Nops, Riversiders, Smoggies, Teessiders, Washers.

Scarlet Runners was the first nickname of Huddersfield Town A.F.C. Founded in West Yorkshire in 1908, the club first adopted all-red shirts, then blue, but did not arrive at the now-traditional blue-and-white stripes until 1913. The Historical Football Kits website records the nickname and the red shirt worn in 1908–9. See also Colnesiders, Terriers, Town.

Scholars is a nickname for clubs originally affiliated to an educational institution. Variant terms are Academicals and Dons. The examples are:

- Cambridge Regional College F.C., founded in 2006; Wikipedia.
- Chasetown F.C., who were founded in 1954 as Chase Terrace Old Scholars (from Chase Terrace High School in Staffordshire); W1994–2013. See also Chase.
- Loughborough University F.C., founded in Leicestershire in 1920, originally as Loughborough College; Wikipedia.
- Potters Bar Town F.C., founded in Hertfordshire in 1960 as Mount Grace Old Scholars F.C., for former pupils of that school. The 'Old Scholars' was dropped in

1984, then the change to Potters Bar Town came in 1991. The nickname appears on the club's badge; W1996–2013. See also Grace.

⚽ Team Bath F.C., founded in Avon in 1999 for Bath University; Wikipedia. See also Crescents, Team.

School of Science is a nickname for Everton F.C., apparently based on a comment from footballer Steve Bloomer (1874–1938) who called the club's style of playing 'scientific' in 1928. Recorded in Pickering 1994. See also Bitters / Bitter Blues, Black Watch, Bluenoses, Blues, Dogs of War, Merseysiders, Moonlight Dribblers, People's Club, Toffees/Toffeemen.

Scorries is the nickname for the Highland side, Wick Academy F.C., founded in 1893. The nickname uses the Caithness dialect word for 'Seagulls', Wick being a seaside town. The word is inexplicably missing from Scots and Gaelic dictionaries, but its meaning is widely acknowledged on the internet. Contrast with 'Seagulls' for English, Welsh and Irish seaside towns. Recorded in RS1995–2012, SFHA.

Scotia is the nickname of Balgonie Scotia A.F.C., founded in Coaltown of Balgonie, Glenrothes, Fife, in 1896. The nickname and suffix is the Latin name for Scotland (compare other Latin nation names Britannia, Caledonia, Cambria, Hibernia); Wikipedia.

Scots is the nickname of Scot F.C., founded at the Scots Sports and Social Club in Milton Keynes, Buckinghamshire in 1981; W1994–7.

Scow is the nickname of Tata Steel F.C., founded at Port Talbot in Glamorgan in 1954. The word originates as an acronym for the original steel company, the club being first called 'Steel Company of Wales A.F.C.' In the 1978–9 season the club was renamed British Steel A.F.C., later becoming Corus Steel F.C., Wikipedia.

Scummers is a derogatory nickname for Southampton F.C., from supporters of Portsmouth F.C. Apart from the obvious meaning of 'scum', people of no value, and the sense that scum floats on water, so it *could* be used for sailors if one wished to be insulting, there is a possibility of some cultural heritage behind the name. Pickering 1994 records the nickname and applies it to Southampton *supporters*. Ferris 2005 (and Kevin Mitchell in *The Observer*, 23 January 2005) say SCUM could be an acronym for Southampton Company [or City] of Union Men, and the name refers to an industrial dispute before the First World War [or the 1930s], in which Portsmouth workers remained steadfast and Southampton workers gave in to the employer's position, but there are profound doubts as to the truth of the story, as both writers admit, not least because the actual dispute does not seem to be recorded. Southampton supporters allegedly reply to the insult by calling Portsmouth 'The Skates' (q.v.), but neither of these terms are used by real Royal or Merchant Navy men, who have the greatest of respect for each other. Both nicknames originate entirely in banter between rival supporters and are unknown outside that context. 'Scum', however, is known more widely for other clubs, from rival fans. See also Ale House Brawlers, Saints.

Scunny is a nickname for the town of Scunthorpe, and is often heard as an unofficial nickname for Scunthorpe United F.C. The club's mascots are Scunny Bunny and Scunny Hunny Bunny. They're rabbits. Room 2006 is one source which cites the nickname and applies it to the football club. See also Iron, Nuts.

Seadogs was a nickname of Scarborough F.C. (1879–2007) and is now used by the new Scarborough Athletic F.C. (2007), who also take the badge, logo and red strip of the older club. The badge features a striking image of a calling seagull, and Sammy Seagull was the club mascot. A seadog is an old nickname for an experienced seafarer; W2000–07 for the old club, W2008–13 for the new. See also Boro, Seasiders, Town.

Seagulls is a nickname for clubs whose home is beside the sea. See also Scorries for an equivalent meaning from north Scotland. The clubs are:

☺ Aberystwyth Town F.C. Although the normal nickname for this club is 'The Seasiders', the Seagulls variant appears on an old enamel badge recorded in AFBC . See also Aber, Black and Greens, Seasiders.

☺ Bray Wanderers A.F.C., founded in 1942, reforming a club of 1922. The club is based in the seaside resort of Bray, Co. Wicklow. Recorded in RI2006. See also Seasiders.

☺ Brighton and Hove Albion F.C., founded in Sussex in 1901, obviously because of the seaside location of these neighbouring resorts, but according to Ferris 2005 the nickname was initially adopted in 1975 as a rhyming response to chants of the nickname of Crystal Palace, 'The Eagles', but the switch to this nickname does not occur in Rothmans until RY1978/9 (continuing then to SSY2012/13). See also Albion, Dolphins, Flippers, Seasiders, Seaweed, Shrimps, Tesco's.

☺ Cardiff Metropolitan University F.C. founded as UWIC Inter Cardiff F.C., in a merger in 2000 between Inter Cardiff F.C. and UWIC F.C., renaming in 2012. 'Seagulls' is recorded for this club in W2001 and for the present club on Wikipedia. The nickname was used earlier by Inter Cardiff (see below). See also Diffs / Div's, Inter / International, Sheep.

☺ Colwyn Bay F.C., founded in 1885; W1994–2013, RW1994–2011; the town is a popular seaside resort on the North Wales coast. See also Bay, Harbourmen, Seasiders.

☺ Inter Cardiff F.C., established in a merger in 1990, and briefly renamed as Inter Cable-Tel F.C. in 1996–9 (see below, under Sully), recorded with the Seagulls nickname in W1994–2000 and RW1994–8.

☺ Mousehole F.C., founded in Cornwall in 1922; W1992–4.

☺ Rhyl F.C., founded in Clwyd in 1878, recorded in W1980/1. See also Beavers, Lillies, Lilywhites.

☺ Saltburn Athletic F.C., founded in the Bor. of Redcar and Cleveland in 1998. The club has a logo of a flying seagull and the nickname is printed in the April 2013 edition of the community magazine *Talk of the Town*.

☺ Sully F.C., which merged with A.F.C. Cardiff in 1990 to form Inter Cardiff F.C. In 1996 it renamed itself as Inter Cable Tel F.C., reverting to Inter Cardiff in 1999 (see the entries above). Then in 2000 the club merged with UWIC F.C. to form the new UWIC Inter Cardiff F.C. This present club still preserves the seagull badge which originated with Sully; Wikipedia. A Sully badge recorded in AFBC has the nickname. See also Diffs / Div's, Inter / International, Sheep.

☺ Weston-super-Mare A.F.C. Founded in Somerset in 1887, reformed in 1948, the club plays in black-and-white strip (seagull colours?) but the name obviously comes from the town's status as a major seaside tourist resort; W1988–2013. See also Seasiders.

Seahawks is the evocative nickname of Portstewart F.C., founded in Co. Londonderry in 1968. 'Seahawk' is a name used for ospreys and for several species of skua, seagull-like birds, and a stylised bird appears on the club badge; so on this understanding the nickname is comparable to 'Seagulls', used for several other seaside clubs. However, the word was also popularised as the title of Rafael Sabatini's 1915 novel and the 1940 Errol Flynn film about an English privateer of the time of the Spanish Armada, *The Seahawk*. The word is also used for an American football team and several brands of military hardware. Recorded in RNI2007.

Seahorses is the nickname of Whitley Bay F.C., founded in 1897, originally as W.B. and Monkseaton F.C., renamed to W.B. Athletic from 1950 to 1958, when 'Athletic' was dropped. There is a seahorse on the club badge and the town is a coastal resort at the mouth of the River Tyne, but seahorses are also used as supporters for the coat of arms of Newcastle United F.C. and for the city of Newcastle, so there is a strong local association with the seahorse (another local club, Kennek Roker F.C., one of the ancestor clubs of Sunderland Ryhope Community Association, had a badge showing a seahorse before its merger in 1999: AFBC); Wikipedia. See also Bay.

Seals has been an unofficial nickname for two clubs, from the appealing sea lion. The clubs are:

☺ Aston Villa F.C., from the perspective of West Bromwich Albion supporters (www.baggies.com) or from Birmingham City (Football Fans Census, 2003). Allegedly, Villa supporters were once witnessed clapping at arms' length, stamping the floor and shouting "Villa!" in a falsetto voice, all reminiscent of performing sea lions to those who wished to see it that way (and thus also mocking the official Villa nickname of Lions). See also Claret and Blues, Lions, Perry Bar Pets, Villa / Villans / Villains.

☺ Chester City F.C., founded in 1885, folding in 2010, the club's home ground was The Stadium in Sealand Road from 1906 to 1990, from which the nickname comes. It featured on the club's badge 1974–83 in the form of an image of two playful seals; Rothmans only cites it for a similar period, in RY1973/4–84/5. According to Wikipedia, 'Seals' has been re-adopted by the new Chester F.C., founded in 2010, but it has not yet appeared in printed directories. It makes a late appearance in Pickering 1994. See also Blues, Cestrians, City, Ivies, Magpies, Romans.

Seasiders is a nickname for clubs which are beside the sea, in a town which is a popular tourist resort. The examples are:

● Aberystwyth Town F.C., founded in Ceredigion in 1884. The university town and cultural centre (holding the National Library of Wales) is also a popular summer seaside resort; RW1994, W1995–2005. See also Aber, Black and Greens, Seagulls.

● Afan Lido F.C., founded in the Co. Bor. of Neath Port Talbot at Aberavon in 1967. The nickname is used in the *South Wales Evening Post* on December 16, 2008. See also Lidos.

● Bangor F.C., founded in Co. Down in 1918. The club in this seaside town has a seagull on its badge and plays in the seaside colours of blue and yellow. Recorded in *Stedfast* April 1963 (as 'The Sea-siders'), and RI1997, RNI2007, AFBC.

● Blackpool F.C., from the famous Lancashire resort. One variant name for supporters of the club is Seaside Barmy Army. The nickname appears early, in BoF1905–6; also on the 1936 Thomson 'stamp', in G1956–76, Churchill 1958 and on the 1959 Sweetule card, Richards 1960, SWSCYB 1962–3, Avis 1966–70, and in RY and SSY from 1976/7 to 2012/13. See also Atomic Boys, Donkey Lashers, Merry Stripes, 'Pool, Tangerines.

● Bournemouth F.C., recorded in Avis 1954, though the later editions (1966–70) cite the familiar Cherries and Cherry Bees (q.v.).

● Bray Wanderers F.C., founded in Co. Wicklow in 1942. Recorded in RI1997. See also Seagulls.

● Bridlington Town A.F.C., founded in East Yorkshire in 1918, originally as Bridlington Central United but called Town before the club was listed in W1979/80, reformed in 1994; the nickname appears in W1991–4 and W2007–13. See also Town.

● Brightlingsea United F.C., founded in Essex in 1928 in a merger between B. Town (1919) and B. Athletic (1908); the club merged with Regent Park Rangers in 2005 to form B. Regent; this nickname appears in W1989–90. See also Oystermen, Seasiders, Tics, United.

● Brighton and Hove Albion F.C., recorded in Avis 1954–70 and G1976. See also Albion, Dolphins, Flippers, Seagulls, Seaweed, Shrimps, Tesco's.

● Cemaes Bay F.C., founded in 1976 on Anglesey, recorded in W1997. See also Bay, Demolition Squad.

● (F.C.) Clacton, founded in Essex in 1892 as Clacton Town; recorded in W1979/80–2005 for Town and W2008–13 for the modern club. See also Lilywhites.

● Clevedon Town F.C., founded near Bristol in 1880; W1979/80, W1982/3–80, W1994–2013.

● Colwyn Bay F.C., founded in North Wales in 1885; recorded in W1980/81. See also Bay, Harbourmen, Seagulls.

⚽ Dawlish Town A.F.C., founded in Devon in 1889, originally as Dawlish Argyle; W1987–90 and W2010–11. See also Argyle.

⚽ Dunbar United F.C., founded in East Lothian in 1925; Wikipedia.

⚽ Felixstowe and Walton United F.C., founded in 2000 in a merger between Felixstowe Port and Town (1890) and Walton United (1895); Felixstowe is a Suffolk resort; W1983/4–2000 for F. Port and Town; W2001–13 for the new club.

⚽ Folkestone Invicta F.C., founded in Kent in 1936; W2007–13. See also Invicta.

⚽ Girvan F.C., founded in 1947 in South Ayrshire; Wikipedia. See also Amateurs.

⚽ Marske United F.C., founded in 1956. This North Yorkshire (Redcar and Cleveland) town is a seaside resort, and the club colours of blue and yellow also suggest the local sand and sea; W1997–2013. See also Codheads.

⚽ Minehead A.F.C., founded in Somerset in 1889; recorded in W1982/3–5. See also Blues.

⚽ Newcastle F.C., founded in Co. Down in 1977. The Northern Ireland club is beside the sea; Wikipedia.

⚽ Porthcawl Town Athletic F.C., founded in 1947; recorded in RW1998 and on a badge in AFBC..

⚽ Prestatyn Town F.C., founded in the Denbighshire seaside resort in 1910; recorded in RW2011 and Wikipedia. See also Campers.

⚽ Saltcoats Victoria F.C., founded in 1881 (reformed 1911) in North Ayrshire; Wikipedia, SFHA.

⚽ Scarborough F.C., founded in 1879, closed in 2007 and succeeded by Scarborough Town F.C.; another major resort on the North Yorkshire coast. The club had a magnificent seagull badge but does not seem to have ever been nicknamed 'Seagulls'; Wikipedia. See also Boro, Seadogs, Town.

⚽ Selsey F.C., founded in West Sussex in 1903; W1989–90 and W1993. See also Blues.

⚽ Southend United F.C., from the famous Essex resort. Recorded in Avis 1954 (but later editions have other nicknames). See also Blues, Shrimpers.

⚽ Weston-super-Mare F.C., founded in Somerset in 1948. Recorded in W1979/80–87. See also Seagulls.

⚽ Welshpool Town F.C., founded in Powys in 1878. This nickname is recorded for this club six times, in W1997–9 and W2003–5, whereas the Robinson guides record the ground name Maes y Dre as a nickname in RW1994–2000/1. Both are errors, the club is really nicknamed 'The Lilywhites'. It is difficult to imagine a location in Wales, or even anywhere in Britain, that could be further from the coast as Welshpool. The *sounds* of the two names are too different to have caused confusion, but it is conceivable that 'Maesydre' in unclear handwriting could easily have been misread as 'Seasiders'. See also Lilywhites, Maes y Dre.

⚽ Whitby Town F.C., founded in 1880, from the famous North Yorkshire tourist resort and fishing community; the club went through a variety of names and mergers before the final change in 1949; recorded in W1979/80–87 and W1992–2013 and Barton 1984 & 1985. See also Blues, Town.

Seaweed is an unofficial nickname for Brighton and Hove Albion F.C., from the perspective of Crystal Palace Supporters (recorded on the 2003 Football Fans Census). The nickname makes a mocking reference to both the seaside location and the official nickname of the club, with 'weed' suggesting valuelessness. See also Albion, Dolphins, Flippers, Seagulls, Seasiders, Shrimps, Tesco's.

Sedge is the nickname of the West Yorkshire village club Liversedge F.C., founded in 1910. A short form of the place-name, recorded in W1982/3–86 and W1993–2013.

Seedgrowers is the nickname of Coggeshall Town F.C., founded in Essex in 1878. The nickname is recorded in the title of the club history by John Alston: *The Seedgrowers Centenary: a History of One Hundred Years Football at Coggeshall 1878–1978*; also recorded in W1989 and on the club's website. The club's home ground has been called 'The Crops' since 1960, but the nickname probably refers to the 1878 foundation by the local seed-growing business of J. J. King & Sons.

Seedhillers is recorded in Dobson 1973 as a nickname for Nelson F.C., founded in Lancashire in 1881. The Seedhill area of the town is the location of the football ground (used by the club 1905–68); Dobson recorded that the 'h' was silent and that the nickname was being used at the time for the town generally. See also Admirals, Blues.

Seven is the nickname for Seven Sisters A.F.C., founded in Neath Port Talbot Co. Bor. in 1910. The place-name records the seven sisters of the founder of the coal mine the settlement grew around (recognised as a place-name in 1882), but the Welsh version of the place-name is Y Sefn, so the nickname could be based on this, or simply a short form of the place-name. The club website records that the club was called Seven Sisters Old Blues after a reformation in 1919–20; Wikipedia and club's own website.

Shack is a nickname for Irlam F.C., founded near Salford in 1969, originally as a works side for employees of the engineering firm Mitchell, Shackleton & Co. A short form of Shackleton, punning with the affectionate term for a delapidated house; Wikipedia. See also Mitchell's.

Shakers is the official nickname of Bury F.C., founded in Lancashire in 1885. It is recorded early, in BoF1905–6, and is said to date from the 1892 Lancashire Senior Cup final against Blackburn Rovers: "The then chairman of the club (Mr. J. T. Ingham) exclaimed: "We'll give them a shaking up; in fact, we are 'The Shakers'!". The phrase was an expressive one, was instantly seized upon by the club's supporters, and soon became widely used" Virtually the same words are repeated on the 1933 Ogden card and in Johnston 1934, but slight variations to the quote have occasionally appeared. Despite the club being formed in 1885 from members of the

Wesleyan and Trinitarian free churches, there has never been any suggestion that the nickname is related to the eighteenth-century nonconformist group, The Shakers. The expression is the same as the phrase 'Movers and Shakers', for those who shake the foundations of convention (which appears in print shortly before the 1892 match, in O'Shaughnessy's 1874 poem 'Ode'). Later recorded in the 1936 Thomson 'stamp' album, Churchill 1958 and Norris 1959. Despite the idea that the pamphlet would be authoritative to *squelch* any argument, Vernon 1970–1 gives a known error and then adds another: "Bury are known as the Shakers because the whole team shook at the knees when they qualified for the cup in 1903" and "Squelch! It's because they inflicted the greatest margin of defeat in any Cup Final by beating Derby 6–0!" Dobson 1973 gives the 1892 explanation and adds that sometimes the nickname is also applied generally to the people of Bury. Also recorded in G1956–76, Richards 1960, AA 1960, SWSCYB 1962–3, Avis 1966–70, and throughout RY and SSY from 1970/1 to 2012/13. See also Bucketshakers, Grave Diggers.

Sham is a nickname for Walton and Hersham F.C., founded in Surrey in 1945 as a merger of clubs from these neighbouring towns. The nickname is taken from the last syllable of Hersham, though it sounds derogatory. However, the punk-rock band from Hersham, Sham 69, popularised it after taking it from a damaged sign celebrating the successful 1969 season. One of their songs was 'Hersham Boys'; Wikipedia. Avis 1966–70 records the club as 'Swans and Robins', which suggests that Hersham originally took 'The Robins' nickname. See also Swans, Swans and Robins, Waltz.

Shamrocks was the nickname of Retford Town F.C., founded in Nottinghamshire in c.1948. The shamrock is the clover and a national symbol of Ireland, and the club colours were green and white; the nickname must express an Irish element in the club's history and an admiration for the Dublin side Shamrock Rovers. However, this club folded during the 1985–6 season and the explanation for the nickname can only be guessed at; recorded in Avis 1966–70 and W1983/4–6. Retford Town's official name was reused when BRSA Retford (formed in a 1993 merger of Retford Rail and Eaton Hall College) renamed itself R. Town in 2001 (FCHD). Neither club is related to R. United.

Shannocks is the nickname for anyone living in the seaside town of Sheringham in Norfolk, also used for Sheringham F.C, founded in 1897. The nickname is proudly displayed on the club badge. The nickname is of uncertain etymology, but all discussions accept that it refers to Sheringham people as wild and reckless and may have something to do with fishing. 'Shanny' is a Norfolk dialect word for 'scatter-brained', but it seems likely that this is not an independent word but an adaptation of the town nickname (shanny meaning Shannocks-like). Local bookseller Peter Cox explained that a shannock is also a local name for one of the edible species of North Sea fish (it is unclear which: haddock was popular in the nineteenth-century and has a similar ending to the nickname, but herring is more like the place-name) and that

Sheringham fishermen had a reputation for wild and reckless sailing in their pursuit of those fish. This would make sense, linking quarry and pursuer together with the same name, and using a single trading activity as a metaphor for a whole town is also a normal route for a nickname. The *sh–* alliteration can only have encouraged the association; Wikipedia records the nickname for the club.

Sharks is the nickname for Sharpness A.F.C., founded in Gloucestershire in 1900. The locality is a harbour on the River Severn, but the nickname appears simply to be a play on the place-name, either because of its opening sound or because the teeth of this fearsome predator have a reputation for sharpness; W1985–6.

Shaymen is the main nickname of F.C. Halifax Town. Founded in West Yorkshire in 2008 as a successor to the bankrupt Halifax A.F.C. (1911), the new club reuses the older nickname, based on the old home ground of The Shay at Shay Syke, Halifax. *Shay* is an Anglo-Saxon word meaning a small wood, a thicket or a grove; RY1980/1–93/4, RY1998/9–2002/3 and SSY2004/5–08/9; W1994–8 and 2003–8 record it for the older club, W2011–13 for the new. See also Town.

Sheep is an unofficial nickname for two clubs. The clubs are:

🙂 Cardiff Metropolitan University F.C. founded as UWIC Inter Cardiff F.C., in a merger in 2000 between Inter Cardiff F.C. and UWIC F.C., renaming in 2012 (both clubs originating in 1990). The nickname seems to record nothing other than the large number of sheep in Wales; Wikipedia. See also Diffs / Div's, Inter / International, Seagulls.

🙂 Derby County F.C., as recorded on the Football Fans Census website for 2003, from the perspective of Nottingham Forest supporters. The nickname is a play on the official nickname, The Rams (q.v.).

Sheers is the nickname of Sheerwater F.C., founded in Surrey in 1958, a pluralised short form of the place-name, W2009–13.

Sheik City is an unofficial nickname for Manchester City F.C., from its ownership since 2008 by an investment company owned by H.H. Sheik Mansour bin Zayed Al Nahyan of Abu Dhabi. The nickname is not in any way offensive, it might even have started factually as 'The Sheik's City', but its use by supporters of rival clubs is probably motivated by resentment at the investment capital the new owner has brought, making City one of the richest football clubs in the world. The nickname appears in online journalism. See also Bitters / Bitter Blues, Blues, Citizens, City, Council Housers, Man, Massives, Stockports.

Shells is an alternative nickname for Shildon A.F.C., as a pun on the first syllable of the place-name; Wikipedia. See also Railwaymen.

Shels is a nickname for Shelbourne F.C., founded in Dublin in 1895; a pluralised short form of the place-name. Recorded in Avis 1966–70, RI 1997. See also Aul Reds, Real Reds, Reds.

Shelties is the nickname for the Shetland Isles' Official Football Team (or 'Representative Football Team') when it plays in the international Island Games (founded in 1989). The nickname is also used for the Shetland Sheep Dog and the Shetland Pony, and is a popular nickname for the island group itself; Wikipedia.

Shine was the nickname for Shinewater Association F.C., based in East Sussex. The club disappeared in a merger in 2003, forming Eastbourne United Association F.C.; W1994–6. For Eastbourne and the new club, see U's, United.

Shiners is the nickname for South Normanton Athletic F.C., founded in 1980. The website for the Derbyshire club gives the traditional explanation: "The nickname 'Shiners' derives from the mid 1750s when South Normanton was at the heart of the ribbed stocking industry. The people involved in this craft worked long hours sitting at their windows on wooden stools, so much so, that the backsides of their trousers became very shiny, making them instantly recognisable as coming from the South Normanton area. Since then local people have been referred to and called 'Shiners'." Whether this is ultimately correct or not, the name certainly refers to anyone from South Normanton, and it is now a local street name, Shiners Way. A shiner is also a word for a black eye, and one wonders if the true sense might be 'bruisers', meaning people who regularly get into a fight rather than wearing out their clothing in ceaseless toil. Printed in W2008 but the entry in W2002 records the name of the club programme as *The Shiner*. See also Athletic.

Shipbuilders is the nickname for at least two clubs, one present and one in the past, for a coastal location noted for its ship-building industry. The clubs are:

☺ Barrow A.F.C., founded in 1901. Barrow-in-Furness in Cumbria has long been a major ship-building town; recorded in Avis 1966–70. Dòbson 1973 gives the nickname as one for the town rather than the club. The club's badge illustrates a submarine, many of which have also been built here. See also Bluebirds, Strawberries, Ziggers.

☺ East Craigie F.C., established in 1880 in Dundee, a major port and ship-building centre, though the last Dundee ship was built in 1981; Wikipedia, SFHA.

Shipyard is the nickname of Burntisland Shipyard Amateur F.C., founded in Fife in 1925; club's own website.

Shipyarders is a nickname for Cammell Laird F.C., founded in 1907, originally as the Cammell Laird Institute team. Cammell Laird is a major ship-building firm in Birkenhead, who have long specialised in building Royal Navy warships; one is displayed on the club badge; Wikipedia. See also Camels, Lairds.

Shire is a nickname for two Scottish clubs which take a county name in their official name. Although there are no teams actually representing shires, sometimes a club is named from a county, or is a 'county borough'. See also 'Wee County'. The two clubs are:

☺ East Stirlingshire F.C., founded in Falkirk in 1880, originally as Bainsford Britannia but switching to the present name in 1881. The nickname emphasises the county because sometimes the club name is shortened informally to East Stirling, implying a base in Stirling. Recorded through RY1972/3–SSY2012/13 and in RS1993–2012.

❧ Glasgow Perthshire F.C., founded at Possilpark in Glasgow in 1890 and named after the Glasgow Perthshire Society; Wikipedia, SFHA.

Shoe Army is an unofficial nickname of Northampton Town F.C., reflecting the town's major shoe-making industry, and also suggestive of the huge scale of this industry in the town's history. The 1905–6 *Book of Football* uses 'Bootdom' as a nickname for the town. See also Cobblers, Tayn, Town.

Shopmates is the nickname of Raunds Town F.C., founded in Northamptonshire in 1946. The town has a traditional boot and shoe industry, and in this case the nickname records the widespread use of home-based workshops (rather than large factories) to make the shoes. Home-working was also common in the weaving industry of the West Riding of Yorkshire. Presumably the name also shows that the workshops employed small teams of workers rather than just individual families; W1985–2013.

Shots was an alternative nickname of the former Aldershot F.C. (1926–92) and is the official nickname of the successor Aldershot Town F.C. (1992). The nickname is a short form of the place-name, but it is entirely appropriate for both a football club and Aldershot's main livelihood as an army garrison town. G1956–76, Churchill 1958, Harvey 1959, Richards 1960 and Avis 1966–70 all record both 'Shots' and 'Soldiers'; W1993–2008 and RY1970/1–92/3 and SSY2004/5–12/13 just 'Shots'. See also Soldiers.

Shrews is a nickname for two clubs with the letters 'shrew' in their place-name; though the original element means 'scrubland' in the case of Shrewsbury and 'sheriff' in the case of Shrewton:

❧ Shrewsbury Town F.C., founded in 1886 as a successor to previous teams called Shropshire Wanderers and S. Castle Blues, the club only adopted the shrew as a badge in 1983–93 (and very stylish); first recorded in *Panini's Football Yearbook 1988/89–89/90* and then in RY1989/90–96/7. See also Blues, Salop, Town.

❧ Shrewton United F.C., founded in Wiltshire in 1946; Wikipedia.

Shrimpers is a nickname for seaside clubs which have a nearby shrimping industry. See also Shrimps. The clubs are:

❧ Brighton and Hove Albion F.C., see Shrimps, below.

❧ Harwich and Parkeston F.C., founded in Essex in 1877; Avis 1966–70, W1979/80–2010.

❧ Morecambe, see under Shrimps.

❧ Southend United F.C., founded in Essex in 1906, as a successor to previous teams; the club badge has a shrimp and wavy lines representing the sea. Recorded in G1956–76, Churchill 1958, Harvey 1959, Richards 1960, AA 1960, Avis 1966–70, and throughout RY1970/1–SSY2012/13 as 'Shrimpers'. Jeffrey 1961 argued that the nickname came from the club's crest. See also Blues, Seasiders.

Shrimps is a nickname for two clubs in coastal locations where there is a shrimp industry. See also Shrimpers. The clubs are:

☻ Brighton and Hove Albion F.C., according to G1956–65, Churchill 1958, Harvey 1959, Richards 1960, AA 1960, Avis 1966–70 and Vernon 1970–1 and RY1970/1, before they took the name Seagulls. Avis uniquely records the nickname as 'Shrimpers'. The nickname also appears late, in Pickering 1994. See also Albion, Dolphins, Flippers, Seagulls, Seasiders, Seaweed, Tesco's.

☻ Morecambe F.C. Founded in 1920 in the town overlooking the extensive sands of Morecambe Bay with its internationally-famous shrimp industry, the club adopted a striking shrimp image for its new crest in 2010. Recorded in W1979/80–2007 and SSY2004/5–12/13.

Shrivy is the nickname of Shrivenham F.C., founded in 1900. To *shrive* is to bless, to forgive, and it is believed that the name of this Oxfordshire village refers to land which has been allotted by charter or decree to the church (Mills 1991). A friendly short form recorded in W2008–13.

Shunters is recorded in Jeffrey 1961 as an alternative nickname for Swindon Town F.C., who are also called 'The Railwaymen' in that source. Shunting is what old locomotives do in their retirement. See also Moonrakers, Robins, Shunters, Spartans, Swindle.

Side is a nickname for clubs with the letters '–side' in their official name; a rather satisfying nickname for a football side. The clubs are:

☻ Barkingside F.C., founded in London in 1889, as a short form of the official name, equally suitable for the stadium name, Oakside; Avis 1966–70, W1983/4, Miller & Wright 1996.

☻ Deveronside F.C., founded in Banff in 1977; Wikipedia, SFHA.

☻ Longside F.C., founded in Aberdeenshire in 1947; Wikipedia, SFHA.

Signals was a nickname for Cardiff Hibernian F.C., when they were founded as the 53rd Signals F.C. They joined the Cardiff Combination League in 1963, changing name in 1967 and the nickname is used on the League website history pages. The club originally had a British Territorial Army origin. See also Hibs.

Sileby is a nickname for Northampton Sileby Rangers F.C., founded in Northampton in 1968 as a works side for the Sileby Engineering Co. The club appears to have dropped 'Northampton' from its name for three years: printed in W2002–4, W2005–7 (for Sileby Rangers), W2008–13. See also Rangers, Vans.

Silkmen is a nickname for clubs which are based in towns once prominent in the silk industry. The clubs are:

☻ Flint Town United F.C., founded in 1886; recorded in RW1994–2011 and W1995–9. A large factory opened in Flint in 1908, originally making artificial silk for the British Glanztoff Manufacturing Co. See also Town.

☻ Macclesfield Town F.C. The origins of the Cheshire club go back to 1876; Macclesfield F.C. was formed in 1919, reborn again in 1946 as Macclesfield Town. The nickname comes from Macclesfield being a major centre for the silk industry in the nineteenth century, at one time having 120 mills and dye houses. Recorded in

Avis 1966–70, W1979/80–97 and W2013 and through RY1997/8–SS2012/13.

Singers was a nickname for Coventry City F.C., presumably only in the club's early years as they were founded in 1883 as Singers F.C., for employees of the Singer's Cycle Works, but renamed in 1898. The nickname is recorded late, in Vernon 1970–1 and in RY1983/4. See also Bantams, Blackbirds, Citizens, Peeping Toms, Sky Blues, Wheelmen.

Sjoke City is a derogatory unofficial nickname for Stoke City F.C., from the perspective of Port Vale supporters, and recorded on the 2003 Football Fans Census website. The nickname is a play on words, the spelling suggesting an Icelandic place-name because an Icelandic consortium called 'Stoke Holding' owned the club between 1999 and 2006. The pun also cleverly suggests a shortened spelling of 'it's a joke'. See also City, Clayheads, Jolly Green Giants, Potters.

SK is a nickname for South Kilburn F.C., founded in London in 2005; the initialism is printed in W2012–13 and appears on the club badge. See also South.

Skates is recorded on the 2003 Football Fans Census website, in Ferris 2005, and by Kevin Mitchell in *The Observer*, 23 January 2005, as a derogatory unofficial nickname for Portsmouth F.C. The expression is said to come from Southampton supporters, who exploit a preposterous myth that Royal Navy sailors who were at sea for many months would relieve their frustrations by using the mouth of the skate fish. However, as a nickname for sailors, it just cannot have been that widely known because two Royal Navy warships have been named HMS *Skate*. Portsmouth supporters allegedly call Southampton 'Scummers' (q.v.), but these terms are virtually unknown amongst real Royal or Merchant Navy men, who have the greatest of respect for each other. The two names come entirely from the banter of rival supporters. See also Pompey.

Skem / Skemmers is the nickname of Skelmersdale United F.C., founded in Lancashire in 1882. Although the *l* in the place-name is pronounced, the short form sounds better without it. Recorded in W1979/80–80/1 and W1994–8 as 'Skemmers'; W1982/3–6, W1990 and W1999–2013 as 'Skem'. See also United.

Skinners is a nickname for two clubs, both based on their ground name. The clubs are:

- Bishop's Cleeve F.C., founded in Gloucestershire in 1905. The club used to play on a field called Skinner's Field (because it was either owned by a Mr Skinner or it was a place where animals were skinned), in a location where Voxwell Road and Cheltenham Road are now (thanks to local informant John Burton); W1997–2007. See also Villagers.

- Worcester Park F.C., founded in London in 1921. The name is from the Skinners Field Ground at which they play; W2010 and W2012–13. See also Park.

Skull and Crossbones was the suffix and nickname of an early club in Rhyl, North Wales, from the 1870s. The club is recorded on the website of Rhyl F.C. The players had this forbidding pirate symbol on their black shirts, no doubt taken as an amusing reference to Rhyl's seaside location, but a photograph by Phil Stead on Flickr shows modern supporters with a black skull-and-crossbones banner proclaiming 'Rhyl FC West End Boys'; Huws 2013.

Skunks are delightful black-and-white animals which have a defence mechanism which strikes fear in all potential predators, their famous ability to spray a noxious smell. The animal is untouchable, and therefore makes a superb nickname for a club which plays in these colours, especially in stripes like the animal. However, the word is often used in a derogatory sense (I can't imagine why), so there are only two uses of the nickname, one official and one unofficial, and both referring to the players' black-and-white strip:

☻ Collingwood F.C., founded in Belfast in 2003. The club plays in black and white but not in stripes; the nickname is so closely associated with the club that it is often used as an official name on the internet.

☻ Newcastle United F.C., as an unofficial nickname from the perspective of Sunderland supporters (recorded on the 2003 Football Fans census website). See also Barcodes, Cartoon Army, Entertainers, Frenchcastle, Geordies, Magpies, Toon, Tyneside Professors, Tynesiders.

Sky Blues is a nickname for clubs which play in a sky-blue coloured strip. The examples are:

☻ Ballymena United F.C., founded in Co. Antrim in 1928, reformed as United in 1934. The club's nickname and strip (light-blue shirts and socks, white shorts) are in tribute to the famous Glasgow side (see Rangers as Blues or Light Blues); Wikipedia. See also Braidmen, Light Blues, United.

☻ Barkingside F.C., founded in London in 1889, who also play in a pale sky-blue strip; Wikipedia. See also 'Side.

☻ Cambrian and Clydach Vale Boys and Girls Club F.C., founded in 1965, originally as Cambrian United; recorded in RW2011. See also Cambrian.

☻ Coventry City F.C. Founded in 1883 as Singers F.C. (by employees of the Singer's cycle works), they changed the name to Coventry City in 1898 and in the same year adopted the sky-blue strip from which the nickname derives. The strip was changed in 1922 but revived by Manager Jimmy Hill in 1962, the same year he wrote the Sky Blue supporters' song. It is claimed on Wikipedia that the nickname also dates from 1962. It is recorded in G1965–76, throughout RY and SSY from 1970/1 to 2012/13, except for the odd entry in RY1983/4; G1965–76. See also Bantams, Blackbirds, Citizens, Peeping Toms, Singers, Wheelmen.

☻ Forfar Athletic F.C., founded in 1885. The club originally played in a dark blue; sky blue was introduced in stripes in 1935; replaced by green 1955–67, restored to blue in 1968, but the colours have rarely been sky blue on its own (see Historical Football Kits website). Recorded in RY1982/3–92/3, RS1993–5 and SSY2012/13. See also Loons.

☻ Magherafelt Sky Blues F.C., founded in Co. Londonderry in 1970. The club plays in both sky-blue and navy-blue colours, and consciously took the name and strip inspiration from Coventry City; Wikipedia.

- Minehead A.F.C., founded in Somerset in 1889; recorded in W1979/80. One of the club badges illustrated in AFBC records 'Royal Blues' as another alternative. See also Blues, Seasiders.

Slave Traders is an unofficial nickname for Bristol City, given by arch rival Swindon Town supporters (who are called by City fans Swindle or Swinedon). It points out an unpleasant truth about Bristol's real history and is widely distributed in football forums on the internet. See also Babes, Cider Army, City, Eighty-Twoers / 1982 Ltd, Reds, Robins, Turnips, Wurzels.

Sleeping Giants is a nickname for Hawick Royal Albert F.C., founded in Roxburghshire in 1947. The nickname is recorded in Wikipedia and is clearly an expression of the supporters' faith in the club's future prospects. See also Albert, Royalists (and Dossers for a probable similar meaning).

Smallheath is an unofficial nickname for Birmingham City F.C., from the perspective of Aston Villa supporters (Football Football Fans Census, 2003). The nickname mocks the original name and location of the club (see discussion in the entry under Blues) by suggesting it has a very small fanbase. See also BLose, Blues, Brum, Heathens.

Smoggies is an unofficial nickname for Middlesbrough F.C., and one increasing in popularity amongst the fans, though it was initially coined by rival supporters in satire of the allegedly high levels of pollution in this great northern industrial centre; Wikipedia. See also Boro, Cleveland Cowboys, Ironsiders, Nops, Riversiders, Scabs, Teessiders, Washers.

Smokies is a nickname for Arbroath F.C., founded in Angus in 1878. The nickname refers to the famous Arbroath Smokie which is a smoked haddock, and now a protected brand under European Union laws for local dishes; SSY2012/13. See also Red Lichties.

Snipes is the nickname of three related clubs in the vicinity of Sutton-in-Ashfield, Nottinghamshire. Kings Mill Reservoir is very close to the town and snipes are a common visitor to this lake, but they must also have been a common visitor in earlier days because the bird featured on the coat of arms of the former Sutton-in-Ashfield Urban District Council. The clubs are:

- Ashfield United F.C., founded in 1885, originally as Sutton Town, recorded in Avis 1966–70 and W1994–7. Although the recent renaming to Ashfield United was a result of a sponsorship deal with Ashfield District Council in 1992, the record in Avis shows that an earlier renaming had taken place in the 1960s.
- Sutton Town F.C., founded in 1885 but renamed at least twice as Ashfield United; W1979/80.
- Sutton Town A.F.C., refounded in 2007 and readopting the earlier nickname. An earlier reforming in 2002 adopted the nickname 'Town' (W2006–7).

Social is a nickname for three clubs associated with social clubs. The clubs are:

☺ Billingham Town F.C., founded in Co. Durham in 1967, originally as B. Social F.C., based at a social club; the nickname is in W1985–2007. See also Billy Town, Sound.

☺ Prescot B.I. F.C., founded in Merseyside in 1946; W1982/3–1983/4. The 'B.I.' in the name represented the B.I.C.C. [British International Championship Club] Ltd Athletic and Social Club. The football club seems to disappear after 1985.

☺ Wednesfield F.C., founded in the West Midlands in 1961, originally as W. Social F.C.; W1982/3–90. See also Cottagers.

Sodgers was an unofficial nickname for the Third Lanark Athletic Club; recorded in Potter & Jones 2011, p. 251. The word is a Scots variant for 'soldiers', known since the eighteenth century, and this club originally had a military origin with the Third Lanark Rifle Volunteers. See also Hi-Hi's, Redcoats, Thirds, Volunteers, Warriors.

Sodyheads was apparently the nickname for Kinnaird F.C., founded in Stirlingshire in 1888, closed 1889. The nickname is recorded on the reliable source, SFHA, but it is a mystery.

Soldiers was a nickname of Aldershot F.C. (1926–92), according to Churchill 1958, Harvey 1959, Richards 1960, Avis 1966–70 and Vernon 1970–1; from the town's main livelihood as an army garrison town. See also Shots.

Sols was a proposed nickname for Sunderland A.F.C. in the competition to find a new name after the 1997 move to the new stadium, the Stadium of Light. SOL is an acronym on these initials, but it is also the Spanish word for sun, so also punning with the first syllable of the place-name. According to Ferris 2005, the stadium itself is built on the site of the Monkwearmouth Colliery, closed in 1993, which had a sign at its exit reading 'Into the Light'. See also Bank of England Club, Black Cats, Lads, Light Brigade, Mackems, Miners, Rokerites / Rokermen, Sund-Ireland, Team of All the Talents, Wearsiders.

Sons is the nickname for Dumbarton F.C., founded in 1872. The nickname refers to the famous Rock of Dumbarton, an impressive volcanic plug rising right next to the club's home ground, and the popular expression that anyone born in Dumbarton is a 'son of the rock'. The rock is considered elephant-shaped (and it is!) and so an elephant and castle forms the stylish badge of the club. Recorded in Johnston 1934 and SWSCYB 1962–3 as 'Sons of the Rock'; the fuller form is also used in Potter & Jones 2011, but 'The Sons' has long been the usual style for the nickname; RS1993–2012, RY1972/3–SSY2012/13.

Sooty is recorded as an affectionate nickname for Atherton Collieries A.F.C., founded in Lancashire in 1916, and recorded on the club's own website. Although the name would have a natural association with coal miners, it is difficult to believe that it could have pre-dated the popular children's radio and television star, the glove puppet *Sooty*. There is also a Lancashire association with the puppet, for Harry Corbett bought him from a stall in Blackpool in 1948 and some of the original broadcasts came from Manchester. See also Colls, Colts, Miners, Welfare.

Sorters is the nickname of Faversham Town F.C., founded in Kent in 1884. The nickname is a pun on the name of the home ground, Salters Lane, using the local pronunciation to blur the distinction between sorters and salters, but perhaps with the suggestion that the club will 'sort out' any opponent; Wikipedia. See also Creeksiders, Lilywhites, Town.

Sound is listed as a nickname for Billingham Town F.C. in Barton 1984 & 1985, but this name does not appear in any other source. Although 'sound' is an expression meaning 'reliable', the club was originally founded as B. Social F.C. in 1967 and in W1994 (and later editions) the nickname appears as 'Social'. 'Sound' must therefore be an error arising from a misreading of someone's handwriting (the letters are a very similar shape). See also Billy Town, Social.

Souters is the nickname of Selkirk F.C., founded in the Scottish Borders in 1880. The nickname takes the nickname of the people of Selkirk itself, which means in Scots 'Cobblers' (as in the Northampton shoe makers' nickname). The word is an Old English one, which also survives in English street names (Souters Lane in Chester). Recorded in RS1993–7, 2000–1, SFHA.

South is the nickname for two clubs with the word South in their official names. The clubs are:

- South Kilburn F.C., founded in London in 2005; Wikipedia. See also SK.
- South Liverpool F.C., founded in the late 1890s and reformed in 1935. Recorded in W1979/80–91.

Southbankers is a nickname for Corsham Town F.C., founded in Wiltshire in 1884. The club's home ground is called Southbank; Wikipedia. See also Peacocks, Reds.

Southern is the nickname for Edinburgh Southern A.F.C., founded in 2001; a short form of the official name; Wikipedia.

Spamen is the nickname of Llandrindod Wells A.F.C., founded in Powys in 1883. The Welsh town became a popular spa town in the mid eighteenth century. The town itself is sometimes nicknamed Llandod, which may be used occasionally to refer to the football club; Wikipedia. See also Blues.

Spaniards is the nickname for Rushen United F.C., founded at Port Erin, Isle of Man, in 1910. The nickname is based on the Spanish Head promontory at the southern tip of the parish mainland. The place-name is based on the belief that there was a Spanish Armada shipwreck there; Wikipedia.

Spanners is an unofficial nickname for Millwall F.C., from the perspective of Charlton Athletic supporters, and recorded on the 2003 Football Fans Census website. The nickname refers to an incident when one of the club's own fans threw a spanner on to the pitch; the nickname is now quite commonly used but the incident itself is not dated. See also Dockers, Lions.

Spartans is a football club suffix, in honour of the people of Ancient Greece who were noted for their extreme toughness and single-minded military prowess. The OED records uses of 'Spartan', to mean 'Sparta-like', from 1644 onwards. In sport, the nickname satisfies the need to express 'classicalism', but with a no-nonsense effectiveness. It is also the name of the London Spartan League (1907), merged into the Spartans South Midlands Football League in 1997, and is used for the Czech side Prague Sparta (1893) and Russian Spartak Moscow (1935). Spartan clubs are:

⚽ Blyth Spartans F.C., founded in Northumberland in 1899; recorded as a nickname in Avis 1966–70, W1979/80–86, W1995–2013; Barton 1985.

⚽ Bridgnorth Spartans Junior F.C., founded in Shropshire in 1987; club website.

⚽ Spartans Junior F.C., founded in Edinburgh in 1951. The club badge shows the head of a Spartan warrior; club website.

⚽ Swavesey Spartans F.C., founded in Cambridgeshire in 1989; club website.

⚽ Swindon Spartans F.C., founded in Wiltshire in 1881, but renaming as 'Town' in 1883. See also see Moonrakers, Railwaymen, Robins, Swindle.

⚽ Twyford Spartans Youth F.C., founded in Devon in 1976; club website.

Spelly is the nickname of Spelthorne Sports F.C., founded in Middlesex in 1922. A friendly short form printed in W2012–13.

Speysiders is the nickname for Rothes F.C., founded near Elgin in 1938. The town is on the banks of the River Spey. Recorded in RS1993–2012, SFHA.

Sphinx is the nickname of Coventry Sphinx F.C. The club was founded in 1946, originally as a works side for employees of the Armstrong Siddeley Motor Company, which used the sphinx as a badge. The cars started to be made in the 1920s when all things Egyptian were extremely popular (the discovery of Tutankhamun's tomb was in 1922). The last Armstrong cars were made in 1960, at which the club relaunched as Sphinx F.C., changing to the present name in 1994. The ground is now named Sphinx Drive and a stylish sphinx appears on the club's badge; W2008–13.

Spice Boys was a temporary unofficial nickname for several players in Liverpool F.C., during the late 1990s. The nickname is in ironic contrast to the successful pop group, the Spice Girls, and first appears in *The Daily Mail* in 1996, when there were rumours that player Robbie Fowler was dating 'Baby Spice', one of the group's members. It flourished in a spirit of sarcasm because the pop group was successful and the nickname mocks playboy lifestyles with what was actually a lacklustre performance, but it was also reinforced by several social connections between the players and the group. On 1 February 2013 BBC Radio mentioned that French journalists call David Beckham 'Le Spice Boy'. He is, of course, married to 'Posh Spice', from the pop group. See also Anfielders, Culture Club, Kop / Kopites, Liddellpool, Mariners, Merseysiders, Micky Mousers, Pool, Reds.

Spicky is the nickname for Spixworth F.C., founded in Norfolk in 1964, originally as Norwich Union, renaming as AFC Norwich in 2009, Spixworth United in 2009 and the present name in 2010. The nickname is a friendly short form based on the place-name's pronunciation, and it appears on the club's own website.

Spiders is a nickname for two Scottish clubs which wear black- (or dark-blue) and-white hoops. It originated with Queen's Park F.C., whose hoops are particularly narrow, suggesting spiders' webs. Although it is definitely the narrow lines which are the source of the nickname, Scottish clubs perhaps also enjoy an extra encouragement to take the nickname, from the famous story of Robert the Bruce and the spider. The nickname has also been assumed by an Isle of Man club. The clubs are:

- Downfield F.C., founded in Dundee in 1912. The club wears black-and-white hoops, though today they are not particularly narrow. Wikipedia records the nickname and adds the detail that Queen's Park donated a set of strips to the club when they first started, so the nickname really does refer to the same strip as the famous Spiders; also SFHA.

- Malew A.F.C., founded in the village of Ballasalle, Malew, on the Isle of Man in 1922. The club plays in narrow red-and-black stripes. Although there are Manx folktales about spiders, none of them seem to be associated with this parish, so the nickname seems to be based on the strip, even though the stripes are not particularly narrow; Wikipedia.

- Queen's Park F.C., founded in Glasgow in 1867, and the oldest surviving Association Football Club in Scotland. The nickname refers to the unusually narrow dark-blue-and-white hoops first adopted by the club in 1873 and worn more-or-less ever since, the lines of which are so narrow that they really do look like spiders' webs. The club's programme is called *The Spider*. Recorded early, in BoF1905–6 (pp. 152, 158), and on the 1936 Thompson 'stamp', the 1959 Sweetule card, in SWSCYB 1962–3, Avis 1966–70, through RY1972/3–SSY2012/13 and RS 1993–2012, Pickering 1994. See also Amateurs, Glorious Hoops, Q.P., Queen's.

Spireites is the nickname of Chesterfield F.C. The current club was founded in 1919 as Chesterfield Municipal F.C., after a succession of previous clubs dating back to 1867, and it became independent of the council and dropped its unusual suffix in 1920. An earlier club was called Chesterfield Town (1884–1915) and this club was normally nicknamed 'Town', but BoF1905–6 uses 'Team of the Crooked Spire' for it (p.216). Chesterfield is famous for the astonishing crooked spire on the church of St Mary and All Saints. Johnston 1934 uses the form 'Team of the Crooked Spire' for the present club. The spire first appeared on the club's badge in 1978. The current badge shows it in a fetching stylised form alongside the club's initials. At some time between 1934 and 1956 the nickname became 'Spireites'. Recorded as 'Spireites' in G1956–65, Richards 1960, Avis 1966–70, and in RY and SSY from 1971/2 to 2012/13. See also Blues, Cheaterfield, Team of Surprises, Town.

Spitfires is a nickname for two clubs with an association with the famous Supermarine Spitfire aircraft. These are:

- Castle Vale F.C., founded in 1964, originally as The Horshoe, from the Birmingham pub which was their headquarters; then various renamings until the present name in 2005. The club had a spitfire on its badge and was close to Castle Bromwich Aerodrome where some 300 new spitfires a week were tested before delivery to the RAF, during the Second World War. The club folded in 2012. There was a handsome image of a Spitfire on the club's badge; Wikipedia. See also Kings.

⚽ Eastleigh F.C., because the aeroplane was built in nearby Southampton and flown for the first time from Eastleigh Aerodrome in 1936. The site is now Southampton International Airport and a modern replica of the Spitfire stands outside the entrance. The club was founded in 1946, originally as Swaythling Athletic, renamed Eastleigh in 1980; W2006–13.

Sporting is an appropriate nickname for clubs with this word in their official name. It is so used on the club website of Sporting Bengal United F.C., founded in London in 1996. See also Bengal Tigers.

Sports is a nickname for clubs with the word 'Sports' in their official name, usually because they are associated with a general sports club or play on a general sports field. Examples are:

⚽ Eastbourne Borough F.C., due to their previous name of Langney Sports F.C. Founded in 1964 as Langney (a district of Eastbourne), the Sports suffix was added in 1968 and the whole name changed to Eastbourne Borough in 2001. The club has a distinctive red badge which shows a local Martello Tower; W2002–6 and SSY2009/10–11/12. See also Borough.

⚽ Easington Sports F.C., founded in 1945 in Banbury, Oxfordshire; the nickname is used on the club's own website. See also Clan.

⚽ Fishguard Sports A.F.C., founded in Pembrokeshire in 1947. The nickname appears in match reports from 1972–3 on the 'Pembrokeshiresport.co.uk' website.

⚽ Hullbridge Sports F.C., founded in 1947; Wikipedia. See also Bridge.

⚽ Langney Sports F.C., founded in East Sussex in 1966, at the Langney Sports Club in Eastbourne; W2001.

⚽ Longwell Green Sports F.C., founded in Gloucestershire in 1966; W2006–9. See also Green.

⚽ Mickleover Sports F.C. Founded in Derbyshire in 1948, the team plays on the Mickleover Sports Ground; W2006–13.

⚽ Ransome Sports F.C., founded in Suffolk in 1948, originally as Fisons F.C. The club was originally a works side, representing until recently the Ransomes Engineering company, and this connection is still honoured with the appearance of a tractor on the club badge, but the club is now independent; Wikipedia.

⚽ Woodley Sports F.C., founded in Greater Manchester in 1970, originally as Woodley Athletic. Woodley Sports Centre was established in 1953 as a club for the Bredbury Steel Works; W2007–10. The club renamed as Stockport Sports in 2012. See also Saxons, Steelmen.

⚽ Woodstock Sports F.C., founded in Kent in 1927 as Norton Sports and only changing its name to Woodstock in 2011; Wikipedia.

Spots was a temporary nickname for Bolton Wanderers F.C. in 1884 when the club adopted a white shirt with large red spots on it (illustrated on the Historical Football Kits website, and mentioned in Ballard & Suff 1999, p. 421). See also Noblot /

Notlob, Reds, Savage Six, Trotters, Wanderers, Whites / Whitemen.

Spurs is a popular football club nickname, based on the 'Hotspur' word in the name of Tottenham Hotspur F.C., and it is now a world-wide football club name element in its own right (as is also the fuller form, Hotspur, q.v.). The word refers to the spurs, sharp metal points, added to the feet of fighting cocks in the cruel sport of cock-fighting (or added to the feet of horse-riders to allow them to 'spur on' the horse to run faster), and it came to the Tottenham club from the nickname of Harry Hotspur, or Henry Percy, the fifteenth-century Northumberland aristocrat who is a character in Shakespeare's *Henry IV* and *Henry V* plays, because the club played on land owned by the Percy family. Harry Hotspur was famed for his fighting prowess and his own love of cock-fighting, and the word has come to suggest an athletic dynamism. Cock-fighting was banned in England and Wales as long ago as 1835. The Holyhead club uniquely presents Hotspur as a wasp, after a quote from Shakespeare. British and Irish clubs with this nickname are:

- Fleet Spurs F.C., founded in Hampshire in 1951. The club has a fighting cock, with spurs, on its badge; Wikipedia.
- Gildersome Spurs F.C., founded in 2000 at the G. Sports Centre near Leeds (with a junior side, G. Spurs Junior, founded earlier, in 1977); club's own website.
- Holyhead Hotspur F.C., founded on Anglesey in 1990; Wikipedia. The badge of the club (AFBC) shows a friendly wasp, which records a quote from Act 1 of Shakespeare's *Henry IV Part One*, when the Duke of Northumberland calls Hotspur a 'wasp-stung and impatient fool'. See also Harbourmen.
- Newton Abbot Spurs F.C., founded in Devon in 1938. W2008–9.
- Tottenham Hotspur F.C. Founded in 1882 as Hotspur F.C., the club was based on land owned by the Northumberland Percy family. Since at least 1901 a gamecock has been the club's symbol, and the bird on the badge today still has spurs on its legs. The nickname is recorded in BoF1905–6, the 1933 Ogden card, Johnston 1934, the 1936 Thomson 'stamp', Avis 1954–70, G1956–76, Churchill 1958 and Richards 1960, and throughout RY1970/1–SSY2012/13. See also Lilywhites, Super Spurs, Yids / Yid Army.

Squatters is an insulting unofficial nickname for Bristol Rovers F.C., from the perspective of Bristol City supporters (recorded on the 2003 Football Fans Census). The nickname mocks the fact that the club rented its home ground rather than owned it. See also Arabs, Black Arabs, Gas / Gasheads, Pirates, Purdown Poachers, Rovers, Tesco's.

Squirrels is the nickname of Formby F.C., founded in 1919, originally as Formby United. This Merseyside club boasts a red squirrel on its badge, and the town is one of the last refuges of the British red squirrel, in the local National Trust reserve. That such an association should become the club nickname just goes to show how much football cares about these things; W1980/1–2013.

Staggies is the nickname for Ross County F.C., founded in Dingwall (Ross and

Cromarty) in 1929. The nickname is a friendly form of Stags. The image of the proud Highland stag was greatly popularised by prints of the 1851 painting 'Monarch of the Glen' by Sir Edwin Landseer, but it was adopted by the club in tribute to its use by the Seaforth Highlanders regiment (active 1881–1961). A stag appears on the club badge. The nickname appears in a typical Scots 'friendly' form and is recorded in SSY2005/6–12/13. See also County.

Stags is a common football club nickname, usually for clubs associated with forests, but occasionally the explanation may be from local heraldry or the name of a local pub. The stag, also called a buck (q.v.), is a symbol of male athleticism (the sense in which it is used for 'stag nights'). The use of stags as metaphors for forests is widespread, not only because stags live in forests but because their antlers suggest the branches of trees; a 'stag's head tree' is even used as a common description for a particular tree shape. The examples are:

- Ashton and Backwell United F.C., founded in Somerset in 2010 in a merger between Backwell United and the youth section of Ashton Boys F.C. The club has taken the nickname of the former Backwell side. This area near Bristol is one of luxuriant woodland, though the nickname may also have been generated as a play on bucks and Back–; Wikipedia.
- Ashtree Highfield F.C., founded in Oldbury, Birmingham, in 1918, first as Smethwick Highfield and renaming again to Sandwell Borough before folding in 2001; W1987–8. The nickname here seems to reflect the tree element in the place-name, rather than immediate vicinity to forestry. See also Trees.
- Backwell United F.C., founded in Somerset in 1911; the club merged with Ashton Boys F.C. in 2010 to form Ashton and Backwell United; Miller & Wright 1996, W1998–2008; a Backwell United badge in AFBC shows a stag. See also Reds.
- Chingford F.C., founded in Essex and recorded in Avis 1966–70. Several clubs have come and gone using the Chingford name and it is not clear which of these is recorded in Avis. The location is within the borough of Waltham Forest and close to Epping Forest, where stags exist.
- Esh Winning F.C., founded in Co. Durham in 1967. The location is near the Ragpath Wood, and a stag appears on the club badge; W2005–13. See also Esh.
- Holker Old Boys F.C., founded in Barrow-in-Furness, Cumbria, in 1936. The club has a stag on its badge and the locality is close to forested areas; Stags is the main nickname of this club, recorded on Wikipedia and the club's own web publicity. See also Cobs.
- Ickleford F.C., founded in Hertfordshire in 1918. Although the club is listed in the early Williams directories without a nickname, the enamel badge of the club showed a stag in an unusual sitting position, strongly suggesting that the club was nicknamed The Stags. Here, the nickname may have been a play on harts / Hertfordshire. The club is recorded on the FCHD between 1984 and 1995.
- Kimberley Town F.C., founded in Nottinghamshire in 1886. Like Mansfield (see

next), the location is close to Sherwood Forest; W1982/3–6 and W1994–2002.

- Maidenhead Town Youth F.C., founded in Berkshire in 1946. Here there is no particular forest association, so the nickname appears to have been used as a metaphor for athleticism. This appears to have been the club which was formed in a renaming of Maidenhead Social in 1974, and which folded in 1990 (FCHD). The nickname is recorded in W1983/4–6.

- Mansfield Town F.C. since about 1924. Founded in 1897 as Mansfield Wesleyans, the club changed its name to Town in 1910. The stag image appeared as a badge on the shirts in 1961. Stags are common in Sherwood Forest (and Mansfield traditionally claims to be the centre of the Forest's ancient boundaries), and a stag is a supporter on the coat of arms of the borough of Mansfield. Recorded in G1956–76, Churchill 1958, Norris 1959, Richards 1960, AA 1960, Avis 1966–70; throughout RY1970/1–SSY2012/13 and in W2009–13. See also Yellows.

- Midhurst and Easebourne F.C., founded in 1946. The club has a stylised jumping stag on its badge and the location is amongst the luxuriant Sussex woodland; Wikipedia.

- Rossendale United F.C., founded in Lancashire in 1898, folded in 2011; the club had a stylised stag's head on its badge and its location was in the Forest of Rossendale. Staghills Road was near the club's ground, but it is not clear if the nickname was based on this; W1980/1–2011. See also Dale, Rossy.

- Smethwick Highfield F.C., founded in West Midlands in 1918, originally as S. Town, renaming as Ashtree Highfield in 1986, and Sandwell Borough in 1989, but folding in 2001 (FCHD). The nickname is not easy to explain because it is in a highly urbanised location, the club also carried the nickname of The Trees after the 1986 renaming, but the pun would not work for the earlier club name; W1983/4–6. Stags is also recorded for Ashtree, above, and see also Trees.

- (A.F.C.) Totton, founded in Hampshire in 1975 as a merger between Totton F.C. (1886) and Totton Athletic. The club has a stunning badge of a stag's head with a football. The club's location is on the edge of the New Forest, famous as a royal deer-hunting park since the eleventh century; W1994–2013.

- Verwood Town F.C., founded in 1920. The Dorset place-name means 'fair wood' (Beuboys in a document of 1288, for 'beau bois': Mills 1991) and the town is close to the Hampshire border and the New Forest. A stag with a football is on the club badge; Wikipedia.

- Waltham Forest F.C., founded in London in 1964, originally as Pennant F.C., renaming as Walthamstow Pennant in 1988, renaming as Leyton Pennant in 1995 and finally as the present name in 2003; the nickname follows the forest meaning; W2008–13, though, earlier, a programme illustrated in W2006 is called We are the Stags. See also Lilywhites, Pennant.

- Walton Casuals F.C. Founded in Surrey in 1948, the club has a prominent stag's head with horns on its club badge, but the usual forest association does not apply to the Walton-on-Thames area. It may be that the choice of badge and nickname was arbitrary, or that it came from a military regiment (the club was founded by ex-servicemen); W1998–2013 (but not 2006–7). See also Casuals.

Stanley / Stanleyites are nicknames for the Cheshire club Accrington Stanley F.C. The first is a current nickname for the new team founded in 1968, and the second was apparently used in the 1890s for the old team, which folded in 1966, though 'Stanley' is recorded for the old team as well: Richards 1960, Avis 1966, W1979/80–96 and SSY2004/5–6/7 all have Stanley. The famous suffix was originally adopted because one of the ancestor clubs, Stanley Villa, was based in Stanley Street. A badge in AFBC displays the motto 'On Stanley on'. See also Owd Reds, Reds.

Stans is an unofficial nickname for Bradford Park Avenue A.F.C., from supporters of Bradford City. The club folded in 1974, but was revived in 1988. Before the revival, supporters of Bradford City published a cartoon depicting 'Boring Stan the Avenue Fan', and after the revival the derogatory term Stans had new life. Pickering 1994. See also Avenue.

Star is a nickname for several clubs, each of which have 'Star' in their official names, for several different reasons. Some are related to business names, others perhaps celebrate the traditional use of the 'North Star' for navigation, as they are northern clubs, others perhaps simply suggest brilliance, and in one case it is a place-name. See also 'Stars' for clubs which take the nickname in the plural. The clubs are:

☺ Crumlin Star F.C., founded in Co. Antrim before 1953 (when they won the Junior Cup). The club has a star on its badge; club's own website.

☺ Dalbeattie Star F.C., founded in Dumfries and Galloway in 1900, folded 1948 and reformed 1976. Recorded in RS1996–7, SFHA. See also Rabbits.

☺ Fleet Star F.C., founded at Gatehouse of Fleet in Dumfries and Galloway in 1948; the club's website states the club was formed in a merger of clubs called Fleetside Rovers and White Star; online match reports use it as a nickname, SFHA.

☺ Knowle North Star F.C., a temporary renaming of the West Midlands club Knowle F.C. between 1983 and 1985; W1983/4–6. The reason for the change of name is unknown, but was probably under a sponsorship. See also Robins.

☺ Loughview Star F.C., founded in Co. Down in 1961, merging with Holywood Town (1972) in 1983 to form Holywood F.C.; Wikipedia.

☺ Newcastle Blue Star F.C., founded in Tyneside in 1930, originally as a works side but it is surprisingly unclear exactly what works they represented. The blue star was a trade mark of Newcastle Breweries, appearing on bottles of 'Newcastle Brown Ale' after 1928, since when it has often appeared as an unofficial emblem of the city of Newcastle. They were called N.B.S. until 1973 when they became B.S. Welfare, then just B.S. in 1979 and N.B.S. again in 1986. Between 1994 and 1999 they were RTM Newcastle before returning to their original name. The club folded in 2009. The club appears without a nickname in W1987–94; as 'Star' (for RTM) in W1995–

8 and in W1999–2009, but Wikipedia records an additional nickname 'The Aristocrats', q.v.

⚽ Newtongrange Star F.C., founded in Midlothian in 1890; Wikipedia. See also Nitten.

⚽ Peterborough Northern Star F.C., founded in 1905 as Northern Star, a works team for two brickyards known as Northern (in the village of Eye, near Peterborough) and Star (in Peterborough). In the 1950s the club was known as Eye United but took the present name in 2005; Wikipedia. See also Eyes.

⚽ Seaham Red Star F.C., founded in Co. Durham in 1973. The club was renamed Seaham Colliery Welfare Red Star between 1978 and 1984. The club started as a Sunday morning pub side, though it is not clear if the original name refers to the pub or some other aspect of the locality. Recorded in Barton 1984 & 1985, W1982/3–7 and W1992–2013.

⚽ Solway Star F.C., founded in Annan (Dumfries and Galloway), in 1911. The club folded in 1947. The Historical Football Kits website records the club and uses the nickname.

⚽ Star F.C., based in Gloucestershire, founded in 1965, originally as a works side for Eagle Star, the insurance company. The club renamed after loosing its links with its origins in 2004; club's own website.

⚽ Star F.C., founded in Shropshire in 1947, originally as a works side for Lawson Mardon Star, then Star Aluminium F.C. The name is listed as a nickname in W2002.

⚽ Star Hearts A.F.C., founded in the Fife village of Star in 1962. The club's website uses 'Star' rather than 'Hearts' in its texts; in this instance the nickname is a place-name related to the word 'stair', for a crossing over wetland (see Simon Taylor et al., *The Place-Names of Fife*, vol. 2, Donington, 2008).

Stars is a nickname for clubs which take the plural form of Star in their official name (see also 'Star'). See Huws 2013 for further examples in Wales. The clubs are:

⚽ Continental Stars F.C., founded in Birmingham in 1973, originally as Villa Star, name changed in 1975 (and briefly Handsworth Continental Star in 2001–2). The club website describes the club as 'a beacon' and it has an emphasis on multi-culturalism. The star on the club badge is in the shape of the Star of David; Wikipedia.

⚽ Cwmbach Royal Stars F.C., founded in Rhondda Cynon Taf in 1969, but with earlier clubs going back to 1923. The club has a star-of-David-type star on its badge; club website, Huws 2013.

⚽ Dock Stars F.C., the original name for Pembroke Borough when founded in 1906. The vicinity has major docks; several shipping companies have 'Star' in their names, but it is uncertain if there is connection with the early club, the suffix might even have been suggested by the pronunciation of 'docksters'. See also Borough, Magpies for the later club.

⚽ Newtown A.F.C., in its early years after its foundation in Powys in 1875 as

Newtown Whitestars. The term 'white star' is technically the type of star of our own sun, and is used in the official name of three other present-day clubs, in Belgium, Peru and Poland. Other than association with primary brilliance, there seems no particular reason for the choice of name; cited on Wikipedia as 'Stars' in 2011, changed to 'The White Stars' in 2012. See also Batmans, Robins.

- Oxford United Stars F.C., formed in Co. Londonderry in 1937, recorded in RNI2007; Wikipedia records the alternative 'Oxford Stars'. See also U2s.
- Swan Stars A.F.C., founded in Eastbrook, Vale of Glamorgan, in 1954, the club was based at the Swan Hotel. The old club badge shows swans' heads and a star, but it may be that the suffix was taken as an adaptation of the word 'Swansters', for those from the Swan. At a later date the club renamed as Dinas Powys; club website. See also Ravens.
- Treowen Stars F.C., founded in Monmouthshire in 1926. Recorded in RW1995–2000.
- Troed-y-Rhiw Stars F.C., founded at Merthyr Tydfil before 1908, when the club won the South Wales Amateur Cup. The club was reformed as T. F.C., after the First World War, and again reformed in 1993, but folded in 2012. The club's own website records that 'Stars' was used in the early years before the club renamed as Troedyrhiw F.C. (the name often appears without hyphens) See also Rhiw.

Steelmen is a nickname for clubs originally associated with steel factories, or towns with substantial steel industries. The clubs are:

- Appleby Frodingham F.C., established in North Lincolnshire in 1920, reformed in 1990. The village is very close to the major steel plants of Scunthorpe. W1982/3–6, 2011–13.
- Bilston Town F.C., founded in West Midlands in 1894. Bilston Steelworks closed in 1979; recorded in W1979/80, 1986–2002. Avis 1966–70 has 'United' as the nickname. The club took the present name in 1983. See also Borough.
- Brymbo F.C., founded at Wrexham in 1943; recorded in RW1996–2011. The club was originally called B. Steelworks F.C., but the works closed in 1990. For a short period the club was called Brymbo Broughton F.C. (see RW1998). The reserve side is nicknamed 'The Wanderers' in RW1995, but this is probably an error.
- Consett A.F.C., founded in 1899, originally as Consett Celtic. Consett Ironworks was the main employer in this Co. Durham town from 1837, and provided the first ground for the club. They were nicknamed 'The Ironworkers' (q.v.) until 1967. 'Steelmen' is the nickname in W1979/80–2013, Barton 1984 & 1985.
- Corby Town F.C. Founded in 1948 as the successor to a steelworks side from Stewart & Lloyds, the name honours the dominance of the steelworks in the town's economy. The British Steel Corporation took over in 1967 but it is now part of Corus; Addis 1995 reprints newspaper articles of 1947 which use the nickname for the older club (pp. 15–16). Recorded in Avis 1966–70, W1979/80–2013.
- Motherwell Football and Athletic Club, founded in 1886. The famous Scottish club

has a steelworks on its badge and its home town was once itself nicknamed 'Steelopolis' during the industry's heyday. The steelworks here closed in 1992 and the nickname is a later commemoration. Recorded in the 1936 Thomson 'stamp' album, RS2009–12 and SSY2012/13. See also Dossers, Well.

- ☺ Parkgate F.C., founded in 1969 as the British Steel Corporation Parkgate F.C., near Rotherham, South Yorkshire. The club renamed as Parkgate in 1994; W1994–2013. See also Gate.
- ☺ Port Talbot Town F.C., founded in 1901, originally as P.T. Athletic. The nickname reflects the major importance of the steel industry in the Neath Port Talbot Co. Bor.; recorded in RW 2011. See also Blues.
- ☺ Pressed Steel F.C., founded in Cowley, Oxford, in 1927, for the Pressed Steel Company which made car bodies; the date of foundation from Williams appears to be that of the company rather than the club; W1983/4–87.
- ☺ Woodley Sports F.C., founded in Greater Manchester in 1970, originally as W. Athletic. W. Sports Centre was established in 1953 as a club for the Bredbury Steel Works; W2011–12, but the nickname is earlier, appearing in the title of programmes illustrated in W2004–6. The club renamed as Stockport Sports in 2012. See also Saxons, Sports.

Steels is the nickname for Stocksbridge Park Steels F.C. Founded in South Yorkshire in 1986, in a merger between the local British Steel plant side and the Oxley Park Sports F.C., the nickname derives from the steel industry in the town (see also Blades for another Sheffield side commemorating the steel industry); W1992–2013. See also Foxes.

Stingers is the nickname of Chalfont Wasps F.C., founded in Buckinghamshire in 1922. The team plays in the 'wasp' colours of black-and-yellow stripes with black shorts and socks, and the nickname expresses what wasps do to their victims; W2001–13.

Stockports is an unofficial nickname for Manchester City F.C., coined by Manchester United supporters, on the perception that most City supporters live outside the centre of Manchester, in the SK post code district; used in internet forums. See also Bitters / Bitter Blues, Blues, Citizens, City, Council Housers, Man, Massives, Sheik City.

Stoke is a nickname for Basingstoke Town F.C., founded in 1896; a short form of the place-name, recorded in W1979/80–2006. The club also has a mascot, one Stokie the Dragon (whose name puns on the stoking of fires). See also Blues, Camrose Blues, Dragons.

Ston is a nickname of Pumpherston F.C., founded in West Lothian in 1990 (reforming an older club of 1896); a short form of the place-name; Wikipedia. See also Pumphy.

Stoners is the nickname for Shenstone Pathfinder F.C., founded in Staffordshire in 1968. The nickname appears on several websites and is a pluralised short form of the place-name. The club's unique suffix is an interesting one, suggesting leadership.

Stones is a nickname for clubs with 'stone' in their official name. The clubs are:

- ☺ Addlestone F.C., founded in Surrey in 1885, which became A. and Weybridge Town in 1980, but which closed in 1985; recorded in W1979/80–85.
- ☺ Blackstone F.C., founded in Stamford, Lincolnshire in 1891, originally as Rutland Ironworks F.C., then Mirrlees Blackstones in 1920, then the present name from 1998. The club used to be a works side for the substantial foundry and metalworking industry known as Blackstones, but is now an independent club; W1989–98 for Mirrlees, W1999–2013 for Blackstone.
- ☺ Dagenham and Redbridge F.C., founded in 1992. The nickname appears in Smith 1992/93–95/6. The nickname was inherited from Leytonstone (next entry) but was soon replaced by 'The Daggers'. See also Daggers, Reds.
- ☺ Leytonstone F.C., founded in 1886. Recorded in Avis 1966–70, W1979/80. The club amalgamated with Ilford in 1979 to form Leytonstone & Ilford (1979–87), then absorbed Walthamstow Forest to form Redbridge Forest (1988–92); then merged with Dagenham to form Dagenham and Redbridge ('The Daggers'). W1980/1–9 records it for L & I; W1990–2 and Pickering 1994 record the nickname for Redbridge Forest. See also Cedars, Ford/s.
- ☺ Maidstone United F.C., founded in Kent in 1897, closed in 1992, and immediately reborn as Maidstone Invicta, soon renamed as United. Because fossils are stones, it is a pleasure to observe that the club may be the only one in the world to have a dinosaur on its coat of arms. The Maidstone Iguanodon was discovered in 1834 and added to the town's arms as a supporter in 1949, where it looks quite magnificent. Recorded in Avis 1966–70, W1979/80–89, RY1989/90–92/3 and, for the new club, W2004–11 and W2013.
- ☺ Redbridge Forest, see Leytonstone.
- ☺ Wealdstone F.C., founded in Middlesex in 1899. A pluralised short form of the place-name recorded in Avis 1966–70, W1983/4 and W1988–2013. See also Royal Stones, Royals.

Stony is the nickname for Stony Stratford Town F.C., founded in Buckinghamshire in 1947; Wikipedia.

Storks is the nickname of Padiham F.C., founded in Lancashire in 1878, reformed 1949. The stork comes from the crest on the Burnley coat of arms, where it is a heraldic pun representing the local Starkie family, who were prominent in both Burnley and Padiham. The Stork Hotel in Burnley also exploits the pun, and a handsome stork appears on the club's badge; W1982/3. See also Caldersiders.

Stow is a nickname for Stowmarket Town F.C., founded in Suffolk in 1883. The first element in the place-name is an Anglo-Saxon word for a settlement containing an important church or a meeting place, and in this case there was also a market; W1988–2005. See also Gold 'n' Blacks.

Strathie is a nickname for Strathspey Thistle F.C., founded in Grantown-on-Spey in 1993; SFHA. See also Jags, Thistle.

Strawberries was a nickname for two clubs for different reasons. The clubs were:

- Barrow A.F.C., founded in Cumbria in 1901. Here, the nickname refers to the club's first ground, 'The Strawberry Ground'. Strawberry growing is important in the local economy. The club has never played in red shirts. The nickname is recorded in *Stedfast* in October 1964. See also Bluebirds, Shipbuilders, Ziggers.
- Tiptree United F.C., founded in Essex in 1933 and merging with Maldon Town (1946) in 2009. The club occasionally played in red shirts, but both this and the alternative name 'Jam Makers' came from the town's leading employer, Wilkin & Sons, makers of fine preserves since 1885; W1995–2000. See also Blues, Hoops, Jam Makers.

Straw-Hatters / Straw-Plaiters were earlier nicknames for Luton Town F.C., from the major straw-plaiting and hat-making industry in the town. The form 'Straw-Hatters' is recorded on the 1933 Ogden card set. Recorded in G1956–76, Avis 1954–70 and Pickering 1994 as 'Strawplaiters'; Churchill 1958 (as 'Straw-plaiters'). See also Hatters, Lilywhites, Lootown, Lutonians, Reds.

Streamers is the nickname of Coldstream F.C., founded in the Scottish Borders in 1895. The short form of the place-name nevertheless suggests a fast-paced side. Recorded in RS1993–2001, SFHA.

Street is the nickname for at least three clubs with this word in their official names. The clubs are:

- Andover New Street F.C., founded in Hampshire in the 1890s, originally as New Street F.C., then changing to St Mary's Swifts, then New Street in 1895 and the present name in 2001. The club still has a swift on its badge despite the length of time since it was called Swifts; Wikipedia.
- Bridgend Street F.C., founded in Splott, Cardiff in 1899; the nickname appears on the club's own website.
- Park Street F.C., founded in the village near St Albans, Hertfordshire before 1982; W1993.

Stretton is the nickname of Church Stretton Town F.C., founded in Shropshire in the 1930s. Wikipedia and various club websites refer to this club as 'Stretton'.

Strikers was the nickname and suffix of Newport City Strikers L.F.C., established in 1991, originally as Newport County L.F.C., but also at one point named Cardiff City Bluebirds. The present name was taken after a falling out with Cardiff City, in 2006, so it is not quite clear if the impressive suffix was meant sportingly or politically; club website, Huws 2013.

Stringers is the nickname of Hailsham Town F.C., founded in 1885. The nickname dates from 2000 and refers to the traditional rope-making industry of this Sussex town. The club's badge is a design composed of string; W2004–13. See also Town.

Stripes is a nickname for clubs which play in a striped strip. The clubs are:

- Bath City F.C., for the black-and-white stripes of the shirts; W2000–3. See also City, Romans.

☺ Presteigne St Andrews F.C., founded in Powys in 1897; recorded in RW2011. The club plays in red-and-black striped shirts with black shorts. See also Saints.

☺ Stevenage Town F.C., folded in 1968 but recorded in Avis 1966. The club was replaced with S. Athletic F.C., recorded in Avis 1970. This club then closed in 1976 and was succeeded by Stevenage F.C. in 1976, renamed Borough 1980–2010; the new club played for a while in traditional red-and-white stripes but no longer do so; nevertheless, Stripes is recorded as their nickname too in Miller & Wright 1996. See also Boro.

☺ West Bromwich Albion F.C., founded in 1878. The unofficial nickname appears on Wikipedia and is said to be used occasionally by supporters. Today the stripes are dark blue and white, but other combinations were used in their early years (see Historical Football Kits website). See also Albion, Baggies, Bennies, Boing!, Nigger Minstrels, Sandwell Town, Strollers, Tatters (for a possible connection), Team of Boys, Tesco's, Throstles, W.B.A.

☺ Tooting and Mitcham United F.C., founded in London in 1932, from the black-and-white striped shirts which they adopted in 1956; Wikipedia. See also Half-Halfs, Lilywhites, Terrors, Tooting Terrors.

Strollers is a football club name suffix suggesting self-confident, comfortable travelling. Clubs with this suffix include:

☺ Bloxwich Strollers F.C., founded in West Midlands by 1893, folded in 1934; the club reformed for the 1952–3 season, till 1955–6; refounded again in 1985–6, briefly calling themselves Little Bloxwich Strollers, finally closing in 1998 (facts from Andrew Poole, Bloxidge Tallygraph website).

☺ Civil Service Strollers F.C., founded in 1908, originally as Edinburgh Civil Service F.C. The club badge shows a pen and quill with a football. The nickname appears in RS1993–2001 and SFHA.

☺ Clabby Strollers F.C., formed in 1995 as a breakaway from Fivemiletown United in Co. Tyrone; Wikipedia.

☺ Wednesbury Strollers F.C., an early club founded in Staffordshire in 1875 and disappearing after 1882. This appears to be the earliest use of the expression; Wikipedia, BoF1905–6.

☺ West Bromwich Albion F.C. founded in 1878 as W.B.Strollers before taking the Albion suffix in 1880. The word is used as a nickname ('The Strollers') in BoF1905–6 (p.136). See also Albion, Baggies, Bennies, Boing!, Nigger Minstrels, Sandwell Town, Stripes, Tatters (for a possible connection), Team of Boys, Tesco's, Throstles, W.B.A.

Students is a nickname for clubs connected to universities. The clubs are:

☺ Aberystwyth University F.C.; the team represents the Students' Union rather than the university itself. Huws 2009 records that the club's playing field was acquired in 1906, suggesting that the club was formed around that time; Wikipedia gives the nickname. See also Aber Uni.

☢ Bangor University F.C. (of uncertain date). The nickname is recorded on Wikipedia. See also Green Army.

☢ University College Dublin A.F.C., founded in 1895, originally as Catholic University Medical School F.C. The club changed its name in 1908 when the university took over the medical school. The fanzine is called *Student Till I Graduate*. Recorded in RI1997, 2006. See also College.

Stumpites is an older nickname for Boston United F.C., recorded in Avis 1966–70. The Lincolnshire town is famous for the 'Boston Stump', the tallest parish church tower in Britain, visible at a great distance across the fens. See also Pilgrims.

Stute is the nickname of Institute F.C., founded in the Drumahoe area of Derry in 1905. The club was originally founded at the Presbyterian Working Men's Institute (itself founded in 1882) by players from the closed North End Olympic F.C. Recorded in RI1997, RNI2007. See also Pilgrims, United.

Stutes is the nickname of Histon F.C., from its foundation in Cambridgeshire in 1904 as a club for the Histon Institute. When the Institute closed in 1957, the football club survived and renamed itself Histon F.C., but kept the nickname, a pluralised short form of Institute. The club reached national fame in 2009, when it beat Leeds United in a live television broadcast; W2004–13 and SSY2008/9–11/12.

Suburbs was the nickname of Porth Tywyn Suburbs F.C., founded in Carmarthenshire in 1921, originally as Burry Port Garden Suburbs F.C. Recorded in RW1995–2000.

Suds is the nickname for Amalgamated F.C. Sudbury, formed in Suffolk in 1999 in a union between S. Town (1885) and S. Wanderers (1958). It is unique for the 'A.' in A.F.C. to stand for Amalgamated rather than Association or Athletic; a pluralised short form of the place-name; Wikipedia. See also Borough, Town, Wanderers, Yellows.

Sulphurites is a nickname for Harrogate Town F.C. First founded in North Yorkshire in 1914, reformed in 1935 as Harrogate Hotspurs, and then 'Town' after the Second World War, the club has distinctive yellow-and-black colours. Harrogate is a spa town and its waters were noted for their healthy sulphur content, a mineral which is bright yellow, the shade of the strip. Hence the club was first nicknamed the Sulphur and Blacks, then the Sulphurites; W1980/1 and Miller & Wright 1996 have the nickname. See also Town.

Sun is the nickname for Sun Postal Sports F.C., formed in Hertfordshire in 1995 in a merger between Sun Sports (1898) and Watford Postal Services F.C. The Sun Engraving Company in Watford was the original home of the team, and the Postal club was a team formed from the Royal Mail sorting office. The club badge shows a shining sun together with a postal frank mark; Wikipedia records the nickname.

Sund-Ireland was a temporary unofficial nickname for Sunderland A.F.C., coined by some of the fans, during the 2006–7 season when the owners, the management and the squad had a large number of Irish men; Wikipedia. See also Bank of England Club, Black Cats, Lads, Light Brigade, Mackems, Miners, Rokerites / Rokermen,

Sols, Team of All the Talents, Wearsiders.

Sunset City is a nickname for Peel A.F.C., founded on the Isle of Man in 1888. The nickname is that of the cathedral city of Peel, which is on the west coast of the island, so it experiences sunsets over the Irish Sea. The nickname is not officially adopted by the club, but it is one of two nicknames for the city which are frequently used for the club in journalism (e.g. *Isle of Man Today*, 27.9.2011). See also Peelites.

Super Greens is a nickname for Birtley Town F.C., founded in 1993. The club near Gateshead play in green-and-white hooped shirts, white shorts and green socks; Wikipedia. See also Hoops, Green and White Army.

Super Greens for Torrington F.C., see 'Supergreens', below.

Super K is the nickname of Kello Rovers F.C., founded at Kirkconnel in Dumfries and Galloway in 1903. The K is an initialism for Kello; Wikipedia. See also Rovers.

Super Owls was the nickname of Endsleigh F.C., founded in Cheltenham, Gloucestershire, before 1984, when they became a Saturday side. The club was founded by the Endsleigh Insurance Company (established 1965) which had an owl as its trade logo until 1997. The company was originally established to provide insurance for students, so the owl logo was adopted as a symbol of 'wisdom'. The football club renamed as EFC Cheltenham in 1998, and disappears from the FCHD after 1999; Miller & Wright 1996, W1998–9.

Super Spurs was a nickname for Tottenham Hospur F.C. in 1961, when they won both the FA Cup and the League Championship. The nickname is recorded in Pickering 1994, who adds that the expression was still being heard in the late 1960s. See also Lilywhites, Spurs, Yids / Yid Army.

Super Whites is a nickname for the Birkenhead-based Tranmere Rovers F.C., though they wore blue shirts until 1962 (and blue again 1987–7). A mainly-all-white strip has been worn since 1987 (see Historical Football Kits website). The club was founded in 1884 as Belmont F.C. but changed the name to Tranmere Rovers by the start of the 1885 season; Wikipedia. See also Rovers.

Superblues was a nickname for Ipswich Town A.F.C., from the successful Bobby Robson years (1969–82); widely used in internet journalism. See also Binners / Binmen, Blues, Town, Tractor Boys, Witches.

Superdaffs, see Daffodils.

Supergreens is a nickname for Torrington F.C., founded in Devon in 1908. The club wears Celtic-like green and white hoops and white shorts; W1987–90 as Super Greens, W1994–2007 as Supergreens. See also Torrie.

Superhoops, for Queens Park Rangers F.C.; see under **Hoops**.

Sven's Men was a nickname for the English national football team during the managership of Sven-Goran Eriksson (2001–6). It is a neat rhyming phrase and was frequently used by journalists, who have also deployed it for clubs managed by Sven after 2006. See also Class of '66, Roy's Boys, Sassenachs, Three Lions.

Swallows is the nickname for Llandysul F.C., founded in Ceredigion at an uncertain date, but the team were divisional winners of the Ceredigion League in 1948–9. The nickname is used on the club's own website and the bird appears on the club's badge. The bird is abundantly present in the vicinity, which seems to be the reason for the nickname. The bird is surprisingly rare as a football nickname, but there are other examples in Africa and Malta; club website, Huws 2013.

Swanselona was a punning unofficial nickname for Swansea City A.F.C., during their successful Premiership season of 2011–12, when fans compared them to the world-famous Barcelona side; Huws 2013. See also Elyrch, Jacks, Swans.

Swans is a nickname for at least thirteen clubs, some as a pun on the place-name, some because of the presence of swans in the location, also as a metaphor for a riverside location, and some for local heraldic reasons. The clubs are:

- Barton Town Old Boys F.C., founded in North Lincolnshire in 1995, in a merger between B. Town (1880) and B. Old Boys (1959). The club badge shows the new Humber Bridge, and swans are known here. On the opposite bank of the river is the village of Swanland, though Mills 1991 explains this as recording a Viking personal name; W2008–13.

- Braddan A.F.C., founded in Douglas, Isle of Man, in 1923. The club has a flying swan on its badge, and swans are found on the rivers which flow into Douglas; Wikipedia.

- Buckingham Athletic F.C., founded in Buckinghamshire in 1933, originally as B. Juniors and changing name to Athletic in 1939; the club badge shows a stylish heraldic swan, based on the coat of arms and flag of the county of Buckinghamshire. Swans have been a badge of the county since they were used by the Duke of Buckingham in the fifteenth century; W1991–9. See also Ath.

- Egham Town F.C., founded in Surrey in 1963 as the late reformation of an old club, the Runnymead Rovers (1877–1939). The location is near the Thames; W1995–7 and Miller & Wright 1996. See also Sarnies, Town.

- Llanfairfechan Athletic F.C., in Conwy Co. Bor., Wales. The club no longer exists and the nickname is assumed because an enamel badge of the club, dated 1997, recorded in AFBC, shows two swans with a football. The modern Llanfairfechan Town F.C. does not appear to have a nickname.

- Newington Youth Club F.C., founded in Belfast in 1979, originally as Jubilee Olympic (unknown reason). See also 'Ton.

- Newport Pagnell Town F.C., founded in Buckinghamshire in 1963, originally as Newport Pagnell Wanderers, changing name in 1972. The club has a handsome stylised swan on its badge and the bird is the traditional symbol of the county of Buckinghamshire; a swan also appears as the crest of the town's arms, and the town was built at the confluence of the rivers Ouzel and Ouse; W1993–2013.

- Slimbridge F.C., founded in 1902. The club shows a stylised swan on its badge (partly composed of the letters AFC); the nickname is recent and refers to the famous bird sanctuary established in this Gloucestershire village by Sir Peter Scott;

W2006–13.

⊕ Staines Town F.C. Established in 1892, the name is taken from the two swans on the town's coat of arms, which are also used by the club, and the birds are a traditional feature of this Thameside town; W1979/80–2013. See also Leghorns, Linos, Massive, Old Lagonda, Town.

⊕ Stapenhill F.C., founded in Staffordshire in 1947, reformed in 2009. The club badge shows two stylised swans and the town, near Burton-on-Trent, has a riverside location; W1993–2002.

⊕ Storrington F.C., founded in West Sussex in 1920. Although the original place-name is believed to record storks (Mills 1991), swans are also a frequent visitor to the village and feature in street names and an hotel name. The club has a stylised swan on a blue badge; W1989–90, W1993–6 and W2006–9. See also Blues.

⊕ Swanage Town and Herston F.C., founded in 1966, in a merger of S. Town and H. Rovers. The Dorset club has a swan on its badge and the nickname clearly derives from the place-name (which does actually refer to swans in its original meaning, see Mills 1991); W1987–96.

⊕ Swansea City A.F.C., recorded on the 1933 Ogden cigarette card for Swansea Town (1912) as "an obvious sobriquet which does not require any explanation". The word is merely a pun, however, for the first syllable in the English name for the Welsh Abertawe, which actually records the Scandinavian personal name Sweyn. The club has played in a mainly all-white strip for the whole of its existence and was renamed 'City' when Swansea became a city in 1970. Cyril the Swan is the famous mascot. Recorded in the Thomson 'stamp' 1936, Avis 1954–70, G1956–76, Churchill 1958, Richards 1960, AA 1960, RW 1994–2011 and throughout RY1970/1–SSY2012/13. See also Elyrch, Jacks, Swanselona.

⊕ Walton and Hersham F.C. Founded in a merger in 1945, a swan appears on the club badge and the bird is a natural association for the riverside location of Walton-on-Thames. Recorded in W1979/80–2013. See also Sham, Swans and Robins, Waltz.

Swans and Robins was a nickname for Walton and Hersham F.C., founded in Surrey in 1945 as a merger of clubs from these neighbouring towns. Although 'Swans' is retained as a nickname (Wikipedia, and see previous entry), Avis 1966–70 records the club as 'Swans and Robins', which suggests that Hersham originally took the 'Robins' nickname as Walton is the location nearer the river. The club today has a beautiful badge which displays both a swan and a robin, and the club plays in a nearly-all-red strip. See also Sham, Swans, Waltz.

Sweeney is an unofficial nickname for A.F.C. Guildford City. 'Sweeney' is Cockney rhyming slang for 'Metropolitan Police Flying Squad' (from Sweeney Todd). It was used as the title of a popular television drama of 1975–8, the connection being the 1975 prosecution of the Guildford Four, who were forced to confess to crimes they had not committed by aggressive police interrogation, like that in the television series; Wikipedia. See also City, Guild, Pinks.

Swifts is both a popular football club suffix and can be a nickname for the clubs so called. There seems no particular reason for a club to call itself The Swifts, other than the desire to be associated with the bird's speed, elegance and untouchability. Huws 2013 lists several more Welsh examples. The clubs with Swifts as a nickname are:

☙ Bangor Swifts F.C., founded in Co. Down in 1970. The club has a stylised swift on its badge; Wikipedia.

☙ Bolehall Swifts F.C., founded in 1953 in Staffordshire; there is a swift on the club badge; W1987–2005.

☙ Dungannon Swifts F.C., founded in Co. Tyrone in 1949. The club shows a swift on its badge. Recorded in RI1997, RNI2007.

☙ Heybridge Swifts F.C., founded in Essex in 1880. The club also has a stylish red swift as a badge; W1986–2013. See also Black and Whites.

☙ Jeanfield Swifts F.C., founded in Perth in 1928. The club has a swift on its badge; Wikipedia, SFHA.

☙ Leyton F.C., founded in Essex in 1997 in a reformation of the older club of 1868. The club is normally called 'The Lilywhites', but this alternative nickname is recorded on Wikipedia, for an unknown reason. See also Lillies, Lilywhites.

☙ Markethill Swifts F.C., founded in Co. Armagh in 1989; Wikipedia.

☙ Monkton Swifts F.C., founded in Pembrokeshire in 1955; the nickname appears in match reports from 1970–1 on the 'Pembrokeshiresport.co.uk' website. Twitter uses the variant 'Mighty Swifts'.

☙ Sport and Leisure Swifts F.C., founded in Belfast in 1978. The club took the name of the Ulster Sport and Leisure Club in a sponsorship deal. The business has long gone, but the club keeps the name; 'Swifts' was added when a number of players from a folded club called Belfast Swifts joined the club in the 1980s; club's own website.

☙ Stourport Swifts F.C., founded in 1882. The club badge has a black swift on a yellow background; W1985 and W1993–2013.

☙ Walsall F.C., formed in 1888, as W. Town Swifts F.C., in a merger of W. Town (1877) and W. Swifts (1879). The swift suffix was dropped as long ago as 1895 but the bird continues to be used on all the club's badges (a very stylish modern one for 2010–11); Wikipedia. See also Saddlers.

Swindle is one of the more polite unofficial nicknames for Swindon Town F.C., as used by Bristol City supporters. A less polite version is 'Swinedon' from the same source, an internet forum, whereas Oxford United call Swindon 'Scumdon'. See also Moonrakers, Railwaymen, Robins, Spartans.

Swinford was the nickname for Oldswinford Football and Sports Club, founded in the West Midlands in 1955. In 1993 Oldswinford renamed as Brierley Hill Town, and renamed again as Brierley and Hagley Alliance in 2001; the 'Lions' nickname is recorded in W1994–2005, the 'Swinford' nickname in W1985–90. See also Lions.

SYCOB is a nickname for Beaconsfield SYCOB F.C., founded in Buckinghamshire in

1994, in a merger of B. United (1921) and Slough YCOB (entering adult leagues in 1947); SYCOB stands for Slough Youth Centre Old Boys, and it is listed in W1998–2002 as an alternative nickname for the club. See also Rams.

Synners is the distinctive nickname of Billingham Synthonia F.C., founded in 1923 and the only club named after a brand of agricultural fertiliser. Synthonia is synthetic ammonia, made by ICI in Billingham in Co. Durham. Recorded in W1979/80–2013 and Barton 1984 & 1985.

T's was the nickname for Tring Town F.C., founded in Hertfordshire in 1889. The initialism is recorded in W1985–6 and W1997–2004, but the Smith directories for 1993/4–95/6 list it as Ts and W1994–6 and Miller & Wright 1996 list it as 'Tee's'. None of the forms quite suggest 'Two T's', so it remains ambiguous whether it refers to Tring or Town. The club folded in 2003 and its assets were absorbed by Tring Athletic.

T'Colliers or T'Pitmen is recorded in Dobson 1973 as a nickname for the people of Wigan in Lancashire, and also for Wigan Athletic F.C. The nickname uses the Lancashire dialect version of 'The' and records the town's coal-mining industry. See also Athletic, County, Latics, Pie-Eaters / Pies.

Tadders is the nickname for Tadley Calleva F.C., founded in 1989, originally as Tadley F.C. The Hampshire side added 'Calleva', from the Roman name of the nearby Roman town of Silchester, *Calleva Atrebatum*, in 2004; Wikipedia.

Taffs / Taffys are nicknames of Taffs Well A.F.C., founded in 1946. Taff's Well is a place near Cardiff and the name records the local River Taff and a spring. This river flowing through the national capital is also the source of the derogatory nickname for Welshmen as 'Taffies', but it is a real place-name and this nickname is a short form of the club's official name; recorded in RW1995–2011. See also Wellmen.

Tage was the nickname of the Staffordshire side, Armitage F.C. (1946), reformed in 1990 as Armitage 90 F.C., folded in 1996; a short form of the official name, recorded in W1979/80 for the old club, and W1994–6 for the new. See also Blues.

Talbot is a nickname for Cambusnethan Talbot A.F.C., founded in North Lanarkshire in 1999. The suffix is a surname, famously used for the Talbot brand of cars between 1903 and 1992, but the connection here may be similar to the case of Auckinlock Talbot (see under Bot); Wikipedia. See also Camby Talbot.

Tangerine Barmy Army is the nickname of Ayre United A.F.C., founded in Andreas, Ayre, Isle of Man, in 1967. The club plays in a tangerine-and-black strip; Wikipedia.

Tangerines is a nickname for clubs which play in an orange-coloured strip. A variant name on the same theme is Satsumas (q.v.). The clubs are:

☘ Ashford Town F.C., founded in Middlesex in 1958. The club plays in orange-and-white stripes with black shorts; W2010–11. See also Ash Trees.

☘ Blackpool F.C. Founded in 1887, the club adopted their striking tangerine-coloured strip for the 1923–4 season. This was on the recommendation of referee Albert

Hargreaves who had officiated at a Holland-Belgium match and was impressed by the Dutch colours, also used for the Dutch royal family (as in William of Orange and from him adopted as the colour of protestant groups in Northern Ireland, though there is no sectarian suggestion in the Blackpool choice). During the First World War the club adopted the colours of the Belgian flag, out of support for Belgian refugees in the town. Supporters of Blackpool are nicknamed Tangerine Army and Seaside Barmy Army, but used to be called the Atomic Boys (q.v.). The nickname is recorded in G1956–76, Churchill 1958 (along with Seasiders), but Rothmans has only 'Tangerines', 1970/1–75/6 and then switches to 'Seasiders'. See also Atomic Boys, Donkey Lashers, Merry Stripes, 'Pool, Seasiders.

- Diss Town F.C., founded in Norfolk in 1888. The team plays in orange shirts and socks with black shorts; W1992–2013.
- Dundee United F.C., founded in 1909, originally as D. Hibernian, after the demise of D. Harp and D. Wanderers. The club first adopted the tangerine kit colours in 1969. Harvey 1959 cites the club as 'The Blues' but this must be an error because the kit was black and white in the 1950s (see Historical Football Kits website); RY1970/1–72/3. See also Arabs, Terrors.
- Wellington A.F.C., founded in Somerset in 1896; orange shirts; Wikipedia. See also Town, Wellie.

Tanners is cited as a nickname for two clubs, one correctly and one probably in error. The clubs are:

- Leatherhead F.C. Founded in Surrey in 1946 in a merger of L. Rose (1907) and L. United. The nickname is a play on 'leather' in the place-name; W1979/80–2013.
- Maidenhead United F.C., founded in Berkshire in 1870. The club is persistently nicknamed 'The Magpies' in W1981–2012 but it appears as 'Tanners' in Smith 1991/2–1955/6 and in Pickering 1994. This appears to be a simple typesetting error, caused perhaps by the proximity of Leatherhead in the Isthmian League, though its repetition is intriguing. See also Magpies, United.

Tarn is a nickname for Fleet Town F.C., founded in Hampshire in 1890, expressing a local pronunciation of 'Town'. The nickname appears in Miller & Wright 1996. See also Blues, Town.

Tartan Army / Terriers are nicknames for the Scotland National Football Team, first formed in 1870, for the first 'international', held against England. 'The Tartan Army' is also used for supporters. 'Tartan' refers to the unique Scottish national dress, and 'Terriers' to the popular Scots Terrier dog, also known as a Scottie. 'Army' is recorded in Pickering 1994. See also Blues, Bravehearts, Thistle, Wembley Wizards.

Tatters is an unofficial nickname for Wolverhampton Wanderers F.C., from the perspective of West Bromwich Albion supporters. According to www.baggies.com it originates in a local expression for dubious scrap metal dealing, though generally the phrase is used for clothing rags (in Green 1998 the term refers to those who collect rags for recycling). One wonders if there is here a response to the Baggies nickname, which may have originated as a comment from rivals on dishevelled clothing amongst the supporters and players of W.B.A. See also Buckley Babes, Dingles, Wanderers, Wolves.

Tavy is a nickname for Tavistock A.F.C., founded in Devon in 1888. A friendly short form of the place-name; W1994–2005. See also Lambs.

Tayn is an unofficial nickname for Northampton Town F.C., the spelling recording the local pronunciation of 'town'. In 2011 Wikipedia had it as 'Tayn', but in 2012 the spelling was 'Teyn'. Both, however, would be pronounced the same. See also Cobblers, Shoe Army.

Team is an unofficial nickname for clubs using the French naming style, where noun and adjective are reversed. The style suggests Olympic usage and is a recent fashion. Clubs are:

⚽ Team Bath F.C., founded in Avon, 1999; Wikipedia records that the expression 'Team Bath' is used for all the university's sporting operations. See also Crescents, Scholars.

⚽ Team Bury F.C., founded in Suffolk in 2005; Wikipedia. See also Blues.

⚽ Team Northumbria F.C., founded in 1999, renamed 2003, based at Northumbria University in Newcastle-upon-Tyne; Wikipedia now records 'Team North' as a nickname for this club, together with an initialism, TN. See also Tynesiders.

⚽ Team Solent F.C., founded in 2008, Southampton Solent University's side; Wikipedia.

⚽ Team Swansea: of uncertain date, but also called 'Swansea University Mens F.C.' The name is recorded for a match against Birchgrove Colts on 26 January 2013.

Team of All the Talents was a nickname for Sunderland A.F.C. during a succession of successful seasons before 1900. It is recorded in BoF1905–6 and on the 1933 Ogden cigarette card. In Appleton 1960 it is applied to the years 1889–98 but BoF1905–6 says the club was universally known by this phrase by 1896; Avis 1954–70. See also Bank of England Club, Black Cats, Lads, Light Brigade, Mackems, Miners, Rokerites / Rokermen, Sols, Sund-Ireland, Wearsiders.

Team of Boys was a nickname for the successful West Bromwich Albion team in the early 1930s. The nickname is recorded in Pickering 1994 and refers to the relative youth of the players. See also Albion, Baggies, Bennies, Boing!, Nigger Minstrels, Sandwell Town, Stripes, Strollers, Tatters (for a possible connection), Tesco's, Throstles, W.B.A.

Team of Millionaires was a nickname for the early Irish club, Freebooters F.C., founded in Dublin and an early member of the Irish Football Association after 1880, but closed in 1906. The expression is recorded in Johnston 1934 (p. 32) and seems simply to have been a play on the 'piracy' sense of 'Freebooter'. The official name has been assumed by a modern club in Co. Kilkenny. See also Freebooters.

Team of Surprises is recorded as a nickname for Chesterfield Town F.C., founded in Derbyshire in 1884, folding in 1915, in BoF1905–6, p. 216. The club is also cited in that source as having the nickname 'Team of the Crooked Spire', also used for the successor team, founded in 1919. This variant appears to be a play on the spire nickname, and refers to the club's fame as one which often produced surprising results despite a relative lack of resources. See also Blues, Cheaterfield, Spireites, Team of Surprises, Town.

Team of the Crooked Spire, see Spireites.

Team of the Eighties is recorded in Pickering 1994 as a nickname for Crystal palace F.C., used in the popular press for the club in c.1980, after their great achievements during the 1970s. See also Eagles, Glaziers, Palace.

Team with No Boots was an unofficial nickname of Crusaders F.C., founded in Belfast in 1898. The nickname was coined by the manager Roy Walker (1989–98) and referred to the relative poverty of the club (but which was irrelevant to their impressive performance); Wikipedia. See also Crues, Hatchetmen.

Teddy Bears is a nickname for Rangers F.C., founded in Glasgow in 1872. The unexpected name comes from rhyming slang. First, Rangers is abbreviated to 'Gers, this gets pronounced Gairs, and *then* it rhymes with bears. For similar phrases, see Candy Rock, Tin Pail. Recorded in Borlenghi 1999; Wikipedia. For Rangers, see also Blues, 'Gers, Huns, Iron Curtain, Light Blues, Rangers.

Tee's, for Tring Town, see T's, above.

Teessiders is a commonly used unofficial nickname for Middlesbrough F.C., after the river Tees which flows through the town; frequently heard on match commentaries. See also Boro, Cleveland Cowboys, Ironsiders, Nops, Riversiders, Scabs, Smoggies, Washers.

Teg is the nickname for Panteg A.F.C., founded in Torfaen Co. Bor. in 1947 as a works side for the Richard Thomas and Baldwin Steelworks, originally called RTB Panteg, taking the present name in 1972. The nickname is recorded in R1994–6 and is a short form of the place-name.

Teigars is a nickname of Llanberis F.C., founded in Gwynedd in 1890. The club plays in a black-and-amber strip, the traditional tiger colours (though they are not in stripes). The nickname is usually expressed in its Welsh spelling, though with the strange use of the English pluralising –s on the end; club website. See also Beris, Blac and Amber, Darans, Llanbêr, Loco / Locomotives.

Teigns is a nickname for Teignmouth F.C., founded in Devon in 1946. A pluralised short form of the place-name, recorded in W1994–9 and *This is Devon*, 3 May 2010.

Terras is the nickname for Weymouth F.C. Founded in Dorset in 1890, the club adopted a brickish-red or terracotta-coloured strip almost immediately, and it is from this that the nickname comes. The associated social club is called the Terra Cotta Club. Recorded in Avis 1966–70, W1979/80–2013 and SSY2007/8–09/10.

Terriers is a nickname for three clubs whose home has an association with this type of dog. The clubs are:

⚽ Bedlington Terriers F.C., founded in Northumberland in 1949, originally as Bedlington Mechanics and going through two renamings (B. Colliery Welfare and B. United), disbanded and reformed as Town in 1977 before taking the present name in 1980. A pithead and the distinctive Bedlington Terrier dog are displayed on the club badge, and a supporters' chant is "Woof, woof, terriers!" The breed has several alternative names (Rothbury, Northumberland, Gypsy and Miners) but Bedlington is their most-accepted name. They were used in the mines to kill rats; Barton 1984, W1986–90, W2008–13.

⚽ Huddersfield Town F.C., where it has been the official nickname since the 1969–70 season. It is in honour of the Yorkshire terrier pedigree dog breed (see Tykes for a more commonplace Yorkshire terrier), which is not only local, but also a dog noted for its courage and determination. The club mascot is now on the same theme, one Terry the Terrier. The club was called Huddersfield A.F.C until it dropped 'Association' in 2005. Recorded in G1976, RY1971/2–SSY2012/13. See also Colnesiders, Scarlet Runners, Town.

⚽ Scottish National Football Team, in the form 'Tartan Terriers', from the popular Scottish Terrier or 'Scottie' dog. See also Tartan Army, Wembley Wizards.

Terrors is the official nickname of two unrelated clubs, though it is difficult to explain. The name certainly implies a club which will strike terror in the minds of rival teams … and both clubs can offer a 'T' alliteration which might have helped the nickname's adoption. The clubs are:

⚽ Dundee United F.C., founded in 1909, originally as D. Hibernian, after the demise of D. Harp and D. Wanderers. The club's ground is called Tannadice Park, and in 1963 a popular song 'The Terrors of Tannadice' was recorded by Hector Nicol. The club's website states that the nickname was not known before the Second World War, and suggests that it probably dates from the 1949 Scottish Cup win over Celtic, making the nickname appear long before the song. It would seem, therefore, to derive from a spontaneous expression of exuberant joy after a giant-slaying achievement (compare other nicknames like 'Crazy Gang' and 'Lions' arising in similar circumstances). The 1986 Panini sticker presents the nickname as a Dracula-like vampire attacking a player. Recorded in RS1993–2012, and through RY1973/4–SSY2012/13. See also Arabs, Tangerines.

⚽ Tooting and Mitcham United F.C., founded in London in 1932, in a merger between Tooting Town (1887) and Mitcham Wanderers (1912). W1979/80 and W1981/2–86 record it in the form Tooting Terrors; W1980/1 and W1987–2013 as Terrors. There seems to have been no particular reason for the nickname other than to suggest fearsomeness, with alliteration. See also Half-Halfs, Lilywhites, Stripes, Tooting Terrors.

Tesco's is an amusing nickname for three clubs which have on occasion adopted a blue-and-white striped shirt which some observers believe is reminsiscent of the design on the Tesco carrier bag. The three clubs are:

⚽ Bristol Rovers F.C., who adopted a blue-and-white striped and quartered design in 1996 which was nicknamed 'the Tesco shirt' by their own supporters (see Historical Football kits website). See also Arabs, Black Arabs, Gas / Gasheads, Pirates, Purdown Poachers, Rovers, Squatters.

⚽ Brighton and Hove Albion F.C., from the perspective of Crystal Palace supporters, and recorded on the 2003 Football Fans Census website. The club has worn blue and white almost continuously since 1904 (see Historical Football Kits website). See also Albion, Dolphins, Flippers, Seagulls, Seasiders, Seaweed, Shrimps.

⚽ West Bromwich Albion F.C., as a tongue-in-cheek alternative explanation for the origin of the nickname 'Baggies', though the club colours are also the right shade of blue for Tesco. It is recorded as a nickname on the 2003 Football Fans Census, from the perspective of Wolverhampton Wanderers supporters. The right stripes have been worn almost continuously since 1889 (see Historical Football Kits website). See also Albion, Baggies, Bennies, Boing!, Nigger Minstrels, Sandwell Town, Stripes, Strollers, Tatters (for a possible connection), Team of Boys, Throstles, W.B.A.

Tevie Boys is the nickname of Teversal F.C., founded in 1918 and based near Mansfield in Nottinghamshire. The club was reformed in 1986 as T. Miners Welfare. renamed T. F.C. in 2000. The club display a pithead on their badge, and the nickname is a friendly short form of the place-name; W2008–13.

Th' Owd Reds see under Owd.

Theestle is the nickname of Largs Thistle F.C., founded in North Ayrshire in 1889. Here the famous suffix is given a spelling to suggest its local pronunciation; Wikipedia.

Thin Red Line is the nickname of Rhayader Town F.C., founded in Powys in 1884. The club folded in 2006 but was reformed in 2007; it plays in red-and-white shirts with black shorts. The nickname expresses the sense of solidarity of a sporting side in red, but the club tradition is that it originally referred to the red ribbons the club wore across their shirts in the 1880s to distinguish themselves from opponents; recorded in RW1994–2011; Huws 2013.

Thirds was a nickname for the Third Lanark Athletic Club, founded in Glasgow in 1872, originally as The Third Lanarkshire Rifle Volunteers Athletic Club, and closed in 1967. The club renamed itself in 1903, when it became independent of its military origins, and the name has recently been revived as an amateur men's side (2003). Recorded in Avis 1966–70. See also Hi-Hi's, Redcoats, Sodgers, Volunteers, Warriors.

Thistle is an early football club name suffix in Scotland, based on the spiky plant which is one of the national symbols (Scottish clubs also have a general fashion for using flower names). Clubs with this suffix tend to have the nickname 'The Jags', expressing the jagged edges of the plant. One of the earliest surviving clubs with the name is Partick Thistle, founded in 1876 (see Jags). Ayr Thistle was earlier (1872), but merged with a neighbour in 1879. In the following cases, however, the nickname is usually 'Thistle' (and see also Theestle, above):

- ⚽ Ardeer Thistle F.C., founded in Stevenston, Ayrshire, in 1900; Wikipedia, SFHA.
- ⚽ Ayr Thistle F.C., founded in 1872. The club merged with Ayr Academicals in 1879 to form Ayr F.C.; BoF1905–6, Wikipedia.
- ⚽ Bathgate Thistle F.C., founded in West Lothian in 1937; Wikipedia, SFHA.
- ⚽ Bridge of Don Thistle J.F.C., founded in Aberdeen in 1983, originally as Wilsons XI, after the club's founder, renaming Hillhead in 2006 and the present name in 2011; Wikipedia.
- ⚽ Burghead Thistle F.C., founded in Moray in 1889 (1902 on club's own website); Wikipedia.
- ⚽ Dalkeith Thistle F.C., founded in Midlothian in 1892; Wikipedia. See also Jags.
- ⚽ Dalry Thistle F.C., founded in Ayrshire in 1920; Wikipedia.
- ⚽ Dingwall Thistle F.C., founded in Highland sometime between 1929 (when a previous club of the name merged to form Ross County) and 1968–9, when the club were champions of the North Caledonian League; club website.
- ⚽ Kirriemuir Thistle F.C., founded in Angus in 1921; Wikipedia. See also Kirrie.
- ⚽ Livingston F.C., founded in 1943, originally as Ferranti Thistle for an Edinburgh electrical engineering company; the club renamed to Meadowbank Thistle and then relocated to Livingston in 1995. The nickname is recorded in RS1993–5 and RY1989/90–94/5 for Meadowbank; RS 1996–7 and RY1995/6–6/7 for Livingston. See also Lions, Livi, Wee Jags.
- ⚽ Lothian Thistle Hutchison Vale F.C., founded in 1969, originally as an Edinburgh works side. Recorded in RS1996–7, 2000–2001, SFHA.
- ⚽ Meadowbank Thistle, see under Livingston, above.
- ⚽ Scotland National Football Team. Although not normally used for the national side, it is so used in BoF1905–6 (p.227). See also Blues, Bravehearts, Tartan Army / Terriers, Wembley Wizards.
- ⚽ Strathspey Thistle F.C., founded in Grantown-on-Spey in 1993. Recorded in RS2011–12. See also Jags, Strathie.
- ⚽ Tain Thistle F.C., founded in Highland in 1996; club website.
- ⚽ Thistle F.C., was the name of a Scottish club in its own right, based at Braehead Park in Glasgow, founded in 1875, closed after 1894 (Potter & Jones 2011; Wikipedia).
- ⚽ Tulliallan Thistle F.C., founded in Kincardine, Fife, in 1962, closed in 2003; SFHA.

Thorfinn is the nickname and part-official name of Kirkwall Thorfinn F.C., founded in Orkney in 1891. The club is named after Thorfinn Sigurdsson, or Thorfinn the Mighty, the eleventh-century earl of Orkney. The club was founded at a time when medieval subjects were very popular, and Thorfinn was the most famous of the Viking rulers of Orkney; club's own website.

Thoroughbreds is the nickname of Kildare County F.C., founded in 2002 and based at Newbridge. The club is a successor to the previous Newbridge Town, founded in 1959. The nickname uses the popular expression for 'pedigree' horses and records the importance of this affluent county for the Irish horse industry. The county has more stud farms than any other county, and has three important racecourses. Recorded in RI2006.

Thrapo is a nickname for Thrapston Town F.C., founded in Northamptonshire in 1960, originally as Thrapston Venturas. A friendly short form of the place-name, recorded on Wikipedia. See also Town, Venturas.

Three Lions is the nickname for the England National Football Team, first formed in 1870 for the first 'international', held against Scotland. The nickname uses the three lions on the heraldry first adopted by King Richard I, which is also the badge for the side. See also Class of '66, Roy's Boys, Sassenachs, Sven's Men.

Throstles is the long-standing official nickname of West Bromwich Albion F.C. Founded in 1878 as West Bromwich Strollers, the suffix was changed to Albion in 1880. Soon after, the club secretary, Tom Smith, suggested the badge could be a throstle (a thrush) sitting on a crossbar, because the public house in which the team used to change kept one of these birds as a pet. In 1900 the club moved to a new home called 'The Hawthorns' from the large number of hawthorn bushes which were cleared during the building, so the crossbar was changed to a hawthorn branch on the badge. The nickname is recorded early, in BoF1905–6. The 1933 Ogden card records the name, saying "These speckled birds were numerous in the vicinity of the ground", and adding the detail that a throstle in a cage was used as a mascot on match days. Recorded in Johnston 1934, Avis 1954–70, G1956–76, Churchill 1958 and Richards 1960, AA 1960, *Stedfast* December 1964 and throughout RY1970/1–SSY2012/13. See also Albion, Baggies, Bennies, Boing!, Nigger Minstrels, Sandwell Town, Stripes, Strollers, Tatters (for a possible connection), Team of Boys, Tesco's, W.B.A.

Thursdays is a nickname of Abergavenny Thursdays F.C., founded in Monmouthshire in 1927. At the time, Thursday was the half-day closing day for traders, and so the only day on which the club could play. There are other Thursday clubs in Wales (see Huws 2013), and see also Wednesday for a similar coining. Recorded in Avis 1966–70, RW1994–2011. See also Butchers, Pennies.

'Tic is an unofficial nickname for Celtic F.C., founded in Glasgow in 1887. A short form of the official name, widely used on the internet amongst the club's own supporters. See also Bhoys, Celts, Hoops, Lisbon Lions, Quality Street Kids, Tims.

Tics is the nickname of Brightlingsea Regent F.C., founded in Essex in 2005, in a merger between B. United and Regent Park Rangers. The nickname is from one of its ancestor clubs, Brightlingsea Athletic (1908) (which had merged with B. Town in 1928 to form B. United) and is a short form of the suffix. The nickname has lasted a suprisingly long time; W2012–13. See also Oystermen, Seasiders, United.

Tigers is mainly a nickname for clubs which play in black-and-amber striped shirts (or close equivalents). However, two of the clubs are so named for no particular reason.

An attractive variant is the White Tigers (q.v.), used for the white and gold colours of Truro City. The examples are:

⚽ Axminster Town A.F.C., founded in Devon in 1903. The club badge in AFBC (and club's website) records the nickname, and the team plays in black-and-amber stripes.

⚽ Gloucester City A.F.C., founded in 1889; from their distinctive black and amber striped shirts; W1986–2013. See also City, Citizens, Gloucestrians.

⚽ Handcross Village F.C., founded in Sussex in 1978, reforming a club from the early twentieth century. The club plays in amber and black stripes. The club's own website gives the nickname and states that the colours were also used by the ancestor club. An enamel badge appears in AFBC.

⚽ Holbeach United F.C., founded in 1929; the club plays in black-and-amber striped shirts with black shorts and yellow socks, but the club is in the Lincolnshire fens and the nickname may also recall the notorious 'Fen Tigers', possies of men who would make up a 'ran-tan-tan' to exact public humiliation on transgressors against public morality. Recorded in Avis 1966–70; W1982/3–2013.

⚽ Hull City A.F.C. Founded in East Yorkshire in 1904, the club soon adopted the distinctive black-and-amber striped shirts on which the nickname is based, and it was included in the 1933 Ogden cigarette card set, the 1936 Thomson 'stamp', G1956–76, Avis 1954–70, Churchill 1958, Norris 1959, Richards 1960, in SWSCYB 1962–3 and throughout RY1970/1–SSY2012/13. The badge of the club features a handsome tiger head, and the mascot is one Roary the Tiger.

⚽ Hyde F.C. Founded in Greater Manchester in 1885, renaming as Hyde United in 1919, reverting to the original name in 2010. The club has never played in the black-and-amber tiger colours. The club's website explains "Hyde's nickname, the Tigers, was adopted at the end of the 1960s when they were founder members of the Northern Premier League. They were expected to struggle but fought like tigers for two seasons and finished seventh and eleventh. However, the club could not compete financially and returned to the Cheshire League in 1970." Recorded in W1979/80–2013.

⚽ Kildrum Tigers F.C., founded in Co. Donegal in 1948. The club badge shows a stylised tiger head in black and yellow, while the team itself plays in red-and-black stripes, sufficiently suggestive of tigers. The club's own website gives a history and uses the nickname.

⚽ Kingsbury London Tigers F.C., established in 2006, in a merger of London Tigers (1997) and Kingsbury Town (1919); W2010–11. The club reverted to the London Tigers name at the end of the 2011 season (see below). For Kingsbury Town, see Kings, Mustard Pots and Town.

⚽ Leyland Motors F.C., founded at Leyland in Lancashire in 1920. 'The Tigers' nickname is recorded in W1982/3–1986; at the time the club played in amber-and-navy-blue strip, not quite the Tiger colours, but navy blue is sufficiently dark to appear black against the amber. See also Motormen.

⚽ Llanberis F.C., but see under the Welsh spelling: Teigars, Y.

⚽ London Tigers F.C., founded in 1986, merging in 2006 with Kingsbury Town (1919), but reverting to its original name in 2011. The club is attached to the community sports organisation of that name; it has a strong Bangladeshi membership and no doubt took the Tigers name to evoke Asian splendour, but it also plays in the traditional tiger colours, amber shirts and black shorts and socks, though not in stripes. The club badge shows suitable scratch marks; W2012–13.

⚽ Mardy Tigers L.F.C., founded in Mardy, Abergavenny, in 2009. The nickname is used on the club's own website. 'Mardy' is an English dialect word meaning 'stroppy', or 'unco-operative' but no pun is intended here, it is a place-name.

⚽ Neath Port Talbot Tigers F.C., founded in Glamorgan in 2004. The club is a consciously multi-ethnic side, but the 'Tigers' name may have been adopted as a suitable symbol for the Asian element in the membership (as also used for London Tigers). The club badge shows a leaping tiger; club's own website.

⚽ Prescot Cables A.F.C., founded in Merseyside in 1884. The club has gone through several renamings but has retained the 'Tigers' nickname throughout, and it plays in a black-and-amber strip. Recorded in W1979/80 for P. Town; W1982/3–6 for P. Cables; W1993–7 for P. AFC; and W1998–2013 for P. Cables. See also Cables.

⚽ Saltdean United F.C., founded in Sussex in 1966. The club plays in black and red stripes; W1993–2007.

⚽ Tenterden Tigers Junior F.C., founded in Kent in 1996. The club plays in yellow and black and the nickname also appears in the official name. The present club is a youth side but it has an older Tenterden F.C. (1890) in its ancestry; club's own website.

⚽ Turton F.C., founded in Lancashire in 1871, and the county's oldest surviving club. The club plays in blue and white, so the reason for the nickname is not known; Wikipedia

⚽ Willesden F.C., founded in London in 1946. The nickname is recorded in W1980/1 but the club strip at the time was blue-and-white stripes, with 'all red' listed in W1978/9 and 1979/80, so the reason for the nickname is not clear. The club was dissolved in 1981.

⚽ Worksop Town F.C., from their black-and-amber shirts. Founded in 1861, the club claims to be the fourth oldest club in the UK. The club badge features a splendid tiger head. Recorded in Avis 1966–70, W1979/80–2013.

Timbers is the nickname of Handrahan Timbers F.C., founded in the West Midlands in 1982, sponsored by the W. J. Handrahan & Son timber company; W1993–2003.

Tims is a nickname for Celtic F.C., founded in Glasgow in 1887. The nickname derives from a generic term for Catholic Irish immigrants to Glasgow in the nineteenth century, Tim Malloys, based on an allegedly typical name for such a person. The nickname used to have criminal associations (rival Protestant gangs were called Billyboys), but is still popular. Rhyming slang (Tim Malloys / Bhoys) encourages its use for both club and supporters. The first two editions of the *Rothmans Football Yearbook* (RY1970/1–71/2) cite it as the official nickname. See also Bhoys, Celts, Hoops, Lisbon Lions, Quality Street Kids, 'Tic.

Tin Pail is the nickname of the Glasgow (Tollcross) side, Vale of Clyde F.C., founded in 1873. The nickname appears to be Glaswegian rhyming slang, using the standard expression for a metal bucket, simply because Pail rhymes with Vale. As with 'Teddy Bears' for 'Gers, there need not be any association between the nickname and the official name other than a chance similarity in the sound of only one word in the nickname; Wikipedia, SFHA. See also Cabbage, Candy Rock, Jam Tarts, and Teddy Bears for other such expressions.

Tinmen is the nickname of Truro City F.C., founded in Cornwall in 1889, from the fame of the Cornish tin mines; Wikipedia. See also City, White Tigers.

Tinners is the nickname for St Just F.C., founded in Cornwall before 1959 (FCHD). The nickname refers to the fame of the Cornish tin mines (see also The Tinmen for Truro); W1992–5.

Tipples was the nickname for Tower Hamlets F.C., founded in London before 1989 as K.P.G. Tipples F.C., renaming as 'Tower Hamlets (Tipples)' in 1991 (FCHD, and so listed in W1992–3 without a nickname). The club appears in W1994–5 as Tower Hamlets with Tipples as a nickname. An on-line forum suggests that the name referred to a local public house called 'Tipples', presumably as a sponsor. This pub was a temporary renaming of the 'Salmon and Ball', which had once been part-owned by football legend Bobby Moore. The club disappears after 1995.

Tirion is a nickname of Bryntirion Athletic F.C., founded in Bridgend Co. Bor., Wales, in 1956; a short form of the place-name, recorded on Wikipedia in 2012, the nickname there had been 'Bryn' in 2011. See also Athletic, Bryn.

Tish is the nickname for St Ishmael's F.C., founded in Pembrokeshire, apparently recently, internet references to it seem to start in 2011. The nickname is one generally used for the village, and is clearly derived from 'St Ish'. The nickname was used for the club by Pembrokeshiresport.co.uk on 2 August 2012; Huws 2013.

Tivvy is the nickname for Tiverton Town F.C., founded in Devon in 1913, originally as T. Athletic, the nickname is a friendly short form of the place-name. Recorded in W1979/80–90 and W1994–2013. See also Lacemen.

TN, see Team Northumbria under 'Team'.

TNS is a nickname and abbreviation for The New Saints F.C., founded in 2004, in a merger between Oswestry Town F.C. (Shropshire) and Total Network Solutions F.C. Total Network Solutions was the Welsh club Llansantffraid F.C. (nicknamed 'The Saints', founded in 1959 at the Powys border town of Llansantffraid-ym-Mechain), which agreed to take its sponsor's name in 1996. In 2006 the sponsorship lapsed and the club adopted a new name which had the same initials, but one which honoured the nickname traditions of the two original clubs; Wikipedia. See also Blues, Saints.

Toffees / Toffeemen is the famous nickname for Everton F.C. Although there is some doubt over the origins of the name, the two alternative theories are very similar. One is that it is named after a sweetshop called Ma Noblett's, near the Goodison Park stadium and the eighteenth-century lock-up called Prince Rupert's Tower which features on the club's crest. This shop sold Everton Mints, but an alternative shop is Ye Anciente Everton Toffee House, run by Ma Bushell, also in the centre of Everton near the tower and the Queen's Head Hotel. In 1879 the decision was made here to change the name of the club from St Domingo's (founded in 1878 by members of St Domingo's Methodist Church, Everton) to Everton F.C. Ferris 2005 states that Ma Bushell was the original inventer of the Everton mint, but who lost trade after the club moved to Goodison Park, and who responded by getting permission to distribute her toffees inside the ground at match days. The nickname might actually originate in the Everton Mint alone, rather than the nearby toffee shops. The association is commemorated by the Toffee Lady mascot who walks round the perimeter of the pitch throwing free Everton Mints into the crowd before a match starts at Goodison Park. The early sources give the nickname as "The Toffee's", in BoF1905–6 , or 'The Toffees', in the 1933 Ogden card set (both these suggest Ye Anciente Toffee House as the explanation). Also recorded in the 1936 Thomson 'stamp', G1956–76, the 1959 Sweetule card (which gives Mrs Noblett and states she is the inspiration behind the club mascot), Churchill 1958, Norris 1959, Richards 1960, SWSCYB 1962–3 and Avis 1954–70 (spelled Toffies in Avis). However, in the *Rothmans Football Yearbooks* the nickname appears as 'The Toffeemen' from RY1970/1 to 1982/3. This form is continued in the Williams League Directories 1985–95. Rothmans, however, moves to 'The Toffees' in RY1988/9 and so continues to SSY2012/13. See also Bitters / Bitter Blues, Black Watch, Bluenoses, Blues, Dogs of War, Merseysiders, Moonlight Dribblers, People's Club, School of Science.

Toffeemen was the nickname for Lovells Athletic F.C., a works side for the G. F. Lovell and Co. Ltd confectionary firm, based in Newport, Gwent, formed in 1918, folded with the firm in 1969. The company was famous and made the 'Toffee Rex' brand. A short history of the club by Ade Williams appears on the internet, which includes the nickname; Huws 2013.

Ton/s is a nickname for clubs which have this place-name element in the official name, as a short form. The element just means a settlement, a village, an estate, but as a nickname it suggests a team of frightening weight. When it is a separate word, the T requires an extra stress in pronunciation, almost emphasising the 'weight' meaning with an expletive thud. The effect is quite visceral, giving this simple nickname an extra dimension. The nickname might appear in the plural, 'Tons'. The clubs are:

- Bitton A.F.C., founded in 1892. Although the club itself is uncertain of the origins of the nickname, it is clearly a short form of the place-name, similar to many other such in this dictionary. *Ton* can be used as a slang word for the number hundred, but the idea that "other fans assigned it because the locals of Bitton were deemed upper class" seems to be stretching the coincidence too far; W2011–13. See also Boyds, River Boys.

🌐 Brightons F.C. (as 'Tons'), founded in Falkirk in 1990 (cited in an internet source in 2011, not accessible in 2012).

🌐 Clapton F.C., founded in London in 1878; the nickname is 'Tons'. The club originally played as Downs F.C., on Hackney Downs, but changed to Clapton in 1879; W1979/80–2013.

🌐 Greenock Morton F.C., founded in 1874 (as Morton, renaming in 1994); a short form of the second name, which is the name of the first patron of the club, local builder James Morton, either directly or from Morton Terrace, where many of the first players lived. Recorded throughout RY1970/1–SSY2012/13 and RS 1993–2012. See also Pride of the Clyde.

🌐 Morton, see under Greenock Morton.

🌐 Newington Youth Club F.C., founded in Belfast in 1979; Wikipedia. See also Swans.

🌐 Ton Pentre A.F.C., founded in 1935 in Rhondda Cynon Taf; W1994–7. See also Bulldogs, Rhondda Bulldogs.

🌐 Tongwynlais F.C., founded in 1935; recorded in RW1994. The place-name is pronounced 'Ton-Gwynlais', making the short form an easy adaptation. The opening phrase in Welsh means a portion of unploughed land (Owen & Morgan 2007).

Tonics is the nickname for Hindsford A.F.C., founded in Greater Manchester in 1926. The club's website uses the nickname but does not explain it, but records that the club was founded in the midst of the 1926 Miners' Strike by bored miners, without any funds or ground to play on, but soon establishing a name for themselves in local football. The nickname seems therefore to refer to the therapeutic joy which the club brought to its local community in hard times. The club badge shows a deer leaping over a watercourse, adapted from the place-name (deer and ford), but this does not seem ever to have inspired a nickname.

Toon is often used to represent a Northern pronunciation of 'Town' and has been adopted as a nickname for three clubs. The clubs are:

🌐 Alnwick Town F.C., founded in Northumberland in 1879. The club is nearly always recorded without a nickname, but 'The Toon' is printed in W1986.

🌐 Ballymoney United F.C., founded in Co. Antrim in 1944. The club has also had the former names Coronation Blues and B. Athletic and the nickname expresses the Ulster pronunciation; RNI2007. See also United.

🌐 Newcastle United F.C., using the local Geordie pronunciation. The nickname is more often heard for the supporters as Toon Army; Wikipedia. See also Barcodes, Cartoon Army, Entertainers, Frenchcastle, Geordies, Magpies, Skunks, Tyneside Professors, Tynesiders.

Tooners is a nickname for Cove Rangers F.C., founded in Aberdeenshire in 1922. The nickname uses the Northern English and Scots pronunciation of town and means 'towners'. See also Highland Dynamite, Wee Rangers.

Toonsers is the nickname of Dufftown F.C., founded in 1890 in Banffshire. The Northern expression for 'town dwellers' or 'townies' is here presented in the local Scots dialect.

Toosey is a nickname for St Osyth F.C., founded in Essex in 1951. The nickname is based on a popular nickname for the town, a friendly form of the place-name; printed in W1988. See also Saints.

Tooting Terrors was a nickname for Tooting and Mitcham United F.C., founded in London in a merger in 1932; recorded thus in W1979/80–86, and later as Terrors in W1987–2012. The survival of the T.T. form suggests that it may have been used by Tooting alone before the merger, but there seems to have been no particular reason for the nickname other than to suggest fearsomeness. See also Half-Halfs, Lilywhites, Stripes, Terrors.

Tops is a nickname for Coulsdon Town F.C., founded in London in 1968, originally as Reedham Park, then Netherne (1992), then C. Town (2006) before a merger with Salfords in 2007 generated the new name C. United, but the club reverted to the name of C. Town in 2011. The delightful nickname is recorded for United in W2009–10 and it almost certainly refers to the name of the club's earliest ground, which was at Higher Drive Recreation Ground, a play on tops / higher. See also C's.

Torrie is a nickname for Torrington F.C., founded in Devon in 1908; W1994–2007. See also Supergreens.

Tots is the nickname of Totnes and Dartington F.C., founded in Devon in 2005, in a merger of T. Town and D. Sports Club; a pluralised short form, used in *This is Devon*, 3 May 2010.

Totts is the nickname of Totternhoe F.C., founded in Bedfordshire in 1906. A pluralised short form recorded in W1983/4 and W1994–2001.

Tower is used as a nickname for First Tower United F.C., founded in 1920 on the island of Jersey, recorded in W2001 (p. 1022) and also on the club's website.

Towerites was the nickname of the old New Brighton Tower F.C., which existed 1897–1901, named from a prominent building in this Lancashire seaside resort. In 1923 the club was re-established and took the nickname Rakers (q.v.).

Town is a football club name element for a club which wishes to emphasise its links with its home town. It is often used to refer to the club on its own, and has been noticed in the following 141 examples:

- Abingdon Town F.C., founded in Oxfordshire in 1870. The nickname appears in W1980/1, W1983/4–90. See also Abbots, Over the Bridge.
- Alcester Town F.C., founded in Warwickshire in 1927, originally as Alcester Juniors, renaming in 1953; the club folded after appearing in W1993–4, but a flourishing youth side, Alcester Athletic, succeeded them.
- Alton Town F.C., founded in Hampshire in 1947; the club merged with Alton Bass in 1990; W1980/1. For the present club of the same name, see Brewers.

✪ Amesbury Town F.C., founded in Wiltshire in 1904. This side is noted for having played its first match in a field beside Stonehenge, spawning later stories that they had used the monument for goalposts. Recorded in W1997. See also Blues.

✪ Amlwch Town F.C., founded in Anglesey in 1897; Wikipedia.

✪ Ammanford A.F.C., founded in 1991 in a merger of A. Town and A. Athletic; although the suffix is now dropped from the official name, the nickname was inherited from the older club; recorded in RW1994–2011. See also Blackbirds.

✪ Ampthill Town F.C., founded in Bedfordshire in 1881; W1994–8.

✪ Ashton Town A.F.C., founded in 1953 in Greater Manchester, originally as Makerfield Mill; Wikipedia.

✪ Athlone Town F.C., founded in Co. Westmeath in 1887. Recorded in RI1997, 2006.

✪ Baldock Town F.C., founded in Hertfordshire in 2006, adopting the name of an earlier club of 1905–2001. The club is based at the Knights Templar Sports Centre and have a knight on their badge, but do not seem to have used this symbol as a nickname; Wikipedia records 'Town'. See also Reds.

✪ Banbridge Town F.C., founded in Co. Down in 1947; Wikipedia.

✪ Barnoldswick Town F.C., founded in Lancashire in 2003, in a merger between B. United and B. Park Rovers; used on the club's own website as well as Wikipedia. See also Barlick.

✪ Barnstaple Town F.C., founded in Devon in 1904, originally as Pilton Yeo Vale, but renamed as early as 1905; Avis 1966–70. See also Barum.

✪ Beckenham Town F.C., founded in Kent in 1971; W1983/4–93. See also Becks, Reds.

✪ Bewdley Town F.C., reformed in Worcestershire in 1978; Wikipedia. See also Comrades and Vics for previous incarnations.

✪ Bexley United F.C., originally the Kent club Bexleyheath Welling; Wikipedia dates the club as c.1952–76; the nickname is recorded in Avis 1966–70.

✪ Billericay Town F.C., founded in Essex in 1880; recorded in W1979/80–2013. See also Blues, Ricay.

✪ Bracknell Town F.C., founded in Berkshire in 1896, originally as B. Wanderers. W1987–8. See also Robins.

✪ Bridgend Town F.C., founded in South Wales in 1954; used in W1981/2–82/3. See also Brewery Boys, Bridge.

✪ Bridgnorth Town F.C., founded in Shropshire in 1949; W1979/80–2005. See also Meadow Men.

✪ Brighouse Town F.C., founded in West Yorkshire in 1963; W2011–13.

✪ Bromyard Town F.C., founded in Herefordshire in 1893; Wikipedia.

✪ Caldicot Town F.C., founded in Monmouthshire in 1953; recorded in RW1994– 2011. The suffix is also used as a nickname on the club's own website.

✪ Camberley Town F.C., founded in Surrey in 1895, originally as St Michael's

Camberley F.C., then Camberley and Yorktown, and merging with Camberley Wanderers in 1967, to form the present club; W1979/80 and W1985–2013. See also Krooners, Reds.

- Carlton Town F.C., founded in Nottingham in 1903, originally as Sneinton F.C., changing name in 2002; W2008–13. See also Millers.
- Carmarthen Town F.C., founded in 1948; recorded in W1997–2005, RW1998–2011. See also Old Gold.
- Castletown Metropolitan F.C., founded in the ancient capital of the Isle of Man in 1904 (today the capital is Douglas). Here, the nickname is a short form of the place-name; Wikipedia
- Cheadle Town F.C., founded in Greater Manchester in 1961, originally as Grasmere Rovers; Wikipedia.
- Chesterfield Town F.C., founded in Derbyshire in 1884, folding in 1915; BoF1905–6; Wikipedia. See also Blues, Cheaterfield, Spireites, Team of Surprises, Town.
- Cinderford Town A.F.C., founded in Gloucestershire in 1922; W1980/1, W1983/4, W1994–2009. See also Foresters.
- Cirencester Town F.C., founded in Gloucestershire in 1889; W1982/3–90. See also Centurions, Ciren.
- Congleton Town F.C., founded in Cheshire in 1901; W1982/3–5. See also Bears, Humbugs.
- Crawley Town F.C., founded in West Sussex in 1896; W1981/2–5. See also Red Devils, Reds.
- Cwmbrân Town A.F.C., founded in Torfaen Co. Bor. in 1951; W1987 and W1994–2005, RW1994–2003. See also Crows.
- Daventry Town F.C., founded in Northamptonshire in 1886. The club's programme is called *Town Talk* and the nickname is listed in W2011–13.
- Deal Town F.C., founded in Kent in 1908, renaming as Town in 1920. W1983/4–2013. See also Dealers, Fivers.
- Devizes Town F.C., founded in Wiltshire in 1883, originally as Southbroom; W1987–90, W2005–9.
- Downham Town F.C., founded in Norfolk in 1881; W1992–2013. See also Saints.
- Earlestown F.C., originally founded in 1885 at Newton-le-Willows in Merseyside, disbanded in 1911; a new club of the same name was formed in c.1949 and their nickname is recorded in Avis 1966–70. The FCHD does not record the club after 1964.
- Eastbourne Town F.C., founded in Sussex in 1881, originally as Devonshire Park, renaming as Eastbourne before 1890 and adding the Town suffix in 1971; since 2007 'Town' has been the preferred nickname but it does occur earlier: W1987–93, W2008–13. See also Bourne.
- Edgware Town F.C., founded in London in 1939, dissolved in 2008; Avis 1966–70 and Smith 1991/2–95/6. See also Wares.

⚽ Egham Town F.C., founded in Surrey in 1963 as the late reformation of an old club, the Runnymead Rovers (1877–1939); W1985–2008. See also Sarnies, Swans.

⚽ Ellesmere Port Town F.C., founded in Cheshire in 1948, folded 1978, refounded in 1992, folded again in 1994; recorded in Avis 1966–70, W1994. See also Port.

⚽ Enderby Town F.C., founded in Leicestershire in 1900; the club renamed as Leicester United in 1986 but folded in 1996; W1979/80. See also United (for Leicester).

⚽ Exmouth Town F.C., founded in Devon in 1933; W1982/3–2006. See also Blues.

⚽ Fairford Town F.C., founded in Gloucestershire in 1891; W1987–2013.

⚽ Falmouth Town F.C., founded in Cornwall in 1950; W1981/2–2005. See also Ambers.

⚽ Fareham Town, founded in Hampshire in 1946; W1981/2–2008. See also Robins.

⚽ Farnborough Town F.C., founded in Hampshire in 1967, the club reformed after bankruptcy in 2007 as Farnborough; W2003–8. See also Boro, Yellows.

⚽ Farnham Town F.C., founded in Surrey in 1912; W1986–90, W1997–2013.

⚽ Faversham Town F.C., founded in Kent in 1884; W1979/80–2003. See also Creeksiders, Lilywhites, Sorters.

⚽ Fivemiletown United F.C., founded in Co. Tyrone in 1898; Wikipedia.

⚽ Fleet Town F.C., founded in Hampshire in 1890; W1982/3–3/4. See also Blues, Tarn.

⚽ Flint Town United F.C., founded in Flintshire in 1886; recorded in W1994. See also Silkmen.

⚽ Folkestone Town F.C., founded in Kent in 1945, renaming as Folkestone in 1968, as F. and Shepway in 1974, and as F. Town in 1980 before folding in 1990. Recorded in Avis 1966–70 for Folkestone Town, W1979/80–81/2 for Folkestone & Shepway, W1982/3–91 for F. Town.

⚽ Garforth Town A.F.C., founded in West Yorkshire in 1964 and adopting the Town suffix in 1985; Miller & Wright 1996 record 'Town' as a nickname. See also Miners.

⚽ Goole Town F.C., founded in East Yorkshire in 1912, changing the name to Goole A.F.C. in 1997; W1981/2–96. See also Badgers, Vikings.

⚽ Hailsham Town F.C., founded in Sussex in 1885; W1989–90. See also Stringers.

⚽ Halifax A.F.C., founded in West Yorkshire in 1911, dissolved in 2008. Richards 1960 and Avis 1966–70 record this earlier nickname, as did RY1970/1–79/80; Wikipedia also records it for the new FC Halifax Town. See also Shaymen.

⚽ Halstead Town F.C., founded in Essex in 1879; W2001–13.

⚽ Hanwell Town F.C., founded in 1920 in the London borough of Ealing; W1994–2006. See also Geordies, Magpies.

⚽ Harborough Town F.C., founded in Leicestershire in 1975; Wikipedia.

⚽ Harpenden Town F.C., founded in Hertfordshire in 1891; W1994–2013. See also Harps.

⚽ Harrogate Town F.C., founded in North Yorkshire in 1914, reformed in 1935 as

Harrogate Hotspurs, and then 'Town' after the Second World War; W1980/1 and W1998–2013. See also Sulphurites.

💠 Harrow Town F.C., formed in Greater London in 1933 as Roxonian F.C., it was renamed Harrow Town in 1938, then as H. Borough in 1967. The nickname is recorded in Avis 1966.

💠 Hastings Town F.C., now renamed Hastings United F.C. The present club dates to 1894, formed as Rock-a-Nore F.C., then changing to H. and St Leonards Amateurs in 1921 and Hastings Town in 1979, renaming to United in 2002; W1991–2002 as 'Town'. See also Arrows, Claret & Blues, U's, United.

💠 Hatfield Town F.C., founded in Hertfordshire in 1886; W1994–6. See also Blue Boys.

💠 Henley Town F.C., founded in Oxfordshire in 1871; W2001–11. See also Lilywhites.

💠 Hinckley Town F.C., founded in Leicestershire in 1958 as Westfield Wanderers, renaming as Town in 1972 and merging with H. Athletic to form H. United in 1997; W1992–7. See also Eagles, Knitters, Robins, United.

💠 Holmfirth Town F.C., founded in West Yorkshire in 2010; included here in the absence of any known nickname.

💠 Hounslow Town F.C., formed in 1946, renaming as Hounslow F.C. in 1966; the nickname is recorded in Avis 1966–70 and W1979/80–90. The club merged with Feltham in 1995 as a short-lived Feltham and Hounslow.

💠 Hucknall Town F.C. Founded in Nottinghamshire in 1945, originally as Hucknall Colliery Welfare F.C., renamed 'Town' in 1987; W1995–2013. See also Colliers, Yellows.

💠 Huddersfield Town F.C., in widespread use until 'The Terriers' was adopted during the 1969–70 season. Harvey 1959 has no nickname, but it is recorded in Richards 1960, Avis 1966–70, the first *Rothmans Yearbook*: RY1970/1, and a late appearance in Goodall 1982 (p. 220). See also Colnesiders, Scarlet Runners, Terriers.

💠 Hythe Town F.C., founded in Kent in 1910, reforming as Hythe United in 1992, reverting to Town in 1995; W1979/80, W1992, W2006–13. See also Forters, Reds.

💠 Irlam Town F.C., founded in Greater Manchester before 1976, folded after 1995; W1982/3–5.

💠 Ipswich Town F.C., founded in Suffolk in 1878. The nickname is recorded as an alternative to Blues throughout RY1970/1–SS2012/13.

💠 Kendal Town F.C., founded in Cumbria in 1919 as Netherfield A.F.C., taking the present name in 2000; W2003–12. See also Field.

💠 Kingsbury Town F.C., founded by ex-servicemen in London in 1919, merging with London Tigers in 2006, to form Kingsbury London Tigers (see Tigers), renamed London Tigers in 2011. W1981/2–8 and W1994, Smith 1991/2–95/6. See also Kings, and Mustard Pots.

☻ Knighton Town F.C., founded in Powys in 1887; recorded in RW1994–8. See also Borderers, Radnor Robins.

☻ Leighton Town F.C., founded in Bedfordshire in 1885; Smith 1992/3–95/6. See also Buzzards, Reds, Sand Dobbers.

☻ Llandudno Town F.C., founded in 1988 according to the club's badge, but with earlier clubs back to 1878; the nickname is recorded in RW1994–7 but nowadays the club is frequently called just Llandudno F.C., without a suffix or a nickname.

☻ Llangollen Town F.C., founded in 1908; recorded in RW2011.

☻ Llanidloes Town F.C., founded in Powys in 1875; recorded in RW2011. See also Daffodils / Daffs / Superdaffs.

☻ Longford Town F.C., founded in Co. Longford in 1924; RI1997 and 2006, and club's own website. See also De Town.

☻ Loughborough Athletic and Football Club, founded in Leicestershire in 1886, folded in 1900. The Wikipedia article for this club says that it is often referred to as Town despite there being no evidence that it was ever so called. The nickname and false suffix is used in Pickering 1994. 'Town' could still have been the nickname with L.A.F.C. the official name.

☻ Lydney Town F.C., founded in Gloucestershire in 1911; W1982/3–5 and W2008–13.

☻ Lymington Town F.C., formed in Hampshire in 1876. The club merged with Wellworthy Athletic in 1986 to form Lymington A.F.C., and then merged with New Milton in 1998 to form Lymington and New Milton. Meanwhile, a breakaway Lymington Town also reformed in 1998 and is nicknamed Town. In 2007, the merged club changed its name to New Milton Town; Wikipedia. See also Linnets.

☻ Maldon Town F.C., formed in Essex in 1946, merging with Tiptree United in 2009, to form Maldon and Tiptree (see Blues, Hoops, Jam Makers, Strawberries); W1990 and W2001–7 cites 'Town' for Maldon, and Wikipedia continues to list 'Town' as a nickname for the new club. See also Blues.

☻ Manortown United F.C., founded in Dublin in 1969; Wikipedia. See also United.

☻ Melksham Town F.C., founded in Wiltshire in 1876; W1985–90.

☻ Mexborough Town Athletic, F.C., founded in South Yorkshire before 1885, as M. F.C., the club adopted the Town and Athletic suffixes in 1974. The club is now called A.F.C. Sportsman Rovers. Recorded in W1989. See also Athletic, Boro, Pocket.

☻ Mildenhall Town F.C., founded in Suffolk in 1898; W1992–2000. See also Hall, Yellows.

☻ Morriston Town A.F.C., founded in Swansea in the 1940s, originally as Midland Athletic; Wikipedia.

☻ Newbury Town F.C., founded in Berkshire in 1887, dissolved in 1995. The new Newbury F.C. (established 2002) has recently renamed itself Town and has 'Town' on its badge; W1979/80–96 for the old club, Wikipedia and club website for the new.

⚽ Newry Town F.C., founded in Co. Down in 1923; recorded in RI1997. The town itself became a city and the club renamed as City in 2004; no nickname is listed in RNI2007; the club folded in 2012 but it is hoped that it will be reformed; Wikipedia. See also Bordermen.

⚽ Northampton Town F.C., founded in 1897. The nickname is used in BoF1905–6. See also Cobblers, Shoe Army, Tayn.

⚽ Northallerton Town F.C., founded in North Yorkshire in 1895; W1994–2013.

⚽ Old Woodstock Town F.C., founded in Oxfordshire in 1998 in a merger of Woodstock Town (c.1910?) and Old Woodstock (1920). The club is placed here in the absence of any known nickname; Wikipedia.

⚽ Oldham Boro F.C., founded in Greater Manchester in 1964, originally as Oldham Dew, a works side for the building contractors George Dew. The club renamed as O. Town in 1985, and then as O. Boro in 2009; the nickname appears on Wikipedia.

⚽ Omagh Town Football and Athletic Club, founded in Co. Tyrone in 1962, originally as O. Celtic (1962–9). Recorded in RI1997, FBD. The club folded in 2005.

⚽ Ossett Town F.C., founded in West Yorkshire in 1936; Avis 1966–70, W2006–13. See also Golds, Unicorns.

⚽ Oswestry Town F.C., founded in 1860 in Shropshire but playing in the Welsh leagues; 'Town' is listed in W2003. In 2006 the club merged with Total Network Solutions and is now called The New Saints (see under Saints). See also Blues.

⚽ Pershore Town 88 F.C., founded in Worcestershire in 1988, in a merger between P. United, P. Rec. Rovers and P. Bullets; W1994–2005 and on the club website.

⚽ Petersfield Town F.C., founded in Hampshire in 1993 as a successor to P. United (1889). Placed here in the absence of a nickname. The club launched a competition to find a new nickname in 2011, but no conclusion was reached. For the old club, see also Reds, United.

⚽ Polegate Town F.C., founded in East Sussex in 1915, originally as Polegate Comrades, later P. United and Polegate F.C. since the 1930s. The club was reformed as Town in 2006. The entry is placed here in the absence of a known nickname, but the club's website shows that 'Town' is in a different colour on the club badge (suggesting it is the nickname), and the club's history gives the side who re-established the club in 2006 the nickname 'The Refounders'.

⚽ Radstock Town F.C., founded in Somerset in 1895; W1982/3–90. See also Miners, Rads, Reds.

⚽ Reading Town F.C., founded in Berkshire in 1966, originally as Lower Burghfield F.C.; W2006–13.

⚽ Ringwood Town F.C., founded in Hampshire in 1879, originally as R. Hornets, reformed as R. Comrades in 1918, taking the name 'Town' in 1936; Wikipedia. Inserted here in the absence of any other known nickname for the club.

⚽ Romsey Town F.C., founded in Hampshire in 1886; W1998.

❀ Rugby Town F.C., founded in Warwickshire in 1956, originally as Valley Sports. The present name dates from 2005 and it appears as a nickname in W2007–9. See also Valley.

❀ Runcorn Town F.C., founded in Cheshire in 1968, originally as Mond Rangers, renaming in 2005; Wikipedia.

❀ Ruthin Town F.C., founded in 1951; recorded in RW2011. See also Blues, Ruths / The Ruthless.

❀ Seaford Town F.C., founded in East Sussex in 1889; W1993–6. See also Dockers.

❀ Sevenoaks Town F.C., founded in Kent in 1883; W2011–13. See also Oaks.

❀ Sherborne Town, founded in Dorset in 1894. The club is placed here in the absence of a known nickname.

❀ Shettleston Juniors Football and Athletic Club, founded in Glasgow in 1903; Wikipedia, SFHA.

❀ Shifnal Town F.C., founded in Shropshire in 1964; W1982/3–6. See also Reds.

❀ Shirebrook Town F.C., founded in Nottinghamshire in 1985, originally as S. Colliery, renaming in 1993; 'Town' is used as a nickname on the club's own website. See also Brook.

❀ Shirley Town F.C., founded in West Midlands in 1926, originally as West Shirley Athletic, renaming 1974 (FCHD); W1983/4.

❀ Shrewsbury Town F.C., recorded throughout RY1970/1–SSY2012/13 See also Blues, Salop, Shrews.

❀ Sleaford Town F.C., founded in Lincolnshire in 1968; W2010–13. See also Greens.

❀ Soham Town Rangers F.C., founded in Cambridgeshire in 1947, in the merger of S. Town and S. Rangers; W1988–2013. See also Rangers.

❀ Southall Town F.C., founded in Middlesex in 2000, folded in 2004; W2003–4. See also Wood.

❀ St Helen's Town A.F.C.; founded in Lancashire in 1903 but reformed in 1946; W1979/80–85 (as 'Town Ground', clearly the ground name in error), as 'Town' in W1986, W1994–13. See also Saints.

❀ Stafford Town F.C., founded in Staffordshire in 1976; W1995–2004. See also Reds.

❀ Staines Town F.C., established in Surrey in 1892; Avis 1966–70. See also Leghorns, Linos, Massive, Old Lagonda, Swans.

❀ Stamford A.F.C., founded in Lincolnshire in 1986; occasionally used to distinguish the club from the other Stamford side, Blackstones, though not recorded in print (thanks to Kevin Troop). See also Daniels.

❀ Stratford Town F.C., founded in Warwickshire in 1944 (named as Stratford Town Amateurs, 1964–70); W1987–2006, W2009–13.

❀ Tamworth F.C., founded in Staffordshire in 1933; W1994–2005. See also Lambs, Reds.

❀ Thatcham Town F.C., founded in Berkshire in 1894; W1982/3–83/4. See also Kingfishers.

☻ Thetford Town F.C., founded in Norfolk in 1883; W1987–91 and Miller & Wright 1996. See also Brecklanders.

☻ Thrapston Town F.C., founded in Northamptonshire in 1960. The club motto is *Oppido Servire*, or 'service to the town' and 'Town' is used as a nickname on the club website. See also Thrapo, Venturas.

☻ Tipton Town F.C., founded in West Midlands in 1948, originally as Ocker Hill United; Wikipedia.

☻ Wallingford Town F.C., founded in Oxfordshire in 1922; the club merged with W. United in 1995; W1983/4–95. See also Wally.

☻ Warminster Town F.C., founded in Wiltshire in 1885; W1987–90. See also Red and Blacks.

☻ Warrington Town F.C., founded in 1949, originally as Stockton Heath Albion, renamed Warrington in 1961; W1992–2013. See also Levers, Warriors, Wire/s, Yellows.

☻ Wellington A.F.C., founded in Somerset in 1896; W1987–90 (the club itself wrongly called Town here though the nickname seems valid). See also Tangerines, Wellie.

☻ Whitby Town F.C., founded in North Yorkshire in 1880; Smith 1993–4. See also Blues, Seasiders.

☻ Witney Town F.C., founded in Oxfordshire in 1885, replaced by W. United in 2001; W1994–7. See also Blanketmen.

☻ Witham Town F.C., founded in Essex in 1947; W1987–2013.

☻ Wivenhoe Town F.C., founded in Essex in 1925; W1982/3 and W1987. See also Dragons.

☻ Wokingham Town F.C., founded in Berkshire in 1875; W1979/80–2004. The club merged with Emmbrook in 2004. See also Oakey, Satsumas.

☻ Woodford Town F.C., founded in Greater London in 1937. The club folded in 2003; W1980/1–93. See also Woods.

☻ Woodley Town F.C., founded in Berkshire in 1904; W2010–13.

☻ Wrexham F.C. Founded in what is now Wrexham Co. Bor. in 1872, reformed in 1883; Wikipedia. See also Red Army, Red Dragons, Robins.

Towners is a nickname for Enfield Town F.C., which was founded in 2001 as a breakaway group from Enfield F.C. still existed (that team reformed in 2007 as Enfield 1893 F.C. and is nicknamed The E's); W2003–13 and Wikipedia. See also ET's.

Townies is a nickname for two clubs, as a pluralised friendly form of 'Town'. The clubs are:

☻ Kentish Town F.C., founded in the London borough of Camden in 2003; one of the few uses of 'Town' where it appears in the original place-name; W2011–13.

☻ Nuneaton Town F.C. between 1894 and 1937. It was founded in Warwickshire in 1889 as Nuneaton St Nicholas, but renamed 'Town' in 1894, succeeded by

Nuneaton Borough F.C. in 1937. The current Nuneaton Town was born in 2008; Wikipedia, for the earlier club. See also Boro, Nuns, Saints.

Tractor Boys is a recent nickname for Ipswich Town A.F.C. The name refers to the agriculture which is the mainstay of the local economy, and seems to have been first used in the 1998–9 season. It became very popular in 2000–1 during the club's period in the Premiership; it allows journalists to adopt headlines like "Tractor Boys Plough On" (*Daily Telegraph*, 2 February 2002). The club's badge has featured a stylish Suffolk Punch white horse playing with a football, since 1972, also emphasising the local economy. A traditional rivalry with Norwich is called the East Anglian Derby, but this is nicknamed the Old Farm Derby (a humourous allusion to the Old Firm Derby in Glasgow, again emphasising the local agriculture). The nickname never appeared in the *Rothmans Yearbook*, but is printed in SSY2003/4–12/13. See also Binners / Binmen, Blues, Superblues, Town, Witches.

Tractormen is a nickname for Massey Ferguson F.C., based at Coventry and founded in 1956, originally as a works side for the factory making the tractors; W2005.

Trams is the nickname of Croydon F.C., founded in Greater London in 1953, originally as Croydon Amateurs. The nickname only dates from 2000, when the Croydon Tramlink system was installed, which runs beside the home ground, though it also seems to be a humorous contrast with 'The Rams' of Croydon Athletic; W2001–13. See also Blues.

Trawler Boys is a nickname of Lowestoft Town F.C., founded in Suffolk in 1887 and renamed 'Town' in 1890. The Suffolk town is a famous port, fishing community and seaside resort; the nickname is only lately recorded, so it may have been coined in response to the 'Tractor Boys' of Ipswich; W2011–13. See also Blues.

Trawlermen is the nickname for Fleetwood Town F.C. Founded in 1997 (but earlier clubs go back to 1908), the nickname is a strong reminder of the importance of the fishing industry to this Lancashire coastal town. An anchor appears on the club's badge, and the club's supporters are nicknamed the Cod Army. Recorded in SSY2012/13–12/13. See also Cod Army, Fishermen, Reds.

Traws is a nickname for two Welsh clubs as a short form of the place-name: Trawsfynydd F.C. in Powys (1946–57) and Trawsgoed F.C. in Ceredigion; Huws 2013.

Trees is a nickname for clubs with these letters in their official name. The clubs are:

☻ Ashtree Highfield F.C., founded in Oldbury, Birmingham, in 1918, first as Smethwick Highfield, renaming in 1986 and renaming again to Sandwell Borough in 1989 before folding in 2001; a short form of the place-name which continued to be used for Sandwell; W1989 (for Ashtree), W1990–2001 (for Sandwell). See also Stags.

☻ Rowntree Mackintosh F.C., founded as Rowntree as a works side for the famous chocolate factory in York before 1897, they renamed after the company's merger with Mackintosh in 1969, and then became Nestlé Rowntree in 1988. The Trees nickname is recorded in W1982/3–6. See also Jo Row, Rowntrees.

⊛ Sandwell Borough, see under Ashtree Highfield, above.

Tribesmen / Tribal Army are nicknames for Galway United F.C., founded in Co. Galway in 1937, originally as G. Rovers. The nickname refers to the famous 'Tribes of Galway', which were the fourteen merchant families who dominated the commercial and political life of the city between the thirteenth and nineteenth centuries. The expression is said to have been coined by members of Cromwell's army, originally in a derogatory spirit, but it is now a nickname commonly used with pride for the whole county of Galway. Recorded in RI1997, 2006. See also Maroon Army.

Trickies is a nickname for Northwich Victoria F.C., founded in Cheshire in 1874. Obviously suggesting a side that is tricky to play against, the nickname probably comes from a rhyming phrase such as "Tricky Vickies"; W1989–90 and W1999–2013. See also Greens, Vics.

Tricky Trees is a recent nickname for Nottingham Forest F.C. Founded in 1865, the club was called Forest from the outset from their use of the Forest Recreation Ground (1865–79). The Forest in the ground name is derived from Sherwood Forest. The club badge features a prominent single tree with the word Forest beneath it. Recorded in Pickering 1994. See also Forest/Foresters, Garibaldi Reds, Pied Pipers, Reds, Robin Hoods.

Trinity is a nickname for two clubs with the religious word Trinity in their official names. The clubs are:

⊛ Gainsborough Trinity F.C. Founded in Lincolnshire in 1873 as a church side for Holy Trinity church, it was first called Trinity Recreationists; Wikipedia. See also Blues, Holy Blues, Recreationists.

⊛ Sutton Trinity F.C., founded in Nottinghamshire in 1908. Sutton-in-Ashfield has a Trinity Methodist church, with which the club must have had a connection; W1982/3–83/4. The club seems to have disappeared after 1987.

Trins was the nickname of Ettingshall Holy Trinity F.C., founded in Wolverhampton in 1920, originally as a church side. In the club's early years it played in a league called the Wednesbury Church and Chapel League; a pluralised short form of the last word, recorded in W1994–2005. The club has folded.

Triple A's is the nickname for Chirk A.A.A.F.C., standing for Amateur Athletic Association; founded in 1876 at Wrexham Co. Bor.; Wikipedia. See also Colliers.

Trojans was the nickname for Monaghan United F.C., founded in Co. Monaghan in 1979, as recorded in RI1997, and still in use in archived match reports on the internet from 2005. It was replaced with a short form of the place-name (and so appears in RI2006). Trojans is a popular official name for sporting clubs. The Derry-based Trojans F.C. (see Blues) has a badge with a classical helmet and a Latin motto *Unus Sumus* ('we are one'), showing that the suffix is best understood in the same classical context as names like Corinthians and Spartans. As a nickname for a club with no classical suffix, however, the sense would be that of the Trojan Horse, suggesting a dangerous threat from outsiders, newcomers to the scene, all entirely relevant ideas for a sporting side (and the sense of intrusion is why the nickname is now used for computer spy-bugs). The place-name is pronounced 'Monahan', raising the possibility that a rhyming phrase may have encouraged the initial use. See also Grecians for another nickname based on the Siege of Troy. See also Magic Mons / Mons.

Trotters is a nickname for two clubs, and probably uses the colloquial expression for wandering or running, rather than the use of the word for pigs' or sheep's feet (which, of course, has the same ultimate meaning). The nickname originates with Bolton Wanderers. The two clubs are:

⚽ Bolton Wanderers F.C., founded in Greater Manchester in 1874, originally as a church side called Christ Church F.C. The nickname remains ambiguous, and was so in its early usage. It simultaneously carries three meanings: the sense of 'Wandering'; the name of a local food dish using sheep's feet (called trotters); and it may have been a nickname generally used for the people of Bolton before the football club.

(1) Trotters, meaning 'those who trot, or walk', is a mainstream English word but is more popular in the North than the South, and still widely used in Lancashire, so it could easily have been used to express the club suffix, with no double meaning intended. The club tradition is that the Wanderers suffix came after a falling out with the local vicar in 1877, which resulted in the loss of the club's ground; the club was unable to find a permanent replacement pitch until 1895, at Burnden Park, and so were 'wandering' for eighteen years. 'The Trotters' nickname would therefore be a local, slightly humorous, reference to this situation. However, the 1905–6 *Book of Football* gives a slightly different explanation: "The name [Wanderers] was suggested by the fact that they had to wander [from the Christ Church Sunday School building, for meetings] to a neighbouring hostelry, the Gladstone Hotel, near Pike's Lane" (p.114).

(2) Trotters is certainly a local food dish, made from sheep's feet, but attempts to explain how it could have transferred to the football club are difficult. The 1933 Ogden card gives the explanation as "Boiled sheeps' feet, familarly known as trotters, are supposed to be a favourite dish with the people of Bolton, and the story runs that on the occasion of one famous match a big supply was provided for visitors. Piles of sheeps' feet were displayed in the shop windows and they created such an impression that the Wanderers were at once dubbed the 'Trotters'. The nickname still survives although it is not as commonly used as some years ago." However, the card features on its cartoon an image of a tramp, strongly suggesting that the artist was thinking on the 'wandering' lines even if the text gives a different idea. Other references are also ambiguous: Johnston 1934 uses both Trotters and Wanderers as nicknames in the same entry, and the amusing Vernon 1970–1 pamphlet has "Bolton are called The Trotters after their founder who was a pork butcher." and "Squelch! Nonsense.

It's because they never stop running." The nickname appears in Churchill 1958 and Richards 1960; and on the 1959 Sweetule card (with 'tripe and trotters' being a popular Bolton dish as the explanation), and in Norris 1959, also for the local dish. Another story, that during the nineteenth century one of the pitches was adjacent to a piggery, is unconvincing. There is no easy way to link the local dish to the football club and those who have done so seem to be thinking of the 'wandering' meaning at the same time.

(3) There is no doubt that the expression had a specific local meaning before the football club, which could have developed into a general nickname for the people of Bolton. Transfer to the football club would be a natural process, if there could be certainty that the expression really was a nickname for the people of Bolton. Dobson 1973 summarises references from nineteenth-century dialect dictionaries and memoirs showing that 'to trot' was a South Lancashire expression meaning "to joke, satirize, provoke, mislead by way of amusement to the trotter" (from Samuel Bamford, *Dialect of South Lancashire...* (1854, revised edition of his *Tawk o' Seawth Lankeshur*, of 1850)). Dobson then cites accounts of two, more localised, 'trotting' incidents, one at Whittle in Bolton in 1855 and another recalled in Henry Marriott Richardson's *Reminiscenses of Forty Years in Bolton* in 1884. Shawcross 1961 favours this theory and states that 'Trotters' is a general nickname for the people of Bolton. If it was a nickname, meaning 'The Tricksters' or 'The Jokers', it would be entirely in keeping with other such nicknames in Britain (compare, for example 'Tykes', recorded in 1811 as a 'Yorkshire clown'). The etymology of the word is not clear. It perhaps derives from exactly the same mainstream word, because there is a sense that joke tellers 'pull legs' or take people 'for a ride'. Ferris 2005 says that "the team was once full of pranksters and therefore given the Old English name *trotter*, which meant 'practical joker'." But no such Old English word is known to have existed.

So, the nickname does not quite escape its ambiguity, but it is best explained as a combination of (1) and (3), with the local food dish discounted altogether. Recorded in the 1936 Thomson 'stamp' album, G1956–76, SWSCYB 1962–3 and Avis 1966–70, throughout RY and SSY from 1970/1 to 2012/13. See also Noblot / Notlob, Reds, Savage Six, Spots, Wanderers, Whites / Whitemen.

Buckley Town F.C., founded in Flintshire in 1978, in a merger between B. Wanderers and B. Rovers. The nickname was no doubt inherited by the present club from Buckley Wanderers. It may have been inspired in tribute to the Bolton nickname but is probably an independent coining meaning 'those who wander', discussed as the first meaning in the previous entry; Wikipedia. See also Bucks, Claymen, Wanderers.

Tudors is the nickname for Hemel Hempstead Town F.C. Founded in 1885 as Apsley F.C., the name changed to the present one in 1955. The club has a distinctive red badge showing an image of Tudor King Henry VIII, who visited the town in 1539 and gave it a royal charter; W2004–13. See also Hemel.

Tuffs is a nickname for Tuffley Rovers F.C., founded in Gloucestershire in 1929; the nickname appears on a badge in AFBC. See also Rovers.

Tulips is the nickname of Spalding United F.C., founded in Lincolnshire in 1921. The town of Spalding is famous for its annual Flower Parade, in celebration of the local bulb-growing and agricultural economy; this event is often called The Tulip Parade, as the flower is a popular choice in the design of the colourful floats which progress through the town during the festival. In 2008 Spalding was host to the World Tulip Summit. The tulip is regularly used as a symbol for the town (e.g., in Christmas lights), and a red tulip is the club's badge. The nickname is longstanding: Addis 1995 reprints a newspaper cartoon of 1951 which uses a tulip to represent the club (p. 37); W1979/80–2013.

Turfs is the nickname for Tregaron Turfs F.C., founded in Ceredigion at an uncertain date (internet coverage seems to start in 2008). The nickname is well-established, appearing on Twitter and in the *Cambrian News* for 15 January 2013. Richard Huws reports that the word was first used for a team in 1919 and it refers to the Cors Caron, or Tregaron Bog, an area used for turf-cutting when peat was a major part of the local economy, and beside which the club played; Huws 2013.

Turfites was an early nickname for Burnley F.C. at about the time of their entry into the English League in 1888–9. It comes from the name of their home ground, Turf Moor, to which they moved in 1883. Recorded in G1956–65, Churchill 1958, Richards 1960, AA 1960, Avis 1966–70, RY1970/1 and Moss 1983. Dobson 1973 adds that the nickname 'Burnley Turfers' has spread to being used generally for people from Burnley. See also Clarets, Dingles, Gene Puddle, Moorites, Royalites, Turfites.

Turks is a nickname for Drogheda United F.C., founded in Co. Louth in 1975, in a merger of D. United (1919) and D. F.C. (1962). The Islamic star and crescent symbols appear on the club badge, taken from the civic arms. Drogheda shares these symbols with the city of Portsmouth and for the same reason, they were both given charters by the 'Crusader' king, Richard I. A similar badge, and the same club colours of claret and blue, are used by a Turkish side, Trabzonspor, which has now become Drogheda's 'brother' team. Their own nickname is 'Black Sea Storm' in Turkish, but the nickname of Drogheda derives from the club badge rather than this friendship; Wikipedia. See also Boynesiders, Drogs / Super Drogs, United.

Turnbull's Tornadoes was an unofficial nickname for the Edinburgh side Hibernian F.C., during the successful years of the Eddie Turnbull management (1971–80); Wikipedia. See also Cabbage, Hibs / Hibees.

Turnips is a derogatory nickname for Bristol City F.C., coined by Plymouth Argyle supporters. Presumably it refers to the importance of agriculture in Somerset, but it may also be a slight pun on the expression 'turn up for the books', or 'turn up for the bookies', which refers to situations where the horses with bets on them fail to win, so the bookies keep their money; internet forums. See also Babes, Cider Army,

City, Eighty-Twoers / 1982 Ltd, Reds, Robins, Slave Traders, Turnips, Wurzels.

Turra is the main nickname for Turriff United F.C., founded in Aberdeenshire in 1954; a friendly short form of the place-name, recorded in RS2011–12. See also United.

Tute is the nickname of East Chevington F.C., founded in Northumberland before the 1946–7 season, when they won the County Junior Cup. The nickname is a short form of 'Institute', for the East Chevington Social Club and Institute in Morpeth. The nickname appears in several on-line match reports from *The Morpeth Herald*.

Tweedsiders is a nickname for Kelso United F.C., founded in Roxburghshire in 1924. Kelso is on the River Tweed. Recorded in RS1993–7, 2000–1, SFHA.

Two Blues is a nickname for clubs which play in a combination of different shades of blue. These shades are often called 'Cambridge and Oxford' blues. The clubs are:

⚽ Arlesey Town F.C., founded in Bedfordshire in 1891. The club plays in a mixed dark-and-pale-blue strip; W2005–9. See also Blues.

⚽ Bishop Auckland F.C., founded in Co. Durham in 1886, from the two shades of pale and dark blue on their strip. The nickname appears as the title of the club programme (e.g. in W2000, p. 280). See also Bishops.

⚽ The 61 F.C. founded in Luton, Bedfordshire, in 1961, for their sky and royal blue combinations. W1994–8. See also Blues.

Tye is the nickname of the Sussex side, Peacehaven and Telscombe F.C., founded in 1923. Telscombe Tye is the full name of the area of common land in which the village lies; W1979/80 and W1987–2005. See also Haven.

Tykes is the main nickname of Barnsley F.C., founded in Yorkshire in 1887, originally as St Peter's F.C., changing name to Barnsley in 1899. 'Tykes' has long been a nickname for Yorkshiremen, and so easily transfers to a Yorkshire club. It is of uncertain origin but is considered to come from an Old Norse word for a dog, *tík*, later used to mean a contemptible dog. The OED records the word in two sources from c.1400, one meaning a dog and the other meaning 'a dog of a man'. As a nickname for Yorkshiremen it also occurs surprisingly early, in the 1699 *New Dictionary of the ... Canting Crew* ("*Yorkshire-Tike*, a Yorkshire manner of Man", Simpson 2010), and in other early sources from 1721 and 1761. In Chappel 1811 it is defined as "a Yorkshire clown". It is also the nickname for Rugby Union club Leeds Carnegie and has been used for the Yorkshire cricket team. The nickname is recorded for Barnsley on the 1933 Ogden card, without explanation, but the cartoon shows a strange bulldog-like mongrel, and this tradition survives in the mascot, Toby Tyke (famous for having cocked his leg against Manchester City supporters on Boxing Day 1996). In Yorkshire speech, the word is definitely used affectionately. Recorded later in Avis 1966–70, G1976 and throughout RY and SSY from 1970/1 to 2012/13. See also Battling Barnsley, Colliers, Reds, Saints.

Tyneside Professors appears to have been an unofficial nickname for Newcastle United, perhaps before the First World War. It is used in an essay by Roland Allen

(1967), concerning the year 1910, which also says they were "the artists and aristocrats of Soccer". Newcastle became a real university city in 1963. See also Barcodes, Cartoon Army, Entertainers, Frenchcastle, Geordies, Magpies, Skunks, Toon, Tynesiders.

Tynesiders is a nickname for at least three clubs based in Tyneside. The clubs are:

⚽ Gateshead F.C. Founded in 1977 but with several previous clubs closing in 1919, 1974 and 1977, the club's descent goes back to South Shields Adelaide Athletic, which made the bold move to Gateshead in 1930. The nickname is recorded in Barton 1984 & 1985, W1987–2013 and SSY2010/11–12/13. The iconic symbol, The Angel of the North statue at Gateshead, now appears on the club's badge. See also Boro, Heed, Laides.

⚽ Newcastle United F.C., used in BoF1905–6 (which does not use 'The Magpies') and recorded in Avis 1954–70 alongside 'Magpies'. See also Barcodes, Cartoon Army, Entertainers, Frenchcastle, Geordies, Magpies, Skunks, Toon, Tyneside Professors.

⚽ Northumbria University F.C., founded in 1999, changing name in 2003 to 'Team Northumbria F.C.'; used in journalism but often as 'South Tynesiders'. See also Team.

U's is a nickname for clubs called United. The examples are:

⚽ Abingdon United F.C., formed in Oxfordshire in 1946; recorded in W1995–2013.

⚽ Cambridge United F.C., founded in 1912, originally as Abbey F.C., from a district of the city, renaming as Cambridge United in 1951. The initialism is recorded in Avis 1966–70; RY1993/4–2002/3 and SSY 2003/4–5/6, W2006–13 and SSY2006/7–12/13. See also United, Wasps.

⚽ Colchester United F.C. Founded in Essex in 1937. Recorded as U's in Avis 1966–70, G1976, Goodall 1982, W1982/3–92, and throughout RY and SSY from 1970/1 to 2012/13 (except for 1991/2). See also Ewes, Grandad's Army, Oystermen.

⚽ Eastbourne United Association F.C., founded in 1894, originally as First Sussex Royal Engineers and changing name several times before adopting E. United in 1951. The club merged with Shinewater Association in 2003. Recorded in W1979/80–2013. A single reference to a nickname 'Raiders' in W1997 appears to be an error. For Shinewater, see Shine. See also Comrades, United.

⚽ Hastings United F.C. The present club dates to 1894, formed as Rock-a-Nore F.C., then changing to H. and St Leonards Amateurs in 1921 and Hastings Town in 1979. In 1985 another club called H. United folded. They had been formed in 1948 and were nicknamed 'The U's', and Town eventually assumed their name and nickname in 2002. Recorded in Avis 1966–70 and W1979/80–5 for the older United, W2010–13 for the new. Interestingly, W1987 records the nickname 'The U' which is definitely for this later club, still called Town at that point. This may be a mistake, or an illustration of how the club was assuming some of the identity of the older United long before they actually renamed. If the nickname is correct, it is a unique form for United. See also Arrows, Claret & Blues, Town, United.

⚽ Oxford United F.C. The Headington club was formed in 1893 and added the word United to its name within a few months, changing to Oxford United in 1960. The U stands for United, not for the University, though even before the change of name, Headington presented itself as the team for the city (its badge in 1949 shows an ox crossing a ford); G1976, RY1976/7–SS2006/7, W2007–10 and SSY2007/8–12/13. See also Boys from Up the Hill, Dons, United, Yellows.

⚽ Sutton United F.C., founded in London in 1898, in a merger between Sutton Guild Rovers and Sutton A.F.C.; W1980/1–2013, Goodall 1982. See also Gambians.

⚽ Thame United F.C., founded in Oxfordshire in 1883; W1986, W1993. See also United, Utd.

⚽ Thanet United F.C., formed in Kent in a temporary renaming of Margate F.C. between 1981 and 1989; W1981/2–1982/3. See also Gate, Islanders, Lilywhites.

U2's is the nickname of the Co. Londonderry club Oxford United Stars F.C., founded in 1937. The nickname appears to pun neatly on the 'U' of the English Oxford United and the 'U2' Dublin-based rock band founded in 1976, though it is not clear whether the 2 stands for the number or the word 'too' spelled in textspeak; Wikipedia. See also Stars.

Undertakers is the nickname of Port Glasgow Juniors F.C., founded in Greenock in 1948, and taking the name of an earlier club of 1880–1912. One suggestion for the nickname is that an early patron was a funeral director, but by far the more obvious explanation is that the club wears black. The earlier club started in all-black before switching to dark blue, and the present club wears black-and-white stripes with black shorts. Nevertheless, 'The Undertaker' is a nickname also found in aggressive sports like wrestling, and suggests a killing performance with style; Wikipedia, SFHA.

Unicorns is a nickname for Ossett Albion A.F.C., founded in West Yorkshire in 1944. A heraldic unicorn's head forms the club badge, but there seems no particular reason for the original choice of the symbol; Wikipedia. See also Albion, Golds.

United is a football club name suffix which is usually deployed when two teams merge to form a single united team, as in the case of Newcastle United (see 'Magpies'), or as a fresh team succeeding from an older one which had been closed down (as in Leeds United and Peterborough United); but sometimes the name is used simply to suggest solidarity. The word can be used as a nickname for any club called United, and has been noticed for the following sixty-one:

⚽ Alness United F.C., founded in Highland (Ross and Cromarty) in 1935; Wikipedia.

⚽ Ardley United F.C., founded in Oxfordshire in 1945; included here in the absence of any other known nickname for the club.

⚽ Annagh United F.C., founded in Portadown, Co. Armagh, in 1963; Wikipedia.

⚽ Ash United F.C., founded in Surrey in 1911; W2008–12. See also Green Army.

⚽ Ashton United F.C., founded in Ashton-under-Lyne, Cheshire, in 1878, originally as Hurst F.C., renaming in 1947; W1979/80 and W1993. See also Robins.

⚽ Banbury United F.C. Founded in 1931 as Spencer Villa, a works club, it became Banbury Spencer in 1934, then Banbury United in 1965. The nickname is listed only once, in W1980/1. See also Gay Puritans, Puritans.

⚽ Bedford United F.C., founded in Bedfordshire in 1957, originally as a works side for the printers Diemer & Reynolds. The nickname is recorded in W1994–2002. In 2002, the club merged with another local club called Unione Sportiva Valerio (named in Italian and adding the surname of the founder, Nicola Valerio). The new club was initially called Bedford United and Valerio, and was still nicknamed United (W2003–6). After 2006, the club adopted the simpler name of Bedford F.C., with no apparent nickname.

⚽ Bexhill United F.C., founded in East Sussex in 2002, in a merger of B. Town and B. A.A.C. ; club's own website. For the predecessor club, see Green Machine.

⚽ Biggleswade United F.C., founded in Bedfordshire in 1959; Wikipedia.

⚽ Ballymena United F.C., founded in Co. Antrim in 1928; RI1997. See also Braidmen, Light Blues, Sky Blues.

⚽ Boston United F.C., founded in Lincolnshire in 1933. Although the 'Pilgrims' nickname was already being used by the time of W1979/80, Goodall 1982 uses the nickname 'United' for this club. See also Pilgrims, Stumpites.

⚽ Brandon United F.C., founded in Co. Durham in 1968; W1994–2013. See also Blues.

⚽ Brightlingsea United F.C., founded in Essex in 1928, in a merger between B. Town (1919) and B. Athletic (1908); the club merged with Regent Park Rangers in 2005 to form B. Regent; this nickname appears in W1990. See also Oystermen, Seasiders, Tics.

⚽ Cambridge United F.C., founded in 1912, originally as Abbey F.C., from a district of the city, renaming as Cambridge United in 1951. The fuller form of the nickname (as opposed to U's) is recorded in RY1970/1–73/4 and RY1983/4–92/3. It seems to appear for the last time in Williams League Directory 1993 and Pickering 1994. See also U's, Wasps.

⚽ CB Hounslow United F.C., founded in London in 1989, and using the initials of their sponsors, the Cater Bank Co. in their official name; Wikipedia.

⚽ Chesham United F.C., founded in Buckinghamshire in 1917, in a merger between C. Generals and C. Town; W1979/80–1991 and Smith 1991/2–1995/6. See also Generals.

⚽ Coagh United F.C., founded in Co. Tyrone in 1970. Recorded in RNI2007.

⚽ Cookstown United F.C., founded in Co. Tyrone in 1976. The club folded before 2008 and is included here in the absence of any known nickname.

⚽ Cranfield United F.C., founded in Bedfordshire in 1904; W1994–6.

⚽ Cumbernauld United F.C., founded in North Lanarkshire in 1964; Wikipedia, SFHA.

- Drogheda United F.C., founded in Co. Louth in 1975, in a merger of D. United (1919) and D. F.C. (1962); RI1997 and RI2006. See also Boynesiders, Drogs / Super Drogs, Turks.
- Eastbourne United Association F.C., founded in Sussex in 1896, originally as First Sussex Royal Engineers, and having several name changes before adopting E. United in 1951. The club merged with Shinewater Association in 2003; Wikipedia. For Shinewater, see Shine. See also Comrades, U's.
- Edinburgh United Juniors F.C., founded in 1955, folded 1956, refounded in 1985; Wikipedia; SFHA.
- Ellon United F.C., founded in Aberdeenshire in c.1890; club's own website.
- Fanad United F.C., founded in Co. Donegal in 1975; Wikipedia. See also Men from the Kingdom.
- Fauldhouse United F.C., founded in West Lothian in 1919; Wikipedia, SFHA.
- Formartine United F.C., founded in Aberdeenshire in 1946. Recorded in RS2011–12.
- Halkirk United F.C., founded in Highland (Caithness) in 1930; included here in the absence of any other known nickname for the club.
- Hastings United F.C. The present club dates to 1894, and is normally nicknamed 'The U's', but Goodall 1982 called it 'United'. See also Arrows, Claret & Blues, Town, U's.
- Hayes and Yeading United F.C., founded in a merger in 2007; SSY2010/11–12/13. See also Dinc/Ding, Missioners.
- Hereford United F.C., founded in 1924 in a merger. 'United' is the nickname recorded in RY1972/3–97/8 and SSY2006/7–12/13, and in Moss 1983. See also Lilywhites, Whites.
- Hinckley United F.C., founded in Leicestershire in 1997, in a merger between H. Town and H. Athletic; W2007–13. See also Eagles, Knitters, Robins, Town.
- Kelso United F.C., founded in the Scottish Borders in 1924; used on club's own website.
- Knowsley United F.C., founded at Huyton in Merseyside in 1984, originally as Kirkby Town, renaming in 1988 after a change of location; W1990. See also Reds.
- Leeds United F.C., so listed in RY1988/9–2002/3. See also Dirty Leeds, Owls, Peacocks, Whites / Mighty Whites.
- Leicester United, founded in 1900 as Enderby Town; the club renamed in 1986 but folded in 1996; W1989–97. See also Town (for Enderby).
- Lincoln United F.C., founded in 1938, originally as L. Amateurs, renaming in 1954; W1982/3–6; W1994–2013.
- Lossiemouth United Junior F.C., founded in Moray in 1960 (or 1962), reforming an earlier club of 1949–59; Wikipedia.
- Maidenhead United F.C., founded in Berkshire in 1870, called United after a merger in 1920; W1979/80. See also Magpies, Tanners.

⚽ Manchester United F.C. Both BoF1905–6 and Johnston 1934 use the phrase 'The United', also Richards 1960, and the nickname occurs as an alternative to 'Reds' in RY1970/1–74/5. The first two volumes of the Williams League Directories, 1985–6, list the nickname as 'United Reds', but this must be a typing error. See also Busby Babes, Coach-Builders, Fergie's Fledglings, Heathens, Man, Manure, Munichs, Outcasts, Reds.

⚽ Manortown United F.C., founded in Dublin in 1969; Wikipedia. See also Town.

⚽ Milton United F.C., founded in Oxfordshire in 1909; W2006–8. See also Miltonians.

⚽ Newmains United Community F.C., founded in North Lanarkshire in 1934, originally as Coltness United, renaming in 2006; club's own website. See also Dahlies.

⚽ North Ferriby United A.F.C., founded in East Yorkshire in 1934; W1982/3–2013. See also Villagers.

⚽ Norton United F.C., founded in Staffordshire in 1989; included here in the absence of any other known nickname for the club.

⚽ Oakley United F.C., founded in Fife in 1964; the club badge shows an oak tree, but the club is included here in the absence of any other known nickname for the club.

⚽ Oxford United F.C., founded as Headington in 1893 and added the word United to its name within a few months, changing to Oxford United in 1960. The normal nickname is 'The U's', but the fuller form appears in RY1970/1–73/4. See also Boys from Up the Hill, Dons, U's, Yellows.

⚽ Petersfield United F.C., founded in Hampshire in 1889, folded in 1993 and replaced by P. Town; W1985–93. See also Reds, Town.

⚽ Ponteland United F.C., founded in Newcastle-upon-Tyne in 1900; used on the club's own website.

⚽ Rye United F.C., founded in Sussex in 1938, in a merger of R. F.C. and R. Old Boys F.C.; W2007–13. Between 2001 and 2006 the club was named Rye & Iden United, and United is the nickname for this club in W2006. See also Quarterboys.

⚽ Scunthorpe United F.C. Formed in North Lincolnshire in 1899, merging with North Lindsey in 1910 to form Scunthorpe and Lindsey United; the suffix is used as a nickname in Fabian & Green 1960 (vol. ii, pp. 407–8). See also Iron, Nuts, Scunny.

⚽ Shawbury United F.C., founded at Wem in Shropshire in 1992; Wikipedia.

⚽ Sheffield United F.C., used as 'The United' in BoF1905–6 (no mention of 'Blades' in this source). See also Blades, Blunts, Cutlers, Laneites, Pigs, Red and White Wizards.

⚽ Skelmersdale United F.C., founded in Lancashire in 1882; Avis 1966–70, W1990. See also Skem / Skemmers.

⚽ St Andrews United F.C., founded in Fife in 1920 (though there were also previous clubs in the city); Wikipedia. See also Ancients, Saints.

⚽ St John's United A.F.C., founded at St John, Isle of Man, in 1947. Included here in the absence of any other known nickname for the club.

- Stornoway United F.C., founded on the Isle of Lewis in 1945, according to the club badge. The nickname 'United' appears on the club's own website. See also Black and Ambers.
- Thame United F.C., founded in Oxfordshire in 1883. The club's nickname is variously listed in Williams as U's (W1986, W1993), Utd (W1985) and United (W1987–2013). See also U's, Utd.
- Tobermore United F.C., founded in Co. Londonderry in 1965; RNI2007. See also Reds.
- Winsford United F.C., founded in Cheshire in 1883; W1981/2–89. See also Blues.
- Woodford United F.C., founded in Northamptonshire in 1946 as a sucecssor to a pre-war club called W. Central; W2003–6. See also Reds.
- Wolverhampton United F.C., founded in West Midlands in 1976, in a merger between Oxley and Whitmore Old Boys. A club badge is illustrated in AFBC.
- Worthing United F.C., founded in Sussex in 1988; W2006–9. See also Mavericks.

Unknowns was the nickname, and part-official name, of Bray Unknowns F.C., founded in 1903, which played at the Carlisle Ground in Bray, Co. Wicklow. The nickname is used in the account of the club in Johnston 1934; the club was successful, but folded after the 1942–3 season.

Urchins is the nickname of A.F.C. Hornchurch, formed in Greater London in 2005 on the closure of Hornchurch F.C., which was also called The Urchins. The older club was founded in 1923 as Upminster Wanderers, changing to Hornchurch and Upminster in 1953 and to Hornchurch in 1961. The name is unusual, suggesting 'boys', but it seems to derive as part-pun, part-acronym, using the last four letters of Hornchurch and three letters from the middle of Upminster; perhaps it started out as 'Churchinster'. Recorded for new and old clubs in Avis 1966–70, W1979/80–2013.

Utd is an abbreviation for United and appears as the nickname for Thame United F.C., founded in Oxfordshire in 1883, in W1985. See also U's, United.

U.U.J. is a nickname for the University of Ulster at Jordanstown F.C., from the club initials; Wikipedia. See also Poly.

Vale is a nickname for several clubs with the place-name element 'Vale', or close alternative, in their names. The examples are:

- Abbey Vale F.C., founded in 1974 at New Abbey, Dumfries and Galloway; Wikipedia, SFHA.
- Darvel F.C., founded in Ayrshire in 1889; Wikipedia, SFHA. See also Juniors.
- Deveronvale F.C., founded in 1938 in Banff (now in Aberdeenshire); the name comes from the local river Deveron. Recorded in RS1993–2012, SFHA.
- Islavale F.C., founded in Keith, Moray, in 1949; Wikipedia, SFHA.
- Laurelvale F.C., founded in Co. Armagh in 1950; Wikipedia.
- Malden Vale F.C., founded in London in 1967; W1986–95.

⚽ Nantlle Vale F.C., founded in 1920 at Penygroes, near Caernarfon. The nickname is a short form of the place-name and is recorded in RW1994–5.

⚽ Parkvale F.C., founded near Portlethen in Aberdeenshire in 1898; Wikipedia, SFHA.

⚽ Port Vale F.C., founded in a meeting at the Port Vale Hotel on Limekiln Road in Stoke-on-Trent, Staffordshire, in 1876. The hotel was named from a local series of ports in a valley along the Trent and Mersey Canal in 1876. The usual nickname is Valiants but this form is recorded in the 1991 Williams League Directory, and on Wikipedia, which adds another variant, *Valeites*, which refers to the home ground of Vale Park, built in 1950. See also Fail, Valiants.

⚽ Pewsey Vale F.C., founded in Wiltshire in 1948; W2005, W2009.

⚽ Raynes Park Vale F.C., founded in London in 1995; W2003–13.

⚽ Rossvale F.C., founded in Bishopbriggs, East Dunbartonshire, in 1976, originally as Woodhill Boys Club. The club needed a new name and formed one from street names Rossie Crescent and Vale Walk. The nickname is used in match reports on the club's own website.

⚽ Vale of Leithen F.C., founded at Innerleithen in the Scottish Borders in 1891. Recorded in RS1993–7, 2000–1, SFHA.

⚽ Vale of Leven Football and Athletic Club, founded in Alexandria, Dunbartonshire, in 1939; Wikipedia, SFHA.

⚽ Vale of Nith F.C., founded in Dumfries in 1880, closed in 1889; the Reserve side seems better documented, for which the SFHA records this nickname and another. See also Zebras.

Valiants is a nickname for three clubs, for slightly different punning reasons. The clubs are:

⚽ Charlton Athletic F.C., founded in London in 1905. In the 1963–4 season, competitions were held amongst the fans for a new nickname and a new badge. The winning nickname was 'Valiants', which expresses courageous struggle but also neatly puns with the name of the home ground, The Valley. To further express this, a new strikingly distinctive badge showed a hand holding an upright sword. The nickname failed to supplant the popularity of 'Addicks' (q.v.) but it appears in RY1973/4–93/4, G1976 and Pickering 1994. See also Addicks, Haddicks, Haddocks, Red Army, Robins.

⚽ Flixton F.C., founded in Greater Manchester in 1960; the nickname may have been entirely an adaptation of the earlier nickname 'Valley Roaders', after the Valley Road ground, or it may be a play on 'Valley Lions', as Lions is another nickname for the club and the symbol on the club badge; W2004–12. See also Flixs, Lions, Valley Roaders.

⚽ Port Vale F.C., as an adaptation of the club name. It is recorded in G1956–76, Churchill 1958, Richards 1960, AA 1960, Avis 1966–70, and throughout RY1970/1–SSY2012/13. By the 1970s the club had a badge showing a valiant knight on horseback. The club's name itself has two sources (see above, under Vale). A local media campaign to change the nickname to 'The Colliers' around 2000 was rejected by the fans. See also Fail, Vale.

Valley is a nickname for Rugby Town F.C., founded in Warwickshire in 1956, originally as Valley Sports. Before long, the club was calling itself VS Rugby, renaming as Rugby United in 2000 and Rugby Town in 2005. 'Valley' is recorded as the nickname for V.S.R. in W1982/3–2000; for United in W2001–5 and for Town in W2010–13. See also Town.

Vallians is recorded in G1956–65, Churchill 1958, Harvey 1959, Richards 1960 and RY1970/1–73/4 as the nickname of Rochdale F.C. (Greater Manchester, 1907). As there is no 'Vale' element in the club's history, and the nickname has two *ll*s, it is clearly an adaptation of 'valley', the meaning of 'dale'. See also Dale.

Valley Roaders was a nickname for Flixton F.C., founded in Greater Manchester in 1960; the nickname is an abstraction from the Valley Road ground; Miller & Wright 1996, W1997–2003. See also Flixs, Lions, Valiants.

Vans is a nickname for Northampton Sileby Rangers F.C., founded in 1968, originally as a works side for the Sileby Engineering Co. The nickname seems an unlikely one, but it refers to a temporary renaming of the club as Northampton Vanaid F.C., after a sponsorship deal with a courier company. The nickname is recorded in W1995–2000 for Vanaid, and in W2001 after the club reverted to its original and present name. See also Rangers, Sileby.

Varsity is a nickname for any university football club, especially used for Oxford and Cambridge sporting sides. It is a colloquial short form of 'university' and first appears in the OED in a poetic context in 1846. It is used in BoF1905–6 (pp.181–3) for the two university Asociation teams.

Venga Boys is the nickname of Venture Community F.C., founded in Wrexham in 1994, originally as Venture Youth; recorded in RW2011. The nickname is a pun on the sound of Venture, easily slurred as 'venga', with the name of an international pop group called 'The Vengaboys', founded in Amsterdam in 1997.

Venturas is the main nickname of Thrapston Town F.C., founded in Northamptonshire in 1960. The nickname refers to the original name of the club, Thrapston Venturas, renamed as Town in 1996. The word is Spanish for 'Good Fortune', a word which appears elsewhere in sport, business names, place-names and personal names; W1995–2013. See also Thrapo, Town.

Vets is the traditional nickname for sporting sides which are called 'The Veterans'. Sometimes veteran sides are temporary groupings of former players, as in Amersham Veterans, from Amersham Town, who played a celebratory match against Celebrity XI in 2007; but there are also clubs called Veterans which are intended for players aged over 35, as with Fylde Coast Veterans F.C., founded in Lancashire in 2010, or over 40, as Trimdon Veterans, based at Sedgefield in Cleveland. An internet search for 'Veterans' and 'F.C.' produces hundreds of examples, with 'Vets' the preferred nickname. The expression is also used for retired soldiers.

Vickers is the nickname of VCD Athletic F.C., founded in Kent in 1916 as Vickers F.C. A foundation in wartime is unusual, but Vickers was a busy armaments factory in Crayford and the club was founded for workers there; the VCD in the current name stands for 'Vickers, Crayford and Dartford'.; 'VCD' appears on the club badge; W2000–13.

Vics is a nickname for clubs with the name of Queen Victoria in their official name (which might come 'secondhand' from a place or district name with this element). The same nickname is often used for pubs called 'The Victoria'. Interestingly, many of the clubs which take this name are recent foundations. Examples are:

⚽ Arbroath Victoria F.C., founded in Angus in 1882; Wikipedia, SFHA.

⚽ Bentley Victoria Welfare F.C., based in South Yorkshire, the club folded in 1987; W1982/3–6.

⚽ Bewdley Town F.C., originally founded as Wribbenhall Victoria in Worcestershire in 1885, soon renaming as Bewdley Victoria and then as B. Comrades after the First World War (no current nickname is known for the club; Wikipedia). See also Comrades, Town.

⚽ Biddulph Victoria F.C., founded in Staffordshire in 1969, originally as Knypersley Victoria; W2003–11. The club folded in 2011.

⚽ Blantyre Victoria F.C., founded in Lanarkshire in 1890; W1982/3, SFHA.

⚽ Borrowash Victoria A.F.C., founded in Derbyshire in 1963; W1982/3–2008.

⚽ Brechin Victoria F.C., founded in Angus in 1917; Wikipedia, SFHA.

⚽ East Cowes Victoria Athletic A.F.C., founded in 1885. The Isle of Wight side has a ground in Beatrice Avenue (named from one of Victoria's daughters), on land which is part of the royal estate of Osborne House, the queen's country retreat; W1994–2000.

⚽ Irvine Victoria F.C., founded in 1904 in Ayrshire; Wikipedia. See also Wee Vics, Westenders.

⚽ Knighton Victoria F.C., founded in Powys in 2010; Wikipedia.

⚽ Knypersley Victoria F.C., founded in Staffordshire in 1969, renaming as Biddulph Victoria in 2002, folding in 2011; W1994–2002.

⚽ Malmesbury Victoria F.C., founded in Wiltshire in 1896, originally as M. Town. The name changed in 1973, adopting the suffix of a Swindon club which had folded; W2001–13.

⚽ Northwich Victoria F.C., founded in Cheshire in 1874, and acknowledged to have been named in honour of Queen Victoria. Recorded in Avis 1966–70, W1979/80–2013 and SSY2004/5–5/6 and SSY2007/8–09/10. See also Greens, Trickies.

⚽ Portgordon Victoria F.C., founded in Moray in 2006, originally as Buckie Victoria, renaming in 2008; Wikipedia.

⚽ Steelend Victoria Junior F.C., founded near Dunfermline, Fife, in 1995; Wikipedia, SFHA.

✪ Whitletts Victoria F.C., founded in South Ayrshire in 1944; Wikipedia, SFHA.

Victors is a unique nickname for a club called 'Victoria', recorded on Wikipedia for Dingwall Victoria United F.C., founded in Ross and Cromarty, Highland in 1905. The club merged in 1929 with Dingwall Thistle, to form the modern Ross County.

Vikings is a nickname for clubs which are proud of the Viking heritage of their area, or which see 'Viking' as a description of a band of roving warriors. Many clubs also have Viking ships on their badges, even if they do not adopt the nickname. The clubs, from all parts of Britain and Ireland, are:

✪ Doncaster Rovers F.C., founded in South Yorkshire in 1879. The club adopted a Viking image as a badge in 1972. The nickname has long been used as an alternative nickname for the club, although it does not appear in print in the mainstream sources. It is the name of a local co-operative for supporters of the club, and appears on t-shirts and in internet forums. As with Goole, Doncaster was never a Viking settlement but was in the Danelaw. It is not clear if the nickname is earlier than the badge or inspired by it, but the adoption of the badge alone shows that 'Vikings' has long been associated with 'Rovers' in the minds of supporters. See also Donny, Rovers.

✪ Dublin City F.C., founded in 1999, originally as Home Farm Fingal, in a split from Home Farm Everton (1928). The club was renamed Dublin City in 2001 but folded in 2006. Recorded in RI2006. Dublin was settled by the Vikings in 841 and soon became an independent Viking kingdom, surviving until it was conquered in 1171. See also Dubs.

✪ Goole A.F.C., founded in East Yorkshire in 1912 as Goole Town, changing to Goole in 1997. The club sports a red badge of a Viking ship. The town of Goole is a modern port on the River Humber. The area was part of the Viking Danelaw, but the town itself is not recorded before the late middle ages, so it is not a Viking settlement or a Viking place-name. However, the nickname is suitable for a seaport, and is also used in several Viking pubs and hotels in the town, and the name of the Marina at Goole; W1989–96; the club programme is called *Viking Review* (see W2004–10). See also Badgers, Town.

✪ Hakin United A.F.C., founded in Pembrokeshire in 1948. The nickname appears in match reports from 1972-3 on the 'Pembrokeshiresport.co.uk' website. The vicinity was one of Viking settlement in the ninth century, including a band led by Hubba who is commemorated in the place-name Hubberston, the parish which includes the village of Hakin. A stylised Viking ship appears on the club's badge and the club's youth side is called the 'Young Vikings'; club website, Wikipedia and Huws 2013.

✪ Oving F.C., founded in West Sussex in 1978. The nickname appears to have been coined as a play on the place-name, either from the suggestion of 'Roving' or based simply on the second syllable, but Sussex has never been an area of Viking settlement; W2000–03.

◉ Sidmouth Town F.C., founded in Devon sometime before 2007, when the club was entered in an online directory. The town is a coastal location, but outside the Danelaw; a Viking ship appears on the badge in AFBC.

◉ Thurso F.C., founded in Caithness (Highland) in 1998. The club sports a Viking badge and this part of Scotland is predominantly Viking in its medieval heritage; Wikipedia. See also Crabs.

◉ Viking Greenford F.C., founded in Middlesex in 1945, originally as Viking Sports, renaming in 2000; W1982/3–99 for the old name, W2000–3 for the new.

Villa / Villans / Villains are alternative nicknames for any club with 'Villa' in the official name, which is usually based on the name of a local feature. The name was certainly popularised by the success of the Aston Villa side. The examples are:

◉ Askern Villa F.C., founded in East Yorkshire in 1924, originally as Askern Welfare, renaming in 2008; W2012–13 (as 'Welly or Villa'). See also Welly.

◉ Aston Villa (and with variants 'Villans' and 'Villains'), founded in 1874 by cricket-playing members of the Villa Cross Wesleyan Chapel in Aston, Birmingham. The club's first home was Aston Park (1874–6) and they have been based at Villa Park since 1897. 'Villa' is a short form of the official name but 'Villans' adapts this, and punningly suggests the third form, and all three have appeared throughout the history of the club. 'Villains' appears in 1933 on the Ogden cigarette card, Churchill 1958, Harvey 1959, Richards 1960 and the 1959 Sweetule card (which has a cartoon of an evil-looking villain). In Johnston 1934, the 1936 Thomson 'stamp' album, G1956–76, SWSCYB 1962–3 and *Stedfast* October 1964 the nickname is 'Villans', though Thomson adds that 'Villains' is used by opposing sides (and the cartoon illustrates highway robbery). Avis 1954–70 has the nickname in the form 'Villa(i)ns' and the 1966 and 1970 editions also have 'The Villa' as an alternative. Pickering 1994 has Villa and Villans; RY1970/1–74/5 has 'Villains', with 'Villans' in RY 1975/6–2002/3 and SSY2003/4–12/13. Finally, if that was not complicated enough, BoF1905–6, AA 1960 and all the Williams League directories 1985–95 print only 'The Villa', so there is no clear chronological sequence in the style of this nickname, all three appear early and recently. See also Claret and Blues, Lions, Perry Bar Pets, Seals.

◉ Boldon Community Association F.C., founded in Co. Durham in 1903, originally as Boldon Villa, and also known as Boldon Colliery Welfare. The nickname is recorded in Barton 1984 & 1985, W1982/3–2005.

◉ Castle Villa Athletic F.C., founded at Castledermot in Co. Kildare in 1969; Wikipedia.

◉ Elburton Villa F.C., founded in Plymouth in 1982; W2008–13.

◉ Fairfield Villa F.C., founded in Hereford & Worcester in 1902, reformed 1959; W1993–5.

◉ Frecheville Community Association F.C., founded in a suburb of Sheffield in 1945; W1982/3–90. The reason for the nickname is not clear, it may be that the impressive Community Association building was nicknamed 'The Villa'.

- Hanworth Villa F.C., founded in Middlesex in 1976; W2009–13 (where it is consistently spelled Vilans). The club badge records it as Villains (AFBC).
- Northwich Villa F.C., founded in Cheshire in 2005, oriognally as Woodley; club's own website.
- Pelsall Villa F.C. (as 'Villains' or 'Villians') founded in West Midlands in 1897, reformed 1961; as 'Villains' in Miller & Wright 1996, as 'Villians' in W1994–2004.

Village is a nickname for clubs with the word Village in their official name (see also Villagers). The clubs are:

- Franklands Village F.C., founded in West Sussex in 1956; W1986–90.
- Garden Village F.C., founded in Swansea in 1922; recorded in RW 2001–11; a short form of the club name. See also Canaries.

Village Lads was a nickname for Farsley Celtic A.F.C., founded in the village near Leeds in West Yorkshire in 1908, and closed in 2010; W1985–6. See also Celts, Little Celts, Villagers.

Villagers is a nickname for clubs which are, or were, based in villages. The clubs are:

- Bishop's Cleeve F.C., founded in Gloucestershire in 1905. It is a village side; W2008–13. See also Skinners.
- Farsley A.F.C., founded in 2010 after the closure of F. Celtic. The previous club was also nicknamed The Villagers, or the Celts, and was founded in 1908 when F. was a village. It is now a suburb of Leeds. The club was considering a change of name to Farsley Celtic Leeds just before closure. Despite the Celtic association, the Farsley side played and play in all-blue colours; W1994–2010 and SSY2008/9 for the old club, W2011–13 for the new. See also Celts, Little Celts, Village Lads.
- Higher Walton F.C., founded in the Lancashire village in 1882 (and surviving in various successor clubs till 2005). The nickname is used in press reports from 1886 to 1892 quoted in the history by Peter Holme, 2006. See also Waltonians.
- Holyport F.C., founded in 1934. The club's home ground is Summerleaze Village, within the Berkshire town of Holyport; W2008–13.
- Ifield F.C., founded in West Sussex in 1950; W1988–90, W1995.
- Long Melford F.C., founded in 1868. Long Melford is a large village in Suffolk with an enormous medieval church more suitable for a city cathedral, but it is a village nevertheless; W2005–13.
- Loughgall F.C., founded in the village near Armagh, Co. Antrim in 1967 (reforming an older club of 1897); recorded in RNI2007.
- North Ferriby United A.F.C., in a village near Hull, East Yorkshire. Founded in 1934, the club has held its own against many teams from larger places and is currently a successful member of the Northern Premier League Premier Division. See also United.
- Wolviston F.C., founded in Cleveland in 1910. The nickname was used on the club's own website in 2012. See also Wolves.

Ville was the nickname of Waterlooville F.C., founded in Hampshire in 1910 and merging with Havant in 1998; W1979/80–98. See also Borough, Hawkes, Magnets.

Violet is the nickname and part official name of Stonehouse Violet F.C., founded in Lanarkshire in 1966, originally as Stonehouse Thistle, changing name in 1969. 'Violet' is a colour and the name of several plants which are so coloured (including, of course, the thistle). Scottish clubs have a fashion for adopting 'flower' names; Wikipedia, SFHA. See also Jags.

Vipers is the nickname for the New Heaton Mersey Vipers Junior F.C., founded on Merseyside in 2010. The club have an image of a snake's head as their badge and the nickname in used on the club's own website.

Vixens is a nickname, and can be an official name, of a women's football club, using the word for female foxes. It is an independent nickname, because the two clubs below are affiliated with men's clubs which do not use the fox as a nickname. Leicester City, however, has a mascot called Vicky the Vixen. The clubs are:

- Bristol Academy Women's F.C., founded in Avon in 1998, originally as Bristol Rovers W.F.C.; Wikipedia.
- Leeds City Vixens L.F.C., founded in West Yorkshire in 1993, which also has a mascot called Vicky the Vixen and fox-head badge; Wikipedia.

Volunteers is recorded as a nickname for the Third Lanark A.C. in BoF1905–6. Founded in Glasgow in 1872, closed in 1967, the club had a military origin, being the Athletic Club of the Third Lanarkshire Rifle Volunteers. See also Hi-Hi's, Redcoats, Sodgers, Thirds, Warriors.

Waders is the nickname of Biggleswade Town F.C., founded in Bedfordshire in 1874. The nickname puns with the last syllable of the place-name to suggest a team which will wade into the game; W1991–2013.

Wagon was the nickname of Derby Carriage and Wagon (Reckitts) F.C., founded in Derbyshire in 1935, playing at the Carriage and Wagon Welfare Ground. The club was originally a works side for the Derby Carriage and Wagon works (built in 1876) which made railway rolling stock, the club adopted the extra name 'Reckitts' in 1988 but it disappears from the FCHD in 1995; W1994–5.

Wakes is the nickname of Bourne Town F.C., founded in Lincolnshire in 1883. The nickname celebrates the eleventh-century freedom fighter Hereward the Wake, opponent of the Norman Conquest, who is also commemorated in the name of the local radio station (Hereward Radio), street names, business names etc.; recorded in W1979/80–2013.

Walkers was the nickname for Tetley Walkers F.C., founded in Warrington, Cheshire in 1974. The club was a works side for the famous brewery (itself formed in a merger in 1960 between Tetley of Leeds (1822) and Walkers of Warrington (1864) and then merging with Ind Coope and Ansells to form Allied Breweries in 1961). The club folded in 2001; W1995–2001.

Wally is the nickname for A.F.C. Wallingford, founded in Oxfordshire in 1995 in a merger between W. Town (1922) and W. United (1934); a friendly short form of the place-name. See also Town.

Walnut Boys is the nickname of A.F.C. Kempston Rovers, originally founded in 1884, but reformed in 2002 in a merger of the Bedfordshire clubs of K. Rovers, K. Colts and K. Town. Explanations for the nickname are not easy to find, but a forum on the Rushden and Diamonds website states that the original ground was on the site of an orchard of walnut trees and strong winds the night before a match had blown the walnuts onto the pitch. When the opposing side turned up, they commented that they would be playing the Walnut Boys today. However, there is a strong association between the town of Kempston and walnuts (which are represented in the civic regalia and street names), so presumably walnut production was once a major part of the local economy; W1982/3–2010 and W2013.

Waltonians was a nickname used for Higher Walton F.C., founded in the Lancashire village in 1882 (and surviving in various successor clubs till 2005). The nickname is used in press reports from 1886 to 1892 quoted in the history by Peter Holme, 2006. See also Villagers.

Waltz is the intriguing nickname of Walton and Hersham F.C., founded in Surrey in 1945, in a merger of clubs from these neighbouring towns. The nickname seems to be a clever pun on the place-names: Walt' followed by a sh' sound easily mutating to z; Wikipedia. See also Sham, Swans, Swans and Robins.

Wanderers is a nickname for clubs with the suffix 'Wanderers' in their official name. There are various traditions that the suffix was used for clubs which originally did not have their own ground, but the name fits the pattern of many such 'travelling' expressions, poetically suggesting bands of roving warriors. The earliest usage may be that of Wanderers A.F.C., in 1864. Not all clubs so-called are necessarily so-nicknamed (there are a great many more, see also Huws 2013); some notable examples are:

- Bolton Wanderers F.C. Founded by a local vicar in Greater Manchester in 1874 as Christ Church F.C., they broke away and became Bolton Wanderers in 1877. The club tradition is that initially they had difficulty finding a permanent pitch to play on (see more discussion under 'Trotters'), but the 1905–6 *Book of Football* states "The name was suggested by the fact that they had to wander [from the Christ Church Sunday School building, for meetings] to a neighbouring hostelry, the Gladstone Hotel, near Pike's Lane" (p.114); on p.148 'The Wanderers' is used as the nickname. See also Noblot / Notlob, Reds, Savage Six, Spots, Trotters, Whites / Whitemen.
- Buckley Town F.C., founded in Flintshire in 1978 in a merger between B. Wanderers and B. Rovers; recorded in RW1994–8. See also Bucks, Claymen, Trotters.
- Burton Park Wanderers F.C., founded in Northamptonshire in 1961, originally as Kettering Park Wanderers; Wikipedia and club's own website.

☺ Caernarfon Wanderers F.C., founded in Gwynedd in 2007, but reusing a name from the 1880s. The suffix is used as a nickname in *The Daily Post* on 11 August 2012 but the club seems now to have folded.

☺ Cray Wanderers F.C., founded in Bromley, London, in 1860; W2012–13. See also Wands.

☺ Dorking Wanderers F.C., founded in Surrey in 1999; Wikipedia.

☺ Drayton Wanderers F.C., formed in Middlesex in 1964, it was briefly renamed Uxbridge Town 1989–92; the club disappears after 2004; W2001–4.

☺ Forth Wanderers F.C., founded in the Lanarkshire village of Forth in 1904; Wikipedia, SFHA.

☺ Ffostrasol Wanderers F.C., founded in Ceredigion by the late 1970s. The club is mentioned on many websites and an enamel badge of the club is recorded in AFBC.

☺ Ipswich Wanderers F.C., founded in Suffolk in 1980, first as an under-14 boys' team, then moving to adults and adopting the Wanderers suffix in 1989; W1992–2013.

☺ Jersey Wanderers F.C., founded on the island in 1894 (though the club badge reads 1905); club's own website.

☺ Kettering Park Wanderers F.C. A newspaper cutting from 1989 reproduced in Addis 1998 (p. 142) uses the suffix as a nickname, also in W1990–2012. In W1991 there is a single usage of 'Park Wanderers'.

☺ Nithsdale Wanderers F.C., founded at Sanquhar, Dumfries and Galloway, in 2001 (reforming an older club of 1897–1964); used as a nickname on Wikipedia. See also Dale.

☺ Quedgeley Wanderers F.C., founded in Gloucestershire in 1994, though the club's website tends to use the initialism QWFC as a nickname.

☺ Shropshire Wanderers F.C., an early pioneer club based in Shrewsbury but frequently playing against Welsh teams in the 1870s, and contributing players to the Welsh national team in 1876. Their FA Cup records run from 1873 to 1878 (FCHD); mentioned in BoF1905–6.

☺ St Cuthbert Wanderers F.C., founded in 1879 in Kirkcudbright, Dumfries and Galloway. Here, the nickname and official name commemorates an ancient wandering. The place-name Kirkcudbright means the 'Church of St Cuthbert'. After the Viking attack on Lindisfarne in 875, the monks carried Cuthbert's mortal remains to several places, including Kirkcudbright, before taking them to Chester-le-Street in 995. The club formed as a church side for the local Catholic St Cuthbert's church. Recorded in RS1995–6. See also Saints.

☺ Sudbury Wanderers, founded in Suffolk in 1958, merging with S. Town in 1999; W1992–9. See also Borough, Suds, Town, Yellows.

☺ Thursday Wanderers F.C., a side formed in 1879 by players at Sheffield F.C. who wished to play on this particular day. The club last appears in the early 1880s (Wikipedia) and is briefly mentioned in BoF1905–6 (p.213).

☼ Wanderers A.F.C., founded in London in 1859, originally as Forest F.C. (from Epping Forest), changing its name to Wanderers in 1864. This club was an extremely successful Victorian side (winners five-times of the earliest F.A. Cup Finals in the competition's first seven seasons, 1871–8), which must have encouraged the spread of the name. The club disappears from the FCHD after 1880 but is known to have survived until at least 1883. In 2009, the club was reformed with the approval of descendants of some of the early players and now competes in the Surrey South Eastern Combination; Wikipedia. See also Foresters.

☼ Wickwar Wanderers F.C., founded in Gloucestershire in 1990. The club's website records previous teams in the town with the suffixes Athletic, Rovers and United, which had the nickname The Brewers in the early decades of the twentieth century.

☼ Wolverhampton Wanderers F.C., founded in a merger in 1879. Although usually nicknamed 'The Wolves', Norris 1959 says "you'll often hear them called the Wanderers in that Soccer-conscious Midlands town." The nickname is recorded early, used in BoF1905–6. See also Buckley Babes, Dingles, Tatters, Wolves.

☼ Woolpack Wanderers F.C., the 'other' Isles of Scilly side, so renamed in 1984, previously The Rovers (not that they could rove or wander very far). There are only two clubs on the islands, which have the world's smallest football league; Wikipedia. See also Gunners.

☼ Wycombe Wanderers F.C., founded in Buckinghamshire in 1887; the use of the suffix is rare for this club but it is so used in Goodall 1982. See also Blues, Chairboys.

Wands is the nickname of Cray Wanderers F.C., founded in Bromley, London, in 1860. The club is one of the oldest in the world, the short form of the suffix allows journalists to use the headline 'Magic Wands' in match reports; W1982/3–2013. See also Wanderers.

Wardens is a nickname for Saffron Walden Town F.C., founded in Essex in 1872. The nickname appears to be an adaptation of the second word in the place-name, though this does not mean 'wardens'; the club's own website does use 'Walden' as a nickname, and also has the initialism 'SWTFC'. The nickname appeared on Wikipedia in September 2012 and may simply be a typing error. See also Bloods, Saffron.

Wares was a nickname of the London side, Edgware Town F.C., founded in 1939, dissolved in 2008, as a pluralised short form of the place-name; W1979/80–2008. See also Town.

Warriors is a good nickname for any sporting club, and is not unlike other names suggesting bands of roving warriors: Crusaders, Rovers, Vikings, Wanderers etc. (and note also the use of Army for supporters). It may be formed as a pun on the place-name, or because of a genuine military ancestry for the club, or for absolutely no reason other than assumed prowess. The clubs are:

☼ Stenhousemuir F.C., founded near Falkirk in 1884, in a breakaway from Heather Rangers. The nickname is said to have been adapted in the late 1880s but, if it had any original justification, the reasons for it are now lost. Recorded in *Stedfast* July 1963, through RY1974/5–SSY2012/13 and in RS1993–2012.

⚽ Third Lanark A.C., founded in Glasgow in 1872, closed in 1967. This particular club definitely had a military origin, being the Athletic Club of the Third Lanarkshire Rifle Volunteers. Recorded in Johnston 1934, on the 1936 Thompson 'stamp' (with a cartoon of Viking warriors), G1956–65 and Harvey 1959, AA 1960, SFHA. See also Hi-Hi's, Redcoats, Sodgers, Thirds, Volunteers.

⚽ Thrapston Warriors AD 2009 F.C., formed in Northamptonshire in 2009 as a youth side, playing in the Weetabix U10 League. The club is included here as an example of Warriors used to suggest 'assumed prowess'; club's own website.

⚽ Warrington Town F.C., founded in Cheshire in 1949, originally as Stockton Heath Albion, renamed Warrington in 1961. Here it is an adaptation of the opening syllables of the place-name; Wikipedia. See also Levers, Town, Wire/s, Yellows.

⚽ Wexford Youths F.C., founded in Co. Wexford in 2007; Wikipedia. See also Youths.

Wars is a nickname of Warlingham F.C., founded in Surrey in 1896. Punning on the first syllable of the place-name, it nevertheless suggests a club with a combative spirit. The village was also a major witness to the Battle of Britain in the skies above it duirng the Second World War; Wikipedia and W2013. See also Hammers.

Washers was a nickname for the short-lived Middlesbrough side, Ironopolis F.C. (1889–94). The word is slang for money, and it refers to the salaried professional status of the club at a time when going professional was controversial. In Appleton 1960 (pp. 82–3), the phrase is attributed to a shipyard worker saying "If you want professionals you must put your washers together" and with the detail that "Early shareholders wore a jet coat pin in the form of a washer with a little jet ball dangling in the centre. The pin was inscribed 'Play up the Washers'." Nevertheless, doubts must be expressed as to whether the club itself accepted the nickname because the word is considered derisory, for small change (see Phythian 1955 and Beale 1989). Perhaps in engineering Teesside it did not have this connotation. See also Boro, Cleveland Cowboys, Ironsiders, Nops, Riversiders, Scabs, Smoggies, Teessiders.

Wasps is usually a nickname for clubs which play in black-and-yellow striped shirts (or other combinations which also suggest the appearance of wasps, the insects come in many colours). Exactly the same colours might generate nicknames like 'Bees', 'Hornets', 'Tigers' or 'Black and Ambers'; some further examples of 'Wasps' appear in Huws 2013. The examples here are:

⚽ Aberdeen F.C., founded in 1903. The club first played in black-and-gold stripes before changing to a red-and-white strip in 1966. Recorded in SWSCYB 1962–3. See also Black and Golds, Dandies, Dons, Red Devils, Reds.

⚽ Alloa Athletic F.C., founded in Clackmannanshire in 1878 (originally as Clackmannan County). Recorded on the 1959 Sweetule card, *Stedfast* November 1963, G1976, in RS 1993–2012 and through RY1974/5–SSY2012/13. The club plays in the wasp colours of gold-and-black hoops. See also County, Hornets.

☺ Cambridge United F.C., founded in 1912, originally as Abbey United, the club has regularly had a distinctive black-and-amber kit, often but not always in stripes (see Historical Football Kits website). The club changed its name to Cambridge United in 1951. The nickname is mentioned on the 'Beautiful History' website. See also United, U's.

☺ Cove F.C., founded in Hampshire in 1897. They play in the wasp colours of yellow shirts and socks and black shorts; Wikipedia.

☺ Dolgellau Amateur F.C., founded in Gwynedd in 1971, in a merger between D. Albion and D. Town; recorded in RW2011. The club plays in black-and-amber striped shirts with black shorts, the traditional wasp colours.

☺ East Grinstead Town F.C., founded in Sussex in 1890. The club plays in black-and-yellow stripes with black shorts and socks; W1983/4–2013.

☺ Newport County F.C. – a proposed nickname during a competition in 1913, based on the amber-and-black strip the club wore from the outset. However, the colours were not arranged in stripes, a possible reason for 'Ironsides' winning the competition instead; Wikipedia. See also Black and Ambers, County, Cromwellians, Exiles, Ironsides, Port.

☺ Sark National Football Team. The nickname has recently appeared on Wikipedia and obviously refers to the Channel Island team's secondary strip of black-and-amber colours. See also Bad Lions, Mad Lions.

☺ Slough Town F.C., founded in Berkshire in 1893. The nickname is recorded in Pickering 1994 and refers to the amber-and-blue hooped shirts the team wore before the Second World War. See also Rebels.

☺ Watford F.C. The nickname is unexpected nowadays, but is recorded in Johnston 1934 with the explanation "The original colours were red, green and yellow stripes, and this led to the club being known as the 'Wasps'." The Historical Football Kits website records this strip for 1898 (and in hoops 1903–9) but also illustrates an earlier red-and-yellow stripes from 1890. See also Blues, Brewers, Golden Boys, Hornets, Horns / 'Orns, Saints, Yellow Army.

Waterfall Men is the nickname of Llanrhaeadr ym Mochnant F.C., founded in 1882; recorded in RW2011. The nickname records the famous waterfall of Pistyll Rhaeadr near this town in Denbighshire, and the first word of the place-name means 'church of the waterfall'.

Waters is the nickname for Virginia Water F.C., founded in Surrey in 1921; a pluralised short form of the place-name, recorded in W1994–5 and on the club website.

Watersiders is the nickname of Blackfield and Langley F.C., founded in 1935. The club is based near Southampton, beside the seawater of the Solent; Wikipedia.

Watt is the nickname is Heriot-Watt University F.C., founded in Edinburgh in 1945, as a short form of the official name. The College became a university in 1966.

Recorded in RS1993–7, 2000–1, SFHA.

Waverley is the nickname of Hawick Waverley F.C., founded in the Scottish Borders (Roxburghshire) in 1980. The club badge (AFBC) shows an image of Sir Walter Scott and the suffix records the title of his first historical novel, *Waverley*, published in 1814 and commemorating the Jacobite Rebellion of 1745. The novel is very much at the heart of Scottish national consciousness; the suffix is used as a nickname on the club's own website.

Waysiders is a nickname for Airdrie United F.C., founded in 2002 as a successor to Airdrieonians F.C. (1878–2002), also used for the old club. The nickname means 'The Roadsiders' and seems to refer to one theory as to the origin of the place-name Airdrie (as the place on the wayside). The town also has a large Wayside Tavern in Chapel Street. Recorded in RS1993–8 and RY1974/5–2002/3 for the old club. See also Diamonds, Excelsior, Onians.

W.B.A. is an initialism for West Bromwich Albion F.C., recorded in Avis 1966–70. See also Albion, Baggies, Bennies, Boing!, Nigger Minstrels, Sandwell Town, Stripes, Strollers, Tatters (for a possible connection), Team of Boys, Tesco's, Throstles.

Wddyn Boys, see Lakesiders.

Wearsiders is an older nickname for Sunderland A.F.C., from their location on the banks of the River Wear. It is recorded early, in BoF1905–6, and on the 1933 Ogden cigarette card, Avis 1954–70, Jeffrey 1961 and *Stedfast* February 1965. See also Bank of England Club, Black Cats, Lads, Light Brigade, Mackems, Miners, Rokerites / Rokermen, Sols, Sund-Ireland, Team of All the Talents.

Weddingmakers was a nickname for Gretna F.C., founded in 1946 and closed in 2008. Gretna Green in Dumfries and Galloway was the famous centre for runaway marriages before a change in Scottish law in 1856, and the town continues to be a popular location for marriages for romantic reasons; Wikipedia. The expression is a slightly awkward one, so it may have been coined as a pun, suggesting the opposite of the popular term 'widowmakers', used for many masculine 'killer' concepts, from military hardware to shockingly butch white vests. See also Anvils, Black and Whites, Borderers, Celebrant, Monochrome, Weddingmakers.

Wednesday is an occasional nickname for Sheffield Wednesday F.C., founded in 1867 as an offshoot from The Wednesday Cricket Club; the football club was called The Wednesday F.C. until 1929, when it took the present name. Wednesday was the day the members played, that being a half-day for local traders; recorded in BoF1905–6 (with the variants 'Sheffielders' and 'Wednesdayites'), Avis 1954–70 and in RY1970/1 (first issue only). See also Blades, Groveites, Owls, Pigs, Wendys.

Wee County is the nickname of Nairn County F.C., founded in the small Scottish county of Nairn in 1914. Recorded in W1982/3, RS1993–2012, SFHA. See also County.

Wee 'Gers is a nickname for smaller clubs in Scotland which are called Rangers, in contrast to the prominent Glasgow side, which is itself nicknamed 'Gers. The clubs are:

- ⚽ Berwick Rangers F.C., founded in Northumberland in 1884 (but playing in the Scottish leagues); SSY2008/9–10/11. See also Black and Gold, Borderers, Dream Team, Rangers, Wee Rangers.
- ⚽ Cambuslang Rangers F.C., founded in Lanarkshire in 1899; Wikipedia. See also Lang.
- ⚽ Kilsyth Rangers F.C., founded in Lanarkshire in 1913; Wikipedia; SFHA has the nickname as just 'Gers'.

Wee Hoops is the nickname of Donegal Celtic F.C., founded in Belfast in 1970. The club's name, nickname and strip are in tribute to the Glasgow Celtic side. The club plays at the Donegal Celtic Park; Wikipedia, recorded in RNI2007 as 'Hoops'. See also Celtic, D.C.

Wee Jags was a nickname for Livingston F.C., founded in Edinburgh in 1943, originally as Ferranti Thistle, renaming as Meadowbank Thistle before a move to Livingston in 1995. The nickname is recorded in RS1993–5 and RY1985/6–94/5 for Meadowbank, RS1996–7 and RY1995/6–6/7 for Livingston. From RS1998 the club is nicknamed Lions. See also Lions, Livi, Thistle.

Wee Rangers is a nickname for two clubs called Rangers, and is clearly used in contrast to the famous Glasgow side. The clubs are:

- ⚽ Cove Rangers F.C., founded in Aberdeen in 1922; Wikipedia. See also Highland Dynamite, Tooners.
- ⚽ Lisburn Rangers F.C., founded in Belfast before 1963 (when they joined the Amateur League); Wikipedia.

Wee Rovers is the nickname of Albion Rovers F.C., founded in Coatbridge in North Lanarkshire in 1882. The nickname means 'The Small Rovers' and is in contrast to the only other mainstream Scottish team called Rovers, Raith Rovers. Recorded in RS1993–2012 and RY1973/4–SSY2012/13.

Wee Vics is the nickname of Irvine Victoria F.C., founded in 1904 in Ayrshire. The nickname must be in contrast to Arbroath Victoria (see 'Vics'). The club plays at the Victoria Park ground in Irvine; Wikipedia, SFHA. See also Vics, Westenders.

Welders is the nickname for Harland and Wolff Welders F.C., founded in Belfast in 1965 as a works side for the long-established (1861) shipbuilding works. Recorded in RNI2007.

Welfare, in England and Wales, is a name from the Miners' Welfare movement, administered by a royal commission between 1920 and 1951. It developed benefits such as baths, canteens, educational scholarships, social clubs, recreational grounds and football clubs in mining communities across the country. The football sides usually adopted the word 'Welfare' in their official name, because they were attached to Miners' Welfare Clubs (some formed from surviving clubs long after the nationalisation of the coal industry and the closure of the Commission). In Scotland, the word usually refers to the Scottish Welfare Football Association, set up in 1918, and responsible for sporting activities in communities throughout Scotland, not necessarily mining ones. The Scottish organisation still exists and some five hundred amateur clubs are affiliated to it. Variant nicknames include Wellie, Wells, and Welly, but 'The Welfare' is or has been used for the following clubs:

⚽ Armthorpe Welfare F.C., founded in South Yorkshire in 1926; W1983/4—86. See also Wellie.

⚽ Blidworth Welfare F.C., refounded in Nottinghamshire in 1980; W1982/3–6. See also Hawks.

⚽ Dawdon Colliery Welfare F.C., founded in Co. Durham in 1977; club website.

⚽ Eppleton Colliery Welfare F.C., founded in Co. Durham in 1929, closed in 2005; the ground still exists and is still called the Eppleton Colliery Welfare Ground; W1994–2004.

⚽ Glasshoughton Welfare A.F.C., formed in West Yorkshire in 1964, originally as Anson Sports, renaming in 1976; W1986 and W2012–13. See also Blues.

⚽ Horden Colliery Welfare A.F.C., founded in Co. Durham in 1908; recorded in Avis 1966–70. See also Colliers.

⚽ Llay Welfare F.C., founded in Wrexham Co. Bor. in 1930 and recorded in RW1994–6 and the club's website. The club occasionally uses 'Miners Welfare' in the official name. See also Llay.

⚽ Nostell Miners Welfare F.C., founded near Wakefield, West Yorkshire, in 1928; W2008–13.

⚽ Ryhope Colliery Welfare F.C., founded in Co. Durham in 1956, originally as Ryhope Blue Star; recorded in Barton 1984 & 1985 and W1982/3–6.

⚽ Staveley Miners Welfare F.C., founded in Derbyshire in 1962; W1995–2013.

⚽ Tonyrefail Welfare A.F.C., founded in Rhondda Cynon Taf, probably in 1925 when the Welfare Ground opened. The club is recorded in RW1994–6 but without a nickname.

⚽ Whitehill Welfare F.C., founded in 1953 in Midlothian. Recorded in RS1993–7, 2000–1, SFHA.

⚽ Ynysddu Welfare A.F.C., founded in Caerphilly Co. Bor. in 1947. The club began a merger with Crusaders A.F.C. in 2005, completed in 2008 in the formation of the new Ynysddu Crusaders; internet history of local football dated July 2012.

Well is a nickname for clubs with the place-name element *–well* in their official name. The examples are:

⚽ Glapwell F.C., formed in Derbyshire in 1985; W2008–11.

⚽ Motherwell Football and Athletic Club, founded in 1886. Recorded throughout RY and SSY from 1970/1 to 2012/13; RS 1993–2008, G1976. See also Dossers, Steelmen.

Wellie is a nickname for three clubs, based on the official names. The clubs are:

⚽ Armthorpe Welfare F.C., founded in 1926. The club plays at Welfare Ground in the

374

coalmining village of Armthorpe near Doncaster, where Kevin Keegan was born. The club's badge shows a stylised football with a miner's head on it, and the nickname is a friendly short form of 'Welfare' (q.v.); W1994–2013.

⚽ Great Harwood Town F.C., founded in Lancashire in 1966, originally as Harwood Wellington (after 'The Duke of Wellington' pub), but renaming to G.H.Town in 1978 after the demise of another local club. The nickname can only date between 1966 and 1978. The renamed club folded in 2006 and the nickname is recorded on the club's commemorative website. See also Arrad, Robins.

⚽ Wellington A.F.C., founded in Somerset in 1896; a friendly short form recorded in W2010–13 (where the club is wrongly called 'Town'). See also Town.

Wellies is the nickname of the Herefordshire side, Wellington F.C., founded in 1968; a pluralised friendly short form of the place-name; Wikipedia.

Wellmen is the nickname of two Welsh clubs with the word 'well' in their place-name. The clubs are:

⚽ Holywell Town F.C., founded in Flintshire in 1946 but following earlier clubs called H. United (1905) and H. Arcadians (1929); the nickname is an adaptation of the place-name and is recorded in RW1994–2011, W1994–9. See also Arcadians.

⚽ Taffs Well A.F.C., founded near Cardiff in 1946; Wikipedia. See also Taffs / Taffys.

Wells is a nickname for two clubs, for slightly different reasons. The clubs are:

⚽ Tunbridge Wells F.C., founded in Kent in 1886; a short form of the place-name. Recorded in W1979/80–2013.

⚽ Hemsworth Miners Welfare F.C., founded in West Yorkshire in 1981, following the closure of H. Colliery F.C. in 1980; a pluralised short form of Welfare (q.v.); W2012–13.

Welly is a nickname for two clubs based on the name 'Welfare' (q.v.) in the official name. This particular spelling of the nickname perhaps also carries a pun on kicking (as in "Give it some welly"), itself punning on the Wellington boot.The clubs are:

⚽ Askern Welfare F.C., founded in East Yorkshire in 1924, renaming to Askern Villa in 2008; W2003–5 (as Welly), W2012–13 (as 'Welly or Villa'). See also Villa.

⚽ Ibstock United F.C., founded in Leicestershire in 2005 in a merger between I. Welfare and I. Youth. W2003–5.

Welsh Bluebirds is recorded in Avis 1970 as an alternative nickname for Cardiff City, alongside the more familiar Bluebirds. The nickname was clearly a temporary fashion which did not survive. See also Bluebirds, Dwarfs, Redbirds.

Wembley Wizards was a nickname for the successful side of the Scotland National Football Team after their 5–1 defeat of England at Wembley Stadium in 1928; G1956–76. See also Blues, Bravehearts, Tartan Army / Terriers, Thistle.

Wendys is an unofficial derogatory nickname for Sheffield Wednesday F.C., from the perspective of Sheffield United supporters, as recorded on the 2003 Football Fans Census website. The nickname is a pun on a girl's name and the sound of 'Wednesday'. See also Blades, Groveites, Owls, Pigs, Wednesday.

West is a nickname for some clubs with the element 'West' in their official name. The clubs are:

⚽ Haverfordwest County A.F.C., founded in Pembrokeshire in 1899; as a short form of the place-name. See also Bluebirds, County.

⚽ West Allotment Celtic F.C., founded near Newcastle-upon-Tyne in 1928; W2006– 7. See also Celtic.

⚽ West Auckland Town F.C., founded in Co. Durham in 1893. Recorded in Barton 1984 & 1985, W1982/3–6, W1992–2013.

⚽ West United F.C., based at the South Park Ground in Galway. The locality also has an 'East' club; Wikipedia.

West End is the nickname of Forfar West End F.C., founded in Angus in 1885; club's own website and SFHA.

Westenders is a nickname for three clubs, for reasons of location. The clubs are:

⚽ Gap Connah's Quay Nomads F.C., founded in Flintshire in 1946 as C.W. Juniors, changing to Nomads in 1951; recorded in RW1994–2002 and RW2011 and W1994–2005. The nickname refers to the club's former location at the Halfway Ground on Coast Road, which is to the west of the town centre (see Huws 2009). Huws (pers. com. and 2013) believes that the nickname would also have been used by an earlier club, Connah's Quay and Shotton F.C. (1920–27), which had rented the same ground. The present club moved in 1997. See also Deesiders, Nomads.

⚽ Irvine Victoria F.C., founded in 1904 in Ayrshire. The nickname refers to the club's location on the west bank of the River Irvine, which flows through the town. See also Vics, Wee Vics.

⚽ Somersham Town F.C., founded in Cambridgeshire in 1893. The club's home is the West End Ground; W1995–2004.

Western is an alternative nickname for Treharris Athletic Western F.C., founded in 1889, originally as Treharris Athletic, renaming in 2010 when it merged with Western Hotel F.C. (a club sponsored by the Great Western Hotel in Treharris); based in the Co. Bor. of Merthyr Tydfil. The club may have won the (English) Western League in 1910, but the nickname derives from the merger. See also Lilywhites.

Wet Sham is an unofficial derogatory nickname for West Ham United F.C., from the perspective of Millwall supporters, recorded on the 2003 Football Fans Census website. The nickname is a gentle pun on the official name, reversing only two letters to make two words which connote superficiality. See also Academy of Football, Claret and Blues, Cockney Boys, Eastenders, Hammers, Hamsters, ICF, Irons.

Weys was a nickname for Godalming and Guildford F.C., renamed as Godalming Town in 2005. The nickname is based on the ground name, Weycourt in Godalming, W1995–8. See also G's, Gees, Weys.

Whe Ho is the nickname of the Clydebank side, Yoker Athletic F.C., founded in 1886.

The nickname has long been unexplained but clearly derives from an expression, probably a supporters' chant. A recent internet discussion initiated by Alasdair Galloway produced a consensus that it derived from a shout in Glaswegian dialect, meaning either 'Away' ('Whe ho the wee Yoker') or 'Here we go', both phrases being widely known in football (at Sunderland it's 'Ha' Way the Lads', at Jarrow 'Haway the Roofers'). One contribution said "*Whee-ho the Yoker* was a shout still ... heard in the 1960s ..." The Glaswegian love of rhyming slang is probably the explanation for the final form (ho/yo). Other possibilities, such as a supporters' song based on the Burns patriotic song, 'Scots wha hae' cannot be entirely discounted, but the 'away' explanation seems the most plausible. Even if the general sense of encouragement is clear, the words may not, of course, have a specific meaning. Some phrases, such as the similar 'Yee ha!', 'Whe hey!' and 'Heh Ho!' function as expressions of surprise or joy without having a literal meaning, and the pronunciation of 'Away' might also have been influenced by these; Wikipedia, club's own website and SFHA.

Wheelmen was an early nickname for Coventry City F.C. and refers to their early years. They were founded in 1883 as Singers F.C., for employees of the Singer's Cycle Works, renaming as C. City in 1898. It must be to these cycle wheels that the nickname refers, but the nickname is recorded late, in RY1983/4. See also Bantams, Blackbirds, Citizens, Peeping Toms, Singers, Sky Blues.

Wheelwrights is the nickname for Wheelwright Old Boys F.C., founded in 1932 for old boys of Wheelwright Grammar School, Dewsbury, Yorkshire; club website.

Wherrymen is the nickname of Beccles Town F.C., founded in 1919. It is said in explanation on Wikipedia that the Suffolk town "was once a busy trading town on the River Waveney", though it requires some slurring in pronunciation to make Waveney into Wherry. The final form seems to be a deliberate chime with 'ferrymen'.

White Brigade is a nickname for Annbank United F.C., founded in Ayrshire in 1939; mentioned on the club's own website and SFHA. The club wears white shirts. See also Bankies.

White Horse Men is the nickname of the Wiltshire side, Westbury United F.C., founded in 1920. The nickname refers to the famous eighteenth-century carving of the white horse on the nearby hillside; W1987–2013 (with variants of Horse Men / Horsemen). 'White Horse' is also the official name of several smaller clubs, some based on a similar nearby feature (Abingdon, Biddestone), others based on pub names (Tyne and Wear, Kimpton near Hitchin).

White Men / Whitemen, see under Whites (for Bolton Wanderers).

White Stars, see under Stars (Newtown).

White Tigers is a nickname of Truro City F.C. Founded in Cornwall in 1889, the club plays in an all-white strip with a pale gold for details (and away strip), the colours associated with white tigers; Wikipedia. See also City, Tinmen.

White Wolves is the nickname of Louth Town F.C., founded in Lincolnshire in 2007 after the closure of L. United (The Lions). The club plays in a mainly white shirt with black shorts and socks and has a wolf rampant on its shield. The old club's colour was red. The wolf has long been a badge for the town, appearing on the civic heraldry, and was first used in the arms of one Nicholas de Luda in 1351. It originates in a typical medieval heraldic pun, based on the similarity of the Latin words *lupa* (wolf) and *Luda* (for Louth); W2011–13.

Whites is a nickname for teams which wear white shirts, or an all-white strip. 'The Lilywhites' is also common. The examples are:

- ⚽ Bolton Wanderers F.C. (also The Whitemen), from their traditional white shirt (from 1888–90 and almost continuously since 1892, see Historical Football Kits website); Wikipedia. See also Noblot / Notlob, Reds, Savage Six, Spots, Trotters, Wanderers.

- ⚽ Corinthians A.F.C., founded in Douglas, Isle of Man, in 1930. The club plays in white shirts with black shorts, and has an official name in the sporting 'classical names' tradition. The club badge shows outline Corinthian-style architectural pillars. The club website has the variant form The Mighty Whites; Wikipedia.

- ⚽ Dover Athletic F.C., founded in 1983 as a successor to a long succession of bankrupt predecessors, the club plays in mostly-white shirts and black shorts, and the club badge features the famous White Cliffs of Dover. The club continued with 'Lilywhites' (from a previous club) till 1999 but are now just 'The Whites'; W2000–13. See also Lilywhites.

- ⚽ Fulham F.C., from their adoption of an all-white strip in 1903. Nowadays, however, the shorts are black; Wikipedia. See also Badgers, Cottagers, Lilywhites.

- ⚽ Hednesford Town F.C., founded in Staffordshire in 1880, white shirts and black shorts. Recorded in W1988–90. See also Pitmen.

- ⚽ Hereford United F.C., from the all-white strip adopted from their foundation in 1924, though in 1946 black shorts were introduced (said to have been made from recycled black-out curtains) and the colours have usually had a mixture of black and white since; Wikipedia. See also Bulls, Lilywhites, United.

- ⚽ Leeds United A.F.C. (also Mighty Whites). The club adopted the famous all-white strip in 1961, at the start of the Don Revie management (1961–75), and allegedly this was not as a salute to the white rose of Yorkshire but a salute to the continental champions Real Madrid. Their current badge, since 1984, now features the white rose, but previously it copied the crest of the city of Leeds. 'Whites' is given in the Williams League Directories 1985–95 and in SS2003/4–12/13. See also Dirty Leeds, Owls, Peacocks, United.

- ⚽ Lisburn Distillery F.C., founded in Belfast in 1880. The club was known as Distillery F.C. until 1999 and was originally founded as a works side for the Royal Irish Distillery company. The club plays in an all-white strip. The nickname is recorded in Fabian & Green 1960 (iv, p. 139) for the 1899–1900 season, but whether it was in use that early is not clear, RI1997, RNI2007.

⚽ Molesey F.C., founded in Surrey in 1953; white shirts; W1980/1–90. See also Moles.

⚽ Preston North End F.C., founded in 1880, the club first adopted the white shirts (and blue shorts) from which the nickname comes in 1888; Wikipedia. See also Glasses, Invincibles, Proud Preston / PNE / North End, Lilywhites.

⚽ Salisbury City F.C., founded in 1947, renamed 'City' in 1993; the club plays in an all-white strip; W1990–2013 and SSY2008/9–10/11. See also Lilywhites.

⚽ Yate Town A.F.C. Founded in Gloucestershire in 1906, originally as Yate Rovers, the club was reformed in 1933, and again in 1946 as Yate YMCA, and then as Town in 1959. The club plays in white shirts with blue shorts; W1983/4–91. See also Bluebells.

Wick is the nickname of Eton Wick F.C., founded in Berkshire in 1881; a short form of the official name; W2001–10.

Wickers is the nickname of two clubs, which play in the same Sussex league. Their proximity perhaps raises the question whether clubs should have an away nickname. The clubs are:

⚽ Southwick F.C., founded in Sussex in 1882; W1987–2009.

⚽ Wick F.C., founded in Sussex in 1892; W1985–2013.

Wild Boars, see Boars (Eversley)

Wilderness Boys is the evocative nickname of the new Grimsby Borough F.C., founded in 2003. The club website states that the nickname is because the club had no ground of its own, but they are now established at the new Bradley Community Stadium in Grimsby; W2011–13.

Willows is the nickname of Walsham-le-Willows F.C., founded in Suffolk in about 1890, and repeating the place-name. The club's badge has a stunning image of a willow tree with a football surrounded by the nickname repeated five times.

Windmill Army is a nickname for supporters of North Leigh F.C., founded in Oxfordshire in 1908. The club has an attractive badge of a windmill and there is a famous windmill in the centre of the town; Wikipedia. See also Nor Lye, Windmill Army, Yellows.

Wingmakers is a nickname for Airbus UK Broughton F.C., founded as a works side for the Vickers Armstrong aircraft factory in Flintshire in 1946. The club now has a badge with a modern Airbus flying over a football, and the club ground is called The Airfield; AFBC. See also Planemakers.

Wings is the nickname of Welling United F.C. Founded in London in 1963, the nickname appears to be a contraction of the place-name (w'ing), but the club's badge further expresses this with a proud image of a flying pegasus (a horse with wings); W1982/3–2013. See also Reds.

Winky is the friendly short form nickname for Wincanton Town F.C., founded in Somerset in 1890. The club currently plays in the Dorset leagues and the nickname appears on several county websites. It seems also to have a broader use as a nickname for the town itself.

Winton is the nickname of Ardrossan Winton Rovers F.C., founded in Ayrshire in 1902. The short form of the official name is recorded on Wikipedia, SFHA.

Wire is a nickname for Warrington Town F.C., founded in Cheshire in 1949, originally as Stockton Heath Albion, renamed Warrington in 1961. The name is taken from the town's leading industry since the early nineteenth century, the production of steel wire. The former Wire Works is currently being developed as a retail park. The Rugby League side Warrington Wolves are also nicknamed The Wire (recorded in Dobson 1973). The singular form is used on Wikipedia and on the club's own website, but W1983/4–6, W1991, Smith 1991/2–95/6 and Pickering 1994 record the nickname as Wires. See also Levers, Town, Warriors, Yellows.

Wishy is the nickname of Wishaw Juniors F.C., founded in North Lanarkshire in 1919, originally as Wishaw YMCA, changing name in 1924; a friendly short form of the place-name; Wikipedia.

Witches is a nickname for at least three clubs, either for historical reasons or as a pun on the place-name. The clubs are:

⚽ Ipswich Town F.C. recorded in Avis 1966–70, and clearly as a pun on the sound of the place-name. See also Binners / Binmen, Blues, Superblues, Town, Tractor Boys.

⚽ Middlewich Town F.C., founded in Cheshire in 1998, in a merger of M. Athletic (1952) and M. Town Youth. The nickname is a pluralised adaptation of the last syllable of the place-name; recorded for the earlier club in W1979/80 as 'The Witch', and as 'The Witches' in W1980/1.

⚽ Warboys Town F.C., founded in Cambridgeshire in 1885. The nickname here refers to the notorious trials of the Warboys Witches (Alice Samuel and family), in 1589–93; W1992–2004. A badge showing a flying witch appears in AFBC.

Withy is the nickname for Witheridge F.C., founded in Devon in 1920; a friendly short form recorded in W2008–13.

Wizards is a nickname for Merlins Bridge A.F.C., founded in Pembrokeshire at an uncertain date, but match reports from 1972–3 appear on the 'Pembrokeshire-sport.co.uk' website, and using this and the variant nickname. Under the influence of English pronunciation and the fame of Merlin, the wizard of the Arthurian legends, the place-name here has shifted from the earlier *Mawdlyn's Brydge*, originally referring to a bridge dedicated to Mary Magdalen (Owen and Morgan 2007). See also Bridge.

Wolves is a nickname for at least three clubs with a similar-sounding word in their place-name. All three place-names contain Anglo-Saxon personal names referring to wolves. The clubs are

⚽ Wolverhampton Wanderers F.C., founded in 1877 as St Luke's (school) F.C., they merged in 1879 with another club called The Wanderers and adopted their current name. The nickname is recorded in BoF1905–6, on the 1933 Ogden card, the 1936

Thomson 'stamp', Avis 1954–70, G1956–76, Churchill 1958, Norris 1959, Richards 1960, AA 1960, and throughout RY1970/1–SSY2012/13. The place-name means 'Wulfrun's high farmstead' (Mills 1991). The nickname has since been transferred to related groups such as the Wolves Academy, Wolves Women and the charity Wolves Aid. There is also the famous Wolfie mascot. See also Buckley Babes, Dingles, Tatters, Wanderers.

◎ Wolverton Town F.C., founded in Buckinghamshire near Milton Keynes in 1887, originally as a railways works side, W. L & NWR F.C., renaming as 'W. British Rail' 1948–81, and as W. Town 1981–7. In 1987 they renamed as MK Wolverton, then as AFC Wolverton before folding in 1992. In 2004, W. Town was reborn. The place-name is here considered to refer to a man called Wulfhere (Mills 1991); W1983/4–89. See also MK Wolves, Railwaymen.

◎ Wolviston F.C., founded in Cleveland in 1910. In this case Mills 1991 says that 'Wulf' is the personal name in the place-name; W1994–2005. See also Villagers.

Wolves Sporting is the nickname of Wolverhampton Sporting Community F.C., founded in 2001. Earlier, the club was called Chubb Sports but lost its ground and sponsorship when the Chubb lock company folded. It reformed as Heath Town Rangers in 2001 and then took the present name in 2010; Wikipedia.

Wombles is a friendly nickname for Wimbledon F.C. and its successor A.F.C. Wimbledon, from the famous children's television series *The Wombles of Wimbledon Common*. The discipline of Womble Studies began with Elisabeth Beresford's sequence of five novels (1968–1976) but became a more popular activity after the 1973 television series. It was inevitable that the name should transfer to anything which had a connection with the real Wimbledon. Between 2000 and 2003 the club had a mascot, Wandle the Womble (named from the nearby river Wandle), and the new Wimbledon club now has Haydon the Womble, named by Elisabeth Beresford herself from the name of the nearest railway station. Wombles are small furry long-nosed rubbish-collecting creatures who guard their privacy, living in burrows, a role-model for all of us. Recorded in Pickering 1994 for the old club, W2005–6 for the new. See also AFC / A.F.C., Crazy Gang, Dons (three entries), Franchise F.C.

Wood is a nickname for clubs with the word 'wood' in their official name, though sometimes it takes the plural form 'Woods' (q.v.). The examples are:

◎ Boreham Wood F.C., formed in Hertfordshire in 1948 in a merger between Boreham Rovers and Royal Retournez, the club name has always separated Borehamwood into two words, though it has been a single word since the thirteenth century (see Mills 1991). Recorded in W1979/80–2013.

◎ Evenwood Town F.C., founded in Co. Durham in 1890; W1995–2005. See also Blues.

◎ Shortwood United F.C., founded in Gloucestershire in 1900; the club website and W1983/4–2013 has 'Wood', Wikipedia has 'Woods'.

◎ Southall Town F.C., founded in Middlesex in 2000, folded in 2004. It is not at all clear why the nickname appears as 'The Wood' in W2001–2, it could be a mistake. See also Town.

☺ Thorniewood United F.C., founded in the Lanarkshire town of Viewpark in 1924; Wikipedia, SFHA.

☺ Walsall Wood F.C., founded in West Midlands in about 1915, originally as Walsall Wood Ebenezer Primitive Methodists, taking the present name in 1986; a short form of the place-name, recorded in Wikipedia. See also Prims.

☺ Wrockwardine Wood F.C., founded in West Midlands in 1890. The short form of the official name is used in online match reports.

Wooders is the nickname for Garswood United A.F.C., founded in Cheshire in 1968; Miller & Wright 1996.

Woodpeckers is the nickname for Woodbridge Town F.C., founded in Suffolk in 1885. A pluralised adaptation of the first element in the place-name, the nickname, and a picture of the bird, now appears on the club badge and is recorded in W1993–2013. See also Bridge.

Woods is a nickname for clubs with the element 'wood' in their official name, though it can also take the singular form 'Wood' (q.v.). Known plural forms are:

☺ Colliers Wood United F.C., founded in London in 1874, originally as Vandyke F.C.; W2005–13.

☺ Northwood F.C., founded in London in 1899; the nickname is widely used on the club website and the club badge shows a small forest on a hill; W1982/3–83/4 and W1994–2013.

☺ Woodford Town F.C., founded in Greater London in 1937, folded in 2003. The nickname is recorded on Wikipedia. See also Town.

Woolwich is an unofficial nickname for Arsenal F.C., coined by supporters of Tottenham Hotspur, and recorded in 2003 on the Football Fans Census website. The nickname is a reference to the original location of the club (see discussion under 'Gunners'), but it will have taken its emotive impact as mockery because of the advertising slogans for the Woolwich Building Society. The 1905–6 *Book of Football*, however, uses a similar expression, 'The Woolwichers' (p. 17). See also Boring Arsenal, France, Gooners, Gunners, Invincibles, Lucky Arsenal, Reds, Royals.

Works is recorded in W1994–5 as the nickname for Biwater F.C., founded as a works side at Clay Cross, Derbyshire, in 1952. Although the expression can, like 'the business', mean 'the real thing', here it refers to the former name of the club, Clay Cross Works F.C. The name changed in 1988. The club seems to have folded after 1995 but there have been successor clubs in the town.

Worthians is the nickname of Highworth Town F.C., founded in Wiltshire in 1894; an abstraction from the second element of the place-name; W1994–2013.

Wrens is the nickname for two clubs, based on the official names. The clubs are:

☺ Blackpool Wren Rovers, founded in Lancashire in 1931 as Wren Rovers, adding Blackpool to their name in 1998. Their name and nickname is from the street called

Wren Grove, which was their original base. Recorded in W1979/80 and W1982/3–7 (for Wren Rovers), and W1998–9.

☺ Rainworth Miners Welfare F.C., founded in Nottinghamshire in 1922. The name is an adaptation of the opening syllable of the place-name, pronounced 'Ren'orth' locally. Nevertheless, the more formal sound, 'Rain-worth', is not unknown and a former club badge illustrated in AFBC amusingly shows an umbrella symbol for the club. The modern badge shows a miner's lamp; W2008–13.

Wulfs is the nickname for A.F.C. Wulfrunians, founded in 2005 in Wolverhampton. The club takes its name from the personal name within the place-name (meaning 'Wulfrun's high farmstead' (Mills 1991), and the nickname being a short form of that; Wikipedia and internet match reports.

Wurzels is an unofficial nickname for Bristol City F.C., from the perspective of Bristol Rovers supporters, and recorded on the 2003 Football Fans Census website. There are two possible explanations for the derogatory nickname. One is that it refers to the children's book and television character Worzel Gummidge (a scarecrow famously played by Jon Pertwee in the 1979 series), because he spoke with a Bristol accent (though this accent would equally apply to Bristol Rovers). Also, Worzel has three different heads, one of which is a turnip, which would chime with another of City's nicknames. The alternative explanation is perhaps more likely, that it refers to the Somersetshire folkband The Worzels (founded 1966), one of whose successful songs, 'I am a Cider Drinker', would also chime with another of City's unofficial nicknames. The two different spellings of Worzel or Wurzel are so easily confused they cannot be considered evidence, and the coiners of the nickname could easily have had both meanings in mind. See also Babes, Cider Army, City, Eighty-Twoers / 1982 Ltd, Reds, Robins, Slave Traders, Turnips.

Wyesiders is a nickname for Builth Wells F.C., founded in Powys in 1879 or 1883, from the club's location on the river Wye. The nickname is used frequently for the club on the internet, as in a match report against Carno on 28 October 2010. The river is a long one and the nickname also appears for Hereford Rugby Club and for Newbridge-on-Wye F.C. founded in 1920 in Powys (Huws 2013). See also Ambers, Black and Ambers, Bulls.

Y-Fronts was an unofficial nickname for York City F.C. in the 1970s. Although they have been on sale in the UK since 1938, men's Y-front underpants became really popular in the 1970s; the nickname is based on a bold new shirt design adopted between 1974 and 1978 when York City placed a large Y (for York) across the whole of the shirt fronts, as a celebration of their promotion to the dizzy heights of the Second Division. The symbol was dropped after relegation to the Fourth Division in 1978. The modern badge of the club still retains a prominent Y dividing the shield; Wikipedia, Historical Football Kits website etc. See also City, Minstermen, Yorkies.

Yachtsmen is a nickname for two clubs in places associated with yachting. The clubs are:

⚽ Cowes Sports F.C., founded on the Isle of Wight in 1881. The location has been the home of international yacht racing since 1815; Miller & Wright 1996, W2008–13.

⚽ Wroxham F.C., founded in Norfolk in 1892, does not have a coastal location, but is in the Norfolk Broads and is the home of the Norfolk Broads Yacht Club. The club badge shows a stylised arrangement of sails; W1992–2013.

Yellamen is the nickname of Ascot United F.C., founded in Berkshire in 1965. The club plays in yellow shirts and socks with blue shorts. As with the next entry, the name expresses the local pronunciation of yellow; W2011–13 (as 'Yellaman'; Wikipedia has the plural form).

Yellas is a nickname of the Surrey club, Westfield F.C., founded in 1953, who play in yellow shirts with black shorts and socks. The name gives the local pronunciation of 'Yellows'; Wikipedia. See also Field.

Yellow Army is a nickname for two clubs who wear yellow shirts:

⚽ Canvey Island F.C., from their yellow shirts and pale blue shorts; Wikipedia. See also Gulls, Islanders.

⚽ Watford F.C., after their adoption of a golden shirt in 1959, which changed to yellow in 1976; Wikipedia. See also Blues, Brewers, Golden Boys, Hornets, Horns / 'Orns, Saints, Wasps.

Yellow Boys is the nickname for Penmaenmawr Phoenix F.C., founded in Conwy Co. Bor. in 1973. The club plays in yellow shirts; recorded in RW1994–5.

Yellow Canaries was the nickname of C.P.D. Trefeurig and District United, based at Banc-y-Darren in Ceredigion from 1948 to 1953. The nickname is recorded in Huws 2010. The club played in 'old gold' shirts with navy blue shorts. The Welsh language version of the nickname is Y Caneris Melyn.

Yellows is a nickname for clubs which play in a yellow shirt or an all-yellow strip. Examples are:

⚽ A.F.C. Sudbury, formed in Suffolk in 1999 in a merger between Sudbury Town (1874) and S. Wanderers (1958), the yellow shirts and nickname were inherited from the former Town side (though Borough was their preferred nickname); W2008–13. See also Borough, Suds, Town, Wanderers.

⚽ Farnborough F.C., founded in Hampshire in 1967, originally as Farnborough Town, the club reformed after bankruptcy in 2007 and play in an all-yellow strip (with blue trim); Wikipedia. See also Boro, Town.

⚽ Hucknall Town F.C. Founded in Nottinghamshire in 1945, originally as Hucknall Colliery Welfare F.C., renamed 'Town' in 1987, they play in yellow shirts; Wikipedia. See also Colliers, Town.

⚽ Invergordon F.C., founded in Highland (Ross and Cromarty) in about 1910. The club plays in yellow shirts; Wikipedia.

⚽ Isle of Man National Football Team, which represents the island in the international Island Games (founded in 1989); plays in a yellow shirts with red shorts; Wikipedia.

⚽ Lancing F.C., founded in West Sussex in 1941, originally as L. Athletic; yellow shirts with blue shorts; W1994–2002. See also Lancers.

- Mansfield Town F.C., founded in Nottinghamshire in 1897, from the dominance of yellow in their strip colours; Wikipedia. See also Stags.
- Mildenhall Town F.C., founded in Suffolk in 1898; the club plays in amber and black; W1992–2000. See also Hall, Town.
- North Leigh F.C., founded in Oxfordshire in 1908; yellow shirts; Wikipedia and club's own website. See also Millers, Nor Lye, Windmill Army.
- Oxford United F.C. The gold shirts and black (later Oxford-blue) shorts were adopted in the 1950s when the club was still called Headington, and the colours are still mainly gold; Wikipedia. See also Boys from Up the Hill, Dons, U's, United.
- Southport F.C., founded in 1881 in Merseyside, due to their distinctive yellow strip, but which they only adopted in 1954; Wikipedia. See also Port, Sandgrounders.
- Trefonen F.C., founded in Shropshire in 2008. The club plays in yellow shirts and socks, with green shorts (colours which generate the nicknames Canaries and Daffodils for other clubs); Wikipedia. See also Pitmen.
- Warrington Town F.C., founded in Cheshire in 1949, originally as Stockton Heath Albion, renamed Warrington in 1961. The club plays in yellow shirts and socks; Wikipedia. See also Levers, Town, Warriors, Wire/s.

Yeltz is the nickname of Halesowen Town F.C., founded in West Midlands in 1873. The explanation is that *Yeltz* is a nickname for anyone from Halesowen and is based on the local pronunciation of the place-name, traditionally pronounced something like *'Ellzowen*, making what looks like a radical change of the initial H to Y far more natural, and this difference in pronunciation is known for other words in the local dialect. Another example is the famous Black Country word for 'I am', *yam*, which has generated a nickname for speakers of the dialect, the Yam-Yams (from a Birmingham perspective). The unexpected 't' might well recall an earlier pronunciation: a document of 1745 listed on the website of Worcester Record Office mentions 'William Sadler of Halce Owen', suggesting some extra sound used to be in the place-name where the t now appears in the nickname (for historical linguistic reasons 'c' can sometimes adapt to 't', as in 'pretence' and 'pretentious').

The dialect is certainly the right explanation for the nickname, but an alternative story needs to be mentioned as it is now circulated on the internet. It is said that a Hungarian player with the unlikely name of Pungus Catfich, who played for the club in the late 1940s, would lapse into Hungarian or German in the heat of the moment. His call of "Yeltz, Albert, yeltz!" is said to have meant something like "Over here, Albert, on my head!" So, possible explanations would be German *Jetzt!* meaning "Ready! Pass it here!" (the opening j is pronounced as y, the e is pronounced long, which could have led an English audience to assume a medial l in the word, and the final t is silent, leaving z as the final sound); or Hungarian *Jeles!*, pronounced 'yelesh', meaning "Excellent! Well done!" or *Játssz!*, meaning "Play! Come on!" In the last case, the á vowel is also pronounced long, also possibly suggesting a medial l to an

English audience. The more plausible word is the German *Jetzt*, as most Hungarians were fluent in German (because of the dual monarchy of Austro-Hungary before 1918) (thanks to Bernard Adams and colleagues in the Hungarian Translators' Association). Like all good myths, the story has just enough credibility to ensure its survival, but it is highly likely that it is entirely invented: no independent evidence for the player seems to exist, and two famous 1950s Hungarian footballers, Ferenc Puskás and Sándor Kocsis, had names which seem to be the inspiration for Pungus Catfich. Recorded in Avis 1966–70, W1979/80–2013.

Yids / Yid Army / Yiddos is an unofficial nickname for supporters of Tottenham Hotspur F.C. Although the name 'Yid', based on Yiddish, the Jewish dialect of German, is usually used as a term of abuse, in the context of Tottenham it is entirely respectable and courageous. In 1936, the British Fascist Party leader Oswald Mosley led a racist march in Tottenham, where the local football team had a large number of Jewish supporters. In order to show solidarity with the Jewish supporters, the non-Jewish fans adopted the name 'The Yids' as a nickname. When racist supporters of other teams used the term in their chants at matches, its effect was therefore compromised. According to Ferris 2005, the nickname was first used only in the 1980s, but this must (surely?), have been a revival of an older club tradition. See also Lilywhites, Spurs, Super Spurs.

YM is a nickname for clubs which have been affiliated to the YMCA, or Young Men's Christian Association, during their history. The clubs are:

⚽ Horsham YMCA F.C., founded in Sussex in 1898; W1988–90 as Y.M., W1993–2013 as YM's.

⚽ Kirkcaldy YM Junior F.C., founded in Fife in 1969; Wikipedia, SFHA.

⚽ Newport YMCA A.F.C., founded in 1973 in a merger between the Newport Central YMCA and Newport Pill YMCA; RW1996.

Yo-Yo Club is a nickname for a club which regularly moves up and down the league divisions, gaining promotion and relegation in rapid succession. Many teams have been so called, but it seems only Stirling Albion have so far earned the phrase as a semi-official nickname (see next entry). The Germans have another delightful expression, 'escalator clubs'.

Yo-Yos is a nickname for Stirling Albion F.C., founded in 1945. The nickname refers to the movement of the club between the leagues in the 1950s and early 1960s, encouraging the proverbial expression "Going up and down like Stirling Albion". Nowadays, the club is a successful mainstream Scottish team; Wikipedia. See also Albion, Binos.

Yorkies is a nickname for York City F.C. It is not just a pun on the city place-name (also used generally for people from York). Yorkie chocolate bars were made by Rowntree's, the historic city employer, and were renowned for their chunky masculinity, not least in their advertising. The brand is now owned by Nestlé, now based in York and a sponsor to the football club. The Bootham Crescent stadium was renamed Kit-Kat Crescent 2005–10, in thanks for Nestlé sponsorship. Yorkie the Lion is the club mascot; Wikipedia. See also City, Minstermen, Y-Fronts.

Young Dons, for Donington F.C., see under Dons.

Young Dragons is a nickname for the Wales National Football Team, under-21s side; Wikipedia.

Young Guns is the nickname of Caerau Ely F.C., founded in 1955 near Bridgend, South Wales. The nickname is an increasingly popular expression, which became more widely known after its use for the title of the 1988 film about Billy the Kid. The meaning here need be no more than 'good shooters'; Wikipedia.

Youths is a nickname and part official name for Wexford Youths F.C., founded in Co. Wexford in 2007; Wikipedia. See also Warriors.

Yowes is the intriguing nickname of Lanark United F.C., founded in 1920. The word is Scots for ewes, female sheep, but the reason for it is not immediately obvious. The word is used in a famous Burns poem, 'Ca' the yowes tae the knowes' ('Take the ewes to the hills'), but there is no local connection to the poem. Lanark is the location of a major livestock auction, where ewes are regularly sold, and the most common Scottish sheep, the Black Face, has a Lanark variety (compare the Aylesbury Ducks and the Dorking Chicks for other nicknames formed from a local breed of a common animal). But the most likely explanation has to be the sound of the word. The Scots pronunciation of Yowes in the Burns poem chimes with knowes, so it is pronounced just as it is spelled, but 'ewes' is often pronounced in Scotland in the same way as in England, so the nickname is a colourful spelling of the sound 'U's', for United, a nickname already known elsewhere. This pun has also occurred in England in an unofficial nickname for Colchester United in Essex (see Ewes and U's). The importance of the local livestock industry no doubt encouraged the nickname to be expressed in the famous Scots spelling; SFHA.

Zebras is a nickname for clubs which play in black-and-white stripes. It is the preferred nickname for such design on the continent, but in Britain and Ireland the more common nickname is Magpies (q.v.), even though magpies do not have stripes. The 'Zebra' clubs are:

- Brigg Town F.C., founded in Lincolnshire in 1863. Brigg is famous for its annual horse-trading fair, so perhaps the club took this nickname as suggesting the striped horse; black-and-white striped shirts, black shorts; W1982/3–2013.
- Cefn Druids F.C., founded in Wrexham in a merger in 1992; recorded in RW1994. Black shorts with black-and-white striped shirts. See also Ancients, Druids.
- Leith Athletic F.C., founded in Edinburgh in 1887, folded in 1955. A new club of the same name was formed in 1996. The nickname is recorded on SFHA for the old club. See also Athletic and Black and Whites, for the new club.
- Rainham Town F.C., founded in Essex in 1945, closed 1994. By the time of W1979/80, the club had adopted an all-red strip, but this nickname is recorded in Avis 1966–70, presumably for an earlier strip. See also Reds.

⚽ Vale of Nith F.C., founded in Dumfries in 1880, closed in 1889; the Reserve side seems better documented, for which the SFHA records this nickname and another. The Reserve side at least played in black-and-white stripes. See also Vale.

Zeplins is the nickname of Cuffley F.C., founded in Hertfordshire in 1958. The nickname commemorates a famous incident at Cuffley on 3 September 1916 when a German airship was shot down. It was not a Zeppelin but the Schütte-Lauz SL–11, but 'Zeppelin' has long been a generic term and the craft was even reported as a Zeppelin in the press at the time. The German pilots were given a military funeral at Potters Bar, film of which survives. The club badge shows a stag's head with a burning airship and a biplane above it. Wikipedia records the variant form 'The Zeps', 'Zeplins' is the form recorded in W1993–6.

Ziggers was a nickname for Barrow A.F.C., founded in Cumbria in 1901. An interesting word, but the story is surreal. A zigger is an old army kit bag, so called because of the zig-zag (or criss-cross) cords used to tie it up (like boot laces). The club tradition in the 1950s and '60s was for one of these bags to be painted in the club's blue colours and paraded around the ground as a mascot before a match at the home ground of Holker Street. Photographs of the mascot are available on the internet. The supporters would chant a song "Zigger, Zigger – Zagger, Oi, Oi, Oi!" (or Zigger-Zagger, Zigger-Zagger, Oi, Oi, Oi!). Modern versions of the song are alleged to have racist overtones and it has become associated with the Chelsea Shed Boys (q.v.), but there is no reason to suppose that these applied in Barrow-in-Furness at the time of the tradition, not least because the expression has two possible uses in mainstream football: **(1)** recent editions of Brewer's *Dictionary of Phrase and Fable* (Room 1999) say that 'zigger-zagger' was the name of the revolving racket which used to be used by football fans to generate noise (this definition, however, is not found anywhere else and seems to be an error). **(2)** The expression was clearly a supporters' chant independently of the Barrow tradition; it appears throughout Peter Terson's play, *Zigger Zagger* (first performed in 1967, printed by Penguin in 1970), and it seems to refer to the zig-zag pattern of the ball passing from one player to another in its rhythmic progress towards the goal (another expression for a similar idea is 'the old one-two', an expression borrowed from boxing). The supporters' chant encourages the players to adopt this movement, as well as suggesting to opponents that they are about to be overcome. The army kit bag must therefore have been adopted as a mascot because it shared a name which was already current in football culture. The word was adopted as the name of the club magazine, *The Zigger*, in 1967 (same year as the play), and is today used for the newsletter. Inexplicably, this beautiful word is missing from the OED and other standard dictionaries; recorded for Barrow in W1990. See also Bluebirds, Shipbuilders, Strawberries.

APPENDIX ONE:
WORDS USED AS CLUB SUFFIXES

Included here are words which are commonly attached to club official names, if they are not part of the club's place-name or institution name. I have not included unique examples if the word itself is also unique to the club (such as Chenecks, which could never be used for another club), but I have included unique examples which refer to a more general cultural inheritance (such as Rob Roy, which could easily be adapted by another club). The list only includes examples from clubs which are mentioned in the Dictionary. Suffixes are frequently used as nicknames in their own right. Occasionally they appear as prefixes; some clubs use more than one expression.

Academical/s
Academy
Adelaide
Aelwyd
Albert
Albion
Alexandra
Alliance
Alma
Alpha
Amateur/s
Amateur Athletic Association
Ancient/s
Angels
Antelope
Arabs
Arcadians
Argyle
Association Football Club
Athletic
Athletic Club
Athletico
Belles
Belvedere
Blackbirds
Bluebell

Bohemians
Bon Accord
Boro / Borough
Boys
Boys and Girls Club
Britannia
Brotherhood
Buds
Burgh
Caledonia/n/ns
Cambrian
Casuals
Cavaliers
Celtic
Centaurs
Charterhouse
Cherrypickers
Church
Citadel
City
Civil Service
Club
Clwb Pêl-Droed
College
Collieries
Colts

Community
Comrades
Corinthians
Coronation
Cougars
County
Cowboys
Crusaders
Dazzlers
DDSS (Discharged and Demobilised
    Soldiers and Sailors)
Decimals
Diamonds
District
Dodgers
Dominoes
Dons
Draconians
Dragons
Druids
Dynamo/e/s
Eagles
Elite
Ex-Schoolboys
Falcons
Football Club
Former Pupils
Freebooters
Gabriels
Genesis
Girls
Gothic
Grasshoppers
Guild
Gunners
Gymnasium
Harlequins
Harp/s
Harriers
Hearts
Heathens

Herd
Hibernian/s
Hornets
Hotspur
Institute
Inter / International
Invicta
Ironopolis
Ironsides
It's Just Like Watching Brazil
Ivanhoes
Jets
Junior/s
Ladies Football Club
Lammas
Left Overs
Leisure Centre
Linnets
Lionesses
Lions
Manor
Marine
Mechanics
Methodists
Metropolitan
Mills
Miners
Miners Welfare
Mission
Motors
Municipal
National Football Team
Nomads
North / ern
Old Boys
Old Scholars
Olympic
Orient
Panthers
Pegasus
Pennant

Phoenix
Pickwicks
Primitive Methodists
Primrose
Progressive
Pumas
Racing Club
Radicals
Ramblers
Rangers
Recreation /ists
Red/s
Remnants
Representative Football Team
Rifles
Rob Roy
Rocks
Romulus
Rovers
Royal
Royal British Legion
Saints
Saracens
Saxons
Scotia
Senior
Shamrock
Skull and Crossbones
Sky Blues
Social Club
Spartans
Sphinx
Sporting
Sportiva/o
Sports
Spurs
Stanley
Star/s
Strollers
Suburbs
Supermarine

Swifts
Team
Terriers
Thistle
Thorfinn
Thursdays
Tigers
Tornadoes
Town
Trinity
Trojans
United
University
Vale
Venturas
Veterans
Victoria
Vikings
Villa
Village
Violet
Vipers
Wanderers
Warriors
Wednesday
Welfare
Whitestars
Wolves
Women's Football Club
XI (eleven)
Youth/s
Youth Centre

APPENDIX TWO:

THE UNIVERSE OF FOOTBALL:

SUBJECTS IN THE NICKNAMES

Abbreviations, acronyms and short forms are mainly excluded from this list because they do not contain a subject. The real reason for the nickname may not always reflect the subject content here (birds, for instance, are often used to describe colour) and sometimes the relevance is by association rather than specific statement. Only nicknames are included here, but the club's official name may also contain ideas (such as 'The 61 F.C.' being a number and a year). The journey through the universe, from 'Age' to 'Youth', illustrates football's place at the heart of humanity.

Age: Ancients, Aul Reds, Dinosaurs, Dodgers, Druids, Grand Old Team, Grandad's Army, Old Boys, Old Invincibles, Old Lions, Old Reds, Old 'Uns, Owd Reds, Vets. *See also* Youth.

Agriculture: *see* Food and Food Industry.

Alcohol: Ale House Brawlers, Brewers, Brewery Boys, Cider Army, Fed, Landlords, Tipples, Tonics, Wurzels.

Americanisms: Armadillos, Batmans, Beach Boys, Bluebirds, Braves, City Slickers, Cleveland Cowboys, Cougars, Cowboys, Cutters, Eric Cartman's Barmy Army, Greenbacks, Indians, Jags (for the cat / car), Krooners, Micky Mousers, Panthers, Pennant, Pilgrims, Pompey, Pumas, Skunks, Young Guns.

Amphibians: Salamanders.

Animals: *see under* Amphibians, Birds, Fish and Other Marine Animals, Human Beings, Insects and Spiders, Mammals, Palaeontology, Snakes.

Architecture: Abbey, Bont, Brickies, Bridge, Bridgers, Bridges, Brig, Briggers, Broch, Builders, Castle, Castlemen, Church, Cottagers, Council Housers, Demolition Squad, Fort, Forters, Frenchcastle, Gable Endies, Gate, Gates, Hall, Houses, Levers, Mighty Del, Mill, Minstermen, Moatmen, Moatsiders, Over the Bridge, Palace, Pier, Priory, Priorymen, Quarterboys, Roofing, Shack, Spireites, Squatters, Stumpites, Terras, Tower, Towerites, Villa / Villans / Villains, Windmill Army.

Arts: Culture Club. *See also* Colours (Descriptive), Literature, Music, Poetry.

Astronomy: Atomic Boys, Aurora, Crescents, Moonlighters, Star, Stars, Sun, Sunrise City, White Stars.

Athletics: Athletic, Aths, Harriers, Latics, Sporting, Sports. *See also* Other Sports.

Birds: Blackbirds, Bluebirds, Budgies, Buntings, Buzzards, Canaries, Chicken-bree

Team, Chickens, Chicks, Cock 'n' Hens, Cock Robins, Cockerels, Cocks, Cormorants, Cranes, Crows, Cuckoos, Curlews, Drake's Ducklings, Ducks, Eagles, Eaglets, Elyrch, Eosiaid, Fergie's Fledglings, Finch, Finches, Gulls, Harriers, Hawks, Henrun, Hens, Kestrels, Kingfishers, Larks, Leghorns, Linnets, Magpies, Mallards, New Robins, Nightingales, Owls, Peacocks, Pelican, Penguins, Pewits, Piod, Pheasants, Radnor Robins, Ravens, Redbirds, Robins, Rookettes, Rooks, Roosters, Rwsters, Seagulls, Seahawks, Scorries, Snipes, Storks, Super Owls, Swallows, Swans, Swans and Robins, Swifts, Throstles, Welsh Bluebirds, Woodpeckers, Wrens, Yellow Canaries.

Body Parts: Bloods, Bones, Chelsea Headhunters, Eyes, Flippers, Gills, Hearties, Hearts, Heed, Horns, Jaggy Bunnets.

Books: Barcodes, Press, Printers. *See also* Literature, Poetry.

Cats: *see under* Mammals.

Classicalism: Apollo, Arcadians, Centurians, Cestrians, Corinthians, Corinths, Corries, Draconians / Dracs, Excelsior, Gladiators, Grecians, Gymns, Olympic, Pegasus, Pic, Pompey, Pompey Ladies, Romans, Roms, Spartans, Trojans.

Clothes: Baggies (?), Bonnets, Cobblers, Corsetmen, Glasses, Glovers, Hatters, Pockets, Rags, Redcoats, Souters, Straw-Hatters / Straw-Plaiters, Tatters (?), Y-Fronts.

Colours (Descriptive): All Whites, Amber and Blacks, Ambers, Aul Reds, Blac and Amber, Black and Ambers, Black and Gold/s, Black and Greens, Black and Red Army, Black and White Army, Black and Whites, Blue and Whites, Blue Army, Blues, Buffs, Claret and Blues, Clarets, Dark Blues, Emerald Greens, Emeralds, Flying Blues, Gold and Black Army, Gold 'n' Blacks, Golds, Green, Green and Blacks, Green and Reds, Green and Golds, Green and White Army, Green Army, Greens, Holy Blues, Lilywhites, Light Blues, Lurgan Blues, Marigolds, Maroon Army, Maroons, Mighty Blues, Mighty Whites, Monochrome, Old Gold, Orange Army, Pink and Chocolate, Pinks, Real Reds, Red and Blacks, Red and Blues, Red and Greens, Red and White Wizards, Reds, Saffron, Salmoners, Satsumas, Scarlet Runners, Sky Blues, Super Greens, Super Whites, Superblues, Supergreens, Tangerines, Terras, Two Blues, Violet, White Brigade, White Men / Whitemen, Whites, Yellamen, Yellas, Yellow Boys, Yellows.

Colours (Metaphorical): Atomic Boys, Badgers, Bantams, Barcodes, Batmans, Bit o'Red, Black Arabs, Black Cats, Black Dogs, Black Dragons, Black Watch, Blackbirds, Bloods, Blue Belles, Blue Boys, Blue Imps, Bluebells, Bluebirds, Blueboys, Bonny Blues, Buzz, Canaries, Candystripes, Cards, Cherries, Chocolates, Cock Robins, Crows, Daffodils, Dolly Blues, Doms, Emeralds, Garibaldi Reds, Golden Boys, Green Lions, Green Machine, Greenbacks, Hornets, Humbugs, Ivies / Ivys, Leafe, Lilywhites, Lobsters, Magpies, Marigolds, Mustard Pots, Pansies, Peacocks, Peas, Penguins, Peppermints, Piod, Poppies, Radnor Ravens, Red Army, Red Devils, Red Dragons, Red Imps, Red Lichties, Red Lions, Red Rebels,

Redbirds, Redcoats, Redmen, Robins, Robins, Rooks, Salamanders, Salmoners, Satsumas, Scarlet Runners, Skunks, Spiders, Stingers, Strawberries, Supherites, Swans, Swans and Robins, Tangerine Barmy Army, Tangerines, Teigars, Terras, Tesco's, Thin Red Line, Tigers, Undertakers, Violet, Wasps, Welsh Bluebirds, White Horse Men, White Stars, White Tigers, White Wolves, Yellow Army, Yellow Canaries, Zebras.

Computers: Barcodes.

Criminals: Ale House Brawlers, Bad Boys, Bankers, Cheaterfield, Donkey Lashers, Freebooters, Highwaymen, Lambs, Pirates, Skull and Crossbones, Stab City, Sweeney, Swindle, Villains. *See also* Law and Order, Pirates.

Dancing / Body Movements: Boing!, Can Cans, Shakers, Waltz.

Days of the Week: Thursdays, Wednesday, Wendys.

Defence Studies: *see* Military.

Dialect: Ar Tarn, Bonny Oodle, Braw Lads, Brig, Briggers, Cabes, Cattachs, Chicken-bree Team, Cobbydalers, Darreners, De Town, Dokens, Doonhamers, Hive, Jaggy Bunnets, Jaggy Nettles, Loons, Mackems, Medda, Niseachs, Nitten, Nor Lye, Norn Iron, Owd Reds, Peasy, Posset, Red Lichties, Rouslers, Sassenachs, Scorries, Shannocks, Shiners, Smokies, Sodgers, Souters, Sweeney, T'Colliers or T'Pitmen, Tarn, Tayn, Theestle, Toon, Tooners, Toonsers, Trotters, Tykes, Whe Ho, Wurzels, Yeltz, Yowes.

Directions: East, Eastenders, Mids, North, North End, Orient, South, Southern, West, West End, Westenders.

Diseases and Medicine: Bitters / Bitter Blues, Jaggy Bunnets, Mental Hospital, Tonics. *See also* Body Parts, Obesity Studies.

Dogs: *see under* Mammals.

Economics: *see* Manufacturing and Industry and Trade, Money, Poverty.

Educational: Aber Uni, Academy, Academical, Acas, Accies, Alma, College, Dandy Dons, Dons, Glasgow Uni, Poly, Prog, Scholars, School of Science, Students, Super Owls, Tyneside Professors, Varsity, Watt, Young Dons.

Electricity: Atomic Boys, Diamonds, Dynamo/s, Dynamoe/s, G's, Lights, Mo's, Moes, Powermen, Red Lichties.

Elitism: Aristocrats, Cavaliers, Earls, Excelsior, Laird/s, Landlords, Lords, Peacocks, Posh, Tyneside Professors. *See also* Politics, Republicanism, Royalty.

Emotions: *see* Fear and Courage, Happiness.

Entertainment: Entertainers, Gooners. *See also* Television / Radio / Cinema / Theatre.

European Union Studies: Albion, Britannia, Bucketshakers, Comrades, Constitution, Danes, France, Frenchcastle, Grecians, Huns, Inter / International, Iron Curtain, Islanders, Khaki Chums, Romans, Spaniards, Wars. *See also* Money.

Fear and Courage: Braves, Terrors, Tooting Terrors, Valiants.

Fish, Other Marine Animals and Fishing Industry: Addicks, Anchormen,

Bloaters, Cod Army, Codheads, Crabs, Dolphins, Fish, Fish Suppers, Fishermen, Flippers, Gills, Haddicks, Haddocks, Herrings, Lobsters, Mariners, Mullets, Musselmen, Oystermen, Penwaig, Pikes, Red Lichties, Seahorses, Seals, Shannocks, Sharks, Shrimpers, Shrimps, Skates, Smokies, Trawlerboys, Trawlermen.

Flags: Pennant.

Flowers: *see* Plants.

Folklore: Cuckoos, Curfews, Dollies, Druids, Fingal, Ghosts, Monkey Hangers, Moonrakers, Pedlars, Peeping Toms, Pied Pipers, Poachers, Robin Hoods, Roys, Wakes, White Horse Men. *See also* Dialect, Mythical and Supernatural, Religious Expressions.

Food and Food Industry: Addicks, Almonds, Baker Boys, Bakers, Berrypickers, Biscuit Boys, Biscuitmen, Biscuiteers, Bloaters, Brewers, Brewery Boys, Butchers, Cabbage, Candy Rock, Candystripes, Cheesemen, Cherries, Cherrypickers, Chicken-bree Team, Chickens, Chippy, Chips, Cider Army, Cock 'n' Hens, Cod Army, Codheads, Cooks, Corn, Cornies, Crabs, Doughboys, Farm, Farmer's Boys, Fed, Field, Fields, Filberts, Fish Suppers, Fishermen, Flourmen, Gingerbread Men, Gingerbreads, Haddocks, Ham Bappers, Hammies / Hams, Henrun, Hens, Herd, Herrings, Humbugs, Jam Boys, Jam Makers, Jam Tarts, Jam Town, Jambos, Jammies, Jolly Green Giants, Lobsters, Mangos, Manure, Merry Millers, Mullets, Mushrooms, Musselmen, Mustard Pots, Natives, Nurserymen, Nuts, Orchard, Orchardmen, Oystermen, Peas, Penwaig, Peppermints, Pie Eaters / Pies, Pie Men, Poachers, Quality Street Kids, Red Lichties, Rowntrees, Salts, Sarnies, Satsumas, Seaweed, Shannocks, Shrimpers, Shrimps, Smokies, Spice Boys, Strawberries, Synners, Tangerines, Toffees / Toffeemen, Tractor Boys, Tractormen, Trawler Boys, Trawlermen, Turnips, Walnut Boys, Windmill Army, Yorkies.

Furniture: Cabes, Cabinetmakers, Chairboys.

Geographical Terms: Ar Tarn, Aurora, Bankers, Bankies, Bay, Beach Boys, Belvedere, Borderers, Bordermen, Boro, Borough, Broch, Broch United, Brook, Brooksiders, Burgh, Burn, Burnie, Bury, Capitals, City, City Devils, City Gents, City Slickers, Coasters, Colony, Common, Commoners, Countrymen, County, Covies, Dale/s, Dalers, Deans, Down, Drove, East, Eastenders, End, Farm, Fenmen, Ferry, Field, Fields, Fleet, Ford/s, Forest, Foresters, Gate, Glebe, Glens, Green, Grove, Hamlet, Haven, Heartlanders, Heath, Hill, Hill Club, Hillians, Hillmen, Hills, Hive, Inter / International, Islanders, Junction, Lakesiders, Lane, Little Club on the Hill, Locals, Main, Manor, Marine, Maze, Mead, Meadow Men, Mids, Mighty Moor, Moorlanders, Moors, New Towners, Newtowners, North, North End, Orient, Over the Bridge, Paraders, Parishioners, Park, Parkies, Pennies, Pens, Plain, Point, Pool, Pools, Port, Portites, Ports, Rec, Riversiders, Road, Roaders, Rockies, Rocks, Row, Royal Stones, Stones, Seasiders, Seaweed, Shire, Side, Sons (of the Rock), South, Southern, Street, Suburbs, Tarn, Tayn, Ton/s, Toon, Tooners, Toonsers, Town, Towners, Townies, Vale, Valley, Vallians,

Village, Village Lads, Villagers, Ville, Waterfall Men, Waters, Watersiders, Waysiders, Wee County, Well, Wellmen, Wells, West, West End, Westenders, Wick, Wickers, Wood, Wooders, Woods.

Geology: Baggies, Brickies, Dabbers, Claymen, Rockies, Rocks, Royal Stones, Salts, Sand Dobbers, Sandgrounders, Spamen, Stoners, Stones, Sulpherites, Turfs. *See also* Palaeontology, Precious Metals and Stones.

Geometry: *see* Shapes.

Ground Names and Features: Anfielders, Belvo, Camrose Blues, Cottagers, Crofters, Crows, Dennyboys, Dens Parkers, Evans Bevan Boys, Forters, Galabankies, Groveites, Hedgemen, Jolly Boys, Kirkby Roaders, Kop / Kopites, Kopettes, Laneites, Larks, Lowfielders, Millers, Moles, Moatmen, Moatsiders, Moorites, Paraders, Parishioners, Pennies, Planters, Rakers, Rec, Riversiders, Roaders, Rokerites / Rokermen, Seals, Shaymen, Skinners, Sols, Sorters, Southbankers, Strawberries, Tops, Turfites, Valiants, Valley Roaders.

Happiness: Dandies, Dandy Dons, Edinboro Darlings, Entertainers, Gala, Gay Puritans, Happylanders, Jolly Boys, Jolly Green Giants, Merry Millers, Merry Stripes.

Human Beings: Bad Boys, Belles, Bhoys, Blue Boys, Blueboys, Boyos, Boys from Rathbone Street, Boys from up the Hill, Boys in Green, Braves, Braw Lads, Brotherhood, Chelsea Headhunters, Citizens, Cits, City Gents, City Slickers, Clan, Cleveland Cowboys, Commoners, Comrades, Cowboys, Crew, Dandies, Dinasyddion, Dossers, Exiles, Fenmen, Gents, Lads, Landlords, Lankies, Locals, Loons, Man City / Man U, Nomads, Pensioners, People's Club, Social, Sons, Tribesmen / Tribal Army, Unknowns, Urchins, Village Lads, Wardens, Wilderness Boys.

Iceland: Sjoke City, Thorfinn, Vikings. *See also* Fish, Other Marine Animals and Fish Industry.

Insects and Spiders: Ants, Bees, Buzz, Cricketts, Grasshoppers, Hornets, Mosquitoes, Spiders, Stingers, Wasps.

Institutions: Aelwyd, Brotherhood, Civil, Club, College, Constitution, Curfews, Fed, Firm, Franchise, Guild, Lawmen, Lawyers, Legion, Legionnaires, Lodge, Met, Pensioners, People's Club, Police, Poly, Social, Stute, Stutes, Tute, Welfare, Wellie, Wells, Welly, YM.

Insults: Bad Lions, Bitter Blues, Bitters, BLose, Cheaterfield, Council Housers, Dirty Leeds, Fail, Franchise, Gene Puddle, Hamsters, Mad Lions, Manure, Rent Boys, Sadford, Savage Six, Scabs, Scummers, Seaweed, Sham, Sheep, Sjoke City, Skates, Skunks, Slave Traders, Squatters, Stans, Swindle, Tatters, Turnips, Wendys, Wet Sham, Wurzels, Yids / Yid Army / Yiddos.

Kitchen Appliances: Blades, Cutlers, Kets / Kettles, Marigolds, Mustard Pots, Potters.

Language: *see* Dialect, Geographical Terms.

Law and Order: Bad Boys, Lawmen, Lawyers, Met, Police, Sweeney. *See also* Criminals, Pirates.

Literature (includes Biblical): Darans, Famous, Famous Five, Ghosts, Hearts, Honest Men, Ivanhoe, Minstermen, Picks, Rabs, Rechabites, Waverley, Wombles, Yowes.

Lizards: Dinosaurs, Lizards.

Mammals: Antelopes, Armadillos, Badgers, Bears, Beavers, Boars, Brox, Bucks, Bulls, Camels, **Cats** (*also* Bad Lions, Bengal Tigers, Black Cats, Cattachs, Cougars, Green Lions, Jags, Lionesses, Lions, Lisbon Lions, Livy Lions, Mad Lions, Old Lions, Panthers, Pumas, Teigars, Three Lions, Tigers, White Tigers), Colts, Deranged Ferrets, Deres, *dogs* (Black Dogs, Bulldogs, Doggy, Dogs Of War, Harriers, Rhondda Bulldogs, Seadogs, Shelties, Tartan Army / Terriers, Terriers, Tykes), Dolphins, Donkey Lashers, Ewes, Foxes, Goats, Hamsters, Harbour Rats, Hares, Lambs, MK Wolves, Moles, Monkey Hangers, Otters, Pigs, Rabbits, Rams, Seals, Sheep, Shelties, Shrews, Skunks, Squirrels, Staggies, Stags, Thoroughbreds, Vixens, White Horse Men, White Wolves, Wild Boars, Wolves, Wolves Sporting, Yowes, Zebras.

Managers, Owners or Players: Buckley Babes, Busby Babes, Chelski, Clarkie's, Coad's Colts, Crazy Gang, Culture Club, Dicko's, Drake's Ducklings, Fergie's Fledglings, Fowlers, Iron Curtain, Jackburn, Leishman's Lions, Liddellpool, Lisbon Lions, Mitchell's, Pied Pipers, Roy's Boys, Sven's Men, Turnbull's Tornadoes, Wembley Wizards.

Manufacturing and Industry and Trade: Airportmen, Anvils, Baggies, Bakers, Belters, Berrypickers, Biscuit Boys, Biscuitmen, Biscuiteers, Blades, Blanketmen, Blast, Blasties, Bleachers, Bloaters, Blunts, Boatmen, Brakes, Brewers, Brewery Boys, Brickies, Bullets, Butchers, Cabes, Cabinet Makers, Cables, Camels, Chairboys, Cheesemen, Chemists, Cherrypickers, Cider Army, Clayheads, Claymen, Coalmen, Cobblers, Cod Army, Codheads, Colliers, Colliery, Colls, Cornies, Corsetmen, Cutlers, Dabbers, Dentals, Dockers, Dolly Blues, Doughboys, Engineers, Ferrytoun, Fishermen, Flourmen, Foresters, Foundry, Foundrymen, Fulshie, Furnacemen, Gas, Gasheads, Gasmen, Gingerbreads, Gingerbreadmen, Glassboys, Glassmen, Glaziers, Glovers, Gravelmen, Hammers, Harbour Rats, Harbourmen, Hatters, Iron, Irons, Ironsiders / Ironsides, Ironworkers, Jam Boys, Knitters, Lacemakers, Lacemen, Lawnmowers, Lights, Linos, Lockmen, Loc's, Locies, Loco/s, Locomotives, Magnets, Mariners, Marketmen, Mechanics, Mechs, Merry Millers, Milkmen, Mill, Millers, Mills, Miners, Motormen, Motors, Musselmen, Nailers, Natives, Needles, Nops, Nurserymen, Nuts and Bolts, Oilers, Oilmen, Orchardmen, Oystermen, Paintmen, Parras, Pie Men, Pitmen, Planemakers, Planemen, Potters, Powermen, Press, Printers, Quarrymen, Radicals, Rads, Rail, Railwaymen, Red Lichties, Rollers, Roofing, Saddlers, Sand Dobbers, Scabs, Scow, Seedgrowers, Shiners, Shipbuilders, Shoe Army, Shopmates,

Shrimpers, Shunters, Silkmen, Singers, Skinners, Slave Traders, Smokies, Sooty, Souters, Spamen, Spitfires, Steelmen, Steels, Straw-Hatters / Straw-Plaiters, Stringers, Synners, T'Colliers or T'Pitmen, Tanners, Tatters, Timbers, Tinmen, Tinners, Toffees / Toffeemen, Tractor Boys, Tractormen, Trams, Trawler Boys, Trawlermen, Undertakers, Vans, Vickers, Walnut Boys, Welders, Wheelmen, Wheelwrights, Windmill Army, Wingmakers, Wire, Works, Yorkies.

Marriage: Anvils, Celebrant, Civil, Weddingmakers.

Mathematics: Decies, Pars, Thirds. *See also* Numbers, Shapes, Years.

Medievalism: Alfredians, Archers, Arrows, Barum, Bravehearts, Castle, Castlemen, Celtic, Celts, Cestrians, Clan, Crusaders, Curfews, Firm, Frenchcastle, Goths, Heathens, Ivanhoe, Knights, Landlords, Martyrs, Moatmen, Moatsiders, Quarter-boys, Saints, Salop, Saras, Saxons, Spurs, Super Spurs, Thorfinn, Tribesmen / Tribal Army, Turks, Vikings, Wakes, Witches, Wizards. *See also* Architecture, Religious Expressions, Saints.

Military: Admirals, Archers, Army, Arrows, Barmy Army, Black Watch, Braves, Buffs, Bullets, Castle, Castlemen, Cavaliers, Centurians, Commandos, Comrades, Coms, Cutters, Dick-Kerr's, Fed, Fizzers, Fort, Frenchcastle, Garrison, Generals, Gladiators, Grandad's Army, Guardsmen, Gunners, Highland Dynamite, Home Guard, Khaki Chums, Knights, Lancers, Legion, Legionnaires, Light Brigade, Lochgelly Sodgers, Marines, Maroon Army, Orange Army, Parras, Peaceful Warriors, Raiders, Rams, Rangers, Rebel Army, Red Army, Redcoats, Rifles, Sailors, Sappers, Seadogs, Shots, Sodgers, Soldiers, Tangerine Barmy Army, Tartan Army / Terriers, Tribesmen / Tribal Army, Turks, Vickers, Volunteers, Warriors, Wars, Yellow Army, Zeplins.

Money: Bank of England Club, Bankers, Bucketshakers, Chelski, Chicken-bree Team, Greenbacks, Jackburn, Money Men, Moneys, Moonlighters, Pennies, Plastics, Sheik City, Team of Millionaires, Washers, Woolwich. *See also* Poverty.

Music: Beach Boys, Beganifs, Bels, Can Cans, Drum, Harp, Harps, Krooners, Linnets, Nigger Minstrels, Pied Pipers, Singers, Spice Boys, U2, Venga Boys, Waltz, Wurzels.

Mythical and Supernatural: Black Cats, Black Dogs, Black Dragons, City Devils, Devils, Dragons, Druids, Fairies, Ghosts, Griffins, Imps, Lady Imps, Magic Mons, Pegasus, Red Devils, Red Dragons, Red Imps, Sphinx, Unicorns, Wands, Wembley Wizards, Wings, Witches, Wizards, Young Dragons. *See also* Folklore.

National Symbols: Bulldogs, Black Dragons, Daffodils, Dragons, Druids, Harp, Harps, Jags, Lions, Red Dragons, Shamrocks, Tartan Army / Terriers, Theestle, Thistle, Three Lions, Wee Jags, Young Dragons.

Nationalities (Includes Regional): Albion, Arabs, Argyle, Bengal Tigers, Black Arabs, Bohemians, Bohs, Bravehearts, Brazil, Britannia, Bulldogs, Caledonia/n/s, Caley, Calies, Cambrian, Celtic, Celts, Chelski, Clan, Cleveland Cowboys, Cockney Boys, Cumbrians, Danes, Exiles, Fifers, France, Frenchcastle, Gambians,

Goths, Grecians, Gypsies, Hibees, Hibernian, Hibs, Highland Dynamite, Huns, Indians, Kingdom Boys, Little Brazil, Little Celts, Locals, Men from the Kingdom, Mighty Belfast Celtic, Norn Iron, Our Wee Country, Paisley Brazilians, Russians, Saras, Sassenachs, Saxons, Scotia, Sheik City, Shelties, Sjoke City, Spaniards, Spartans, Sund-Ireland, 'Tic, Trojans, Turks, Vikings, Welsh Bluebirds, Yids / Yid Army / Yiddos. *See also* Place-Names Overseas.

Nicknames for Places and Peoples: Arky-Penarky, Arrad, Bacachs, Baggies, Barlick, Barum, Becks, Beganifs, Belters, Blades, Black Cats, Blasties, Blue Toon, Bonnie Oodle, Brum, Buddies, Buttercups, Cattachs, Cauther, Cestrians, Clayholers, Cobbydalers, Cockney Boys, Darreners, Donny, Dumps, Geordies, Happylanders, Heartlanders, Invicta, Jacks, Kingdom Boys, Leythers, Mackems, Men from the Kingdom, Monkey Hangers, Niseachs, Posset, Proud Preston, Sandgrounders, Scunny, Shannocks, Shelties, Shiners, Smokies, Sons (of the Rock), Souters, Stab City, Sunset City, Toosey, Tribesmen / Tribal Army, Trotters, Tykes, Yeltz, Yids / Yid Army / Yiddos, Yorkies.

Nuclear Power: Atomic Boys. *See also* Electricity, Science.

Numbers: Alpha/s, Decies, Fivers, Seven, Thirds, Trinity, Triple A's, Two Blues. *See also* Years.

Obesity Studies: Chippy, Chips, Chocolates, Heavies, Pie Eaters / Pies, Pie Men.

Other Sports: Archers, Athletic, Aths, Bantams, Colts, Cricketts, Darts, Doms, F1, Floggers, Flyers, Flying Blues, Foxes, Foxhunters, Gladiators, Gowfers, Harriers, Harry Wragg's, Heavies, Hotspur, Huntsmen, Hurlers, Ice Kings, Jockeys, Krooners, Latics, Lidos, Pars, Racers / Racing, Ramblers, Rec, Recreationists, Rifles, Scarlet Runners, Sporting, Sports, Spurs, Team, Thoroughbreds, Tics, Waders, Yachtsmen.

Palaeontology: Dinosaurs, Rockies, Rocks, Royal Stones, Stoners, Stones.

Performance (Good): Big Club, Biz, Bravehearts, Bully Wee, Crazy Gang, Culture Club, Darans, Dazzlers, Dream Team, Excelsior, Invicta, Invincibles, Jolly Green Giants, Lions, Lucky Arsenal, Shakers, Sorters, Stingers, Team of All the Talents, Team of Millionaires, Team of Surprises, Terrors, Tigers, Tops, Trickies, Venturas, Vics, Victors, Works. *See also* Primacy.

Performance (Poor): Bad Lions, Bantams, Bitters, Bitter Blues, BLose, Bluenoses, Boring Arsenal, Bucketshakers, Cartoon Army, Cheaterfield, Dirty Leeds, Dwarfs, Fail, Mad Lions, Pars, Posh, Yo-Yo Club, Yo-Yos.

Personal Names: Annies, Daniels, Dons, Foxes, Gabs, Geordies, Habbies, Jacks, Laides, Mikes, Pat's, Peeping Toms, Peters, Pompey, Rechabites, Robin Hoods, Roy, Roy's Boys, Sven's Men, Thorfinn, Tims, Wulfs.

Philosophy: Grecians. *See also* Religious Expressions, Republicanism.

Pirates: Black Arabs, Bucks, Freebooters, Hearties, Highwaymen, Pirates, Skull and Crossbones, Team of Millionaires.

Place-Name Elements: *some are included under* Geographical Terms.

Place-Name Errors (Folk Etymologies): Adders, Dragons, Eagles, Maglonians, Mallards, Oakey, Oaks, Owls, Ravens, Sound, Wolves.

Place-Names Overseas: Bengal Tigers, Bohemians, Bohs, Brazil, Corinthians, Corinths, Danes, France, Gambians, Goths, Grecians, Lisbon Lions, Little Brazil, Munichs, Paisley Brazilians, Russians, Spaniards, Spartans, Trojans, Turks. *See also* Nationalities.

Plants: Bluebells, Buds, Buttercups, Daffodils, Daffs, Dahlies, Daisies, Dokens, Fern, Haws, Hedgemen, Ivies / Ivys, Jaggy Nettles, Jags, Lilies / Lillies, Lily, Lilywhites / Lillywhites / Lily Whites, Marigolds, Moss, Nettles, Nurserymen, Pansies, Poppies, Rose, Saffron, Seaweed, Seedgrowers, Superdaffs, Theestle, Thistle, Tulips, Turfs, Turnips, Violet, Wee Jags. *See also* Trees.

Poetry: Honest Men, Yowes. *See also* Literature, Rhyming Phrases.

Politics: Bravehearts, Cavaliers, Comrades, Croms, Cromwellians, Garibaldi Reds, Iron Curtain, Iron Ladies, Ironsiders, Libs, Loyals, Mavericks, Moles, Outcasts, Pie Eaters / Pies, Rabs, Radicals, Raiders, Rebel Army, Rebels, Red Army, Scabs, Squatters, Wars, Washers, Welfare, Wellie, Yids / Yid Army / Yiddos. *See also* Elitism, Poverty, Republicanism, Royalty.

Pollution: Chemists, Gas / Gasheads, Smoggies, Sooty.

Poverty: Baggies (?), Pie Eaters / Pies, Rags, Tatters, Team with No Boots, Tonics. *See also* Money.

Precious Metals / Stones: Black and Ambers, Black and Golds, Diamonds, Emeralds, Gold and Black Army, Gold 'n' Blacks, Golds, Old Gold, Panners, Rubies.

Primacy: A's, Alpha/s, F1, Tops, Triple A's, Victors. *See also* Performance (Good).

Proverbial Expressions: Arabs, Bad Boys, Bairns, Bonny, Cats, Dokens, Famous, Honest Men, Shakers, Sleeping Giants.

Religious Expressions: Abbey, Abbots, Angels, Baptists, Bishops, Blue Cross, Bones, Brotherhood, Cardinals, Charterhouse, Church, Churches, City Devils, Cross, Crues, Crusaders, CTK, Darans, Devils, Dublin Saints, Friars, Gabs, Gay Puritans, Generals, Grace, Grave Diggers, Guardians, Gurus, Heathens, Holy Blues, Holy City Boys, Kirk, Kirks, Martyrs, Messengers, Methodists, Minstermen, Missioners, Nuns, Pilgrims, Prims, Priory, Priorymen, Puritans, Quakers, Quarterboys, Rechabites, Saints, Saras, Shrivy, Spireites, Stumpites, Trinity, Undertakers, Wilderness Boys, Witches.

Republicanism: Comrades, Croms, Cromwellians, Iron Curtain, Rebel Army, Rebels, Red Army.

Rhyming Phrases: Cabbage, Fail, Harry Wragg's, Jam Tarts, Jam Town, Jambos, Jammies, Jo Row, Landlords, Pennies, Pesda, Rookie Cookie, Roy's Boys, Salmoners, Stans, Sven's Men, Sweeney, Teddy Bears, Tims, Tin Pail, Trickies. *See also* Poetry.

Rivers: Bankers, Bankies, Bannsiders, Barrowsiders, Boyds, River Boys, Boynesiders,

Brettsiders, Brook, Brooksiders, Burn, Burnie, Caldersiders, Colnesiders, Corribsiders, Creeksiders, Creesiders, Dee, Deesiders, Dons, Leesiders, Merseysiders, Pride of the Clyde, Rhiewsiders, River Boys, Riversiders, Roesiders, Speysiders, Taffs / Taffys, Teessiders, Tweedsiders, Tyneside Professors, Tynesiders, Waterfall Men, Watersiders, Wearsiders, Wyesiders.

Routeways: Bont, Bridge, Bridgers, Brig, Briggers, Drove, Ford/s, Gate, Over the Bridge, Road, Street. *See also* Rivers, Transport.

Royalty: Albert, Alex, Alfredians, Berts, Cavaliers, Crown, Faithfuls, Geordies, Guardsmen, Ice Kings, Imperial, Kingdom Boys, Kings, Laides, Loyals, Palace, Queen's, Queens, Royal Stones, Royalists, Royalites, Royals, Tudors, Vics, Victors, Wee Vics.

Saints: Aggie, Ants, Candy Rock, Dublin Saints, Fish, Gabs, Geordies, Guardians, Jimmies, Lukes, Martyrs, Mikes, Pat's, Peters, Saint Peters, Saints, TNS, Toosey.

Science: Atomic Boys, Gene Puddle, School of Science. *See also* Astronomy, Geographical Terms, Geology, Numbers, Paleontology, Precious Metals and Stones, Shapes, Technology.

Seaside Fun: Candy Rock, Donkey Lashers, Marine, Pier, Rocks, Sandgrounders, Scorries, Seagulls, Seahawks, Seahorses, Seals, Seasiders, Seaweed, Shells.

Shapes: Barcodes, Crescents, Cross, Diamonds, Edge, End, Glorious Hoops, Half-Halfs, Half Hoops, Hooky, Hoops, Merry Stripes, Spots, Star/s, Stripes, Superhoops, Wee Hoops.

Size (Big): Big Club, Jolly Green Giants, Heavies, Lankies, Massive, Massives, Mighty, Mighty Belfast Celtic, Mighty Blues, Mighty Del, Mighty Moor, Mighty Whites, Mighty Willow, Sleeping Giants.

Size (Small): Bantams, Bully Wee, Colts, Dwarfs, Grasshoppers, Little Brazil, Little Celts, Little Club on the Hill, Micky Mousers, Minnows, Our Wee Country, Wee County, Wee 'Gers, Wee Hoops, Wee Jags, Wee Rangers, Wee Rovers, Wee Vics.

Sleep: Dossers, Knappers, Peaceful Warriors, Sleeping Giants.

Snakes: Adders, Vipers.

Social Sciences: *see* Educational, Elitism, Institutions, Marriage, Money, Nationalities, Politics, Poverty, Republicanism, Royalty.

Suffixes: *see Appendix One.*

Supporters: Arabs, Atomic Boys, Baggies (?), Barmy Army, Bitters, Bluenoses, Boing!, Chelsea Headhunters, Cod Army, Gas / Gasheads, Gooners, Hatters, ICF, Kop / Kopites, Kopettes, Massive, Massives, Pie Eaters / Pies, Pirates, Red Army, Road, Scummers, Stans, Stockports, Straw-Hatters / Straw-Plaiters, Tartan Army / Terriers, Tims, Toon, Windmill Army, Yids / Yid Army / Yiddos, Yorkies, Ziggers.

Sweets: Candy Rock, Candystripes, Humbugs, Peppermints, Quality Street Kids, Rowntrees, Yorkies.

Technology: Barcodes, Brakes, Cables, Engineers, Lawnmowers, Lights, Lockmen,

Mechanics, Mechs, Nuts and Bolts, Planemakers, Planemen, Powermen, Wire, Works. *See also larger lists under* Manufacturing and Industry and Trade, Transport.

Teeth: Dentals, Gnashers, Sharks.

Television / Radio / Cinema / Theatre: Annies, Batmans, Bay / Bay Enders, Bennies, Binners, Bluebirds, Dingles, Eastenders, Entertainers, Eric Cartman's Barmy Army, Gooners, Harlequins, Herby, Micky Mousers, Quality Street Kids, Quins, Sooty, Wombles, Young Guns.

Toys: Micky Mousers, Sooty, Teddy Bears, Tops, Yo-Yo Club, Yo-Yos, Ziggers.

Transport: Airmen, Airportmen, Anchormen, Boatmen, Coach-builders, Ferry, Ferrytoun, Harbourmen, Highwaymen, ICF, Jags, Jets, Junction, Loc's, Locies, Loco/s, Locomotives, Marine, Motormen, Motors, Oilers, Oilmen, Old Lagonda, Planemakers, Planemen, Port, Portites, Ports, Rail, Railwaymen, Rollers, Sailors, Seadogs, Shipbuilders, Shipyard, Shipyarders, Shunters, Slave Traders, Spitfires, Supermarines, Talbot, Tractor Boys, Tractormen, Trawler Boys, Trawlermen, Trams, Wingmakers, Vans, Wagon, Wheelmen, Wheelwrights, Wherrymen, Wingmakers, Wings, Yachtsmen, Yorkies, Zeplins. *See also* Travel.

Travel: Bohemians, Bohs, Camels, Crusaders, Freebooters, Gypsies, ICF, Nomads, Pilgrims, Pirates, Raiders, Rangers, Roaming Brigade, Rovers, Strollers, Trotters, Vikings, Waders, Walkers, Wanderers, Warriors, Waysiders, Wee 'Gers, Wee Rangers, Wee Rovers, Wilderness Boys. *See also* Transport.

Trees: Acorns, Almonds, Ash Trees, Cedars, Dealers, Filberts, Firs, Forest, Foresters, Laburnums, Leafe, Leaves, Mangos, Mighty Willow, Nuts, Oak, Oakey, Oakmen, Oaks, Orchard, Orchardmen, Robin Hoods, Timbers, Trees, Tricky Trees, Walnut Boys, Willows, Wood, Wooders, Woodpeckers, Woods. *See also* Plants.

Vietnam War: Cutters.

Warfare: *see* Military, Vietnam War, Weapons.

Water: Marine, Pool, Pools, River Boys, Water, Waterfall Men, Watersiders, Well, Wellmen, Wet Sham. *See also* Fish, Other Marine Animals and Fishing Industry, Geographical Terms, Rivers, Seaside Fun, Weather.

Weather: Arabs, Darans, Ice Kings, Sols, Turnbull's Tornadoes.

Weapons: Blades, Bullets, Cutters, Daggers, Gunners, Hatchetmen, Highland Dynamite, Shots, Stab City, Young Guns.

Weird and Wonderful: Baggies, Boing!, Crazy Gang, Dazzlers, Fizzers, Ghosts, Hi-Hi's, Whe Ho, Wizards, Ziggers.

Women: Annies, Belles, Blue Belles, Dick-Kerr's, Donny Belles, Iron Ladies / Ironesses, Lady Imps, Lionesses, Llani Ladies, Nuns, Pompey Ladies, Rookettes, Vixens, Wendys, Witches.

Years: Class of '66, Eighteen-Eighty-Three, Eighty-Twoers, Team of the Eighties.

Youth: Babes, Bhoys, Blue Boys, Blueboys, Boyos, Busby Babes, Braw Lads, Colts, Drake's Ducklings, Fergie's Fledglings, Golden Boys, Juniors, Lads, Lambs, Team of Boys, Urchins, Young Dons, Young Dragons, Young Guns, Youths.

SOURCES AND BIBLIOGRAPHY

WEBSITE LIST
Club websites are too numerous to list. Mainstream ones, some used far more often than others, are:

communigate.co.uk/ne/teesspeak
Dictionary of the Scots Language: dsl.ac.uk
footballcrests.com
Football Club History Database: www.fchd.info (FCHD)
footballfanscensus.com
Historical Football Kits: historicalkits.co.uk
Oxford English Dictionary: oed.com (OED)
scottish-football-historical-archive.com (SFHA)
thebeautifulhistory.wordpress.com
Welsh Football Data Archive: www.wfda.co.uk
wikipedia.org

BIBLIOGRAPHY: TITLES REFERRED TO AS ABBREVIATIONS

AA Anglo-American Chewing Gum Ltd. (Halifax, West Yorkshire), 'Famous Soccer Clubs', series of waxed wrappers (1960) and 'Noted Football Clubs' (1961).

AFBC [Association of Football Badge Collectors], *Football Badge Directory 2009* (in four parts: *English League*; *English Non League*; *Scottish League including Channel Islands, Eire, Northern Ireland, Scottish Non League, Welsh Non League*; *Football Associations of the British Isles and Ireland* (Liverpool: the Association, 2009) [these 'directories' are catalogues of badges, presented as photocopied images in alphabetical order but undated; the production is several hundred pages of loose A4 sheets, unbound].

BoF 1905–6 *The Book of Football. A Complete History and Record of the Association and Rugby Games*, issued in 12 parts, October 1905 to March 1906; facsimile reprint by Desert Island Books, Southend on Sea, 1997, reprinted 2005).

FCHD: see website list.

G (+ date) Golesworthy. Maurice, *The Encyclopaedia of Association Football* (London: Robert Hale, 1956; 7th edn, 1965; 12th edn, 1976).

OED: see website list.

RI (+date/s) Robinson, John, *The Supporters' Guide to Irish Football 1997* (Cleethorpes: Soccer Books, 1996); *The Supporters' Guide to Eircom FAI Clubs 2006* (Cleethorpes: Soccer Books, 2006).

RNI (+date/s) Robinson, John, *The Supporters' Guide to Northern Irish Football* (Cleethorpes: Soccer Books, 2007).

RNL (+dates), Robinson, John, *The Supporters' Guide to Non-League Football* (Cleethorpes: Soccer Books).

RS (+date/s) Robinson, John, *Scottish Football Supporters' Guide and Yearbook* (Cleethorpes: Soccer Books).

RW (+date/s) Robinson, John, *The Supporters' Guide to Welsh Football* (Cleethorpes: Soccer Books, 1994–).

RY (+ date/s) *Rothmans Football Yearbook 1970–71* (London: Queen Anne Press, 1970); continued annually; title changed in 2003 to *Sky Sports Football Yearbook 2003–2004* (SS) and published by Headline since 1992.

SFHA: see website list.

SS: *Sky Sports Football Yearbook*, see under RY for *Rothman's Football Yearbook*.

SWSCYB 1962–3, *Sheffield Wednesday F.C. Supporters' Club Year Book 1962/63* (Sheffield, 1962), 'Football Club Nicknames', p. 37.

W (+ date/s) Williams, Tony, *The F.A. Non-League Football Annual 1978–79* (London: Queen Anne Press, 1978); followed by *1979–80* (same publisher, 1979) and *1980–81* (Hungerford: Tony Williams, 1980). The format and title then changed to *Rothmans F.A. Non-League Football Yearbook 1981–82* (Aylesbury: Rothmans Publications, 1981); followed by *1982–83* (1982) and *1983–84* (1983). Everything then changed again to: *FA Non-League Directory 1985* (London: Newnes Books, 1984); followed by *1986* (1985). The format and publisher then changed to *Non-League Directory 1987* (no place, Tony Williams Publications, 1986). The series switched to the familiar red covers for the *1988* edition and the word 'Club' was added to the title, followed by annual editions to *2013* (2012). The back cover of the 25th anniversary *2003* volume shows a sequence of wrappers from the entire series.

WL (+ date/s) Williams, Tony (ed.), *The League Club Directory 1985* (Feltham: Newnes Books, 1984); succeeded by *Football League Club Directory 1986* (London: Guild Publishing, 1985), then *Football League Club Directory 1987* (Tony Williams Publications, 1986); the series then mutated to *Barclays League Club Directory 1988*, published by Tony Williams, then with the same title published by *The Daily Mail* till *1991*, then published by Burlington Publishing for *1992* and *1993*; then mutating again to *Endsleigh Football Club Directory 1994* (published by Harmsworth Active, last appearing for *1995*); eleven volumes in total.

BIBLIOGRAPHY: TITLES REFERRED TO BY AUTHOR AND DATE

Adrian, Alec, *Dunkirk Sportsmen* (Ilfracombe: Stockwell, 1943).

Allen, Roland, 'The Year Barnsley Disorganised the Tyneside Professors', in Leslie Frewin (ed.), *The Saturday Men. A Book of International Football* (London: Macdonald, 1967), pp. 253–6.

Appleton, Arthur, *Hotbed of Soccer. The Story of Football in the North East* (1960, reprinted

London: Sportsmans Book Club, 1961).

Avis, F.C., *Soccer Dictionary* (London: F. C. Avis, 1954, 1966, 1970).

Ayto, John and Crofton, Ian (eds), *Brewer's Britain and Ireland* (London: Weidenfeld & Nicolson, 2005).

Ballard, John & Suff, Paul, *World Soccer. The Dictionary of Football. The Complete A–Z of International Football from Ajax to Zinedine Zidane* (London: Boxtree, 1999).

Barnes, Jon, *Grantham Town Football Club. The History* (Grantham, 2003).

Barton, Bob (ed.), *Northumbrian Football Yearbook 1984–85* (Newcastle upon Tyne, 1984); new edition *Northumbrian Football Yearbook 1985–86* (1985).

Beale, Paul, *A Concise Dictionary of Slang and Unconventional English, from A Dictionary of Slang and Unconventional English by Eric Partridge* (London: Routledge, 1989).

Borlenghi, Patricia, *Football Crazy! All You Need to Know about Football* (London: Bloomsbury Children's Books, 1999).

Chappel, C., *A Dictionary of Buckish Slang, University Wit and Pickpocket Eloquence* (London: C. Chappel, 1811; facsimile reprint by Studio Editions, 1994).

Churchill, R. C., *Sixty Seasons of League Football* (Harmondsworth: Penguin Books, 1958).

Coates, Richard, 'A Typology of Football Club Names in the British Isles', in *Papers from the 22nd International Congress of Onomastic Sciences, Pisa, 2005*, vol. 2 (Pisa, 2008), 557–67.

Coates, Richard, 'Pompey as the Nickname for Portsmouth', *Nomina*, 32 (2009, *recte* 2011), 59–74.

Coates, Richard, and Rachel Sutton-Spence, 'Football Crazy? Place-Names and Football Club-Names in British Sign Language', *Nomina*, 34 (2011, *recte* 2013), forthcoming.

Delahunty, Andrew, *Oxford Dictionary of Nicknames* (Oxford: OUP, 2003).

Dobson, Bob, *Lancashire Nicknames and Sayings* (Clapham: Dalesman Books, 1973).

Dolan, Terence Patrick, *A Dictionary of Hiberno-English. The Irish Use of English* (Dublin: Gill & Macmillan, 1998).

Dunk, Peter (ed.), *Panini's Football Yearbook 1988–89* and *1989–90* (London: Panini Publishing Ltd., 1988 and 1989).

Easterbrooke, Basil, 'What's in a Name?', *Soccer Gift Book 1969–1970* (London: Longacre Press, 1969), pp. 84–6.

Fabian, A. H. and Green, Geoffrey (eds), *Association Football*, 4 vols (London: Caxton Publishing, 1960).

Ferris, Ken, *Football Terms and Teams* (Manchester: Carcanet Press, 2005).

Flanagan, Deirdre and Flanagan, Laurence, *Irish Place Names* (Dublin: Gill & Macmillan, 1994).

Frewin, Leslie (ed.), *The Saturday Men. A Book of International Football* (London: Macdonald, 1967).

Goodall, G. R., *FA Cup Non-League Giant-Killers Annual (1945–1982)* (London: Goodall Publications, 1982).

Green, Jonathon, *Cassell's Dictionary of Slang* (London: Cassell, 2005, new edition of the work of 1998).

Guinness n.d., c.1999, *The Guinness Book of Football* (London: Guinness Publishing, c.1999).

Harvey, Charles (ed.), *Encyclopædia of Sport* (London: Sampson Low, Marston and Co. Ltd., 1959).

Holme, Peter, *Play up, Higher Walton! Football in a Lancashire Village from 1882 to 2005* (Blackpool: Landy Publishing, 2006).

Huws, Richard E., *Caneris Melyn Trefeurig / Trefeurig's Yellow Canaries 1948–1953* (Tal-y-bont: the author, 2010).

Huws, Richard E., *The Football and Rugby Playing Fields of Wales* (Tal-y-bont; Y Lolfa, 2009).

Huws, Richard E., *The Football and Rugby Team Nicknames of Wales* (Donington: Paul Watkins, 2013)

Huws, Richard E., *The Footballers of Borth and Ynys-las, 1873–1950* (Tal-y-bont: the author, 2011).

Jeffrey, Gordon, 'Those Nicknames!', in *All Stars Football Book* (Manchester: World Distributors Ltd., 1961), 67–70, reprinted in Leslie Frewin (ed.), *The Saturday Men. A Book of International Football* (London: Macdonald, 1967), pp. 249–52.

Johnston, Frank, *The Football Encyclopædia. A Historical and Statistical Review of the Game of Football since it became a National Sport* (London: Associated Sporting Press, 1934).

Jolly, Rick, *Jackspeak. The Pusser's Rum Guide to Royal Navy Slanguage* (Torpoint: Palamanando Publishing, 1989).

Jones-Baker, Doris, 'Nicknaming in Popular Nomenclature of English Places', *Nomina*, 5 (1981), 57–61.

Long, Harry Alfred, *Personal and Family Names. A Popular Monograph on the Origin and History of the Nomenclature of the Present and Former Times* (London: Hamilton, Adams & Co., 1883).

McCarra, Kevin, *Scottish Football. A Pictorial History. From 1867 to the Present Day*, Clydesdale Bank Heritage series no. 2 (Glasgow and Edinburgh: Third Eye Centre and Polygon Books, 1984).

Miller, Kerry and Wright, James (eds), *The Non-League Football Year Book 1996–97* (no place: Paper Plane Publishing, 1996) [only volume published].

Mills, A. D., *A Dictionary of English Place-Names* (Oxford, OUP, 1991, new edn 1998); many reprints since.

Mills, A. D., *A Dictionary of London Place-Names* (Oxford, OUP, 2001).

Moss, Robert Hutton, *The Book of Football Lists. An Encyclopedia of Football Facts* (London: W. H. Allen, 1983).

Norris, Peter, 'I wonder why', *Charles Buchan's Football Monthly* (March, 1959), p. 35.

Ogden: *Football Club Nicknames*, set of 50 cigarette cards issued by Ogden's Tobacco Co., 1933; reprinted by Hignett, 1933 and Imperial, 1997.

Owen, Hywel Wyn, and Morgan, Richard, *Dictionary of the Place-Names of Wales* (Llandysul: Gomer Press, 2007).

Phythian, B. A., *A Concise Dictionary of English Slang* (London: Hodder & Stoughton, 6th impression, 1991).

Pickering, David, *The Cassell Soccer Companion. History. Facts. Anecdotes* (London: Cassell, 1994; revised editions 1995, 1998).

Potter, David and Jones, Phil. H., *The Encyclopaedia of Scottish Football* (Durrington: Pitch Publishing, 2011) (esp. pp. 251–2).

Quinion, Michael, *Port Out, Starboard Home and Other Language Myths* (London: Penguin Books, 2004).

Reaney, P. H. and Wilson, R. N., *A Dictionary of English Surnames* (Oxford: OUP, 1997)

Richards, Harold, *The Way There. A Soccer Encyclopaedia* (London: Stanley Paul, 1960).

Rivet, A. L. F. and Smith, Colin, *The Place-Names of Roman Britain* (London: B. T. Batsford, 1979)

Robinson, John, *Supporters' Guide to Welsh Football 1994* (Cleethorpes: Soccer Book Publishing, 1993); subsequent editions for 1998, 2011.

Robinson, John, *Scottish Supporters' Guide and Yearbook 2011*, 18th edn (Cleethorpes: Soccer Book Publishing, 2010).

Robinson, John, *The Supporters' Guide to Northern Irish Football*, 4th edition (Cleethorpes, Soccer Books, 2007).

Room, Adrian, *Brewer's Dictionary of Names* (London: Cassell, 1992).

Room, Adrian (ed.), *Brewer's Dictionary of Phrase and Fable* (London: Cassell, 1999).

Room, Adrian, *Dictionary of Sports and Games Terminology* (Jefferson, N.C.: McFarland, 2010).

Room, Adrian, *Nicknames of Places. Origins and Meanings of the Alternate and Secondary Names, Sobriquets, Titles, Epithets and Slogans for 4600 Places Worldwide* ((Jefferson, North Carolina: McFarland and Co., 2006).

Seddon, Peter J., *A Football Compendium. An Expert Guide to the Books, Films & Music of Association Football*, 2nd edn (Boston Spa: the British Library, 1999).

Seddon, Peter, *Football Talk. The Language and Folklore of the World's Greatest Game* (London: Robson Books, 2004); chapter 21 is on nicknames, pp. 202–14.

Shawcross, Fred, 'Soccer Nicknames', in *The Book of All Sports*, ed. W. J. Hicks (London: News Chronicle Book Department, 1961) , p. 56.

Simpson, John (ed.), *The First English Dictionary of Slang, 1699* (Oxford: Bodleian Library, 2010) [new edition of *A New Dictionary of the Terms Ancient and Modern of the Canting Crew in its Several Tribes, of Gypsies, Beggers, Thieves, Cheats, &c.*].

Sims-Kimbrey, J. M., *Wodds and Doggerybaw. A Lincolnshire Dialect Dictionary* (Boston: Richard Kay, 1995).

Smith, Bruce (ed.), *The Playfair Non-League Football Annual 1991–92* (London: Macdonald Press, 1991); then *1992–93* (1992); then reformed as *Non-League Football Pocket Annual 1993–94* (London: Words on Sport, 1993), then *1994–95* (1994) and

1995–96 (1995).

Stead, Phil, *Red Dragons. The Story of Welsh Football* (Talybont: Y Lolfa, 2012).

Sweetule: *Football Club Nicknames*, set of 25 'cigarette cards' issued by Sweetule Products Ltd., Redcliffe, Manchester, 1959.

Stedfast 1963–1965: a series of cartoons in the monthly *Stedfast Magazine*, published for The Boys' Brigade by Stedfast Publishers, London.

Thomson, D. C. (publisher), set of 'stamps' for a football album issued with *Adventure* magazine, 1936.

Twydell, Dave, *Defunct F.C. Club Histories and Statistics: Bedford Town, Chippenham United, Guildford City, Pegasus, Symmingtons / Market Harborough Town* (Harefield: the author, n.d., c.1988).

Urdang, Laurence, *A Dictionary of Names and Nicknames* (Oxford: OUP, 1991).

Vernon, Leslie (ed.), *Club Colours and Nicknames* (London: Esso Squelcher Books [no. 7 of 16], n.d., 1970–1).

Weekley, Ernest, *An Etymological Dictionary of Modern English* (London: John Murray, 1921).

Williams, Tony, *The Guinness Non-League Football Fact Book* (Enfield: Guinness Publishing, 1991).

INDEX OF CLUB OFFICIAL NAMES

Andover New Street, see Street

Annagh United, see United

Annan Athletic, see Athletic, Black and Golds, Galabankies

Annbank United, see Bankies, White Brigade

Annfield Plain, see Plain

Anstey Nomads, see Nomads

A.P.V. Peterborough City, see Bakers

Apollo Juniors, see Apollo

Appleby Frodingham, see Steelmen

Appledore, see Fishermen

Arbroath, see Red Lichties, Smokies

Arbroath Victoria, see Vics

Archdales '73, see Dales

Ardeer Thistle, see Thistle

Ardley United, see United

Ardrossan Winton Rovers, see Winton

Ards, see Red and Blues

Ards Rangers, see Rangers

Ardstraw Bridge, see Bridge

Arlesey Town, see Blues, Two Blues

Armadale Thistle, see Dale

Armagh City, see Eagles

Armitage, see Blues, Tage

Armthorpe Welfare, see Welfare, Wellie

Army Crusaders, see Crusaders

Arniston Rangers, Arnie, 'Gers

Arnold, see Saints

Arnold Kingswell, see Kings

Arnold Town, see Eagles

Arsenal, see Boring Arsenal, France, Gooners, Gunners, Invincibles, Lucky Arsenal, Reds, Royals, Woolwich

Arthurlie, see 'Lie

Arundel, see Mullets

Ascot United, see Yellamen

Ash United, see Green Army, United

Ashfield, see Field

Ashfield United, see Snipes

Ashford, see Ash Trees, Tangerines

Ashford Town / United, see Nuts and Bolts

Ashington Community, see Colliers

Ashton and Backwell United, see Stags

Ashton Athletic (Manchester), see Ash/Ashes

Ashton Town, see Town

Ashton United, see Robins, United

Ashtree Highfield, see Stags, Trees

Askern Villa / Welfare, see Villa, Welly

Aston Villa, see Claret and Blues, Lions, Perry Bar Pets, Seals, Villa / Villans / Villains.

Aston Villa Ladies, see Lady Villans

Ashton-under-Lyne, see Robins

Ashton United, see Robins, United

Athersley Recreation, see Penguins

Atherstone Town, see Adders

Atherton Laburnum Rovers, see L.R., Laburnums, Panthers, Rovers

Atherton Collieries, see Colls, Colts, Miners, Sooty, Welfare

Athlone Town, see Town

Auchinlock Talbot, see Bot

Aveley, see Blues, Millers

Avon (Bradford), see Firm

Axbridge Saxon, see Saxons

Axminster Town, see Tigers

Aylesbury, see Moles

Aylesbury United, see Ducks

Aylestone Park, see Park

Ayr Academicals, see Academical

Ayr Parkhouse, see Parkies

Ayr Thistle, see Thistle

Ayr United, see Honest Men

Ayre United, see Tangerine Barmy Army

Bacup Borough, see Borough, Buttercups, Lilywhites

Back, see Bacachs, Blues

Backwell United, see Reds, Stags

Badshot Lea, see Baggies

Old Team, Mighty Belfast Celtic

Belgrave Wanderers, see Bels

Bellshill Athletic, see Hill

Belper Town, see Nailers

Belvedere, see Belvo

Bemerton Heath Harlequins, see Quins

Benburb, see Bens

Benfield Park, see under Newcastle
Benfield

Bentley Victoria Welfare, see Vics

Berkhamsted, see Berko, Comrades,
Lilywhites

Berriew, see Rhiwsiders

Berwick Rangers, see Black and Gold,
Borderers, Dream Team, Rangers,
Wee Gers, Wee Rangers

Bethesda Athletic, see Pesda

Bethnal Green United, see Green Army

Bettws, see Blues

Betws Blackbirds, see Blackbirds, Town.

Bewdley Town, see Comrades, Town,
Vics

Bexhill Town, see Green Machine

Bexhill United, see United

Bexley United, see Town

Bicester Town, see Foxhunters

Biddulph Victoria, see Vics

Bideford, see Robins

Biggleswade Town, see Waders

Biggleswade United, see United

Bilborough Pelican, see Pelican

Billericay Town, see Blues, Ricay, Town

Billingham Synthonia, see Synners

Billingham Town, see Billy Town, Social,
Sound

Bilston Community College, see College

Bilston Town, see Borough, Steelmen,
United

Binfield, see Moles

Birmingham City, see BLose, Bluenoses,
Blues, Brum, Heathens, Smallheath

Birtley Town, see Hoops, Green and
White Army, Super Greens

Bishop Auckland, see Bishops, Two Blues

Bishop Sutton, see Bishops

Bishop's Cleeve, see Skinners, Villagers

Bishop's Stortford, see Bishops, Blues

Bishopmill United, see Bish

Bitton, see Boyds, River Boys, Ton

Biwater (Clay Cross), see Works

Blaby and Whetstone Athletic, see Athletic

Black Country Rangers, see Rangers

Blackburn Rovers, see Blue and Whites,
Dingles, Highwaymen, Jackburn,
Plastics, Riversiders, Rovers

Blackheath Electromotors / Electrodrives,
see G's

Blackpool, see Atomic Boys, Donkey
Lashers, Merry Stripes, 'Pool,
Seasiders, Tangerines

(A.F.C.) Blackpool, see Mechs/Mechanics

Blackpool Wren Rovers, see Wrens

Blackstones, see Stones

Blackwell Miners Welfare, see Miners

Blackwood Dynamo, see Dynamo/s

Blaenau Festiniog Amateurs, see
Amateurs, Comrades, Quarry Men

Blairgowrie, see Berrypickers, Blair

Blakenall, see Lions, Nall

Blandford United, see Royals

Blantyre Celtic, see Celtic

Blantyre Victoria, see Vics

Bletchley Town (two clubs), see Blues,
City, Gladiators, Moles

Blidworth Welfare, see Hawks, Welfare

Bloxwich Town, see Kestrels

Bloxwich United (2001), see Griffins

Bloxwich United (2006), see Red Lions

Blyth Spartans, see Spartans

Bo'ness United, see B.U.'s

Bodedern Athletic, see Boded

Bodmin Town, see Black and Ambers

Brislington, see Bris

Bristol Academy Women's, see Vixens

Bristol City, see Babes, Cider Army, City, Eighty-Twoers / 1982 Ltd, Reds, Robins, Slave Traders, Turnips, Wurzels

Bristol Manor Farm, see Farm

Bristol Rovers, see Arabs, Black Arabs, Gas / Gasheads, Pirates, Purdown Poachers, Rovers, Squatters, Tesco's

Britannia, see Britannia

Briton Ferry Athletic / Llansawel, see Athletic, Ferry

Broadbridge Heath, see Bears

Brockenhurst, see Badgers

Brockmoor Pickwicks, see Lions (under Brierley Hill Alliance).

Brocton, see Badgers

Brodsworth, see Broddy

Bromham, see Owls

Bromley, see Lilywhites, Ravens

Bromsgrove Rovers, see Greens, Rovers

Bromsgrove Sporting, see Rouslers

Bromyard Town, see Town

Brora Rangers, see Cattachs

Broughty athletic, see Fed/s

Broxbourne Borough V. and E., see Boro, SAVE

Broxburn Athletic, see Brox, Burn

Brymbo, see Steelmen

Bryntirion Athletic, see Athletic, Bryn, Tirion

B.S.C. (Parkgate), see Gate

Buchanhaven Hearts, see Hearties

Buckie Rovers, see Rovers

Buckie Thistle, see Hoops, Jags

Buckingham Athletic, see Ath, Swans

Buckingham Town, see Robins

Buckland Athletic, see Bucks

Buckley Town, see Bucks, Claymen, Trotters, Wanderers.

Budleigh Salterton, see Robins

Bugbrooke St Michaels, see Badgers

Builth Wells, see Ambers, Black and Ambers, Bulls, Wyesiders

Buncrana Hearts, see Hearts

Bungay Town, see Black Dogs

Buntingford Town, see Buntings

Burgess Hill Town, see Hillians

Burghead Thistle, see Thistle

Burnham, see Blues

Burnham Ramblers, see Ramblers

Burnley, see Clarets, Dingles, Gene Puddle, Moorites, Royalites, Turfites.

Burntisland Shipyard Amateur, see Shipyard

Burscough, see Linnets

Burton Albion F.C., see Albion, Brewers

Burton Park Wanderers, see Wanderers

Burton United, see Crofters

Bury, see Bucketshakers, Grave Diggers, Shakers

Bury Town, see Blues

Bushey Rangers, see Rangers

Bustleholme, see B's

Buxted, see Bux.

Buxton, see Bucks

Caberfeidh, see Caber

Cadbury Athletic, see Athletic

Cadbury Heath, see Heathens

Caddington, see Oaks

Cadoxton Imps, see Imps

Caerau 'Athletic', see Athletic, Riverboaters

Caerau All Whites, see All Whites

Caerau Ely, see Young Guns

Caerleon, see Romans

Caernarfon Borough, see Borough

Caernarfon (or Carnarvon) Ironopolis, see Canaries, Nops

Caernarfon Town, see Canaries

Caernarfon Wanderers, see Wanderers

Caerphilly, see Jackdaws

Caersws, see Amateurs, Bluebirds

Caldicot Town, see Town

Caledonian, see Caley

California Youth, see Boars

Calne Town, see Lilywhites

Camberley Town, see Krooners, Reds, Town

Cambrian and Clydach Vale Boys and Girls Club, see Cambrian, Sky Blues

Cambridge City, see City, City Devils, Lilywhites, Town

Cambridge Regional College, see Scholars

Cambridge United, see U's, United, Wasps

Cambridge University, see Varsity

Cambridgeshire University Press, see Press

Cambuslang Rangers, see Lang, Wee 'Gers

Cambusnethan Talbot, see Camby Talbot, Talbot

Camelford, see Camels

Camelon, see Mariners

Cammell Laird, see Camels, Laird/s, Shipyarders

Cannock Chase, see Prog

Canterbury City, see City

Canton Liberals, see Libs

Canvey Island, see Gulls, Islanders, Yellow Army

Cardiff Academicals, see Accies

Cardiff City, see Bluebirds, Dwarfs, Redbirds, Welsh Bluebirds

Cardiff Civil Service, see Saints

Cardiff Corinthians, see Alpha, Cards, Corinthians, Corries

Cardiff Draconians, see Draconians / Dracs

Cardiff Hibernians, see Hibs, Signals

Cardiff Institute H.E., see Archers

Cardiff Metropolitan University, see Diffs / Divs, Inter / International, Seagulls, Sheep

Carlisle United, see Blues, Cumbrians, Foxes

Carlton Town, see Millers, Town

(F.C.) Carlow, see Barrowsiders

Carluke Rovers, see Jam Town, Rovers

Carmarthen Town, see Old Gold, Town

Carno, see Greens

Carnoustie Panmure, see Gowfers

Carrick Rangers, see 'Gers, Rangers

Carshalton Athletic, see Robins

Castell Alun Colts, see Colts.

Castle Vale, see Spitfires

Castle Vale King's Heath, see Kings

Castle Villa Athletic, see Villa

Castlebar Celtic, see Castlebar, Celtic

Castleton Gabriels, see Angels, Castlemen, Gabs, Garrison, Guardians, Messengers

Castletown Metropolitan, see Town

Causeway United, see Blues

Cavaliers, see Cavaliers / Cavs

CB Hounslow United F.C., see United

Cefn Druids, see Ancients, Druids, Zebras

Celtic, see Bhoys, Celts, Hoops, Lisbon Lions, Quality Street Kids, 'Tic, Tims

Celtic Nation, see Gilly

Cemaes Bay, see Bay / Bay Enders, Demolition Squad, Seasiders.

Chadderton, see Chaddy

Chaddesley Corbett, see Ravens

Chalfont St Peter, see Saints

Chalfont Wasps, see Stingers

Chantry Grasshoppers, see Grasshoppers

Chard Town, see Robins

Charlton Athletic, see Addicks, Haddicks, Haddocks, Red Army, Robins, Valiants

Chasetown, see Chase, Scholars

Chatham Town, see Chats

Chatteris Town, see Lilies

Cheadle Town, see Town

415

Cheddar, see Cheesemen

Chelmsford City, see City, Clarets

Chelsea, see Blues, Chelsea Headhunters, Chelski, Drake's Ducklings, Pensioners

Cheltenham Saracens, see Saras

Cheltenham Town, see Robins, Rubies

Cherry Orchard, see Orchard

Chertsey Town, see Curfews, Curlews, Town

Chesham United, see Generals, United

Cheshunt, see Ambers

Cheslyn Hay, see Hay

Chessington and Hook United, see Blues, Chessey

Chester City, see Blues, Cestrians, City, Ivies, Magpies, Romans, Seals

Chesterfield, see Blues, Cheaterfield, Spireites, Team of Surprises, Town

Chester-le-Street Town, see Cestrians

Chickerell United, see Chickens

Chichester City, see Chi, City, Lilywhites

Chimney Corner, see Corner

Chingford, see Stags

Chinnor, see Biz

Chippenham Town, see Bluebirds

Chippenham United, see Firs, United

Chipping Norton Town, see Chippy, Magpies

Chipstead, see Chips

Chirk A.A.A., see Colliers, Triple A's.

Chorley, see Magpies

Christ the King, see CTK

Church Stretton Town, see Stretton

Cinderford Town, see Foresters, Town

Cirencester Football Academy, see Academy

Cirencester Town, see Centurions, Ciren, Town

Cirencester United, see Herd

Civil Service Strollers, see Strollers

Clachmannan, see Clacks

Clachnacuddin, see Clach, Lilywhites

(F.C.) Clacton, see Lilywhites, Seasiders

Clacton Town, see Seasiders

Clandown, see Dons

Clanfield, see Robins

Clapham Rovers, see Hybrid Club, Rovers

Clapton, see Tons

Cleethorpes Town, see Owls

Clevedon Town, see Seasiders

Clifton, see All Whites

Cliftonville, see Reds

Clitheroe, see Blues

Clyde, see Bully Wee

Clydebank, see Bankies

Clydebank Rovers, see Little Brazil, Rovers

Clydesdale Harriers, see Harriers

Clyst Rovers, see Rovers

Coagh United, see United

Coalville Town, see Ravens

Cobh Ramblers, see Ramblers

Cobham, see Hammers

Cockfosters, see Fosters

Coedpoeth United, see Coedy

Coffin Dodgers, see Dodgers

Cogan Coronation, see Cogan

Cogenhoe United, see Cooks

Coggeshall Town, see Seedgrowers

Colby, see Moonlighters

Colchester United, see Ewes, Grandad's Army, Oystermen, U's

Coldstream, see Streamers

Coleraine, see Bannsiders, Lilywhites

Coleraine Olympic (new club), see Olympic

Coleshill Town, see Colemen / Coalmen, Coleshillites, Colts, Greens, Rabbits

Colletts Green, see Green

Collier Row, see Row

Collier Row and Romford, see Boro

Colliers Wood, see Woods

Colne, see Reds

Colne Dynamoes, see Dynamoes

Colney Heath, see Magpies

Colony Park, see Colony

Coltness United, see Dahlies

Colwyn Bay, see Bay, Harbourmen,
Seagulls, Seasiders

Colwyn Celts, see Celts

Comber Recreation, see Rec

Comberton Crusaders, see Crusaders

Concord Rangers, see Beach Boys, Rangers

Congleton Town, see Bears, Humbugs,
Town

Connah's Quay and Shotton, see
Deesiders, Nomads, Westenders

Consett, see Steelmen

Continental Star, see Stars

Conwy United, see Musselmen

Cooksbridge, see Bridge, Cooks

Cookstown Olympic, see Olympic

Cookstown United, see United

Corby Town F.C., see Ironworkers,
Steelmen

Corinthian Casuals, see Amateurs, Casuals,
Corinthians, Pink and Chocolate

Corinthian, see Corinthians

Corinthians, see Whites

Cork Bohemians, see Bohs

Cork City, see City, Leesiders, Rebel
Army

Cornard United, see Ards

Corrib Celtic, see Corribsiders

Corsham Town, see Peacocks, Reds,
Southbankers

Corwen Amateurs, see Reds

Cottesmore Amateurs, see Amateurs

Coulsdon Town / United, see C's, Tops

Cove, see Wasps

Cove Rangers, see Highland Dynamite,
Tooners, Wee Rangers

Coventry City, see Bantams, Blackbirds,

Citizens, Peeping Toms, Singers, Sky
Blues, Wheelmen

Coventry Copsewood, see G's

Coventry Sphinx, see Sphinx

Cowdenbeath, see Beath, Blue Brazil,
Brazil, Cowden, Fifers, Miners

Cowes Sports, see Yachtsmen

Cradley Heath, see Heathens

Cradley Town, see Hammers, Lukes

Craigmark Burntonians, see Mark

Craigneuk, see Craigie

Craigroyston, see Craigie

Cranborne, see Cranes

Cranfield United, see United

Cranleigh, see Cranes

Crawley Down Gatwick, see Anvils

Crawley Town, see Red Devils, Reds,
Town

Cray Valley Paper Mills, see Mills

Cray Wanderers, see Wands, Wanderers

Creetown, see Ferrytoun

Crendon Corinthians, see Corinthians

Crescent Rovers, see Rovers

Crewe Alexandra, see Alex, Railwaymen,
Robins

Crichton, see Dynamo/s (under
Blackwood)

Cricklade Town, see Crick

Crockenhill, see Crocks

Croesyceiliog Association, see Cockerels,
Croesy

Cromer Town, see Crabs

Crook Town, see Black and Ambers

Crossgates Primrose, see Rose

Crowborough Athletic, see Boro, Crows

Crown Scissett, see Crown

Croxley Guild of Sport, see Dicko's

Croydon, see Blues, Trams

Croydon Athletic, see Rams

Croydon Common, see Cock Robins,
Robins

Croydon Municipal, see Lions

Cruden Bay, see Bay

Crumlin Star, see Star

Crumlin United, see Crumlin Boys

Crusaders (Belfast), see Crues, Hatchetmen

Crusaders (London), see Crusaders

Crystal Palace, see Eagles, Glaziers, Palace, Team of the Eighties

Cuffley, see Zeplins

Cullompton Rangers, see Cully, Rangers

Culter, see Deesiders

Cumbernauld United, see United

Cumnock Juniors, see Nock

Cupar Hearts, see Hearts

Curzon Ashton, see Blues, Curzon, Nash

Cwmbach Harriers, see Harriers

Cwmbach Royal Stars, see Stars

Cwmbrân Celtic, see Celts

Cwmbrân Town, see Crows, Town

Cwmfelinfach Colts, see Colts

Dafen Welfare, see Bluebirds

Dagenham and Redbridge (etc.), see Daggers, Reds, Stones

Daisy Hill, see Cutters, Daisies

Dalbeattie Star, see Rabbits, Star

Dalry Thistle, see Thistle

Dalton Crusaders, see Crusaders

Darlaston Town, see Blues, Darlo

Darlington, see Darlo, Eighteen-Eighty-Three (1883), Quakers

Darlington Cleveland Bridge, see Bridge

Darlington Railway Athletic, see R.A., Railwaymen

Dartmouth, see Darts

Dartford, see Darts

Darvel, see Juniors, Vale

(A.F.C.) Darwen, see Anchormen, Darreners, Salmoners

Daventry Town, see Town

Daventry United, see Motormen

Dawdon Colliery Welfare, see Welfare

Dawlish Town, see Seasiders

Deal Town, see Dealers, Fivers, Town

De Havilland, see DH

Debenham Leisure Centre, see Hornets

Deeping Rangers, see Rangers

Defaid Du, see Bad Boys

Denaby United, see Colliers, Reds

Derby Carriage and Wagon (Reckitts), see Wagon

Derby County, see County, Rams, Sheep

Derby County Ladies, see Ewes

Dergview, see Derg, Constitution (or Constitutes)

Dereham Town, see Magpies

Derry City, see Candystripes

Desborough Town, see Ar Tarn

Deveronside, see Side

Deveronvale, see Vale

Devizes Town, see Town

Dick, Kerr's Ladies, see Dick-Kerr's

Didcot Town, see Railwaymen

Dinas Powys, see Ravens, Stars

Dingwall Thistle, see Thistle

Dingwall Victoria United, see Victors

Dinnington Town, see Dinno

Diss Town, see Tangerines

Dock Stars, see Stars

Doddinghurst Olympic, see Olympic

Dolgellau Amateur, see Wasps

Dolphin, see under Dolphins

Doncaster Rovers, see Donny, Rovers, Vikings

Doncaster Rovers Belles Ladies, see Belles, Donny Belles

Donegal Celtic, see Celtic, D.C., Wee Hoops

Donington, see Dons

Dorchester Town, see Magpies

Dorking, see Chicks

Dorking Wanderers, see Wanderers

Douglas and District, see D&D
Douglas High School Old Boys, see
  DHSOB
Dover, see Lilywhites
Dover Athletic, see Lilywhites, Whites
Downes Sports, see Builders
Downfield, see Spiders
Downham Town, see Saints, Town
Draperstown Celtic, see Celtic, D.C., Half
  Hoops
Drayton Wanderers, see Wanderers
Drogheda United, see Boynesiders, Drogs
  / Super Drogs, Turks, United
Droylsden, see Bloods
Drumaness Mills, see Mills
Drumchapel Amateur, see Drum
Drumcondra, see Drums
Dublin City, see Dubs, Vikings
Dudley Sports, see Pie Men
Dudley Town, see Duds, Robins
Dufftown, see Toonsers
Dulwich Hamlet, see Hamlet
Dumbarton, see Sons / Sons of the Rock
Dumbarton Academy Former Pupils, see
  Accies
Dumfries High School Former Pupils, see
  Dumfries F.P.'s
Dundalk, see Lilywhites
Dundee, see Blues, Bonnets, Dark Blues,
  Dee, Dens Parkers
Dundee North End, see Dokens
Dundee United, see Arabs, Tangerines,
  Terrors
Dundee Violet, see Pansies
Dundela, see Duns, Henrun
Dundonald, see Duns
Dundonald Bluebell, see Bluebells
Dunfermline Athletic, see Dumps, Fifers,
  Leishman's Lions, Pars
Dungannon Swifts, see Swifts
Dunipace Juniors, see Pace

Dunkirk, see Boatmen
(A.F.C.) Dunstable, see O.D.'s
Dunstable Town, see Blues
Dunstan Federation Breweries, see Fed
Dunstan UTS, see Fed
Duntocher Hibernian, see Hibs
Durham City, see Citizens, City
Dyffryn Banw, see Banw
Dynamo Blues, see Blues
Dynamo Star, see Mo's
Eaglesham Amateurs, see Hammies, Hams
Earlestown, see Town
Earlswood Town, see Earls
Easington Colliery, see Colliery
Easington Sports, see Clan, Sports
East Chevington, see Tute
East Cowes Victoria Athletic, see Vics
East Craigie, see Shipbuilders
East End, see End
East Fife, see Fifers / The Fife
East Grinstead Town, see Wasps
East Ham United, see Hammers
East Kilbride, see EK, Jags
East Preston, see EP
East Stirlingshire, see Shire
East Thurrock United, see Rocks
East United, see East
Eastbourne Borough, see Borough, Sports
Eastbourne Town, see Bourne, Town
Eastbourne United, see Comrades, U's,
  United
Easthouses Lily Miners Welfare, see
  Houses, Lily
Eastleigh, see Spitfires
Eastwood Hanley, see Blues, Potters
Eastwood Town, see Badgers
Ebbsfleet United, see Fleet
Ebbw Vale, see Cowboys
Eccleshall, see Eagles
Eccleshall Comrades, see Comrades
Eccleshill United, see Eagles

Edinburgh Athletic, see Crew

Edinburgh City, see City, City Slickers

Edinburgh Southern, see Southern

Edinburgh University, see Burgh

Edgware Town, see Town, Wares

Egham Town, see Sarnies, Swans, Town

Elburton Villa, see Villa

Elgin City, see Black and Whites, City

Ellesmere Port and Neston, see Portites

Ellesmere Port Town, see Port, Town

Ellesmere Rangers, see Rangers

Ellon United, see United

Elmore, see Eagles

Ely City, see Robins

Ely Crusaders, see Crusaders

Ely Rangers, see Diffs / Divs, Floggers, Griffins

Emberton, see Rams

(A.F.C.) Emley, see Pewits

Enderby Town, see Town, United (under Leicester)

Endsleigh, see Super Owls

Enfield 1893, see E's

Enfield Town, see ET's, Towners

England National Football Team, see Class of '66, Roy's Boys, Sassenachs, Sven's Men, Three Lions

Englefield Green Rovers, see Rovers

Eppleton Colliery Welfare, see Welfare

Epsom and Ewell, see E's

Erith and Belvedere, see Deres

Erith Town, see Dockers

Esh Winning, see Esh, Stags

Eton Manor, see Braves, Manor

Eton Wick, see Wick

Ettingshall Holy Trinity, see Trins

Evans and Williams, see Albies

Evenwood Town, see Blues, Wood

Eversley, see Boars

Everton, see Bitters / Bitter Blues, Black Watch, Bluenoses, Blues, Dogs of War, Merseysiders, Moonlight Dribblers, People's Club, School of Science, Toffees/Toffeemen

Evesham United, see Robins

Ewell Saxons, see Saxons

Excelsior, see Excelsior

Exeter City, see Grecians

Exmouth Town, see Blues, Town

Eyemouth United, see Fishermen

Eynesbury Rovers, see Rovers

F1 Racing, see F1

Fairfield Villa, see Villa

Fairford Town, see Town

Fakenham Town, see Ghosts

Falkirk, see Bairns

Falmouth Town, see Ambers, Town

Fanad United, see Men from the Kingdom, United

Fareham Town, see Robins, Town

Farleigh Rovers, see Foxes

Farnborough / Town, see Boro, Town, Yellows

Farnborough North End, see Covies, North End

Farnham Town, see Town

Farsley / Farsley Celtic, see Celts, Little Celts, Villagers, Village Lads

Faversham Town, see Creeksiders, Lilywhites, Sorters, Town

F.C. United of Manchester, see FC, FCUM, Red Rebels

Feckenham, see Millers

Felinfach, see Milkmen

Felinheli, see Felin

Felixstowe and Walton United, see Seasiders

Feltham, see Blues, Flyers

Feltham and Hounslow Borough, see Blues, Boro, Flyers

Ferndale Athletic, see Athletic, Fern

Ferryhill Athletic, see Latics

Ffostrasol Wanderers, see Wanderers
Finchampstead, see Finch, Finches
Finchley, see Finches
Finn Harps, see Harps
First Tower United, see Tower
Fisher (and Fisher Athletic), see Club, Fish
Fishguard Sports, see Sports
Fivemiletown, see Town
Flackwell Heath, see Heathens
Fleet Spurs, see Spurs
Fleet Star, see Star
Fleet Town, see Blues, Tarn, Town
Fleetwood Town, see Cod Army,
    Fishermen, Reds, Trawlermen
Fletton United, see Brickies
Fleur-de-Lys, see Flower
Fleur-de-Lys Welfare, see Flower
Flint Mountain, see Mountain Men
Flint Town United, see Silkmen, Town
Flixton, see Flixs, Lions, Valley Roaders,
    Valiants
Fochabers, see Bears
Folkestone Invicta, see Invicta, Seasiders
Folkestone and Shepway, see Town
Folkestone Town, see Town
Ford Motors, see Motors
Ford Sports, see Motormen
Ford United, see Motormen, Reds (as
    Redbridge)
Forest, see Foresters, Wanderers
Forest Green Rovers, see FGR, Green,
    Green Army, Lawnmowers, Little
    Club on the Hill, Rovers.
Forfar Albion, see Albion
Forfar Athletic, see Loons, Sky Blues
Forfar West End, see West End
Formartine United, see United
Formby, see Squirrels
Forres Mechanics, see Can Cans
Forres Thistle, see Jags
Fort William, see Fort

Forth Wanderers, see Wanderers
Ffostrasol Wanderers, see Ffrosty,
    Wanderers
Franklands Village, see Village
Fraserburgh, see Broch
Fraserburgh United, see Broch United
Frecheville Community F.C., see Villa
Freebooters (two clubs), see Freebooters,
    Team of Millionaires
Friar Lane and Epworth, see Lane
Frickley Athletic, see Blues
Frimley Green, see Green
Frome Town, see Robins
Fryston C.W., see Colliers, Colliery
Fulham, see Badgers, Cottagers,
    Lilywhites, Whites
(A.F.C.) Fylde, see Coasters
Fylde Coast Veterans, see Vets
Gabalfa Draconians, see Draconians /
    Dracs
Gainsborough Trinity, see Blues, Holy
    Blues, Recreationists, Trinity
Gala Fairydean, see Braw Lads, Dean,
    Fairies, Gala
Galmpton United and Torbay Gentlemen,
    see Gents
Galway Bohemians, see Bohs
Galway Hibernians, see Hibs
Galway United, see Maroon Army,
    Tribesmen / Tribal Army
Gap Connah's Quay Nomads, see
    Deesiders, Nomads, Westenders
Garden Village, see Canaries, Village.
Garforth Town, see Miners, Town
Garrison Gunners, see Gunners
Garswood United, see Wooders
Garw Athletic, see Athletic
Gateshead, see Boro, Heed, Laides,
    Tynesiders
Gateshead Clarke Chapman, see Clarkie's
Gedling Miners Welfare, see Miners

Gildersome Spurs, see Spurs
Gillford Park, see Gilly
Gillingham F.C., see Gills
Gillingham Town, see Gills
Girvan, see Amateurs, Seasiders
GKN Sankey, see Blues
Glan Conwy, see Jolly Boys
Glantraeth, see Glan
Glapwell, see Well
Glasgow Perthshire, see Shire
Glasgow University, see Glasgow Uni
Glasshoughton Welfare A.F.C., see Blues,
    Welfare
Glastonbury Town, see Dollies, Killman
Glebe Rangers, see Glebe
Glenafton Athletic, see Afton, Glens
Glenavon, see Lurgan Blues
Glenbuck Cherrypickers, see
    Cherrypickers
Glentoran, see Cock 'n' Hens, Glens
Glenrothes, see Glen
Glentanar, see Glens
Glossop North End, see Hillmen
Gloucester City, see Citizens, City,
    Gloucestrians, Tigers
Godalming Town, see G's
Godalming and Guildford, see G's, Gees,
    Weys
Godmanchester Rovers, see Goddy.
    Goody, Rovers
Golspie Sutherland, see under Cattachs
Goole, see Badgers, Town, Vikings
Gorleston, see Cards, Greens
Gornal Athletic, see Peacocks
Gosport Borough, see Borough
Gothic F.C., see Goths
Goytre United, see Goyts
GPT (Coventry), see G's
Graham Street Prims, see Prims
Grange Albion, see Albion
Grange Harlequins, see Quins

Grantham Town, see Gingerbreads
Grasshoppers, see Grasshoppers
Gravesend & Northfleet United, see Fleet
Grays Athletic, see Blues, Boys from
    Rathbone Street, Gravelmen / G-Men,
    Grays
Great Harwood Town, see Arrad, Robins,
    Wellie
Great Wakering Rovers, see Rovers
Great Yarmouth Town, see Bloaters
Greenock Morton, see Pride of the Clyde,
    'Ton
Greenwich Borough, see Boro
Gresford Athletic, see Athletic
Gresley Rovers, see Moatmen, Rovers
Gretna, see Anvils, Black and Whites,
    Borderers, Celebrant, Monochrome,
    Weddingmakers
Gretna 2008, see Black and Whites
Greyfriars (various), see Friars
Grimethorpe M.W., see Colliers
Grimsby Borough, see Wilderness Boys
Grimsby Town, see Fishermen, Mariners
Guernsey, see Green Lions
Guernsey Rangers, see Rangers
Guernsey Rovers, see Rovers
Guildford City, see City, Guild, Pinks,
    Sweeney
Guilsfield F.C., see Gills, Guils
Guisborough Town, see Priorymen
Guiseley, see Lions
Guru Nanak Gravesend, see GNG, Gurus
(C.P.D.) Gwalchmai, see Gwalch
Gymnasium, see Gymns
Hade Edge, see Edge
Hadleigh United, see Brettsiders
Hafod Brotherhood, see Brotherhood
Hailsham Town, see Stringers, Town
Hakin United, see Vikings
Halesowen, see Yeltz
Halesowen Harriers, see Harriers,

Lilywhites
Halifax A.F.C., see Shaymen, Town
(F.C.) Halifax Town, see Shaymen, Town
Halkirk United, see United
Hall Road Rangers, see Blues, Rangers
Hall Russell United, see Halls
Hallam, see Countrymen
Hallen Athletic, see Armadillos
Halstead Town, see Town
Hamilton Academical, see Academical,
  Acas, Accies
Hampstead Heathens, see Heathens
Hampton and Richmond Borough, see
  Beavers, Borough
Hams Hall, see Powermen
Hamworthy United, see Hammers
Handcross Village, see Tigers
Handrahan Timbers, see Timbers
Handsworth, see Amber and Blacks
Hanwell Town, see Geordies, Magpies,
  Town
Hanworth Villa, see Villans
Harborough Town, see Town
Harefield United, see Hares
Haringey Borough, see Borough
Harland and Wolff Welders, see Welders
Harlech Town, see Castlemen
Harlow Town, see Hawks, Lilywhites,
  Owls
Harpenden Town, see Harps, Town
Harrogate Railway Athletic, see
  Locomotives, Rail
Harrogate Town, see Spurs (for discussion
  of Hotspur), Sulphurites, Town
Harrow Borough, see Boro, Reds
Harrow Town, see Town
Harrow Hill, see Harry Hill, Hill
Harrow Hill Rovers, see Borough
  (Hounslow), Rovers
Harrowby United, see Arrows
Hartlepool United, see Dockers, Monkey

Hangers, Pool, Pools
Hartley Wintney, see Row
Harwich and Parkeston, see Shrimpers
Harworth Colliery Institute, see Reds
Haslingden, see Hassy
Hassocks, see Robins
Hastings Town, see Arrows, Claret and
  Blues, Town, U's
Hastings United (old and new clubs), see
  Arrows, Claret & Blues, Town, U's,
  United
Hatfield Main, see Main
Hatfield Town, see Blue Boys, Town
Havant and Waterlooville, see Borough,
  Hawks, Magnets, Ville
Haverfordwest County, see Bluebirds,
  County, West
Haverhill Rovers, see Reds, Rovers
Hawarden Rangers, see Rangers
Hawick Royal Albert, see Albert,
  Royalists, Sleeping Giants
Hawick Waverley, see Waverley
Hay St Mary's, see Saints
(A.F.C.) Hayes, see Brook
Hayes, see Missioners
Hayes and Yeading United, see Dinc /
  Ding, Missioners, United
Haywards Heath Town, see Bluebells,
  Heath
Hazells (Aylesbury), see Printers
Headington Amateurs, see A's
Heanor Town, see Lions
Heart of Midlothian, see Edinboro
  Darlings, Famous, Hearts, Jam Tarts,
  Jambos, Jammies, Maroons
Heath Hayes, see Hayes
Heather St Johns, see Saints
Heaton Rifles, see Rifles
Heavitree Social United, see Heavies
Hebburn Town, see Hornets
Hednesford Town, see Pitmen, Whites

Helston Athletic, see Blues

Hemel Hempstead, see Hemel, Tudors

Hemsworth Miners Welfare, see Wells

Hendon, see Dons, Greens

Hengrove Athletic, see Grove, Hens

Henley Town, see Lilywhites, Town

Herbrandston, see Herby

Hereford United, see Bulls, Lilywhites,
     United, Whites

Herne Bay, see Bay

Herriot-Watt University, see Watt

Hertford Town, see Blues

Hertfordshire Rangers, see Rangers

Heston Rovers, see Rovers

Heybridge Swifts, see Black and Whites,
     Swifts

Hibernian, see Cabbage, Hibs / Hibees,
     Turnbull's Tornadoes

Higham Town, see Lankies

Higher Walton, see Villagers, Waltonians

Highgate United, see Gate, Reds

Highmoor-Ibis, see Mighty Moor / Moor

Highworth Town, see Worthians

Hill of Beath Hawthorn, see Haws

Hillingdon Borough, see Blues, Boro,
     Hillmen

Hinckley Athletic / Town / United, see
     Eagles, Knitters, Robins, Town,
     United

Hindsford, see Tonics

Histon F.C., see Stutes

Hitchin Town, see Canaries

Hoddesdon Town, see Lilywhites,
     Lowfielders

Holbeach United, see Tigers

Holbrook Sports, see Brookies

Holker Old Boys, see Cobs, Stags

Hollington United, see Old Lions

Holly Lane '92, see Lane

Holmer Green, see Greens

Holmesdale, see Dalers

Holmfirth Town, see Town

Holsworthy, see Magpies

Holt United, see Bulls

Holwell Sports, see Holwell

Holyhead Hotspur, see Harbourmen,
     Spurs

Holyport, see Villagers

Holywell Arcadians, see Arcadians

Holywell Town, see Wellmen

Holywood, see Star (under Loughview)

Home Farm Everton, see Farm

Hook Norton, see Brewery Boys, Hooky

Horden Colliery Welfare, see Colliers,
     Welfare

Horley Town, see Clarets, Hammers

(A.F.C.) Hornchurch, see Urchins

Horndean, see Deans

Horsham, see Hornets

Horsham YMCA, see YM

Horwich R.M.I., see Leythers, Locos,
     Railwaymen

Hounslow Borough, see Borough

Hounslow Town, see Town

Hucknall Colliery Welfare, see Colliers

Hucknall Town, see Town, Yellows

Huddersfield Town, see Colnesiders,
     Scarlet Runners, Terriers, Town

Hull City, see Tigers

Hullbridge Sports, see Bridge, Sports

Hungerford Town, see Crusaders

Huntingdon Town, see Croms

Huntingdon United, see Green and Reds

Huntley & Palmers, see Biscuit Boys

Huntly, see Black and Golds

Hurley Daw Mill, see Mill

Hurlford United, see Ford

Hurstpierpoint, see Hurst, Point

Hyde / United, see Tigers

Hythe and Dibden, see Boatmen

Hythe Town, see Forters, Reds, Town

Ibstock United / Welfare, see Welly

Kings Norton Town, see Nomads

Kingsbury London Tigers, see Tigers

Kingsbury Town, see Kings, Mustard Pots,
 Town

Kingsley Olympic, see Olympic

Kingstonian, see K's

Kinnaird, see Sodyheads

Kinnoull, see Noull

Kintbury Rangers, see 'Gers, Rangers

Kirby Moxloe, see Kirby

Kirkcaldy YM, see YM

Kirkham and Wesham, see Coasters

Kirkintilloch Rob Roy, see Rabs, Roy

Kirkley and Pakefield, see Kirks, Royals

Kirkwall Rovers, see Rovers

Kirkwall Thorfinn, see Thorfinn

Kirriemuir Thistle, see Kirrie, Thistle

Kiveton Park, see Park

Knaphill, see Knappers

Knebworth, see Mighty K's, Orange Army

Knighton Town, see Borderers, Radnor
 Robins, Town.

Knighton Victoria, see Vics

Knockbreda, see 'Breda

Knowle, see Robins, Star

Knowle North Star, see Star

Knowsley United, see Reds, United

Knutsford, see Robins

Knypersley Victoria, see Vics

Lambourn Sports, see Ams

Lanark United, see Yowes

Lancaster City, see Dolly Blues

Lancing, see Lancers, Yellows

Langford, see Reds

Langley Park Welfare, see Park

Langney Sports, see Sports

Largs Thistle, see Theestle

Larkhall Thistle, see Jags, Larkie

Larkhill Athletic, see Larks

Larne, see Harbour Rats

Launceston, see Clarets

Launton Sports, see Riversiders

Laurelvale, see Vale

Laxey, see Miners

Leamington, see Brakes

Leamington Hibernian, see Hibs

Leatherhead, see Tanners

Leavesden Hospital F.C., see Leaves

Leeds City, see City

Leeds City Vixens Ladies, see Vixens

Leeds United, see Dirty Leeds, Owls,
 Peacocks, United, Whites / Mighty
 Whites

Leek County School Old Boys, see Old
 Boys

Leek Town, see Blues

Left Overs Sports Club, see LOSC

Leicester City, see City, Filberts, Fosse /
 Fossites, Foxes, Ice Kings, Nuts

Leicester United, see United (and see
 Enderby Town)

Leicester YMCA, see Beavers

Leigh Genesis, see Leythers, Locos,
 Railwaymen

Leighton Town, see Buzzards, Reds, Sand
 Dobbers, Town

Leiston, see Blues

Leith Athletic, see Athletic, Black and
 Whites, Zebras

Lesmahagow, see 'Gow

Letchworth Garden City, see Bluebirds

Letchworth Garden City Eagles, see Eagles

Letcombe, see Brooksiders

Letterkenny Rovers, see Rovers

Leverstock Green, see Green

Lewes, see Rooks

Lewes Ladies, see Rookettes

Lewis United, see Hoops

Lex XI, see Lawmen

Leyland Motors, see Motormen, Tigers

Leyton, see Lillies, Lilywhites, Swifts

Leyton Orient, see CO's, O's, Orient

Leyton Pennant, see Lilywhites, Pennant,
    Stags
Leyton-Wingate, see Lilywhites
Leytonstone, see Cedars, Stones
Leytonstone and Ilford, see Ford/s, Stones
Lightwater Pumas, see Pumas
Limavady United, see Lims, Roesiders,
    United
Limerick, see Blades, Blues, Lims
Lincoln, see Amateurs
Lincoln City, see Deranged Ferrets, Imps
    / Red Imps
Lincoln Ladies, see Lady Imps
Lincoln Moorlands Railway, see Moors
Lincoln United, see United
Lindfield Rangers, see Rangers
Linfield, see Blues
Linlithgow Rose, see Rose, Rosey Posey
Lisburn Distillery, see Whites
Lisburn Rangers, see Wee Rangers
Liskeard Athletic, see Blues
Lisvane-Heath Hornets, see Hornets
Little Common, see Common
Littlehampton Town, see Marigolds
Liverpool, see Anfielders, Culture Club,
    Kop / Kopites, Liddellpool, Mariners,
    Merseysiders, Micky Mousers, Pool,
    Reds, Spice Boys
(A.F.C.) Liverpool, see Kopettes, Reds
Liversedge, see Sedge
Liverton United, see Lilies
Livingston, see Lions, Livi / Livi Lions,
    Thistle, Wee Jags
Llanberis, see Beris, Blac and Amber,
    Darans, Llanbêr, Loco / Locomotives,
    Teigars.
Llanboidy, see Foxes
Llandegfan Antelope, see Antelopes
Llandrindod Wells, see Blues, Spamen
Llandudno Junction, see Junction,
    Railwaymen

Llandudno Town, see Town.
Llandyrnog United, see Dyrni
Llandysul, see Swallows
Llanelli, see Reds
Llanelli Radicals, see Radicals
Llanfairfechan Athletic, see Swans
Llanfairpwll, see Chocolates
Llangefni Town, see Cefni, Dazzlers
Llangollen Town, see Town
Llanidloes Ladies, see Llani Ladies
Llanidloes Town, see Daffodils / Daffs /
    Superdaffs, Town
Llanrhaeadr ym Mochnant, see Waterfall
    Men
Llanrwst United, see Roosters, Rwsters
Llansantffraid Village, see Saints
Llanwddyn, see Lakesiders
Llanybydder, see Eosiaid, Yr
Llanymynech, see Exiles
Llay Royal British Legion, see Legion
Llay Welfare, see Llay, Welfare
Lliswerry Athletic, see Lizards
(A.F.C.) Llwydcoed, see Coed
Lochee Harp, see Harp
Lochee United, see Bluebells
Lochgelly Albert, see Berts
Lochgelly DDSS, see Lochgelly Sodgers
Lochgelly United, see Happylanders
Lochore Welfare, see Lo'hore
London Caledonians, see Calies
London Colney, see Blueboys
London Maccabi Lions, see Lions
London Tigers, see Tigers
Long Eaton United, see Blues
Long Melford, see Villagers
Long Sutton Athletic, see Magpies
Longford Town, see De Town, Town
Longside, see Side
Longwell Green Sports, see Green, Sports
Lordswood, see Lords
Lossiemouth, see Coasters

Lossiemouth United, see United

Lothian Thistle Hutchison Vale, see Thistle

Loughborough, see Luffs

Loughborough Dynamo, see Dynamo,
  Moes

Loughborough Town, see Town

Loughborough University, see Scholars

Loughgall, see Villagers

Loughview Star, see Star

Louth Town, see White Wolves

Louth United, see Lions

Lovells Athletic, see Toffeemen

Lower Maze, see Black and Red Army,
  Maze, Mills

Lowestoft Town, see Blues, Trawler Boys

Loxwood, see Magpies

Ludgvan, see Hurlers

Ludlow Town, see Knights

Lugar Boswell Thistle, see Jaggy Bunnets

Luncarty, see Bleachers

Lurgan Celtic, see Bhoys, Hoops

Luton Town, see Hatters, Lilywhites,
  Lootown, Lutonians, Reds, Straw-
  Hatters / Straw-Plaiters

Lydney Town, see Town

Lye Town, see Flyers

(AFC) Lymington, see Linnets

Lymington Town, see Town

Lyndhurst, see Foresters

Macclesfield Town, see Silkmen

Machynlleth Town, see Maglonians

Maesglas, see Blues

Maesteg Park Athletic, see Park

Maesycwmmer, see Druids, Maesy

Magherafelt Sky Blues, see Sky Blues

Maghull, see Blues

Maidenhead Town Youth, see Stags

Maidenhead United, see Magpies, Tanners,
  United

Maidstone Invicta, see Stones

Maidstone United, see Stones

Maine Road, see Blues, Road

Malden Vale, see Vale

Maldon and Tiptree, see Blues, Hoops,
  Jam Makers, Strawberries, Town

Maldon Town, see Blues, Town

Malew, see Spiders

Malmesbury Victoria, see Vics

Maltby Main, see Miners

Manchester Arcadians, see Arcadians

Manchester City, see Bitters / Bitter
  Blues, Blues, Citizens, City, Council
  Housers, Man, Massives, Sheik City,
  Stockports

Manchester United, see Busby Babes,
  Coach-Builders, Fergie's Fledglings,
  Heathens, Man, Manure, Munichs,
  Outcasts, Red Devils, Reds, United

Manders, see Paintmen

Mangotsfield United, see Field, Mangos

Manor Thistle, see Crew

Manortown United, see Town, United

Mansfield Town, see Stags, Yellows

March Town United, see Hares,
  Railwaymen

Marchwiel Villa, see Lions

Mardy Tigers, see Tigers

Margate, see Gate, Lilywhites

Marine, see Lilywhites, Mariners

Market Drayton Town, see Gingerbread
  Men

Market Harborough Town, see Huntsmen,
  Linnets

Markethill Swifts, see Swifts

Marlow, see Blues

Marlow United, see Flying Blues

Marske United, see Codheads, Seasiders

Marsden, see Cuckoos

Martin Baker Sports, see Baker Boys

Maryhill, see Hill

Massey Ferguson, see Tractormen

Matlock Town, see Gladiators

Nantwich Town, see Dabbers

Neath Athletic, see Eagles

Neath Port Talbot Tigers, see Tigers

Needham Market, see Marketmen

Nefyn United, see Herrings, Penwaig.

Neilston Juniors, see Farmer's Boys

Nelson, see Admirals, Blues, Seedhillers

Nelson Cavaliers, see Cavaliers / Cavs

Ness, see Niseachs

Nestlé Rowntree, see Jo Row, Rowntrees, Trees

Netherfield, see Field

New Bradwell St. Peter, see Jimmies, Peters, Saint Peters

New Brighton, see Rakers, Towerites

New College Academy, see College

New Heaton Mersey Vipers Junior, see Vipers

New Mills, see Millers

New Milton Town, see Linnets

New Quay, see Mackerel Men

Newark Town, see Peaceful Warriors

Newbridge-on-Wye, see Bridge, Wyesiders

Newburgh, see Burgh

Newbury Town, see Town

Newcastle, see Seasiders

Newcastle Benfield, see Lions, Saints

Newcastle Blue Star, see Aristocrats, Star

Newcastle Emlyn, see Emlyn

Newcastle It's Just Like Watching Brazil, see Brazil

Newcastle Town, see Castle

Newcastle United, see Barcodes, Cartoon Army, Entertainers, Frenchcastle, Geordies, Magpies, Skunks, Toon, Tyneside Professors, Tynesiders.

Newhall United, see Blues

Newhaven, see Dockers

Newington Youth Club, see Swans, 'Ton

Newmains United Community F.C., see United

Newmarket Town, see Jockeys

Newmilns, see Lacemakers

Newpark Olympic, see Olympic

Newport City Strikers, see Strikers

Newport Civil Service, see Civil

Newport Corinthians, see Corinthians

Newport County A.F.C., see Black and Ambers, County, Cromwellians, Exiles, Ironsides, Port, Wasps

Newport YMCA, see YM / YMCA.

Newquay, see Peppermints

Newton Abbot, see Reds

Newton Abbot Spurs, see Spurs

Newton Aycliffe, see Acorns, Aycliffe

Newton Heath LYR, see Coach-Builders, Heathens

Newton St Cyres, see Saints

Newton Stewart, see Creesiders

Newtongrange Star, see Nitten, Star

Newtown, see Batmans, Robins, Stars.

Newry City / Town, see Bordermen, Town

Neyland, see Nomads

Nithsdale Wanderers, see Dale, Wanderers

North Ferriby United A.F.C., see United, Villagers

Northampton ON Chenecks, see Chenecks

Northampton Sileby Rangers, see Rangers, Sileby, Vans

Northampton Spencer, see Millers

Northampton Town, see Cobblers, Shoe Army, Tayn, Town.

Northern Nomads, see Nomads, Roaming Brigade

Northfield Town, see Cross

North Greenford United, see Blues

North Leigh, see Millers, Nor Lye, Windmill Army, Yellows

North Ormesby Sports, see Doggy

Pegasus Juniors, see Redmen, Reds

Pegham, see Lions

Pelsall Villa, see Villains / Villians

Pembroke Borough, see Borough, Magpies, Stars

Pencoed Athletic, see Coed

Penhill, see Hill Club, PYC

Penicuik Athletic, see Cuikie, Rookie Cookie

Penmaenmawr Phoenix, see Yellow Boys

Penn and Tylers Green, see Penn

Pennant, see Lilywhites, Pennant, Stags

Penparcau, see Arky-Penarky

Penrhiwceiber Rangers, see Rangers

Penrhyncoch, Lions, Penrhyn, Roosters

Penrhyndeudraeth, see Penrhyn

Penrith, see Blues, Cumbrians

Penryn Athletic, see Borough, Pens

Pentwyn and Llanedeym Dynamos, see Dynamo/s

Penybont United, see Bont

Penycae, see Cae

Penzance, see Magpies

Peppard, see Pepps

Pershore Town 88, see Town

Peterborough Northern Star, see Eyes, Star

Peterborough United, see Brickies, Posh

Peterhead, see Blue Toon

Peterlee Newtown F.C., see Newtowners

Petersfield Town / United, see Reds, Town, United

Petershill, see Peasy

Pewsey Vale, see Vale

Phoenix Bessemer, see Phoenix

Phoenix Park, see Park

Pickering Town, see Pikes

Pilgrims, see Pilgrims

Pilkington XXX, see Glassmen, Pilks

Plymouth Argyle, see Argyle, Green Army, Pilgrims

Plymouth Parkway, see Parkies / Parkway

Plymstock United, see Reds

Polegate Town, see Town

Polesworth North Warwick, see Poles

Polkemmet Juniors, see PJs

Pollok, see 'Lok

Pontardawe Town, see Ponty

Pontefract Collieries, see Colls

Ponteland United, see United

Pontlottyn Blast Furnace, see Blast

Pontprennau Pumas, see Pumas

Pontrhydfendigaid and District, see Bont

Pontyclun, see Clun

Pontypridd Town, see Dragons, Ponty

Poole Borough, see Hornets

Poole Town, see Dolphins

Port Glasgow Juniors, see Undertakers

Port Talbot Town, Blues, Steelmen

Port Vale, see Fail, Vale, Valiants

Portadown, see Ports

(A.F.C.) Portchester, see Porchey, Royals

Portfield, see Field

Portgordon Victoria, see Vics

(Athletic F.C.) Porth, see Black Dragons

Porth Tywyn Suburbs, see Suburbs

Porthcawl Town Athletic, see Seasiders

Porthleven, see Fishermen

Porthmadog, see Port, Porth

Portishead Town, see Posset

Portland United, see Blues

Portsmouth, see Blues, Pompey, Sailors, Skates

Portsmouth Ladies, see Pompey Ladies

Portsmouth Royal Navy, see Sailors

Portstewart, see Seahawks

Potters Bar Crusaders, see Crusaders

Potters Bar Town, see Grace, Scholars

Potton United, see Royals

Prescot Cables / Town, see Cables, Tigers

Prescot B.I., see Social

Pressed Steel, see Steelmen

Gabs, Garrison, Guardians, Messengers

Rogerstone, see Ivanhoe, Rogie Aces

Rolls Royce Engines, see Rollers

Roman Glass St George F.C., see Romans

Romford, see Boro

Romsey Town, see Town

Romulus, see Roms

Ross County, see County, Staggies

Ross Town, see Riversiders

Rossendale United, see Dale/s, Rossy, Stags

Rossington, see Locals

Rossington Main, see Colliery

Rossvale F.C., see Vale

Rosyth, see Rec

Rotherham County, see County

Rotherham United, see Millers / Merry Millers

Rothes, see Speysiders

Rothes Decimals, see Decies

Rothesay Brandane, see Danes

Rothley Imperial, see Imps

Rothwell Corinthians, see Corinthians / Corinths

Rothwell Town, see Bones

Rowntree Mackintosh, see Jo Row, Rowntree, Trees

Royal Albert, see Albert

Royal Engineers, see Sappers

Royal Marines, see Commandos, Marines

Royston Town, see Crows

RTM Newcastle, see Aristocrats, Star

Ruabon Druids, see Druids

Rugby Town / United, see Town, Valley

Ruislip Manor, see Manor

Runcorn, see Corn, Linnets

Runcorn Linnets, see Linnets

Runcorn Town, see Town

Rushall Olympic, see Olympic, Pics

Rushden and Diamonds, see Annies, Diamonds, Russians

Rushden and Higham, see Lankies

Rushen United, see Spaniards

Rustington, see Blues

Rustington Otters, see Otters

Rutherglen Glencairn, see Glens

Ruthin Town, see Blues, Ruths / The Ruthless, Town

Ryde Sports, see Reds

Ryhope Colliery Welfare, see Welfare

Ryhope Community, see CA, Ryes

Rye United, see Quarterboys, United

Ryton and Crawcrook Albion, see Albion

Saffron Walden, see Bloods, Saffron, Wardens

Saintfield United, see Saints

Salford City, see Ammies

Salisbury City, see Lilywhites, Whites

Salisbury Saxons, see Saxons

Saltaire, see Salts

Saltash United, see Ashes

Saltburn Athletic, see Seagulls

Saltcoats Victoria, see Seasiders

Saltdean, see Tigers

Saltney Town, see Bordermen

Salts (Saltaire), see Salts

Sandridge Rovers, see Ridge, Rovers

Sandhurst Town, see Fizzers

Sandiacre Town, see Saints

Sandridge Rovers, see Ridge

Sandwell Borough, see Stags, Trees

Sandy Albion, see Albion

Sark National Football Team, see Bad Lions, Mad Lions, Wasps

Sauchie Juniors F.C., see Sauchie

Sawbridgeworth Town, see Robins

Saxons, see Saxons

Scarborough, see Boro, Seadogs, Seasiders

Scarborough Athletic, see Seadogs

Scarborough Town, see Boro, Seasiders, Town

Solihull Moors, see Moors

Solway Star, see Star

Somersham Town, see Westenders

Sonning Common Peppard, see under
    Pepps

South Bank F.C., see Bankers

South Kilburn, see SK, South

South Liverpool, see South

South Normanton Athletic, see Athletic,
    Shiners

South Park, see Barmy Army

South Shields, see Laddies / Laides,
    Mariners

South Shields Cleadon Club, see Club

Southall, see Fowlers

Southall and Ealing Borough, see Hall

Southall Town, see Town, Wood

Southam United, see Saints

Southampton, see Ale House Brawlers,
    Saints, Scummers

Southend Manor, see Manor

Southend United, see Blues, Seasiders,
    Shrimpers

Southport, see Port, Sandgrounders,
    Yellows

Southwick, see Wickers

Spalding United, see Tulips

Spartans Junior, see Spartans

Spelthorne Sports, see Spelly

Spennymoor Town, see Moors

Spixworth, see Spicky

Splott Albion, see Albion

Sport and Leaisure Swifts, see Swifts

Sporting Bengal United, see Bengal Tigers,
    Sporting

Sporting Devils, see Devils

Sporting Fingal, see Fingal, Ravens

(A.F.C.) Sportsman Rovers, see Athletic,
    Boro, Pockets, Town.

Squire's Gate, see Gate

St Agnes, see Aggie

St Albans City, see Saints, City

St Andrews, see Saints

St Andrews United, see Ancients, Saints,
    United

St Anthony's, see Ants

St Asaph City, see Saints

St Austell, see Lilywhites

St Bernards, see Saints

St Blazey, see Green and Blacks, Saints

St Clears, see Saints

St Cuthbert Wanderers, see Saints,
    Wanderers

St Duthus, see Saints

St Francis Hospital, see Mental Hospital,
    Saints

St Francis Rangers, see Rangers, Saints

St George's, see Geordies

St Helen's Town, see Saints, Town

St Ippolyts, see Saints

St Ishmael's, see Tish

St Ives Town, see Saints

St James's Gate, see Gate

St John's United, see United

St Johnstone, see Saints

St Just, see Tinners

St Leonards, see Blues, Saints

St Leonards Stamcroft, see Blues

St Margaretsbury, see Athletic, Bury

St Mary's (three clubs), see Saints

St Mirren, see Black and White Army,
    Buddies, Paisley Brazilians, Saints

St Neots, see Saints

St Osyth, see Saints, Toosey

St Patrick's Athletic, see Pat's, Saints

St Peters (St Albans), see Saints

St Roch's, see Candy Rocks

Stafford Rangers, see Boro, Rangers

Stafford Road, see Roaders

Stafford Town, see Reds, Town

Staines Lammas, see Blues

Staines Town, see Leghorns, Linos,

Swavesey Spartans, see Spartans

Swindon Athletic, see under Hill Club, PYC

Swindon Corinthians, see Corinthians

Swindon Supermarine, see Marine

Swindon Town, see Moonrakers, Railwaymen, Robins, Spartans, Swindle

Symingtons, see Corsetmen

Tadcaster Albion, see Brewers

Tadley Calleva, see Tadders

Taffs Well, see Taffs / Taffys, Wellmen

Tain Thistle, see Thistle

Talgarth Rovers, see Rovers

Tamworth, see Lambs, Reds, Town

Tandragee Rovers, see Rovers

Tarff Rovers, see Rovers

Tarleton Corinthians, see Corinthians

Tata Steel, see Scow

Taunton Town, see Peacocks

Tavistock, see Lambs, Tavy

Tayport, see Port

Team Bath, see Crescents, Scholars, Team

Team Bury, see Blues, Team

Team Northumbria, see Team, Tynesiders

Team Solent, see Team

Team Swansea, see Team

Technogroup Welshpool Town, see Lilywhites

Teignmouth, see Teigns

(A.F.C.) Telford, see Bucks, Lilywhites

Telford United, see Bucks, Lilywhites

Tenterden Tigers, see Tigers

Terenure College, see 'Nure

Tetley Walker, see Walkers

Teversal, see Tevie Boys

Thackley, see Reds, Dennyboys

Thame United, see U's, United, Utd

Thames Polytechnic, see Poly

Thamesmead Town, see Mead

Thanet United, see Gate, Islanders, Lilywhites, U's.

Thatcham Town, see Kingfishers, Town

The 61 FC, see Blues, Two Blues

The New Saints, see Blues, Saints, TNS

Thetford Town, see Brecklanders, Town

Third Lanark Athletic Club, see Hi-Hi's, Redcoats, Sodgers, Thirds, Volunteers, Warriors

Thistle, see Thistle

Thornaby, see Blues

Thorne Colliery, see Colliery

Thorniewood United, see Wood

Thornton Hibernian, see Hibees, Hibs

Thorpe Athletic, see Athletic

Thrapston Town, see Thrapo, Town, Venturas

Threave Rovers, see Rovers

Three Bridges, see Bridges

Thurrock, see Fleet

Thursday Wanderers, see Wanderers

Thurso, see Crabs, Vikings

Tilbury, see Dockers

Tipton Town, see Town

Tiptree United, see Blues, Jam Makers, Strawberries

Tirydail Cowboys, see Cowboys

Tiverton Town, see Lacemen, Tivvy

Tividale, see Dale/s

Tobermore United, see Reds, United

Toddington Rovers, see Rovers

Tokyngton Manor, see Manor

Tolka Rovers, see Rovers

Tollcross United, see Cross

Ton Pentre, see Bulldogs, Rhondda Bulldogs, Ton

Tonbridge Angels, see Angels

(A.F.C.) Tondu, see Robins

Tongwynlais, see Ton

Tonyrefail Welfare, see Welfare

Tooting and Mitcham United, see Half-Halfs, Lilywhites, Stripes, Terrors,

Tooting Terrors

Torpoint Athletic, see Gold and Black Army, Point

Torquay United, see Gulls, Magpies

Torrington, see Supergreens, Torrie

Total Network Solutions, see Saints

Totnes and Dartington, see Tots

Tottenham Hotspur, see Lilywhites, Spurs, Super Spurs, Yids / Yid Army

Totternhoe, see Totts

(A.F.C.) Totton, see Stags

Tow Law Town, see Lawyers

Tower Hamlets, see Tipples

Trafford, see North

Tralee Dynamos, see Dynamos, Kingdom Boys

Tranmere Rovers, see Rovers, Super Whites

Trawsfynydd, see Traws

Trawsgoed, see Traws

Tredomen Athletic, see Engineers

Trefeurig and District United, see Yellow Canaries

Trefonen, see Pitmen, Yellows

Tregaron Turfs, see Turfs

Treharris Athletic Western, see Lilywhites, Western

Treowen Stars, see Stars

Trimdon Veterans, see Vets

Tring Athletic, see Athletic

Tring Town, see T's, Tee's

Triplex, see Glassboys

Troed-y-Rhiw, see Rhiw, Stars

Trojans, see Blues, Trojans

Trowbridge Town, see Bees

Truro City, see City, Tinmen, White Tigers

Tuam Celtic Athletic, see Hoops

Tuffley Rovers, see Rovers, Tuffs

Tulliallan Thistle, see Thistle

Tunbridge Wells, see Wells

Turriff United, see Turra, United

Turton, see Tigers

Twyford Spartans, see Spartans

Tynecastle, see under Cross

Tytherington Rocks, see Rocks

Tywyn / Bryncrug, see Cormorants

U.C.L. Academicals, see Academicals, Accies

(A.F.C.) Uckfield, see Oaks

Uckfield Grasshoppers '81, see Grasshoppers

Union Mills, see Millers

Unione Sportiva Valerio, see Bedford United

United Services Portsmouth, see RN

University College Dublin, see College, Students

University of Ulster at Jordanstown, see Poly, U.U.J.

University of Wales in Cardiff, see Archers

Upton Town, see Emeralds

UWIC Inter Cardiff, see Diffs / Div's, Inter / International, Seagulls, Sheep

Uxbridge, see Reds

Uxbridge Town, see under Drayton Wanderers

Vale of Clyde, see Tin Pail

Vale of Leithen, see Vale

Vale of Leven, see Vale

Vale of Nith, see Vale, Zebras

Vale Recreation, see Green and Golds, Rec

Valley Sports, see Valley

VCD Athletic, see VCD, Vickers

Vauxhall Motors (Ellesmere Port), see Motormen

Vauxhall Motors (Luton), see Motors

Verwood Town, see Stags

Viking Greenford / Sports, see Vikings

Virginia Water, see Waters

Vosper Thorneycrofts, see Boatmen

VS Rugby, see Valley

Wadebridge Town, see Bridgers

Wakefield, see Bears, Pewits

Wakehurst, see Magpies

Wales National Football Team, see
Dragons, Young Dragons

(A.F.C.) Wallingford, see Wally

Wallingford Town, see Town

Walsall, see Saddlers, Swifts

Walsall Wood, see Prims, Wood

Walsham-le-Willows, see Willows

Waltham Abbey, see Abbey, Abbots

Waltham Forest, see Lilywhites, Pennant,
Stags

Walthamstow Avenue, see A's, Avenue

Walthamstow Pennant, see Lilywhites,
Pennant, Stags

Walton and Hersham, see Sham, Swans,
Swans and Robins, Waltz

Walton Casuals, see Casuals, Stags

Wanderers, see Foresters, Wanderers

Wantage Town, see Alfredians

Warboys Town, see Witches

Ware, see Blues

Warlingham, see Hammers, Wars

Warminster Town, see Red and Blacks,
Town

Warrenpoint Town, see Point

Warrington Town, see Levers, Town,
Warriors, Wire/s, Yellows

Washington, see Mechanics

Waterford United, see Blues

Waterloo Rovers, see Rovers

Waterlooville, see Borough, Hawks,
Magnets, Ville

Waterlows, see Printers

Watford, see Blues, Brewers, Golden
Boys, Hornets, Horns / 'Orns, Saints,
Wasps, Yellow Army

Watton United, see Brecklanders

Waunfawr, see Beganifs

Wealdstone, see Royal Stones, Royals,
Stones

Wednesbury Old Athletic, see Old 'Uns

Wednesbury Strollers, see Strollers

Wednesfield, see Cottagers, Social

Wellesbourne, see Bourne

Welling United F.C., see Reds, Wings

Wellingborough Saxon, see Saxons

Wellingborough Town, see Doughboys

Wellingborough Whitworths, see
Flourmen

Wellington (Herefordshire), see Wellies

Wellington Amateurs, see Ams

Wellington (Somerset), see Tangerines,
Town, Wellie

Wellington Town (Shropshire), see
Lilywhites

Wells City, see City

Welshpool Town, see Lilywhites, Maes y
Dre, Seasiders

Welton Rovers, see Rovers

Welwyn Garden City, see Citizens

Welwyn Pegasus, see Pegasus

Wembley, see Lions

West Allotment Celtic, see Celtic, West

West and Middle Chinnock, see Chinnocks

West Auckland, see West

West Bromwich Albion, see Albion,
Baggies, Bennies, Boing!, Nigger
Minstrels, Sandwell Town, Stripes,
Strollers, Tatters (for a possible
connection), Team of Boys, Tesco's,
Throstles, W.B.A.

West End, see End

West Ham United, see Academy of
Football, Claret and Blues, Cockney
Boys, Eastenders, Hammers,
Hamsters, ICF, Irons, Wet Sham

West Thurrock, see East Thurrock

West United, see West

Westbury United, see White Horse Men

440

Wolverhampton Wanderers, see Buckley Babes, Dingles, Tatters, Wanderers, Wolves

Wolverton Town, see MK Wolves, Railwaymen, Wolves

Wolviston, see Villagers, Wolves

Wombourne Olympic, see Olympic

Woodbridge Athletic, see Magpies

Woodbridge Town, see Bridge, Woodpeckers

Woodford Town, see Town, Woods

Woodford United, see Reds, United

Woodley Hammers, see Hammers

Woodley Sports, see Saxons, Sports, Steelmen

Woodley Town, see Town

Woodstock Sports, see Sports

Wooldale Wanderers, see Bonnie Oodle

Woolley Miners Welfare, see Colliers

Woolpack Wanderers, see Wanderers

Woolwich Town, see Dockers

Wootton Bassett, see Bassett

Wootton Blue Cross, see Blue Cross

Worcester Athletico, see Emeralds

Worcester City, see Blues, City, Dragons, Faithfuls, Loyals, Royals

(AFC) Worcester Olympic, see Olympic

Worcester Park, see Park, Skinners

Workington, see Reds

Worksop Parramore, see Parras

Worksop Town, see Tigers

Wormley Rovers, see Robins

Worsbrough Bridge Athletic, see Bridge, Briggers

Worthing, see Rebels, Red Army

Worthing United, see Mavericks, United

Wren Rovers, see Wrens

Wrexham, see Red Army, Red Dragons, Robins, Town

Wrockwardine Wood, see Wood

Wroxham, see Yachtsmen

(A.F.C.) Wulfrunians, see Wulfs

Wycombe Wanderers, see Blues, Chairboys, Wanderers

Wythenshawe Amateurs, see Amateurs

Yate Town, see Bluebells, Whites

Yaxley, see Cuckoos

Yeading, see Dinc / Ding, Missioners, United

Yeovil Town, see Casuals, Glovers

Yiewsley, see Blues

Ynys-las Gunners, see Gunners

Ynysddu Crusaders, see Crusaders

Ynysddu Welfare, see Welfare

Yoker Athletic, see Whe Ho

York City, see City, Minstermen, Y-Fronts, Yorkies

Yorkshire Amateur, see Ammers, Hammers

Yorkshire Main Colliery, see Main.